JESUIT LIFE &
MISSION TODAY

Jesuit Life & Mission Today

The Decrees of the
31st–35th General Congregations
of the Society of Jesus

John W. Padberg, S.J.
Editor

The Institute of Jesuit Sources
Saint Louis

No. 25 in Series 1: Jesuit Primary Sources in English Translation

This North American publication of the documents of the Thirty-first through the Thirty-fifth General Congregations of the Society of Jesus was edited by John W. Padberg, S.J., director of the Institute of Jesuit Sources. It is a complete authorized English-language version of the following official texts as published in Rome by the General Curia of the Society of Jesus in the *Acta Romana Societatis Iesu (AR):*

1. *Decreta Congregationis Generalis XXXI . . . annis 1965–1966 (AR 1967)*

2. *Decreta Congregationis Generalis XXXII . . . annis 1974–1975 (AR 1975)*

3. *Decreta Congregationis Generalis XXXIII . . . anno 1983 (AR 1984)*

4. *Decreta Congregationis Generalis XXXIV . . . anno 1995 (AR 1995)*

5. *Decrees of General Congregation XXXV . . . anno 2008 (AR 2009)*

Library of Congress Control Number: 2009920151

ISBN 978-1-880810-69-7 cloth

  978-1-880810-70-0 paper

©2009 The Institute of Jesuit Sources
  3601 Lindell Boulevard
  St. Louis, MO 63108
  tel: 314-633-4622
  e-mail: ijs@jesuitsources.com
  www.jesuitsources.com

CONTENTS

INTRODUCTION

A general congregation is the highest authority, the ultimate governing body in the Society of Jesus. It is also the most representative instance of the Society's current understanding of itself, its life, and its mission in the context of its *Constitutions,* its history, its spirituality, and the world in which it seeks to serve the Lord. That is why this volume, containing the results of the work of the five most recent general congregations, bears the title *Jesuit Life and Mission Today.* At the same time, 450 years link the general congregations of this volume to their predecessors. The first such congregation took place in 1558; the most recent Thirty-fifth Congregation convened in 2008. While they may, indeed, share some long-standing characteristics with those past gatherings, these last five congregations also clearly differ from the previous thirty in ways that will be pointed out later in these pages. An English-language translation from the Latin texts of the decrees of the first thirty congregations, from 1558 to 1957, was published in 1994.[1] This volume carries forward that project for the Thirty-first through Thirty-fifth Congregations in 1965–66, 1974–1975, 1983, 1995, and 2008.

Members of the Society of Jesus will know what a general congregation is in general, what it is for, how it works, and what the last five congregations have done. But since there will be other readers for this volume who are not Jesuits, a brief account of such matters may be helpful here. This introduction is meant to provide some factual information about congregations in general, about the five most recent such meetings, and about the decrees produced by them. It is neither a commentary on nor a history of those congregations.

At this point a commentary, whether the work of one or of many hands, would still be too close in time to events, especially to the most recent Thirty-fifth General Congregation. And a commentary here would either be so brief as to be quite inadequate or so lengthy as vastly to increase the size and complexity of this volume.

Although the decrees of each congregation are preceded by a so-called "Historical Introduction," or "Historical Preface," excerpted from the official minutes of the congregation, a full history of these five congregations in the strict

---

[1] John W. Padberg, S.J., Martin D. O'Keefe, S.J., and John L. McCarthy, S.J., *For Matters of Greater Moment: The First Thirty Jesuit General Congregations* (Saint Louis: The Institute of Jesuit Sources, 1994).

sense of that term cannot be written yet. Any such history would include research not only on the decrees of the congregations but also on those official minutes, on proposals accepted and rejected, on activities and reports of the Jesuit participants internal to the congregations and of personages external to it, such as other Jesuits and officials of the Church. Such a history, if it were to be true to the subject, would also have to involve judgments about those participants, both external and internal, many of whom are still alive or recently deceased, and about their actions. Such judgments, however fair and nuanced they tried to be, might also have to call into question what such people did and why and how they did it.

A general congregation meets essentially for two purposes: first, to elect a new superior general of the Society if the former one has died or has asked permission to resign; secondly, to deal with matters of greater importance in the life of the Society. This institution of general congregations finds its remote origin in a foundational (in several senses of the word) experience of the ten men who were to be the founders of the Society of Jesus.[2]

In 1538, seeking to serve the Lord in and through the Church, they had offered themselves to Pope Paul III. He readily accepted their offer of service and almost immediately sent them off on a variety of missions. They soon realized that this dispersal could lead to the breaking-up of their still informal but very close companionship. So after a series of prayerful and frank meetings, in the spring of 1539 they unanimously resolved to bind themselves together by a vow of obedience to one of their members as superior of the group and to constitute a religious order if the Pope accepted their request and formally established them as such. The so-called "Formula of the Institute," the proposal they eventually presented to the Holy See, is the fundamental rule of the Society. It provided for a "council which must necessarily be convoked to establish or change the *Constitutions* and for other matters of more than ordinary importance."[3]

The *Constitutions* of the Society, especially its eighth part, is the primary source of information about a general congregation; for example, its occasion, membership, place and time of assembly, and manner of reaching decisions. On those foundations one congregation after another has elaborated and modified increasingly detailed *formulae* or procedural norms, such as one will find in decrees of several of the congregations included in this volume. As to when such a meeting should be held, the *Constitutions* declare that "it is presupposed that for

---

[2] Their names and lands of origin are as follows: Ignatius of Loyola, Francis Xavier, Diégo Laínez, Alphonse Salmerón and Nicolás Bobadilla (Spain); Simão Rodrigues (Portugal); Paschase Broët and Jean Codure (France); Pierre Favre and Claude Jay (Savoy). All were graduates of the University of Paris.

[3] "Formula of the Institute," 2, in *The Constitutions of the Society of Jesus and Their Complementary Norms,* ed. John W. Padberg, S.J. (Saint Louis: The Institute of Jesuit Sources 1996), p. 5.

the present it does not seem good in our Lord that such a congregation should be held at definite intervals or very frequently,"[4] and so the Society has never established set times for it; however, for some years in past centuries, the Holy See prescribed recurrent congregations at nine-year intervals. Present practice calls for a congregation to be held for the election of a general superior; in addition, a general may summon one to deal with matters of greater moment for the whole Society or by a meeting of a so-called congregation of procurators, now held every four years precisely to determine whether the state of the Society calls for a general congregation.

According to the "Formula of the Institute," "the council [congregation] . . . should be understood (according to the explanation in our *Constitutions*) to be the greater part of the entire professed Society which can be summoned without grave inconvenience."[5] But almost from the beginning it became clear that such a group could in no way be thus summoned and assembled;[6] and so from the First General Congregation on, the actual membership has consisted of the provincial superiors of all the provinces of the Society, those holding several of the major offices at the Curia (the Roman headquarters of the Society), plus a specified member of delegates chosen from each province. Today those delegates are elected by provincial congregations held in each of the provinces.

The day-to-day activities of a general congregation are detailed in its written *Acta* or minutes prepared by an elected secretary and reviewed by the members. The subject matter of a congregation is basically the *postulata* or topics proposed for deliberation and action that come from the members of the Society individually or more formally through a vote of a provincial congregation or from the delegates themselves. Committees or commissions, set up in accord with the subject matter of the *postulata*, prepare a proposed decree and present it to the whole congregation for discussion, amendment, and finally, after further discussion if necessary, for a vote. A favorable majority of a public vote makes such a document a formal enactment, or *decretum*, of the general congregation, applicable to the whole Society. The modalities of its application in the ensuing years are the responsibility of the superior general and of the provincials through whom he acts.

The decrees of the last five congregations are strikingly different in form and tone from those of the previous thirty congregations, as is immediately evident to anyone comparing their texts as found respectively in *Matters of Greater Moment* and in the present volume, *Jesuit Life and Mission Today*. The overwhelming majority of the decrees in the former volume are in the form of brief,

---

[4] *Constitutions,* no. 677 (p. 330).

[5] "Formula," no. 2 (pp. 5–6).

[6] *Constitutions,* no. 682 (pp. 332–333).

simple, terse, dry texts, most often imposing a particular obligation or prohibiting a specific action. The decrees in this volume, beginning with the Thirty-first Congregation and continuing through the Thirty-fifth, are in many cases quite lengthy and complex, in some cases almost poetic, mandating specific activities often only in administrative matters, seeking instead to evoke responses of mind and will and heart on the part of members of the Society by citing the deepest sources of Jesuit imagery and spirituality in Scripture and in the *Spiritual Exercises*.

In addition to the historical introduction or preface and the decrees themselves, the last five congregations have also mandated the inclusion of several accompanying documents in their published material, especially documents from the Holy See, such as addresses by the pope to members of a congregation or communications from offices of the Holy See, or addresses and homilies by Father General. Earlier congregations seldom contained such complementary documents. Finally, in the present volume the material for each congregation includes an alphabetical list of its members and the provinces to which they belong.

When the decrees themselves, up through the Thirtieth Congregation, were officially published (in Latin alone), it was regularly noted that they were "ad usum nostrorum tantum" (for the use of Ours [i.e., Jesuits]) alone. From the Thirty-first Congregation on, their decrees and associated material, such as membership lists, are readily available. They provide extraordinary primary-source material not only for future authors of historical studies but also for those interested in subjects ranging from religious life to political science, from spirituality to sociology, from theology to demographics.

What follows will very briefly describe the context and the decrees of each congregation in turn.

The Thirty-first Congregation (1965–1966) took place in the context and atmosphere of the Second Vatican Council. Most unusually, it extended over two sessions, the first in the spring and summer of 1965 as the council itself was preparing to hold its fourth session, the second in the fall of 1966, a year after the conclusion of the council. It elected as superior general Father Pedro Arrupe, by birth a Spaniard but a longtime member of and at that time provincial of the Japanese Province. He was the first Basque since Saint Ignatius to govern the Society. The congregation took seriously the recommendation of the council that religious congregations return to their sources, their original charism, for inspiration, and bring up to date the life and structures of their communities and apostolates, that is, work toward *aggiornamento*, as the council expressed it. It also had to deal with to an unprecedented two thousand *postulata* from all over the Society. In response, it proclaimed its desire that the Society "take a very close look at its own nature and mission in order that, truthful to its own vocation, it can renew itself and adapt its life and its activities to the experiences of the Church and the needs of contemporary humankind."[7] It did so in a series of fifty-six decrees on an abundant variety of topics ranging, for example, from the mission of the Society today to the distinction of grades and the formation of Jesuits; from religious life in general and each of the vows in particular to the subject of reading at table; from the task of the Society regarding atheism to topics of the apostolate, such as the better choice and promotion of ministries to the Jesuit priestly apostolate; from ecumenism, the social apostolate, the apostolate of education, scholarly work and research to cultivating the arts in the Society; from details on congregations to the office of General.

The Thirty-second Congregation (1974–1975) affirmed the work of the previous congregation and in answer "to the many requests received from all parts of the Society for clear decisions and definite guidelines concerning our mission today . . . respond [ed] as follows: The mission of the Society of Jesus today is the service of faith of which the promotion of justice is an absolute requirement. For reconciliation with God demands the reconciliation of people with one another." This was intended to orient in a clear way the apostolic life of the Society. Even though the congregation asserted immediately that "in one form or another, this has always been the mission of the Society,"[8] quoting in support of that claim the "Formula of the Institute,"[9] this statement generated more discussions and debates within and outside the Society in the ensuing years than any other decree of any of these five congregations. The congregation's sixteen decrees were all grouped into four general categories: the Society's response to the challenges of our age, development of the apostolic body of the Society, witness to the Gospel in today's circumstances, and structures of congregations and government.

A serious problem arose at this meeting, when the topics that the congregation thought it had to take up included the desirability and possibility of extending the so-called "fourth vow" to all the members of the Society. This obligation stemmed from the expressed desire of the previous congregation to that effect and the large number postulata it had received on the subject. The Holy See wished the congregation not to take up this matter. But a series of unclear communications and missed signals and misunderstandings, too complicated to go into here, between the congregation and the Holy See brought tensions and hurt

---

[7] GC 31, d. l, no. 1 (1/) (In this volume, p. 47). Each decree has its own set of numbers internal to that decree. In this edition, however, **boldface** numbers followed by a slash (/) have been added at the beginning of a passage, running consecutively from the first paragraph to the last of a congregation's decrees. In this case, **1**/ refers to the first paragraph in the decrees of GC 31.

[8] GC 32, d. 4. nos. 1–3 (47/–48/; in this volume, p. 298).

[9] See the somewhat more extended account in *Together as a Companionship,* by John W. Padberg, S.J. (Saint Louis: The Institute of Jesuit Sources, 1994) passim. especially pp. 88–91.

feelings on both sides. The upshot was that the congregation could do nothing to bring about such an extension.

The Thirty-third Congregation began on September 2, 1983. It took place amid a series of unusual events in the two years before it convened. Already in 1980 Father Arrupe had informed Pope John Paul II of his desire to resign his office because of advancing age. The Pope asked him to postpone this move. Then, on August 7, 1981, Father Arrupe suffered a serious stroke. On October 5 of that same year, the Pope, in a quite unprecedented move, named Father Paolo Dezza, an Italian Jesuit, as his personal delegate to govern the Society and to see to the long-term preparation for a congregation. Father Dezza had long been an official in the Society, and for many years he had served as advisor to or member of Vatican offices. Slightly less than five months later, on February 27, 1982, in a meeting with all the provincials of the Society, the Pope said that he was confident that a congregation could be convoked later that year. On December 8, 1982, Father Dezza did summon a congregation to commence in the following September. Its major task was twofold—to deal with the proposed resignation of Father Arrupe and to elect a new superior general.

On September 3 the congregation accepted Father Arrupe's resignation and expressed its gratitude to him in "thunderously protracted applause." On September 13, 1983, on the first ballot it elected as superior general of the Society Father Peter-Hans Kolvenbach. Originally from the Netherlands, Father Kolvenbach, a member of the vice-province of the Near East, had done special studies in linguistics, taught at St. Joseph University in Beirut, and served as superior of his vice-province; at the time of his election, he was rector of the Pontifical Oriental Institute in Rome.

It soon became clear that the congregation did not want to produce a lengthy series of documents. It first dealt with some necessary governance material on province and general congregations and confirmed the norms on poverty approved *ad experimentum* by the Holy See at the end of the previous congregation. In addition to those matters, it decided to produce a single major decree *(decretum unicum),* which came to be entitled "Companions of Jesus Sent into Today's World." The decree's first part dealt with the life of Jesuits as members of the Society and the second part with its apostolic efforts. In addition to speaking of the experiences of the Society, the context in which it worked, and the summons and requests that had come from recent popes, the decree reaffirmed the Society's mission as expressed in the two previous congregations, called for fidelity to its "way of proceeding," and spoke of the prerequisites for credibility in its life and mission.

Almost ten years later, in September 1992, Father Kolvenbach announced his intention to hold another general congregation. The Thirty-fourth Congregation opened on January 5, 1995. Its central concern was the revision of the law proper to the Society. Over several years "an extensive and meticulous work of preparation" for such a revision had been going on. Its success was evident in the way its individual segments were presented, considered, discussed, and approved at various times in the course of the Thirty-fourth Congregation. This all led to a final approval of clarifications and revisions in the text of the *Constitutions* and its publication along with the *Complementary Norms to the* Constitutions. As for the twenty-six more particular decrees of the congregation, they were grouped into five major sections, along with an introduction and a conclusion. After the introduction describing the Society as "united with Christ on mission," the Society looked at that mission itself in the first section, and at its members as servants of Christ's mission. That mission included the service of faith and the promotion of justice as set down in the Thirty-second and confirmed in the Thirty-third Congregation; but here it broadened and deepened that mission to include, as inextricably linked and intertwined in it, inculturation and interreligious dialogue. The four other major groupings of decrees, are entitled "Aspects of Jesuit Life for Mission," dealing with matters internal to the life of the Society; "In the Church," treating of the Jesuit attitudes of service in the Church, ecumenism, cooperation with the laity in mission, and Jesuits vis-à-vis the situation of women in church and civil society. The particular and detailed list of decrees in the next two sections, entitled "Dimensions and Particular Sectors of Our Mission" and "Structures of Government," can be seen in the table of contents of the congregation itself further on in this volume, as is true of all the other congregations. Finally, the conclusion developed a set of eight "characteristics of our way of proceeding."

The Thirty-fifth General Congregation began on January 7, 2008. The immediate circumstance that led to the congregation was the request by Father Kolvenbach that a general congregation accept his resignation and then move to the election of a new superior general. As he himself said on January 8, when he proffered that resignation, "I feel that the Society of Jesus has the right to be governed and animated by a Jesuit in full capacity of his spiritual and corporal gifts and not by a companion whose energies will continue to diminish because of his age— soon eighty years old—and because of the consequences of that age, especially in the area of health." [10] On January 14, with affection for Father Kolvenbach and gratitude for all he had done for the Society, the congregation voted to accept his resignation.

After four days of prayer, reflection, and one-on-one discussions among the delegates themselves, the congregation on January 19 elected as superior general of the Society of Jesus Father Adolfo Nicolás. A Spaniard by birth, he entered the Society in 1953, went to Japan in 1960, and after ordination and graduate studies returned to Japan to become a professor of systematic theology in Tokyo. Successive responsibilities followed: he was called to serve as director of the East

---

[10] *GC* 35, Historical Introduction (in this volume, p. 716).

Asian Pastoral Institute in Manila, rector for Asian Jesuit students of theology there, provincial of Japan, work among poor immigrants in Tokyo, and, in 2004, president of the East Asian Jesuit Assistancy Conference of provincials.

The congregation adopted six decrees. The first was a response to two actions by Pope Benedict XVI—a letter of January 10 to Father Kolvenbach as the congregation began and an address to its members at a meeting with him on February 21. Both the letter and especially the meeting and his address to the delegates were characterized by expressions of warm affection for and confidence in the Society. The congregation in turn responded in its first decree with a promise to serve the Church "with renewed vigor and zeal."

The other five decrees treated respectively identity, mission, obedience, governance, and collaboration. The second decree dealt with "rediscovering the charism of the Society." In language at times poetic, it reflected on what it is to be a Jesuit. It affirmed as fundamental to any Jesuit "an experience that places him, quite simply, with Christ at the heart of the world." The third decree, on "challenges to our mission today," made clear that the Jesuit response is a continuing commitment to the service of faith and the promotion of justice in which inculturation and interreligious dialogue must be ever-present elements. Such a response demands reconciliation with God, with one another, and with creation. This last-named obligation involves a more explicit concern about globalization and ecology than previous congregations had expressed. The fourth decree affirmed that obedience in the life of the Society is grounded in a desire "to be sent on mission in the image of the Son and so to serve the Lord in companionship." Hence the famous so-called "fourth vow" of obedience, requiring "total availability to serve the Church wherever the pope sends us." The fifth decree on governance in the Society, far more a "nuts and bolts" document then any of the others, is important in helping "to give a body to the spirit," by attempting to better organize central governance in Rome as it affects the several geographic regions of the Society, its provinces, and its local communities. All this it did by setting down principles and practices that should guide "governance at the service of universal mission." Finally, the last decree affirmed more strongly than ever before "collaboration at the heart of mission"—collaboration with laity, with other religious, with people who share Jesuit values, if not in some instances their beliefs.

To conclude then: The decrees of the last five general congregations contained in this volume are both a summing-up and a moving forward. They sum up a special chapter in the history of the Society of Jesus from 1965 to 2008. Those five congregations all took place in the short-range and long-range aftermaths of Vatican II, and they wrote the beginning of a new chapter in that history. GC 31 in 1965–1966 elected Father Pedro Arrupe as superior general and took seriously the recommendation of the council that religious congregations return to their sources for inspiration and bring up to date the structures of their communities and apostolates. GC 32 in 1974–1975 affirmed the work of the previous congregation and its famous statement that the "mission of the Society of Jesus today is the service of faith of which the promotion of justice is an absolute requirement," and it oriented in a special way the external or apostolic life of the Society. The illness of Father Arrupe occasioned GC 33 in 1983, which elected Father Peter-Hans Kolvenbach as general. GC 34 in 1995 both strongly reaffirmed that earlier mission statement and broadened it to include interreligious dialogue and inculturation. Its most important accomplishment was to provide for the Society a set of current norms governing how it was to live and work, norms that are complementary to the Jesuit *Constitutions* themselves. Father Kolvenbach convoked GC 35 to submit his resignation because of the diminution of the energy and health he needed to carry out his responsibilities as general superior. The congregation accepted that request and, in a sense, closed a chapter of more than forty years in Jesuit history. In electing the new general, Father Adolfo Nicolás, and producing its six decrees, GC 35 moved the Society forward to build on the accomplishments of those four decades for Jesuit life and mission today.

John W. Padberg, S.J.

Editor

In the 450th year since the
    First General Congregation of the Society of Jesus.

Abbreviations Used in the Footnotes

AA	*(Apostolicam Actuositatem) Decree on the Apostolate of the Laity.* Vatican II, 1965
AAS	*Acta Apostolicae Sedis*
ActRSJ	*Acta Romana Societatis Iesu*
AG	*(Ad Gentes) Decree on the Church's Missionary Activity.* Vatican II, 1965
AR	*Acta Romana Societatis Iesu*
CCEO	*Code of Canon Law for the Eastern Churches*
CD	*(Christus Dominus) Decree on the Bishops' Pastoral Office in the Church.* Vatican II, 1965
CIC	*Code of Canon Law*
CollDecr	*Collectio Decretorum Congregationum Generalium Societatis Iesu.* 1961
Coll. d.	*Collectio Decretorum Congregationum Generalium Societatis Iesu.* 1961
Cons(t.)	*Constitutiones Societatis Iesu*[1]
ConsMHSJ, I	*Monumenta Constitutionum praevia.* Sources and records previous to the texts of the *Constitutions*
D.	Decree
DH	*(Dignitatis Humanae) Declaration on Religious Freedom.* Vatican II, 1965
DV	*(Dei Verbum) Dogmatic Constitution on Divine Revelation.* Vatican II, 1965

---

[1] For references to the *Constitutions of the Society of Jesus,* see, for example, *The Constitutions of the Society of Jesus and Their Complementary Norms: A Complete English Translation of the Official Latin Text* (St. Louis: Institute of Jesuit Sources, 1996).

EE	*Spiritual Exercises of St. Ignatius (=SpEx)*
Epit	*Epitome Instituti Societatis Iesu, 1962*
ES	Motu Proprio *Ecclesiae Sanctae,* 1966
ET	Pope Paul VI, Adhortatio Apostolica "Evangelica Testificatio," June 29, 1971. *AAS* (1971), p. 497 sq.
FI	*Formula of the Institute of the Society of Jesus*[2]
FGC	*Formula of a General Congregation*
FPG	*Formula of a Provincial Congregation*
GC	General Congregation of the Society of Jesus
GE	*(Gravissimum Educationis) Declaration on Christian Education.* Vatican II, 1965
GenExam	*General Examen*[3]
GS	*(Gaudium et Spes) Pastoral Constitution on the Church in the Modern World.* Vatican II, 1965
LG	*(Lumen Gentium) Dogmatic Constitution on the Church.* Vatican II, 1964
MHSJ	Monumenta Historica Societatis Jesu
MI	Monumenta Ignatiana
MNAD	*Epistolae P. Hieronymi Nadal*
n(n).	Number(s)
NA	*(Nostra Aetate) Declaration on the Relationship of the Church to Non-Christian Religions.* Vatican II, 1965
NC	*Normae Complementariae Constitutionum Societatis*
NG	*Normae Generales de Studiis*
OC	*Obros Completas de S. Ignacio de Loyola*

---

[2] References to the *Formula of the Institute* present a special problem, in that several ways of numbering them have been employed in the course of the centuries. The numbers used here are those employed in *The Constitutions of the Society of Jesus and Their Complementary Norms,* cited above.

[3] References to this document can be found in *The Constitutions of the Society of Jesus and Their Complementary Norms,* cited in n. 1 above.

OE	*(Orientalium Ecclesiarum) Decree on Eastern Catholic Churches.* Vatican II, 1964
OT	*(Optatam Totius) Decree on Priestly Formation.* Vatican II, 1965
PC	*(Perfectae Caritatis) Decree on the Adaptation and Renewal of the Religious Life.* Vatican II, 1965
PL	*Patrologia Latina*
PO	*(Presbyterorum Ordinis) Decree on theMinistry and Life of Priests.* Vatican II, 1965
SC	*(Sacrosanctum Concilium) Constitution on the Sacred Liturgy.* Vatican II, 1963
SpEx	*Spiritual Exercises of St. Ignatius*
UR	*(Unitatis Redintegratio) Decree on Ecumenism.* Vatican II, 1964

THE 31st GENERAL CONGREGATION OF THE SOCIETY OF JESUS

May 7–July 15, 1965

and

September 8–November 17, 1966

LETTER OF PROMULGATION FROM FATHER GENERAL

To the Whole Society

Reverend Fathers and dear Brothers in Christ,

Pax Christi

The decrees of the Thirty-first General Congregation I am sending with this present letter in the name of that Congregation to all the provinces, vice-provinces and missions so that they might be published in the houses of the Society.

In virtue of the powers given to me by the General Congregation[1] I have suspended until January 1, 1968, the date on which Decree 11, on the norms of promotion to last vows, takes effect. This is so that the advancement to final vows of all of those who pronounce such vows after that date might be adapted to these new norms, but not how-ever the advancement of those who take final vows before that date. All the rest of the decrees, in accord with the norm of the Formula of the General Congregation,[2] *enter into force from the date of this present letter.*

I commend myself earnestly to your Sacrifices and prayers,

The servant of all of you in Christ,

Pedro Arrupe
General of the Society of Jesus

Rome, February 15, 1967

---

[1] See D. 56, n. 2, 3°e.

[2] *Formula* C.G., n. 144, §2, 3°.

A

HISTORICAL PREFACE

TO THE DECREES

OF THE 31st GENERAL CONGREGATION

Excerpted from the Official Minutes of the Congregation

HISTORICAL PREFACE TO THE DECREES
OF THE 31st GENERAL CONGREGATION

Excerpted from the Official Minutes of the Congregation

When Very Reverend Father John Baptist Janssens died on October 5, 1964, at the beginning of his nineteenth year as General of the Society of Jesus, Reverend John L. Swain was the same day formally appointed Vicar-General of the Society, in accord with the will left by Fr. Janssens. Father Swain, upon the advice of the Fathers Assistant, announced in his letter of November 13 of the same year that the General Congregation was to take place during the next year, 1965. However, he did not set a specific date for its convocation because of the uncertainty about when the fourth session of the Second Vatican Council would be held and also because of the interval needed to complete the preparations for the work of the Congregation which Father Janssens had begun. In another letter dated January 13, 1965, Father Vicar, again with the consent of his Assistants, set May 6 as the date for the gathering of all the delegates in Rome, so that the first formal session of the Congregation might be held on the following day.

On the day appointed all the members of the Congregation were present in Rome at the curia and at the house of writers next door except for the provincials and the electors of both of the provinces of Poland. (From these provinces the provincials and two of the electors were able to come before the third full meeting of the Congregation. For the other two electors, two substitutes were provided.) Also unable to be present were the provincial and the electors of the province of Bohemia and all of the delegates to the Congregation from the province of Hungary and the vice-provinces of Lithuania and Rumania as well as from the missions of Latvia and Estonia. The provincial of Hungary and the vice-provincial of Slovakia were each able to designate a single priest to serve in their stead. In order that these localities of the Society might be present in some way at the Congregation, Father Vicar named as procurators Fathers Wenceslaus Fert from the province of Bohemia and Father Bruno Markaitis from the vice province of Lithuania. In the same way, in order to take advantage of their intimate knowledge of affairs, Father Vicar also named Father Thomas Byrne who had previously held the office as substitute Assistant, and Father Paul Mailleux, the delegate of Father General for the Byzantine Rite.

1. The Beginning of the Congregation
(From the Minutes, Acta 1)

On May 7, 1965, the first Friday of May, after the delegates had been received in audience by the Supreme Pontiff, Paul VI, and had received his apostolic benediction, all of the members of the Congregation, that is, all the electors who were present and who had a proven right to be there, entered the assembly hall of the Congregation in the order assigned. After the hymn to the Holy Spirit and the accompanying prayers were recited, the Congregation by unanimous vote declared itself full and legitimate. After this, one of the electors, about whose right to be present some doubt had arisen and who for this reason had been left waiting outside the hall, was admitted to the applause of all those present.

Then Father Vicar gave the prescribed address in which he rendered an account of all that had been done after the death of the General, and he spoke specifically of the preparation for the Congregation and exhorted all those present to that peace, harmony, and faithfulness by which this one desire might flourish amid such diversity of opinion: that the Society of Jesus, faithful to the spirit of its founder, might fully respond to the needs of the Church.

After the appropriate voting, Father Pedro M. Abellan, a delegate from the province of Toledo, was elected Secretary. He was also at the same time the Procurator General of the Society. As Assistant Secretary the Congregation elected Father Aloysius Renard from the province of Southern Belgium. The other details normally pertaining to the election of the General of the Society were, with the approval of the Congregation, deferred in order that before that election certain problems might be discussed.

2. The Election of the Deputies "ad detrimenta"
(From the Minutes, Acta 2)

Once the prior meetings of the assistancies had been held, in which, according to the norms of the *Formula,* names of candidates could be proposed, on May 8 the following were elected as deputies "ad detrimenta" in several ballots and a single counting of the votes: From the Italian Assistancy, Father Paolo Dezza, delegate from the Venice-Milan province; from the German Assistancy, Father Anthony Pinsker, delegate from the Austrian province; from the French Assistancy, Father Antoine Delchard, delegate from the province of Northern France; from the Spanish Assistancy, Father Lucio Craveiro da Silva, the provincial of Portugal; from the English Assistancy, Father Angus MacDougall, provincial of Upper Canada; from the American Assistancy, Father John J. McMahon, delegate from the New York province; from the Slavic Assistancy, Father John G. Fucek, provincial of Croatia; from the Southern Latin American Assistancy, Father Anthony Aquino, provincial of Central Brazil; from the Indian Assistancy, Father Edward

Mann, provincial of Bombay; from the Northern Latin American Assistancy, Father Henrico Gutierrez Martin del Campo, delegate from the province of Southern Mexico; from the East Asian Assistancy, Father Leo Cullum, delegate from the Philippine province.

Since the Supreme Pontiff had wanted to meet with all the delegates to the Congregation before the Congregation itself began, there was no need to designate certain members to go to him now in order to ask the papal blessing.

3. The Election of Father General
(From the Minutes, Acta *3–8)*

1. Since some postulata had proposed that before the election of the General certain questions should be treated, and especially the question of the length of office of the General, the Congregation thought that in order to proceed to a peaceful election it was necessary to consider this question attentively before the election itself. Therefore, with the inclusion of the delegates who were present for the Congregation only for business and not also for elections, that is the procurators, a discussion took place during five sessions both on the duration of the office of Father General as well as on the prior question of whether the Congregation had the power to pass laws before the election of the General. Finally, on May 17, the Congregation decided not to pass any decree at that time but, once the election had been finished, to examine the matter thoroughly and to make decisions in the plenitude of its power.

2. It was decided, therefore, that the four days for the gathering of information were to begin on the next day, May 18, and, in accord with the proposal of the Vicar, Father Maurice Giuliani, delegate from the Paris province, was selected to give the exhortation on the day of election itself. For the job of "Inclusor," that is the one who formally locks the members of the Congregation in the hall, Father George Bottereau, the Superior of the Curia, was chosen. In accord with the provisions of the *Formula,* the judges who would deal with any question of "ambition" were, besides Father Vicar, the oldest professed from each of the assistancies, that is Fathers Paolo Dezza, Petrus van Gestel, Jean M. Le Blond, Severian Azcona, William J. Murphy, Joannes B. Kozelj, Isidore Griful, Melchior M. Balaguer, Francis Robinson and Leo Cullum.

3. On May 22, in accord with all the prescriptions of the *Formula* drawn from the Constitutions and from the decrees of previous General Congregations, Reverend Father Pedro Arrupe was by majority vote on the third ballot elected Superior General of the Society. He had been up to that time provincial of the province of Japan. A formal certification of this election was passed immediately and signed by the Vicar-General. Without any delay Father Paolo Molinari, the

Postulator General of the Society, informed the Holy Father and he sent to the new General and to the whole Society his special blessing.

4. The Election of the Secretaries and the Deputies for the Screening of Postulata
(From the Minutes, Acta 9)

1. After the election of the General, the delegates who were not formally electors were called back to the hall, that is the Secretary of the Society, Father James W. Naughton, the Treasurer General, Father Romulus Durocher, and the Procurators, Fathers Thomas Byrne, Wenceslaus Fert, Paul Mailleux and Bruno Markaitis.

2. By majority votes in secret ballots the following were then elected. First, on a separate ballot, as Secretary of the Congregation, Father Pedro M. Abellan who had also previously been elected secretary for the election of the General. Then on a single ballot his two assistants, Fathers John A. McGrail, provincial of Detroit, and Vincenzo Monachino, delegate from the Roman Province.

3. After the meeting of the various Assistancies, the following were elected deputies for the screening of postulata: From their respective Assistancies: Italian, Father Roberto Tucci, delegate of the Neapolitan province; German, Father Francis von Tattenbach, delegate of the Upper German province; French, Father Maurice Giuliani, delegate of the Paris province; Spanish, Father Victor Blajot, delegate of the Bolivian province; English, Father Piet Fransen, delegate of the Northern Belgian province; American, Father John G. Ford, delegate of the New England province; Slavic, Father Stephan Dzierzek, provincial of the Greater Polish province; Southern Latin American, Father Ferdinand Larrain, delegate of the province of Chile; Indian, Father Aemilius Ugarte, delegate of the province of Madurai; Northern Latin American, Father Aloysius Achaerandio, delegate of the Central American vice-province; East Asian, Father Charles McCarthy, delegate of the Far Eastern province.

5. The Commissions on Substantive Affairs
(From the Minutes, Acta 9, 10, 16, 42, 45, 92)

In order better to carry on the work of the Congregation, Father General together with the deputation for screening postulata, to which the Congregation had entrusted this, set up six commissions. Many of them were later divided into subcommissions and even the subcommissions finally into sections. These commissions and subcommissions were as follows:

First Commission: Governance

Subcommissions:

1. Governance in general
2. Universal governance
3. Governance of provinces
4. Congregations

Second Commission: Ministries and Apostolate

Subcommissions:

1. The ordering of ministries in the whole Society
2. Foreign missions
3. Education and the scientific or scholarly apostolate
4. Pastoral ministries and ecumenism
5. Social apostolate and communications media

Third Commission: Studies of Jesuits

Subcommissions:

1. Formation in general
2. The ordinary course of studies
3. Special studies

Fourth Commission: Religious Life

Subcommissions:

1. The nature and purpose of religious and apostolic life in the Society today
2. The vows in general
3. Poverty
4. The spiritual life
5. Spiritual formation
6. Tertianship
7. Common life and discipline

Fifth Commission: Preservation and Renewal of the Institute

Subcommissions:

1. The substantials of the Institute
2. Admission to the Society and to holy orders and dismissal from the Society

3. Grades in the Society

4. Temporal coadjutors

5. Knowledge of the Institute

Sixth Commission: **The Mission of the Society Today**

In order that the apportionment of the members of the Congregation to the various commissions and subcommissions might be easier and more acceptable, each member was asked to indicate quite freely what commission he would prefer to work on, and the deputation for assigning commission membership took account of these wishes.

Later other commissions or groups or committees were set up. For example, there were a special commission which was to help in writing the texts of decrees, a commission on procedure, a group of canonists who would be of help especially to the first and fifth commissions, a group of experts who were charged with the stylistic editing of the language of the decrees and putting them in order, a group of experts to revise the *Formulas* of the Congregation, and other groups of delegates established for taking care of whatever necessary work arose.

6. The Two Sessions of the Congregation
(From the Minutes, Acta *33–35, 38, 41–43, 46, 49–51, 54, 57, 58)*

1. What had never before happened in the history of the Society occurred at this Congregation. It was divided into two sessions. The Congregation took into account the tremendous amount of work generated by the more than 1,900 postulata, the grave and serious nature of the questions to be treated, the immense expectations of the entire Society, the imminence of the fourth session of the Second Vatican Council and other conditions of both the circumstances and the times. It examined various proposals (for example: establishing a group of deputies who, with the authority of the Congregation would complete the work it had begun, or the calling of another General Congregation within three to five years). Finally after two months of work the Congregation decided to adjourn temporarily on July 15, 1965, and to continue its work in September of the following year, 1966 (cf. d. 49). Later in a letter of Dec. 8, 1965, to all major superiors, the General set September 8, 1966, as the date for convening the second session. At the same time he gave to the members of the Congregation the opportunity for a triduum of spiritual recollection on the 5th, 6th and 7th of the same month at the Curia itself.

2. During the time between the sessions the work of the Congregation did not cease. Either through letters or by frequent meetings of delegates with other Jesuit experts a variety of reports was prepared and sent to all the members of the Congregation or distributed to them at the beginning of the second session.

3. After the triduum of recollection in which Father General himself proposed the material for the points for meditation on each of the days, the Congregation began again on September 8, 1966, the feast of the Nativity of Our Lady. The same members were present who had been there at the first session and in addition the new regional assistants and provincials who had in the meantime been named by Father General. Absent, however, were the provincials and delegates from Poland who had not been able to obtain permission from their government to come. Also absent were Fathers Frederic Buuck, delegate from the Lower German province; Edward Mann, former provincial of Bombay; John Rocha, former Assistant for Southern Latin America; John Sehnem, former provincial of Southern Brazil; Anton Pinsker, delegate from the province of Austria; and Jean Richard, former provincial of Montreal, all of whom were hindered by illness or some other obstacle. The following were also absent at first, but they all later arrived: Fathers John Terpstra, provincial of the Netherlands; Daniel Villanova, provincial of Sicily; John Correia Afonso, provincial of Bombay; Leo Rosa, provincial of Venice-Milan; Abdallah Dagher, delegate of the vice-province of the Near East; and Ferdinando Larrain, delegate of the province of Chile.

4. In both sessions there were the same secretaries, deputations and commissions. But since Fathers Anton Pinsker and Edward Mann who had been deputies "ad detrimenta" in the first session were now absent, in their place were elected Father John Schasching, provincial of Austria from the German Assistancy, and Father Melchior M. Balaguer, delegate of the province of Bombay from the Assistancy of India.

7. Procedural Matters and Public Information Matters
(From the Minutes, Acta 1, 2, 4, 5, 10, 12, 17, 46, 48, 50–52,
54, 56, 61, 62, 87, 88, 92, 96, 98)

1. In order to save time in so large a Congregation and with such an amount of work to be done, certain methods of procedure were adopted right from the beginning which in certain matters differed from the norms of the *Formula of the Congregation* or added to those norms. The following are the more important examples. Each delegate had permission to speak only once in the same plenary session on the same business (later the amount of speaking time was cut down to seven minutes); for the balloting on substantive matters red and green electric lights were generally used, the results of which were electronically calculated; the Acta or minutes of the sessions were not read publicly but each of the members of the Congregation received copies of them (see *Formula of the General Congregation,* nn. 16, 24, paragraph 2, 121); the "Relationes praeviae," that is the first formal reports, and the definitive judgments (see *Formula of the General Congregation,* n. 119) were prepared by subcommissions but they were approved by the chairman of the commission and by the chairmen of all of the subcommissions of that com-

mission; the chairmen of the various commissions helped Father General in arranging all of the work.

2. In the second session, at the suggestion of the special commission on the manner of proceeding which had been set up toward the end of the first session, the Congregation, first as an experiment and then definitively, approved new rules or norms, the most important of which were the following: *(a)* Father General named as Vice Chairman of the sessions Fathers Paolo Dezza, the General Assistant; Jean Calvez, delegate of the province of Paris; and George P. Klubertanz, delegate of the province of Wisconsin. They helped him in preparing and chairing the sessions of the Congregation. *(b)* Those speakers who before a session had asked permission to speak were given seven minutes. Those who during a session sought that permission (see *Formula of the General Congregation,* n. 121), received five minutes. *(c)* During the discussion any member of the Congregation could propose "a motion of order" which, if the Congregation approved it, could change the order of the agenda which had been proposed by the chairman and the vice chairmen. *(d)* Speakers were allowed to propose amendments to the text of a decree and these amendments were voted on before the full text itself came to a vote. *(e)* The commissions and subcommissions could have "open sessions" in which any of the members of the Congregation could be present and speak but could not vote unless they were themselves members of that commission or subcommission. *(f)* Some Fathers who were not members of the Congregation were brought in to help write the Acta or the minutes of the Congregation. They received permission to attend the plenary sessions.

3. As far as vernacular languages went, from the beginning of the Congregation approval was given to speakers to use English, French, Spanish and Italian provided that beforehand they provided a Latin summary of their speech. Very few, however, made use of this permission.

The question of using "simultaneous translations" was more than once taken up. Toward the end of the first session the Congregation decided that such a system was not to be introduced for the present Congregation. But they recommended to Father General that he study the whole thing with a view toward the next general congregation. In the second session, at the proposal of the commission on procedure, the Congregation first gave its approval to use simultaneous translations in the "open sessions of the commissions" and later to use them as an experiment in six of the plenary sessions.

4. Since not a few people asked that in some way Jesuits and also non-Jesuits might be kept informed of the actions of the Congregation, while at the same time the *Formula of the General Congregation* (n. 25 paragraph 3) as well as the freedom of the Congregation and of the delegates demanded a certain caution, right from the beginning the Congregation set up an "Information Office" after

a consideration and discussion of the matter. It was made up of Fathers who were not members of the Congregation but who did have permission to attend its sessions. Newsletters written by them were reviewed according to a set of norms by a commission of delegates which had been established for that purpose by Father General. There were also regulations for the news which the delegates themselves sent out privately.

8. The Introductory Decrees
(From the Minutes, Acta 32, 33, 38, 49, 105–108)

The General Congregation wished to preface its decrees with three documents which serve as a sort of general introduction:

1. First, "The Mission of the Society of Jesus Today" (d. 1): The first draft had been prepared in the first session by Commission VI. In the interval between sessions a mixed commission made up of members from the fourth and the sixth commissions was set up which, with the help of many other experts and after several attempts, worked out a new text. Once the comments of the delegates had been received at the beginning of the second session, this new text was again revised and after discussion was approved by the Congregation on November 16, 1966.

2. Secondly, "On the Renewal of Our Law" (d. 2): This decree sets forth the principles and conditions which are to be observed in the renewal of our law. The subcommission on the substantials of the Institute prepared this decree. After the usual deliberation and discussion, it was approved at the same time as the first decree.

3. Thirdly, "The Task of the Society with Regard to Atheism" (d. 3) : The sixth commission worked out the text for this decree in the first session in order that the Society might immediately take on the responsibility asked of it by the Supreme Pontiff in his audience on May 7, 1965, "in order that with all your united strength you might oppose atheism most forcefully." The decree was approved on July 5, 1965, and on July 15 by a unanimous vote the Congregation decided on its immediate promulgation so that without delay the Society could put in the public domain its response to the will of the Supreme Pontiff.

9. The Conservation and Renewal of the Institute
(From the Minutes, Acta 52–54, 57)

Not a few postulata which were sent to the Congregation asked either explicitly or implicitly that it be easier to deal with changing the substantials of the Institute, not excepting those which are contained in the *Formula of the Institute.* On the other hand, other postulata, out of fidelity to the spirit of St. Ignatius, insistently wanted the Congregation to declare that our Institute maintained its full force and obligation even in our times. The Congregation therefore thought that it had to act on the revision of decrees 12–16 of the Collection of Decrees. Having taken on this most serious of questions, the subcommission on the substantials of the Institute prepared two reports. However, because of the length of time needed for their research work, the reports could not be discussed in full session although they had been given to the members in the first period of the Congregation. In the interval between the two sessions, after consulting with other experts, the draft of a decree was written from the material in those two reports and discussions were held on that draft in the usual way in the second session. This discussion, however, brought on a new revision of the draft out of which finally came the definitive text which the Congregation approved on September 19, 1966 (d. 4). In that decree, because of certain extrinsic difficulties, the Congregation did not want to retain the old prohibition against introducing changes in the text of the Constitutions themselves as written by Ignatius, but they expressly committed this matter to the judgment of the General. In addition, the Congregation wanted Title I in the future edition of the collection of decrees to be called "The Institute and its parts," and section III which is to be entitled "The conservation and renewal of the Institute," to be placed before section II which is entitled "Interpretation and dispensation from the Institute."

10. The Distinction in Grades
(From the Minutes, Acta *33–35, 37, 38, 42–43, 55–59, 61, 62, 65, 67–73)*

1. This was one of the most serious and one of the most lengthily treated questions in the Congregation. There was a very large number of postulata about it, and they came either from the provincial congregations or from individual Jesuits. Some of them simply wanted to abolish the distinction of grades in the Society. Others wanted its opportuneness at least to be subject to judgment. Yet others asked that it be preserved absolutely unchanged. Some vehemently complained about the norms presently used for the promotion to solemn profession. . . . Given the situation and the time available, the subcommission on grades consulted with experts in law and history, investigated the origin of grades and their establishment, and their development in the old and in the restored Society. It examined the arguments set forth on either side of the question and it proposed to the Congregation various solutions. A very large number of written comments came from the members of the Congregation, and after discussion in many plenary sessions, the Congregation finally came to this conclusion in its first period: *(a)* A decree would not be passed on removing the distinction of grades between the professed and spiritual coadjutors. *(b)* There was to be no decision that all the scholastics would first take the vows of the spiritual coadjutor and that some of them could later be promoted to the solemn profession. *(c)* The current norms for admission to the profession were to be revised. *(d)* It was rec-

ommended to Father General that he set up a commission with the responsibility to investigate the whole problem; this investigation was to include the advantages and disadvantages of granting the solemn profession also to temporal coadjutors (see d. 5 n. 2).

2. But, among other things, between the two sessions of the Congregation two documents of the Church were published, namely the conciliar decree "Perfectae Caritatis" and the apostolic letter "Ecclesiae Sanctae." At least to some members of the Congregation this seemed to change the whole state of the question; to others, however, it seemed that the distinction of grades in the Society was repugnant neither to the mind nor to the will of the Church. Because of all this, in September, 1966, the controversy started up again. So that everybody might knowledgeably carry on discussion on the disputed questions, first of all, a group of eleven experts prepared an informational report on the principal points in law which had to be considered with reference to this question. Then four speakers were designated, one by one. Two of them were to give the reasons for removing the distinction of grades and two the reasons for retaining it. Besides this, everyone had plenty of opportunity to speak. A day of consideration, of reflection and prayer was then provided for and all were urged to offer Masses and prayers to God by which they might ask light to find His will in so important and serious a decision. Finally on October 7th, the feast of Our Lady of the Rosary, in secret ballots the Congregation decided the following: *(a)* The grade of spiritual coadjutor was not to be here and now suppressed, nor were "Definitors" to be set up who could decide together with Father General on the suppression of this grade either in law or in practice. *(b)* But immediately after the conclusion of this 31st General Congregation a commission was to be established which was to investigate the whole question of the grade of spiritual coadjutor and which would inform the next congregation of procurators about the results of its research in order that the congregation of procurators might decide whether a general congregation should be called in order to deal with this matter (see d. 5 n. 1). *(c)* A discussion was to begin immediately on revising the norms for promotion to the grade of professed of four solemn vows.

11. The Permanent Diaconate
(From the Minutes, Acta *43, 45, 48, 81–83, 90)*

The question of whether to allow perpetual deacons in the Society was brought up in some postulata in connection with the question of temporal coadjutors. Toward the end of the first session the Congregation decided that the whole question ought to be more accurately investigated in the light of the teachings of the Council and the question of the distinction of grades in the Society. This was done by the appropriate subcommission and by a certain number of experts. Their proposals were discussed in the second session, and the Congregation judged that it ought not to act on the question of introducing the permanent diaconate into the Society at the present time, but rather that it ought to remove whatever obstacles might stand in the way of it being later introduced, committing that to the prudence of the General (d. 6). As for the religious vows which would be pronounced by such deacons, whether in the future they would be the vows of the temporal coadjutors or the spiritual coadjutors, the Congregation did not pass a decree because the function of deacons was not yet clearly defined in the documents of the Church, and because the Holy See intended to give further details on this for all religious.

12. Temporal Coadjutors
(From the Minutes, Acta *43, 45, 48, 60-63, 79, 104, 105)*

The fact that the number of temporal coadjutors in the Society has been in constant decrease from the beginning of the twentieth century was not the only reason why the General Congregation began to take up this problem. Very many postulata asked for such a treatment, and they desired that the nature of the vocation of the temporal coadjutor would be more clearly defined, that the esteem for this vocation should be shown in actual practice, that the coadjutor brothers would have access to more types of responsibilities and, for these reasons, that their formation—spiritual, cultural and technical—might be further developed. Having all of this before them, the subcommission on temporal coadjutors prepared a draft of the decree and after receiving the comments of the Fathers, corrected it and presented it for debate. The Congregation did not wish to take a vote on this draft in the first session in order that so serious a question could be considered at greater length and allowed to mature. Therefore, with the help of other designated experts a new draft of the decree was written in the interval between the two sessions. Research also took place into what temporal coadjutors themselves from various regions of the Society thought about their vocation and about a decree from the Congregation. These opinions along with the new draft decree were given to the members of the Congregation in the second session. After the usual written comments the question was again discussed in plenary sessions. Finally the Congregation voted on October 12, 1966, on a definitive text and on amendments which had been proposed by the delegates (d. 7). As far as the name of the grade itself, the Congregation decided that in the Latin decree itself the name "coadiutor temporalis" was to be retained but in the vernacular languages it could be translated according to the custom or usage of each region.

13. The Spiritual Formation of Jesuits
(From the Minutes, Acta *82–86, 106, 107, 114)*

The Congregation received more than 160 postulata in which, for a variety of causes, some complained about the way in which in our times young Jesuits were being formed in the spiritual life. Toward the end of the first session the Fathers of the Congregation received a first report prepared by the appropriate subcommission in which the principles and characteristics of Ignatian spirituality were recalled and in which practical applications to be made here and now for each period of formation were proposed. Because of the lack of time the question could not be pursued any further. In the interval between the sessions there were meetings of masters of novices and of spiritual fathers from many Assistancies. With their opinions taken into account, the subcommission wrote a new report in the second session and distributed it. There was an "open session" of the subcommission with simultaneous translation. From the remarks which were made at that session and from the written comments of the members of the Congregation, the subcommission revised the report and opened it up to discussion, making the comment that the nature of the decree was pedagogical and not doctrinal. The main intention was that it deal in an appropriate manner with the spiritual difficulties of the young Jesuits of our times. In the discussion, quite a few amendments were proposed, and they were voted on too. Finally, a definitive text was approved on November 4 and 5, 1966. A verbal change in that text was allowed as a result of an "intercession" proposed on November 11 (decree 8).

14. The Formation of Scholastics Especially in Studies
(From the Minutes, Acta 30–32, 39)

The postulata which dealt with the academic formation of Jesuits numbered around 300. Commission III took very attentive account of them and thought it was better to prepare a single decree which would treat organically of all the material. For many questions this decree would satisfy the desires expressed in the postulata; for other questions which could not immediately be solved, it would provide opportune guidelines. Although a general congregation can indeed revise the decrees of prior congregations, and can even change the Constitutions, it cannot derogate from the universal laws of the Church. Such laws, for example, are the apostolic constitution "Sedes Sapientiae" which, up to the present, still obliges all religious, and the conciliar decree "Optatam Totius" which pertains to all priests. As far as academic degrees go, by decree of the Second Vatican Council, the law on ecclesiastical academic degrees, that is the apostolic constitution "Deus Scientiarum Dominus" is to be revised. Since, for this reason, it is not yet clear what studies will be required in the future for individual degrees, the Congregation was unwilling to set down determinate norms. It did establish this general norm, that Jesuits commonly should acquire those degrees in philosophy and theology which they are able to acquire by our curriculum of studies. Besides, since when it comes to studies, there are many rapid changes in the world and in the Church and, since one region differs from another very greatly, it was difficult to set down laws which were too precise. Wherefore, at the proposal of the commission, the Congregation was satisfied to set down general norms and to put off further determination of those norms either to a new Ratio Studiorum which would apply to the whole Society or to regional orders of studies which were to be prepared soon for the various regions of the society. Therefore, the Congregation gave to Fr. General, with the advice of the commission which was to be set up to revise the Ratio Studiorum, the power even to revise those decrees of preceding general congregations which could not be squared with the new conditions of our times and circumstances. For this reason the decree which had been prepared, discussed and approved in the first session was, by the will of the Congregation immediately promulgated by Fr. General on July 13, 1965 (decree 9).

15. On the Vows of Scholastics and Their Dismissal from the Society
(From the Minutes, Acta *37, 38)*

Some postulata indicated that difficulties were to be found in the present regulations of vows after two years, and they proposed that this regulation either should be accommodated to the norms of the common law of the Church or should be changed in some other way. Other postulata saw a certain defect in fairness in the dismissal of scholastics and coadjutors according to the norms of the rescript of the Holy See of Aug. 10, 1959. Into both types of difficulties an appropriate subcommission looked carefully, and it prepared and distributed a report, but since this would touch the specific papal law of the Society, the question first was asked whether the Congregation even wished to discuss the matter. In both cases, the majority of the members of the Congregation voted negatively.

16. The Third Probation
(From the Minutes, Acta *39, 40, 46)*

The postulata which dealt with this central point of our Institute, rather than opposing the institution of the third probation itself, brought up instead questions of the concrete way in which in our times it is put into effect or pointed out difficulties in its external structure. The subcommission on the third probation, which was made up of eight tertian instructors, after looking at all of this very carefully, decided, first, that that external structure was neither necessary to obtain the purposes set down in the Constitutions and pontifical documents nor was it prescribed by the general congregations, but that it only came from the ordinances and instructions of previous Fathers General. The commission saw in addition that hardly anything could be set down for the whole Society before a careful investigation of the ways in which, for our times and conditions, other structures would better help obtain those same ends in various regions. So it proposed to the Congregation the draft of a decree in which it confirmed the importance of the tertianship and gave rather general norms for the way in which its external structure might be renewed. This renewal was to be effected after taking account of the appropriate experiments by which the General could see what ought to be set down for the whole Society. This the Congregation approved of in the first session on July 13, 1965 (decree 10).

17. Admission to the Religious Vows
(From the Minutes, Acta *43, 55, 82 84, 104, 118, 121, 123)*

1.   In accord with the will of the Congregation as it was made clear in both sessions (see above n. 10), the subcommission on grades, with the help of certain experts, prepared a first report on the new norms to be observed in promotion to last vows. The tenor of that proposal was that, supposing a sufficient theological knowledge, the reason for admission to the solemn profession of four vows would consist especially in the outstanding apostolic capabilities of the candidate himself, which would be shown in the obvious evidence of his practice of virtue and in his uncommon aptitude, proven by experience, for one of the ministries of the Society. When the Congregation later decided that a decree on removing the distinction of grades was not to be passed, the question of the norms for promotion to last vows was taken up again. After the proposal of the subcommission had been examined and discussed in the usual way and finally after taking account of the comments and the amendments of the members of the Congregation, it was voted approval on November 3, 1966 (decree 11).

2.   As to what pertains to the rite to be observed in the pronouncing of vows, the Congregation, in response to a particular postulate, committed to Father General on November 17, 1966, the task of preparing an ordination for the whole Society to be used on an experimental basis (decree 12).

18. The Religious Life
(From the Minutes, Acta *17, 33–38, 43, 44, 46–48,*
77, 80, 81, 99–101, 105–123)

1.   *Religious life in general*—The Congregation judged it opportune to start its decrees on the adaptive renovation of religious life in the Society by a preface "on the religious life in general." The Congregation excerpted that preface from a rather longer document on the teachings of the Council on religious life and their application to the Society, which the appropriate subcommission had prepared and which had undergone discussion. Later, with the approval of the Congregation, the subcommission withdrew that document because there was still rather difficult work yet to be done on it which could not be done because of the imminent end of the Congregation. So this briefer introduction, after being discussed and amended in the usual way, was approved by the Congregation on November 16, 1966 (decree 13).

2. *On Prayer*—In the first session the particular subcommission prepared a report on spiritual life in the Society, which proposed solutions to the wishes expressed in the postulata. This report, revised according to the written comments of the delegates, was discussed in three sessions, but there was not time to finish the work. At the time of the interval between sessions, a large number of experts in history, spiritual theology, and psychology were questioned, and their written responses went out to all of the members of the Congregation. In the second session, it seemed opportune to separate the question of prayer from the other questions connected with it (spiritual formation, the vows, community life, and discipline . . .) which were going to be treated in other decrees. The subcommission on spiritual life again prepared the draft of a decree. On this draft there was discussion through almost five whole plenary sessions. After more than 80 speakers had been heard, the document went back to the subcommission which had been increased in size by two more members. However, since they were preparing a definitive text, it seemed best to know what the opinion of the majority of the members of the Congregation would be as to the rule of an hour of daily prayer. At the request of the subcommission, a secret written straw ballot or indicative vote was taken. In accord with the tenor of this ballot, the subcommission then revised the draft of the decree. Again public discussion ensued, so that the members of the Congregation could propose amendments. Finally, the revised draft and the amendments which had been proposed were voted on November 14, 1966. But on the following days three "intercessions" were made about n. 11 of the decree. Two of those "intercessions" were rejected on November 17. The third, however, was agreed to by the Congregation. Finally, a further vote took place on the whole of section 11 which had been amended in accord with that third intercession, and it received approval by a large vote (decree 14).

3. *Devotion to the Sacred Heart of Jesus*—There were not a few postulata on this matter. Also, experts were consulted in the period between the two sessions. Nonetheless, because the desires expressed in the postulata would have entailed a long and difficult theological investigation which exceeded the scope of the labors of the Congregation, the subcommission on the spiritual life judged that a formal decree ought not to be passed, but rather that it ought to be recommended to Father General that he promote a theological and pastoral study of this devotion. However, in the general discussion it was clear that this was not satisfactory to many of the members of the Congregation, and finally when it came to a vote on November 17, 1966, in the very last meeting of the Congregation, it approved by a very large majority vote the text of the decree proposed in the course of an amendment (decree 15).

4. *Chastity*—The subcommission on vows, following in the steps of the Second Vatican Council and after consulting many other Fathers who are experts in moral theology, canon law, and psychology, prepared a report during the period

between the two sessions of the Congregation and sent it to all the members. Once they had in hand their comments, the subcommission wrote a draft of the decree in the second session, and it was discussed in plenary meetings. The principal point of discussion was, whether in the brief amount of time available, a document could be prepared which would satisfy the demands of the Society. The greater part of the Congregation decided that a decree should be passed but that its general tenor should be completed by a study done by experts, and they committed to the care of Father General this study (decree 16).

5. *Obedience*—Not a few postulata complained of the crisis of obedience of the Society of today. Some of those postulata desired that the principles of Ignatian obedience should again be affirmed. Others asked that there should be an explanation of the relationship of those principles to the progress of biblical, psychological, and sociological scholarship. Others requested that a special commission be set up by Father General which would investigate the whole problem. The subcommission on vows already in the first session tried to prepare a report which in some way would respond to these desires. But after the conclusion of the Second Vatican Council, there was an obvious need for calling together a group of experts with whose help a draft of a decree might be prepared. So in the period between the two sessions, eleven experts of varying opinions and tendencies were consulted who, first of all, sent in written positions papers. Later, they met with the chairman and with the other members of the subcommission and prepared a second report which was sent to all the members of the Congregation. With these comments in hand, a final draft was written in accord with the comments. This draft was the object of discussion in plenary sessions. In the report, the chapter on the difficulties which might arise from the demands of conscience, as it was so-called, was omitted. However, it became clear in the discussion that this omission did not meet the approval of many of the members of the Congregation. Therefore, once the discussion was finished, the Congregation on November 11,1966, voted on all the parts of the decree except for n. 10. Later, on the 16th of the same month, they approved paragraph 10 to which the subcommission had restored the paragraph on the difficulties of conscience (decree 17).

6. *Poverty*—Besides the work of the commissions which had been set up at the order of the 29th and 30th general congregations, there existed an abundant amount of explanatory material which had been prepared before the Congregation by a particular expert. With the help of these documents, the subcommission on poverty prepared eight reports. They were as follows; the way of proceeding in this matter, the general principles of our poverty, the vow of not relaxing poverty, common life, collective poverty, remuneration for work, the gratuity of our ministries, foundations. After the members had commented, the draft of a decree was prepared which, after the usual discussion, the Congregation approved in the first session on July 10, 1965 (decree 18). On July 13, by majority vote the

following were elected definitors: Fathers Antoine Delchard, delegate from the province of northern France; Jesus Diaz de Acebedo, delegate from the province of Loyola; Joseph Gallen, delegate from the province of Maryland; and Antonio Leite, delegate from the province of Portugal. According to n. 20 of the decree, they were to prepare a draft of an adaptive renewal and redoing of all of our law on poverty. Father General was later to promulgate this decree and put it into practice as an experiment until the next general congregation. Since, however, the decree would touch the *Formula of the Institute* as it was approved by the Holy See "in forma specifica," an account of what had been done was prepared and sent to the Supreme Pontiff. After consulting with the Sacred Congregation for Religious, he responded through a letter of His Eminence, the Cardinal Secretary of State, on June 6, 1966, kindly approving and confirming what had been done (see document 3).

7. *Common life and religious discipline*—The appropriate subcommission had prepared several documents. In the first session of the Congregation, the members received a first report, but they were unable to enter into discussion on it. In the interval between sessions, a second report was prepared and quite a few experts were consulted who sent in their written comments. After further remarks from the delegates of the Congregation had been received, the subcommission wrote a draft of the decree on which discussion took place in the second session in September, 1966, in the course of several meetings. Nonetheless, the Congregation thought that the whole draft ought to be more accurately redone, and, for this reason, they sent it back to the subcommission again. The subcommission, with an increase in membership, redid the whole draft, and, again, there was discussion on it in November. Finally, the decree was approved on November 17 in the two last meetings of the Congregation (decree 19).

8. *Reading at Table*—*a.* In some postulata, the proposal came up to revise the present norms for reading at table, but the subcommission on knowledge of the Institute, to whom the question was referred, after considering the nature of the proposal and the fact that it was rather a matter of Father General's power, as well as the difficulty of writing general laws for such a great variety of places, judged that the whole thing ought to be committed to him. This judgment the Congregation approved in the last session (decree 20, n. 1).

b. Father Janssens, in accord with the mind of the 30th general congregation, had changed the custom of reading the Summary of the Constitutions at table every month to the reading of it three times a year as long as rule n. 53 of the same Summary (about reading it monthly in private) still remained in force. Some complained in their postulata that because of this prescription knowledge of the Constitutions would decrease, and others proposed some remedies. Since, however, this pertained to the responsibility of Father General, and since besides, another decree had committed to him a revision of the rules (see decree 19, nn.

14–16), the subcommission on knowledge of the Institute thought that the whole thing should be referred to his prudent judgment and action. This proposition the Congregation also agreed to in the last session.

19. The Better Choice and Promotion of Ministries
(From the Minutes, Acta *23, 39–41, 48)*

1. In the light of postulata which looked only to some aspects of our apostolates, the subcommission on the choice of ministries judged that thought should be given to the adaptation of our total apostolate. Because of this, it proposed to the Congregation a general report on the apt choice and arrangement of ministries. Once it had received comments from the members of the Congregation, the subcommission prepared the text of a decree on which there was discussion in the first session and which was voted acceptance on July 14, 1965 (decree 21).

2. Many postulata asked that major superiors be helped in their better choice of ministries by commissions of experts, a situation which did not seem to have been provided for sufficiently in decree 50 of the 30th general congregation. The present Congregation, after the matter had been examined by a subcommission and, as usual, discussed in plenary sessions, thought it opportune to recommend the setting up of commissions on the choice and arrangement of ministries, not only for the individual provincials but also for regional gatherings of provincials. This, therefore, was decided on the same date, July 14, 1965 (decree 22).

20. Our Priestly Apostolate
(From the Minutes, Acta *66, 73–75, 87, 102, 108)*

In this decree (decree 23), the Congregation wished to respond to many postulata. In some of them, the fear was expressed lest the present-day Society be too much given over to apostolic works of the temporal order which were rather the work of laity than of priests. Those postulata asked that our priests occupy themselves, especially in the ministry of the word of God and in the administration of the sacraments. Other postulata, on the contrary, expressed the desire that the Society declare that priesthood in the Society could be exercised not only in the direct care of souls but also in other works which were ordered to the good of the Church, for example, in scholarly research, in the education of youth, in the social apostolate. In the first session of the Congregation, the sixth commission prepared a report which, however, did not satisfy many of the participants in the Congregation. During the fourth session of the Second Vatican Council, a rather broad inquiry was made among the conciliar experts who were members of the Society and who were then at Rome. Later, a meeting with these experts was held in order that, among other things, this situation might be examined. With their help, some of the members of the Congregation prepared a second report which was sent to all of the members. After comments, a special subcommission was set up in the second session. It redid the whole text of the proposed draft before it went into discussion. Once the discussion was held, the Congregation approved this text with some amendments on October 19, 1966 (decree 23). There was later, however, a formal "intercession" which dealt with n. 6 of the decree, on the works which pertain to a priest by his very ordination. In order to avoid false interpretations, the Congregation corrected that number on November 7.

21. Mission Service
(From the Minutes, Acta 41, 61, 63–65, 92, 107)

1.   To satisfy those who were asking either about the purpose and nature of our missionary work or about other questions of the missionary action of the present day Society, the Congregation preferred to pass a general decree rather than to give response to individual questions or wishes. With this in mind, toward the end of the first session, a draft was prepared and distributed to the members of the Congregation, but, because of the lack of time, there was no opportunity for discussion. After the first session of the Congregation, however, the conciliar decree, "Ad Gentes" and more recently the apostolic letter "Ecclesiae Sanctae" appeared, and several experts drawn from the whole Society were asked their counsel. Once having received their judgments, the subcommission on foreign missions redid the whole draft. The members of the Congregation had their say in the discussion periods and proposed amendments. Finally, on October 22, 1966, the balloting took place, and the decree was approved in its latter form (decree 24).

2.   There were seven postulata on the subject of more easily permitting journeys of missionaries back to the province of their origin. One of these postulata was sent and signed by all of the major superiors of East Asia. There was no obstacle to this in the decrees of preceding general congregations. Therefore, it seemed sufficient to the subcommission to declare that trips of this kind ought to be considered something normal for the benefit of the mission and of the missionaries and to recommend to Father General to set more specific norms in this matter. This judgment was approved by the Congregation on November 5, 1966 (decree 25).

22. Ecumenism
(From the Minutes, Acta 77–79, 101, 102, 115)

Four postulata publicly expressed the wish that the spirit and work of ecumenism be promoted in the Society. In the first session of the Congregation, a report was prepared along with a very brief draft of a decree, but there was no time for discussion. Later, a certain number of the delegates, along with some experts on ecumenical and conciliar matters drafted another report which was sent to all of the members of the Congregation. At the beginning of the second session, a new subcommission was set up which, again, redid the text in the light of the comments of the delegates and of experts and in the light of the great diversity of circumstances in the various regions of the world. The draft was discussed in plenary session, and, once the discussion was over with, Augustin Cardinal Bea, the head of the Secretariat for the Union of Christians, who had been invited by Father General, gave a talk to all the members of the Congregation. Finally, on November 2, 1966, the decree was approved (decree 26).

23. Pastoral Institutions
(From the Minutes, Acta 43, 44, 95–97, 116)

In the first session of the Congregation, inquiry was undertaken and discussion took place in the plenary sessions about accepting the care of souls in parishes as was proposed in several postulata. There was no time, however, to come to a vote on this. In the period in between the sessions, two reports were prepared by the appropriate subcommission, one on pastoral institutions, especially on the Apostleship of Prayer and the Marian Congregations or Sodalities, the other on apostolic work in parishes. These reports were sent to the members of the Congregation and after their comments had come in and the Secretariats of the Apostleship of Prayer and the Sodality had been consulted, three separate chapters were written by three groups of delegates in the second session out of which the draft of the decree was fashioned. The usual general discussion took place and the definitive text of the decree was approved by the Congregation on November 14, 1966 (decree 27).

24. The Apostolate of Education
(From the Minutes, Acta 97–100, 115, 123)

There were not a few postulata which asked the Congregation to set forth accurately our task of teaching students in colleges in the light of the characteristics of our vocation and in the light of the theological doctrine on the character and office of the priest in the Church. These postulata were seriously considered in the first session of the Congregation. Later, at the end of January, 1966, some of the delegates met, and after examining the earlier work and the recommendations made by prefects of study and also listening to several experts, they prepared a report which was sent to all the members of the Congregation. Because of the importance of the matter, this report occasioned many comments; some called into doubt the very usefulness of this apostolate and others concerned themselves with particular problems in it. Therefore, a subcommission on education, after speaking of more general matters, decided to insert in the text of the decrees, along with norms appropriately adapted to our day, the norms also given in the decrees of previous congregations. This draft underwent quite a bit of discussion in the second session of the Congregation, in this instance using as an experiment simultaneous translations. About 40 of the members of the Congregation spoke and almost 60 amendments were proposed. Balloting took place on all of this on November 12, 1966, and the definitive text was then approved (decree 28). However, several "intercessions," were made which sought a somewhat more accurate way of expressing matters in two places in the decree, and the Congregation accepted these two "intercessions" on the 17th of the same month.

25. Scholarly Work and Research
(From the Minutes, Acta 65, 66, 68, 69, 103)

This question was touched upon in many postulata, either directly or indirectly. In the first session of the Congregation, the matter was looked into in the light of the office and the responsibilities of priest, and in that light a draft was prepared and distributed to the members of the Congregation. Many comments ensued and at the beginning of the second session a specific subcommission was set up which prepared a new report in two sections. The first of them set forth a sort of rationale for a decree, and the second gave the text of a decree in five chapters. After the usual discussion, the subcommission went back to revising the decree 40 in the light of the amendments and proposals of the speakers, and, for this reason, the first chapter was divided into two paragraphs in order that more emphasis might be given to the question of the sacred sciences. The decree as thus revised was approved by the Congregation on November 2, 1966 (decree 29).

26. Cultivating the Arts in the Society
(From the Minutes, Acta 112–114, 119)

Some of the members of the Congregation asked that the Congregation acknowledge by a specific decree the apostolic values of the liberal arts. A subcommission, therefore, was set up which prepared a report. In the report it pointed out what place the arts of this type should have in the history of the Society and in the documents of the Church. In confirmation of the latter, the subcommission adduced the conciliar decree "Gaudium et Spes," n. 62. It also contended that those arts exercised a great influence in our day on the minds of men because of the prominent place which the communications media have in present day life. In these contents, it proposed the text of a decree, which after discussion in the general sessions, was agreed upon by the Congregation on November 15, 1966 (decree 30).

27. Interprovincial Houses in Rome
(From the Minutes, Acta 100, 102–104, 106, 118)

In order to respond to the postulata which asked that the houses in Rome which were immediately dependent upon the General might be more generously provided for, the subcommission on education already in the first session prepared a report on the nature and on the conditions of these houses, along with draft recommendations, and gave it to the members of the Congregation. In order to examine this matter more accurately, a special subcommission was set up in the second session, which prepared another draft decree. After the usual discussion, this draft was accepted by the Congregation on November 15, 1966 (decree 31).

28. The Social Apostolate
(From the Minutes, Acta 23, 24, 32)

Although the three previous general congregations, 28, 29 and 30, had occupied themselves with the social apostolate, nonetheless in order to repair certain defects in our legislation on social matters and to respond to postulata, the appropriate subcommission proposed to the Congregation that, presupposing and confirming antecedent decrees, it also pass a new decree in which certain aspects of the social apostolate would be more distinctly defined. This was done in the first session of the Congregation and in accord with the established procedural norms, the new decree was discussed and then approved on July 1, 1965 (decree 32).

29. Relations with the Laity
(From the Minutes, Acta 63–66, 82, 100–103, 112)

In several of the decrees of the Congregation mention is made of the laity and of their collaboration in our apostolate. In the light of the decisions and the teachings of the Second Vatican Council and of the wishes expressed by many Jesuits in their postulata, it seemed necessary to pass a specific decree, with this especially in mind, that Jesuits might appropriately adapt to the teachings of the Second Vatican Council the way in which they related to the laity. Toward the end of the first session, a subcommission on the laity was set up which in the interval between the sessions prepared the draft of a decree. At the beginning of the second session, after having received the comments of the members of the Congregation, the subcommission thought it appropriate to open to discussion two different decrees, the one, more general, on the relationship of the Society to laypersons and their apostolate, and the other on a closer juridical bond between the Society and certain laypersons. This second question touched not only upon the apostolate but also upon other aspects of our Institute.

The first decree after the usual discussion and amendments was approved on October 14, 1966 (decree 33).

With reference to the other problem, after discussion and in the light of the extraordinarily large variety of conditions in the various regions of the Society, it seemed more appropriate to leave the whole matter to the judgment and the prudence of the General. This was approved by the Congregation on November 10, 1966 (decree 34).

30. The Mass Media
(From the Minutes, Acta 18, 32)

1.   In the light of some of the postulata and the ordinations of Very Rev. Father John B. Janssens, already in the first period of the Congregation it seemed opportune to pass a decree on this matter. It would bring together and arrange the norms which up to the present had been established and would strengthen them by a new declaration on the part of the Society (decree 35). To this, the Congregation added a special recommendation of the Vatican radio station which had been entrusted to the Society by the Supreme Pontiff (decree 36). Both of these decrees were approved on July 1, 1965.

2.   Two postulata treated of the opportuneness of setting up at the curia of the General an information center for the purpose of collecting and disseminating news which would be useful for our apostolates. After the matter was considered and examined by the appropriate subcommission and discussed in full assembly, the Congregation decided that this proposition was to be recommended to Father General (decree 37).

31. The General Congregation
(From the Minutes, Acta 47, 52, 53, 55, 58–60, 75, 76, 108, 109, 120)

1.   A certain number of postulata proposed that a general congregation be summoned at specifically stated times, for example, every six years. After the matter had been investigated by the subcommission on congregations, it seemed that the reasons which, at the time of St. Ignatius, held that a general congregation should not take place at specific times were still valid. The difficulties which had been set forth in several of the postulata could be sufficiently obviated by the congregations of procurators and by the provincial congregations, the functions of which had now been increased. Besides, the fuller communication between head and members could be brought about through the congregations of provincials, through the "relatores" elected in the provincial congregations, through the trips by Father General to the various provinces and the journeys of the provincials to Rome. After consideration of all of this, the Congregation decided on July 14, 1965, that the general congregations were not to be summoned at set intervals.

2.   Quite a few postulata also dealt with restricting the number of members in a general congregation. They also dealt with a more equitable "representation" of the provinces, with granting to vice-provincials the right to come ex officio to general congregations either with or without an elected member. Even before the present Congregation, a particular expert had undertaken a full and accurate investigation of this matter. In the first session of the Congregation, the subcommission on congregations prepared a report and, after receiving comments, revised it. In it several methods were thought up and elaborated upon to solve what

is not an easy question. In the second session of the Congregation, the discussion went on through plenary meetings, but finally on September 22, 1966, the Congregation decided that in the next, i.e., the 32nd general congregation, the rules presently in force should be observed, namely, at that congregation there would be present from each of the provinces the provincial along with two elected members, but from the independent vice-provinces, the vice-provincial was not to come ex officio, neither with another delegate who had been elected in the congregation of the vice-province nor without such a delegate.

3. The experience of this present Congregation and many postulata were persuasive on the need of preparing more accurately the material to be dealt with in the congregation and on the need of having present at the congregation itself experts for all the more difficult matters. The appropriate subcommission studied this matter and prepared a report in the first session. The discussion on this was held on November 19, 1966. A decree, with certain amendments which had been proposed during the course of the discussion, was passed on November 16, 1966 (decree 38).

4. Since the apostolic letter "Ecclesiae Sanctae" which had been published by the Supreme Pontiff, Paul VI, on August 6, 1966, prescribed that in order to promote the adaptive renewal of each individual religious institute, a special general chapter should be held within two or at the most three years, whether this chapter be an ordinary or an extraordinary one, the question arose whether this present 31st General Congregation satisfied the prescription of the Holy Father or whether another general congregation had to be called. The question was examined in the usual way. Six special experts were consulted. A report was prepared by a subcommission. Members of the Congregation gave their written comments. Discussion took place in the plenary sessions. The Congregation, however, decided that it was not its part to vote on this matter but rather that the Sacred Congregation for Religious ought to be asked about it. On November 12, 1966, the Sacred Congregation replied during the course of our second session that the present Congregation fulfilled those requisites which the apostolic letter, "Ecclesiae Sanctae," had set forth (see document 4).

32. Congregations of Procurators and Provincials
(From the Minutes, Acta 15, 16, 42, 85, 89, 90, 93)

Some postulata asked for the suppression of the congregation of procurators; others asked that it be more appropriately adapted. Already in the preparations for this General Congregation, Rev. Father Janssens had posed the question, and research had been undertaken by an expert. In the first session of the Congregation, the subcommission on congregations prepared a report and after the usual comments and the discussion in general sessions, the matter was proposed to the Congregation by stages. On July 9, 1965, the Congregation decreed the following: The congregation of procurators was not to be suppressed. It was, however, to be renewed or adapted in its purpose and in its members. *(a)* As for the purpose of the congregation, besides the vote on whether to call or not to call a general congregation, consultation was to be held under the leadership of Father General about the circumstances and the activities of the whole Society. *(b)* As far as the members go, alternatively to Rome were to come procurators who had been elected in provincial congregations, and provincial superiors (who, however, were obliged to follow the vote of their own provinces if that vote was to call a general congregation). When the provincials did thus meet, another member of the Society was to be elected who could be either a professed father or a spiritual coadjutor. He was to send a written report to Rome and, at the judgment of Father General, could be called to Rome. Finally, the Congregation extended all of these provisions to the independent vice-provinces. In the second session of the present Congregation, a subcommission, relying specifically upon certain historical facts which previously could not be considered, proposed that the whole question be reintroduced, but the Congregation did not approve of this. Therefore, certain added questions alone were considered. On October 24, 1966, it was decided that the meeting of provincials every six years with the General and his assistants and counselors was to be called the "Congregation of Provincials." It was also decided that the first meeting to be called after the present General Congregation would be a congregation of procurators elected in their own provincial congregations. Finally it was decided that if, after the "votes" of the provincial congregations and of the congregations of independent vice-provinces had been received in Rome, and it was certain from those votes that there was an affirmative majority for calling a general congregation, the congregation of provincials would de jure not be held (decree 39).

33. The Provincial Congregation
(From the Minutes, Acta *19–23, 42, 83, 85–88, 97–99, 114, 115, 119, 120, 123)*

The rules presently in force on the make-up of the provincial congregations had for a long time displeased many Jesuits. Therefore, it is hardly to be wondered at if many postulata brought up this question. In the preparation for the General Congregation, Father Janssens had already proposed the problem and an expert had done research on it. In the first session of the present Congregation, three principal solutions were proposed by the subcommission on congregations: a limit on the age of those who were to be delegates, a proportionate representation from age levels, and an antecedent or previous election. Once the matter, as usual, had been examined and discussed, on July 9, 1965, the Congregation decided the following: *(a)* The legislation presently in effect was to be reformed and some limitation on the number of members to be called to the congregation was to be retained. *(b)* There was to be no age limit on the members, nor was there to be a distribution of delegates according to age; rather, preference was to be given to some kind of antecedent election. There were many further specifications to be determined; they were examined in the second session. After the preliminary vote had been taken which, according to the *Formula of the General Congregation,* defines those points for which a two-thirds majority vote is needed for passage, on October 22, 1966, the Congregation decided on the following specifications for the election to a provincial congregation: *(a)* Not only the professed of four vows but also the formed spiritual and temporal coadjutors would have the same right to active voice (the right to vote) in the election; however, the scholastics who were priests and who had finished theology were not to have this right to vote as some had proposed. *(b)* Not only the professed of four vows but also the spiritual coadjutors, would have passive voice (the right to be voted for), so that the number of spiritual coadjutors in a provincial congregation could be the same as but could not exceed the number of professed. On November 12, going yet further, the Congregation decided that even the formed temporal coadjutors would have passive voice, with the proviso that at the most five of them could be members of the congregation and that at least one of them had to be present as a member. Finally, there were a certain number of complementary questions which came up and on which the Congregation voted in the last session, November 17th (decree 40 and 51).

34. Governance in General
(From the Minutes, Acta *17–19)*

The document on governance in general was prepared by the appropriate subcommission; written remarks were handed in and a discussion was held in several plenary sessions. From these discussions, it was evident that the questions dealt with there would better and more accurately be treated in the decrees on the religious life, especially the decree on obedience, and because of this, it seemed much less useful to pass a separate decree on governance in general.

35. Governance of the Whole Society
(From the Minutes, Acta *3–7, 12-16, 20–26, 30, 32–34, 41, 46, 49,*
53, 55, 56, 58, 60, 66)

1. *The Superior General—(a)* On the question of the length of office of the Superior General of the Society—as was said above in number 3—there had already before his election been discussion in several sessions. After the election the Congregation confirmed the Constitutions, which state that the Superior General is to be elected for life. After the matter had been considered in the usual way by a subcommission and had been discussed in several plenary sessions, clearer norms were set down for his resignation from office, and decree 260 of the *Collectio Decretorum* was reworded. Both of these were approved on July 8 and 13, 1965,

and the Congregation voted on the text of the decree on July 15, adding to it the right to promulgate it immediately (decree 41).

(b) Lest the General lack the help he needs for the complexity and amount of business with which he deals, after a certain number of postulata had been examined by a subcommission and after the discussion in the plenary sessions, the Congregation on July 8, 1965, approved the addition of a fourth paragraph to decree 262 of the *Collectio Decretorum* (retaining the third paragraph about a substitute vicar-general). By this, the General has the right to nominate a vicar-general as a helper as often as this seems necessary or convenient to him (decree 41, n. 3).

(c) Some postulata expressed the desire that Father General would visit various regions and provinces of the Society, at least when there would be more serious business at hand. After considering the advantages and disadvantages, the Congregation decided to recommend those journeys to the General (decree 42).

2. *The Vicar-General nominated at the death of the General*—With the necessity of preparing well for a general congregation, something which the members of this Congregation were much aware of, and with the number of general assistants now set at four, questions arose on the function of the vicar-general at the death of the general. These questions, which had been proposed in two postulata, were examined by the subcommission on universal governance during the period between sessions of the Congregation and after comments by the members of the Congregation, they underwent discussion in the second session. On October 17, 1966, the Congregation decided upon the changes which were to be introduced into the office of the vicar-general (decree 43).

3. *The General Assistants*—With the growth of the Society and the growth, therefore, in the number of assistants, not a few inconveniences followed from the usage which began right at the first general congregation that the same persons be assistants "ad providentiam" and "ad consilium." Father Janssens acted on this matter in preparation for the Congregation and a study was done by an expert. Besides, almost 70 postulata were sent to the Congregation. The subcommission on the governance of the whole Society, after it had examined attentively the Constitutions of the Society and its history, thought out several solutions and proposed them to the Congregation. After an antecedent straw ballot or indicative vote in order to ascertain the mind of the Congregation, the subcommission prepared a report, and, after the usual comments, submitted for discussion its final judgment. Lengthy discussion took place on the question. Finally, on June 24, 1965, the Congregation decreed the following: *(a)* Only four assistants would be elected by the congregation; they would exercise the providence of the Society toward the General; they would be the consultors of the General in the canonical meaning of the term. The other counselors (general counselors, regional assistants and expert counselors) would be named by Father General. *(b)* The length

of office of those four general assistants, in accord with the norms of the Constitutions, would not be limited; they would be elected to serve until the election of a new general, in such a way, however, that others could take their place in accord with the revised norm of decree 269 of the *Collectio Decretorum;* the general congregation, even one which would be called simply to deal with business, would always be able to elect new general assistants. *(c)* These provisions would explicitly be labeled "experimental" until the next general congregation. Once the vote had been taken, Father General declared that on this occasion he would name as general counselors those whom the congregation would elect general assistants. There was an "intercession" on the length of office of general assistants, but when the vote was taken, in neither case was there the two-thirds majority necessary to change the Constitutions. Finally, on June 28, 1965, the text of the decree on the general assistants was approved. The second session of the Congregation added a certain number of declarations in order to clear up some doubts: Decree 264 of the *Collectio Decretorum* was simply suspended until the next general congregation; the approval of the assistants and of the provincials in designating a new general assistant outside of the general congregation would be required for the validity of such a designation (decree 44, 1).

4. *The other Counselors of Father General*—In the voting on the general assistants, the existence of other counselors had already been approved, but further specifications were necessary. The question was proposed and discussed, and on July 1, 1965, the Congregation decided the following: *(a)* The General would have general counselors who would help him especially in those things which were of more universal moment to the Society; regional counselors who would help him especially on the affairs of a particular region; and expert counselors who would help him especially in specific or special questions. *(b)* The four assistants "ad providentiam" would be called "General Assistants." The counselors on matters of more universal moment to the Society would be called "General Counselors." The counselors on the affairs of individual regions would be called "Regional Assistants" and the rest would be called "Expert Counselors." *(c)* Regional assistants would be named after hearing the advice of the provincials of the region and, if they were to be named during a general congregation, upon hearing the advice also of the delegates of that region or assistancy (decree 41, n.2).

5. With a change in the situation of the assistants, a doubt arose about their right to attend the congregations of the Society. After the customary examination and discussion, the Congregation decided that the new norms were to be observed until the next general congregation could give a final judgment about this experiment (decree 44, III).

6. Visitors—*(a)* A particular postulatum proposed that decree 274 of the *Collectio Decretorum* should be revised in order to avoid doubts or difficulties

which could come up. After the usual examination and discussion, the Congregation decided on September 17, 1966, to agree to this suggestion (decree 45; I).

(b) Some postulata dealt with the office itself of the visitor. Documents of the law and history of the Society were consulted in dealing with the question. However on July 8, 1965, the Congregation decided that nothing was to be changed in our legislation on visitors, but it recommended to the General that visitors should not keep their office too long nor should they enjoy indefinite authority or jurisdiction (decree 45, n.2).

36. The Election of the General Assistants and the Nomination of the Other Counselors of Father General
(From the Minutes, Acta *24, 27–30, 33, 41)*

1. Once the question of general assistants had been solved, and after the four days of information gathering, and after the other prescriptions of the *Formula* had been carried out, in three sessions and by separate votes on June 29, 1965, the Congregation elected the following as general assistants: Father Paolo Dezza, elector of the province of Venice-Milan (second ballot); Father Vincent T. O'Keefe, elector of the province of New York (first ballot); Father John L. Swain, who had just recently fulfilled the office of assistant and of vicar-general (second ballot); and Father Andrew Varga, substitute for the provincial of Hungary (third ballot).

2. On June 30, with those members also present who could be part of the Congregation only for the business of the Congregation, on the third ballot Father John L. Swain was elected admonitor of the superior General.

3. Father General, as has been said, named as general consultors those whom the congregation had elected as general assistants. Afterwards, after he had heard the advice of the provincials and delegates of each of the assistancies, he named the following as regional assistants on July 8th: For Italy, Father Hyginus Ganzi, from the province of Turin; for Germany, Father Mario Schoenenberger, from the vice-province of Switzerland; for France, Father Maurice Giuliani, from the province of Paris; for Spain, Father Victor Blajot, from the vice-province of Bolivia; for the English assistancy, Father Andrew Snoeck, from the province of northern Belgium; for the American Assistancy, Father Harold Small, from the province of Oregon; for the Slavic Assistancy, Father Anton Mruk, from the province of lesser Poland; for the southern Latin American Assistancy, Father Candido Gavina, from the province of Argentina; for India, Father Jerome D'Souza, from the province of Madurai; for the northern Latin American Assistancy, Father Emanuel Aceves, from the province of North Mexico; for the East Asian Assistancy, Father Herbert Dargan, from the province of Ireland.

37. The Governance of Provinces and Houses
(From the Minutes, Acta *16–18, 24, 30, 44, 47, 77–81, 95, 103, 104, 112, 121, 123)*

1. *Provincials*—Many postulata dealt with provincials, either to give them greater power or to aid them in receiving more help from consultors and experts, or to encourage inter-provincial cooperation. Since it belonged to the office of the General to grant greater power to the provincials, the Congregation on July 12, 1965, took the following actions: *(a)* Certain decrees by which provincials were obliged to seek the consent of Father General it wanted revised. *(b)* It recommended to Father General that in accord with his prudence he give wider powers to the provincials, and that the provincials, after they had been in office for a certain time, should be called to Rome so that they could consult with Father General and be better prepared to rule the province in accord with the mind of St. Ignatius. *(c)* It recommended to the provincials that they make better use of commissions or committees of experts and of consultors meetings of the province in which other fathers and brothers could be of help according to the subject matter to be dealt with. *(d)* It recommended that regulation 825, paragraph 3, of the Epitome be changed so that the office of admonitor to the provincial need not necessarily be entrusted to his socius. *(e)* Finally, it approved the text of the decree on provincials (decree 46).

2. *Local superiors*—A report was prepared in the first session of the Congregation and comments on it came from the members of the Congregation. Later, however, it seemed preferable not to pass a separate decree about local superiors but rather to treat the subject in other decrees, specifically in the decree on the life of obedience in the Society.

3. *The selection of consultors*—In the Society, differently than in other religious institutes, the consent or the advice of consultors is generally not required for the validity of the actions of superiors. However, in order to adapt itself to the mind of the Holy See as expressed in the apostolic letter "Ecclesiae Sanctae," the Congregation passed a decree on November 10, 1966, defining the way in which members of the Society would have a truly effective part in the selection of consultors. After an "intercession" the words "truly effective" which had been removed from the decree were again put back into it (decree 47).

4. *Inter-provincial cooperation*—This matter was deliberated on at length. In the first session of the Congregation, the appropriate subcommission had prepared a report and received comments on it, and discussion had gone on in full assembly. But at that point nothing was decided on because, at the request of certain of the delegates, the Congregation judged that the matter was not yet mature and should be postponed until the second session. A new report was prepared in the interval and it was discussed through several meetings in the second session. Finally, on October 25, 1966, a decree was approved (decree 48).

38. The Formulas of the Congregations

(From the Minutes, Acta 3, 7, 11, 12, 17, 20, 23–25, 48, 59 , 60, 64, 89–91, 107, 114, 115)

1. After the usual deliberations, the Congregation decided on June 9, 1965, what was to be changed in numbers 25, 118, and 124 of the *Formula of the General Congregation* so that the procedures for maintaining secrecy and for deciding on certain changes in the Institute could be defined. On November 16, 1966, it also approved certain amendments to number 116 which dealt with sending postulata to a general congregation (decree 50).

There was also question of changing the ceremonies connected with the election of the general, as two postulata proposed. The subcommission drew up various suggestions for discussion. However, since the conditions in which future elections would take place were not at all clear, especially in the matter of liturgical laws which were then in process of change, the Congregation on September 27, 1966, decided that it was enough to drop chapter 6 in title 3 of the *Formula of the General Congregation* and to add in number 56, a paragraph according to which the order and procedure for the day of election would be proposed by the vicar and approved by the congregation (decree 50).

There was also deliberation on the power of a general congregation before the election of the General himself, but since the matter needed further investigation and there were more serious and pressing questions, no decision was taken.

2. *The Formula of the Provincial Congregation*—Besides those points which dealt with the composition of the congregation, which were treated in number 33 above, this Congregation introduced certain other changes as follows:

(a) On June 27, 1965, changes in numbers 3 and 92, lest the provinces which were undergoing persecution would be totally absent from the congregation.

(b) On November 16, 1966, changes in numbers 28, 74, 81, 86, dealing with postulata and the matters to be treated in a congregation.

(c) On November 5, 1966, changes in numbers 29, 39, 43, 55, and 76, defining minor questions (decree 51).

3. Toward the end of the Congregation, a committee of experts was set up which was to take care of revising the several formulas of the congregations. However, since, besides the changes prescribed by this Congregation itself, there would be others which would have to be introduced either as necessitated by the legislation of the Congregation or as requested by certain postulata, and since there was not enough time to examine and approve each and every one of them, the Congregation gave to the General the responsibility and the power to finish this work of revising the formulas, with the deliberative votes of those members

of the general curia who by reason of their office had a right to attend a general congregation (decree 52).

39. The Catalog of Censures and Precepts
(From the Minutes, Acta 110, 111, 119)

It was asked that the catalog of censures and precepts imposed upon Jesuits should be revised (*Collectio Decretorum*, nn. 303–315). Since this was a question of rather complicated legal matters which would need some research, especially historical research, and since it was foreseen that in the new code of canon law the part dealing with penalties was being revised, the Congregation decided, after hearing the report of a committee of canonists and after discussion, that it was enough to delegate this power to Father General (decree 53).

40. The Censorship of Books
(From the Minutes, Acta 111, 119)

Some postulata proposed the revision of the norms on previous censorship of books. A committee of canonists prepared a report which was discussed in plenary session. Since the commission which was to deal with the Ratio Studiorum still had to do research on the norms dealing with doctrine to be held in the Society, and since we could not know what laws would be set down on this matter by the Church in the new code of canon law, the question could not at present be decided. In order to provide some remedy for current difficulties, the Congregation recommended this matter to Father General, and gave him the necessary power to adapt the particular norms of our law after he had consulted experts and the general assistants (decree 54).

41. The Abrogation or Revision of Certain Decrees
(From the Minutes, Acta 120, 121, 123)

The present Congregation, after the usual research and deliberation, revised certain decrees in the *Collectio Decretorum,* which had been approved in 1923. For example, on the preservation and renewal of the Institute, on the studies of our scholastics, on poverty. However, there were requests that still other decrees for various reasons be revised or be taken out of the collection. Agreeing with this request, the Congregation passed decree 55. Numbers 2 and 3 of that decree it approved on July 12, 1965. Number 1 it approved on November 17, 1966 (decree 55).

42. Powers Granted to Father General
(From the Minutes, Acta 49, 123)

The following were in addition to the powers and delegations which were set forth in other decrees :

1. At the end of the first session of the Congregation for this one time alone, the Congregation gave Father General the power to change provincials for a proportionately grave reason before the end of the Congregation. This carried the proviso, however, that anyone who had finished his term of office of provincial in that period would, nonetheless, still retain the right of coming to the General Congregation in the second session, and that anyone who was during that time newly appointed a provincial also had the right to come to the Congregation with the full and complete rights of a delegate.

2. Since the legislative work of the 31st Congregation was very large and simply could not, therefore, always provide for all of the implications which these new decrees and the other dispositions relative to our law might entail, the Congregation gave Father General the power, with the deliberative vote of the members of the general curia who by reason of their office had a right to attend a general congregation, to abrogate or to modify decrees of prior general congregations which could not be reconciled with the decrees of this Congregation (decree 56, n.)

3. As previous general congregations had been in the custom of doing, so also at the end of each session this Congregation gave to the General under certain conditions the power to dissolve colleges and professed houses, the right to approve the Acta or minutes of some of the sessions, and the right to polish stylistically the statutes or decrees of the Congregation (decree 56, n.2).

43. Other Acts of the Congregation

(From the Minutes, Acta *11, 12, 20, 34, 43, 74, 81, 83, 92, 96, 104,105, 109, 112)*

1. Since colleges can be sold, dissolved, or transferred only by a general congregation (see the *Formula of the Institute,* 2, and the *Collectio Decretorum,* n. 281), the Congregation was asked for permission to suppress Beaumont College in the English province and the college of Livorno in the Roman province. But at the request of delegates from several assistancies, since these were individual instances and very complex ones, the Congregation committed the care of the affair to Father General with full power to decide in accord with his own prudent judgment.

2. In each of the sessions of the Congregation, permission was given to certain members to leave early, either because of serious business which they had on hand which could not brook delay or because of ill health. Those members were :

a. In the first session: Fathers Emmanuel Antunes, delegate from Portugal (from the 20th meeting); Wenceslaus Feřt, procurator from Bohemia (from the 35th meeting); Aloysius del Zotto, delegate from Kerala (from the 44th meeting);

b. In the second session: Fathers Pedro B. Velloso, delegate from Central Brazil (from the 73rd meeting); Josef Curie, delegate from Croatia (from the 76th meeting) ; Emmanuel Antunes, delegate from Portugal (from the 89th meeting); Mauritio Eminyan, delegate from Malta (from the 92nd meeting); John Thomas, delegate from Wisconsin and Eusebio Garcia Manrique, delegate from Aragon (from the 102nd meeting); John Foley, former provincial of Wisconsin (from the 108th meeting); Jean LeBlond, delegate from Northern France and Daniele Villanova, provincial of Sicily (from the 112th meeting); Jose Arroyo, delegate from Toledo (from the 118th meeting).

To other of the delegates permission was granted to be absent from one or another session.

3. The cut-off day for proposing new postulata was set for June 9, 1965, for all of those who were not actually members of the Congregation, and November 13, 1966, as the end of the work of the Congregation approached, even for those who were members of the Congregation.

44. The Benevolence of the Supreme Pontiff Toward the Congregation
(From the Minutes, Acta *1, 11, 105, 110, 120)*

The Supreme Pontiff, Paul VI, twice wished to speak personally to the members of the General Congregation. On the morning of May 7, 1965, before the sessions began, he invited the whole Congregation to the Vatican and expressed his best wishes and paternal hopes (see Document 1). Toward the end of the Congregation, on November 16, 1966, he graciously concelebrated Mass with Father General and five others of the members of the Congregation in the Sistine Chapel in the presence of all the other members of the Congregation. In his talk, sincerely and with great affection he expressed his anxieties and his confidence in the Society (see Document 2). Besides, several times in each session of the Congregation and in the period between the sessions he wanted to be informed by Father General about the course of its work and to look at the decrees of the Congregation. The Congregation, in a letter of November 16, 1966, expressed its thanks to him (see Document 5).

45. The End of the Congregation
(From the Minutes, Acta *49, 123)*

On November 17, 1966, the General Congregation came to an end. It had previously interrupted its meetings on July 15, 1965, and had taken them up again on September 8, 1966.

In the last meeting of each session, Father Severiano Azcona, who was previously been an assistant and who was oldest in order of profession, spoke in the name of all the members of the Congregation in offering thanks, first of all, to

God, and then to our Father General and to all who had helped toward the successful outcome of the Congregation. Then Father General spoke, and, after he had briefly described the sum total of the work of the Congregation, he gave encouragement to everyone to work effectively to put into practice the decrees and the ordinances of the Congregation so that the hoped for renewal of the Society might thereby take place.

Finally, the members were asked whether they wished to declare the Congregation ended, and after they had responded with a unanimous "yes," they recited the hymn, "Te Deum Laudamus," and all made their way home.

Thus, at the end of the 123rd meeting, after 141 days of work (70 in the first session and 71 in the second session), after many meetings of commissions and experts held in the interval between the two sessions of the Congregation, at eight in the evening on November 17, 1966, the 31st General Congregation, the twelfth in the restored Society, came to an end. May God bless the labors of this Congregation for His greater glory.

B

DECREES OF THE

31st GENERAL CONGREGATION

I

INTRODUCTORY DECREES

DECREE 1

The Mission of the Society of Jesus Today

1. On the Life and Mission of the Society in This New Era

1/   In this "new age" in which the human race now finds itself,[1] the Society of Jesus, according to the spirit of the whole Church, which is itself in process of renewal, recognizes the difficulties with regard to its goal and plan of life which are arising from the changes that have taken place in man's way of living and thinking. At the same time it recognizes the opportunities which arise from the new developments in our world and those which flow from the renewal of the Church that has been begun by the Council. It intends, therefore, to take a very close look at its own nature and mission in order that, faithful to its own vocation, it can renew itself and adapt its life and its activities to the exigencies of the Church and the needs of contemporary man.

2/   The nature and the special grace of our vocation are to be discovered above all in the dynamic development of the Society from its earliest historical beginnings.

2. The Origin of the Society in the Experience of the Spiritual Exercises

3/   For this history has its beginnings in the Spiritual Exercises which our holy Father Ignatius and his companions went through. Led by this spiritual experience, they formed an apostolic group rooted in charity, and in which, after they had taken the vows of chastity and poverty and had been raised to the priesthood, they would offer themselves as a holocaust to God for whose praise and honor they had given up all that they had.[2]

4/   They had heard the invitation of Christ the King and had followed it; for that reason they not only dedicated themselves entirely to labor, but desiring to become outstanding in every service of their king, they made offerings of greater worth and importance;[3] so that they would be sent under the banner of

---

[1] GS 4

[2] See *Deliberatio primorum Patrum* (a. 1539), *Cons*MHSJ, I, 2.

[3] See *SpEx,* The Kingdom of Christ (97).

Christ by Him into the entire world, spreading His teachings among all degrees and conditions of men.[4]

3. The "Mission" under the Roman Pontiff

5/ In this spirit they had offered and dedicated themselves and their lives to Christ our Lord and to His true and legitimate vicar on earth; so that he as Vicar of Christ might dispose of them and might send them where he judged that they could bear greater fruit.

6/ But the first mission entrusted to them by Pope Paul III was one that was likely to scatter the group of Fathers in all directions. Therefore, after many deliberations in which they tried to distinguish between various spiritual inspirations and weigh the reasons for each side carefully, these first Fathers decided that they should not break up "a society united in God," but rather gradually strengthen it and stabilize it by making themselves into a unified body. Indeed they judged it more expedient to give their obedience to one of their number that they might more successfully and perfectly carry out their first desire of fulfilling the divine will in all things. Thus also the Society would be more securely preserved.[5]

4. The "Missionary" Constitution of the Society of Jesus

7/ Thus it came about that the promise made to God of obeying the Roman Pontiff with regard to all missions turned out to be "our beginning and first foundation."[6]

8/ Such an offering expressed the consummation of that knowledge of Christ which they had acquired in the Exercises, and united and drew that first apostolic band together in one body. It was in order to fulfill this offering more completely that the Society, as a mode of life, had its beginning under the Constitutions.

---

[4] See *SpEx,* The Two Standards (145). In the deliberation on poverty Ignatius listed among its advantages: "13. Esta (la pobreza) elegiendo todos diez, nemine discrepante, tomamos por cabeza al mismo Jesu nuestro Criador y Senor para yr debaxo de su bandera para predicar y exortar, que es nuestra profesion." *Cons*MHSJ, I, 80, No. 13.

[5] See *Deliberatio primorum Patrum, Cons*MHSJ, I, 7. In order that the true value of obedience in the Society may become more clear, this should be noted: in the beginning obedience was rather *ad intra* for the body of the Society, since "missions" came directly from the Holy Father. The power to send Jesuits to the Christian faithful was given to Father General by Pope Paul III in 1542, but the power to send them to infidels was not given until 1549 in the Bull *Licet Debitum.* And this was done even though some of the first members were opposed (see ibid., p. 395). From that time on obedience in the Society acquired its full apostolic or "missionary" sense and consequently its supreme importance.

[6] *Declarationes circa missiones* (1544–45), *Cons*MHS], I, 162.

9/ The first steps of the Society were directed by Ignatius himself in the way of the Lord by his spiritual experience, in accordance with which he interpreted the course of events in the light of their relation to God. The result was that Ignatius founded the Society as an organization which would continually renew itself in the Church through the inner vigor of the Exercises and under the vitalizing impulse of the Spirit to fulfill those things which its vocation and its mission to promote the divine glory and the greater service of souls demanded.

5. New Developments in the History of Man

10/ The history of four centuries, with its fluctuations between honor and humiliation, has cast a rather penetrating light upon the nature of the Society and its originating idea. With whatever degree of fidelity to its vocation and mission the apostolic works of the Society were begun and carried on, nonetheless on the one hand they show an internal dynamism in the attitude of universality and flexibility, while on the other hand the limitations and deficiencies of its individual members stand revealed.

11/ Today, however, our Society, along with the whole Church, finds the conditions of human history profoundly changed.[7] The members themselves share in the contemporary "social and cultural transformation," and the new ways of living which arise from socialization, urbanization, industrialization, and ever widening communication among men, and they do not fail to participate in the changed ways of thinking and feeling and weighing the values of human life. They experience also the fact that a keener sense of liberty has developed and that there is a more universal desire for the "full and free life"; they realize therefore at the same time that the conditions which affect religious life have been changed.[8]

12/ For they are conscious on the one hand of that purifying of the religious life which, according to the Second Vatican Council, flows from the "more critical faculty of judging" which has grown up in our day.[9] They are conscious as well of the grave problems which can be found among many, even among Christians, arising from the crisis to which the Gospel itself and the Church's doctrine have been exposed because of modern criticism and contemporary philosophy. And they cannot avoid hearing the widespread criticism that the teaching and life of the Christian estrange him from the world and its struggles,[10] while at the same time great multitudes are still compelled to live a life unworthy of the human person and the human race itself remains without any true unity.

---

[7] See GS 1.

[8] See GS 4, 6, 7, 9.

[9] See GS 7.

[10] See GS 34

13/　　They are also acutely aware that they are surrounded by various sorts of atheistic teachings and especially by that humanism which contends that "liberty consists in this, that man is to be an end unto himself, the sole artisan and creator of his own history" and that "this freedom cannot be reconciled with the affirmation of God."[11] Often, too, they feel in themselves also that ambivalent desire of their contemporaries to perfect themselves as men.

6. The Need for Revitalizing the Mission of the Society

14/　　But all the members of the Society, firmly grounded in faith, in company with all other Christians, lift their eyes to Christ, in whom they find that absolute perfection of self-giving and undivided love which alone completely reconciles man to God and to himself. For unless men adhere to Christ and follow the way which He shows, they desire and seek in vain for that full realization of themselves which they long for in their undertakings.

15/　　From this love for Christ, the Society offers itself completely to the Church in these needs, so that the Supreme Pontiff, as the Vicar of Christ, may "send" all its members into the vineyard of the Lord.

16/　　Thus the Society will try to be of assistance to the Church according to the measure of the grace of its vocation, while the Church itself is helping the world so that the kingdom of God may come and the salvation of the human race may be achieved. Our Lord, with whose name our Society has been signed and under the standard of whose cross it desires to serve the kingdom of His love, is Himself the goal of human history, the point to which the desires of history and civilization converge, the center of the human race, the joy of all hearts and the fulfillment of all seeking. "Enlivened and united in His Spirit, we journey toward the consummation of human history, one which fully accords with the counsel of God's love: 'To re-establish all things in Christ, both those in the heavens and those on the earth' (Eph. 1.10)."[12]

7. The Need of Renewal and Adaptation in the Society

17/　　In order that our Society may more aptly fulfill in this new age its mission under the Roman Pontiff, the 31st General Congregation has striven with all its power so to promote a renewal that those things may be removed from our body which could constrict its life and hinder it from fully attaining its end, and that in this way its internal dynamic freedom may be made strong and vigorous, and ready for every form of the service of God.

---

[11] GS 20. See decree 2 (on atheism).

[12] GS 45.

DECREE 2

THE RENEWAL OF OUR VOWS

18/ 1. The adaptation and renewal of our way of living and acting extends itelf, as it should, even to the body of laws which contain the spirit and end of the Society and also describe its structures and govern its apostolic action. Although the Council and the post-Conciliar documents invite us to this renewal, they carefully and clearly distinguish between fundamental or permanent elements of the Institute (whether this is understood as a way of living or as a collection of laws), and elements which are contingent and therefore changeable in response to the circumstances and needs of various times.

19/ 2. The former, since they flow either from the very nature of the evangelical counsels,[1] or constitute the specific nature of our Institute,[2] are to be conserved as having a perennial value. At the same time, however, they are to be renewed by a continuous return to the sources of all Christian life, to the spirit of the founder, and to the originating inspiration of the Institute.[3] Contingent elements, however, should be so skillfully adapted that the religious life is purified of foreign elements and freed from those that are obsolete.[4] Indeed, with a view to this end experiments in matters at variance with our own law may be instituted prudently by legitimate authority, or even in matters at variance with the common law, insofar as the Holy See, in suitable cases, will permit.[5]

20/ 3. The 31st General Congregation has approached the task of adapting and renewing the Society in this manner, called by our mother the Church and under her guidance, and in a certain continuing tension between the faithful desire of retaining what is permanent and ought to remain as fundamental, and the

---

[1] See Paul VI, Address *Magno gaudio,* To the general chapters of some religious families, etc., May 23, 1964, *AAS* 56 (1964) 567; *ActRSJ* 14 (1964) 408.

[2] These proper elements, as being specific and to be preserved, are described in various ways: "the integral mind of the founder," (Paul VI, ibid., p. 569), "the proper nature and discipline of the institute" (loc. cit.), "the integral spirit of the rules" (loc. cit.), "individual character" (PC 2, c), "the spirit of the founder, as also . . . the particular goals and wholesome traditions which constitute the heritage of each community" (PC 2, b) ; see ES II, 12a; "the proper spirit" (ES II, 31) ; "the end, nature, and character of the institute should be preserved" (ES II, 6); see ES II, 33 and 40; also PC 20; "the primitive spirit" (ES II, 16 §3).

[3] See PC 2.

[4] ES II, 16 §2.

[5] ES II, 6, 7, 8.

vital necessity of adapting the Institute to those circumstances in which its life is led and its mission is carried out.

21/   Thus it has determined that the entire government of the Society must be adapted to modern necessities and ways of living; that our whole training in spirituality and in studies must be changed; that religious and apostolic life itself is to be renewed; that our ministries are to be weighed in relation to the pastoral spirit of the Council according to the criterion of the greater and more universal service of God in the modern world; and that the very spiritual heritage of our Institute, containing both new and old elements, is to be purified and enriched anew according to the necessities of our times.

22/   4.   Finally, since every true law seeks to enunciate the will of God, and since this will can be manifested under the inspiration of the Holy Spirit through subjects as well as through superiors and congregations, the Holy See properly urges full and free consultation of all members as a means of helping and directing the work of the congregation.[1] Indeed, as much as time and the circumstances of its convocation permitted, our present Congregation has enjoyed this help.[2]

23/   But since a suitable renovation cannot be made once and for all but must be continually promoted,[3] consultation can be employed even more extensively in the future,[4] both with a view to the preparation of future general congregations, and in order that the Superior General together with his council may make use of it for carrying on the renewal of the Society in virtue of the faculties granted him by the Holy See until the next congregation.[5]

---

[6] ES II, 4.

[7] See Letter of Reverend Father Vicar-General, December 15, 1964, *ActRSJ* 14 (1964) 525-26.

[8] ES II, 19.

[9] See *Formula of the Provincial Congregation,* N. 28, §§1–2; *Formula of the General Congregation,* Nn. 116–17.

[10] ES II, 7–8.

DECREE 3

THE TASK OF THE SOCIETY REGARDING ATHEISM

I. The Spread of Atheism and the Mandate of the Holy Father

24/ 1. The glory of God, as the goal of all creation, and man's own good require that he acknowledge, reverence, and serve God. Hence, the danger of atheism which faces so many men today should greatly stimulate the companions of Jesus to offer a purer witness of religious life and a more zealous devotion to apostolic work. The denial of God is no longer, as in former centuries, an isolated phenomenon; it has become widespread, affecting entire social groups and nations. In some countries, atheism is systematically spread by public authority, thereby violating the rights of man to the free investigation of truth and the practice of religion. In many more regions, the denial of God or indifference to religion has directly or indirectly infected the cultural and social life. The Supreme Pontiff Paul VI, on the occasion of the gathering of the Fathers for the 31st General Congregation, committed to the Society, in view of its special vow of obedience, the task of resisting atheism "with forces united."[1] Each Jesuit, therefore, earnestly though humbly, should take part in this task by prayer and action, and each should be grateful that he can thus better serve "his Lord alone and the Church, His spouse, under the guidance of the Roman Pontiff, the Vicar of Christ on earth."[2]

II. The Understanding of Atheism and Its Causes and of the Motives of Atheists

25/ 2. All Jesuits, whatever their particular apostolic work, should give more attention to atheists and try to reach a better understanding of atheism and of indifference to religion. They should examine the different kinds of atheism, both systematic and practical, and should understand them as well as possible.

26/ 3. They should also distinguish its causes, such as the relationship which the modern denial of God has to all the changes taking place in the material and social condition of mankind; or those "complex and multiple" causes which may exist "in the minds of atheists, so that one should be cautious in passing judgment on them";[3] or those social injustices which, especially in developing countries, in-

---

[1] Paul VI, Address to members of 31st General Congregation, May 7, 1965.

[2] *FI* Julius III, n. 2.

[3] ES, *AAS* 56 (1964), 652.

cline many men to accept the atheistic doctrines which are connected with programs of social revolution.

III. Some Difficulties Urged against Belief in God and How to Deal with Them

27/ 4.   To overcome the difficulties which are raised against faith, often even among believers, Jesuits should take appropriate action, not for any political reasons, but purely from apostolic motives.

28/ 5.   Many difficulties arise from this, that "there is a demand that the world of divine realities be presented in a higher and purer way than has been the custom in some imperfect forms of speech and worship."[4] Jesuits should therefore try to purify the presentations of God and to promote a truly personal adherence to the faith among believers.

29/ 6.   There are also some atheists, "gifted with a greatness of spirit," who are motivated by impatience with "the mediocrity and desire of personal advantage which infect so many parts of human society in our times."[5] Jesuits therefore should make every effort to see that faith may always lead to a genuine love of neighbor, a love that is practical and social-minded.

30/ 7.   On the other hand, the legitimate aspiration toward the autonomy of the sciences and of human enterprise is often carried to such a point that it arouses objections against the acknowledgement of God; indeed, some men present abandonment of religion as man's path to freedom. Therefore, our aim must be to let faith penetrate the concrete totality of life. It should be made clear that the Christian life does not turn away from developing the world. In fact, human values, cultivated without pride, and the universe itself, cleansed of the corruption of sin, illuminated and transfigured, will have their place "in that eternal and universal kingdom" which Christ will restore to the Father at the end of time.[6]

IV. The Character of Our Way of Life

31/ 8.   These means should be applied by members of the Society first of all in their own lives. Each should constantly cultivate an awareness of God who is living, working, and loving, an awareness which the Exercises of St. Ignatius impart through the meditation on the Foundation and the Contemplation for Obtaining Love. And, as far as possible, what God is should be made evident in the entirety of the Jesuit way of living and acting, namely, by taking on that basic at-

---

[4] ES, *AAS* 56 (1964), 652.

[5] ES, *AAS* 56 (1964), 653.

[6] See 1 Cor. 15:24.

titude which the incarnate Word of God revealed throughout His life and especially in His supreme sacrifice, the attitude which the Exercises aim at, beginning with the contemplation on the Kingdom of Christ.

32/ 9. Because atheists, estranged as they are from the environment of the religious world, will mainly judge us by our lives and actions, our way of living and acting must be entirely sincere and free from all appearance of pride or pretense.

V. The Formation of Jesuits

33/ 10. The formation of Jesuits should be adapted so as to establish and promote this kind of spiritual life and a sincere and fraternal manner of acting. Scholastics should also be trained to understand the mentality of atheists and their theories, and they should be furnished with appropriate information, especially in the scholarly disciplines dealing with man, presented in modern terms. Care should also be taken that, as far as this is possible, those especially who come from an entirely Christian environment can, in good time, have some personal contacts with atheists.

VI. The Right Order of Our Ministries and Their Adaptation to the Task Comissioned by the Holy Father

34/ 11. The mandate of resisting atheism should permeate all the accepted forms of our apostolate so that we may cultivate among believers true faith and an authentic awareness of God. But we must also direct a greater part of our efforts, more than we have in the past, to nonbelievers, and we must search for and experiment with new ways for coming into closer and more frequent contact with atheists themselves, whether they belong to those parts of society which are most in need or to those which are culturally more advanced.

35/ 12. With regard to the areas where atheism is being spread, we should concentrate on aiding the developing regions, where religious life is liable to greater and more abrupt disturbances because of the faster rate of change.

36/ 13. In the light of the principal causes of atheism, it is clear that we must emphasize both the social and the university apostolates, either at our own or in secular universities.

37/ 14. The vigorous intellectual efforts of all our scientists, philosophers, and theologians are also called for, and there should be a continuing cooperation among Jesuit scholars in various disciplines, especially the sciences dealing with man.

38/ 15. In our schools, the modern atheistic positions should be explained and subjected to careful evaluation, not by indulging in empty polemics, but by promoting the most accurate critical understanding of the atheists' arguments and ways of thinking.

39/   16. Jesuits should approach atheists with the firm conviction that the divine law is written in the hearts of all men and with the belief that the Holy Spirit moves all men to the service they owe to God their creator. Both by a style of proclamation adapted to each person, combined with religious respect, and by a brotherly witness borne in the concrete details of living and acting, Jesuits should work to remove obstacles and to help atheists find and acknowledge God.

40/   17. All superiors should see to it that our apostolate is constantly adapted to this end. It is especially recommended to Father General that in conversation with the Holy Father he try to obtain a clear knowledge of his mind with regard to the task he has committed to us and that, with the advice of experts, he direct the entire apostolate of the Society in carrying out that mission as effectively as possible.

II

THE INSTITUTE IN GENERAL

DECREE 4

THE PRESERVATION AND RENEWAL
OF THE INSTITUTE

I. Introduction

41/ Since "the most important work to which the General Chapters should devote their chief attention consists in carefully adapting the laws of their Institute to the changed condition of the times . . . but in such wise . . . that the specific nature and discipline of the Institute is preserved intact,"[2] the General Congregation, heartily desiring to open up the road, and provide the juridical principles for the adaptation of our body of laws, as mentioned in the Introductory Decree, determines and decrees the following changes in the *Collection of Decrees.*

2. On the Institute and Its Parts

42/ This new decree is to be inserted at the beginning of the Prooemium of the Collection of Decrees:

43/ The term "Institute of the Society" means both our way of living and working,[3] and the written documents in which this way is authentically and legitimately proposed.[4] Among these documents some are laws properly so called; others set forth the legitimate traditions of the Society.[5]

44/ To maintain faithfully the grace of our vocation as described in the Institute, the Spiritual Exercises of our holy founder stand in first place, both as a

---

[2] Paul VI, Address *Magno gaudio,* to the general chapters of some religious families, etc., see AAS 56 (1964) 569. ActRSI 14 (1964)410.

[3] See Paul III, *Regimini Militantis;* Julius III, *Exposcit Debitum: Formula of the Institute* of Paul III, 1, 9; *Formula of the Institute* of Julius III, 1, 2, 9; *Cons.* [134, 152, 186, 398, 686, 603] ; etc. Note that the use of roman or italic type for textual changes in previous decrees is different in the official Latin editions of the documents of the 31st and 32nd General Congregations. This English translation has followed the same usages as the official Latin texts.

[4] See *CollDecr* 7.

[5] E.g., St. Ignatius, *Letter on Obedience;* see *CollDecr* 7 §1, 2°.

perennial source of those interior gifts upon which depends our effectiveness in reaching the goal set before us,[6] and as the living expression of the Ignatian spirit which must temper and interpret all our laws.

45/ §1. The *Formula of the Institute,* or fundamental Rule of the Society has primacy of dignity and authority in the Institute.[7] It was set down first by Paul III,[8] then more exactly and in greater detail by Julius III,[9] was approved *in forma specifica* by many of his successors, and has obtained in a special way the status of pontifical law.

46/ §2. There are also other laws of the Institute which have obtained the status of pontifical law, but not all have been approved by the Holy See in the same way; hence they enjoy varying degrees of dignity and authority.

47/ §3. Apostolic Letters, rescripts, and indults issued for the Society also pertain to the pontifical law specific to the Society.

3. On the preservation and renewal of the Institute

48/ In the *Collection of Decrees* decrees 12-16 are to be changed in this way:

49/ Decree 12—§1. The substantials, or fundamentals, of our Institute are, first, the matters contained in the *Formula* of Julius III.[10] For the *Formula* exhibits the fundamental structure of the Society, based, with the help of grace, on Gospel principles and the experience and wisdom of our holy Father Ignatius and his companions.[11] Accordingly, as the *Formula* itself recommends, all Jesuits should strive to keep before their eyes this image of their Institute, which is a way to God, as long as life lasts.[12]

50/ §2. Secondly, among the substantials are included also those matters without which the substantials of the *Formula* can be preserved with great difficulty or not at all.[13] General congregations have the power to declare which matters are substantial, and have done so at times;[14] moreover

---

[6] *Cons.* [813].

[7] *Formulas of the Institute* of Paul III and Julius III.

[8] Paul III, *Regimini Militantis.*

[9] Julius III, *Exposcit Debitum.*

[10] GC 5, D. 44, 58.

[11] See the beginning of the Bulls of Paul III and Julius III.

[12] *Formula of the Institute* of Julius III, 1.

[13] GC 5, D. 44, 45, 58.

[14] GC 5, D. 58; GC 27, *CollDecr* 13, b.

the General has the same power, to be exercised in matters of practice on a temporary basis.

51/ Decree 13 is abrogated.

52/ 53 Decree 14—§1. The general congregation can declare the meaning of the substantials of the *Formula of the Institute,* but cannot change them on its own authority.[15]

53/ §2. Let substantials outside the *Formula of the Institute* continue to have the same stability they have previously enjoyed, except perhaps where the general congregation shall have determined that the connection of any one of them with the *Formula* has been notably weakened.

54/ §3. In matters which are not substantial, the Constitutions can and sometimes should be changed by the general congregation, but such a change should not be decreed definitively without a previous experiment or without a very clear reason.[16]

55/ §4. Decrees of general congregations, as well as rules and ordinations drawn up by the generals, even if inserted in the Collection of the Institute, not only may be changed by the aforesaid authorities in accordance with the competence of each, but it is their duty to provide for the continuing adaptation of them to the needs of the times.[17]

56/ §5. Every adaptation of the Institute should aim at always establishing whatever seems to contribute most, all things considered, to the knowledge, love, praise, and service of God, and to the salvation of souls. For our holy Father Ignatius laid down as the foundation, or first criterion, of all our laws the greater glory of God and the help of souls.[18]

57/ Decree 15—§1. It is permitted to the provincial congregations to treat of the substantials of the Institute, provided there are serious reasons, and in accordance with the norms laid down in the *Formula of the Provincial Congregation.*

58/ §2. In sending postulata to the general or provincial congregation, all Jesuits should bear in mind the above decrees; and let each, with due love of the patrimony of the Society and with due regard for his own responsibility, propose what he desires for the renewal and adaptation of the Institute,

---

[15] *Formula of the Institute* of Julius III, 2. GC 1, D. 16.

[16] GC 1, D. 16.

[17] *Cons. Prooemium in Declarationes et Annotationes Constitutionum* [136].

[18] *GenExam* and *Cons,* passim.

realizing, moreover, that the light necessary for making such postulata will be obtained not only from dialogue but most of all from prayer.

59/ Decree 16—Customs contrary to our law are not permitted in the Society.

4. On censures and precepts pertaining to the preservation of the Institute

60/ The 31st General Congregation abrogates the precept of holy obedience in No. 306 of the *Collection of Decrees*; and commissions Father General to petition the Holy See, insofar as this is necessary, to revoke the penalties in No. 305 of the *Collection of Decrees*. For it is the desire of the Congregation that a love and longing for all perfection may lead all Jesuits to the genuine preservation and increase not only of the body but also of the spirit of the Society.[19]

DECREE 5

THE DISTINCTION OF GRADES

61/ 1. The General Congregation decrees that, immediately after the close of the 31st General Congregation, a commission should be set up which will study the whole matter of suppressing the grade of spiritual coadjutor, either in law or in practice, and which will report on it to the next congregation, either of provincials or of procurators, in order that it may decide whether a general congregation should be summoned to deal with this matter.

62/ 2. The General Congregation recommends that the commission which is to study the entire problem of the distinction of grades should extend its study to include the advantages and disadvantages involved in granting solemn profession also to the temporal coadjutors.

---

[19] See *Cons.* [602, 813].

DECREE 6

The Permanent Diaconate

63/ 1. Gladly complying with the will of the Church which orders the restoration of the permanent diaconate in Eastern Churches where it has fallen into disuse[2] and also in the Western Church, where, in the judgment of the bishops and with the approbation of the Holy See, such a restoration may tend to the good of souls,[3] the 31st General Congregation declares that there is no obstacle preventing our Society, as far as it depends on us, from being helped in the future by certain members who would work permanently in the sacred order of the diaconate for the service of the Church.

64/ 2. But the General Congregation entrusts this matter of permanent deacons to Father General for prudent experimentation, according to the mind of the Church, where it is needed for the good of souls, as, for example, in our houses of the eastern rites in which it is not permitted for a priest to exercise the functions of a deacon in the celebration of liturgical offices

---

[2] See OE 17.
[3] See LG 29, AG 16.

DECREE 7

THE BROTHERS

65/ 1. Since it is of the greatest moment that all Jesuits truly understand the nature of the Jesuit brothers' vocation in order that they may be properly integrated into the life of the Society, it seemed clear to the 31st General Congregation that the principal task to be accomplished with respect to the brothers was clearly to state the nature of their vocation and the practical applications which flow from it. The result will be that all members of the Society, even at the cost of a complete change of mind,[2] may be truly of "one heart and one mind,"[3] and all, enjoying one and the same vocation apart from the priesthood, may together and in the spirit of our founder dedicate themselves totally to the mission of the Church.[4]

66/ 2. Since apostolic activity belongs to the very nature of the religious life in Institutes devoted to the apostolate,[5] the whole life of a brother must be called apostolic by reason of the specific consecration which they make to God through vows in the body of the Society. But beyond that, the brothers have a full share in the special apostolic nature of the Society, which pertains to all its members. For that reason their activity in the Society is to be defined by the same principles which define the apostolic service of the whole Society, namely, through its attention to the greater service of God and the universal good. Thus it is that, through various talents and activities—all its members being united in one spirit by the bonds of love and obedience[6]—the Society is to enjoy the presence of Christ, perform His tasks, and manifest His coming.[7]

67/ 3. Those offices and functions of the brothers which are described in the Institute have a true apostolic value and are to be performed in a spirit of cooperation. It is by works such as these that the religious intimacy and calm of the

---

[2] See the letters of Fr. Janssens, October 30, 1959, *ActRSJ* 13(1959) 628; and August 31, 1964, *ActRSJ* 14 (1964) 553 ff.

[3] AA 4, 32 (cited in PC 15).

[4] See PC 6.

[5] See PC 8.

[6] *Cons.* [821].

[7] See PC 15.

Society's houses, the fraternal union in the service of Christ,[8] the dedication of scholastics to their studies, and especially the mobility and freedom of priests in the ministries[9] are more perfectly maintained. Such offices are to be committed to the brothers with the fullest possible responsibility.

68/   Furthermore, in the service of the Society,[10] administrative offices may be given them, even in our communities and with respect to other Jesuits, always excluding, of course, the power of jurisdiction.

69/ 4. Moreover, following precedents in both the old and the restored Society, in addition to the offices mentioned above and in accordance with the judgment of superiors, brothers properly undertake those other tasks for which they may have a God-given talent and in which they may be of assistance and example "for the help of souls."[11] Among such tasks are teaching, practicing the liberal and technical arts, laboring in the fields of science and in whatever other areas their work, according to circumstances and places, may prove more useful in attaining the end of the Society.

70/   In all the above mentioned ways the brothers, as men consecrated to God, show that only in the spirit of the beatitudes can the world be transfigured and offered to God;[12] and in the Society they make a great contribution to the good of the Church.

71/ 5. Since the Society wishes that the brothers be brought closely into both the social and liturgical life of the community as well as into its works,[13] as befits companions who live the religious life in the same family, fraternal union and communication are to be fostered more and more among Jesuits by all the means which a discerning love may dictate.[14]

72/ 6. To this end the following will also be conducive: *(a)* the avoidance of every social distinction in community life; *(b)* the sharing, on the part of all Jesuits, in common domestic tasks, always with consideration for the greater service of God and the help of souls; *(c)* progressive participation on the part of the

---

[8] See LG 43.

[9] *Cons.* [149] ; ES II, 27.

[10] *Cons.* [148].

[11] *Cons.* IV, Prooemium, 1 and A [307-8].

[12] See LG 31.

[13] See PC 15.

[14] See what is said on this subject in decree 19, nn. 1–8 (Community Life).

brothers in consultations; *(d)* the observance of the decisions of the 31st General Congregation regarding their participation in congregations.[15]

73/ 7. The formation of brothers is to be entrusted to men who are carefully selected and diligently prepared.[16] They are to be taught especially to devote their lives to the service of the Church in the following of Christ. In order, however, that they may fulfill their duties and perform their functions more perfectly in the circumstances of modern life, their formation is to be spiritual, doctrinal, and technical, even confirmed with suitable degrees. This formation is to be carried out in suitable houses and is to be continued throughout life in accordance with each one's abilities.[17] The diversity which can result from this will contribute greatly to all the varied and necessary ministries which are to be carried on with one and the same spirit, supposing, of course, the preservation of indifference and availability for any offices whatsoever. "There are varieties of graces but one and the same Spirit."[18]

74/ 8. In order that all this may be conveniently put into execution, Father General is to establish a commission of experts. It will be their function: (a) to study more profoundly and to propound the theology of the vocation of the religious who is not destined for the priesthood in theSociety;[19] (b) to advise Father General on practical experiments to effect the application of this decree; (c) to propose general guidelines for the formation of brothers, which ought to be adapted by provincials for their respective areas; (d) to revise the rules and regulations concerning the brothers according to the spirit of this decree.

---

[15] See decree 40, nn. 2, 4; ES II 27.

[16] See PC 18.

[17] Loc. cit.

[18] 1 Cor. 12:4.

[19] See ES II 16 § 2.

III

THE FORMATION OF JESUITS

DECREE 8

The Spiritual Formation of Jesuits

75/   To all Jesuits the General Congregation fraternally proposes the following norms as a kind of spiritual pedagogy, ardently desiring that each Jesuit may become that instrument joined to God which is demanded by our religious and apostolic vocation.

I. General Norms

76/ 1. Since all spiritual progress is the work of divine grace, it is essential that each one should dispose himself to implore that grace by humble prayer and to respond to it with docile obedience in all his actions.

77/ 2. Spiritual formation will assist Jesuits, as they grow in faith, hope, and love, to follow Christ ever more closely and become ever more intimately conformed to him according to the grace of our vocation. But since, though called to perfect love, we are still sinners, our following of Christ must take the form of continual conversion to him.

78/   This progressive conformity to Christ can take place only on condition that we humbly listen to his word in Scripture, continually draw life from his sacraments, and follow him as present in the Church.

79/ 3. Our following of Christ will be more genuine and intimate the more intent each Jesuit is on adopting that manner of serving Christ peculiar to this Society, which precisely "desires to be distinguished by the name of Jesus."[2] Let all, then, learn to esteem this vocation as God's gift and adhere to it loyally. And let those attitudes of mind be cultivated which St. Ignatius held most dear: personal love for the poor and humble Christ, filial devotion to our Lady His mother, sincere zeal for souls, fortitude in undertaking even more difficult enterprises for God's glory, a readiness for service founded on obedience and self-denial, the ability to find God in all things, development of skill in the discernment of spirits, ease in initiating spiritual conversation with others, a concern for thinking with the Church. . . .[3]

---

[2] *Formula of the Institute,* n. 1.

[3] See *SpEx* 146–47, 352–70; *Cons.* [288, 547, 648, 729, 813].

80/ 4. The Society's apostolic objective is to be considered the principle which regulates the entire formation of our members. It should, therefore, inspire their formation in prayer, the aim of which is to fashion men who will seek God in everything, as well as that formation in the religious and apostolic life whereby Jesuits are trained to become "prompt and diligent" in sharing Christ's redemptive mission in the Church with a magnanimity that embraces ever greater tasks and bears every adversity with steady cheerfulness.[4]

81/ 5. For the sake of each one's spiritual growth, we should all cooperate actively in a spirit of fraternal love, bearing one another's burdens according to the measure of each one's grace and the work entrusted to each one by the Society. All should therefore have high regard for the account of conscience to superiors, which has been held in such honor by the Society's long tradition, for conversation with the spiritual father, and also for fraternal gatherings which, if they promote a common seeking of God's will, bring spiritual joy, encouragement, and apostolic fruitfulness to all.

82/ 6. It should not be forgotten that the process of formation, a progressive and never completed work, is to take the form of an organic development in the various stages of formation, such that the spiritual life is never split off from the affective, intellectual, or apostolic life. Let us rather be directed by that discerning charity which St. Ignatius teaches us and seek to be able to recognize and choose the will of God in every situation.

83/ 7. Following the pedagogy of the Exercises, spiritual formation should fashion men who have true freedom and maturity of spirit, who feel themselves to be freer, the closer they are dedicated through obedience to the will of God. This divine will is concretely revealed to us especially by the inner promptings of grace and the direction of superiors, as well as by the example of our brothers, by the demands of our apostolic work, of common life, and of our rules, and by the contingencies of our own life and the spiritual needs of our time.

84/ This objective is unattainable apart from the constant cultivation of a spirit of initiative and responsibility within obedience, and of self-denial in working together at a common task. This, as St. Ignatius rightly perceived, can be obtained only through experience, which makes it necessary during the time of formation to provide opportunity for all to advance in freedom and maturity.

85/ 8. Since St. Ignatius so strongly recommends to us a right intention,[5] Jesuits do well to cultivate sincerity, which is not genuine unless it be combined with loyalty to those norms given us by the Church and the Society in accordance

---

[4] See *SpEx* 91, 97–98; *Exam* [101–102], *Cons.* [547, 621].

[5] *Cons.* [288, 360, 618, 813].

with the promises we have freely made. Thus all should be convinced that subjective sincerity must find its complement in objective loyalty.

86/ 9. Since conditions in the modem world demand firmer foundations for the spiritual life, it is necessary that from the very beginning the scholastics and brothers be educated continually and progressively to a deeper knowledge of the mystery of Christ based on Holy Scripture and the liturgy, as well as on the Society's traditional devotion to the Sacred Heart of Jesus, and on the teaching concerning the Church and other theological themes, always with the same purpose in view, that faith, hope, and love be together nourished and strengthened.[6]

87/ In mission lands it will help to enlist their rich heritage of sound morality and ascetical and mystical aspiration for the spiritual formation of Jesuits.

88/ 10. Human virtues are to be held in high esteem because they make the apostolate more fruitful and religious life happier; among these virtues are "goodness of heart, sincerity, strength of mind and constancy, diligent care for justice, politeness, and other virtues which the Apostle Paul commends."[7]

89/ 11. As other general congregations have already declared, special care must be paid to the selection of superiors and those who serve as fathers and masters of the spiritual life, so that the most capable men may be chosen for these offices which are more important than any other whatsoever. It is vitally important to be sure that, over and above knowledge and virtue, they are especially endowed with those human and spiritual gifts whereby they can inspire communities, foster fraternal cooperation, and help all towards greater spiritual maturity in discerning God's ways. What must be looked for, therefore, is openness of spirit, ease in dialogue, and abundant talent in these men whose essential task is to stimulate and attract their brethren by means of new things and old.

90/ 12. For any spiritual pedagogy to be fruitful it has to be adapted to those for whom it is meant to be used. Hence it will be up to the superiors and those groups in provinces and regions which care for the formation of Jesuits to seek, under Father General's direction, those means which are better accommodated to different situations. Throughout the indications set forth in the following chapters, this continued quest for adaptation is always presupposed.

II. The Novitiate

91/ The content of this chapter pertains alike to the scholastics' and the brothers' novitiate. It will only be necessary to introduce such differences of method as are required by the different modes of one and the same service to which all

---

[6] OT 8, 14; PC 2.

[7] PO 3; see Phil. 4, 8.

are called. Whether the scholastics and brothers have the same master or different ones, care must be had to obtain a common formation.

92/ This initial stage of formation is defined by its twofold purpose: it is a time at once of probation and of formation, during which the grace of vocation should be cultivated and during which it should already manifest its fruitfulness.

93/ 13. To this end, sufficient human maturity is a requirement for candidates. Experience has shown, however, that in our own time affective maturity has become more difficult for adolescents. Deficiencies in this regard are difficult to detect, especially in candidates who in other respects are mature and intellectually gifted. According to circumstances, opportune provision must be made for this serious difficulty:

94/ —by instituting a more searching examination of candidates, adapting the instructions given by St. Ignatius to our own times and having recourse when necessary to the recommendations of men skilled in psychology. The secrecy of consultation, the candidate's freedom, and the norms established by the Church are, however, to be strictly safeguarded;

95/ —by postponing, when it seems advisable, the time of admission. In such cases the applicants can be recommended to certain selected fathers who will help them towards obtaining maturity in their vocation while they prepare for entrance into the novitiate by means of studies and apostolic experiments.

96/ 14. A vocation is then to be tested by various experiments which, in St. Ignatius' view, constitute the specific characteristic of the Society's novitiate. To achieve their purpose, however, these must place the novices in those circumstances wherein they can give evidence of "what they really are"[8] and show how they have made their own the spiritual attitudes proper to our vocation. New experiments, therefore, which fulfill this purpose today, ought to be prudently and boldly pursued.

97/ 15. The primacy in the novices' formation should be given to the Spiritual Exercises, since of all the experiments they are the chief and fundamental one. Let them, therefore, be well prepared for, made at the most advantageous time, and presented in all their force and spiritual vigor. For it is by means of them that the novices are introduced into the heart, as it were, of their vocation, so perceiving its distinctive grace that they are able to bear witness to it.

98/ 16. Education towards familiarity with God in prayer should be carried out in the apostolic atmosphere of the Exercises. The daily exercises of piety should tend to arouse personal love for Christ and teach the seeking of famil-

---

[8] Gonçalves da Cámara, *Memoriale,* 257, MHSI, I, 678.

iar communion with God in all things. Care should also be taken that the novices clearly understand how the different means presented in the Constitutions themselves (examinations of conscience, prayer, meditation, reading . . . [277])[9] serve to complement one another. These modes of prayer ought to be nourished by assiduous reading of Sacred Scripture and participation in the sacred liturgy. The novices will thus be introduced more deeply into the common prayer of the People of God and each one's sacramental life will be more abundantly fruitful. Primacy in this sacramental life belongs to the Eucharist, which from the start should be made our life's vital center. The sacrament of penance, moreover, should be cultivated in such a way that it retains its theological and ecclesial value and exerts its full effect on spiritual progress in the way of the Lord.

99/ 17. This familiarity with God depends on self-denial, a spirit of recollection, and peace of mind. In these times it not infrequently happens that conditions of life are such as to engender, even unconsciously, a certain disquiet or anxiety of mind which makes a life of prayer more difficult despite good will. All therefore need to understand how, in addition to a living faith, emotional balance, humble acceptance of oneself, trust in others, and freedom of mind constitute for each one virtually fundamental conditions for the enjoyment of true and familiar converse with God.

100/ 18. The practice of community life should both develop the brotherhood of our members and benefit the affective maturity of the novices. This supposes that the novitiate community is already a brotherhood in the Spirit, which imparts to true friendship that perfection of charity to which the vow of chastity is itself ordered. The more fraternal is community life, the more will the novices grasp its meaning and its demands and feel themselves to be a part of the whole Society.

101/ In the same spirit a suitable sharing of life and work should be fostered between the scholastic and coadjutor novices, whereby they can be familiarly known and helped in esteeming and realizing their own vocation. In external matters such as food, clothing, and lodging, there should be complete equality.

102/ 19. Education towards a discerning charity by means of spiritual direction and obedience supposes that complete trust and freedom prevail between Father Master and the novices. A further necessity is that the novitiate's way of life be not so rigidly determined that the novices, lacking in all initiative, can hardly ever practice spiritual discernment, or even obedience itself, except in the form of a passive and impersonal submission.

103/ 20. Formation in self-denial will be more authentic the more closely the novices follow in the footsteps of Christ who took the form of a servant. Self-

---

[9] *Cons.* [277].

denial will be exercised primarily, humbly and simply, in the everyday demands of our vocation. Particular mortifications should, however, be undertaken, under the guidance of obedience, as indicated by the individual's requirements, the Church's call, and the world's needs. Let the novices learn, in theory and by practice, so to shape their life by austerity and sobriety that, being "really and spiritually poor," they may be that sign "highly esteemed today" which the Church desires.[10]

104/ 21. During the time of novitiate, the doctrinal elements referred to in No. 9 comprise both a deeper initiation into the mystery of Christ and a fuller knowledge of the sources of the Society's spiritual doctrine and manner of life, chiefly to be drawn from the Society's history and the examples of its saints. Faults and deficiencies should not, however, be systematically overlooked, in order that the novices may be more ready to follow in the footsteps of our better members and more aware of their responsibility to the Society.

105/ Instruction should be given from the outset to the scholastic novices concerning the priestly character of their vocation, and to the novice brothers concerning the religious and apostolic character of their vocation and the meaning and value of work in accordance with the decree on the brothers.

106/ 22. Although entrance into the novitiate should entail a real separation from the life previously led in the world, superiors should nevertheless provide that the novices, while consistently maintaining a spirit of recollection, should have sufficient social contact with their contemporaries (both within and outside the Society). Likewise the necessary separation from parents and friends should take place in such a way that genuine progress in affective balance and supernatural love is not impeded.

107/ For this purpose the novitiate should, as far as possible, be located in a place where the novices' probation can be conducted according to the manner of life proper to the Society.

108/ 23. Since spiritual progress requires living conditions which stimulate rather than crush human virtues, care must be taken to prevent the novitiate's being so remote from reality that novices' difficulties are there overlooked rather than solved. The more the novices are stimulated to assume responsibilities with prudent and discerning charity, the more successfully will they acquire spiritual maturity and the more freely will they adhere to their vocation.

109/ 24. Since human development does not proceed at the same pace in everyone, if, when the time of noviceship is ended, some of the novices, well endowed with the qualities requisite for this vocation, still have not shown suffi-

---

[10] PC 13.

cient maturity, major superiors should not hesitate to use the faculty given them by our law and postpone the taking of first vows or even extend the noviceship for a time by the introduction of some longer experiment.[11]

110/ 25. It will benefit the spiritual, intellectual, and affective formation of the novices if they are associated with some other selected men besides Father Master who at certain times can assist him in his work, in order to provide the novices with a richer and fuller image of the Ignatian vocation.

111/ 26. The master of novices is to be assisted in acquiring ever better knowledge of the mentality of the candidates, so that he can adapt to it his spiritual pedagogy and the structural features of the novitiate. It is especially the provincial's role to help him in this task, providing him with the collaboration of experts and fostering meetings between masters of novices and those who, within or outside the Society, are devoted to the formation of youth.

III. The Brothers' Spiritual Formation after the Novitiate

112/ 27. After the completion of the noviceship, the brothers' formation should be continued until tertianship, both in the juniorate[12] and afterwards with various experiments and assignments. Thus the technical, cultural, and doctrinal formation which renders them more apt for the service of God will be closely conjoined with spiritual development.

113/ 28. Where it has not been done already there should be instituted during the time of juniorate a complete and well-adapted course in theology as a principal discipline. There should also be among the other disciplines suitable instruction concerning "ways and habits of thought and opinion in contemporary social life."[13]

114/ 29. After the juniorate the brothers should be sent to those houses where their progressive spiritual training can be provided for more easily. The superior of the house should have the greatest care for their formation and should provide them with appropriate means for developing their personal spiritual life at the same time that he entrusts them with increasing responsibility. He should especially urge their active and conscious participation in liturgical celebrations, particularly of the Eucharist.[14]

---

[11] See *Exam* [100]; *Cons.* [514].

[11] See GC 30, D. 41.

[13] PC 18.

[14] See SC 7, 10.

115/ They should have a qualified spiritual father who is seriously devoted to their care. Under his direction they should receive spiritual instruction by way of rather frequent conversations and private reading.

116/ 30. A short course or program on spiritual and doctrinal formation should be set up each year especially for those brothers who have not yet completed tertianship. On such occasions, following a closely integrated program, lectures are to be offered on Sacred Scripture, liturgy, theology, or social doctrine.

IV. The Scholastics' Spiritual Formation after the Novitiate

117/ 31. The vocation tested and strengthened during the novitiate should continue its growth throughout the whole time of formation. Accordingly it is necessary for there to be an appropriate transition and continuity between the noviceship and subsequent formation, and between various stages of the latter. Intellectual formation and the genuine integration of human values can assume full meaning and importance only if they are accompanied by deeper knowledge and love of Christ, so as to bring about a unification of the whole personality.

118/ 32. All ought therefore to read carefully what is said of formation in general in the decree on the training of scholastics especially in studies (Chapter I) and strive to put it faithfully into effect. Moreover, the scholastics should persuade themselves that the best way to union with God and the proper preparation for the priesthood are to be found in seriously striving to live the spirit of our vocation.

119/ 33. Wise and competent spiritual fathers are to be chosen, who can offer fraternal help to the scholastics during their time of study to achieve a true discernment of spirits.

120/ All the fathers who reside in houses of formation should also feel that each in proportion to his office shares in the task of providing for the scholastics' spiritual growth and their apostolic preparation.[15] Indeed, everyone in the province should be ready to offer generous help to the formation of our men.

121/ It is further to be hoped that in particular regions meetings will be held, either independently or in collaboration with groups concerned with intellectual and pastoral formation, to develop an organized survey of spiritual training for the whole program of formation.

122/ 34. Throughout all of their formation the scholastics should keep in view the priestly character of our vocation, with the result that study, prayer, and all other activities may be imbued with a desire of serving God and the Church with priestly love

---

[15] See OT 5.

for men. Especially before they come to theology, they should be provided with opportunity to secure a deeper understanding of their priestly calling.

123/ 35. A life of prayer should be cultivated which is suitable for a time of study. Each one should therefore earnestly seek, with the spiritual father's help, a way of prayer which has vitality for him. To this end they should carefully search out among the different ways of prayer proposed by the Exercises, namely, meditation, contemplation, *lectio divina,* liturgical and vocal prayer, those which best lead them to God. This personal effort, pursued with constancy, will be a great help to the scholastics in acquiring familiarity with God.

124/ The annual Spiritual Exercises are to be regarded as the spirit which animates our formation and brings us to fuller awareness of our vocation. The scholastics should learn to apply the rules and principles of the Exercises to those difficulties which are likely to arise during the time of studies. The scholastics should be permitted on occasion during their formation to make the Spiritual Exercises alone under the direction of an experienced spiritual father so as to have freer and more fruitful communion with God and respond with fuller and more ready availability to the promptings of the Holy Spirit.

125 36. The scholastics should recall that the virtues required by intellectual labor, such as attention, humility, readiness to serve, constancy, patience and tolerance of adversity, and love of truth, open up to them a most fitting way of finding God in studies.

126/ It should also be kept in mind that the time of studies, undertaken according to the spirit of our vocation, provides valuable opportunities for obedience joined to personal initiative, for affective maturity and charity, and for a life that is poor and devoted to labor. The life of a scholastic should, therefore, be so arranged that occasions are not lacking for the truly responsible exercise of these virtues, so that Jesuits may personally experience the meaning of the evangelical counsels.[16]

127/ 37. At the same time that the scholastics, impelled by an apostolic spirit, seek to know the world with its aspirations and values, which today are so often alien to faith, let them earnestly nourish their own faith and each day shape their intellect more to the mystery of Christ, lest otherwise there should gradually develop a most serious divorce of human wisdom from faith. "Above all, let Sacred Scripture be daily in their hands, so that from reading and meditating the divine Scriptures they may learn 'the surpassing knowledge of Jesus Christ' (Phil. 3:8)."[17]

---

[16] See OT 9.

[17] PC 6.

128/ 38. Finally, scholastics, who are greatly affected by the aspirations and movements of our time, must respond to them as spiritual men, with humble loyalty to the Society. Thus by their vigor and alertness they will make a much desired contribution to the Society's renewal and adaptation.

129/ 39. During the time of teaching or experiments, treated in the decree on the training of scholastics especially in studies (No. 30), care is to be taken that the scholastics' spiritual life not only does not thereby suffer damage, but on the contrary that it derive therefrom a proper growth. For inasmuch as such experiments represent at once testing and formation, their particular circumstances should contribute to that full apostolic and religious maturity to which the entire education of Jesuits is directed.

130/ 40. The scholastics should therefore be seriously concerned to seek their own spiritual growth and to adapt it more closely to the particular conditions of an apostolic life. If in the process they experience greater difficulties in prayer and work, let them learn to overcome these with magnanimity and patience in the Lord.

131/ 41. Superiors should take care that only those apostolic works are entrusted to the scholastics which are consistent with their spiritual progress. Let them provide the spiritual help which such a time most requires. Thus superiors should see to it that the scholastics are accepted in a brotherly spirit into the community of members already formed, and that they are assisted by some suitable spiritual father so that these experiments strengthen them in their vocation.

132/ Scholastics are not, however, to be sent to such experiments before they have acquired the doctrinal formation which will enable them to fulfill them profitably. Special care should be taken of those destined for secular studies that they may secure a doctrinal formation adapted to their particular studies and requirements.

V. Tertianship

133/ Since the General Congregation has already promulgated a decree on tertianship, urging instructors to undertake experiments with a view to rendering it more profitable, only its place and importance in the organic process of the fathers' and brothers' formation are treated here.

134/ 42. Tertianship aims at perfecting the formation of the affections[18] and testing whether the tertian, imbued with the Society's spirit, shows promise of continuing to make progress himself and of helping others in the Lord.

---

[18] See *Cons.* [516]; see *Polanci Complementa,* II, *Industria* 5 [Ser. 1], 744.

135/ 43. The expression school of affection[19] characterizes that institution in which members of the Society are so "filled with love of the true doctrine of Christ"[20] that they "progress in the Spirit and seriously follow Christ our Lord" and "love and ardently desire to put on the Lord's own clothing and insignia for his love and reverence."[21] This schooling consists in concrete and personal contact with the things of the Society, consisting on the one hand in a vital confrontation with the Institute both in documents and in religious and community life itself, and on the other hand in actively participating in various experiments, first in the Spiritual Exercises, so as to develop a deeper practice of prayer (and in it "to seek God and direct all their affection towards the Creator"),[22] and then in other experiments, which in the case of the priests should be of a pastoral nature, so that they may be practiced in the discernment of spirits while working in the varied circumstances of the world.

136/ 44. To bring this about it will help most if the tertians have an instructor who is in the first place a genuine spiritual teacher and who will examine the experiences undergone in the course of formation and help each one by means of the rules of the discernment of spirits to find his own way to greater progress.

137/ 45. The greatest benefit is rightly expected from this final probation, namely, for each one to bring to completion the desired synthesis of spiritual, apostolic, and intellectual formation which makes for the fuller integration in the Lord of the whole personality, in keeping with the Society's objective as St. Ignatius described it: "that, since they themselves have made progress, they may better help others to make spiritual progress to the glory of God and of our Lord."[23]

VI. Continuing Formation

138/ 46. Closely following the Church, which, in liturgical renewal, biblical and theological reflection, and attention to the changing conditions of the times, is led by the Holy Spirit to complement the wisdom of antiquity by means of new developments, all, even those who have already completed their formation, should strive constantly to draw from these sources renewal for their own spiritual lives. Their apostolic activity will thus be enabled to answer more effectively the needs of the Church and of men.

---

[19] *Cons.* [516].

[20] *SpEx* 164.

[21] *GenExam* [101].

[22] *Cons.* [288].

[23] *Cons.* [516].

139/ 47. The means commended by our Institute are therefore to be carefully preserved (the annual Exercises, recollections, etc.). Prudently adapted to the requirements of age or spiritual condition, these means are purged of all taint of formalism and exert their proper effect. Those new means should also be adopted (special courses, meetings, etc.) which commonly serve to promote renewal in the contemporary Church. It will be up to superiors to provide opportunities for these, especially for those men who are usually kept from them by duties and occupations.

140/ 48. It is likewise desirable that for the Society as a whole as well as for its particular regions, the tools necessary for spiritual formation may be made available also in vernacular languages, as, for example, St. Ignatius' works and the texts of our spiritual tradition, theological writings of outstanding worth, news about enterprises undertaken in other regions, etc. Thus will the whole Society be enabled to accomplish in common the study and discernment of the will of God, which is the principle and goal of all spiritual growth, so that all "may learn to live in close and familiar fellowship with the Father through his Son Jesus Christ in the Holy Spirit."[24]

---

[23] OT 8.

DECREE 9

The Training of Scholastics Especially in Studies

I. Training in General

141/ 1. The training of the scholastics should be apostolic in its orientation; namely, that Jesuits may be able "with the help of God to benefit both their own souls and those of their neighbor."[2] Therefore, the scholastics, called by Christ our Lord to serve the universal Church as future priests, should prepare themselves, with the help of divine grace, "for the defense and propagation of the faith and the growth of souls in Christian life and doctrine."[3] The result should be that, living in close familiarity with God, through a profound understanding of the faith and a vital knowledge of men, they will become true ministers of Christ, who make the presence of God felt in the modern world.

142/ 2. There should be an organic unity in the whole training of the scholastics. Thus, beginning with the novitiate and throughout the entire course of studies there should be a close integration of spiritual formation, the work of study, and apostolic activity. All who have charge of the training of Jesuits, either in government or in teaching, should diligently and harmoniously work together for this integration.

143/ 3. The scholastics should base their lives on the principles of the spirituality of the Society, as explained in the decrees on the spiritual life. They should strive for the fullness of Christian life in charity. They should practice a true self-denial, especially in faithful application to study, should come to an intimate knowledge and a generous observance of the Constitutions, and should continuously foster, in intimate prayer and the mysteries of the sacred liturgy, a personal union with Christ their Lord, who calls them to share in his priesthood.

144/ 4. In the whole course of training, apostolic experiments of a suitable nature should be undertaken. These experiments should be carefully directed by experts, who are themselves so filled with the priestly and pastoral spirit that the training, both spiritual and intellectual, will be filled with that same spirit. An

---

[2] *Cons.* [351].

[3] *Formula of the Institute,* n. 1.

additional help to this end will be frequent meetings with those who are already working in the apostolate.

145 5. Provision should be made in each stage of the training for personal maturity, especially of the emotions; the advice of trained psychologists should be used when it is necessary. In this way, the balanced development of the spiritual, intellectual and affective life will be secured, and the true maturity of the whole person will be achieved.

146/ 6. The scholastics, in their whole course of studies, should try to develop a sense of genuine and sober responsibility, rejecting every form of immaturity which would make them unable to face the difficulties of life. Therefore, frequent occasions should be given them for exercising responsibility, in leading the spiritual and intellectual life more actively and spontaneously, in doing some work in the house, and in vigorously carrying on various apostolic experiments as well.

147/ 7. Great care should be taken that each scholastic be directed according to his own gifts, both natural and supernatural. At the same time a sense of solidarity and collaboration should be fostered in the whole period of training, so that every trace of that egoism which is rightly criticized may be removed from our training.

148/ 8. The discipline of common life is to be embraced from the inner law of love, as a necessary element in our training; namely, to follow the divine will faithfully in daily life, to promote solid personal maturity, to practice the duties of charity toward fellow religious. Let the practice of this discipline be such that the scholastics, following Christ their Lord and Master in humble reverence and obedience, may enjoy the true freedom of the children of God in the Holy Spirit.

149/ 9. Care is to be taken that the number of scholastics in the houses of formation be not too large, so that mutual relations can be spiritual and fraternal, the discipline may be that of a family, and the government truly paternal.

150/ 10. True dialogue should exist between superiors, professors, and scholastics. It should be possible for all to express opinions and make suggestions with openness and candor. Thus in the final decision, which belongs to the superior, there will be closer consensus and obedience, and a filial spirit and fraternal communion of mind will grow continuously within the community.

151/ 11. The scholastics should have suitable contacts with outside university groups, with clerics and religious, and also with laymen both of their own and of other nations. This, of course, should be arranged with prudence. In this way, ridding themselves of nationalism and every other form of particularism, they will acquire the universality of mind and openness toward different forms of culture and diverse civilizations and mentalities which our apostolic vocation demands.

152/ 12. The entire training of the scholastics should be inspired by the spirit of the Second Vatican Council as manifested in its constitutions and decrees, namely in the constitutions on the Church and the Sacred Liturgy and in the decrees on priestly formation, on the appropriate renewal of the religious life and on ecumenism.[4]

II. On Studies

153/ 13. The purpose of studies in the Society is apostolic, as is the purpose of the entire training. Through their studies the scholastics should acquire that breadth and excellence in learning which are required for our vocation to achieve its end.

154/ 14. The education given through our studies is both general and special: the general education which is necessary for all priests in the Society; the special education which is daily more necessary for the various tasks for which Jesuits are to be prepared. Their general education should give to the minds of the scholastics that Christian vision which will illuminate the entire field of future special study and work, and also bring light to others with whom they work.

155/ 15. To insure that the intellectual formation of Jesuits is ordered to meet the needs of the times, the entire *Ratio Studiorum* shall be revised. Considering the great diversity of regions and circumstances, this *Ratio* shall determine only general norms. It should have due regard both for the laws of the Church (those now in force as well as those to be passed by the Council or after the Council) and for the laws passed by the present General Congregation. The new *Ratio Studiorum* can depart from the decrees of preceding general congregations as this is opportune, until the next general congregation makes a final decision. In the meantime, some definite experiments, with the approval of Father General, can be carried on; the results of these experiments are to be accurately reported to the commission on the *Ratio Studiorum*.

156/ 26. In the different regions, it will be the task of the (group of) provincials to have a special *Ordo Studiorum* drawn up, which will adapt and fill out the general norms, considering the special circumstances of each region. These special Ordinations, which must be approved by Father General, are to be regularly revised, so that the training of Jesuits may always correspond to the apostolic needs of each region.

A. *The General Curriculum of Studies*

157/ 17. Before they begin philosophy and theology, the scholastics should have completed that training in letters and sciences which in each nation is re-

---

[4] See LG, SC, OT, PC, UR.

quired before specialization is begun. Their knowledge of Latin should be sufficient for them to understand and use with ease the sources of the sacred sciences and the documents of the Church. This training in letters and sciences, if it has not been completed before entrance into the Society, shall be completed in the novitiate; and, if necessary, in the juniorate.

158/ 18. In those provinces in which, according to their special Ordinations, higher studies are pursued in the juniorate, they should be capable of developing in the juniors a well-balanced religious and human maturity, and they should give them as well a vital knowledge of man and of the modern world. This humanistic training is to be achieved by the study of ancient and modern literature, and also of history and the sciences. Furthermore, the juniors should endeavor early to develop their aesthetic sense. It is urgently desired that the scholastics early in their studies learn one or more modern languages in addition to their own. Finally, in the entire course of studies, but especially in the juniorate, the scholastics should practice those means of expression which are suited to the people of our age. Skilled in the arts of writing and speaking, they can become better preachers of the Gospel of Christ.

159/ 19. Since in modern civilization, the audio-visual media are most effective in moving the souls of every class of people, the scholastics shall have suitable opportunities for access to them, and also of learning how they can be used successfully in the apostolate.

160/ 20. In the novitiate or the juniorate or at least in the beginning of the course of philosophy, the scholastics shall receive an appropriate introduction to the mystery of Christ and the history of salvation; this should give them a vision of the meaning, order, and apostolic purpose of all their studies; it should likewise help to ground their own religious life in faith, and strengthen them in their vocation. The methodical reading of Holy Scripture shall be begun with a gradual initiation in the novitiate. Likewise, throughout the whole course of training they shall learn to take an active part in the liturgy, and come to understand it more deeply.

161/ 21. The courses in philosophy and theology shall be so fitted to each other, and the disciplines shall be so arranged, that all of them harmoniously work together to attain the apostolic end of our studies. This end will not be obtained in the Society unless apostolic men trained as well as possible in these studies are prepared. Therefore, as a general rule, our scholastics should work for those academic degrees in philosophy and especially in theology, which can be obtained in our course of studies and help towards our apostolic purpose.

162/ 22. All scholastics shall study philosophy for at least two years. The introduction to the mystery of Christ is to be their guiding light; the patrimony of a perennially valid philosophy is to be the foundation of their thinking. Thus they can be brought to a personal and truly philosophical reflection on human existence, and especially on Christian existence. This reflection should take account of the progress of both philosophy and science, and try to respond to the vital problems of contemporary men, especially of those who have a greater influence in the territory. Through this reflection they should gain an insight into the whole of reality according to its metaphysical structure; it should lead to a knowledge of God, and in this way prepare the way for theology.

163/ 23. The instruction in theology for all scholastics shall be given for four years. This instruction shall be pastoral, in the sense that by an accurate study of the sources and by an investigation of the meaning of the faith, the scholastics shall so deeply penetrate the richness of divine revelation, that the word of God will nourish their own personal spiritual life and will be able to be effectively communicated in the priestly ministry to the people of their own time. They shall seriously study Sacred Scripture, so that it will be the very soul of all the other disciplines, by means of accurate exegesis and a suitable doctrinal synthesis. To reach this deeper understanding of the faith, so necessary for our times, they shall reverently, without preconceived opinions, study the relation of the mysteries among themselves as well as their relation to the urgent philosophical questions of their time. In all this they shall loyally follow in the footsteps of the Fathers both of the East and of the West and of the great Doctors of the Church.

164/ 24. Separate classes for long and short course are not required in theology. Nonetheless, individual care should be given to the scholastics so that they will be better trained according to their individual aptitudes and their special future assignments.

165/ 25. The programs of the entire philosophical and theological curriculum shall be revised, so that disciplines can be taken in their entirety, the matter be distributed more systematically, unnecessary repetitions can be avoided, obsolete questions can be omitted, and those which have an influence at the present time can be treated more profoundly. New disciplines should not be lightly introduced, but rather new questions should be taken up in the appropriate places in already existing disciplines. For the social formation of the scholastics, in addition to special courses, care is to be taken that in other philosophical and theological disciplines their social aspect and dimension be developed more fully.

166/ 26. The methods of teaching shall be revised. The hours of class shall be reduced when circumstances require it; correspondingly, the active participation of the scholastics shall be increased, and encouragement shall be given to their mutual cooperation, under the personal direction of the professors, in seminars, written papers, private study, and small groups.

167/ 27. It is also desirable that each scholastic, under the direction of the prefect of studies, find some field of specialization according to his individual talent; he should work on this in the time left over from the ordinary studies; he should foster a personal interest in studies, and prepare himself remotely for his own future apostolate in the modern world.

168/ 28. Examinations should be genuine tests. According to the norms to be determined in the *Ratio Studiorum,* they can be both oral and written; but in a principal discipline they may not be merely written. The examiners shall make a personal and free judgment; it is permissible for them to consult together after the examination. Examinations can be repeated once; but those who do not pass the second examination in a principal discipline lose the right both to a licentiate and to the profession in the Society.

169/ 29. The matter for the *examen ad gradum* is the whole of theology. Philosophical questions are to be included insofar as they are related to theological ones. The examination will last one hour and a half, and the candidate shall be examined by each examiner for about twenty minutes. This examination also can be repeated once. It is permissible, however, for the examiners to consult together; they can make their judgment also from knowledge they have outside the examination and can take account of the grades given through the entire course; therefore these grades should be available to the examiners.

170/ 30. Regency can be made after philosophy, or, where it seems better, deferred until after theology, or omitted, or joined with special studies. But when it is omitted, care should be taken to secure the purpose of the regency by various apostolic works. These works should be set up during the entire period of training (see No. 4), especially during the annual vacation, arranged with prudence, without harm to studies, and under the direction of a man of experience.

171/ 31. Ordination to the priesthood, especially when regency does not take place before theology, can suitably be deferred, according to the special norms to be approved by Father General for the needs of a particular region.

172/ 32. In the houses of study there should not be too many scholastics for the reasons given in No. 9. But since a sufficient number of professors, a good library and other scholarly helps are necessary for intellectual training, schools and faculties should not be multiplied; but, where this can be conveniently done, let there be several religious communities, the scholastic members of which attend the same school or faculty. Indeed, let there be concern, as far as it is possible, that our houses of study be built near university centers, so that the scholastics can also have the advantage of other professors and libraries; care should be taken, however, that their training, far from being injured thereby, become better.

B. Special Studies

173/ 33. Since it is daily more necessary that not only those who are destined to teach, but also those who exercise other ministries of the Society, have special preparation, the provincials should provide for the training of an ample number of competent men for the various tasks, keeping in mind both the needs of the apostolate and the talents and preference of the scholastics.

174/ 34. Those who are to have special studies should be chosen carefully and in good time; they should be directed by a special prefect of studies even during the period in which they are still following the general curriculum; they should devote themselves to their specialization generously and exclusively, and continue in it so that, as far as possible, they become outstanding.

175/ 35. Likewise, those who are destined for administrative functions in large houses, especially in houses of study, should have some advance preparation. This may include special studies, and, in any case, it presupposes the natural and supernatural gifts required for such offices. This is especially true for treasurers of large houses or provinces.

176/ 36. Special care should be given to the preparation of spiritual fathers of Jesuits and of externs. This can be done in special courses in Rome or elsewhere, or privately, under the direction of a trained, experienced man, or with some other suitable preparation, according to decree 40 of the 30th General Congregation. This is especially true of those destined to be masters of novices and instructors of tertians.

177/ 37. Those who are to teach the sacred sciences in major seminaries and especially in Jesuit faculties, should take special studies either in the international institutes in Rome or in other universities, as the provincial, with the advice of experts, shall think best. They are to obtain the appropriate academic degrees, especially ecclesiastical ones, and to be well prepared for teaching.

178/ 38. Scientific and technical advancement is a major factor in our times. The positive sciences exert an ever increasing influence on the mentality of men and on the very structure of our daily lives. Hence those who are destined for scientific research and for teaching the secular sciences should have special training to fit them for the scientific apostolate which is so very important. In fact, the Society should have men with doctoral degrees who become truly eminent in these fields.

179/ 39. Men skilled in pastoral work should also be trained with special studies. This will enable them to promote the proper arrangement of our ministries and their adaptation to modern times and special circumstances.

180/ 40. Those who are destined for other regions, in addition to the general preparation, should, where it is necessary, have a specialization before they go to that region, with a view to the circumstances of that region.

C. Doctrine and Teaching

181/ 41. The purpose of our studies is to train Jesuits to proclaim and transmit the truth revealed in Christ and entrusted to the Church. Our teaching therefore should faithfully adhere to what "was once given to the holy men of the faith,"[2] and should be such that, accommodating itself to changing ways of speaking and thinking, and adapting itself to the diverse cultures of the whole world, it can continually revivify that faith in the hearts of men.

182/ 42. Let Jesuits put their trust in the strength of the divine truth, and in that inner unction of the Holy Spirit which leads the Church of Christ to all truth. Therefore let them join to their studies a close familiarity with God, and in this secure way they will be safe from timidity as well as from thoughtless innovation. Let them in all matters see that their knowledge is well-grounded, according to the norms which the Holy See has given us.

183/ 43. Professors should bear in mind that they do not teach in their own name, but that their mission is in the Church and from the Church, and that they are joined in charity in the Society of Jesus. Hence they should let themselves be guided by the mind and will of the Church, show proper respect for the teaching authority of the Church, and have regard for the building up of the faith in their students and in all the faithful. At the same time they should keep in mind those who are separated from us.

184/ 44. Let both professors and scholastics faithfully adhere to and diligently study the word of God in Scripture and Tradition. Let them also have high regard for the holy Fathers and other Doctors, and for those authors of the Society who are highly regarded in the Church. Let them follow principally the mind and principles of St. Thomas; his works should be well known to them.

185/ 45. Professors should clearly distinguish between matters of faith to be held by all and teachings approved by the consent of theologians. Probable, new, and merely personal explanations are to be proposed modestly.

186/ 46. For more secure and profitable progress in doctrine, it will be very helpful if the professors freely and sincerely communicate to their colleagues their new ideas, even before they are published. Thus, if necessary, they can be corrected, and can perhaps also be of benefit to others.

---

[2] Jud. 3.

187/ 47. The scholastics during their course of studies should learn, under the direction of their teachers, to read critically and use prudently the works even of non-Catholics, especially of those who have great influence on the modern mind. Thus they should learn how to retain what is good, and correct what is unacceptable.

DECREE 10

TERTIANSHIP

188/ 1. The 31st General Congregation, having a high regard for the institution of the third probation, which is defined by our holy Father St. Ignatius in the Constitutions and praised in apostolic letters and the documents of the Society, and yet at the same time aware of the difficulties which beset the third probation, seeks its adaptation and renewal. This renewal, which should help to achieve more efficaciously the purposes intended by the founder himself, should be carried out according to the norms of the Second Vatican Council, the principles of the religious life, and the apostolic goal of the Society, which are proposed in other documents of this Congregation.

189/ 2. This renewal will be especially brought about by the particular care taken to acquire an interior knowledge and personal experience of the spirit of the Spiritual Exercises and the Constitutions,[2] and to put this spirit into one's own prayer and apostolic action.

190/ 3. But since many modern difficulties concern the concrete ways in which the practice of this institution of the third probation is carried out, the Congregation, considering the different circumstances in different countries, concludes that for the present new experiments are to be attempted with regard to the structure of the third probation before anything is definitively decided for the whole Society.

191/ 4. Therefore, in the different regions it shall be the duty of the provincials and instructors to try new methods and suitable experiments, with the approbation of Father General, so that the purposes set down in the Constitutions[3] and in the Bull *Ascendente Domino* may be achieved again in our time. It is understood, moreover, that these purposes are to be renewed and adapted, in the light of the principles enunciated by this Congregation, to the circumstances of different regions.

192/ 5. These experiments should be carried on for three years, or longer if Father General sees fit. When this period is finished, there shall be a meeting, which will be able to judge about the results of these experiments and shall be a help to Father General in writing a new Instruction and in revising the rules of the instructor.

---

[2] *CollDecr* 156.

[3] *Cons.* [514, 516], 126

DECREE 11

Norms for Promotion to Final Vows

193/ The General Congregation, desiring to meet requests of very many postulata that the claim to profession of four vows should be based more on the overall religious and apostolic capability of a man, supposing of course that he has suitable knowledge of theology, lays down by way of experiment the following revision of the norms for profession of four vows:

194/ 1. Decree 158 of the *Collection of Decrees* shall be revised to read:

All who are to be advanced to final vows must be outstanding in that following of Christ prooosed to us in the gospels since this is the ultimate norm of religious life;[2] such men are those who:

1° regularly and for the most part, in ordinary matters, act according to the demands of virtue that is rooted in love of Christ, and are expected to do the same under more difficult circumstances if they occur;

2° humbly accept corrections concerning faults they have committed in religious life and generously strive to improve;

3° driven on by love, live more and more for Christ and His Body which is the Church,[3] and in the daily practice of virtue bear witness both to their fellow Jesuits and to others of the new life that is had through the redemption of Christ.[4]

195/ 2. Decree 160 of the *Collection of Decrees* shall be revised to read :

In order that a man may be admitted to the solemn profession of four vows the following are required:

1° a high level of virtue in conformity with decree 158, one that is positively proved and evident to the extent that it stands out as a good example to others."[5] A deficiency in this regard cannot be supplied by any other endowments.

---

[2] See PC 2, *a.*

[3] See PC 1.

[4] See LG 44.

[5] See *GenExam* [12] ; *Cons.* [819].

2° sound judgment and prudence in action,[6] as well as tested and basic strength of character;

3° a more than ordinary talent for our ministries;[7]

4° a high level of learning in conformity with decree 118 (of which §3 has been abrogated) or other outstanding endowments in conformity with Nos. 3 and 4 below;

5° the priesthood;[8]

6° at least thirty-three years of age;[9]

7° at least ten full years in the Society in addition to the years spent in initial studies of philosophy and theology in the Society;[10]

8° at least three full years, after the completion of the course in theology and in addition to tertianship and to special studies, if any were made, spent in carrying out ministries or offices.

196/ 3. Decrees 161 and 162 of the *Collection of Decrees* and decree 36 of the 28th General Congregation are abrogated, and in their place a new decree is enacted which reads:

§1. Provided always that the requirements contained in No. 2 are kept, those men can be admitted to the solemn profession of four vows without an examination *ad gradum* who have a doctorate or licentiate or some other equivalent degree in the sacred sciences, or who have engaged in these sciences with success either in teaching or writing.[11]

§2. In each individual case it is necessary that the provincial and his consultors have proof of the candidate's high level of learning.

197/ 4. Decree 163 of the Collection of Decrees shall be revised to read:

§1. Provided always that the requirements contained above in No. 2 are kept, those men can be admitted to solemn profession without an examination ad gradum who show outstanding apostolic or ministerial capability. Such are:

---

[6] See *Formula of the Institute* of Julius III, 9.

[7] See ibid; *GenExam* [12] ; *Cons.* [308, 819].

[8] See *GenExam* [12].

[9] See GC 8, D. 7, 33.

[10] See GC 9, D. 42; GC 13, D. 9; GC 16, D. 20.

[11] See GC 7, D. 96; GC 30, D. 68.

1° those who have shown noteworthy talent in governing or preaching or writing;[12]

2° men who are proficient in literature or the sciences and who have received higher academic degrees or who have taught successfully at an advanced level;[13]

3° those who have filled any post or ministry proper to the Society in an outstanding way that has won general acclaim.

§2. In each individual case it is necessary that the provincial and his consultors have proof of the outstanding apostolic and ministerial capability of the candidate, in addition to his adequate theological learning.

198/ 5. A new decree is enacted which reads:

Provincials and their consultors, when they are treating of those to be advanced to final vows, should inquire whether some spiritual coadjutors or approved scholastics deserve to be proposed to the General for the grade of the professed in conformity with Nn. 3 and 4 above. If any such are discovered, evidence of the sort specified in §2 of these decrees should be gathered, as well as all other personnel reports, so that they can be sent to the General. This can be done not only once but repeatedly.

199/ 6. Decree 165 of the *Collection of Decrees* shall be revised to read:

No men should be admitted to the grade of formed coadjutor, whether spiritual or temporal, unless:

1° they have risen above mediocrity in virtue in conformity with decree 158;

2° they have shown sufficient talent for the works and ministries that are proper to the Society;[14]

3° if they are brothers, they have completed ten years of religious life and thirty-three years of age; if they are approved scholastics, they have completed the time in the Society and are of the age specified in No. 2, 6°, 7° and 8° above.

200/ 7. The General Congregation recommends that:

1° the whole process for gathering personnel reports, whether for admission to theology, or for advancement to holy orders, or to final vows, or to an office of government should be thoroughly studied and reviewed;

---

[12] See GG 7, D. 33; GC 13, D. 19.

[13] See GC 6, D. 15; GC 7, D. 33, n. 6; GC 29, D. 33.

[14] *Cons.* [522].

2° the provincial and his consultors, when they are to pass on someone for advancement to the grade of professed, should have available:

a. a complete transcript of grades received in examinations throughout the course of philosophy as well as theology;

b. full information on other advanced studies, whether made in the Society or outside of it;

c. an accurate report of the ministries and works in which the candidate has engaged, along with judgments on his success, etc.

DECREE 12

THE VOW CEREMONY

201/   The 31st General Congregation entrusts to Father General the task of drafting an Ordination for the whole Society, at least for the purpose of experimentation, concerning:

a. concelebration at the pronouncing of last vows;

b. the use of the vernacular in the pronouncing of first vows;

c. the presence of at least close relatives at the pronouncing of first vows, and similar details.

IV

RELIGIOUS LIFE

DECREE 13

RELIGIOUS LIFE IN GENERAL

202/ 1.   The Second Vatican Council profoundly investigated the mystery of the Church in relation to the conditions of our times. In that investigation it cast a special light upon the religious profession of the evangelical counsels both as a means of attaining sanctity by special grace and as a way of fulfilling service to God and man.

203/ 2.   Inserted by baptism into the Mystical Body of Christ, strengthened by confirmation with the power of the Holy Spirit, and consecrated into a royal priesthood and a holy people,[2] we receive a more special consecration for the divine service in the Society of Jesus by the profession of the evangelical counsels, so that we may be able to bring forth richer fruits from the grace of baptism.[3]

204/ 3.   Since the goal to which the Society directly tends is "to help our own souls and the souls of our neighbor to attain the ultimate end for which they were created,"[4] it is necessary that our life—of priests as well as scholastics and brothers—be undividedly apostolic and religious. This intimate connection between the religious and apostolic aspects in the Society ought to animate our whole way of living, praying, and working, and impress on it an apostolic character.

205/ 4.   To attain this end which the Society places before itself and "for the conservation and growth not only of the body . . . but also of the spirit of the Society . . . those means which join the instrument with God and dispose it to be rightly governed by the divine hand are more efficacious than those which dispose it towards men."[5]

206/ 5.   For the spiritual life is a participation in the life of the most holy Trinity dwelling within us so that we may be made conformed to the image of the Son of God "so that He may be the firstborn among many brethren,"[6] for the glory of God.

---

[2] See AA 3.

[3] See LG 44.

[4] *Cons.* [307].

[5] *Cons.* [813].

[6] Rom. 8. 29.

207/ This life involves the whole man and all his activities, by which he as a Christian corresponds to every impulse received from God. It does not consist only in individual acts of devotion, but ought to animate and direct our whole life, individual and community, together with all our relations to other persons and things. It is nourished and fostered by every grace by which God turns to us and communicates Himself to us, especially by His word and the sacraments of Christ.

208/ We for our part respond by the obedience of faith in which we give ourselves freely to God, "offering the full submission of intellect and will to God who reveals,"[7] celebrating as the high point of our life the sacred liturgy of the Lord's Eucharist, participating in the sacraments of Christ, and offering ourselves through love in all our actions, especially those which are apostolic, and all our hardships and joys.

209/ 6. In order to promote the adaptation and renewal of religious life among all Jesuits, the 31st General Congregation has made these decrees in the spirit of the Second Vatican Council.

---

[7] DV 5.

DECREE 14

Prayer

Introduction

210/ 1. The Second Vatican Council, encouraging the work of renewal in the Church, wishes every Christian, and particularly all priests and religious, earnestly to advance in the spirit of prayer and in prayer itself.[2] At the same time, difficulties and doubts, both theoretical and practical, are raised against prayer and these cause no little harm to the Society. Hence the General Congregation considers that it must recall the importance of prayer and propose specific orientations on the manner and conditions of prayer in the Society so that superiors and each individual member may be able to weigh their responsibilities in God's presence.

211/ 2. Our entire spiritual life is in Christ Jesus. We share, of course, the adoptive sonship of God which all the faithful have through faith and baptism, but belong in a special way to God through our consecration as religious in the Society which our founder wished to bear the name of Jesus. We desire to know only Christ Jesus who, sent forth from the Father, consummated the work of saving creation by His life, death, and resurrection. Risen now and exalted by the Father, He draws all things to Himself through the Holy Spirit whom He has sent into the world, so that in Him all may be one as He and the Father are one. Thus, through the grace of our vocation, at once both religious and apostolic, we share in the salvific work of Christ, partaking more fully and intimately of Christ's own love for the Father and for all men, for He loved us unto the end and gave Himself as a ransom for all. Here, then, is our vocation, to love the Father and His children, to work with Christ in His Church for the life of the world that the Father may receive greater glory, to strive towards our goal in the Spirit—this is the ever flowing font of the joy of our charity and the offering of our strength.

212/ 3. The Spiritual Exercises of our father St. Ignatius are both the heritage of our spirituality and the school of our prayer. They indeed open the way through which we may penetrate ever deeper into the mystery of salvation which in turn feeds our lives as apostles in the world. For it is faith, progressively encompassing all reality, that must permeate us as persons if we are to give authentic witness to the living presence of Christ the Lord. The witness is what we seek in mental

---

[2] See PC 5-6; PO 18; OT 8; ES II, 21.

prayer as we enjoy God's presence and try, with the aid of His grace, to see all things in the light of Christ. Through mental prayer our individual lives receive clarity and meaning from the history of salvation, are set against the background of God's speaking to us, and hopefully are enriched with that freedom and spiritual discernment so necessary for the ministry of the Gospel. These reasons apply to all religious involved in the world of today, which far too often ignores its God. For these religious, formal prayer is a precious chance to see the unity of creation and to refer creation to the Father. Our own men, conscious of our special task of challenging atheism, find further apostolic significance in prayer as it fosters in us a sense of the living God and an encouragement of our faith.

213/ 4.　The Jesuit apostle goes from the Exercises, at once a school of prayer and of the apostolate, a man called by his vocation to be a contemplative in action. For the closer and more firmly we bind ourselves to Christ, denying self-love in our association with His salvific work, the more fully do we adore the Father in spirit and truth and the more effectively do we bring salvation to men. Witnesses to Christ in our apostolate, we see Him praying always to the Father, often alone through the night or in the desert. We, too, must enjoy familiar conversation with Him in continuous and in formal prayer. This very intimacy with Christ forges a union of our life of prayer and our life of apostolic work. Far from living two separate lives, we are strengthened and guided towards action in our prayer while our action in turn urges us to pray. Bringing salvation to men in word and deed through faith, hope, and love, we pray as we work and are invited to formal prayer that we may toil as true servants of God. In this interplay, praise, petition, thanksgiving, self-offering, spiritual joy, and peace join prayer and work to bring a fundamental unity into our lives. Truly this is our characteristic way of prayer, experienced by St. Ignatius through God's special gift nourished by his own generous abnegation, fiery zeal for souls, and watchful care of his heart and senses. He found God in every thing, every word, and every deed. He relished God's omnipresence. If the Jesuit apostle is to live this intimate marriage of prayer and action in today's world, he must return each year to the school of the Exercises, so that, spiritually renewed, he may take up his work again with deeper faith and love.

214/ 5.　The People of God, in whom Christ shows us the way to the Father, are our people. Hence the prayer of every Christian is rooted in the prayer of the Church and flowers into liturgical action. Thus the celebration of the Eucharist is the center of the life of the apostolic religious community, bringing fraternal union to its perfection and blessing every apostolic endeavor with the waters of holiness.

215/ 6.　Since it has pleased the Father to speak to men both in His Son, the Word Incarnate, and in many ways in Scripture, the Bible, a treasure bestowed by the Spouse on His Church to nourish and guide all men, is truly the ever-flowing font of prayer and renewal of religious life. In each of us, as the whole tradition of the Church attests, Holy Scripture becomes our saving word only when heard in prayer that leads to the submission of faith.[2] *Lectio divina,* a practice dating back to the earliest days of religious life in the Church, supposes that the reader surrenders to God who is speaking and granting him a change of heart under the action of the two-edged sword of Scripture continually challenging to conversion. Truly we can expect from prayerful reading of Scripture a renewal of our ministry of the word and of the Spiritual Exercises, both of which derive their vigor from our familiarity with the Gospel. And, since the word of God comes to us in the living tradition of the Church, our scriptural reading can never be improved apart from revived interest in the Fathers and the outstanding spiritual writers, especially those of the Society. Nor can we ever forget that spiritual reading played a key role in the conversion of St. Ignatius. Similarly, our theological studies, which ought to be continued through our entire apostolic life, should be united to prayer to lead us to an ever deeper experience of the Lord.

216/ 7. Those means which unite us to God and aid us in helping souls are mentioned in the Constitutions as "integrity and virtue, especially love, purity of intention in serving God, familiarity with God in spiritual exercises of devotion, and sincere zeal for souls for the glory of Him who created and redeemed them."[3] Hence our father St. Ignatius urges us to advance "in zeal for solid and perfect virtue and spiritual matters,"[4] pointing out how vital it is for each of his men to seek that manner and kind of prayer which will better aid him progressively to find God and to treat intimately with Him. With brotherly union, each Jesuit and his superior must collaborate in this humble and oft-repeated search for the divine will.

217/ Every one of us, therefore, must keep some time sacred in which, leaving all else aside, he strives to find God. Through prayer he must seek to develop his spiritual life. In his dialogue with God he will grow in knowledge of God's ways with him, of the choices God desires him to make, of the apostolate God has for him, of the height and manner of perfection to which God lovingly invites him. His prayer thus becomes a truly vital activity whose progressive growth evidences increasingly the action and presence of God in him. His prayer teaches him and tries him in faith, hope, and charity through which we seek, love, and serve God progressively in all things.

218/ Prayer, then, becomes not only a matter of obeying our religious rule, acceptable as that is to God, but also a personal reply to a divine call. Prayer is thus a faithful response to the law of charity towards God and men which the Holy

---

[2] See DV 25.

[3] *Cons.* [813].

[4] Loc. cit.

Spirit has written in our hearts. The charity of Christ urges us to personal prayer and no human person can dispense us from that urgency.

219/ 8. To live his life of prayer, which in the Society is never separated from apostolic action, each of us must first deny himself so that, shedding his own personal inclinations, he may have that mind which is in Christ Jesus. For while on the one hand, prayer brings forth abnegation, since it is God who purifies man's heart by His presence, on the other, abnegation itself prepares the way for prayer, because only the pure of heart will see God. Progress in prayer is possible for those alone who continually try to put off their misguided affections to ready themselves to receive the light and grace of God. This continual conversion of heart "to the love of the Father of mercies" is intimately related to the repeated sacramental act of penance.[5]

220/ Self-denial, which disposes us for prayer and is one of its fruits, is not genuine unless amid the confusion of the world we try to keep our hearts at peace, our minds tranquil, and our desires restrained. Abnegation for us will consist chiefly in fidelity as we daily live our first consecration to God and remain faithful to Him even in insignificant details. Growth in prayer and abnegation necessarily implies spiritual discernment by which a man is willing to learn from God, so that these gifts appear more clearly externally while they strike deeper roots into his inner life.

221/ Though modern living seems to make it hard for us to provide these conditions for true prayer, with trust in God we must try courageously to actualize these aids to prayer in our own lives. Then we can truly serve our neighbor better.

222/ 9. Superiors must actually lead the way in this matter of growth in prayer, inspiring by their example, helping their men, encouraging them, and aiding their progress. If their leadership is to be truly spiritual, they must understand the consciences of their men and get to know them through dialogue which is based on mutual trust. Further, it is the superior's function to promote the prayer life of the entire community as well as the individual's and to provide those conditions which favor prayer. He should see that the daily order and house discipline give each enough time for his customary prayer and its preparation and aid him to pray better.

223/ Spiritual fathers, as well as superiors, show the true charity of Christ towards those placed in their charge when they guide them and aid them in this art of prayer, at once most difficult and divine.

---

[5] See PO 18.

Decree

224/ 10. Liturgical celebrations, especially those in which the community worships as a group, and above all the celebration of the Eucharist, should mean much to us. For it is the Eucharistic sacrifice, the highest exercise of the priesthood, that continually carries out the work of our redemption, and for this reason, priests are strongly urged to celebrate Mass every day,[6] for even if the faithful are unable to be present, it is an act of Christ and of the Church.[7] Concelebration, by which the unity of the priesthood is appropriately manifested, is encouraged in our houses when allowed by the proper authority, while each priest shall always retain his right to celebrate Mass individually.[8] Priests themselves extend to the different hours of the day the praise and thanksgiving of the Eucharistic celebration by reciting the divine office.[9] Hence our priests should try to pray attentively[10] and at a suitable time[11] that wonderful song of praise[12] which is truly the prayer of Christ and that of His Body to the Father."[13]

225/ 11. The General Congregation wishes to remind every Jesuit that personal daily prayer is an absolute necessity.

226/ But the Congregation, recognizing the value of current developments in the spiritual life, does not intend to impose upon all indiscriminately a precisely defined universal norm for the manner and length of prayer.

227/ Our rule of an hour's prayer is therefore to be adapted so that each Jesuit, guided by his superior, takes into account his particular circumstances and needs, in the light of that discerning love which St. Ignatius clearly presupposed in the Constitutions.

228/ The Society counts on her men after their formation to be truly "spiritual men who have advanced in the way of Christ our Lord so as to run along this way," men who in this matter of prayer are led chiefly by that "rule . . . which discerning love gives to each one," guided by the advice of his spiritual father and the approval of his superior.[14]

---

[6] See PO 13.

[7] See PO 13.

[8] See SC 57.

[9] See PO 5.

[10] See SC 90.

[11] See SC 94.

[12] See SC 84.

[13] See SC 84.

[14] *Cons.* [582].

229/ All should recall that the prayer in which God communicates Himself more intimately is the better prayer, whether mental or even vocal, whether it be in meditative reading or in an intense feeling of love and self-giving.

230/ 12. As for what concerns the approved scholastics and brothers in particular, account should be taken of the following:

1° During the entire time of their formation they should be carefully helped to grow in prayer and a sense of spiritual responsibility towards a mature interior life, in which they will know how to apply the rule of discerning love which St. Ignatius prescribed for his sons after the period of their formation.

231/ 2° To foster this growth, the Society retains the practice of an hour and a half as the time for prayer, Mass, and thanksgiving. Each man should be guided by his spiritual father as he seeks that form of prayer in which he can best advance in the Lord.[15] The judgment of superiors is normative for each.[16]

232/ 3° In the communities in which they live, since these are ordinarily more tightly structured and larger in numbers, the daily order should always indicate clearly a portion of the day fixed by superiors, within which prayer and preparation for it may have their time securely established.

233/ 13. The exercise of prayer known as examination of conscience, aptly designated by St. Ignatius to develop purity of heart, spiritual discernment, and union with God in the active life, should be made twice daily. The Society, following its approved tradition, recommends that it last a quarter of an hour.

234/ 14. The prayerful reading of Scripture is a spiritual exercise that all should highly esteem and faithfully perform. As we read, we should try to deepen our familiarity with the word of God, to listen carefully to His voice, to sharpen our perception of salvation history in which the mystery of Christ is foretold, fulfilled, and continued in His Church. We should truly seek and find Christ in the pages of the Fathers and of all Christian writers, especially Jesuits.

235/ 15. Insofar as their apostolic character permits it, Jesuit communities should be united daily for some brief common prayer. The particular form should be approved by the provincial according to norms to be established by Father General. The prayer should take into account the greater needs of the whole world, the Church, the Society, and the community itself. Moreover, for the faithful fulfillment of their apostolic vocation both communities and individuals should cherish daily converse with Christ the Lord in visiting the Blessed Sacrament.[17]

---

[15] See decree 8 (spiritual formation of Jesuits), 35 §1.

[16] See *Cons.* [342].

[17] See PO 18.

236/ 16. The Spiritual Exercises should be made yearly by all, according to the method of St. Ignatius,[18] for eight successive days.[19] Adaptations may be allowed because of particular circumstances; the provincial is to be the judge of the merits of each case. More general adaptations which affect an entire province or assistancy are to be submitted to Father General for approval. The circumstances of the annual retreat (such as silence, recollection, a location removed from ordinary work) should be managed in such a way that the Jesuit is able truly to renew his spiritual life through frequent and uninterrupted familiar conversation with God.

237/ 17. Decrees 52, 55, 81 of the *Collection of Decrees* are to be modified according to Nos. 10 to 16 of the above.

---

[18] See *CollDecr* 55 §3.

[19] *CollDecr* 55 §1.

DECREE 15

DEVOTION TO THE SACRED HEART OF JESUS

238/ 1. The Second Vatican Council has shed a brilliant new light upon the mystery of the Church, but this mystery is perceptible only to eyes directed in faith to the eternal love of the Incarnate Word. For Christ, who "thought with a human mind, acted by human choice, and loved with a human heart,"[2] sacrificed Himself in human love that He might win as His bride the Church which was born from His side as He slept on the cross.

239/ 2. The Church finds a splendid symbol for this love, at once human and divine, in the wounded heart of Christ, for the blood and water which flowed from it aptly represent the inauguration and growth of the Church[3] and solicit our response of love. Devotion to the Sacred Heart, as proposed by the Church, pays tribute to "that love which God has shown us through Jesus, and is also the exercise of the love we have for God and for our fellow-men,"[4] effecting that interpersonal exchange of love which is the essence of Christian and religious life. This is why devotion to the Sacred Heart is regarded as an excellent and tested form of that dedication "to Christ Jesus, king and center of all hearts, which our age urgently needs, as Vatican II has insisted."[5] This should be the concern of the Society above all, both among its own members and in its apostolic ministry, not only because of our long and venerable tradition but also because of the very recent recommendation of the Roman Pontiff.

240/ 3. For these reasons the General Congregation readily embraces the wishes of the Supreme Pontiff; it recalls the decrees of earlier congregations concerning devotion to the heart of Christ[6] and urges all members of the Society to "spread ever more widely a love for the Sacred Heart of Jesus and to show all men by word and example that the renewal of minds and morals, as well as the increased vitality and effectiveness of all religious institutes in the Church, which are called for by the

---

[2] GS 22.

[3] See LG 3.

[4] Pius XII, *Haurietis Aquas, AAS* 48 (1956) 345.

[5] Paul VI, *Investigabiles Divitias, AAS* 57 (1965) 300.

[6] See *CollDecr* 223, 286 §1 ; GC 23, D. 46, n. 1; GC 26, D. 21; GC 28, D. 20; GC 30, D. 32.

Second Vatican Council, ought to draw their chief inspiration and vigor from this source."[7] In this way we shall more effectively make the love of Christ, which finds its symbol in the devotion to the Sacred Heart of Jesus, the center of our own spiritual lives, proclaim with greater effect before all men the unfathomable riches of Christ, and foster the primacy of love in the Christian life.

241/ 4. It is no secret, however, that devotion to the Sacred Heart, at least in some places, is today less appealing to Jesuits and to the faithful in general. The reason for this is perhaps to be found in outmoded devotional practices. Therefore our theologians, men experienced in spirituality and pastoral theology, and promoters of the apostolate of the Sacred Heart of Jesus are urgently asked to search out ways of presenting this devotion that are better suited to various regions and persons. For, while preserving the essential nature of the devotion, it would seem imperative to set aside unnecessary accretions and adapt it to contemporary needs, making it more intelligible to the men of our time and more attuned to their sensibilities.

242/ 5. The General Congregation also recommends that Father General encourage these studies. He will then be in a position to assist the whole Society to a better renewal of its religious and apostolic spirit.

---

[7] Paul VI, *Disserti Interpretes, ActRSJ* 14 (1965) 585.

DECREE 16

CHASTITY IN THE SOCIETY OF JESUS

243/   The mental attitude of men today and the new ways in which our ministry must be fitted into their lives give rise to new problems which touch upon our consecration to God through the vow of chastity. But since these problems are not yet mature enough for a fully balanced and wise solution, the 31st General Congregation recommends to Father General that, as soon as he deems it opportune, he entrust to experts a study on the apt assimilation of advances in the fields of theology, psychology, and pedagogy, and on their application to the direction of Jesuits, so that they may ever more surely persevere in perfect chastity.

244/   Moreover, the Congregation, after attentive study of the documents of the Second Vatican Council, and mindful of its own decrees on the spiritual life and the formation of Jesuits, proposes and enacts the following declarations and norms.

245/ 1.   God, pouring forth his charity in our hearts through the Holy Spirit, confers upon some in the Church the gift of consecrated chastity,[2] a sign of charity and likewise a stimulus to it, whereby they may more easily devote themselves with an undivided heart to Him alone and to the service of His kingdom.[3] Therefore, chastity "for the sake of the kingdom of heaven,"[4] to which by both His example and His calling Christ invites us, and which we as religious profess,[5] following the lead of so many saints, should, as the Church repeatedly urges and as our founder expressly declares, be "perfectly observed" by us.[6]

246/ 2.   Our contemporaries, to whom we are sent[7] and with whom we deal in fraternal fashion,[8] are freshly pondering the meaning and value of human love

---

[2] See Rom. 5.5; Matt. 19.11; 1 Cor. 7.7.

[3] See LG 42.

[4] Matt. 19:12.

[5] See LG 46; PC 12.

[6] *Cons.* [547].

[7] See *Cons.* [163, 603] ; see PO 16; GS passim.

[8] See PO 3.

and of the entire sexual life. To them we wish to offer the sincere, simple, and pru-dent[9] testimony of our consecrated chastity.

247/ 3.   For the vow of chastity, inspired by charity, in a new and wonderful way consecrates us to God, and engages us in a new and eminently human state of life, which renders the heart singularly free and inflames it with charity towards God and all men. The life of chastity consecrated to God is, moreover, a living sign of that future world in which the children of the resurrection "will neither marry nor take wives,"[10] and likewise a most suitable means "for religious to spend themselves readily in God's service and in works of the apostolate."[11]

248/ 4.   Accordingly, in our Society, not only poverty and obedience, but chastity also is essentially apostolic. It is not at all to be understood as directed ex-clusively to our personal sanctification. For, according to the whole intent of our Institute, we embrace chastity as a special source of spiritual fruitfulness in the world.[12] Through it, full dominion of our energies, both bodily[13] and spiritual,[14] is retained for a prompter love and a more total apostolic availability towards all men.[15] Moreover, the profession of chastity for the sake of the kingdom of heaven is of itself a true preaching of the Gospel, for it reveals to all men how the king-dom of God prevails over every other earthly consideration, and it shows won-derfully at work in the Church the surpassing greatness of the force of Christ the King and the boundless power of the Holy Spirit.[16]

249/ 5.   On the other hand, chastity vowed to God through celibacy implies and requires of us a sacrifice by which we knowingly and willingly forego en-trance into that family relationship wherein husband and wife, parents and chil-dren, can in many ways, even psychologically, attain mutual fulfillment. Hence, our consecration to Christ involves a certain affective renuntiation and a solitude of heart which form part of the cross offered to us by Jesus as we follow His foot-steps, and which closely associate us with His paschal mystery and render us shar-ers of the spiritual fertility which flows from it. The vow of chastity, then, on the indispensable condition that it be accepted with a humble, joyous, and and firm spirit as a gift from God, and be offered as a sacrifice to God, not only does not

---

[9] See Matt. 10.16.

[10] Luke 20.35.

[11] PC 12, PO 16.

[12] See LG 42.

[13] See 1 Cor. 7.4.

[14] See 1 Cor. 7.32–33.

[15] See PC 12.

[16] See LG 44.

diminish our personality[17] nor hamper human contacts and dialogue, but rather expands affectively, unites men fraternally, and brings them to a fuller charity.[18]

250/ 6. However, that a man may dare to enter upon this vocation of love in the Church, he will necessarily require:

a. lively faith, for only with the help of faith can the meaning and worth of that higher love be understood which, through consecration, takes up the affections of the personality of a man or woman and transcends its natural expression;

b. a sound balance in affective life, constantly becoming more perfect, whereby the conscious and subconscious impulses and motivations of the entire personality are integrated to pave the way for a fully human commitment;

c. and finally, in our days particularly, an informed choice, freely, explicitly, and magnanimously made, of the properly understood excellence and worth of chastity consecrated to Christ. For through chastity a man, by the oblation of his whole body and soul, devotes himself to the Lord, [19] and by a genuine act of assent takes up the gift of a vocation to establish a relationship of the love of friendship and charity which goes beyond the fullness of Christian marriage.

251/ 7. Besides, in order that perseverance in one's vocation throughout life may be obtained, and that the love once consecrated may grow unceasingly, it is necessary:

a. continually to nourish that original lively faith through familiar converse with God, though contemplation of Christ's mysteries, and through vital assimilation to Him in the sacraments, both of penance, whereby we are made progessively more pure and at peace, and of the Eucharist, whereby we come to form one heart and one spirit with the people of God;

b. to sustain the initial resolve of persevering and growing in love, by fostering charity and the ready union of souls which flourish "when in common life true fraternal love thrives among its members";[20]

c. to strengthen the pristine desires of serving God in this vocation through truly responsible apostolic labor, which in the course of years should be adapted constantly, as far as possible, to the progressive development of one's personality;

---

[17] See LG 46, see GS 41.

[18] See LG 44, PO 16, OT 10.

[19] See OT 10.

[20] PC 12; see LG 43.

d. to protect constancy of will, both by a vigorous prudence, which leads individuals and communities "not to presume on their own resources, but to practice mortification and custody of the senses,"[21] and by mutual confidence between subjects and superiors, which contributes wonderfully to renewal of the account of conscience, so much recommended;[22]

e. to renew incessantly the strong desire of persevering, through humble and simple devotion to the Blessed Virgin Mary, who by her chaste assent obtained divine fecundity and became the mother of beautiful love.

252/ 8. Therefore, the 31st General Congregation proposes and commends the following.

a. All should cultivate close friendship with Christ and familiarity with God, for in this world, no one lives without love. But when our contemporaries question or fail to understand what our love is, we should offer them a fitting reply through the witness of a life of consecrated chastity, and at the same time with humble and persevering prayer we should beg for ourselves and our confreres the grace of personal love for Christ.

253/ For our Father Ignatius experienced this grace, so permeating his entire personality that he bound his brethren to himself as friends and by his personal affability led countless men and women to God.

254/ In the Spiritual Exercises he wished to urge the imploring of this grace, so that throughout the meditations and contemplations on the mysteries of the life, death, and resurrection of our Lord Jesus Christ, and in the application of the senses to them he would have us beg to know interiorly the Lord "who for me was made man, so that I may love Him the more, and follow Him more closely."[23]

255/ *b.* Still, all should keep in mind that love consecrated by chastity should constantly grow and approach the mature measure of the fullness of Christ.[24] It is, consequently, not a gift bestowed once and for all, mature and complete, at the beginning of one's spiritual life, but such as by repeated decisions, perhaps serious ones, should steadily increase and become more perfect. Thus the heart is more and more cleansed of affections not yet sufficiently understood, until the man adheres totally to Christ through love.

---

[21] PC 12; see PO 16.

[22] See *Cons.* [551].

[23] *SpEx* 104.

[24] See Eph. 4.13.

256/ Such love of Jesus our Lord impels a person likewise to genuine human love for men and to true friendship. For chastity for the sake of the kingdom of heaven is safeguarded by fraternal friendship and in turn flowers forth in it. Hence also, we should regard as the precious apostolic fruit of ever more perfect love of friendship that mature, simple, anxiety-free dealing with the men and women with whom and for whom we exercise our ministry for the building up of the body of Christ.[25]

257/ *c.* But to attain the perfect liberty of chaste love, besides the familiarity with God mentioned above, all the supernatural and natural helps available should be used.[26] Among these, however, those contribute more to the faithful fulfillment of one's oblation of chastity which are positive, such as probity of life, generous dedication to one's assigned task, great desire for the glory of God, zeal for solid virtues and spiritual concerns,[27] openness and simplicity in activity and in consulting with superiors, rich cultural attainments, spiritual joy, and above all true charity. For all these things will of their nature more easily bring a man to the really full and pure love for God and men which we earnestly desire.

258/ *d.* Nevertheless, mindful of the above-mentioned solitude of heart which constitutes part of the cross embraced through our vocation to follow Christ, and of our frailty which from youth to old age necessarily accompanies the development of chaste love,[28] we cannot forget the ascetical norms which the Church and the Society in their wide experience maintain and which dangers against chastity require today no less than in the past.[29] So we should diligently stand firm against desires which might lessen a just and wholesome dominion over our senses and affections.

259/ *e.* Finally, sustained by the grace of God and mortified at all times,[30] we should generously and strenuously devote ourselves to apostolic labor and know how to participate with moderation in the human contacts which our ministry involves, our visits and recreations, our reading and study of problems, our attendance at shows, and use of what is pleasurable, so that the testimony of our consecration to God will shine forth inviolate.

260/ 9. As for superiors,

---

[25] See Eph. 4.12.

[26] See PO 16.

[27] See *Cons.* [813], PO 11.

[28] See 2 Cor. 4.7.

[29] See PO 16, PC 12.

[30] See 2 Cor. 4.7 f.; 6.3 f.; Col. 3.1 f.; *GenExam* [103].

a. Let them know first of all that no one is to be admitted to the Society whom they consider ill-suited for consecrated chastity.[31] Accordingly, they should study and faithfully fulfill what the Church tirelessly enjoins in this respect.[32] Therefore, they should carefully inquire "about the free consent of the candidates, their moral fitness, physical and psychic health, and tendencies which might have been transmitted from their family."[33] And especially, "since the observance of total continence intimately involves the deeper inclinations of human nature, candidates should not undertake the profession of chastity nor be admitted to its profession except after a truly adequate testing period, and only if they have the needed degree of psychological and emotional maturity."[34] Proof of this is to be found particularly in a certain stability of spirit, in an ability to make considered decisions, and in an accurate manner of passing judgment on events and people.[35]

261/ *b.* The superiors, together with spiritual fathers thoroughly trained for their task, should see to it that Jesuits in the course of their formation be educated in the matter of sex in a suitable, positive, and prudent manner, so that they may properly know and esteem not only the meaning and superiority of virginity consecrated to Christ, but also the duties and dignity of Christian marriage.[36] Moreover, they should be manfully armed in advance, so as to be able vigorously to surmount the various crises of maturation.

262/ *c.* Likewise, superiors and spiritual fathers alike should manifest the utmost solicitude for the spiritual life of each individual, aware that they must give an account of all of them before God. Hence they should try to see fully and, as it were, to anticipate the psychological problems, the fatigue and difficulties, the wavering, weaknesses, and temptations which Jesuits, either in conversation or in any sort of contact, manifest more or less clearly. These they should perceive and evaluate accurately; what is more, they should show themselves ready to re-examine a man's aptitude for our vocation before permitting that further steps in it be made.

263/ *d.* Let superiors, exercising due firmness and putting aside a kindness which might better be called cruelty, take care that those who are unfit or doubtful-

---

[31] *Cons.* [163, 179].

[32] CIC 571 2; 575 §1; 973 §3; OT 6; see *Cons.* [205, 819]; *Instruction of the Sacred Congregation of Religious,* February 2, 1961, Nos. 29–31; GC 28, D. 24; Rev. Fr. Ledochowski, in *ActRSJ* (1951) 127–28; Rev. Fr. Janssens, *De indole votorum, ActRSJ* (1959) 623–625; *De perseverantia, ActRSJ* 14 (1965) 445–451.

[33] See QT 6.

[34] See PC 12.

[35] See OT 11.

[36] See OT 10.

ly suitable be not advanced to vows or to orders. Thus, for example, someone who so lives separated from the others in the community that he raises a positive doubt about his aptitude for ready companionship with Jesuits or for apostolic contacts with his neighbors, should be directed to some other way of serving God.

264/   And in our times, those who hold fast to a firm doubt regarding the value and worth of the vow of chastity and of celibacy are not to be judged fit for religious life and the priesthood.

263/   *e.*   Solicitous, attentive, and with much trust, superiors should be at the service of the recently ordained priests and brothers who are beginning to work in the vineyard of the Lord, as also of those who for a long time engage in arduous special studies, so as to make them conscious that they form a true part of their communities.

266/   Superiors should lovingly endeavor to lead back those whom they see or sense to be drawing away from the community. And all Jesuits should be prepared to cooperate with superiors in their solicitude, discreetly but in good time making known to them the difficulties and temptations of their confreres.[37]

Conclusion

267/   10.   Finally, with superiors taking the lead, whose duty it is to be present and available, to encourage their brethren, and to offer them solicitous care, and with the cooperation of subjects, there will reign in the community through the wholehearted efforts of everyone the fraternal charity which, with participation in the same Eucharist, will make us all one united body. That charity, moreover, purifies our hearts of all feeling of envy, hostility, or bitterness. It so disposes us to bear each other's burdens and to treat one another with reverence that we may feel a generous love for one and all in the community and at the same time conduct with all a profitable and fruitful dialogue.

---

[37] See *GenExam* [63].

DECREE 17

THE LIFE OF OBEDIENCE

I. Introduction

268/ 1. The General Congregation, solicitous to take into account the signs of the times according to the mind of the Church,[2] and conscious of the social change in our day which gives rise to a new awareness of the brotherhood of men and a keener sense of liberty and personal responsibility, along with an excessively critical attitude and an overly naturalistic view of the world, has thought it necessary to express its mind on obedience, which is a hallmark of the Society and her principle of vitality. The Congregation considers this new situation "not in the spirit of fear, but of power and of love and of prudence"[3] as a fitting occasion and challenge for the Society's renewal in the spirit and practice of obedience. It is convinced, moreover, that the way to the grace of our vocation will be opened not by natural means alone, whether philosophical, psychological, or sociological, but ultimately under the light of faith alone, "with the eyes of the mind enlightened."[4]

II. Obedience in the Society: Apostolic by Nature

269/ 2. Impelled by love of Christ, we embrace obedience as a distinctive grace conferred by God on the Society through its founder, whereby we may be united the more surely and constantly with God's salvific will,[5] and at the same time be made one in Christ among ourselves. For the Society of Jesus is a group of men who seek close union with Christ and a share in the saving mission which He realized through obedience unto death. Christ invited us to take part in such a mission when, bearing His cross, He told St. Ignatius at La Storta, "I will that you serve Us." Through obedience, then, strengthened by vow, we follow "Jesus Christ still carrying His cross in the Church militant, to whom the eternal Father gave us as servants and friends, that we may follow Him with our cross"[6] and be

---

[2] See GS 4, 11.

[3] 2 Tim. 1.7.

[4] Eph. 1.18.

[5] See PC 14.

[6] *Monumenta Patris Nadal* (in MHSJ), IV, 678; see V, 296.

made His companions in glory. We render service to Christ as He lives and works in the Church. Nor could our Society be sealed with the name of Jesus were it not fully committed to the service of the Church, which is the society of the Son of God, Christ Jesus our Lord.[7] Now through the vow of obedience our Society becomes a more fit instrument of Christ in His Church, unto the assistance of souls for God's greater glory. Hence, neither our religious life nor our apostolic action can survive or be renewed unless we hold firmly to sincere obedience.

III. The Superior as Representing Christ

270/ 3. The first Fathers of the Society held the unshaken conviction that "they had no other head than Christ Jesus, whom alone they hoped to serve,"[8] and they solemnly sanctioned this fact in the *Formula of the Institute,* affirming that they wanted "to serve the Lord alone."[9] In the same *Formula,* however, they already expressly declared that "they are serving the Lord alone and the Church His spouse, under the Roman Pontiff," understanding that they offer obedience to Christ Himself when they obey the visible head of the Church. Moreover, in the deliberations of the first Fathers, all decided unanimously that they should obey not only the Vicar of Christ, but also the superior chosen from among them, "so that we can more sincerely and with greater praise and merit fulfill through all things the will of God."[10] St. Ignatius repeatedly states this, that every superior is to be obeyed "in the place of Christ and for the love of Christ."[11] For Christ, as head and shepherd of the Church, is truly present in lawful superiors. The Church is the sacrament of salvation and unity,[12] i.e., the visible sign of His invisible presence and power. Therefore He is present in him who as Vicar of Christ "presides over the universal Church,"[13] and by whose ministry "the whole multitude of believers . . . is maintained in unity."[14] He is likewise present in a special way in religious superiors, who under the Roman Pontiff lawfully govern the community of their brethren, and by whose ministry "the community is gathered as a true family in the name of the Lord."[15] For them also, then, the promise of the Lord holds

---

[7] See 1 Cor. 1.9.

[8] *Fontes narrativi de S. Ignatio* (in MHSJ), I, 204.

[9] See *Formula of the Institute,* 1.

[10] *Deliberatio primorum Patrum,* 4, *Cons*MHSJ, I, 4.

[11] See *GenExam* [83, 85]; *Cons.* [286, 424, 547, 551].

[12] See LG 1, 48.

[13] First Vatican Council, DS 3063.

[12] First Vatican Council, DS 3051.

[15] PC 14.

good: "He who hears you, hears me,"[16] so that in faith we can hear in their commands the voice of Christ commanding. Rightly, therefore, are we said to serve the Lord alone when we obey superiors in the Church.[17]

IV. Authority to Be Exercised in the Spirit of Service and of Discerning Love

271/ 4. After the example of Christ, whose place he holds, the superior should exercise his authority in a spirit of service, desiring not to be ministered unto, but to serve;[18] he should be the servant of all, set over a family of fellow servants, in order to serve by his governing. Resplendent in his ruling should be the kindness, meekness, and charity of Christ,[19] who, bearing the likeness and authority of the Father, became the brother and companion of us all to live among us and labor with us. While he maintains sincere interior reverence, he should exercise simplicity in his way of speaking, so that the friendly concord of Christ with His apostles may come to view. And yet superiors should learn how to blend necessary rectitude and strictness with kindness and meekness,[20] desiring more to serve their brethren than to please them. Hence government in the Society should always be spiritual, conscious before God of personal responsibility and of the obligation to rule one's subjects as sons of God and with regard for the human personality,[21] strong where it needs to be, open and sincere. Superiors should reckon their direction of Jesuits, both as a community and as individuals, more important than any other tasks to be done. Superiors should be appointed who, as far as possible, are gifted with true personal authority, so that they can stir subjects to voluntary obedience, and so that the subjects may willingly agree to be guided by them.

272/ 5. In the exercise of authority, however, the gift of discretion or of discerning love is most desirable.[22] To acquire this virtue, so necessary for good government, the superior should first of all be free from ill-ordered affections[23] and be closely united and familiar with God,[24] so that he will be docile to the will

---

[16] Luke 10.16.

[17] See *Formula of the Institute,* 1.

[18] See Matt. 20.28.

[19] See *Formula of the Institute,* 6.

[20] See *Cons.* [727].

[21] See PC 14.

[22] See *Cons.* [161, 219, 269, 423, 624, 729].

[23] See *Cons.* [222, 726].

[24] See *Cons.* [723].

of Christ, which he should seek out with his subjects and authoritatively make manifest to them. Besides, he ought to know thoroughly our ways of acting, according to our Institute. Keeping in view, then, our end, which is none other than the greater service of God and the good of those who engage in this course of life,[25] he should command the things which he believes will contribute towards attaining the end proposed by God and the Society,[26] maintaining withal due respect for persons, places, times, and other circumstances.[27]

273/ 6. But in order that he may more easily discover the will of God, the superior should have at hand able advisers and should often consult them. He should also use the services of experts in reaching decisions on complex matters. This will the more easily enable members of the Society to be convinced that their superior knows how, wants, and is able, to govern them well in the Lord.[28] Besides, since all who work together in God's service are under the influence of the Holy Spirit and His grace, it will be well in the Lord to use their ideas and advice so as to understand God's will better. Superiors in the Society should readily and often ask for and listen to the counsel of their brethren, of a few or of many,[29] or even of all gathered together, according to the importance and nature of the matter. Superiors should gratefully welcome suggestions which their fellow Jesuits offer spontaneously, with a single desire of greater spiritual good and the better service of God, but the duty of the superior himself to decide and enjoin what ought to be done remains intact.[30]

274/ 7. It is also advantageous to the Society that the superior leave much in his orders to the prudence of his confreres, making liberal use of the principle of subsidiarity. To the extent that they make the spirit of the Society their own, especially if they are men long proven in humility and self-denial, individuals are to be allowed suitable freedom in the Lord. And finally, the universal good itself will sometimes demand that, in the manner of urging what has been commanded, account be taken also of human frailty.

275/ 8. This truly spiritual government, whereby Jesuits are directed by superiors with discerning love rather than through external laws, supposes communication between the two which is as far as possible plain and open. The superior should endeavor to make his mind clearly known to his confreres and understood

---

[25] See *Cons.* [746].

[26] See *Formula of the Institute,* 6.

[27] See *Cons.* [746].

[28] See *Cons.* [667].

[29] See *Con.s* [221, 810]; *Cons*MHSJ, I, 218–219.

[30] See PC 14.

by them; and he should take care that they, according to the nature and importance of the matter and as their own talents and duties require, share more fully in his knowledge and concern both for the personal and community life of Jesuits and for their apostolic labors. The religious, for his part, should try to make himself known, with his gifts and limitations, his desires, difficulties, and ideas, through a confiding, familiar and candid colloquy, about which the superior is held to strict secrecy. In this way an account of conscience is obtained which is sincere and open in form, and not reduced to a formal, periodic inquiry about actions already performed.[31] That kind of friendly and confidential conversation, one that is frankly spiritual and aims at promoting the apostolic objective of our vocation and the religious sanctification of the apostle, will constitute the dialogue that is fundamental and essential for the wholesome progress of our Society. Hence it is the mind of the Congregation that the account of conscience in its proper sense should remain and be strengthened as a general practice. But it is charity which should inspire it, as St. Ignatius wished, with any obligation under pain of sin always precluded.

V. Obedience to Be Offered with Complete Availability in a Personal, Responsible Way

276/ 9.   The Society's members, as the Constitutions provide, should show respect and inward reverence for their superiors, and in the Lord should love them from the heart.[32] To them they should leave the full and completely free disposal of themselves, desiring to be guided not by their own judgment and will,[33] but by that indication of the divine will which is offered to us through obedience. Jesuits, mindful that they are part of a Society which is wholly dedicated to Christ and His Church, should for their part primarily direct their labors under the guidance of the Holy Spirit for the service of the whole Church and Society.

277/   Obedience is to be offered by all promptly, cheerfully,[34] and in a supernatural spirit, as to Christ. In this spirit, all should make their own the superior's command in a personal, responsible way, and with all diligence "bring to the execution of commands and the discharge of assignments entrusted to them the resources of their minds and wills, and their gifts of nature and grace," "realizing that they are giving service to the upbuilding of Christ's body according to God's design."[35] Hence, not just any sort of obedience is expected of us, but an obedi-

---

[31] See *Cons.* [551].

[32] See *Cons.* [284, 551] ; PC 14.

[33] See *Cons.* [618–619].

[34] See *Cons.* [547] ; *Letter on Obedience,* 12.

[35] PC 14.

ence full and generous, of the intellect, too, insofar as possible, rendered in a spirit of faith, humility, and modesty.

278/ 10. Our holy Father St. Ignatius desired that we should all excel in the virtue of obedience.[36] Accordingly, with all our force and energy we should strive to obey, first, the Sovereign Pontiff, and then the superiors of the Society, "not only in matters of obligation, but also in others, even at the mere hint of the superior's will, apart from any express command."[37] We are to respond with perfect obedience in all things where there is not manifestly any sin.[38] Nor may a subject refuse to obey because he thinks it would be better to do other things, or because he believes he is led along lines by the inspiration of the Holy Spirit.

279/ It happens more often nowadays that a member of the Society will sincerely consider that by a dictate of conscience he is forbidden to follow the superior's will, for he thinks that in a given case he is morally obliged to the contrary. Now it is true that no one may act against the certain dictates of his conscience. Still, conscience itself requires that in its formation attention be paid to all the factors which merit consideration in judging the morality of a decision, such as the universal good of the Church and the Society, which may be at stake, as well as the rights of others and the special obligations and values of religious life, which were freely assumed. Only a consideration of the whole reality can bring about a well-formed conscience. A member of the Society, therefore, should sincerely ponder the matter before the Lord, and present his reasons to his immediate or higher superior. It will then be the duty of the superior to weigh these reasons with an open mind, to review the case, and finally urge or withdraw the command.[39] But if the subject cannot be induced in this way to accept with a good conscience the decision of the superior, he may request that the whole question be referred to the judgment of certain persons, even non-Jesuits, to be chosen by common consent.[40] If after such a decision, however, no solution is reached which the Jesuit thinks he can follow without sinning, the superior, having consulted higher superiors as the case may merit, should provide for the course of action which seems more advisable in view of both the good of the whole Society and the good of the individual Jesuit's conscience. But a man who, time after time, is unable to obey with a good conscience, should take thought regarding some other path of life in which he can serve God with greater tranquility.

---

[36] See *Cons.* [547] ; *Letter on Obedience,* 2–3.

[37] *Cons.* [547].

[38] See *Cons.* [284, 549].

[39] See *Cons.* [543, 627] ; *Letter on Obedience,* 19.

[40] See *GenExam* [48-49] ; MHSJ, XII, 680.

280/ 11. Obedience is the ordinary means by which God's will is made clear to the members of the Society. However, it does not take away, but rather by its very nature and perfection supposes in the subject the obligation of personal responsibility and the spirit of ever seeking what is better. Consequently the subject can, and sometimes should,[41] set forth his own reasons and proposals to the superior. Such a way of acting is not opposed to perfect obedience, but is reasonably required by it, in order that by an effort common to both superior and subject the divine will may more easily and surely be found. For obedience of judgment does not mean that our intellect is bereft of its proper role, and that one should assent to the superior's will against reason, rejecting the evidence of truth. For the Jesuit, employing his own intelligence, confirmed by the unction of the Holy Spirit, makes his own the will and judgment of superiors, and with his intellect endeavors to see their orders as more conformed to the will of God.[42] He diverts his attention from a fretful consideration of the opposite reasons, and directs it solely to positive reasons intrinsic to the matter or to motives which transcend this order, namely, values of faith and charity. For practical matters are at issue, in which almost always there remains some doubt as to what is most fitting and more pleasing to God. Theoretical certitude or very high probability about the objective superiority of a given solution is not to be awaited before a superior can authoritatively impose it; nor are the reasons for a course of action always and everywhere to be given the subject that he may devote himself wholeheartedly to the goals and works assigned to him. For the final reason for religious obedience is the authority of the superior. Trust is to be placed in Christ, who by means of obedience wishes to lead the Church and the Society to the ends He proposes.

281/ 12. Thus understood, obedience is not opposed to the dignity of the human person who obeys, nor to his maturity and liberty,[43] but rather strengthens such liberty[44] and admirably fosters the progress of the human person by purification of heart and assimilation to Christ and His mother.[45] For sons of the Society in the light of faith find the foundation of obedience in the example of Christ. Just as the Son of God "emptied himself, taking the form of a servant, being born in the likeness of men"; just as He humbled himself and became obedient unto death, even death on a cross,"[46] so also do members of the Society from love for Christ and to gain souls, "offer the full dedication of their own will as a sacrifice of

---

[41] See PO 15; *GenExam* [92, 131]; *Cons.* [543, 627].

[42] See *Cons.* [284, 550, 619].

[43] See PC 14.

[44] See LG 43.

[45] See LG 46.

[46] Phil. 1.7–8.

self to God."[47] Thus they bind themselves entirely to God, beloved above all, and by a new and special title dedicate and consecrate themselves to His service and honor, bearing witness to the new freedom whereby Christ has made us free.[48]

VI. Obedience as a Bond of Union

282/ 13   The Society "can neither be preserved nor governed, and so it cannot attain the end to which it aspires for God's glory, unless its members be united to each other and with their head."[49] This will be effected mainly by "the bond of obedience, which unites individuals with their superiors, and these among themselves and with the provincials, and all with Father General."[50] But union and obedience are founded on charity, for "if the superior and his subjects are strongly united with God's sovereign goodness, they will easily be united with one another."[51]

Impelled by the same charity, all "should show reverence and render obedience in accord with Church law to bishops because of their pastoral authority in the particular churches and for the union and harmony necessary in apostolic labor."[52] In this way Jesuits are proven to be true sons of the Church and contribute to the building up of the Body of Christ.[53]

---

[47] PC 14.

[48] See Gal. 4.31.

[49] *Cons.* [655].

[50] *Cons.* [821].

[51] *Cons.* [671].

[52] LG 45.

[53] See Eph. 4.12.

DECREE 18

POVERTY

I. Introduction

283/ 1.   The 31st General Congregation, having carefully considered the need of adaptation and renewal of the Institute in regard to poverty, has decreed by its own authority that it be undertaken according to the norms defined below.

II. Directive Norms on Evangelical and Religious Poverty in the Society of Jesus

284/ 2.   Since the Church of the Second Vatican Council, in its desire to be "the Church of all, but in a special way the Church of the poor,"[2] calls on all the faithful to give an authentic testimony of poverty, and since the world, infected with atheism and closed to the heavenly goods of the kingdom of God, desperately needs this sign, the Society of Jesus, avowing at the same time poverty and the apostolate, in the Church, will try to give this witness of poverty in a more perfect way.

285/   The Society of Jesus is also impelled to this by the innate force of its vocation. For it is a community of disciples of the poor Christ, which has taken up an "apostolic life" to lead men to the kingdom of the Father by the path of poverty of spirit.

286/   To bring about this renewal of our way of poverty, the following declarations are made.

287/ 3.   The spirit of poverty has an essential value in our evangelical and religious life. For it is the spirit of Christ, who "though He was rich, became poor for your sake, to make you rich out of His poverty."[3] Imbued with this spirit, the companions of Jesus in a true consecration "more closely follow and more clearly show the Savior's self-emptying by embracing poverty with the free choice of God's sons."[4] At the same time, they manifest the wealth of the kingdom of God, in that they give up earthly goods and practice charity for the needy, knowing

---

[2] John XXIII, Address. *La grande aspettazione,* Sept. 11, 1962, AAS 54 (1962) 682.

[2] Cor. 8.9.

[4] LG42.

that "our Lord Jesus Christ will provide the necessities of life and dress for his servants who are seeking solely the kingdom of God."[5]

288/ 4.   Our poverty in the Society is apostolic: our Lord has sent us "to preach in poverty."[6] Therefore our poverty is measured by our apostolic end, so that our entire apostolate is informed with the spirit of poverty.

289/ 5.   In order that this poverty may flourish the more, the Society seeks its adaptation and renewal both by a return to the true doctrine of the Gospel and the original inspiration of the Society and by the adaptation of our law to the changed conditions of the times, in such a way that, insofar as it may be necessary, the letter of the norms may be changed, but not the spirit, which must continue undiminished.[7]

290/ 6.   This adaptation and renewal must affect the forms of our poverty as well as the juridical norms, so that these forms may truly suit the mentality, life, and apostolate of our times and give a visible witness to the Gospel. Therefore our contemporary poverty must be especially characterized by these qualities: sincerity, by which our lives are really poor; devotion to work, by which we resemble workers in the world; and charity, by which we freely devote ourselves and all we have for the service of the neighbor.

291/ 7.   Our profession of poverty should be sincere, so that the manner of our life corresponds to this profession. St. Ignatius wanted us to take the criterion for the poverty of our life both from our apostolic end and from the principles of the Gospel, for we are apostles of the Gospel. But since we are apostles of this age, we must pay special attention to the social circumstances of time and place.

292/   If, following in the footsteps of our predecessors, we would wish to give—or repeat—more concisely defined norms, assuming discernment in their application, we should have to say that the character of our poverty in regard to our way of life must be adapted to people of modest means so that our food, clothing, dwelling, and travels are such as are suited to the poor.[8] Where we must make use of larger buildings, travel, or instruments for our work, these should really be, and as far as possible clearly appear to be, necessary instruments intended solely for our apostolate which we use in adherence to our poverty.[9]

293/   The Society really intends to answer the demands of this real, not pretended, poverty.

---

[5] *Formula of the Institute, 7.*

[6] *S. Ignatii Epistolae et Instructiones* (in MHSJ), I, 96.

[7] Paul VI, Address *Magno Gaudio,* May 23, 1964, *ActRSJ* 14 (1964) 410.

[8] See *GenExam* [81] ; GC 30, D. 46, 4°.

[9] See GC 30, D. 46, nn. 2, 4.

294/ 8. The witness of our poverty today most aptly shines forth in our practice and spirit of work undertaken for the kingdom of God and not for temporal gain. This poverty should be filled with activity, by which we resemble men who must earn their daily bread; it should be equitable and just, ordered in the first place to giving each one his due; finally, it should be generous, so that by our labor we may help our poorer houses, our works, and the poor.

295/ 9. Our poverty, then, should become a sign of our charity in that by our lack we enrich others. Nothing should be our own so that all things may be common in Christ. Communities themselves, renouncing their own advantage, should be united to each other by the bond of solidarity. Finally, the parts of the Society should freely become poorer so that they may serve the whole body of the Society. And the bond of charity should not be restricted only to Jesuits, for all men are related to the Mystical Body of Christ. Charity should always crown the obligations of justice by which we are bound in a special way to those who are poorer and to the common good.

296/ 10. All should remember, however, that no community form of poverty nor any outward profession of it will be genuinely Christian unless it is inspired by a highly personal sentiment of the heart, that is, by a spiritual poverty, drawn from a close and constant union with the incarnate Word of God. Therefore, there is a broad field of personal responsibility in which each can more perfectly live his calling to poverty and, within the limits of the common good, express it with discerning love by living more frugally, under the guidance of superiors.

297/ 11. The Society, facing a world in which a large part of mankind lies wounded and despoiled, moved by the love of the Good Samaritan, and conscious of its universal vocation, should subject its apostolate to examination, to see how it may more fully turn itself to those who are abandoned, "to evangelize the poor, to heal the crushed in heart."[10]

III. Directive Norms concerning Common Life in the Society of Jesus

298/ 12. The General Congregation, in its concern about the obligation of religious life and the evangelical witness given by that life in all our apostolic activity, has set itself to define what "common life" means as applied to the Society's poverty so that our communities and individual members may be more accurately guided in really practicing in an always more perfect way personal poverty and communal or collective poverty.

---

[10] Luke 4.18; see *SpEx* 167.

299/ 13. Our community poverty includes two aspects: that "common life" which St. Ignatius derived from a centuries-old tradition and current Church law still sanctions as an essential element for all religious families; and that mode of living which, in the following of Christ as He preached with the apostles, bears the mark of the special calling that ought to characterize the Society's efforts as it works among men for the redemption of the world. Moreover, it is of the utmost importance that an apostle, always following the poor Christ, somehow accommodate himself to the manner of life of those whom he helps, becoming all things to all men.[11] Therefore our every use of material things should be such that by the sharing of these goods in common we not only express and strengthen the unity of heart and mind of all members of the Society, but also, by the tenor of our life, signify to the world our will, both common and personal, to give a witness of evangelical poverty, humbly and fraternally serving all, especially the poor, so that we may gain all for Christ, living as poor men and in externals in a manner common to all.

IV. The Matter of the Vow Not to Relax Poverty

300/ 14. The General Congregation authentically declares the matter of the vow not to relax poverty to be completely defined in this statement: "To bring about an innovation in regard to poverty means to relax it by admitting any revenues or assets for the use of the community, whether with a view to the sacristy, maintenance, or any other purpose, apart from the case of the colleges and houses of probation."[12] Therefore, in virtue of the vow the solemnly professed are obliged only to this: not to grant a stable income to professed houses and independent residences, notwithstanding other more general expressions which are found in the same Declaration.

V. The Fruit of Labor

301/ 15. The General Congregation declares, that in addition to the alms and income admitted by the Constitutions, gain from or remuneration for work done according to the Institute is a legitimate source of material goods which are necessary for the life and apostolate of Jesuits. But we are to select these labors according to the obligations of obedience and the nature of our ministries, avoiding every desire of monetary gain or temporal advantage.

VI. The Gratuity of Ministries

302/ 16. The General Congregation interprets the gratuity of ministries in the Society in the following way:

---

[11] See 1 Cor 9.22.

[12] *Cons.* [554].

a. The nature of gratuity is to be explained in the first instance from its purpose, which is both inner freedom (absence from seeking one's own temporal advantage), outer freedom (independence from the bonds of undue obligation), and the edification of the neighbor which arises from this freedom and from the love of Christ and men.

303/ *b.* This gratuity is not opposed to the acceptance of Mass stipends or alms according to the current law of the Church. But in practice account must be taken of edification and of charity to the poor both in and outside of the Society, according to norms to be established by Father General.

304/ *c.* Exception being made of the special norms for parishes and for a legitimate recompense for travel and other expenses, including sustenance, Jesuits may demand no stipend for their work in spiritual ministries, especially for those mentioned in the beginning of the *Formula of the Institute* of Julius III; they may accept only those which are offered to them. It belongs to Father General to define the norms for this in practice.

305/ *d.* The General Congregation declares that the rights of authors, emoluments, honoraria, grants, and other gifts which are considered to be the fruit of the talents and industry of Jesuits may be accepted; however, in the choice of ministries or works, let Jesuits not be influenced by the intention of making profits.

306/ *e.* Tuition charges for education do not of themselves go against gratuity. Nonetheless, from the very apostolic intention of the Society in the ministry of the teaching and formation of youth and according to the mind of St. Ignatius, we are to try our best, as far as is possible according to the circumstances of time and place, to devise means by which we can return to the practice of teaching without the help of tuition.[13]

VII. Foundations in the Law of the Society

307/ 17. The General Congregation modifies decree 188, §1, in the *Collection of Decrees* thus:

"It is to be understood that those revenues which, according to the Constitutions, may be accepted by a 'house' if they are offered by founders 'in such a way that their disposition is not in the hands of the Society and that the Society is incompetent to institute civil action in their regard,' may be received—either from founders of houses or churches, or from any other benefactor—not only for the purpose of maintenance but also for other similar purposes, such as for the sacristy, for the library, or even for living expenses."[14]

---

[13] See *CollDecr* 193 §§3, 4.

[14] See GC 24, D. 16.

308/ 18. The General Congregation believes that it is expedient to request from the Holy See in favor of the Society the power by which Father General can establish, define, administrate, suppress, and assign non-collegiate foundations, notwithstanding the fact that the common law gives the right and duty to local ordinaries to establish and visit such foundations.

309/ 19. The General Congregation gives a mandate to Father General that, when this power has been obtained, he will by an Ordination establish the norms for setting up foundations for the good of some houses or works, and for a more precise definition of the nature and purpose of some funds which are necessary for the financial life of the Society.

VIII. Procedures

310/ 20. The General Congregation decrees that a commission shall be set up, according to the *Constitutions* VIII, 7, 3 [715], and the *Formula of the General Congregation* (Nos. 125–27), adding some prescriptions which seem appropriate, even though contrary to some of the statutes of the *Formula of the General Congregation;* this commission shall consist of Father General, who has the right to preside, and four *definitores,* on these conditions :

a. The four *definitores* shall be chosen by the General Congregation by a majority of secret votes, each one by a distinct vote, or, if some names shall be proposed by Father General, by a vote (or votes) containing several names; moreover, it shall be in the power of Father General, for a good reason and with the advice of the General Assistants, to accept or even to ask for the dismissal of one of the definitores and to replace him with another.

b. The *definitores* with Father General shall determine matters only with that power which the General Congregation gives to them.

c. Their task will be to prepare in stages a schema of adaptation and renewal, and revision of our entire law concerning poverty.

d. The schema definitively worked out by the commission of *definitores* shall be promulgated by Father General for use and experiment for the whole Society until the General Congregation immediately following this one.

IX. Applying to the Holy See

311/ 21. The General Congregation decides that numbers IV, V, and VI of this decree be submitted to the Holy Father for confirmation, or at least for the purpose of informing him.[15]

---

[15] See the letter of Cardinal Cicognani, June 6, 1966, to Fr. General (communicating the papal approval of the Congregation's decrees on religious poverty and the gratuity of ministries).

DECREE 19

COMMUNITY LIFE AND RELIGIOUS DISCIPLINE

I. Community Life

A. *The Nature of Community Life in the Society of Jesus*

312/ 1. The sense of community evolved gradually in the infant Society. The first members, "friends in the Lord,"[2] after they had offered themselves and their lives to Christ the Lord and given themselves to His vicar on earth that he might send them where they could bear more fruit,[3] decided to associate themselves into one body so that they might make stronger and more stable every day their union and association which was begun by God, "making ourselves into one body, caring for and understanding one another for the greater good of souls."[4] Similarly they agreed later to give their obedience to some superior "so that they might better and more carefully fulfill their first desires to do the divine will in all things,"[5] and gain greater internal cohesion, stability, and apostolic efficacy.

313/ 2. And so community in the Society of Jesus takes its origin from the will of the Father joining us into one, and is constituted by the active, personal, united striving of all members to fulfill the divine will, with the Holy Spirit impelling and guiding us individually through responsible obedience to a life which is apostolic in many ways. It is a community of men who are called by Christ to live with Christ, to be conformed to Christ, to fulfill the work of Christ in themselves and among men. This is the foundation and aim of community life in the Society of Jesus.

314/ 3. The union of minds of the members among themselves and with their head, leading to personal holiness and at the same time to apostolic activity, flows from a love for our God and Lord, Jesus Christ,[6] and is sustained and governed by the same love. When it is strengthened by mutual understanding, this

---

[2] *S. Ignatii Epistolae et Instructiones* (in MHSJ), I, 119.

[3] B. Petri Faber, Ad D. de Gouvea (in MHSJ) I, 132; *Cons.* [605].

[4] *Deliberatio primorum Patrum,* 3, *Cons*MHSJ, I, 3 (a. 1539).

[5] *Deliberatio primorum Patrum,* 8, *Cons*MHSJ, I, 7.

[6] See *Cons.* [671].

love gives a community a way of finding God's will for it with certainty. For this dialogue between superiors and subjects or between the members of the Society, whether it takes place man to man or as a community effort, becomes supernaturally meaningful when it is directed towards finding the divine will, cultivating fraternal love and promoting our work as apostles.

B. The Importance of Community Life for Religious Life

315/ 4. When community life flourishes, the whole religious life is sound. Obedience, for instance, is a very clear expression of our cooperation toward common ends, and it becomes more perfect to the extent that superiors and subjects are bound to one another in trust and service. Chastity is more safely preserved, "when there is a true brotherly love in community life between the members."[7] Poverty, finally, means that we have made ourselves poor by surrendering ourselves and our possessions to follow the Lord.[8] Community life aids and assists us in this surrender in a great variety of ways, and in its own unique way is the support of poverty.[9] When the religious life is thus strengthened, unity and flexibility, universality, full personal dedication, and the freedom of the Gospels, are also strengthened for the assistance of souls in every way. And this was the intention of the first companions.

316/ In addition, community life itself is a manifold testimony for our contemporaries, especially since by it brotherly love and unity are fostered, by which all will know that we are disciples of Christ.[10]

C. Conditions for Community Life

317/ 5. *a.* The principal bond of community life is love,[11] by which our Lord and those to whom He has entrusted His mission of salvation are loved in a single act. By this love, which contains a real offering of one's self to others, a true brotherhood in the Lord is formed, which constantly finds human expression in personal relationships and mutual regard, service, trust, counsel, edification, and encouragement of every kind.

318/ More concretely, the following are increasingly necessary for community life in the Society of Jesus:

---

[7] PC 12.

[8] See Luke 18.28.

[9] See *Cons.* [570].

[10] See John 13.35; PC 15.

[11] See *Cons.* [671].

b. Exchange of information in the community,[12] by which superiors and subjects are kept informed about common works and plans, and help each other with advice.

319/ *c.* Frequent consultation with experts, to share their insights, and frequent consultation among the members of the community, aimed at actively engaging everyone in the process of coordinating and promoting the apostolate, and in other things which pertain to the good of the community.

320/ *d.* Delegation, by which the superior willingly gives the members greater responsibility for special missions and projects, and makes use of the principle of subsidiarity. When responsibility of this kind grows, a common burden is carried by many, and the sense of community is increased.

321/ *e.* Collaboration of every kind, transcending every sort of individualism, which is more necessary in contemporary circumstances than ever before for the apostolate of the Society and a more intimate way of living together.

322/ *f.* A certain order of life which is determined by the conditions of life and work proper to each community. For this is a very apt means for making more efficacious both individual and community work, for making mutual interchange among members easier, and for creating those exterior and interior conditions of silence, recollection, and peace of mind, which are so useful for personal study, reflection, and especially prayer. In addition, it is a complement of charity itself and its realistic expression, as well as a sign of religious consecration and union in the service of Christ.

323/ *g.* A feeling for the whole Society on the part of the members, which transcends local and personal limits, and in many ways helps community life itself, for each individual is included "as a member of one and the same body of theSociety."[13] Therefore, the more clearly the members recognize that they are connected with the whole life and apostolate of the Society, the more community life will become psychologically and spiritually richer.

D. More Concrete Applications

324/ 6. *a.* In relation to the whole Society: The sense of belonging and responsibility of each individual toward the whole Society, which was mentioned in No. 5 *g,* is manifested in a knowledge of our history, our saints, our works, and our men, especially of those who are facing difficulties for the sake of Christ; in main-

---

[12] See *Cons.* [673].

[13] *Cons.* [510].

taining Ignatian mobility and flexibility with a view to helping any region of the Society whatsoever; in the practice of a generous hospitality towards all Jesuits.[14]

325/ *b.* In relation to neighboring houses and provinces: There should be more association between the fathers and brothers of different houses and provinces, so that they can help each other by this association and by the way their experiences complement one another. They should meet more frequently to discuss the apostolate, the religious life, the teaching of the Council, and new questions of theology, in order to improve their knowledge and enable them to act in basic unity. And one house should share with another material goods "so that those which have more may help those which are in need."[15]

326/ 7. In the houses of those who have final vows,

a. Since common prayer, especially the celebration of Mass and devotion to the Eucharist, is very helpful for tightening the bonds of community, all should faithfully fulfill the prescriptions of No. 15 of the Decree on Prayer.

327/ *b.* Our community life should at the same time be improved by our common apostolic work. So we must promote the closest possible cooperation among Jesuits, both by having all or very many in a community devoted to the same work and by making use of small groups, to whom the superior can grant the powers he judges to be helpful for meeting the needs of the apostolate (see No. 5, *d*). Cooperation in work begins and is sustained by previous exchange of information on the community level, by encouraging one another's efforts, and by various forms of consultation (see No. 5, *b-c*) beyond those prescribed in our law.

328/ *c.* Priests, brothers, and scholastics should all associate with one another easily, in sincerity, evangelical simplicity, and courtesy, as is appropriate for a real family gathered together in the name of the Lord.[16] As far as apostolic work or other occupations for the greater glory of God permit it, all of us, "esteeming the others in their hearts as better than themselves,"[17] should be ready to help out in the common household chores.[18]

329/ *d.* The standard of living with regard to food, clothing, and furniture should be common to all so that, poor in fact and in spirit, differences may be avoided as far as possible. This does not prevent each one from having what is necessary for his work with the permission of the superior. But while he applies him-

---

[14] See *CollDecr* 74.

[15] See PC 13; D. 18, n. 9.

[16] See PC 15; ES II, 25.

[17] *Cons.* [250].

[18] See D. 7, nn. 5–6.

self intensely to his own work, let each one also recognize his responsibility for the spiritual help and material sustenance of other members of the community.

330/ e. Customs which are more suitable for monastic life shall not be introduced into our community life, nor those which are proper to seculars; much less, those which manifest a worldly spirit.

331/ Let our relationship with all other men be such as can rightly be expected from a man consecrated to God and seeking the good of souls above all things; and it should include a proper regard for genuine fellowship with all other Jesuits.

332/ Our houses should be open in genuine hospitality even to persons not members of the Society, especially to religious and to those who work with us.

333/ *f.* Keeping in mind apostolic poverty and our witness to those among whom we must live, our houses should be made suitable for apostolic work, study, prayer, relaxation of mind and a friendly spirit, so that Jesuits will feel at home in their own house.

334/ It can be a great help to the simplicity and intimacy of community life as well as to poverty if the house or place where we live and the house or place where we work or even where we study can be conveniently separated.

335/ *g.* After consultation a simple daily order should be established which will suit our apostolic activities and the common good of the members, and which can be adjusted by the superior for good reason.

336/ *h.* Those norms of community life which are to be observed uniformly in the houses of any region should be proposed at a meeting of the provincials, and after the approval of Father General are to be maintained with equal vigor by all the provincials.

337/ 8. In the houses of formation,

a. Our younger members, both scholastics and brothers, are to be prepared for that community life which has been proposed in the preceding numbers as proper to those living in the apostolate. But the pedagogical nature of the years of formation, the nature of the studies or activities in these houses, and the number of members, make some suitable adaptations of community life necessary.

338/ *b.* In houses of formation there should be more room for common participation in some forms of prayer, especially for active and varied participation in a community celebration of the Eucharist, and for some short common prayer every day, to symbolize and deepen the religious bond which unites us in our Lord and by our Lord with the Society, the Church, and the world.

339/ *c.* Each one's sense of community, as a necesary prerequisite for the apostolic life of the Society, should be seriously tested and formed during these years. Candidates and those in the course of training should be examined with special attention to their ability to get along with people; it is to be considered as one of the signs of vocation to the Society.

340/ *d.* The scholastics and brothers should in suitable ways be initiated into their community of work, whether it be in studies or other duties or in the apostolate, maintaining a suitable balance with individual work in depth, especially in studies, a balance which modern conditions seem to make rather difficult to preserve.[19]

341/ At the same time attention must be paid to education for dialogue among themselves and with superiors, for cooperation and obedience, in line with the suggestions made in other decrees of this Congregation,[20] all of which tend to form men who are capable of making the best possible choices, with the help of supernatural illumination and sufficient advice from others.

342/ *e.* A communal life, which according to No. 7, *b-d,* is based on the evangelical spirit of service, work, and authentic poverty, is to be made more perfect by a gradual participation of the young men in offices and consultations. This will help to develop their responsibility and a realistic sense of their vocation, while it shows "who they really are."

343/ *f.* The order of the day, mentioned in No. 5, *f* and No. 7, *g,* is to be faithfully observed particularly in houses of training, in order that due regard may be had for these values: the interior spiritual life which is to be fostered even by external helps; charity, or responsibility for those conditions of silence, recollection, etc., which aid the work, quiet, and prayer of others; the efficacy of personal and community work as well as our living together; the intrinsic and formative value of a well considered rule,[21] and the formative value of fidelity in carrying out those things God entrusts to us by obedience.

344/ *g.* In due proportion and under direction, we should foster relationships between the younger members of different nations, either for the sake of higher studies or to learn modern languages, or for apostolic experiments. This will greatly increase understanding and unity in the Society in the future.

---

[19] See PC 15. [This footnote appears in the Latin original without a specific reference indication in the text itself.]

[20] See D. 8 and D. 9.

[21] See OT 11; *Cons.* [294–295 and 435–436].

II. Religious Discipline

345   9.   The life of the Society, its activity, and more concretely community life in it, is a cooperation of all members flowing from love.[22] But according to the mind of our founder and the desires of the Church, it ought to be defined and ordered by rules. Rules are a safeguard for charity and a sign of the union of members, and they also constitute a real help for human weakness, a stimulus to individual responsibility; and a means of coordinating activities for the common good.

346/   10.   These rules pertain to the whole vital spiritual range of religious obedience, and their application to individuals is subject to the living rule of the direction of a superior. Therefore what this General Congregation has said about obedience, especially in No. 8 of the Decree on the Life of Obedience in the Society, should be recalled again here, since religious discipline in the Society of Jesus ought to be marked with the characteristics of Ignatian obedience. According to the will of the Church and the Vicar of Christ, again manifested to us,[23] rules were written and are to be written to make clear the will of God "in order to make better progress in the way of divine service upon which we have entered."[24] They show us a way of loving which is concrete, constant, and personal, and they give us an externally uniform way of serving others. For the rule prepares us for a closer union with Christ and the Church. It leads us to Christ like a guardian, and therefore it ought to be accepted with that filial love with which it was given[25] and which leads to the liberty of sons.

347/   11.   Understanding the observance of rules in this way, as a movement from love to love, we must say that it is a means of sanctification for everyone,[26] a sanctification indeed ordered toward more fruitful apostolic action.

348/   In addition, it is a way to human perfection, for this kind of observance of rule is neither an empty formalism nor a so-called self-alienation. In fact, since it sometimes requires a renunciation and denial of real values, by which denial we are associated with Christ, it leads to solid personal maturity.[27]

349/   12.   Therefore religious discipline in the Society supposes and produces superiors and subjects who are obedient men, mature in a Christian way.

---

[22] See *Cons.* [671].

[23] See *Cons. Prooemium* [134]; Pius XII, *ActRSJ* 13 (1957) 293; LG 45; PC 4; Paul VI, *AAS* 56 (1964) 565–571; *ActRSJ* 14(1964) 409–410; ES 12–14.

[24] *Cons. Prooemium* [134].

[25] See *Cons.* [602].

[26] See GC 28, D. 22, 3°.

[27] See LG 46, OT 11, PC 14.

350/ For it is the task of superiors to seek diligently the will of God even with the help of advice from others about the most suitable means, and to decide what is to be done,[28] and then to express their decisions clearly. It is also their duty to foster the observance of rules and to adapt them to individuals as circumstances require. The most efficacious means of obtaining this is that they stand before their subjects as living examples who will continually draw the rest to fidelity and generosity in the service of the Lord.

351/ But their greatest duty is to lead their subjects, especially the younger ones, to an ever increasing formation in re-sponsibility and freedom, so that they observe rules not inthe spirit of fear[29] but from an intimate personal conviction rooted in faith and charity.

352/ Subjects, for their part, should foster a love for the rules by constant reading and meditation on the Constitutions, from which they can draw the genuine spirit which should pervade our way of life. In fact, from a familiarity with the text of our founder we can gather what importance many of the rules have for the perfection of our own vocation and for the apostolic mission of the Society, so that with hearts full of love we may set ourselves to observe them.

353/ 13. Discipline, however, is not to be sought in itself and for itself. Its purpose is "to enable us to accomplish God's will in all things more honestly and with greater praise and merit."[30] A dynamic resolve to accomplish this when faced with the variety of constantly new challenges which face the Church should make all, superiors and subjects alike,attentive to the signs of the times. They must read thesesigns with God's help and be ready to propose in due time suitable revisions of the rules, which will remove things which are obsolete and out of place, strengthen what is still vital, and open up paths which are perhaps new and more likely to lead us to our goal.[31]

354/ Rules, however, remain in force until they arc revoked or changed by competent authority.

III. Revision of the Rules

355/ 14. A revision of the rules is entrusted to Father General for completion as soon as possible, according to the principles of the Church,[32] so that some common norms may be established for the whole Society. These will of necessity

---

[28] See PC 14.

[29] See *Cons.* [547, 602].

[30] *Deliberatio primorum Patrum,* 4, *ConsMHSJ,* I, 4.

[31] See ES II, 14, 17.

[32] See ES II, 12–14.

be few in number, rather general, brief, as far as possible expressed in a positive way and organically ordered, and solidly based in theology, so as to signify and bring about the union of the members. It should be left to the provincials to determine with the approbation of Father General more particular norms for individual provinces.[33]

356/ 15. The rules of the Summary and the Common Rules are to be within the competence of the General. Therefore, in the *Collection of Decrees,* decree 3, §2, 3°, the words "Summary of the Constitutions" and "Common Rules" are now deleted.

357/ 16. The General is commissioned to issue Ordinations dealing with the matters presently contained in the *Collection of Decrees,* decrees 48; 52, §2; 61; 65–72. The power is also given to him to suspend, from the day on which he promulgates each Ordination of this sort, the related decrees, until the next congregation, with the consent of the General Assistants.

DECREE 20

Reading at Table

358/ 1. After careful consideration of the reasons advanced for introducing changes in the present directives for reading at table and in light of the variety of circumstances prevailing in various parts of the Society, the General Congregation turns over to Father General the task of making prudent arrangements for the practice in each province or region.

359/ 2. To prevent a decline in knowledge of the Constitutions as a consequence of discontinuing the monthly reading of the Summary of the Constitutions at table, the General Congregation recommends to Father General that he take measures effectively to preserve and foster this knowledge, either by restoring the monthly reading of the Summary, or by determining that key paragraphs of these Constitutions should be read in order at table, or by some other more suitable method.

---

[33] See *Cons. Prooemium* [136].

V

THE APOSTOLATE

DECREE 21

The Better Choice and Promotion of Ministries

360/ 1.   While the 31st General Congregation recognized the hard work that our Society puts into its apostolic ministries, at the same time it notes that our labors have not produced all the results that we could rightly expect, if one considers the proportion between the efforts and the results achieved.

361/   Part of the reason for this is our failure at times continually to renew our apostolic or missionary spirit and to maintain the union which the instrument should have with God,[1] or our neglect of "moderation in labors of soul and body"[2] or a too great scattering of our forces;[3] but the principal reason is our failure adequately to adapt our ministries to the changed conditions of our times.

362/ 2.   Hence, not a few doubts are being raised whether some of our works have become obsolete or are in need of a profound renewal at least in regard to the way in which they are carried on. On the other hand, new fields of apostolic labor invite us, fields which seem to be of very great importance for spreading the faith and imbuing the world with the spirit of Christ and are at the same time entirely in harmony with the particular spirit of our Society. Likewise, other apostolic forces are frequently found in the Church today which in a special way cultivate this or that field of the apostolate, so that our work in almost the same field has lost its note of urgency. Finally, we need to be more available to take on those ministries which answer the urgent pastoral needs of the modern church and the special missions of the Roman Pontiff. For these missions, in keeping with our distinctive spirit, we should be particularly ready.

363/ 3.   Weighing all these points, the General Congregation judges that the Society still retains a capacity for renewal and adaptation to our time. This capacity comes from the unique flexibility given to our Institute by the Holy Spirit and from the varied and widespread experience of our men in so many fields of the apostolate. Renewal and adaptation require a continual revision of the choice and promotion of our ministries. Such a revision moreover answers the express wishes of the Fathers of Vatican II for renewal and adaptation in the religious life.

---

[1] See *Cons.* [813].

[2] See *Cons.* [822].

[3] See GC 30, D. 50, §1.

364/   Therefore, it seems that certain more general orientations should be set down in this matter.

A. The Norms for Renewal

365/ 4. All Jesuits, especially superiors, to whom the choice of ministries belongs "as the most important task of all,"[4] must work very hard at bringing about this renewal of our ministries. The norms for renewal are found in the Constitutions themselves. Much light is shed on these norms by the decrees of the general congregations and the Instructions of the Fathers General. While retaining their perennial validity, these norms must always be rightly applied to historical circumstances. But it is especially from a renewed and profound study of our spiritual heritage that this renewal must be drawn. The Spiritual Exercises of St. Ignatius can pour into us the spirit of magnanimity and indifference, of firm decision and reformation, a renewal, that is to say, of our activity or of the means for reaching our goal more successfully through the light of those well known principles: the greater service of God, the more universal good, the more pressing need, the great importance of a future good and special care of those significant ministries for which we have special talent.

B. Certain Dispositions Required for This Adaptation

366/ 5. In order to use these norms correctly and effectively, there is especially needed that union of the instrument with God which comes from faith and charity. From this union, above all else, comes the efficacy of our apostolate; and this union cannot be supplied for by other gifts of the merely natural order.

367/ 6. This familiarity with God, moreover, because of the union of our apostolate with the mission of the Incarnate Word, calls for not less, but closer involvement in this world. This demands certain dispositions of soul which will better serve this purpose.

368/   *a.* The contemporary world, shaken by such rapid and profound changes, demands of us the capacity to recognize this process. This ability to recognize change is, as it were, the humility that befits us as creatures, a humility that makes us open and faithful to all creation so that, discovering the will of God in these processes, we may bring about a continual renewal and adaptation of our apostolate.

469/   *b.* Besides, the closer social relations now being formed among men and nations, in a world that is on its way to becoming unified, demand of us the spirit of fraternal dialogue, mutual reverence and a sense of complementarity and collaboration in action.

---

[4] Fr. Janssens, Letter on Our Ministries, *ActRSJ* 11 (1947) 299–336.

370/ *c.* livelier awareness of human progress and of temporal values, the abuse of which frequently leads to a denial of religion and of God Himself, is a consideration also of great importance in the apostolate. For in apostolic work, whose true goal is to announce to men the mystery of Christ who is at work in us and in the world, it is man in his entire life and concrete existence who must be reached.

C. Our Cooperation with Others in the Apostolate

371/ 7.   In keeping with the mind of Vatican II in its theological and pastoral teaching, the provincials are invited to a close collaboration with those whom the Holy Spirit has placed to rule the church of God.[5] Keeping ourselves available in the first place to the Holy See, let all Jesuits and especially superiors propose to themselves "to follow the plans, judgments and works of the hierarchy and to bring them to completion and be animated by the dynamic spirit of fellowship."[6] Therefore, let our works be harmonized with the pastoral programs of the bishops, especially by means of our collaboration as religious with the conferences of bishops. Let us be eager to render apostolic service to priests and to those aspiring to the priesthood.

372/ 8.   Collaboration with other religious is also to be commended, keeping intact, however, the character of each order. Spiritual helps which are asked for by other religious societies are to be gladly supplied. For this purpose the conferences of major superiors will be of great service.

373/ 9.   An extensive and sincere collaboration with the laity is likewise to be commended. For in the works of our Society, our own responsibility for their inspiration, orientation and direction must be shared in a certain definite way by the laity. In the expanse, moreover, of the whole Church, serious care must be fostered to help the laity to grow and become true men and Christians, fully conscious of their own responsibility toward the Church and the world. This is especially true of those lay persons (men and women) who, because of their greater importance for the universal good of the Church, deserve special spiritual attention.Finally, contacts of true friendship with the laity in secular associations and in the multiple circumstances of daily life manifest our attentive presence to the concrete existence of man, express a form of charity and constitute a real beginning of the apostolate; at the same time they will enrich us interiorly and make us more human in exercising our apostolic work.

---

[5] See Acts 20.28.

[6] Paul VI, Address *Sincero animo* to the Fathers of the 31st General Congregation (May 7, 1965) ; Document 1 in this volume and *AAS* 57 (1965) 511–15.

374/ 10. With regard to the universal Church, lastly, let the Society provide cooperation in the same spirit of service, through centers that organize apostolic action.

D. Some Fields of the Apostolate Which Today Deserve Special Attention

375/ 11. The world of our day is marked by certain characteristics, namely, the progress of higher education, the advance of professional life, the increasing proportion of younger people, international organizations and the serious needs of some parts of the world. Hence it comes about that certain fields of modern life have acquired a special urgency, fields that must be considered among the other works laudably carried on by our Society:

a. the field, namely, of higher education, especially in the positive sciences through which scientific research and the technical arts are advanced;

b. the field of labor and professional groups, especially those in greater need;

c. the education of youth, especially that part which, it is foreseen, will have greater influence in the life of the Church and the world;

d. international organizations which aim at bringing together organically every sector of the world, an activity whose importance for the whole of mankind can scarcely be exaggerated;

e. certain geographical regions where the very great increase in population, the rapid evolution in social, economic and political life, hunger and many other miseries of every sort, as well as the bitter struggle between the Christian conception of life and opposed ideologies, demand strong apostolic efforts without delay;

f. in addition, in regions which are traditionally Christian, we must expend a great deal of effort on behalf of those who are called "neopagans," those namely who are infected with either theoretical or practical atheism.

376/ 12. With great eagerness, let all Jesuits undertake those apostolic works which are calculated to implement the constitutions and decrees of Vatican II, always keeping in mind the proper character of our Institute. Missions, moreover, which the Supreme Pontiff may wish to entrust to our Society at any time and in any part of the world, we are to place in the category of the highest priority. Hence, the commission to oppose atheism which Paul VI has given to us, we should accept with grateful eagerness.

377/ 13. Let our entire Society renew its missionary spirit in keeping with the Decree on the Missionary Activity of the Church *(Ad Gentes),* since our Society was founded to spread the faith.

378/ 14. In developing the apostolate of the Society in the world of today, the use and vitalization of the means of social communication should be promoted more every day. These mass media go far toward shaping the modern mind, and they lead us to a manner of expression which is adapted to the temper of present-day man.

379/ 15. Since experience shows that we have not lacked well-ordered norms admirably composed by the Fathers General nor the sincere wish of the whole Society nor decrees calling for an adaptation, we must now use the means that will more effectively put all these forces into operation. For this purpose, besides the awareness which must of necessity be made more sensitive in the whole Society to the urgency of renewal and adaptation in the choice and promotion of our ministries, the setting up of special commissions will be of great service to the Fathers Provincial and even to Father General in the choice of ministries and in organizing our apostolate.

DECREE 22

THE COMMISSION FOR PROMOTING THE BETTER CHOICE OF MINISTRIES

380/ 1.   To promote the better choice of ministries and some long-range planning, a commission should be set up as an aid to the provincial and under his authority.

381/ 2.   The task of this commission will be, after careful study, to advise on an overall review of ministries. This will involve making suggestions as to which ought to be kept or dropped and which ought to be renewed or begun for the first time. We should always keep in mind social conditions and pastoral programs, the supply of apostolic forces that is at hand or hoped for, the more pressing needs, and the help which ought to be given Father General for more universal works.

382/ 3.   The provincial should appoint to such a commission those Jesuits who have sufficient experience in the ministries of the Society, and also experts in those special disciplines (e.g., pastoral theology and the sociology of religion) that are of greater importance for a reconsideration of the matter. If it is necessary, experts from outside the Society, even lay persons, should be called in at the right moment.

383/ 4.   When the commission has in due time gathered its information, it should place before the provincial the conclusions of its investigation and deliberate on them in a meeting together with the consultors of the province at least once a year.

384/ 5.   After everything has been considered in this fashion, it will be the task of the provincial to decide on the reorganization and promotion of ministries and to determine whether or not, if conditions have perhaps changed, further studies by the commission are needed.

385/ 6.   In order to achieve a more effective coordination of the apostolate in a given region, boards of provincials, where they already exist or where it might seem good to set them up, can be greatly helped by a similar interprovincial commission linked with the provincial commissions. In regions that are sufficiently homogeneous, a single interprovincial commission can be instituted in place of commissions for the individual provinces.

DECREE 23

The Jesuit Priestly Apostolate

I. Introduction

386/ 1. From the Society's beginning and throughout its history, Jesuit priests have always given themselves to the ministry of God's word and Christ's sacraments and to other works as well for the sake of churches and nations. Today, too, as members of a single body they are at work in many different fields.

387/ But the manifold changes that mark the present age demand that the Society reassess its works, adapting them to present and, as far as possible, to future circumstances. For relationships within the Church are being profoundly transformed: the laity is assuming its proper active role; the union of priests with each other and with their bishops is coming to the fore; all are being stirred to a sense of responsibility for the good of the Church as a whole. Relationships between the Church and the world, too, are being transformed: for while the lawful autonomy of earthly values is being more expressly recognized,[1] at the same time the intimate connection between the Gospel and the earthly progress and service of the human family is being more vividly perceived.[2] Finally, the proportion of priests to a growing population and its increased needs is being lessened, so that a better distribution of priests is demanded.

388/ Due to these changes, the place and role of the priest is being variously envisioned by many today. Some think the Jesuit priest should be engaged solely in directly pastoral work; others desire that he should be more fully present in the areas where man's secular efforts are being expended. Some hope that the early vigor of the Society will be recaptured if the priestly ministry is purified of all so-called accidental forms; others believe a more universal good will emerge if no limits are placed on the scope of priestly activity.

389/ It is not for the General Congregation to settle theological differences on the priestly role and ministry. We intend, however, to recall some principles of the Catholic faith and of the Jesuit Institute and to draw from them several criteria which may help the Society and its members to determine, according to the talent given each by the Lord of the vineyard and according to their vocation in the Church, what works our priests ought to engage in principally, and what works ought rather to be left to others.

---

[1] See GS 36.

[2] See GS 38.

390/ 2. Some principles pertinent to the matter under dispute and drawn from the teaching of Vatican II will help us resolve this problem.

391/ All members of the People of God share in Christ's priesthood and in the one mission of the Church; but different degrees or states bring different functions, though these are ordered to and complement each other.[3]

392/ Priests "by the power of the sacrament of orders, and in the image of Christ the eternal High Priest . . . are considered to preach the Gospel, shepherd the faithful, and celebrate divine worship. . . . They exercise this sacred function of Christ most of all in the Eucharistic liturgy. . . . For the penitent or ailing among the faithful, priests exercise fully the ministry of reconciliation and alleviation. . . . Exercising within the limits of their authority the function of Christ as Shepherd and Head, they gather together God's family as a brotherhood all of one mind and lead them in the Spirit, through Christ, to God the Father."[4]

393/ This priestly ministry, within the unity of the presbyteral order, embraces various functions: evangelization of non-believers, catechesis, parochial or supraparochial ministry, scientific research or teaching, participation in the life and toil of workers, and many other activities that are apostolic or ordered to the apostolate.[5]

394/ It is indeed characteristic of laymen, passing their lives as they do in the midst of the world and amid secular tasks, that they be led by the spirit of the Gospel to "work for the sanctification of the world from within, in the manner of leaven. In this way they can make Christ known to others especially by the testimony of a life resplendent in faith, hope, and charity."[6] Yet such an apostolate is not theirs alone;[7] priests, too, in their own way, share it, and must, moreover, effectively help laymen in their apostolic task in the Church and the world.[8]

395/ Religious, finally, are called from both the clerical and the lay state to be consecrated and entirely dedicated to loving God above all, and by their special charism within the Church's life to bear witness that "the world cannot be

---

[3] See LG 10, PO 2.

[4] LG 28.

[5] See PO 4, 8.

[6] LG 31; AA 2, 5.

[7] See LG 31, GS 43.

[8] See AA 25.

transfigured and offered to God without the spirit of the beatitudes,"[9] and thus each in his own way will forward the saving mission of the Church.[10]

396/ 3.   The overall guiding norm for our own apostolate, as is clear from our holy founder's special charism,[11] from the *Formula of the Institute*[12] and the Constitutions,[13] and from the Society's living tradition, is the greater service of God and the more universal good of souls, to be striven for in the greatest possible docility to God's will as manifested to us in the Church and the circumstances of each age, but especially through the Roman Pontiff.

397/   The Society itself is made up of various members; "according to the grace imparted to them by the Holy Spirit and the specific quality of their vocation,"[14] some are priests, some not. Yet all with one mind strive for the single apostolic end set before the whole body of the Society.

398/   As for priestly functions, both the *Formula of the Institute* and the Constitutions clearly state that the Society's priests are destined "above all . . . for every form of ministry of the word"[15] and for the administration of the sacraments.[16] Yet other works are not only not excluded but expressly commended to priests,[17] "as shall be judged best for God's glory and the common good."[18]

399/   In defining more accurately the supreme norm of our apostolate, Ignatius says: "Those of the Society may devote their energies to spiritual objectives and also to corporal ones, in which, too, mercy and charity are practiced . . . ; if both cannot be achieved simultaneously, then, other things being equal, the former are always to be preferred to the latter."[19] With the words "other things being equal," St. Ignatius instructs us that the principle of the preeminence of spiritual works is itself subordinate to his supreme and fundamental norm.

400/ 4.   If criteria for our activity are to be derived correctly from the principles given, the following distinctions must be kept in mind..

---

[9] LG 31.

[10] See LG 43.

[11] See *SpEx* 23, 98.

[12] See *Formula of the Institute,* 1, 2.

[13] *Cons.* [603, 622].

[14] *Formula of the Institute,* 1.

[15] Loc. cit.; see *GenExam* [30]; *Cons.* [308, 603, 645] and passim.

[16] See *Formula of the Institute* 1; Cons. [406–407, 642–643].

[17] See *Formula of the Institute* 1; Cons. [623, 650].

[18] *Formula of the Institute* 1; *Cons.* [591–593, 650, 793].

[19] *Cons.* [623].

401/   In dealing with the priesthood, careful distinction must be made between its essential nature as grounded in Christ's institution, and the concrete historical forms in which that nature is, as it were, variously incarnated in divergent cultures, social structures, and patterns of custom. The nature of Christian priesthood is a matter of dogma and thus unchangeable; concrete forms, on the other hand, are to be adapted to the specific contemporary situation, under the inspiration of the Holy Spirit, the guidance of the hierarchy, and according to the standards of prudence.[20]

402/   All Jesuits, scholastics and brothers included (in schools, for instance, and in other communal works), share together in the one total apostolate exercised by the Society as a priestly body. Each priest, however, is called by God through his ordination to exercise his priesthood in the concrete circumstances of his life.

403/   To grasp this priestly vocation more fully, other distinctions must be made. A priest of the Society is a man created by God and placed amid a certain people. He is a man baptized and confirmed and therefore, as a "brother among brothers,"[21] he shares in the priesthood common to all the faithful. Furthermore, he is a religious, and a religious of the Society: as a religious he has by vow consecrated himself to God in the Church to be "an admirable sign of the heavenly kingdom";[22] as a member of the Society, he lives his religious consecration in an apostolic body. He is, in addition, a priest, taken into the presbyteral order, which is in hierarchical communion with the episcopal order at whose head is Peter's successor.

404/   Each priest must integrate all these aspects of his life into a unified, personal, concrete spirituality; he must, with the interior help of the Holy Spirit and under the guidance of superiors, bring them to fulfillment in an organic and vital unity. In priestly activity and spirituality, then, we need to avoid all one-sided solutions and tendencies; for then some single aspect, be it humanistic, religious, or priestly, is so stressed that the others fade into the background because of this stress.

405/   The 31st General Congregation, with the foregoing exposition of principles in mind, establishes the following.

---

[20] See PO 22.
[21] See PO 9.
[22] PC 1.

II. Decree

406/ 5. The manifold activity of priests in the Society flows from the nature and mission of the priesthood and from the distinctive grace and overall guiding norm of our Institute.

407/ 6. Since priests by their ordination as assistants, of subordinate rank, to the episcopal order, are consecrated for the manifold ministry of the word, for the administration of the sacraments, and for the pastoral rule of the family of God, these forms of ministerial apostolate are deservedly to be held in special esteem.

408/ 7. Since, however, Christ, Head of the Church, is integrating the whole world into a kingdom for the Father, it is for the priest, as sign and minister of the Lord's active presence, to be present in or to collaborate with all human efforts which help in establishing the kingdom.

409/ 8. Since today such collaboration is urgently needed in preparing the way for the Gospel and in establishing or extending the Church's presence by scholarly research and teaching, especially in the sacred sciences, by social work and work in communications media, this type of collaboration ought to be regarded as a genuine apostolate for the Society's priests. Especially indeed ought we be concerned with areas critical for the human person as a whole, such as the sciences of man and the education of youth.

410/ 9. Although the General Congregation intends to offer brothers greater opportunity for all such apostolic works and responsibilities as suit their state, and while, on the other hand, it also desires a greater collaboration with laymen in the apostolate, this does not at all imply—as is clear from what has already been said—that the Society's priests are to be diverted from fields more proper to laymen or the brothers.

411/ 10. The choice of one or other apostolate is to be made according to the criteria set down in the Decree on the Better Choice and Promotion of Ministries, where the Ignatian guiding norm is applied to the contemporary situation with a view to reaching the best possible balance in our ministries.

412/ 11. In assigning priests to various ministries, superiors should look, as our founder did, not only to existing apostolic needs, but also to the call and particular gifts of those to be assigned. All, however, should cultivate the greatest possible docility to the divine will and thus be ready to meet the more pressing and universal needs of the Church, expressed to them through superiors.

413/ 12 Priests of the Society whose apostolate lies primarily in areas of temporal concern, united with all other priests in one total priestly ministry for the sake of men,[23] should bring their priesthood to bear upon all their activity, especially through prayer, though the witness of their lives, and through the Holy Eucharist, which "contains the Church's entire spiritual wealth, that is, Christ Himself,"[24] and through which men and all created reality are brought to the Father.

---

[23] See PO 8.

[24] See PO 5.

DECREE 24

MISSION SERVICE

414/ 1. From the "fountain of love" which is God the Father, mankind has been freely created and graciously called to form a community of sons in the Son; for by the mission of the Son, God "determined to intervene in human history in a way both new and definitive."[1]

415/ The only-begotten Son has been sent by the Father to save what was lost, and through the Holy Spirit, to unite men who were redeemed by Him into one Mystical Body which is the Church.

416/ As the Son was sent by the Father, He in turn sent the apostles[2] as heralds of saving charity, giving them this solemn command: "Go, therefore, and make disciples of all nations, baptizing them . . . and behold, I am with you all days, even unto the consummation of the world."[3]

417/ Heeding the mandate of Christ, the Church "continues unceasingly to send heralds of the Gospel until such time as the infant churches are fully established and can themselves carry on the work of evangelizing."[4] Thus, "the specific purpose of this missionary activity is evangelization and the planting of the Church among those peoples and groups where she has not yet taken root."[5]

418/ 2. It was for this task of announcing the Gospel that God in His providence called, along with other heralds of the Gospel, our holy Father Ignatius and his companions. God set their hearts on fire with a zeal which made them desire at first to go to Jerusalem to help nonbelievers.[6] And when this project proved impossible, this same zeal urged them to offer themselves without reservation to the Vicar of Christ so that he might show them what part of the Lord's vineyard stood most in need of their labors.[7]

---

[1] AG 2–3.

[2] See John 20.21.

[3] Matt. 28.19–20.

[4] LG 17.

[5] LG 17.

[6] *Chronicon Societatis Iesu, auctore Joanne Alphonso de Polanco* (in MHSJ), I, 26, 50.

[7] *Cons.* [618].

419/   And so the new-born Society, by this commitment to Christ's Vicar, was established as an apostolic order for work "among believers and nonbelievers"[8] and was made an intimate sharer in the mission mandate of the entire Church.

420/   As part of the pilgrim Church, therefore, the Society has embraced as strongly as it can the Church's universal mission, and is so alive with this missionary spirit that it necessarily communicates to its members a zeal for souls great enough to make both the defense of the faith and its propagation one and the same vocation. The *Formula of the Institute* approved by Julius III described this quite aptly": Whoever wishes to fight under the banner of the cross in our Society . . . should seriously consider himself part of the Society established chiefly for this, that it especially labor for the defense and propagation of the faith. . . ."[9]

421/ 3.   The 31st General Congregation keeps before its eyes those serious words of the Second Vatican Council: "The present historical situation is leading humanity into a new stage. As the salt of the earth and the light of the world, the Church is summoned with special urgency to save and renew every creature."[10] It is also aware of the large segment of mankind that is not yet Christian. Accordingly, this Congregation establishes that the following means be earnestly employed in order that Jesuits may better respond to their own mission calling and to the desires of the Church.

422/ 4.   Jesuits should be convinced that activity aimed at spreading the Church among those groups and peoples where it is not yet fully established is not a work reserved merely for some Jesuits who may have received a kind of second vocation. Rather, all Jesuits, with the same zeal and for the same basic reason, should strive to respond to this mission vocation with largeness of spirit. Every Jesuit, therefore, and not only those who so petition, may be sent to the missions by reason of his vocation to the Society. Those of the Society, moreover, who were born in mission lands ought to be clearly aware of their serious responsibility for planting the Church with deep roots in their own countries. But even these men should be prepared to undertake mission service among other peoples.[11]

423/   Superiors, however, ought to select for the missions those who are men of solid virtue, who are clearly flexible, and who are capable not only of learning languages, but also of fitting into a new culture. Among those chosen

---

[8] *Cons.* [618] ; and the *Formulas of the Institute* approved by Paul III (1540) and Julius III (1550).

[9] Julius III, *Exposcit Debitum* (July 21, 1550).

[10] AG 1.

[11] See AG 20.

there should be some who have the intellectual capacity to become outstanding in the intellectual apostolate, and in scientific, cultural and religious research.[12]

424/ 5. All Jesuits dedicated to missionary activity, according to the spirit of the Second Vatican Council, should try to walk "the same road which Christ walked: a road of poverty and obedience, of service and self-sacrifice to the death, from which death He came forth a victor by His resurrection. For thus did all the apostles walk in hope."[13]

425/ 5. In order that the Society may respond more fully both to the contemporary needs of the Church and to its own essential vocation, every effort should be made to increase the proportion of members in mission work. It is especially desirable that this increase in the missionary activity of the Society develop out of the fostering of vocations in mission lands themselves. Superiors must be convinced, therefore, that this formation of members who come from the newly-established churches themselves is the most important contribution to mission work that the Society can make.

426/ 6. In order to achieve fully the genuine goal of mission activity, Jesuits engaged in this work should be aware of the following:

a. It is according to the spirit of the Second Vatican Council that "the young churches, rooted in Christ and built upon the foundation of the apostles, take to themselves in a wonderful exchange all the riches of the nations which were given to Christ as an inheritance."[14] All Jesuits, therefore, who work among other peoples, should not only treat individual persons with charity, and the positive elements of their religions with reverence,[15] but in everything which does not run counter to Christian faith and sensibility, they should highly esteem the culture, customs and traditions of these peoples.[16]

427/ *b.* The principal means for the work of planting the Church, and the one recommended above all others, is the preaching of the Gospel. But where the direct preaching of the Gospel is for the time being impossible, Jesuits must strive in every other method they use "to bear witness to Christ by charity and by works of mercy."[17]

428/ *c.* The work of education "by means of different kinds of schools, which should be considered not only as an outstanding means for forming and

---

[12] See AG 34; ES III, 22

[13] AG 5; see *SpEx* 95, 98, 167.

[14] AG 22

[15] See NA 2.

[16] See AG 9, 11, 15–16, 18–22, 25–26; GC 30, D. 54.

[17] AG 6.

developing Christian youth, but also as a service of supreme value to men, especially in the developing nations,"[18] should be ranked very high. Education can, in this way, become an excellent form of preaching whereby all the human values found in the culture of those people who are not yet Christian are embraced, raised up, and offered to God the Father through the Church.

429/   For the same reason, students who leave their native land to study abroad and who are very often in need of spiritual assistance should receive brotherly care and attention. Young people of this kind—and others too, whether they be workers or members of other classes—should be helped to fit into the social and Catholic life of the people among whom they dwell. In areas, therefore, where foreigners such as these are found, it recommended that provincials be ready and willing to assign some Jesuits to this kind of work.[19]

430/   *d.* Although no type of ministry is foreign to the Society, nevertheless, those works should be chosen first which are more urgent or more universal. Among these, special mention ought to be made of cooperation in the formation of diocesan clergy, cooperation in the formation of religious men and women, the formation of the laity for the apostolate, the use of communications media, the social apostolate, ecumenical work, by which the reason for scandal arising from the division among Christians is removed, and dialogue with non-Christian religions.[20]

431/   *e.* "For building up of the body of Christ,"[21] cooperation with bishops is important, as is collaboration in a fraternal spirit with both diocesan and religious clergy, and participation in conferences of religious.[22]

432/ 7.   All Jesuits applied to the missions should be thoroughly prepared and sent as soon as possible, although the proper time will depend on the qualities of individuals and the conditions of the regions.

433/   This preparation, for those who are assigned abroad or for those who come from the young churches themselves, should include, according to the needs of each one, a sufficient knowledge of the language, history, culture and religion of the people. All of these are to be kept in mind throughout their entire formation, but especially during the time of philosophy and theology.

434/   Moreover, all Jesuits the world over should be sufficiently instructed in the theology of the missions and should try to nourish their zeal for souls by means of constant communication from the missions.

---

[18] AG 12; see GE 9.

[19] See AG 38; ES III, 23.

[20] See AG 15, 34.

[21] Eph. 4.12.

[22] See AG 33; ES III, 21.

435/ 8. The missionary character of the whole Society should make itself evident in its works. For this reason:

1° *a.* Provinces should consider the mission works that are entrusted to them as an integral part of the province, on the same level as the other works of the province. They should help these mission works with money and men, and with a greater enthusiasm where the needs are more pressing. This applies as well to those areas that have already been erected as independent vice-provinces and provinces.

436/ *b.* After assuming office, provincials should visit the mission works that are under their care in order to acquaint themselves with their needs, and they are to be liberal in extending help to these missions.

437/ *c.* It is recommended that in provinces responsible for mission works there be a father who is knowledgeable in mission affairs and has the missions as his particular responsibility. He will furnish needed advice to the provincial and to the consultors in planning the apostolic works of the province.

438/ 2° Let Jesuits diligently promote the work of the missions among all the faithful, and foster missionary vocations.

439/ 3° It is very important that knowledge of the missions be more and more widely circulated by mission periodicals or even other types of periodicals.

440/ 4° Each Jesuit, according to his own ability, should help to encourage and fulfill the aspirations of those lay people who wish to be of service to the developing nations. The Society throughout the world has the opportunity to instill Christian inspiration into the social and economic endeavors undertaken by various other institutions for the good of those nations.

441/ 5° For better information, coordination, and cooperation among Jesuits and for the benefit of those engaged in mission service, the Mission Secretariat should be enlarged.

442/ 9. The 31st General Congregation desires that the Society for its part offer itself to the service of the Church in its worldwide mission, so that "the splendor of God which brightens the face of Jesus Christ may shine upon all men through the Holy Spirit."[23]

---

[23] AG 42.

DECREE 25

JOURNEYS BY MISSIONARIES

443/ A return to the province of origin is considered something normal for the benefit both of the missions and of the missionaries. With regard to its frequency, the general norms to be established by Father General must be observed, their application according to the situation being left to the provincials.

DECREE 26

ECUMENISM

I. Introduction

444/ 1. Together with all the faithful the Society of Jesus welcomes with filial devotion the Decree on Ecumenism *(Unitatis Redintegratio),* the Decree on Eastern Catholic Churches *(Orientalium Ecclesiarum),* and the Declaration on Religious Freedom *(Dignitatis Humanae)* as they come from the Second Vatican Council. The 31st General Congregation urges that through their prayer and study all members of the Society make the spirit and teaching of these decrees their own. They are to be mindful that the ecumenical frame of mind itself, as well as all ecumenical activity, is founded on the spirit of truth and sincerity, a spirit of progressive interior renewal and especially the spirit of love. They are to pursue with their holy desires and prayers that full unity which the Father Himself is preparing through the Holy Spirit for the Church of Christ, His Son. Let them be aware that they are now being gathered together with other Christians in a genuine form of communion, and together with them they are to realize that they are brothers as well of all who believe in God and adore Him.

445/ 2. The 31st General Congregation, humbly acknowledging the sins against unity committed by members of the Society, whether in the past or in more recent times, joins with the Council itself in recalling the witness of John: "To say that we have never sinned is to call God a liar and to show that His word is not in us."[1] "Thus, in humble prayer, we beg pardon of God and of our separated brethren, just as we forgive those who trespass against us."[2]

---

[1] 1 John 1.10.

[2] UR 7.

446/ 3.   Therefore the 31st General Congregation proposes to offer certain practical directives to Jesuits. These should be applied with due account being taken of each one's training, of local circumstances, and particularly of the directives of the hierarchy.

II. The Ecumenical Education of Jesuits

447/ 4.   For a suitable training of Jesuits in the matter of ecumenism the following recommendations are offered. During the time of their studies, scholastics are to acquire a solid knowledge of the history of the separated churches and communities and of their spirituality. The course in sacred theology provided for the theologians should be in harmony with the ecumenical spirit. Where for various considerations it seems opportune, special courses are to be given in Eastern theology and in that of the Reformation. In the lectures on pastoral theology attention is also to be given to the sometimes very difficult problems which can arise in certain regions from contacts with other religions. Professors are to be sure that the facts of history and of doctrine also are interpreted with calm objectivity.[3] And finally, all are to avoid prejudices and offensive modes of speech, and they are to eliminate entirely "words, judgments and actions which do not truly correspond with the situation of our separated brethren, since they are neither true nor fair, and thus make our relations with them more strained."[4]

448/ 5.   An education in ecumenism is not a matter of the intellect alone, but must be part of one's spiritual formation as well, since a truly ecumenical spirit cannot be had without a change of heart.[5]

449/ 6.   All are to be mindful that personal contact with the separated brethren is of the highest value in wiping out age-old prejudices, in coming to a better knowledge of their faith, their love of Christ, and their spiritual life, as well as the difficulties, even of conscience, which they experience in regard to the Catholic Church.

450/   For this reason, where it can be done fruitfully, professors or ministers of other confessions are, on appropriate occasions, to be invited to give lectures. They are to be received fraternally and Jesuits are to accept their invitations willingly in return.

451/   If, moreover, there is a seminary of another confession near our scholasticate, it can be helpful to provide for the scholastics some opportunity for contacts with their colleagues.

---

[3] See UR 10.

[4] See UR 4.

[5] See UR 7.

452/ 7. Due consideration being had for their religious formation and the offices they hold, brothers are to be informed in the matter of ecumenism so that by prayer, suitable understanding, and such personal contacts as fall to them, they too may participate in this activity of the Society.

453/ 8. Provision is to be made that some of our men are prepared as experts in ecumenical matters according to the requirements of different regions. They are to learn to grasp fully the doctrine and the spiritual life both of Catholics and of separated brethren. Thus they will be equipped to give accurate instruction to our scholastics; to be available with their counsel and collaboration for the works of the province, in the colleges, in the parishes, and the like; to take competent part in ecumenical meetings and, finally, by study and writing, to foster ecumenical theology and contribute to its advance.

III. The Practice of Ecumenism

454/ 9. A dignified and reverent celebration of the liturgy, both of the Eucharist and of the other sacraments, often contributes more to the elimination of prejudice than learned argument. Moreover, where the local bishop permits it, Jesuits are to take part with our separated brethren in some public forms of common prayer, especially prayer for the grace of union. The octave of prayer for Church unity, which is customarily celebrated annually in many places, is warmly recommended to Jesuits.

455/ 10. The study and use of Sacred Scripture is to be encouraged. Of itself this is a great contribution to the unity of Catholics with other Christians.[6] The greater the influence of Sacred Scripture on our spirituality, liturgical worship, and theology, the closer will be the union of all believers in Christ. For then they will be drawing the water of salvation from a common spring.

456/ 11. The Society should stand ready to offer whole-hearted assistance to others within the Church who are engaged in this same work of ecumenism and likewise to receive help from them. Such collaboration is itself a sign of the unity present in the Church and at the same time a source of inspiration for promoting it further.

457/ 12. Ecumenical contacts, whether indirect, through books and periodicals, or direct and personal are to be fostered by Jesuits according to the special circumstances of a locality, a province, or a house.

458/ *a.* Those who work in education are to imbue their students with the ecumenical spirit by their teaching and example. They should make efforts to establish dialogue between their students and those of the separated brethren and to initiate cooperation with them on the institutional level.

---

[6] See UR 21.

459/ In setting up our university programs of scientific research in biblical exegesis, dogmatic theology, Church history, religious sociology, and the like, cooperation with separated brethren is to be sought wherever it seems especially profitable.

460/ *b.* Those who engage in social work or dedicate themselves to works of mercy, or who collaborate in international organizations for peace and unity among nations and for the conquest of world poverty, ought to keep before their minds what a lively sense of justice and sincere love of their neighbor our separated brethren have developed out of their faith in Christ. Cooperation should be sought with them and where it already exists it is to be even further promoted.

461/ *c.* Those who are occupied in the pastoral ministries through work in the parishes, in giving the Spiritual Exercises, etc., should seek to discuss parallel or mutual problems with their counterparts in other churches and communities, and to undertake cooperation with them, even where more difficult questions, such as mixed marriages or the like, are involved.

462/ *d.* Mindful of the scandal given non-Christian peoples by our divisions, those who labor in the missions should foster an ecumenical spirit and cooperation so that insofar as possible, through the common witness of all believers, the light of Christ may shine more brightly among non-Christians and the scandal of division may be lessened by the sincerity of our mutual esteem and charity. On the other hand, vigilant care must be taken that the faithful not be exposed to the danger of syncretism or indifferentism. However, particularly in the case of the cultivated, such danger is to be avoided by means of a solid education in doctrine and in a training directed to a deeper love of the Church rather than through a timorous isolation from other Christians.

463/ 13. Lest they hinder rather than advance the progress of unity, Jesuits must remember that ecumenical work is no easy task and that it is not to be left to the indiscreet zeal of private individuals. "Nothing is so foreign to the spirit of ecumenism as a false conciliatory approach which harms the purity of Catholic doctrine and obscures its assured genuine meaning."[7]

464/ Therefore in ecumenical activity Jesuits are faithfully to observe all the prescriptions and directives of the Holy See and of those whose duty it is to direct the ecumenical movement.

IV. Recommendations to Father General

465/ 14. Moreover, the 31st General Congregation makes the following recommendations to Father General so that in his prudence he may see to it:

---

[7] See UR 11.

1° that there be established a council on ecumenical affairs composed of experts from various nations, and at the same time appoint one of the Assistants or expert advisors as delegate for fostering the ecumenical movement;

466/ 2° that insofar as it can serve the purpose of the promotion of the ecumenical movement, there be established, either by Jesuits alone or in collaboration with others, institutes or houses of study for experts and students, and this in centers renowned for ecumenical studies;

467/ 3° that liturgical texts pertaining to the Society, or other official documents, such as the *Ratio Studiorum* and the like, be revised according to the ecumenical spirit, and in particular that all offensive expressions be eliminated.

DECREE 27

Pastoral Services, Residences, and Parishes

I. Pastoral Services

468/ 1.   Under present circumstances in the Church, those pastoral works or services that have been begun for the greater service of God and the more effective welfare of souls in accordance with the spirit of our vocation are to be renewed and energetically promoted, provided that they still fulfill the end for which they were intended and are approved by the hierarchy. Those should be dropped that cannot be adapted. In arriving at this decision the judgment of the bishops and of lay directors should be taken into account. Jesuits should diligently look for new forms of pastoral services, according to the tradition and spirit of the Society, that answer contemporary needs. For the teaching of the Second Vatican Council on the pastoral apostolate does not imply uniformity, but rather proposes a harmonious plurality of all pastoral undertakings, according to the diversity of the Spirit's gifts.[1]

469/ 2.   So that in this adaptation the spirit of our distinctive calling may flourish in its entirety:

1°   Jesuits themselves especially are to be trained to give the Spiritual Exercises in the true and correct way, and others among the diocesan and religious priests are to be helped to do the same, so that the faithful may be led to an intimate knowledge of the Lord, to love and follow Him more.[2]

470/   2°   All should have a high esteem for, and be keenly mindful of, the mystery of the heart of Christ in the life of the Church. It should be so much a part of their own lives that they can promote the knowledge of it among others in their apostolic activity. In this way the results of different ministries may be daily increased, "for from the side of Christ asleep on the cross there has arisen the wonderful sacrament of the entire Church."[3]

471/   They should also trust in the patronage of the Blessed Virgin Mary in their assigned tasks and activities, and everywhere show more and more clear-

---

[1] See PC 20

[2] See *SpEx* 104; *Cons.* [408–409].

[3] SC 5.

ly the role of the mother of the Savior in the economy of salvation.[4] For in holy Church and in our tradition the Virgin Mary "holds a place which is the highest after Christ and yet very close to us."[5]

472/   3° In all their apostolate, our men in pastoral work, in accordance with the desires of the Second Vatican Council, should share with a generous and open mind in the spirit of liturgical, ecumenical and pastoral renewal as well as the introduction to the faith, and with all their strength propagate this spirit.

473/   4° Our works should begin and be carried on under the guidance of superiors, and not in an individualistic and scattered way. Cooperation should be stressed, both among Jesuits who are working amicably and most eagerly for the same apostolic goal, and with others, religious and diocesan priests and the laity. Jesuits should willingly take part in the pastoral planning proposed by the bishops and collaborate with it in a humble and sincere desire of serving the Church.[6]

474/   5° In the selection and planning of ministries and pastoral services of Jesuits as well as in the determination of the places where such ministries are to be exercised, careful attention should be given to what is contained in the Decree on the Better Choice and Promotion of Ministries. In order that Jesuits may be better integrated into pastoral work today, it is necessary that men working in this field be really suitable and competent, and thus they should be trained:

475/   *a.* on the one hand, by the general training in the course of studies, provision for which has already been made in the Decree on the Training of Scholastics Especially in Studies;

476/   *b.* on the other hand, by special training, so that the Jesuits who are to be assigned to these ministries have a sufficient skill in some pastoral work (e.g., in preaching the word of God, in giving the Exercises, in catechetics, in spiritual guidance, in ecumenical activity, in spiritual theology, in family counseling and dealing with working men, and the like);

477/   *c.* and also by institutes that are to be conducted at regular intervals in their regions, so that the priests who are already working in the ministries may be continually kept up to date in regard to new aids.

---

[4] See LG 55.

[5] See LG 54.

[6] See LG 45; CD 33–35; PC 23, 25; GC 31, D. 48.

II. Residences

478/ 3.   In this decree, "residences" are understood to be communities destined for pastoral work,[7] or for any other apostolic work other than the education of youth, which according to the Constitutions belongs to another class of houses.[8]

479/ 4.   Though these residences are generically of one kind, they can have different names, structures, and ministries, according to the needs of men, times, and circumstances.[9] In them, not only the ministries that are strictly priestly works are carried on, but also all those that, according to our situation[10] and according to the needs of the Church of Christ in the modern world, ought to be accepted, as is set forth in the Pastoral Constitution *Gaudium et Spes.*

480/ 5.   Residences should be "living communities," in which the members feel that they are working for the same goal, and, moved by a common spirit, share with each other their worries and successes. So that this can be done more easily, these communities should not be too large, and should be set up, as far as possible, according to natural grouping by works.

481/   The community should be gathered together at regular intervals under the direction of the superior or of some expert designated by him, to review their work, to investigate in common both their methods and their results, and to study contemporary problems.

482/   The tools needed for their labors should be found in the house, such as books, specialized periodicals, and the like.

483/   Young men engaged in this work should be introduced to their pastoral ministries by experienced priests in a brotherly way.

484/ 6.   The whole house should be so set up that the members can pray, work, and rest according to the demands of their apostolate.[11] Under the direction of the superior, the house discipline should be adapted with the needed flexibility, in accordance with the Decree on Community Life and Religious Discipline.

485/ 7.   According to our Constitutions[12] and also according to the new dispositions of the Council,[13] a house destined for the apostolate ought to be outstanding as a "collective" and "more effective" witness to poverty.

---

[7] See *Epit* 29 §1, 5°.

[8] See *Cons.* [289].

[9] See *Epit* 29 §1, 2°, 5°–7°.

[10] See LG 31; *Cons.* [591].

[11] See PC 15; ES II, 26.

[12] See *Cons.* [555–60].

[13] See PC 13; ES II, 23.

486/   The members who live in the residences can live off the income from their work, in accordance with the Decree on Poverty of the 31st General Congregation, but "they should avoid every appearance of luxury, of excessive wealth and accumulation of possessions";[14] they should cherish the free rendering of ministries,[15] and place their confidence in God alone.[16] They should look for new forms of poverty with diligence and in a concrete way, each according to his fashion, and insist[17] that there be, e.g., a more extensive practice of hospitality, a fraternal sharing of possessions,[18] support of the poor, and so on.

487/ 8.   In accordance with the spirit of the Society, and especially in accordance with the repeated wish of the Church, the General Congregation urgently requests the provincials to establish and promote residences among working men and among the more neglected groups. There, Jesuits in a special way should carry on their apostolate, in various manners, while living their life with the poor Christ.[19]

III. Parishes

488/ 9.   Decree 233 in the Collection of Decrees is abrogated.

489/ 10.   A new decree should be entered in a suitable place to this effect :

1° Our Society freely embraces the wish of the Church expressed by the Second Vatican Council, that the religious who are called on by bishops in accordance with their needs "should lend helpful efforts in various pastoral ministries," no exception being made of parishes.[20]

490/   2° The care of souls in a parish, in general, is no longer to be said to be contrary to the principles of the Constitutions, now that the discipline of the Church in regard to parishes committed to religious has been changed. But because of the seriousness of the matter, it belongs to Father General to judge, all things considered, whether a particular parish is to be accepted or given back. The texts of agreements with local ordinaries about parishes are to be approved by Father General.

IV. Recommendations to Superiors

491/ 11.   Superiors, with the approval of Father General, should insist:

---

[14] PC 13; see *GenExam* [81]; GC 31, D. 18, n. 7.

[15] See *GenExam* [4] ; *Cons.* [565].

[16] See *Cons.* [555].

[17] See PC 13; ES II, 23.

[18] See PC 13.

[19] See GC 28, D. 29, n. 8; GC 29, D. 29, n. 5.

[20] CD 35 §1.

1° that the apostolic services of the province and the region be reviewed by the commission on the review of ministries,[21] so that Jesuits may serve the hierarchy of the Church with greater freedom;

492/ 2° that the directors of works sincerely adapt themselves to contemporary pastoral practice, for example, in giving the Exercises, in popular missions, in the cooperation of Jesuits with a program of renewal of the sodalities or the Apostleship of Prayer in those regions where the bishops and major superiors, having first listened to the lay directors, decide in fraternal harmony to renew them so that they may be more effectively promoted;

493/ 3° that Jesuits have a high esteem for the teaching of Christian doctrine to children and the uneducated, either by themselves or by others, as occasion may offer, in accordance with the tradition of the Society and the vows they have taken; for the promotion of new forms of modern catechetics and introduction to the faith by suitable means; for the giving of spiritual aid in hospitals and prisons;

494/ 4° that there be set up institutes for the training of directors of the Exercises as soon as possible, because of their importance and their necessity for the renewal of our ministries; in these institutes there should be research into the "genuine meaning of the Ignatian text"; indeed, there should be a real "reworking" "of the Spiritual Exercises themselves to unfold their spiritual riches to modern man, and to express them in the concepts of the theology of the Second Vatican Council."[22]

---

[21] See GC 31, D. 22.

[22] See Paul VI, Address of December 29, 1965; Letter to Cardinal Cushing, August 25, 1966 (both documents appear in the *Annuarium S. I. 1966–67*).

DECREE 28

The Apostolate of Education

I Introduction

495/ 1. Throughout the world today, whether in the advanced or in the evolving nations, there is clear recognition of the importance of education for the formation of society and particularly for the initiating of youth into life in the human community. Nothing is more esteemed by political leaders than this education of the citizenry, for without it no nation or state can develop or progress and meet the national and international responsibilities imposed by the needs of this age.

496/ 2. The Church has, therefore, reflected upon "the paramount importance of education in the life of man, and its ever-mounting influence on the social progress of this era"[1] and once again affirmed its own role in the development and extension of education. To fulfill this function the Church wishes to employ all appropriate means. Yet it recognizes that schools are educational agencies of "special importance,"[2] for in these institutions Christian teachers are to promote the renewal of the Church and maintain and intensify her beneficent and salutary presence in the contemporary and, particularly, the intellectual world.[3]

497/ 3. In our day we are witnessing everywhere the rapid emergence of new social forms and the society of the future. When new ideas are so widely sown, it is not hard to discern the birth of new patterns of thought and action in the modern world. The promoters of these new ideas, especially when they work out of centers of higher culture and research, are exercising a mounting influence upon the whole of social culture through highly effective modem means of popularization. But since this influence inclines ever more toward an atheistic and agnostic ideology and makes itself felt particularly in educational centers, the presence of Christians in those centers is of the highest moment if the Church is indeed to make an opportune contribution to the society of the future by forming and educating its mind to reverence for God and in the fullness of Christ.

498/ 4. For many centuries the Society of Jesus, in accordance with its Institute, has diligently exercised its teaching function almost uninterruptedly throughout the world. Now, impelled and inspired by the Second Vatican Council, the Society, through its 31st General Congregation, wishes to confirm the high

---

[1] GE introduction.

[2] GE 5.

[3] GE conclusion.

regard it has for this apostolate of education and earnestly to exhort its members that they maintain unflaggingly their esteem for this significant apostolate.

499/ There are some members of the Society, however, who think that our educational institutions in certain parts of the world have become practically useless and should therefore be given up. There are others who recognize the continued effectiveness of these institutions but believe that there are other ministries in which we could perhaps be even more effective. Hence they conclude that it is necessary, or at least appropriate, to leave the work of formal education to laymen or to religious whose institutes dedicate them exclusively to this apostolate. This Congregation judges that there is no uniform solution for this very real and pressing problem. The solution it requires will necessarily vary according to differences of circumstances. Therefore, it must be determined by superiors, with the aid of their brethren and according to the norms for the choice of ministries as applied to the needs of each province or region.

500/ The intention of this present decree, however, is, in the first place, that the Society may think with the Church concerning the paramount importance and effectiveness of the educational apostolate, particularly in our times. Secondly, it is intended that our schools be outstanding not so much for number and size as for teaching, for the quality of the instruction, and the service rendered to the people of God. Thirdly, we should be receptive toward new forms of this apostolate, particularly adapted to the present age, and we should energetically investigate or fashion these new forms either in our own schools or elsewhere. Finally, for those laymen who generously spend themselves with us in this apostolate, the way should be opened to a wider collaboration with us, whether this be in teaching, administration, or on the board of directors itself.

501-2/ 5. It is evident that we can exercise the apostolate of education in various ways either in our own institutions or by collaborating with others. There is an extensive variety today, whether one is speaking of colleges and universities, or vocational schools, or the so-called normal schools for the training of teachers. Which forms of the apostolate of education the Society should take up is a matter for superiors to decide according to the norms for the selection of ministries. But in making this selection, we should consider the new means of social communication, particularly radio and television. For these are highly effective instruments for new kinds of educational organization and pedagogy since they extend to the widest possible audience and reach those who would otherwise be deprived of schooling. Besides, they are very much in line with the present day "culture of the image."

503/ The Society should have its own educational institutions where resources and circumstances permit and a greater service of God and the Church can be thereby expected. For these schools constitute at least one effective instrument for the promotion of our educational purpose, i.e., the synthesizing of faith and culture. Through these schools a firmer and more lasting social presence in the community is achieved, both because they are a corporate effort and because through the students families are influenced. Thus the school becomes an apostolic center within the community.

504/   If, indeed, there is question of closing schools or of handing them over to others, superiors are to work out the best way of doing this in consultation with the local Ordinary and with the approbation of Father General.

II. Decree

505/ 6.   Let Jesuits have a high regard for the apostolate of education as one of the primary ministries of the Society, commended in a special way by the Church in our time. For the transmission of human culture and its integration in Christ significantly contribute to realization of the goal set by our Lord "that God may be all in all things."[4]

506/ 7.   This apostolate aims to provide a service of love for mankind redeemed by Christ. On the one hand, it aims so to educate believers as to make them not only cultured but, in both private and public lives, men who are authentically Christian and able and willing to work for the modern apostolate.

On the other hand, it aims to provide non-Christians with a humanistic formation directed towards the welfare of their own nation and, at the same time, to conduct them by degrees to the knowledge and love of God or at least to the acceptance of moral, and even religious values.[5]

507/ 8.   Let the provincials see to it that the apostolate of education, along with other ministries, be really and continually adapted to the circumstances of men, time, and place, making use in this of the advice both of experts and of the committee on the choice of ministries. Let the provincials also see to it that really competent men are prepared in education.

508/ 9.   In collaboration with the bishops, other religious, and their fellow citizens, let Jesuits be alert to correlate the Society's activity with the complex of pastoral and educational work in the whole region or nation. Since, moreover, dialogue in this pluralistic world is both possible and desirable, let them also willingly cooperate with other organizations, even if these do not depend either on the Church or the Society. Let Jesuits therefore keep in mind the special importance of collaborating with those international organizations which promote education, especially in the less developed countries.

---

[4] I Cor 15.28; see GE introduction; *CollDecr* 131; GC 28, D. 31, n. 1.

[5] *CollDecr* 136; GC 28, D. 31, n. 1.

509/ 10. *a.* Let students be selected, as far as possible, of whom we can expect a greater progress and a greater influence on society, no matter to what social class they belong.

510/ *b.* In order that this criterion of selection may be equitably applied, Jesuits should firmly advance the claims of distributive justice, so that public aid will provide parents with the real liberty of choosing schools for their children according to their conscience.[6]

511/ *c.* However, until such rights have been vindicated, the Society, in accordance with its Constitutions[7] and traditional practice, must make it easy for talented young people, particularly in the emerging nations, to attend our schools. Therefore, let all Jesuits try to obtain public or private endowments, with the help of our alumni, or of those who are bound to the Society through special friendship or apostolic zeal.[8]

512/ 11. Our educational institutions should be established only when and where they show promise of contributing significantly to the welfare of the Church, and can be furnished besides with an adequate supply of competent Jesuits without harm to the training or studies of our own members.[9] Let superiors inquire whether it is more suitable to open or to retain schools of our own or whether it would be better in some circumstances to teach in public schools, or in schools directed by others.

513/ 12. *a.* The first care of Jesuits should be that Christian students acquire that knowledge and character which are worthy of Christians, along with the letters and sciences. To this end, it will help very much if, in addition to the suitable amount of time given to the teaching of Christian doctrine and religion according to modern methods, Jesuits also offer to the students a good example of hard work and dedication as well as of religious life.[10]

514/ *b.* We should try in a special way to imbue our students with the true charity of Christ, according to the social doctrine of the Church. Let them learn to honor and be grateful to laboring men; let them learn to hunger and thirst for that justice which aims to provide all men with an adequate recompense for new work, that the distribution of wealth be more equitable, that the sharing of spiritual goods be fuller and more universal.[11]

---

[6] See GE 6.

[7] See *Cons.* [478].

[8] See GC 28, D. 31, n. 3.

[9] See *CollDecr* 133.

[10] See *CollDecr* 136 §1.

[11] John XXIII, Mater et Magistra *AAS* 53 (1961) 401–464; GS 29; Fr. Janssens, *ActRSJ* 11 (1949) 720–721.

515/   *c.* Let youth be progressively formed to liturgical and personal prayer. As they come to be more mature, exercises of piety should be proposed to them rather than imposed.

516/   *d.* Selected spiritual and apostolic activities which will really be an efficacious means of character formation, for example the sodalities, should be properly established and directed and esteemed by us all. For they serve to introduce and educate our students in apostolic activities step by step.

517/   *e.* Special importance should be attributed to the spiritual direction of students. For this is an effective way of nourishing a person's sense of responsibility both for the ordering of his spiritual life and for the choosing of an adult vocation in accordance with the divine will. In addition, every effort should be made for a fresh increase of priestly and religious vocations so as to help the Church in its present needs.

518/   *f.* Regarding non-Christian students, care must be taken throughout the whole course of studies and especially in ethics courses that men be formed who are endowed with a sound moral judgment and solid virtues. Therefore in their training, the first rank of importance must be given to the formation of a true and right moral conscience, and at the same time of a firm will to act according to it. For in this way they will be best prepared to have a saving effect on family life and society, and in addition to serve their country and to obtain the reward of eternal life.

519/   13. *a.* Let Jesuits remember that the task of teaching is not restricted to some hours nor only to some persons.[12] Let all give a witness of religious and apostolic life; let all be convinced that the common task is more important than individual success; and let them try continually to renew themselves in spirit and understanding. To this end, superiors should favor research, experiments, the discovery of new methods of teaching, and see to it that the members have libraries, audio-visual aids, conferences by experts, possibilities of attending meetings, and other helps.

520/   *b.* Scholastics and younger brothers who are sent to the colleges should be watched over with special care by superiors and spiritual fathers.[13] They should remember that regency is established for their own growth, and so that their virtue may develop, their character be trained, their gifts manifested, and they themselves may make progress in studies. But the real assistance they provide for the work of education should also be considered, and so they should share in the common responsibility for and the discussion of plans concerning the school, according to its statutes.

---

[12] See *CollDecr* 142.

[13] See *CollDecr* 145.

521/ 14. For its part, the Society should help those many children of the Church who are being educated in non-Catholic schools. Superiors should be mindful of the Church's solicitude in this matter. In their concern for the spiritual formation of all youth, superiors should attentively and willingly listen to bishops who ask for the collaboration of the Society in this ministry, especially in directing Catholic centers for students, in the office of chaplains, and also in teaching in non-Catholic schools.[14]

522/ 15. *a.* Young people who travel abroad for their education, as often happens nowadays, should be attentively helped. This is especially important in the case of those, whether Catholic or not, who are outstanding and can be expected to become leaders when they return to their own country.[15]

523/ *b.* We should maintain a relationship with our former students, the products of our whole educational effort, so that they may take their place in society in a Christian and apostolic way and help one another in their respective tasks. The bond which they have with the Society ought to become closer as time goes on so that their influence assists its work.[16]

524/ 16. Elementary schools may be founded and directed where it is necessary. For they are very important and not contrary to our Institute. Nonetheless they should not be accepted without a real and great need, lest on account of the lack of men a greater good would be hindered. Where they are accepted, so far as possible our priests should have only the teaching of religion.[17]

525/ 17. It is during the period of secondary education that many young people (twelve to eighteen years old) either synthesize religion and culture in themselves or fail to do so and are strongly oriented towards good or away from it. Hence, having weighed the objections often made nowadays against secondary schools by those who would rather restrict themselves to pastoral ministries, the Society again asserts that the teaching of youth according to the principles of our Institute, even in the so-called profane disciplines, is entirely conformed to our vocation and to our sacerdotal character. Indeed, it is the ministry to which the Society up to the present owes most of its growth.[18]

526/ 18. Secondary schools, be they old ones retained or new ones founded, should improve continually. They should be educationally effective as well as cen-

---

[14] See GE 7, 10.

[15] See *CollDecr* 418.

[16] See *CollDecr* 144.

[17] See *CollDecr* 132.

[18] See *CollDecr* 131.

ters of culture and faith for lay cooperators and the families of students and alumni. Thereby they will help the whole community of the region. Let Jesuits also foster a closer cooperation with the parents of students, upon whom the primary responsibility of education rests.[19]

527/ 19. *a.* Each province should have its own *ordinationes* for secondary schools, in harmony with its own needs.[20]

528/ *b.* As far as subject matter is concerned, the education of our students should be in conformity with the genuine cultural tradition of each nation or region, in so-called classical literature, or modern literature, or in science.

529/ Moreover, other schools, such as technical and agricultural schools may well be opened where need or great utility suggest it.[21]

530/ 20. *a.* Subjects should be so taught that the mind of the young is not overwhelmed with a multiplicity of details, and that all their powers may be suitably developed and they may be prepared for higher studies. In addition, our students should be helped so that they can make progress by themselves, and so that there may grow in them firmness of mind, uprightness of judgment and sensibility, aesthetic sense, a capacity to express themselves orally and in writing, a sense of community and of civil and social duty, and depth of understanding.[22]

531/ *b.* Regarding the method of teaching, let there be kept in all fields, as far as is possible, the proper method of the Society which is commended in the *Ratio Studiorum.* Therefore let all be familiar with those principles of sound pedagogy which are set down by our holy father in the Constitutions, Part IV, developed in the *Ratio Studiorum,* and clearly explained by many writers of the Society,[23]

532/ 21. After they have consulted Father General, provincials should decide in light of the circumstances of persons and place, whether daily Mass should be obligatory in our residential secondary schools.[24]

533/ 22. So-called apostolic schools can be kept and, established where, all things considered, they seem to be for the greater glory of God.[25] What is said primarily concerning secondary schools is to be applied also to them.

---

[19] See GE 3.

[20] See *CollDecr* 139.

[21] See *CollDecr* 140 §1.

[22] See *CollDecr* 140 §2.

[23] See *CollDecr* 140 §3.

[24] See GC 30, D. hist. 17, n. 3.

[25] See *CollDecr* 135.

534/ 23. Coeducation in secondary schools is not to be allowed except with the approval of Father General.[26]

535/ 24. *a.* On account of the ever-growing importance of universities and institutions of higher learning for the formation of the whole human community, we must see to it that the Society and its priests are present to this work. Let there be, therefore, an ever greater number of professors prepared for such institutions, whether directed by the Society or by others. These professors should be able not only to teach advanced courses, but also to contribute to scholarly progress by their own research and that of their talented students whom they have trained.[27]

536/ *b.* Among the faculties belonging to our institutions of higher education, theology and philosophy should especially have their proper place to whatever extent they contribute, in various places, to the greater service of God.[28]

537/ *c.* The prohibition in the Constitutions, according to which that part of canon law which serves for contesting suits is not to be touched by Jesuits, is to be thus understood: "unless the General judges that something else is good."[29]

538/ 25. The education of priests, as a work of the highest value, is to be considered one of the chief ministries of the Society. Therefore, the seminarians who attend our universities are to be watched over with special attention, and directors and teachers chosen from among our best men are to be assigned to those clerical seminaries whose direction is accepted by the Society.[30] But if there is question of diocesan seminaries, a definite contract shall be made with the bishop and approved by the Holy See.[31]

539/ Not only youth but adults are to be educated, both for the advancement of their professional lives and for the efforts which make their conjugal, family, and social life more human and Christian, and develop a better understanding of the faith.[32]

540/ *a.* According to the mind of the Second Vatican Council, a close collaboration with the laity is recommended. On the one hand we can give them help in their formation by schools, conferences, spiritual exercises and other suitable works, and by our friendly dealing with them and the testimony of our life.

---

[26] See GC 30, D. hist. 17, n. 1.

[27] See GC 30, D. 51, 1.

[28] See *CollDecr* 137 §1.

[29] See *CollDecr* 137 §2.

[30] See OT5; *CollDecr* 134

[31] See ES I, 30 1 ; *CollDecr* 134.

[32] See GE introduction, 9.

On the other hand, let Jesuits consider the importance for the Society itself of such collaboration with lay people, who will always be the natural interpreters for us of the modern world, and so will always give us effective help in this apostolate. Therefore, we should consider handing over to them the roles they are prepared to assume in the work of education, whether these be in teaching, in academic and business administration, or even on the board of directors.[33]

541/   *b.* It will also be advantageous to consider whether it would not be helpful to establish in some of our institutions of higher education a board of trustees which is composed partly of Jesuits and partly of lay people; the responsibility both of ownership and of direction would pertain to this board.

542/ 28. Men of our time are very interested in new and more adequate intercommunication, by which international union and progress are fostered. Therefore Jesuits should be concerned to promote among their students and alumni and other members of the social community those efforts and means which can lead to a greater and more efficacious collaboration among nations.

543/ 29. Prefects or directors of education should be named who will help the provincials in directing the whole effort of education; they can be so united that the whole Society can enjoy the benefits of the studies and the experiments which are being carried on in various regions of the world.

544/ 30. In each province or region there should be a permanent committee of experts who will help superiors in this apostolate, drawing up and continually adapting regulations concerning our schools, in harmony with each one's needs.[34]

545/ 31. To help Father General in fostering the whole work of education, a secretariat of education should be established. Its task will be to collect and distribute information about the apostolate of education carried on by Jesuits and also to promote alumni associations and periodic conventions.

546/ 32. Decree 141 of the *Collection of Decrees* is abrogated.

---

[33] See GC 31, D. 33.

[34] See *CollDecr* 139; GC 28, D. 31, n. 2.

DECREE 29

Scholarly Work and Research

547/ 1.   *a.*   Jesuits should have a high regard for scholarly activity, especially scientific research properly so called, and they are to view this as one of the most necessary works of the Society. It is a very effective apostolate, entirely in accord with the age-old tradition of the Society from its earliest times.[1] It is a generous response to recommendations that the popes have often repeated, especially during the past hundred years.[2] It is more suited to the needs of the men of our times and an excellent means for opening up and carrying on dialogue with them, including nonbelievers, for establishing confidence in the Church, and for elaborating and teaching a synthesis of faith and life.

548/   *b.*   All of this applies first of all to the sacred sciences and those connected with them, which have the first claim on the scholarly potential of the Society. It applies also to those sciences which are called positive, both those which look to man and society and the mathematical-natural sciences, as well as the technical sciences proceeding from them, which profoundly affect the mentality of our times.

549/ 2.   Those Jesuits, therefore, who are assigned to this work by superiors are to give themselves entirely and with a strong and self-denying spirit to this work, which, in one way or another, makes demands upon the whole man. They are to be on guard against the illusion that they will serve God better in other occupations which can seem more pastoral, and they are to offer their whole life as a holocaust to God. At the same time they should do this in such a way that they do not lose touch with the other apostolic activities of the Society. Finally they are to strive earnestly to show themselves truly religious and priestly men in this schol-

---

[1] Discourse of Father Christopher Clavius ("De modo et via qua Societas Iesu ad maiorem Dei honorem, et animarum profectum augere hominum de se opinionem, omnemque haereticorum in litteris aestimationem, qua illi multum nituntur, convellere brevissime et facillime possit"), (Archivum Romanum Societatis Iesu, Hist.Soc. 5c, fol. 185–87); *Ordination on Training Mathematics Teachers,* by Father Robert Bellarmine, promulgated in 1593 by the authority of Father Claudius Aquaviva (Archivum Romanum Societatis Iesu, Epp. NN. 113, fol 184) ; V. Carafa, Ad Praep. Prov. Austriae, Aug 17, 1647 (Archivum Romanum Societatis Iesu, *Austr.* 5, fol. 1116).

[2] See Leo XII, *Quod divina Sapientia,* Aug. 28, 1824; Bull. Rom.Cont., VIII (Prati, 1854), 95–117; Leo XIII, *Ut mysticam Sponsam,* Mar. 14, 1891; Leonis XIII P.M. Acta, XI, 60–66; Pius XI, Address, *Ecco dilettissimi,* Mar. 12, 1934; *ActRSJ* 7 (1934), 643–648; Pius XII, Address, *Siamo particolarmente,* Sept. 29, 1935; *ActRSJ* 8 (1935), 84–86.

arly work. They should remember that in undertaking this work, they are enlisted in the cause of Christian truth and are serving the people of God either by showing forth the presence of the Church among the men of the scientific community or by enriching the understanding of revelation itself through the progress of human knowledge.

550/ 3. Provincials, for their part, must not be deterred by the demands of other works of the province from applying to this scholarly work, definitively and in good time, men whom they find inclined and in the judgment of experts truly suited, yet well proven in the spiritual life. Once assigned to this work, they are not to be taken away from it without grave reason, especially when they have finished their studies, even post-doctoral work, and have begun to produce. Since many of the positive sciences often require youthfulness for their study if one is to become really outstanding in them, provincials are not to hesitate to propose to Father General suitable changes in the ordinary course of study for the young Jesuits engaged in them as need may dictate, according to the Decree on the Training of Scholastics Especially in Studies. Priests who are applied to these studies are to be mindful that, the more advanced they are in any discipline, the more careful they should be that their knowledge of theology is broad and sound, in order that they may be able to exercise their scholarly apostolate with greater authority and profit.

551/ 4. Superiors, especially higher superiors, are to take care that those applied to work in the scholarly disciplines give themselves primarily to the work of research, study, and writing, and that the necessary leisure and helps are provided for this work. They are to acknowledge that scholars have "a lawful freedom of inquiry and thought and the freedom to express their minds humbly and courageously about those matters in which they enjoy competence."[3] Superiors are to permit them to join national and international professional organizations and to attend their meetings when it seems expedient. Finally they are to encourage Jesuits to work not only in our own centers but also in public universities and scholarly institutions according to the various opportunities and necessities of the region. In this way they will cooperate more closely with laymen in penetrating the whole human culture with the Christian spirit and better ordering the world to God, its ultimate end.

552/ 5. Small periodic meetings of Jesuits who are expert in the different scholarly disciplines, especially those closely related, are recommended to provincials. These should promote interdisciplinary communication from time to time and, after careful study of the condition of the scientific apostolate in each region, procure among themselves greater collaboration of all who are working in the sciences. They should also help superiors with their advice in planning, coordinating, preparing,

---

[3] GS 62.

promoting, and also abandoning scholarly works, in such a way that the effort expended in this apostolate may be directed more efficiently to its end.

DECREE 30

Cultivating the Arts in the Society

I. Introduction

553/ 1.   The Church, which has at all times given most generous encouragement to the arts, today again hails their importance.[1] Indeed, in our day especially works of art can exert a vast influence, whether it be with respect to the growth and unfolding of human personality, or to the development of civil society, or to the mutual union of men, a union that paves the way to union with God.

554/   For the arts provide a special pathway to the human heart. As a result, men are often stirred not only by rational arguments but also by artistic works.

555/ 2.   In times past under the patronage of the Society many outstanding artists, not a few of them members of the Society itself, have achieved greatness in poetry, music, the theater, and architecture. In both the Western world and mission areas, all these arts were eagerly pursued by sons of the Society for the greater glory of God and the welfare of souls. This tradition lives on even in the Society of today. Many modern Jesuits who are themselves artists of repute not only pursue the arts but promote an understanding and deeper appreciation of the Gospel message by this activity.

II. Decree

556/ 3.   The 31st General Congregation, taking into consideration both the tradition of the Society and the signs of the times, and aware of the importance of the arts for building up the kingdom of God, wishes to encourage the activity of its members who toil in this field for the greater glory of God.

557/ 4.   During their training Jesuits should be given opportunities to become acquainted with and to appreciate the arts as part of their general education so that all may be better prepared for the apostolate in today's world. The arts can be a genuine help in this apostolate.

558/ 5.   Measures should be taken to permit those who manifest outstanding talents in this field to develop them and to learn how they can integrate their artistic activity into the context of priestly and religious life. In the missions Jesuits should endeavor to make full use of these arts in the apostolic work of spreading Christ's message.

---

[1] See GS 62.

559/ 6. In addition, mutual communication is recommended among members of the Society who are engaged in artistic activity.

DECREE 31

INTERPROVINCIAL HOUSES IN ROME

560/ 1. The 31st General Congregation, in view of the special importance for the service of the Church of the Pontifical Gregorian University and of its associated Biblical and Oriental Institutes as well, joins with previous Congregations[1] in recommending that the whole Society furnish effective help to these common works through subsidies and especially by training professors for them.

561/ 2. The 31st General Congregation also recommends to all provincials those other works or houses in Rome that either are entrusted to the whole Society, such as the Vatican Radio, the Vatican Observatory, and the Russian College, or render a service to the entire Society, such as the Historical Institute or the College of St. Robert Bellarmine.

562/ 3. All provinces ought to share, according to their resources, in the responsibility for those works which become a concern and charge of the whole Society through the person of Father General. Provincials should keep this obligation in mind and, at fixed times, should give thought to assigning one or other of their men to these works.

563/ 4. Recommendations to Father General:

a. The 31st General Congregation recommends to Father General that he provide for the drawing up of a list, to be sent out to the provincials, of professors and other personnel for whom a need may be foreseen over the next three, five or ten years in these houses in Rome.

564/ *b.* It is recommended to Father General that he set up a permanent administrative council to assist him, particularly with regard to needed funds and personnel, in administering these works placed under his care by the Holy See. This council should include, in addition to the directors of these works, some provincials from different regions.

565/ *c.* It is also recommended to Father General that he set up a council for academic planning, one that will be concerned with reviewing broad academic policies in the light of the needs of the times and that will in this way aid him in directing these works entrusted to him by the Holy See, namely, the Pontifical Gregorian University and its associated Institutes. This council should be made up of members of the University itself and of the Institutes as well as of other Je-

---

[1] See GC 29, D. hist. 17, n. 2; D. 32; GC 30, D. 18, n. 1.

suit or non-Jesuit experts. The function of this council will be to advise Father General on academic policy and planning for these works, within the framework of the statutes of the Gregorian University and the Institutes.

566/ *d.* The General Congregation further recommends to Father General that the statutes of the academic institutions of the Society in Rome be revised with the help of the faculty. At the same time a study ought to be made as to whether the faculty should have a consultative role, and even a deliberative vote in decisions on some matters, so as to play a greater part in the academic government.

567/ 5. Those other houses in Rome that depend directly on Father General but are under the charge of only some provinces, such as the national or regional colleges and the Civiltà Cattolica, are likewise recommended to the attention of the General and those provincials who have a concern in the matter.

568/ 6. Proper care should be shown for the language training and the psychological and spiritual adjustment of those brothers who come to Rome from provinces elsewhere. Moreover, if they are to return again to their own provinces, after having rendered excellent service at Rome, superiors ought to see to it that this return takes place at a suitable time and that they are helped to make a psychological readjustment and to continue to contribute to the work of the apostolate.

DECREE 32

THE SOCIAL APOSTOLATE

569/ 1. The 31st General Congregation wishes to recall to all members of the Society that the aim of the social apostolate is "to provide most men, and indeed all of them insofar as earthly conditions allow, with that abundance or at least sufficiency of goods, both temporal and spiritual, even of the natural order, that man needs lest he feel himself depressed and despised."[1] The scope of the social apostolate is broader, therefore, than the task of exercising our ministries or maintaining social works among workmen or other groups of the same sort that are especially needy. These works, indeed, according to the mind of the 28th General Congregation, decree 29, and the 30th General Congregation, decree 52, are to be promoted with great diligence, especially in those regions that are economically less developed. But the social apostolate strives directly by every endeavor to build a fuller expression of justice and charity into the structures of human life in common. Its goal in this is that every man may be able to exercise a personal sense of participation, skill, and responsibility in all areas of community life.[2]

---

[1] Father Janssens, *Instruction on the Social Apostolate* (October 10, 1949), No. 7, *ActRSJ* 11 (1949) 714.

[2] See John XXIII, *Mater et Magistra* and *Pacem in Terris,* passim.

570/   From this it is clear that the social apostolate is fully in harmony with the apostolic end of the Society of Jesus according, namely, to that distinctly Ignatian criterion by which we should always keep before our eyes the more universal and more enduring good. For social structures, above all today, exert an influence on the life of man, even on his moral and religious life. The "humanization" of social life is, moreover, particularly effective as a way of bearing evangelical witness in our times.

571/ 2.   These things are all the more true because in our day the focal point of the social problem goes beyond the inequality between different social groups to "global" inequalities between sectors of economic life, between regions of one nation, between nations themselves or classes of nations. Again, the social problem today is also a matter of inequalities between different racial groups. And people today are not troubled only by particular questions, for example, about wages or working conditions, about family and social security. They are especially concerned with the massive worldwide problems of malnutrition, illiteracy, underemployment, overpopulation. Thus it is that social action looks more and more to the development of economic and social progress that will be truly human.

572/   The Society of Jesus, which has its home "in every corner of the world," seems suited in a special way to entertain this universal or "catholic" vision of the social apostolate by endeavoring with all its might to see that the less developed regions of the world are helped "in deed and in truth" by the more advanced and that the whole world movement of economic progress is imbued with a Christian spirit. It can do this by contributing as well to establishing the presence of the Church in the great national and international associations and congresses that attempt to bring about such progress.

573/ 3.   Since, finally, every form of the apostolate of the Society of Jesus flows from its mission "for the defense and propagation of the faith and the progress of souls in Christian life and learning," we must be very careful lest the social apostolate be reduced merely to temporal activity. This is all the more necessary because in these activities men are often affected by one-sided "ideologies" and violent passions. Never more than in our day is it necessary, therefore, that that "universal love which embraces in our Lord all parties, even though they are at odds with one another,"[3] should shine forth among the companions of Jesus. Our men should be looking only to this, that they are trying to restore "peace on earth," a peace that is "based on truth, on justice, on love, on freedom." We are not forbidden, therefore, to undertake those things "which tend to infuse Christian principles into public life, provided that means in keeping with our Institute are

---

[3] *Cons.* [823].

employed,"[4] in the light of the Church's teaching and with proper respect for the sacred hierarchy.[5]

574/ 4. In order that those prescriptions concerning the social apostolate already laid down in the decrees of general congregations and in the Instruction on this subject may be more effectively carried out, the 31st General Congregation earnestly recommends that:

575/ *a.* in the planning of apostolic activities, the social apostolate should take its place among those having priority;[6]

576/ *b.* in the entire course of Jesuit training, both theoretical and practical, the social dimension of our whole modern apostolate must be taken into account;

577/ *c.* members who are to be specifically destined for this apostolate should be chosen in good time; provincials should not hesitate to assign some men among them who are endowed with truly outstanding gifts both of mind and judgment and of virtue, and train them in the best universities ;

578/ *d.* social centers should be promoted by provinces or regions according to a plan that will seem better suited to the concrete circumstances of each region and time; these centers should carry on research, social education, both doctrinal and practical, and also social action itself in brotherly collaboration with the laity;

579/ *e.* centers of this kind should be in close contact with one another both for the sake of information and for every kind of practical collaboration. Such collaboration should also be encouraged between centers in developed regions and those in regions which are less developed.

---

[4] *CollDecr* 239 §2.

[5] See GC 28, D. 29, n. 16.

[6] See GC 28, D. 29, n. 5.

DECREE 33

The relationship of the Society to the Laity and Their Apostolate

580/ 1. In its teaching and decrees the Second Vatican Council stressed the just autonomy of earthly affairs, the secular character which is proper and peculiar to the laity,[1] the active part they ought to take in the entire life of the Church, and their duty and right to the exercise of the apostolate.[2] These demand that our Society examine the relationship it has to laymen and their apostolate and that it bring this relationship into greater harmony with the norms and spirit of the Council itself.

581/ 2. Jesuits should be more keenly aware of the importance of the state and vocation of laymen and their apostolate since in many areas of human activity and in many places the Church can be present to the world only through laymen. Let them strive not only to recognize the place which the laity have in the mission of the Church but also to promote it, and to hold in high esteem their just liberty.

582/ The laity help us to understand more fully the world and Christian truth itself, and give us a more vivid sense of our mission "for the defense and propagation of the faith." At the same time they are a stimulus to our own continual conversion.

583/ 3. Therefore we should make efforts to understand better their life, their ways of thinking and feeling, their aspirations and their religious mentality, by means of fraternal dialogue. Jesuits can be present to and serve all men, including unbelievers, by taking an appropriate part in various associations and organizations even on the national and international scale.

584/ 4. Whenever and wherever we are associated with laymen, whether they are young people or adults, we must give an example of lively faith, charity, and a genuine fidelity to the Church, always testifying to the high value of religious life.

585/ 5. There are many ways in which we can be of assistance to the laity. It is especially necessary that we bend all our efforts to forming both youth and adults for the Christian life and apostolate so that they may be able to fulfill their mission and assume their proper responsibility according to the Church's expectations.

---

[1] See GS 36, LG 31.

[2] See AA 3, GS 43.

586/ By means of special instruction and spiritual direction we should communicate to those who can profit by it a fuller understanding of the evangelical life according to the Exercises of St. Ignatius, which are also very well suited to the lay state. Thus they may be able to direct all the acts of their daily professional, familial, and social life with a sincere mind and increased liberty to the greater glory of God, and may be able to discover and fulfill the divine will in all things and in this way devote themselves entirely to the service of their brothers as well. This direction is expected of us especially by the rejuvenated sodalities and the various other associations of laymen who are trying to cultivate an intense Christian and apostolic life according to this spirit.

587/ 6. On the other hand, we ought to help the laity in their apostolate. Jesuits should be prepared to offer their cooperation as counselors, assistants, or helpers in the works which the laity themselves promote and direct.

588/ We should also foster the collaboration of the laity in our own apostolic works. We must not only fully observe the demands of justice toward those who work with us but also establish a cordial cooperation based on love. We must open up to them in various ways a wide participation in as well as responsibility for the direction, administration, and even government of our works, keeping of course the power of ultimate decision in the hands of the Society where it has the ultimate responsibility.

589/ In the same spirit, in order that a greater respect may be had for the responsibility of laymen in the Church, let the Society examine whether some works begun by us might be turned over to competent laymen for the greater good of the Church. In all things we should promote an apostolic brotherhood with the laity, based on the unity of the Church's mission.

590/ 7. Since a closer communion and association exists between us and those laymen who have shared more intimately our spirituality and way of feeling and acting, Jesuits, while maintaining our apostolic freedom, should show their close relationship by carefully preserving our loyalty to them and cultivating a sincere friendship with them, and also by actively showing fraternal hospitality toward them.

DECREE 34

Laymen Linked to the Society by a Closer Bond

591/ Since in some regions of the world there are laymen who desire that the Society of Jesus join them to itself by a tighter bond in order that they may be better able to fulfill their own proper lay vocation in the Church;

592/ And since the Society of Jesus, in fulfillment of the Second Vatican Council, seeks a renewal and adaptation which is at once spiritual and apostolic, making a judicious evaluation of the varieties of vocations for the service of the Church and souls;

593/ The 31st General Congregation urges Father General to study the ways by which such bonds and a more stable and intimate collaboration can be achieved, taking into consideration the experiences of different parts of the world.

DECREE 35

The Mass Media

594/ 1. The presence and influence of the new mass media (radio, films, television) daily grow in intensity and extent in the modern world.

595/ On the one hand, they are for our age the most important means of expression and therefore provide us with very suitable aids to our apostolate in many ministries of theSociety.

596/ On the other hand, the spread of these media to the entire human family so reaches the minds and hearts of men of every age and situation that they have a truly universal influence. As a result, they determine to a great extent what modern men think, even what they do.

597/ 2. It follows, therefore, that these media can no longer be looked on as something directed primarily to the relaxation of the spirit, but rather as the means of expression and mass communication in today's state of men and affairs, one which can to some extent be called a "culture of the image."

598/ 3. The General Congregation, reviewing earlier directives in the light of the Second Vatican Council's decree on the Instruments of social communication,[1] wishes to recommend the following with respect to an apostolate of these new means of communication:

599/ 1° These mass media should be employed as very effective tools in many of our ministries, especially in preaching the word of God and in the training of youth.

600/ 2° Consideration should also be given to the specific opportunity afforded by these media to have an impact, whether with regard to treating questions or to influencing people, where one could not easily be had by other means and forms of the apostolate.

601/ 3° Provision should be made in our formation program for a training in the mass media that is adapted to each period of formation.

602/ 4° Provincials should in good time choose some men who are endowed with a religious spirit and other gifts, so that, after they have become expert at various levels of specialization and have acquired academic degrees, they may become competent in the practice of this apostolate and in directing others in it. Where it might seem useful, a center should he set up as a help in the acquiring of this specialization.

603/ 5° What Father Janssens decreed concerning secretariats on the international, regional and provincial levels should be faithfully carried out, since this is a necessary and effective means of stressing and promoting this kind of apostolate.

DECREE 36

THE VATICAN RADIO STATION

604/ Since the operation of the Vatican Radio Station was entrusted to the Society in a particular way by the Holy Father, it should be helped with the most suitable personnel and means so that it can achieve its special objective. The General Congregation asks Father General to undertake such studies as seem useful in order that he may take prompt and effective care of the matter.

---

[1] See Vatican II, *Decree on the Instruments of Social Communication.*

DECREE 37

INFORMATION SERVICE

605/ The 31st General Congregation recognizes how important it is for the Society and especially for Father General to be informed about all that goes on in the Society or outside of it which in any way affects its life. It recommends that Father General examine the entire question of an information service, both in the General Curia and in the whole Society, and that he take care to have some specialists trained who will be able at a suitable time to set up effective information centers. In addition, the *Memorabilia Societatis Iesu* should be revised. It should be edited in a modern language and contain not only "what makes for edification"[1] but everything that is "worthy of note,"[2] including the problems and difficulties that confront the Society in different parts of the world.

---

[1] *Cons.* [675].

[2] Loc. cit.

VI

CONGREGATIONS

DECREE 38

Preparation for a General Congregation

606/ 1. Father General together with the General Assistants should take care of all long term questions and problems that refer to a future general congregation.

607/ 2. It will help if the province congregations that precede a congregation of procurators or of provincials send to Father General not only the postulata and the reasons for or against calling a general congregation, but also questions and problems to be proposed to the future general congregation.

608/ 3. It is the duty of Father General and the General Assistants to see to it that these questions and problems (mentioned above in Nos. 1 and 2) are put in suitable order and carefully studied and prepared, with the assistance of experts, for the future general congregation. When the time has been fixed for the general congregation, these questions and problems, together with the studies made of them, should be sent to all the provincials for communication in a suitable way to the province congregation.

609/ 4. In a congregation of procurators or of provincials, when Father General makes his report on the state of the Society, he should also take into account these problems.

610/ 5. There should be a sufficiently long interval between all the province congregations and the start of the general congregation.

611/ 6. All postulata sent by province congregations or by private individuals should arrive in Rome several months (at least two months) before the start of the general congregation, as far as circumstances permit and Father General or the Vicar decide. It is allowed, however, for the fathers of the congregation to bring their own postulata in keeping with the *Formula of the General Congregation,* No. 116, §2, and No. 101, §6.

612/ 7. To Father General or the Vicar is entrusted the task of calling experts to Rome as soon as possible after the dateof the general congregation has been officially announced and of setting up preliminary committees to gather together and put in order the postulata and to prepare the order of the agenda for the general congregation. These preliminary committees should be filled out, immediately after the province congregations, with electors chosen from the various assistancies.

613/ 8. When the province congregations are concluded, care should be taken to send information to the preliminary committees about each elector's competence and knowledge of questions to be treated, and the same information should be communicated to all the electors. The purpose of this will be to make it easier to set up the commissions for handling the business of the general congregation.

614/ 9. Father General or the Vicar should see to it that the studies and works of the preliminary committees are organized in proper order and communicated to the provincials and electors.

615/ 10. Since the help of experts is of great importance, when the general congregation has assembled, Father General or the Vicar should see to it that a sufficient number of experts are on hand in Rome who can help the commissions in handling their assignments.

DECREE 39

Congregations of Procurators and of Provincials

616/ 1. Every other third year, in place of procurators elected in the province congregations, all the provincials should meet in Rome in a congregation to be called the Congregation of Provincials; the three-year periods are to be calculated in such a way that the first congregation after the General Congregation will be a congregation of procurators, the second, that of provincials. The congregation of provincials, however, is omitted in that third year in which from the number of "votes" of province congregations in favor of summoning a general congregation, it is already certainly clear that a general congregation must indeed be called.

617/ 2. The purpose of each of these congregations is twofold:

618/ 1° To cast a deliberative vote as to whether or not a general congregation should be called;

619/ 2° To consult with Father General about the state and affairs of the Society as a whole, especially about the more universal undertakings of the apostolate and, when it is a question of provincials, to set up those talks and meetings with Father General that are so important for good government. These congregations have, however, no legislative power.

620/ 3. In casting their vote as to whether a general congregation should be called:

1° The provincials are bound to follow the opinion which was approved by their province's congregation in an instance where that opinion was affirmative, i.e., for calling the congregation, but not if it was negative.

621/ 2° Procurators are never bound to follow the opinion of their province, but they should adopt as their own that opinion which, after considering all the information they received, seems better in the Lord.

622/ 4. In province congregations that precede a congregation of provincials, one *relator* is to be elected from the professed and spiritual coadjutors, other than the provincial, who will inform Father General by letter of the state of the province. It is left to the prudence of Father General to judge whether, besides this written report, the *relator* himself should be called to Rome.

623/ 5. What is said here of provinces and provincials is to be understood also of independent vice-provinces and their provincials.

DECREE 40

PROVINCE CONGREGATIONS

624/ 1. The following have a right to attend a province congregation by reason of office (maintaining also decree 44, n. 11, of the present General Congregation and nn. 21–26 of the *Formula of the Provincial Congregation*):

1° the provincial;

2° all local superiors, whatever their title, who are normally named by Father General;

3° the vice-provincial and vice-superiors in accordance with the *Formula of the Province Congregation;*

4° the treasurer of the province;

5° the consultors of the province.

625/ 2. Besides those who enter by reason of office and those who are summoned by the provincial in keeping with the following number, forty fathers or brothers will assemble for the province congregation who were previously elected in accordance with the rules that follow:

a. In this prior election, all the solemnly professed and formed spiritual and temporal coadjutors who are members of the province have active voice, and unless they are already attending the congregation by reason of office, they also have passive voice.

626/ *b.* The election takes place by means of a form sent to the provincial "soli" in which each elector can write the names of twenty-five candidates. The votes should be personal, that is, based on one's own conscience and knowledge and after mature consideration in prayer before God; it is permitted, however, to ask one or other prudent man in secret for information. The electors should look to the good of the whole province and Society rather than the advantage of some house or some part of the province.

627/   *c.*   The counting of the ballots, after the names of the voters have been removed from them, is done by the provincial with the consultors of the province.

628/   3.   The provincial, with the deliberative vote of the group that counts the ballots, can summon to the congregation three other fathers or brothers, and these attend in addition to the fixed number of forty *(supra numerum)*.

629/   4.   At least half of the members of the congregation, including those who enter *supra numerum,* should be professed of four solemn vows. The formed temporal coadjutors should not number more than five, but at least one of them should be present in the congregation.

630/   5.   In a vice-province congregation, the number of members is twenty, in addition to those who enter by reason of office or by nomination by the vice-provincial. Each elector can write on his form the names of twelve candidates.

VII

GOVERNMENT

DECREE 41

The Office of the General

631/ 1. The 31st General Congregation, after a protracted and full discussion of both sides of the question, reaffirms the prescription of the Constitutions that the General is to be elected for life and not for some fixed term;[1] it has made provision, however, for resignation from this office according to norms in the revised version of decree 260 of the *Collection of Decrees.*

632/ 2. Decree 260 of the *Collection of Decrees* shall be revised to read:

§1. Father General may in good conscience and by law resign from his office for a grave reason that would render him permanently incapable of the labors of his post.

§2. The obligation rests especially on the Fathers Provincial in the sight of God to consider and do what they ought to do for the universal good of the whole Society in those matters that concern Father General;[2] generally, however, unless the matter should be extremely urgent, they will fulfill this duty through the General Assistants.[3]

634/ §3. If at least a majority of the General Assistants, out of their knowledge and love of the Society, shall have decided that Father General ought for a grave reason to resign his office, they should advise him of this through the admonitor.

635/ §4. When Father General, either of his own accord but after consultation with the General Assistants, or after having been so advised by them, shall have judged that it is proper to resign his office, he should ask for a secret vote of the General Assistants and the provincials of the whole Society on the seriousness of the causes. These*f* votes should all be counted in the presence of the General Assistants and the Secretary of the Society. If a majority judges that a general congregation ought to be convoked for the purpose of making provision for the supreme government of the Society, Father General ought then to summon it.

636/ §5. Father General's resignation from office does not take effect until it has been accepted by the Society in a General Congregation.[4]

---

[1] See *Cons.* [719–722] ; see Paul V, *Quantum Religio.*

[2] See *Cons.* [778].

[3] See *Cons.* [782].

[4] See CIC 186–87.

637/ §6. If, after he has been duly advised by the General Assistants, Father General either cannot or is unwilling to resign his office, and if a majority of the same Assistants judge that the welfare of the Society might suffer great harm from quite serious causes, such as very grave illness or senility where there is no hope of improvement in the case:[5]

638/ 1 ° A congregation for electing a temporary Vicar should be summoned in accordance with the *Formula* for such a congregation;

639/ 2° The temporary Vicar thus elected, after consultation with the General Assistants, should as soon as possible, under secrecy, inform the provincials and the two superiors or rectors of each province who are oldest in order of solemn profession of four vows, and ask their votes and those of the General Assistants in order to find out what they think should be done for the welfare of the Society;

640/ 3° When all the votes have been counted in the presence of the General Assistants and the Secretary of the Society, if a majority judges that a general congregation should be convoked, the Vicar ought to summon it; in the meantime, however, he should govern the Society in accordance with the norms of the office of Vicar.[6]

641/ 3. In decree 262 of the *Collection of Decrees,* §4 should be added in these words:

Father General has the right to appoint a Vicar-General to assist him as often as it may seem to him to be necessary or helpful to do so.

DECREE 42

Journeys by Father General

642/ Since trips by Father General to the Society in various parts of the world truly help union of hearts in the Society and are helpful in giving him a fuller knowledge of affairs, such trips from time to time are recommended to him by the General Congregation so that personal and fatherly contact with members of the Society may be fostered.

---

[5] See *Cons.* [773].

[6] See *Cons.* [766–777] ; GC 8, DD. 28-29; GC 12, D. 55.

DECREE 43

The Vicar-General after the Death of the General

643/ 1.   The right and duty of the Vicar-General, after the death of the General, to convoke and prepare for a General Congregation in accordance with norms laid down by the General Congregation is explicitly asserted.

644/ 2.   The rules for the office of the Vicar-General are to be revised so that, where mention is made of a vote of the Assistants, this is to be understood to refer to the General Assistants.

645/ 3.   In the rules for the office of the Vicar-General, No. 7 is to be revised to state that the Vicar-General must have four consultors (in the strict sense, i.e., the General Assistants) appointed by the Society; if one of them is lacking, a substitute shall be designated according to the norm of No. 12 in the rules for the office of Vicar-General.

646/ 4.   The last clause of decree 274 in the *Collection of Decrees* is to be revised to state that the office of Visitors, after a General dies, continues until such time as either the Vicar-General, after consultation with the General Assistants, or the new General shall have decided otherwise.

647/ 5.   Concerning the deliberative vote of the General Assistants (No. 12) and affairs which are not to be brought to a conclusion (Nos. 8–9), it seems better to make no change, especially since (see No. 3 above) a Substitute Assistant can now be appointed in place of that General Assistant who might be named or elected as Vicar.

DECREE 44

Assistants and Consultors of the General

648/ 1. In order that the Society may better exercise its providence with respect to the General according to the norms of our Constitutions, and that the General may be better aided by the advice he needs in directing and deciding the grave matters that come before him,[1] the 31st General Congregation has made the following arrangements which are by way of experiment only and are to be submitted to the judgment of the next General Congregation.

I. General Assistants

649/ 1. Four General Assistants only are elected to carry out the Society's providence with respect to the General.[2]

650/ 2. These four General Assistants have a deliberative or consultative vote in those cases in which the common law requires, even in the Society, that the General must act with the consent of his consultors or listen to their advice.

651/ 3. The General has the right and duty to replace them with others, if, after consultation with the other General Assistants, he judges that, either because of notably impaired strength or for another reason, they are so unequal to their task that it can be foreseen that the Society may thereby be in danger of serious harm.[3]

652/ The General ought, however, immediately to seek the approval of the General Assistants and the provincials after he has passed on to them suitable information about the man he has chosen.

653/ Approval of a majority of the General Assistants and provincials is needed for validity. Therefore, until such time as this majority is established, the new General Assistant does not have the right to cast a vote on matters in which the Institute gives a deliberative vote to Assistants, nor does he have a right to attend congregations, whether a general congregation, a congregation of procurators or provincials, or a congregation to elect a temporary Vicar-General.

654/ 4. If a general congregation convoked *ad negotia* declares its intention of proceeding to the election of new General Assistants, the incumbent Assistants ipso facto leave office, but can be reelected to the same office.

---

[1] See *Cons.* [776–777, 803].

[2] See *Cons.* [779].

[3] See *CollDecr* 269 §2, 3°.

655/ 5. The following is to be added in No. 136 of the *Formula of the General Congregation:* The first two Assistants are to be elected individually by separate, successive ballots in the same session, the third in the following session, the fourth in the third session.

656/ 6. All provisions to the contrary, whether in the *Collection of Decrees,* or in the norms of the *Formula of the General Congregation,* or in the rules of the Assistants, and specifically in decrees 263; 268, §2; 269, §2, 3° and §§4, 5; and in No. 130 of the *Formula,* are suspended until the next general congregation shall have passed judgment on the present provision, which is introduced as an experiment. Decree 264, however, is for the time being simply suspended.

II Other Consultors of the General

657/ 7. These will aid in advising the General:

1° General Consultors, especially in considering matters pertaining to the whole Society;

2° Regional Assistants, especially in considering matters pertaining to different regions of the Society;

3° Expert Consultors, in considering matters, whether pertaining to the whole Society or to principal works of the Society, in which they are experts.

658/ All these can give their advice either individually or gathered in a common consultation, as the General shall ask it of them.

659/ 8. The General Consultors, the Regional Assistants and the Expert Consultors are named by the General; before he names a Regional Assistant, however, he should hear the views of the provincials of that region or assistancy, and if the appointment is made while a general congregation is in session, also of all the other electors of the same region or assistancy.

660/ 9. All provisions to the contrary in the decrees of previous general congregations are suspended until the next general congregation shall have laid down a definitive judgment.

III. Rights of Assistants and Consultors of the General respecting Congregations of the Society

661/ 10. General Assistants, General Consultors and Regional Assistants have the right to attend a general congregation, congregations of procurators or provincials, and a congregation for the election of a temporary Vicar-General. General Assistants, however, attend a general congregation with full rights, i.e., as electors, with the right to vote in the election of the General and General Assistants; while General Consultors and Regional Assistants, attend only *ad negotia.* If any at all of these assistants and consultors are changed or cease functioning in their office during a general congregation, both former and new men keep the same right.

662/ 11.   General Consultors and Regional Assistants by reason of their office have active voice in the congregation of their own provinces.

663/ 12.   Expert Consultors have no right, by virtue of their office, respecting congregations of the Society.

DECREE 45

VISITORS

664/ 1.   Decree 274 of the *Collection of Decrees* is revised as follows:

Father General has the power to send Visitors to provinces when it shall seem good to him and for the length of time and with the authority and jurisdiction that seem good. When a General dies, the office of Visitor continues until such time as the Vicar-General, after consultation with the General Assistants, or the new General shall decide otherwise.

665/ 2.   The General Congregation recommends to Father General that, while our law with regard to Visitors is to remain unchanged, they should not stay in office too long nor enjoy undefined authority or jurisdiction.

DECREE 46

Provincials

666/ 1.   The General Congregation calls to mind that our holy father Ignatius wished indeed that "Father General have all authority for the greater benefit of the Society,"[1] and that from him "as from the head, all power of the provincials should proceed, and descend through them to local superiors and through them down to individual persons.[2] He wished that "for the same reason, in each province Father General should have provincials of demonstrated trustworthiness, since he realizes that the good government of the Society to a great extent depends on them,"[3] and "they should be men of the sort to whom a great deal of power can be entrusted."[4] The power that is given to them either by common law or the Society's law in virtue of their office is "ordinary power."

667/ 2.   In this way Father General, "by sharing his work with them as far as the business permits," can have more leisure and time to attend to more universal matters, and more light to see what must be done about them.[5] Subordination under holy obedience will be better preserved in the whole body of the Society, "the more clearly inferiors understand that they depend immediately on their superiors and that it will be very proper for them, and even necessary, to be subject to them in all things for Christ our Lord's sake,"[6] having persuaded themselves that "their superior possesses the knowledge, the will, and the ability to govern them well in the Lord."[7] Provincials themselves and other superiors should devote themselves with a greater sense of responsibility to the task of government entrusted to them, not seeking to avoid making plans or decisions by themselves, but with a courageous spirit embarking on great undertakings for the divine service and remaining constant in carrying them out.[8]

---

[1] *Cons.* [736].

[2] *Cons.* [666].

[3] *Cons.* [797].

[4] *Cons.* [791].

[5] *Cons.* [797].

[6] *Cons.* [206].

[7] *Cons.* [667].

[8] See *Cons.* [728].

668/ 3.   On this account, provincials should carefully listen to their subjects and direct them in the Lord, taking into consideration the internal knowledge which they have of them.[9] This is especially so with regard to rectors and local superiors whom they ought diligently to aid in carrying out their own function, showing them confidence and sharing broad power with them as the matter may demand.[10] They should also foster in the province religious life, the training of our men, and apostolic ministries, seeking always in all things the greater service of Christ's Church. Moreover, although provincials are appointed to rule their particular provinces, "they should turn their attention to the needs of the whole Society and look on interprovincial and international houses and works as part of their duty and responsibility, and willingly help them according to the measure and proportion worked out by Father General for each of the individual provinces."[11]

669/ 4.   In addition, the obligation rests "especially on the Fathers Provincial in the sight of God to consider and do what they ought to do for the general welfare of the Society" in those matters that concern Father General;[12] as a rule, however, they will fulfill this duty through the General Assistants, unless the matter should be extremely urgent.[13]

670/ 5.   The participation of the provincials in the government of the Society demands that there be "a more frequent personal communication" between the general and the provincials[14] and that Father General "know well, as far as can be, the consciences of the Fathers Provincial,"[15] so that from this intimate knowledge and mutual communication the "necessary" influence of the head may more easily "descend" to the provincials "for the sake of the goal that is set for the Society."[16]

671/ 6.   Therefore, the General Congregation:

    a.   recommends that the personal communication of Father General with the provincials be increased, not only by calling them to Rome some time after they have taken office so that they may discuss things with him, but also by calling together all the provincials of a region or even of the whole Society as he shall judge it to be useful;

---

[9] See *GenExam* [97].

[10] *Cons.* [423–425, 662] ; *Epit* 822.

[11] GC 30, D. 49, n. 2; see *Cons.* [778].

[12] *Cons.* [778].

[13] See *Cons.* [767, 782],

[14] *Cons.* [791]; see *Cons.* [662].

[15] *Cons.* [764].

[16] *Cons.* [666].

b. has revised some decrees of general congregations in which the necessity of seeking the consent of the General was laid down as a requirement;

c. hands over to the prudent judgment of Father General the matter of his habitually sharing broader faculties with the provincials in some affairs.

DECREE 47

Selecting House and Province Consultors

672/ In order that the members of the Society may take a truly effective part in the selection[1] of those who make up councils, the General Congregation decrees that:

1° With regard to the consultors of a house: the provincial should inquire into the opinion of members of the community concerning the current or prospective consultors (this can, as a rule, be done readily during the visitation of a house), and in naming consultors he should give proper weight to the members' judgment.

673/ 2° With regard to the consultors of the province: in their official letters to the general, local superiors, having heard the views of the members of their community, to whom they shall offer a clear opportunity of expressing their minds, shall submit their opinion of the province consultors. They shall state whether these consultors are satisfactory or not, and if they are not, they should indicate others who may seem to them to be suited for this post. The consultors of each house, in their official letters to the general, shall submit a similar opinion.

---

[1] See ES II, 18.

DECREE 48

Interprovincial Cooperation

I. Interprovincial Cooperation

A. Interprovincial Cooperation in General

674/ 1. That open and complete cooperation which is more and more a requisite for apostolic action today and which the Second Vatican Council strongly recommends to religious everywhere, should be promoted among all the Society's members, whatever their province.[1] Wherefore, the 31st General Congregation, in accordance with the 30th General Congregation, which already expressed the same earnest desire in its decree 49, again even more vigorously urges all members to bring about by concrete deeds that cooperation of all the provinces.

675/ 2. Therefore, among us from the very start of our training encouragement should be given to a spirit of union and charity that boldly rejects every brand of particularism and egoism, even of a collective kind, and reaches out readily and generously to the universal good of the Society in the service of God's Church.

676/ 3. The organization and planning of all apostolic labors, whether of a province or a region, or the whole Society, can contribute greatly to cooperation among undertakings, especially those of a similar nature, of the same province, or region, or the whole Society.

677/ 4. Moreover, lest we be satisfied with empty words, each provincial should not look solely to the advantages of his own province, but give as much support as possible to the needs of the weaker provinces and missions that unfortunately lack both the means and instruments of the apostolate, and the resources and funds and especially the men. In addition, each meeting of all the provincials, when it is assembled under the presidency of Father General, is asked especially to treat explicitly of this interprovincial cooperation.

678/ 5. Thus generously observing its primitive tradition and eagerly following the prescriptions of the Second Vatican Council, our Society, like a body that is one and apostolic, will pursue more effectively under the standard of Jesus the one and same end, namely, the fraternal reconciliation and salvation of all men in Christ.

---

[1] See CD 6, PC 23, AG 33, ES I 2, II, 42, 4–3, III, 21, 282

B. Economic Cooperation

679/ 6. The 31st General Congregation, in view of the need for this economic cooperation, asks the *definitores* on poverty to render this cooperation more complete by a new and truly appropriate law so that the fraternal charity of the provincials, which has been demonstrated in different ways (e.g., in supporting scholastics and other ways), may be expressed more easily and more universally. Economic cooperation should not be restricted to offering money and resources; for it can also find fulfillment through collaboration in methods of obtaining help from externs and in ways of using money and resources.

C. Cooperation among Neighboring Provinces

680/ 7. In view of the great importance, urgency, and complexity of interprovincial cooperation, the 31st General Congregation does not wish to impede its progress and establishment by rigid or abstract regulations and recommendations, but strongly endorses the idea that various experiments in different regions be approved by Father General with a view to achieving specific, well-adapted, and effective regional cooperation on the basis of which more suitable laws can be formulated at a later time.

D. Principles to Be Observed in Introducing Experiments

681/ 8. Nevertheless, it seems good that certain principles should be observed so that the development of interprovincial cooperation corresponds completely with the method of governing that is proper to the Society, and that certain experiments, among those that are possible, should receive special recommendation.

1° The provincials:

682/ *a.* Progress in interprovincial cooperation should not so overburden the provincials with a multiplicity of difficult transactions that they abdicate their responsibility toward persons. One of the chief duties of their office is to become well acquainted with all who are ascribed or applied to their province, and competently, sincerely and honestly to adopt decisions that affect these persons and their ministries. For this is a fundamental principle of all government in the Society, which is above all a "Society of love." This government does not consist in administration alone, however effective that may be.

683/ *b.* Whatever these laws for interprovincial cooperation are, they will become useless unless the provincials themselves possess the qualities and endowments so absolutely necessary for the establishment of true and productive collaboration among themselves, that is, that intelligence of mind that can grasp the broader and more profound problems, and those special gifts of character that make for easy and sincere relationships among equals. Father General should, moreover, have these qualities in mind when naming provincials.

2° The board of provincials:

684/ *a.* Meetings of provincials should take place as soon as interprovincial cooperation is begun, whatever form this cooperation may take. For these meetings greatly foster mutual understanding and are a good way by which each provincial can grasp the problems of other provincials and at the same time all can comprehend common problems. By such a method the common good of the whole region can be determined and similarly advanced.

685/ *b.* At times, at least, because of his comprehensive knowledge of the whole region, the presence of the Regional Assistant at these meetings can be profitable in that the meeting may be helped in pursuing its own objectives by the counsels and judgment of the Assistant and the Assistant himself may be in a position to obtain fuller information for Father General.

686/ *c.* The chairman of the board of provincials can be one of the provincials who fills this office for a brief time, e.g., for a year, and with the help of a secretary also attends to the preparation and summoning of the meetings and the execution of their decisions according to the objective goals or prescriptions determined by the board.

687/ *d.* The designation of certain experts to investigate and prepare different questions, e.g., on apostolic planning, social, educational, pastoral affairs, etc., can greatly aid in promoting better interprovincial cooperation. These men may be assembled in some interprovincial commissions and can be called to the provincials' meeting or send in a written report. In this way, interprovincial decisions, which are often of rather great importance, may be made in a more objective fashion and be more suited to the needs.

688/ *e.* A board of provincials has no juridical authority in the Society. Even if the provincials agree on a certain decision, this agreement has no force except from the authority of each provincial, and even here the approval of Father General may be required according to the nature and importance of the question. However, if the provincials do not agree among themselves, the affair should be referred to Father General or to the person mentioned in No. 3° who has the power of decision from either his own or from delegated jurisdiction.

3° Delegations of authority made by Father General:

689/ *a.* Father General, either by himself or through a delegate, solves interprovincial problems insofar as they exceed the power of the provincials.

690/ *b.* To solve a particular problem, Father General can delegate authority to one of the provincials or another father. Such authority, however, should not be delegated too frequently to those whose own office is to serve as an adviser to Father General.

691/ *c.* When interprovincial affairs are so multiplied that their resolution by the means mentioned above becomes increasingly difficult, it is necessary to go further and to initiate more radical and even novel experiments, e.g., through delegation of authority, conferred and determined by Father General, either to different fathers according to the diversity, importance, and urgency of the problems or to only one father, so that the common good of the whole region may be provided for in a more organized fashion.

692/ *d.* However, these or various other methods of further extending interprovincial cooperation should be always so arranged that the common good of the region and unity of action are fittingly achieved, that provincials receive effective assistance, and that the rights of all members are fully safeguarded (namely, those mentioned above in No. 1°, *a*).

II Common Houses

693/ 9. The decisions necessary for the organization of common houses are entrusted to Father General so that norms may be formulated gradually from concrete experience with that flexibility and adaptation demanded by the purposes of those houses.

III. Establishing Houses in the Territory of Another Province

694/ 10. Decree 275 §2 of the *Collection of Decrees* should be revised to read:

Several provinces cannot be established in the same territory according to a difference in language or nationality, nor as a rule can houses of different provinces be established in the same territory. Father General can, however, after hearing the opinions of the provincials concerned, permit the establishment of houses of one province in the territory of another province under conditions approved by him and in favor of those who are suffering persecution on behalf of Christ or for other serious reasons.

VIII

APPENDIX

DECREE 49

The Second Session of the 31st General Congregation

695/ 1. The General Congregation decided the following about the second session of the Congregation:

1° July 15th is set as the last day of the first session;

2° The second session will begin in the month of September 1966.

696/ 2. §1—The commissions which have already been set up will remain the same.

§2—At Rome a coordinating commission is set up, the members of which are Father General, the general assistants, the chairmen of the commissions and the secretary of the General Congregation.

§3—Father General, after consulting with the members of the coordinating commission, will set up a special commission to prepare the rules of procedure for the second session.

699/ §4—The modus agendi of the commissions in the interval between the sessions will be substantially the same as it was in the first session and the small groups convoked in the meantime will complete their business by letter.

700/ §5—A special commission will be set up composed of 12 or 15 members which will convene at stated times in order to complete reports, collect and elaborate upon comments received and prepare definitive position papers.

701/ 3. §1—Father General has the power to change provincials for proportionately grave causes before the end of the General Congregation.

702/ §2—Provincials who in between the two sessions have completed their term of office retain their right of membership at the second session.

703/ §3—Provincials who have been appointed in the time in between sessions are to be summoned to the second session as delegates with full power, that is as "Electors."

704/ §4—Prescriptions §§ 1–3 of this third article are to be understood as applying only at this particular Congregation.

705/ 4. Those provinces which will find the expenses of the second session extremely burdensome will be helped by the General Treasurer of the Society in an appropriate way.

DECREE 50

CHANGES IN THE FORMULA OF THE GENERAL CONGREGATION IN ACCORD WITH THE DECISIONS OF THE PRESENT CONGREGATION

706/ n. 7.—§1.   For the business of the congregation, that is, ordinarily after the election of the General has been completed, the following are to be admitted to the congregation and they have from then on the right of voting in everything except the election of the general assistants:

> 1° the general counselors;
>
> 2° the regional assistants;
>
> 3° the secretary of the Society;
>
> 4° the procurator general of the Society;
>
> 5° the treasurer general of the Society;
>
> 6° the provincials of the vice-provinces and the superiors of missions which have the right to send electors in which a congregation could not be held, if perhaps they are not solemnly professed of the four vows.
>
> 7° Procurators who have been called to the congregation by the general in order to provide more ample information on affairs, or who have been sent by their own provincials with the approval of the general given at least after they have been sent.

707/   §2.   If during the general congregation some or all of the general counselors or the regional assistants are changed, those who have newly been named immediately acquire the right mentioned above in §1, 1° and 2°; those however who have left office do not lose that right for that particular congregation.

708/ n. 25—§3   No one should communicate to others outside of the congregation the things which are done in the congregation except according to regulations which the general or the vicar-general have set down and the congregation has approved.

709/ n. 56   §2 *(addenda)*. Then the order of business and the manner of proceeding on the day of election are proposed to the congregation for its approval according to what the vicar-general has set down with the advice of the general assistants taking into account the norms of the Constitutions, the traditions of the Society and the circumstances of the times.

> nn. 71 — 88: omitted.

710/ n. 11. §1. Not only provincial congregations but also all members of the Society can send postulata to the general congregation. The provincial congregation should not be bypassed without a proportionate reason expressed in the postulatum itself.

711/ §2. A postulatum which touches on some law ought to point out the detriments which have followed or which will follow from the observance of the law and only aftert hat should seek some remedy or propose some solution.

712/ §3. Those who are not members of the congregation should in no wise embroil themselves in the affairs which the congregation is treating nor should they force memoranda or informatory material on the members of the congregation nor urge them to follow this or that opinion.

713/ n. 116 bis—§1. The members of the congregation are not bound to sign their postulata as long as they give them either to the secretary of the congregation or to one of the deputies for screening the postulata. Otherwise they are bound to sign them just like those members of the Society who are not members of the congregation.

714/ §2. In all postulata the following is required:

> 1° that they be written in Latin;

> 2° that they exhibit due seriousness and reverence toward the Institute. For this end it will much help if those who are less knowledgeable about the Institute seek the advice of experts;[1]

> 3° that each postulatum be set out on a separate page adding concisely and clearly the principal reasons for the postulatum. It is by no means prohibited, however, for the position taken in the postulatum to be further and more fully developed in other additional pages.

715/ no. 118 §1. Those prescriptions of the Institute which pertain to pontifical law, either the common law or law proper to the Society, cannot be changed by a congregation unless power to change them has been given to the Society by the Holy See. It will however be lawful to treat of them if the congregation has so decided by a prior majority vote. Before such a prior vote, it is appropriate for the commissions to set forth the meaning of and the reasons for the postulata. Once

---

[1] See GC 31, D. 4, n. 3 (D. 12 §1 and D. 15 §2).

a formal discussion has been finished, the congregation should not go to the Holy See for a change in one of those prescriptions unless two-thirds of the members of the congregation agree to this.

716/ §2. The Constitutions of our holy founder can be changed by the congregation in those matters which are not among the substantials.[2] We are not to treat of changing them except after the congregation has decided that they are to be treated of by a majority vote. Commissions, however, may before this vote set forth the meaning of and the reasons for the postulata. A decree introducing such a change is not valid unless it has been approved by two-thirds of the votes.

717/ n. 124—All decrees are to be passed by a majority vote, keeping the prescriptions of n. 118 intact.

DECREE 51

Changes in the Formula of the Provincial Congegation in Accord with the Decisions of the Present Congregation

718/ n. 3—§7 *(addenda)*. If, because of religious persecution or similar adverse circumstances, a provincial congregation cannot be held nor can a provincial send someone from his province in his place to a general congregation or designate someone to fulfill the function of relator, the general, with advice of the general assistants or the vicar-general in the same circumstances, will name some member of the Society from that province who is professed of the four vows, either as elector who will then become a member of the general congregation with full rights in place of the provincial, or as procurator in a congregation of procurators.

719/ n. 6—§1. The right to attend a provincial congregation belongs by reason of their office to the following:

   1° the provincial;

   2° all local superiors no matter what they are called who ordinarily are named by Father General;

   3° the vice-provincial and vice-superiors but only according to the norms of n. 24–26;

   4° the treasurer of the province;

   5° the consultors of the province.

---

[2] See GC 31, D. 4, n. 3 (D. 14 §3).

720/ §2. The following do not have a right to membership by reason of their office:

> 1° the socius to the provincial;
>
> 2° the instructor of the tertianship;
>
> 3° the master of novices.

721/ n. 7—§1. Besides those who by reason of their office are members of the congregation and those who according to norm n. 6 may have been designated by the provincial, there should be in the congregation forty previously elected fathers or brothers.

722/ § 2. In this preliminary election:

> 1° All the solemnly professed and the spiritual and temporal formed coadjutors who are members of that province have active voice, according to the norm of n. 7 bis.

723/ 2° The same members have passive voice unless they already are coming to the congregation by reason of their office, keeping intact the prescriptions of n. 113.

724/ 3° The election is to be carried out by written ballot sent to the provincial "soli" in two envelopes. The name of the person doing the voting is to be written on the inner envelope but not on the ballot itself.

725/ 4° Each member of the province who is voting can write on the ballot the names of 25 candidates. If someone, however, should know only a few members of the province, it will be enough to write only a certain number of names even if he does not fill out the total number of 25.

726/ 5° The electors ought to look to the good of the whole province and of the Society rather than to obtaining some benefit for a particular house or some other part of the province.

727/ 6° The votes are to be personal, that is, to be cast in accord with one's own conscience and knowledge and seriously thought about in prayer before the Lord. Secrecy is to be observed. However it is licit for the person voting to seek information under the seal of confidentiality from one or another prudent man.

728/ 7° No one is to volunteer information to someone who does not ask for it.

729/ §3. For the validity of this preliminary election it is not required that each and every person who has active voice respond, nor that two-thirds of the electors send in a ballot as long as suitably in advance they have received news of the fact the election is to held.

730/ §4. The counting of the ballots, with the names of the voters removed, is to be done by the provincial with the four consultors of the province. This election commission has the right to resolve doubts on the validity of the whole balloting and of each and every ballot.

731/ §5. After the counting of the ballots, a list should be drawn up of those above who have been elected by the whole province, with no indication of the house to which each belongs.

732/ §6. The provincial may, with the deliberative vote of the election commission, summon to the congregation three other professed fathers or spiritual or temporal coadjutors who are to be designated in the list as "named by the provincial." The provincial is however not so bound to name three people. Those so designated become members of the congregation "supra numerum." However they have the right not only to deal with the affairs of the congregation but also to participate in the elections which take place in the congregation.

733/ §7. At least half the members of the congregation including those who are there "supra numerum" will be professed of the four solemn vows. The formed temporal coadjutors shall not exceed the number of five but there must be at least one of them at the congregation.

734/ N.B. It is further to be determined, according to the norm of decree 52, what is to be done when the number of those who have been elected is not sufficient to complete the set number of 40 Jesuits who are to be members of the congregation.

735/ n. 7 bis *(previously §§2–5 no. 7).*

736/ n. 8—§§1–2 are omitted.

737/ n. 10 is omitted.

738/ n. 16—§1. With reference to impediments which might exist in those elected to the congregation, before the congregation begins the provincial, together with four of the members who are to come to that congregation by right of that office and who can conveniently be called together, will judge them.

739/ n. 21—The Jesuits who are members of the General's curia retain active and passive voice in their own province as do also those who are assigned to a house or a work immediately dependent upon the General. In addition, the secretary of the Society, the general counselors, the regional assistants, the procurator general and the treasurer general as well as the superior of the curia have a right to membership in the congregation of their own province by reason of their office. All of these, however, can be dispensed by Father General from the obligation of attending the congregation.

740/ n. 28—§2.   All members of the Society may in their private capacity offer whatever information they wish to the consultors, to the superior or to anyone who is elected to the congregation, or they can send this material to the congregation itself, keeping however the prescriptions of n. 74 §§2–7.

741/ n. 29—§2.   This is so to be made up that after the name of the provincial are listed all those who have taken final vows, according to the calendar order in which they have made their definitive incorporation into the Society. There is to be no precedence by grade or office. If several have pronounced their final vows on the same day, the earlier place on the list is to be given to the one who has been longest in religious life, and then to the one who is older. If there are some who have all of these characteristics identically, then before each provincial congregation the matter is to be decided by lot by the provincial in the presence of the consultors of the province. Scholastics, if there should be some on this list, are to be ranked in order of length of time in religious life.

742/ n. 3—§2. is omitted *(keeping the prescriptions of n. 86).*

743/ n. 43—§3.   No one should communicate to others outside of the congregation except to those who have been elected or to their substitutes who may have perhaps been absent from the congregation the things which are done in the congregation except according to the norms laid down at the immediately previous general congregation. However, the General or the Vicar-General has the power to further adapt these norms to the particular conditions of a provincial congregation.

744/ n. 55—Eighth, immediately after the two deputies have been elected, the day will be set by a public majority vote on which the election of those to be sent is held. If it seems better to postpone that election, there is no impediment to conducting the affairs of the congregation before the election.

745/ n. 74—§1 *(remains the same).*

746/ §2—These postulata:

1°   If they are destined for the General Congregation should be appropriate to preserving, promoting and adapting the Institute.

747/ 2° *(remains the same).*

748/ §3.   It is not the prerogative of the provincial congregation to deal with persons. If, however, in the course of business persons have to be dealt with indirectly, this is to be done with appropriate and religious modesty.

749/ §4. The provincial congregation may act:

1° On the substantials or the fundamentals of the Institute whenever there are serious reasons to do so,[1] and those reasons ought to be the more serious insofar as the affair more intimately touches our way of life and acting;[2]

2° On other of our laws, observing the same proportion.[3]

750/ §5. A postulatum which touches on some law ought to point out the detriments which have followed or which will follow from the observance of the law and only after that should it seek some remedy or propose some solution.

751/ §6. The members of the congregation are not bound to sign their postulata as long as they give them either to the secretary of the congregation or to one of the deputies for screening the postulata. Otherwise they are bound to sign them just as those who are not members of the congregation.[4]

752/ In all postulata the following is required:

1° that they be written in Latin unless they have been submitted by temporal coadjutors; to the Latin should be added a vernacular translation of the postulatum itself and of at least a summary of the whole proposition or argument.

2° that they exhibit due seriousness and reverence toward the Institute. For this it will help much if those who are less knowledgeable about the Institute seek the advice of experts.[5]

3° that each postulatum be set out on a separate page adding concisely and clearly the principal reasons for the postulatum. It is by no means prohibited, however, for the position taken in the postulatum to be further and more fully developed in other additional pages.

753/ §7. Those who are not members of the congregation should in no wise embroil themselves in the affairs which the congregation is treating nor should they force memoranda or informatory material on the members of the congregation or urge them to follow this or that opinion.[6]

754/ n. 76.—All the postulata which have been sent to the congregation are to be given to the members of the congregation along with the reasons added by the author of the postulatum; it is to be noted which of the postulata the deputation has admitted to consideration and which ones it has rejected.

---

[1] See GC 31, D. 4, n. 3 (D. 15 §1).

[2] See GC 31, (D. 12 §1 and D. 15 §2).

[3] See GC 31, (D. 14 §§3–5).

[4] See GC 29, D. 38, n. 28 §1.

[5] See GC 31, D. 4, n. 3 (D. 12 §1 and D. 15 §2).

[6] See GC 29, D. 38, n. 28 §2.

755/ n. 81.—§2. In order for a postulatum to be considered approved by the congregation when it deals with changing the substantials or the fundamentals of the Institute or the pontifical law proper to the Society or the Constitutions, a twofold vote is required: the first ballot by majority vote is to decide whether the matter should be dealt with; the second ballot by a two-thirds majority vote whether the proposal is approved. It is, however, allowable before the first ballot to set forth the meaning and the reasons for the postulata.

756/ n. 86 bis.—The provincial should take care that those who have sent postulata to the provincial congregation learn in good time what happened to their requests, at least if a postulatum was rejected.

757/ n. 92.—§. *(To be added at the end): (a)* If neither a congregation of a vice-province or mission can be held nor the vice-provincial or superior of a mission can send some professed father in his place, because of religious persecution or other unfavorable conditions, the norm of n. 3 §7 is to observed.

758/ §4. *(To be added at the end):* 3° If neither the congregation of a vice province or a mission can be held nor the vice-provincial or superior of a mission can send some other priest in his place, because of religious persecution or similar unfavorable circumstances, the norm of n. 3 §7, is to be observed.

759/ n. 93.—§1 (remains the same).

760/ §2. Besides those who come to the congregation by reason of office and those who may have been designated by the vice-provincial or the superior of a mission in accord with the norm of §3, the congregation will be made up of 20 fathers or brothers previously elected according to the norm of n. 7, §§2–5, except that each of the Jesuits voting can write on his ballot the names of only 12 candidates.

761/ §3. The vice-provincial or superior of the mission can call to the congregation three other fathers or brothers in accord with norm n. 7 §6.

758/ §4. At least half the members of the congregation including those who are there "supra numerum" will be professed of the four solemn vows. The formed temporal coadjutors shall not exceed the number of five, but there must be at least one of them at the congregation.

DECREE 52

Completing the Work on the Formulas of the Congregations

763/   With respect to the *Formulas* of congregations, the 31st General Congregation:

1°   Orders and empowers Father General, with a deliberative vote of those fathers of the general curia who have a right to attend a general congregation by reason of their office:

a.   to give an authoritative answer to questions that will of necessity arise concerning the next province congregations and congregations of procurators and of provincials by adapting the Formulas of these congregations and, where necessary, even changing them;

b.   either to give provisional answers to juridical questions respecting the next general congregation and its *Formula,* or prepare the questions in such a way that the 32nd General Congregation can itself settle them at its outset.

764/ 2°   Recommends also to the General that he communicate to the fathers of the 32nd General Congregation, in good time before the start of the congregation, the decisions so made and the questions to be settled.

DECREE 53

The Catalog of Censures and Precepts

765/   The General Congregation desires that the universal laws of the Society be observed, but that they be observed according to the spirit and aim proposed by St. Ignatius. This means that "in place of fear of offense there be love and desire of all perfection, and that the greater glory and praise of Christ, our Creator and Lord, be achieved.[1] For this reason the Congregation has decided to review the canonical penalties and precepts in virtue of obedience in the "Catalogue of Censures and Precepts Imposed on Jesuits."[2] Therefore, by this decree it delegates to Father General the following powers:

1°   that according to his prudent judgment, with the deliberative vote of those fathers of the general curia who by reason of their office have a right to par-

---

[1] *Cons.* [602].

[2] See *CollDecr* 303–315.

ticipate in the general congregation, and having taken the advice of experts, he can abrogate the canonical penalties and those precepts that are imposed by the Society's own law;

2° that under the same conditions he has the power of abrogating penalties laid down by the Constitutions,[1] as well as permission to enable him to petition the Holy See in the name of the Society for the abrogation of penalties established by particular pontifical law.[2]

DECREE 54

Prior Censorship of Books

766/ 1.   In order that more effective provision be made for Jesuits to engage with congruous freedom and responsibility in the intellectual apostolate of the press and other forms of mass communications, due consideration being given at the same time to security of doctrine and the interests of the Church and of the Society, the 31st General Congregation recommends and, insofar as necessary, communicates to Father General the power, without prejudice to the general principle of the Constitutions regarding previous censorship of writings, to adapt the particular norms of our own law in this respect, by way of experiment. This he may do according to his own prudent judgment, after consultation with experts and with the general assistants.

767/ 2.   With a view to the same end, it is desirable that the boards of provincials, either of an assistancy or of a region or country, having heard the advice of experts, propose to Father General those adaptations which appear to be more appropriate to their own particular situations and problems.

---

[1] See *Cons.* [695–96]; *CollDecr* 303 §2.

[2] See S. Pius V. *Aequum Reputamus;* Gregory XIII, *Ascendente Domino; Coll-Decr* 307 §1; GC 31, D. 4, n. 4.

DECREE 55

Abrogation and Revision of Certain Decrees

768/ 1.　In the *Collection of Decrees* decrees 21; 75, §3; 78, 768 §1; 231; 232; 290; 293 are abrogated to this extent, that norms contained in them shall continue to stay in force with the authority of Ordinations of the Fathers General,[1] until the General shall decide otherwise.

769/ 2.　Decree 75, §3 of the *Collection of Decrees* should be revised as follows:

Letters written or received by the admonitor of a provincial are not subject to the censorship of the same provincial.

770/ 3.　In decree 212 of the *Collection of Decrees,* the following words should be added:

The General can, however, communicate to provincials the faculty of approving specifications for construction of a new building

DECREE 56

Powers Granted to Father General

771/ 1.　For the proper completion of the legislative work of the 31st General Congregation, Father General is empowered, after obtaining the deliberative vote of those fathers of the general curia who have a right ex officio to attend a general congregation, and without prejudice to the powers given him in other decrees, to abrogate or modify decrees of past general congregations which are seen to be not in accord with the decrees of this 31st General Congregation.

772/ 2.　Moreover, the 31st General Congregation grants to Father General the following:

1°　That he himself, if it should be a matter of necessity, can suppress colleges and professed houses, with the deliberative votes, however, of those fathers of the general curia who have the right *ex officio* to attend a general congregation and of the provincial of the province in whose territory the house to be suppressed is located.

773/ 2°　That the minutes of some sessions that could not be distributed to the Fathers of the Congregation should be approved by Father General and the general assistants.

---

[1] See *CollDect* 4.

774/ 3° That with respect to decrees that must be promulgated after the close of the Congregation, it should be permitted to Father General :

    a. to make whatever corrections seem obviously needed;

    b. to reconcile contradictions, if any are detected, according to the mind of the Congregation, but after having ascertained the deliberative vote of those fathers of the general curia who have a right *ex officio* to attend a general congregation;

    c. to edit the decrees with regard to style;

    d. where necessary, to combine different decrees into one, while preserving the meaning and intent of each;

    e. to fix a *vacatio legis* or delay with respect to enforcement, in the light of circumstances, when promulgating the decrees, especially the decree on new norms for advancement to final vows.

C

DOCUMENTS PERTAINING TO THE GENERAL CONGREGATION

1. Address of His Holiness, Pope Paul VI, to the Members of the 31st General Congregation, May 7, 1965

2. Address of His Holiness Pope Paul VI, to the Members of the General Congregation, November 16, 1966

3. Approval by the Supreme Pontiff of the Decrees of the 31st General Congregation on Religious Poverty and on the Gratuity of Our Ministries

4. Letter of Cardinal I. Antoniutti

5. Letter of the 31st General Congregation to the Supreme Pontiff

1. Address of His Holiness Pope Paul VI to the Members of the 31st General Congregation, May 7, 1965

Beloved Sons:

We are happy to receive you today, dear members of the Society of Jesus, and We greet you with Our warm and heartfelt good wishes.

You have gathered in Rome in accordance with the original law of your Society to form the General Congregation which will choose the successor of Father John Janssens, your Superior General, whose loss We mourn with you. The task before you is a difficult and momentous one, for on it depend the well-being and success, the vigor and progress of your religious Institute.

Weigh with sound and well-informed judgment, with the steady wisdom that comes from true prudence, every element that has a bearing on your decision, and, before all else, invoke the light and guidance of the Holy Spirit in pure and fervent prayer, that your voting may conform to the will of God: "Show us the one whom You have chosen."[1]

For Our part, as We greatly share your concern and unite Our prayers with yours, We earnestly wish that the one to be chosen will meet the highest expectations and fully satisfy the needs of your religious family.

Everyone knows that Ignatius, your holy father and law maker, wanted your Society to be marked by a distinctive characteristic and to achieve results by a zeal rooted in virtue. Founded as the result of his unselfish and heaven-sent inspiration, the Society of Jesus was to be, in his plan, outstanding as the solid bulwark of the Church, the pledged protector of the Apostolic See, the militia trained in the practice of virtue.

Your glorious mark of distinction, the great claim to renown, with which you are endowed, is "to fight for God under the standard of the Cross, and to serve God alone and the Church, His spouse, under the Roman Pontiff, the Vicar of Christ on earth."[2] If, in the fulfillment of this pledge of service, other religious have the duty of serving with loyalty, courage and distinction, you ought to possess these qualities in the highest degree.

---

[1] Act 1.24.

[2] *Formula of the Institute* of Julius III, 1.

The glorious pages of your history proclaim that the ambitions and lives of the sons have matched the ideals of their holy father, and that you have deserved the reputation and glory of being the legion ever faithful to the task of protecting the Catholic faith and the Apostolic See.

Like the heavens with their stars, your Order has gained brilliance from your holy martyrs and confessors, from the Doctors of the Church, Peter Canisius and Robert Bellarmine, and from a countless throng of devout, learned, and zealous men. By word and work, they have taught the lesson of fidelity, and have left to their successors as an imperishable example and a spur the path which they have blazed.

The tenor of your lives, as befits valiant soldiers of Christ, tireless workers beyond reproach, should be based solidly on the holiness of behavior which is characteristic of you, on an asceticism of the gospels, which is austere and noteworthy for its virility and strength. It should be permeated by an unwavering discipline which does not give way before individual inclinations, but instead is prompt and ready, reasonable and constant in all its ways and undertakings. In an army, if a line or unit does not keep to its assigned place, it is like an instrument or a voice out of tune. Your new General will take every care to ensure that your harmony be not disrupted by discordant voices, but rather that you deserve full credit for fidelity and devotion. We are happy to see that most of you partake of this fitting unanimity, and We congratulate you for it.

Therefore, all should take care in their thinking, their teaching, their writing, their way of acting, not to conform to the spirit of the world, nor to let themselves be buffeted by every wind of doctrine[3] and not to give in to unreasonable novelties by following personal judgment beyond measure.

Instead, let each one of you consider it his chief honor to serve the Church, our Mother and Teacher; to follow not his own, but the counsel, the judgments, the projects of the hierarchy and to bring them to fruition; to be animated more by the spirit of cooperation than by that of privilege. The Church recognizes that you are most devoted sons, she especially cherishes you, honors you, and if We may use a bold expression, she reveres you. Now when more than ever, as a result of the decrees of the Second Vatican Council, the extent and the possibilities of the apostolate are seen to be so vast, the holy Church of God needs your holiness of life, your wisdom, your understanding of affairs, your dedication to labor, and she asks of you that, holding on most tenaciously to the faith of old, you bring forth from the treasure of your heart new things and old for the increase of God's world-wide glory and for the salvation of the human race, in the name of Our

---

[3] See Eph. 4.14.

Lord Jesus Christ whom Godhas glorified and to whom He has given a name which is above every name.[4]

Hold fast at all times to the safe protection of this Holy Name, your name too and your special glory. Strive eagerly to make it more widely loved and honored since it is the true, never-failing source of salvation: "For there is no other name under heaven given to men, whereby we must be saved."[5]

We gladly take this opportunity to lay serious stress, however briefly, on a matter of grave importance: We mean the fearful danger of atheism threatening human society. Needless to say it does not always show itself in the same manner but advances and spreads under many forms. Of these, the anti-God movement is clearly to be reckoned the most pernicious: not content with a thoroughgoing denial of God's existence, this violent movement against God attacks theism, aiming at the extirpation of the sense of religion and all that is good and holy. There is also philosophical atheism that denies God's existence or maintains that God is unknowable, hedonistic atheism, atheism that rejects all religious worship or honor, reckoning it superstitious, profitless and irksome to reverence and serve the Creator of us all or to obey His law. Their adherents live without Christ, having no hope of the promise, and without God in this world.[6] This is the atheism spreading today, openly or covertly, frequently masquerading as cultural, scientific or social progress.

It is the special characteristic of the Society of Jesus to be champion of the Church and holy religion in adversity. To it We give the charge of making a stout, united stand against atheism, under the leadership, and with the help of St. Michael, prince of the heavenly host. His very name is the thunder-peal or token of victory.

We bid the companions of Ignatius to muster all their courage and fight this good fight, making all the necessary plans for a well-organized and successful campaign. It will be their task to do research, to gather information of all kinds, to publish material, to hold discussions among themselves, to prepare specialists in the field, to pray, to be shining examples of justice and holiness, skilled and well-versed in an eloquence of word and example made bright by heavenly grace, illustrating the words of St. Paul: "My message and my preachings had none of the persuasive force of 'wise' argumentation, but the convincing power of the Spirit."[7]

---

[4] See Phil. 2.9

[5] Acts 4.12

[6] See Eph. 2.12

[7] I Cor. 2.4

You will carry it out with greater readiness and enthusiasm if you keep in mind that this work in which you are now engaged and to which you will apply yourselves in the future with renewed vigor is not something arbitrarily taken up by you, but a task solemnly entrusted to you by the Church and by the Supreme Pontiff.

Hence in the laws and regulations of your Society, ratified by Paul III and Julius III, there is the following declaration: "All who make the profession in this Society should understand at the time, and furthermore keep in mind as long as they live, that this entire Society and the individual members who make their profession in it are campaigning for God under faithful obedience to His Holiness Pope Paul III and his successors in the Roman pontificate. The Gospel does indeed teach us, and we know from the orthodox faith and firmly hold, that all of Christ's faithful are subject to the Roman pontiff as their head and as the vicar of Jesus Christ. But we have judged nevertheless that the following procedure will be supremely profitable to each of us and to any others who will pronounce the same profession in the future, for the sake of our greater devotion in obedience to the Apostolic See, of greater abnegation of our own wills, and of surer direction from the Holy Spirit. In addition to that ordinary bond of the three vows, we are to be obliged by a special vow to carry out whatever the present and future Roman pontiffs may order which pertains to the progress of souls and the propagation of the faith; and to go without subterfuge or excuse, as far as in us lies, to whatsoever provinces they may choose to send us."[8]

It should be considered fully consistent with this vow and its characteristic obligation that it is not merely a matter binding in conscience, but one that must also shine forth through actions and become known to all.

St. Ignatius, your holy Founder, wanted you to be so; We too want you to be so, being sure that the trust We place in you will be entirely fulfilled. We are confident also that the fulfillment of these wishes of Ours shall yield to the Society of Jesus, in all parts of the world where it struggles, prays and labors, a plentiful harvest of renewed life and excellent merits which God will fittingly reward.

With these heartfelt greetings to you all, members of the Society of Jesus, the festive and happy group that surrounds us today, We impart our apostolic blessing on all of you, on all your undertakings, and on the great hope which sets your hearts on fire for pure and lofty aims to be achieved.

---

[8] *Formula of the Institute of Julius III*, 3.

2. Address of His Holiness Pope Paul VI, to the Members of the General Congregation, November 16, 1966

Beloved sons :

It was Our desire that you concelebrate and share with us in the Eucharistic Sacrifice before departing, each to his own land, at the conclusion of your General Congregation and before setting out from Rome, the center of Catholic unity, for the four corners of the world. We wanted to greet each and every one of you cordially, to hearten and encourage you, and to bless each of you, your entire Society and your various works which you undertake for the glory of God and in the service of Holy Church. We desire to renew in your hearts in an almost palpable and solemn way the sense of the apostolic mandate that characterizes and strengthens your mission, as though it were conferred and renewed by your blessed Father Ignatius, a most faithful soldier of the Church of Christ; or as though Christ Himself, whose vicar We are here on earth in this Apostolic See, unworthily but truly, confirmed and mysteriously aided and extended your mission.

For that reason, We have chosen this place that is sacred and awe-inspiring in its beauty, its majesty and especially in the significance of its paintings. This is a place especially venerable by reason of our prayer pronounced here, a most humble prayer but a Pope's prayer, a prayer which gathers together not only the praise and longing of our spirit but also of the whole Church throughout the world and even of all mankind, which We represent before God through our ministry and to which We bring the message of Him Who is most high. We have chosen this place where, as you know, the destinies of the Church are discerned and decided upon at certain periods of history, destinies which we duly believe are ruled over not by the will of men but by the mysterious and most loving assistance of the Holy Spirit. Here, today, when this most holy rite has been finished We shall invoke that same Holy Spirit for our Holy Church which is summed up, as it were, and represented in our apostolic office, as well as for you, the members and superiors endowed with the authority of your and our Society of Jesus.

By this prayer in which we shall implore the Holy Spirit together, all those things which you have so carefully done during this most important period will receive a special approval. You have subjected your Society and all its works to a critical examination, as though concluding four centuries of its history just after the close of the Second Vatican Council, and beginning a new age of your religious life with a fresh outlook and with new proposals.

This meeting therefore, my brothers and most beloved sons, takes on a particular historical significance in that it is given to you and to us to define by means of reciprocal clarification the relationship which exists and which should exist between Holy Church and the Society of Jesus. Through divine mandate We exercise the pastoral guidance of this Church and sum up in ourselves and represent it. What is this relationship? It is up to you and to us to furnish a reply, which will follow a twofold division:

1. Do you, sons of St. Ignatius, soldiers of the Society of Jesus, want even today and tomorrow and always to be what you were from your beginnings right up to today, for the service of the Catholic Church and of this Apostolic See? There would be no reason for asking this question had not certain reports and rumors come to our attention about your Society, just as about other religious families as well, which—and We cannot remain silent on this—have caused us amazement and in some cases, sorrow.

What strange and evil suggestions have caused a doubt to arise in certain parts of your widespread Society whether it should continue to be the Society conceived and founded by that holy man, and built on very wise and very firm norms? The tradition of several centuries ripened by most careful experience and confirmed by authoritative approvals has shaped the Society for the glory of God, the defence of the Church and the admiration of men. In the minds of some of your members, has the opinion really prevailed to the effect that all human things, which are generated in time and inexorably used up in time, are subject to an absolute law of history as though in Catholicism there were no charism of permanent truth and of invincible stability? This rock of the Apostolic See is the symbol and foundation of this charism.

Did it appear to the apostolic ardor which animates the whole Society that your activities could be made more effective by renouncing many praiseworthy customs pertaining to spiritual, ascetical and disciplinary matters, as though they no longer helped but rather impeded you in expressing your pastoral zeal more freely and with more personal involvement? And so it seemed that the austere and manly obedience which had always characterized your Society, which made its structure evangelical, exemplary and very strong, should be relaxed as though opposed to the human person and an obstacle to alacrity of action. This is to forget what Christ, the Church, and your own school of spirituality have taught in so outstanding a way about this virtue. And so there might have been someone who judged that it was no longer necessary to impose spiritual practices on his own soul, that is, the assiduous and intense practice of prayer, a humble and fervent discipline of the interior life, examination of conscience, intimate conversation with Christ, as though the exterior action were enough to keep the soul wise, strong and pure, and as though such activity could achieve by itself a union of the mind with God. It would be as though this abundance of spiritual resources were fitting only for the monk and not rather the indispensable armor for the soldier of Christ.

Perhaps some have been deceived into thinking that in order to spread the Gospel of Christ they must take on the ways of the world, its manner of thinking and acting, and its worldly view of life. On the basis of naturalistic norms they judged the customs of this age and thus forgot that the rightful and apostolic approach of the herald of Christ to men, who brings God's message to men, cannot be such an assimilation as to make the salt lose its tang and the apostle his own virtue.

These were clouds on the horizon, but they have been dispersed in large measure by the conclusions of your Congregation! It was with great joy that we learned that you, in the strong rectitude which has always inspired your will, after a careful and sincere study of your history, of your vocation, and of your experience, have decreed to hold fast to your fundamental constitutions and not to abandon your tradition which in your keeping has had a continual effectiveness and vitality.

By introducing certain modifications to your rule—this renewal of religious life which was proposed by the Council not only was permissible but recommended—you in no way violated that sacred law by which you are Religious and also members of the Society of Jesus. Rather you remedied your circumstances insofar as they showed the wear of time, and you brought new strength to all the undertakings you will assume in the future so that this happy result will stand forth among all the others which you have decided upon in your laborious discussions; this happy result, We say, which has brought about not only a real conservation and positive increase of the body but also of the spirit of your Society. And, in this regard, We fervently exhort you that also in the future you give pride of place in your program of life to prayer, not turning away from the wise directives which you received from your forebears. From where, if not from divine grace, which flows to us as living water through the humble channels of prayer, of dialog with God, and especially of the sacred liturgy, from where will the Religious draw heavenly counsel and strength for bringing about his supernatural sanctification? From where will the apostle receive the drive, guidance, strength, wisdom and perseverance in his struggle against the devil, the flesh and the world? From where will he draw the love by which he loves souls for their salvation and builds a Church along with the workers who have been entrusted with and are responsible for this mystical building, the Church? Rejoice, dearest sons, this is the way, old and new, of the Christian dispensation; this is the form which produces the true religious disciple of Christ, the apostle in His Church, and teacher of His brothers whether believers or not. Rejoice; our goodwill, indeed our very being, joined in communion with you, comforts and accompanies you.

And thus We should receive your particular deliberations—on the formation of your scholastics, on respect for the teaching and the authority of the Church, on the criteria of religious perfection, on the norms by which your apostolic activity and pastoral works are properly directed, on the correct interpretation of the decree of the Ecumenical Council, on the way by which they are to be put into effect, and on other matters of this kind—as the replies to the question We asked above. Yes, to be sure; the sons of St. Ignatius who are honored by the name of members of the Society of Jesus are still today faithful to themselves and to the Church! They are ready and strong! Arms that are used up and less efficient have been cast aside and they have new ones in their hands along with the same obedience, with the same spirit of dedication, with the same desire for spiritual victories.

2. And now the second question arises, that of determining the relationship of your Society to the Church and in a special way to the Holy See. There is a second question which We can almost read on your lips: does the Church, does the successor of St. Peter, think that the Society of Jesus is still their special and most faithful militia? Do they think this is the religious family which has proposed as its particular purpose not so much one or other Gospel virtue to be cherished, but rather has set out, as a guardian and stronghold to defend and promote the Catholic Church itself and the Apostolic See? Are the goodwill, trust, protection which it has always enjoyed still assured? Does the Church assert through the mouth of him who speaks to you now that it still needs and is honored by the militant ministry of the Society of Jesus? Is the Society still strong and suitable for the work of such widespread and such diverse apostolate of today? Here, my dear sons, is our reply: Yes! We have faith and we retain our faith in you; and thus We give you a mandate for your apostolic works; We show you our affection and gratitude; and We give you our blessing.

In this solemn and historic hour you have confirmed with your new proposals that you wish to cling very closely to your Institute, which, when the restorative work of the Council of Trent burned bright, put itself at the service of the Catholic Church. Thus it is easy and enjoyable for us to repeat the words and acts of our predecessors at this time which is different but no less a time of renewal of the life of the Church, following the Second Vatican Council. It is a joy for us to assure you that as long as your Society will be intent on striving for excellence in sound doctrine and in holiness of religious life and will offer itself as a most effective instrument for the defense and spread of the Catholic Faith, this Apostolic See, and with it, certainly the whole Church, will hold it most dear.

If you continue to be what you have been, our esteem, and our confidence in you will not be lacking.

And the people of God will feel the same about you. For what was the mysterious cause that carried your Society to such great growth and success if not your particular spiritual formation and your canonical structure? And if this formation and structure remain the same and nourish in ever-new strength, virtues and works, the hope for your progressive increase and perennial effectiveness in preaching the Gospel and building modern society is not in vain. Are not the structure of your evangelical and religious life, your history and your character, by which you have been an example to others, your best argument and the most persuasive note of credit to your apostolate? And is it not on this spiritual, moral and ecclesiastical firmness that confidence in your work and also in your collaboration is founded? Permit us to say toward the close of this address that We place great hope in you. The Church needs your help, and is happy and proud to receive it from sincere and dedicated sons as you are. The Church accepts the promise of your work and the offer of your life; and since you are soldiers of Christ, it calls you and commits you to difficult and sacred struggles in His name, today, more than ever.

Do you not see how much support the faith needs today, what open adherence, what clear exposition, what tireless preaching, what erudite explanation, how much testimony full of love and generosity?

Do you not see what opportunities are furnished by modern ecumenism to the servant and apostle of the holy Catholic Church for happily creating close relationships with others, for entering prudently into discussions, for patiently proposing explanations, for enlarging the field of charity?

Who is better suited than you to devote study and effort in order that our separated brethren may know and understand us, may listen to us and with us share the glory, the joy, and the service of the mystery of unity in Christ our Lord?

As for the infusion of Christian principles in the modern world as described in the now celebrated pastoral constitution *Gaudium et Spes,* will it not find among you able, prudent and strong specialists? And will not the devotion which you show to the Sacred Heart be still a most effective instrument in contributing to the spiritual and moral renewal of this world that the Second Vatican Council has urged, and to accomplishing fruitfully the mission entrusted to you to confront atheism?

Will you not dedicate yourselves with new zeal to the education of youth in secondary schools and universities, whether ecclesiastical or civil, something which has always been for you a cause of high praise and eminent merit? You should keep in mind that you have been entrusted with many young persons who one day will be able to render precious service to the Church and to human society, if they have received a sound formation.

And what shall we say of the missions? These missions where so many of your members labor admirably, bend every effort, put up with hardships and strive to make the name of Jesus shine forth like the sun of salvation, are they not entrusted to you by this apostolic see as they were once to Francis Xavier, in the assurance of having in you heralds of the faith sure and daring, full of the charity that your interior life renders inexhaustible, comforting and beyond expression?

And finally, what about the world? This ambivalent world which has two faces: the one is that of the compact entered into by all who turn from light and grace; the other, that of the vast human family for which the Father sent His Son and for which the Son sacrificed Himself. This world of today is so powerful and so weak, so hostile and so well disposed; does not this world call you and us to itself, imploring and urging us to a task to be fulfilled? Does not this world, groaning and trembling in this place, in the sight of Christ, now cry out to all of you: "Come, come; the longing and the hunger of Christ await you; come, for it is time."

Yes it is time, my dear sons; Go forth in faith and ardor; Christ chooses you, the Church sends you, the Pope blesses you.

3. Approval by the Supreme Pontiff of the Decrees of the 31st General Congregation on Religious Poverty and on the Gratuity of Our Ministries

June 6, 1966

Secretariat of State of His Holiness

N. 73533

The Vatican

June 6, 1966

Most Reverend Father:

After the 31st General Congregation of the Society of Jesus, you sent to the Holy Father on July 10 of last year a very gracious letter containing the text of the decrees on religious poverty and on the gratuity of ministries which had been passed by an almost unanimous consent. In that letter you recounted the whole matter and in the name of your members you asked that the Holy Father approve those decrees by his favorable consent.

Since—as you wrote—the norms contained in the *Formula of the Institute* and approved by Julius III of venerated memory in the apostolic letter "Exposcit Debitum" on July 21, 1550, needed to be adapted to current circumstances, your General Congregation, desirous of declaring the meaning of the aforementioned *Formula,* decreed that it was allowable for the members of the Society of Jesus to accept Mass stipends (n. 2), to receive honoraria which might be offered on the occasion of spiritual ministries but that they could not demand them (n. 3), and that for other works undertaken by them (which were not considered strictly spiritual ministries) they could earn a recompense as a fruit of their abilities and their labor (nn. 4–5).

The General Congregation wanted to submit these decrees to His Holiness, since these new regulations approved by the Congregation seemed to depart from the letter of the aforementioned *Formula* or to exceed the power of the General Congregation, by reason of the *Formula,* to declare the meaning of "what could be doubtful in . . . the Institute, including this *Formula.*"

After carefully considering the matter, and after taking into account those conditions which in our times the nature of the ministry and the difficulties of providing for sustenance have brought on, with the advice of His Eminence, Ildebrando Cardinal Antoniutti, Prefect of the Sacred Congregation of Religious,

His Holiness approves and confirms the decrees which you proposed for his examination, abrogating all prescriptions, even if they be worthy of special mention, which are contrary to those decrees. Therefore the *Formula of the Institute* will in this matter in the future be interpreted according to the intention of those decrees which were passed by the General Congregations and approved by Pope Paul VI.

As I gladly take care to let you know of this, so also I inform you that the Holy Father very lovingly imparts to you and to the whole Society of Jesus the apostolic blessing as a token of the gifts of God and as a sign of his good will.

I wish also to take the opportunity to acknowledge myself, as is appropriate,

Devotedly yours:

A. G. Cardinal Cicognani

4. LETTER OF CARDINAL I. ANTONIUTTI

Sacred Congregation of Religious

Prot. N. 6995/66

Rome, November 12, 1966

Most Reverend Father :

This Sacred Congregation has carefully considered the request which your reverence sent to us in your letter of October 30 on the question of whether the General Congregation of the Society of Jesus whose second session is now going on fulfills those requirements which in the apostolic letter "Ecclesiae Sanctae" are set down regarding the special Chapter demanded by the Norms (II.3) The response to the question is:

AFFIRMATIVE, since the second session of the General Congregation is being held after October 11, 1966, on which date the norms began to go into effect which were to carry out the decree "Perfectae Caritatis" of the Second Vatican Council.

This session fully complies with the requirements that a special Chapter be held in accord with the aforementioned norms.

As I inform you of this, I also express my deepest hopes that the decisions and the proposals of the members of the General Congregation will turn out to the good of the Church and of the renowned Society of Jesus, to the greater glory of God.

Devotedly yours in Christ,

Cardinal Antoniutti, Prefect

5. Letter of the 31st General congregation to the Supreme Pontiff

Most Holy Father:

Our 31st General Congregation, happily bringing to an end its two sessions of hard work, rejoices in this opportunity to express to you its deepest feelings and to give you heartfelt thanks for the good will which you showed to us when, as we began our work, you received us in audience and inspired us with a fatherly address and when now, after you have followed our labors with your counsel and your prayers, you wished to bring them to a climax with today's concelebration as a sacred seal.

We well know that we can do nothing more pleasing to you than to offer to you the decrees which we have passed in our General Congregation, religiously following the prescriptions of the Second Vatican Council. We want the Society of Jesus in our age most faithfully to carry out that mission which Ignatius took on among the people of God, eagerly to serve the Church of Christ under the Roman Pontiff. The Society will carefully adapt its apostolic minis-tries both to the wishes of the Holy See and to today's needs, fulfilling in the first place that responsibility to resist atheism with united force which you have in a special way wished to ask of us.

To this end we have taken care to adapt our laws to the new needs of our times. But at the same time, mindful that the effectiveness of our apostolate intimately depends upon our union with Christ, we have tried to renew and encourage the religious life of the Society.

May God grant that we fully put into practice our proposals and that the Society always be for you, Most Holy Father, and for the whole Catholic hierarchy, a strong support in the works of the apostolate. We do not deny that because of human weakness we have sometimes failed in that fidelity which we have promised to the Church and to the Roman Pontiff, and we are sincerely sorry that even from our members have come causes of anguish to you. But your apostolic blessing will ask for us from the Lord the abundant graces by which we shall be able to work better, in a more holy way, more effectively for the glory of God and the good of souls.

Rome, November 16, 1966.

D

MEMBERS OF THE 31st GENERAL CONGREGATION

(In Alphabetical Order

President:

To May 22, 1965: Rev. Fr. John L. Swain

From May 22, 1965: Very Rev. Fr. Pedro Arrupe

Last Name, First Name, and Province

Abellán, Petrus	Toledo
Acevéz, Emmanuel	Northern Mexico
Achaerandio, Aloisius	Central America
de Aldama, Iosephus Ant.	Baetica
Aldunate, Iosephus	Chile
Alf, Iacobus	Buffalo
Antunes, Emmanuel	Portugal
Aquino, Antonius	Central Brazil
Arès, Ricardus	Montréal
Arminjon, Blasius	Southern France
Arroyo, Iosephus	Toledo
Arrupe, Petrus	Japan
Arvesú, Fridericus	Antilles
Azcona, Severianus	Spain
Azevedo, Marcellus	Lesser Goia
Baeza, Franciscus Xav.	Castile

Balaguer, Melchior M.	Bombay
Baron, Ferdinandus	Eastern Colombia
Barry, Brendanus	Ireland
Bednarz, Miecislaus	Lesser Poland
Beltrão, Petrus	Southern Brazil
Birkenhauer, Henricus F.	Detroit
Blajot, Victor	Bolivia
Le Blond, Ioannes-Ma.	Northern France
Boylen, Ioannes R.	Australia
Braganza, Franciscus	Gujarat
Brenninkmeyer, Bernwardus	East Germany
Bresciani, Carolus	Bahia
Briceño, Eduardus	Eastern Colombia
Bru, Ioannes	Western France
Bulanda, Eduardus	Greater Poland
Burkhardt, Franciscus	Far East

243

Buuck, Fridericus	Lower Germany
Byrne, Thomas	England
Calvez, Ioannes	Paris
Cardoso, Armandus	Central Brazil
Carrier, Hervaeus	Quebec
Colli, Ioannes	Turin
Connery, Ioannes R.	Chicago
Connolly, Ioannes F. X.	California
Coreth, Emericus	Austria
Corrigan, Terentius	England
de la Costa, Horatius	Philippines
Crandell, Gulielmus A.	New Orleans
Craveiro da Silva, Lucius	Portugal
Crick, Franciscus	Ranchi
Crowther, Emmanuel	Ceylon
Cullum, Leo A.	Philippines
Čurič, Iosephus	Croatia
d'Oncieu, Eugenius	Southern France
D'Souza, Hieronymus G.	India
Dagher, Abdallah	Far East
Daley, Ioannes M.	Maryland
Dargan, Herbertus	Hong-Kong
De Genova, Ludovicus	Patna
Delchard, Antonius	Northern France
Del Zotto, Aloysius	Kerala
Dezza, Paulus	Venice-Milan
Díaz de Acebedo, Iesús	Loyola
Divarkar, Parmananda C. A.	Bombay
Ducoin, Georgius	Western France
Dupont, Andreas	Madagascar
Durocher, Romulus	Economo General
Dzierzek, Stephanus	Greater Poland

Elizondo, Michael	Argentina
Eminyan, Mauritius	Malta
Fank, Carolus	Upper Germany
Federici, Iulius Caesar	Rome
Fernandes, Laurentius	Madurai
Feřt, Venceslaus F.	Bohemia in dispersion
Fimmers, Augustinus	Northern Belgium
Fiorito, Michael A.	Argentina
Foley, Ioannes J.	Wisconsin
Ford, Ioannes C.	New England
Fortier, Vitus	Quebec
Franchimont, Philippus	Southern Belgium
Fransen, Petrus	Northern Belgium
Freitas, Geraldus	Northern Brazil
Fruscione, Salvator	Sicily
Fuček, Ioannes Gualb.	Croatia
Gallen, Iosephus F.	Maryland
Ganss, Georgius E.	Missouri
Garcia Manrique, Euseblus	Aragon
Gargiulo, Armandus	Naples
Gentiloni, Philippus	Rome
van Gestel, Petrus	Germany
Giampieri, Albertus	Naples
Giuliani, Mauritius	Paris
Gomes, Carolus	Goa-Poona
Gomez Perez, Raphael	Southern Mexico
Gonzalez, Gulielmus	Eastern Colombia
Gonzalez, Emmanuel	Japan
Gonzalez, Ludovicus	Toledo
Gordon, Ignatius	Baetica
Goussault, Iacobus	Western France
Gríful, Isidorus	Uruguay

Guaschetti, Carolus	Turin	Madurga, Marianus	Aragon
Gutiérrez M., Henricus	Southern Mexico	Maher, Gulielmus	England
Harvey, Iulianus	Quebec	Mailleux, Paulus	Byzantine Rite
Hirschmann, Ioannes	Lower Germany	Mann, Eduardus	Bombay
Hogan, Ieremias	Australia	Marcozzi, Victorius	Venice-Milan
Hoing, Iosephus	Northern Belgium	Markaitis, Bruno	Lithuania in dispersion
Hughes, Lachlan	Salisbury	Martegani, Iacobus	Italy
Iglesias, Ignatius	León	Martinsek, Franciscus L.	Patna
Iriarte, Victor	Venezuela	Mazón, Candidus	Aragon
Iturrioz, Iesus	Loyola	McCarthy, Carolus	Far East
Junk, Nicolaus	Lower Germany	McGinty, Ioannes I.	New York
		McGrail, Ioannes A.	Detroit
Kelley, Ioannes I.	Oregon	McMahon, Ioannes I.	New York
Kelly, Franciscus	Australia	McQuade, Iacobus I.	Detroit
Kerr, Ioannes	Ireland	Mejía, Franciscus Xav.	Western Colombia
Klein, Henricus	East Germany	Mertens, Victor	Central Africa
Klubertanz, Georgius	Wisconsin	Messineo, Antonius	Sicily
Kozèlj, Ioannes B.	Croatia	Mirewicz, Georgius	Greater Poland
Kusmierz, Antonius	Lesser Poland	Monachino, Vincentius	Rome
Lacourt, Franciscus	Northern France	Monteiro, Sylvester	Kanara
Lang, Caecilius E.	New Orleans	Moreno Albertus	Northern Latin America
Laramée, Ioannes	Montréal	Mruk, Antonius	Lesser Poland
Larrain, Ferdinandus	Chile	Mueller, Ansgarius	Southern Brazil
Laurent, Philippus	Paris	Murphy, Gulielmus I.	New England
Le Saint, Gulielmus	Chicago	Murray, Ioannes	England
Leary, Ioannes	Oregon	Naughton, James	Missouri
Leite, Antonius	Portugal	O'Brien, Iosephus D.	California
Lemieux, Albertus A.	Oregon	O'Connor, Ioannes V.	New England
Litva, Felix	Slovakia	O'Connor, Paulus L.	Chicago
Maas, Simon	Netherlands	O'Conor, Carolus	Ireland
MacDougall, Angus I.	Upper Canada	O'Keefe, Vincentius T.	New York
Mackenzie, Rodericus	Upper Canada	Ochagavía, Ioannes	Chile

Oñate, Iosephus	East Asia
Orie, Carolus	Indonesia
Pasupasu, Daniel	Central Africa
Pillain, Stephanus	France
Pinsker, Antonius	Austria
Portilla, Henricus	Eastern Mexico
Pujol, Clemens	Tarragona
Ramirez Eduardus	Western Colombia
Reed, Ioannes I.	Buffalo
Reinert, Paulus C.	Missouri
Renard, Aloisius	Southern Belgium
Rentería, Ignatius	Northern Mexico
Riaza, Iosephus M.	Castile
Ribas, Petrus	Tarrgona
Richard, Ioannes	Montréal
Ridruejo, Iosephus	Peru
Roberts, Antonius	Jamshedpur
Robinson, Franciscus	Northern Mexico
Rocha, Ioannes B.	Southern Latin America
Romaña, Antonius	Tarragona
Rondet, Michael	Southern France
Rosa, Leo	Venice-Milan
Rosenfelder, Ricardus M.	Patna
de Roux, Rodulfus	Western Colombia
Ryex, Mauritius	Central Africa
Salaverri, Ioachimus	Léon
Salvo, Hippolytus	Argentina
Schasching, Ioannes	Austria
Schoenenberger, Marius	Switzerland
Segura, Emmanuel	Paraguay
Sehnem, Ioannes B.	Southern Brazil
Shan, Paulus	Far East

Shanahan, Iacobus I.	Buffalo
Shea, Arthurus F.	Philippines
Sheridan, Eduardus	Upper Canada
Silva, Franciscus I.	California
Simmel, Ansgarius	Upper Germany
Small, Haroldus O.	America
Smith, Andreas C.	New Orleans
Smulders, Petrus	Netherlands
Soballa, Gunterus V.	East Germany
de Sobrino, Iosephus A.	Baetica
Sogni, Aemilius	Turin
Sponga, Eduardus A.	Maryland
Swain, Ioannes L.	England
von Tattenbach, Franc	Upper Germany
Tejerina, Angelus	Léon
Terpstra, Ioannes	Netherlands
Thomas, Ioannes L.	Wisconsin
Thro, Linus I.	Missouri
Tobin, Elect,	Jamaica
Troisfontaines, Rogerius	Southern Belgium
Tucci, Robertus	Naples
Ugarte, Aemilius	Madurai
Van Roey, Laurentius	Ranchi
Varaprasadam, Ioannes Ma.	Madurai
Varga, Andreas Subst.	Hungary
Velaz, Iosephus Emman.	Loyola
Velloso, Petrus B.	Central Brazil
Verstraete, Lucas	Ranchi
Villalba, Alphonsus	Ecuador
Villanova, Daniel	Sicily
Vizmanos, Franciscus a B.	Castile
Voss Gustavus	Japan
Wautier, Albertus	Calcutta

THE 32nd GENERAL CONGREGATION

OF THE

SOCIETY OF JESUS

December 2, 1974—March 7, 1975

LETTER OF PROMULGATION
FROM FATHER GENERAL

To the Whole Society

Reverend Fathers and dear Brothers in Christ,

Pax Christi

The decrees of the Thirty-second General Congregation which the Supreme Pontiff had asked to be sent to him at the end of the Congregation so that he might consider them before their publication, he has recently returned to me through His Eminence, Jean Cardinal Villot, Secretary of State. Together with the decrees I received from Cardinal Villot on May 2 a letter and some special recommendations with regard to certain of the decrees, which the Holy Father sends to us in order that we might take account of them in putting the decrees into effect. [See pp. 392–395 for this letter.]

Now therefore by this present letter I am sending the decrees of the Thirty-second General Congregation, in the name of the Congregation itself, to all the provinces, vice-provinces and missions, so that they might be published to all the houses of the Society in accord with the norms of the Formula of the General Congregation.[1] *The decrees enter into force from the day of their promulgation, that is, from the date of this present letter, which is being sent along with the formal communication of the decrees.*

The Supreme Pontiff, who followed the work of the Congregation "with keen, loving and personal concern,"[2] desires that these decrees "be put into effect according to the needs of the Society, with the hope that your worthy Jesuit brothers may draw strength from these decrees as they continue their progress in genuine fidelity to the charisma of St. Ignatius and the Formula of the Institute."[3]

The General Congregation itself was very solicitous about arranging for the implementation of these decrees. It asserted that they could not be put into practice

---

[1] Form. Congr. Gen., n. 144, §2, 1°.

[2] Letter from the Cardinal Secretary of State to Father General, May 2, 1975.

[3] Ibid.

without "the cooperation of all Jesuits under the leadership of their Superiors,"[4] and they thought it necessary for this that the documents be "commended to personal reading and community dialogue in a spirit of prayer and discernment."[5]

Only in this way can the decrees of the Thirty-second General Congregation be a strong instrument for that hoped-for renewal and adaptation of our Society to the contemporary needs of the Church and of the world. I would also ask, as far as I am concerned, that along with the decrees all will wish to consider with the greatest attention the documents of the Holy See which pertain to the Congregation, especially the address given by the Supreme Pontiff on December 3, 1974, and the recommendations which in his name are attached to the letter sent to us by His Eminence, the Cardinal Secretary of State on May 2.

In brief: it is our responsibility to put into practice with the greatest fidelity and with a ready disposition these decrees along with the recommendations of the Holy Father, so that what the General Congregation decided, with the Lord's inspiration and under the fatherly guidance of the Vicar of Christ on earth, may have happy results for our whole Society and for all those for whom the Society desires to work in the vineyard of the Lord.

With the intercession of Mary, Mother of the Society, let us try ardently to beg the Lord for a faithful fulfillment of the decrees.

I commend myself to your Sacrifices and prayers.

The servant of all of you in Christ,

Pedro Arrupe
General of the Society of Jesus

Rome, May 8, 1975
Feast of the Ascension of Our Lord Jesus Christ

---

[4] GC 32, Introductory Decree, no. 10.

[5] Ibid., no. 9.

A

HISTORICAL PREFACE
TO THE DECREES
OF THE
32nd GENERAL CONGREGATION

Excerpted from the Official Minutes of the Congregation

HISTORICAL PREFACE TO THE DECREES
OF THE 32nd GENERAL CONGREGATION

Excerpted from the Official Minutes of the Congregation

1. Steps Taken Prior to the Congregation Itself

The 32nd General Congregation was formally summoned by Very Reverend Father General Pedro Arrupe in his letter of September 8, 1973.[1] However, preparations for the Congregation had been going on long before its convocation, and the first steps in that preparation began already in 1970.

In the 65th Congregation of Procurators, September 17–October 6, 1970, Father General said that although the procurators had decided that a General Congregation was not immediately to be called, that is, within a year and a half, nonetheless he was aware that they had clearly enough indicated that a new General Congregation ought to be held within a few years because of the problems of contemporary change and that for such a Congregation there ought to be a longer preliminary preparation than Society law would allow in the case of a formal convocation of a Congregation by a decision of the procurators.[2] He therefore announced that such preparation was to begin immediately, and, indeed, that this preparation was to arise from an effort in depth and breadth to assimilate the Ignatian spirit, to engage in reflection in common and to experience a conversion of the whole Society. The General Congregation itself was to be, as it were, the final step or the juridical expression of such an effort.[3]

A few months later, after consultation with the provincials, Father General set up a preparatory commission of six members: Father Jean Calvez (Atlantic France Province) as chairman, along with Fathers Parmananda Divarkar (Bombay), Walter Farrell (Detroit), Johannes G. Gerhartz (Lower Germany), Luciano Mendes de Almeida (East Central Brazil), and Tomas Zamarriego (Toledo).[4] Over a period of almost three years this commission worked in preparing studies, with the help of almost thirty task forces, on those points which, as a result of consultations

---

[1] *ActRSJ,* XVI, 109–115.

[2] *ActRSJ,* XV, 613.

[3] *ActRSJ,* XV, 616 and 620–621.

[4] *ActRSJ,* XV, 631–634, 721, and 755.

in the whole Society, it seemed necessary to treat, as well as in fostering reflection on those matters on the level both of communities and of provinces.

Several times in the course of those years, Father General himself wrote to the Society about the coming Congregation. Especially on December 25, 1971, he sent a letter about spiritual discernment to be used in common preparatory reflection.[5] Then on April 22, 1972, in light of the progress of this preparatory reflection, he announced that he had decided, with the approval of the Supreme Pontiff, that the Congregation of Provincials which would have been held in 1973 was not going to be called.[6]

In addition to this remote preparation the General was also seriously engaged, even after the calling of the Congregation, in its proximate preparation. He ordered that the Provincial Congregations should be completed before the end of April, 1974, in order that there might be for those called to be members of the Congregation a sufficiently long period of time available to spend on final preparations. The members were to be in Rome on December 1, 1974. As a result, therefore, the postulata sent by the Provincial Congregations could, toward the end of May, 1974, be arranged by topics and sent to all the members of the Congregation.

In accord with decree 38, n. 7, of the 31st General Congregation,[7] three preliminary committees were called to Rome to finish the preparatory work. Those committees dealt with poverty (toward the end of July), with studies (at the beginning of September), and with the preparation of a list of points which were first to be treated and with other final preparatory matters (from the 18th of November on).

2. The Beginning of the Congregation, the Regulations on Publicity and on Procedural Matters
(*From the Minutes,* Acta 1, 11, 15)

The General Congregation was convoked in Rome at the General Curia of the Society of Jesus.

Present in Rome on the designated day, December 1, 1974, were all the members of the Congregation except one, the elector of the vice-province of Rumania. In that vice-province, just as in four other provinces or vice-provinces (Hungary, Bohemia, Lithuania, and Slovakia), provincial congregations could not be held. However, there was one member of the General Congregation from each of these four places; he was appointed either by the major superior of the

---

[5] *ActRSJ,* XV, 767–773.

[6] *ActRSJ,* XV, 878.

[7] *ActRSJ,* XIV, 970.

province or vice-province or by Father General according to the norms of the *Formula of Provincial Congregations,* no. 95, §§2–3.

Three procurators ad negotia were appointed by Father General as members of the Congregation from the province of New York[8] and one from the independent region of Cuba.

The first session was held on the morning of December 2, 1974. Father General began by reading a selection from Sacred Scripture on the action of the Holy Spirit in the Church. All immediately spent some time reflecting on these texts, and then the hymn *Veni Creator* was sung. After Father General had greeted the assembled members, they decided that the Congregation should not be delayed in waiting for the absent elector from the vice-province of Rumania. The Congregation by a unanimous vote then formally declared itself fully and legitimately in session.

After that, the first action taken was to approve of simultaneous translations from the plenary sessions. From this point on, during the whole Congregation there were simultaneous translations from six languages (English, French, German, Spanish, Italian, and Latin) into three languages (English, French, and Spanish). Approximately twenty Fathers and Scholastics worked tirelessly in taking turns as translators under the direction of Father Nicolás Rodríguez Verastegui (Leon).

Father General then spoke at length on the responsibilities of the Congregation, on the great expectations which the members of the Society had, about the attitude of spiritual discernment and prayer to be employed in the Congregation, and on the fundamental motive of our hope, a motive thoroughly theological and in accord with the Spiritual Exercises of St. Ignatius and the Constitutions.

Following this, the Congregation turned to the approval of the regulations for public information proposed by Father General: it set up the Office of Information under the direction of Father Donald Campion (New York). During the whole Congregation this office prepared and published news releases in five languages—English, French, German, Spanish, and Italian. The Congregation also appointed a group of delegates who would exercise supervision over the Office of Information. Provisionally, the group was made up of five Fathers designated by Father General: Fathers Stefan Bamberger (Switzerland), William Daniel (Australia), Julien Harvey (French Canada), Juan Ochagavia (Chile), and Roberto Tucci (Naples). After two weeks they received definitive appointments, and Fathers Tomas Zamarriego (Toledo) and Stefan Moysa-Rosochacki (Lesser Poland) were added as members.

---

[8] *ActRSJ,* XV, 103.

Provisionally and experimentally the "Additions" to the procedural formula (the "rules of order") were approved. They had been worked out before the Congregation and sent to the members before they arrived in Rome. These additions rounded out the *Formula of the General Congregation* without changing it. If one looks at the norms of procedure which were used in the 31st General Congregation,[9] these present additions introduced certain new practices especially through the use of small groups of members, set up by language (often two languages) or by Assistancy. These groups were used at the beginning of deliberations on matters of greater moment before those matters came to the Aula (where the Congregation held its plenary sessions) for further and final action. The "Additions" also provided that at the beginning of its work the Congregation would decide upon a list of points to be treated first in order of priority in such a way that no other points would be brought up for deliberation by the Congregation as a whole except by a new explicit decision. After some weeks these "Additions" were definitively approved for this present Congregation after they had been slightly modified in accord with suggestions from the procedural commission and from some members of the Congregation.

At the end of the first session the Congregation decided that five Fathers who were not members would be admitted to the meetings of the full Congregation in order to help the secretary of the Congregation in the difficult task of writing the Minutes (the "Acta") of the Congregation.

Later, before noon, meetings of the Assistancy groups were held in order to confer on names for elections to be held by the whole Congregation for Secretary, for his assistants, and for members of the deputations on the state of the Society and on the screening of postulata.

That evening at the Gesu a Mass was concelebrated by all of the members of the Congregation. Hundreds of other Jesuits living in Rome also participated. This was the first of the liturgical celebrations which, along with a variety of groups which gathered for common prayer, became in a way a new characteristic of this Congregation. Every day around noon the Eucharist was celebrated in various languages. In addition there were other special Eucharistic celebrations which took place in the course of the Congregation. Also in the first three days of the Congregation, a fair amount of time was left free especially in order that the delegates might spend time in prayer and spiritual reflection. Material for this prayer and reflection was presented by Father General himself.

3. The Address of the Supreme Pontiff to the Members of the Congregation, and Further Communications from Him to the Congregation

(*From the Minutes,* Acta 6, 10, 11, 15, 25, 26, 29, 30, 54, 55, 61, 63)

---

[9] See *ActRSJ,* 819–820.

On the following day, December 3, the Feast of St. Francis Xavier, the Supreme Pontiff, Paul VI, graciously received the Fathers of the Congregation in audience and gave a very important address on the affairs of the Society.[10]

It is helpful to recall here that already before the Congregation he had expressed his mind on its importance and his expectations, desires, even his will. This he did in letters, both at Easter, 1972, when he first received the announcement that a Congregation was to be called, and on September 15, 1973, at the time of its formal convocation.[11] In the same way, the Holy Father wished to follow its work most attentively throughout its whole course.

Before the Congregation, the postulata sent to it were candidly put before him, and he received Father General in audience on November 21, 1974. Throughout the whole time of the Congregation Father General endeavored to inform him regularly of what was taking place in it.

On his part, on the same day, December 3, on which he received the members of the Congregation in audience, the Supreme Pontiff sent through the Secretary of State a letter[12] in which he let Father General know his mind about the innovation by which the fourth vow might be extended to all members of the Society, even those who were not priests (see n. 15 *infra*). In the course of the month of December he again let Father General know his mind.

Toward the end of January, when he had been informed of the actions of the Congregation in treating of this matter with a view to a possible "representation" (see n. 15 *infra*), the Supreme Pontiff asked for an account of the reasons which had thus moved the Congregation. At the same time he ordered the Congregation to forego any deliberations which could be opposed to the norms contained in his letter of September 15, 1973, and in his address of December 3, 1974. In particular they were to do nothing contrary to what he had made clear in the letter of December 3 from the Secretary of State.

After he had received that account, the Supreme Pontiff sent an autograph letter to Father General on February 15, 1975, in which he confirmed that no change could be introduced relative to the fourth vow. He asked the members of the Congregation again to give most careful consideration to what decisions were to be made in the light of his previous letters and of his address of December 3, 1974, and he requested that decisions already made by the Congregation or soon to be made should be sent to him before their publication.[13] He further

---

[10] See pp. 379–390 below.

[11] *ActRSJ*, XV, 827–829 (Letter of the Cardinal Secretary of State, April 18, 1972); ActRSJ, XVI, 11–15 (Autograph letter of the Supreme Pontiff, September 15, 1973).

[12] See p. 391 below.

[13] See pp. 392–393 below.

explained himself in an audience with Father General on February 20. He expressed fear lest the Congregation would give less weight to those matters concerned with the renewal of the spiritual life and of religious life, lest it look at the problems of the promotion of justice in a socio-economic aspect, in a way that is less in conformity with the proper nature of the Society which is a sacerdotal order, and lest it give insufficient care to correcting certain lamentable deviations in doctrinal and disciplinary matters which had in recent years often been manifested with respect to the magisterium and the hierarchy.

On each of these points referred to by the Supreme Pontiff the Congregation entered into long reflection and prayerful meditation, and it accepted them in a spirit of deep faith and obedience. One can consider, in several points later to be indicated and in the decrees themselves, how the Congregation attempted to meet the expectations of the Supreme Pontiff.

4. Elections and Appointments to the Principal Offices of the Congregation
(*From the Minutes,* Acta 2, 3, 4, 5)

For the beginning of the Congregation, the following are still to be mentioned.

On December 4, Father Johannes G. Gerhartz (Lower Germany) was duly elected Secretary of the Congregation. Fathers Luciano Mendes de Almeida (East Central Brazil) and Simon Decloux (Southern Belgium) were elected Sub-Secretaries.

The following were elected to the deputation on the state of the Society from their respective Assistancies: African, Father Pasupasu (Central Africa); American, Father Michael Buckley (California); Southern Latin American, Father Laercio Dias de Moura (East Central Brazil); Northern Latin American, Father Enrique Gutiérrez (Mexico); English, Father Simon Decloux (Southern Belgium); East Asian, Father Benigno Mayo (Philippines); French, Father Claude Viard (Mediterranean France); German, Father Bernward Brenninkmeyer (East Germany); Spanish, Father Urbano Valero (Castile); Indian, Father Casimir Gnanadickam (Madurai); Italian, Father Paolo Molinari (Turin); Slavic, Father Petar Galauner (Croatia). These twelve members, along with Father General and the four General Assistants, made up the deputation on the state of the Society.

As deputies for the screening of postulata, the following were elected from their respective Assistancies: African, Father Philibert Randriambololona (Madagascar); American, Father Robert Mitchell (New York); Southern Latin American, Father Juan Ochagavía (Chile); Northern Latin American, Father Federico Arvesú (Antilles); English, Father Cecil McGarry (Ireland); East Asian, Father Horacio de la Costa (Philippines); French, Father André Costes (Mediterranean France); German, Father Peter Huizing (Netherlands); Spanish, Father

Manuel Segura (Baetica); Indian, Father José Aizpún (Gujarat); Italian, Father Carlo Martini (Turin); Slavic, Father Tadeusz Koczwara (Greater Poland).

Then, in order to set up the President's Council (Consilium Praesidis), the deputation on the state of the Society elected from among the members Father Jean Calvez; the deputation for screening postulata likewise elected Father Cecil McGarry. The Secretary of the Congregation was *ex officio* a member of that Council. In accord with the "Additions" to the norms of procedure, to these three were added two other members whom Father General (the presiding officer) with his council named as "Moderators" (to help him by presiding over sessions when he so designated them). They were Fathers Robert Mitchell and Roberto Tucci. Father Jean Calvez, already a member of the council, was also named a "Moderator."

5. Selection of Topics "to Be Treated First"

(*From the Minutes,* Acta 6, 7, 8, 9, 10, 12, 13, 14)

Taking into consideration the suggestions produced by the preliminary preparatory committee near the end of November, the Congregation on December 9 and 10 set to work in small groups made up of members able to deal with a particular language or languages and in Assistancy gatherings to determine which topics were to have priority of treatment. The discussion continued in plenary session on December 11 and 12, and finally the matter came to a vote. Out of the forty-six proposed topics on the list, each of the following six got better than half of the votes (in order of number of votes obtained): the criteria of our apostolic service today; the "mission" of the Society as drawn from its apostolic character and purpose; poverty, in its more institutional or juridical aspects; the promotion of justice as a criterion of our life and apostolate; the fourth vow and its relation to the Church and to the hierarchy; formed members of the Society.

Then, at the proposal of certain members, the Congregation agreed to decide, besides, on a first priority or on a priority of priorities, in the sense that it would from the beginning be treated in a rather special manner. As this type of first priority the Congregation selected two topics together, namely, the criteria of our apostolic service today and the promotion of justice. It was thereupon decided to spend two or three days immediately in considering these topics in language groups, in Assistancy meetings, and in plenary sessions. This was done from December 13 to 20 (cf. n. 11 *infra*).

6. The Commissions of the Congregation

(*From the Minutes,* Acta 2, 8, 10, 17, 18)

Although in its first days the Congregation had decided that Father General should set up the necessary commissions along with the deputation for screening postulata, the greater part of them could not be established until decisions had been made on what topics to treat first. However, two special commissions were organized previous to this. They were the commissions on juridical matters (five members) and on procedural matters (seven members).

The commissions to deal with substantive matters ("ad paranda negotia") were set up after the discussion on priorities. There were ten of them, each with a fairly large membership of from fifteen to thirty as circumstances dictated,

    I.   The criteria of our apostolate today

   II.   Mission and apostolic obedience

  III.   Poverty

  IV.   The promotion of justice

   V.   The   fourth vow and relationships with the Church and the hierarchy

  VI.   Formed members

 VII.   Formation of Jesuits

VIII.   Spiritual life, community life, and union

  IX.   Government and Congregations

   X.   Final incorporation and tertianship

At the same time a kind of inter-commission on the identity and charism of the Society was established, made up of members of several commissions. As the Congregation went on, certain other groups or commissions or sub-commissions were set up: on the educational apostolate, on the institutions of higher studies in Rome which are the responsibility of the whole Society, on chastity, on inculturation, on the implementation of the Congregation. Near the end of February, a special committee was also established, made up of four members of the Congregation and of the four General Assistants, the task of which was to compare the documents already prepared by the Congregation with the things asked for in the letter and in the address of the Supreme Pontiff. Most of these groups submitted reports to the consideration and approval of the Congregation just as other commissions did. However, the group which dealt with the institutions of higher studies in Rome submitted their conclusions only to Father General and to a special meeting of provincials, without the Congregation being able to deal with the materials because of lack of time. The sub-commission on the educational apostolate produced two reports, but there was no deliberation on them in the meetings of the full Congregation; this group, however, was able to work at preparing a paragraph on education for the decree on our mission today. The group dealing with chastity worked together with the eighth commission, and in addition gave to Father General for his ordinary government some useful observations on the matter. The commission on implementation of the Congregation's decisions prepared material which afterwards was further worked out in Assistancy meetings.

As for the commissions, it should be added that gradually it became clear that those rather large ones which had been set up at the beginning were laboring under some difficulty. Hence, on January 14, 1975, the Congregation decided that a small editorial committee should be elected for each commission by its members, with the provision that when the definitive revised report *(relatio secunda)* which the editorial committee had prepared was to be presented, the whole commission would present its judgment on it at the same time.

Besides these ordinary commissions, the Congregation had recourse to "Definitors of the second type" in order to deal with postulata on the *Formula of the Provincial Congregation,* except for the question of active and passive voice (the capability of voting or being voted for) in the election of delegates to such a Congregation. That point the Congregation wanted to deal with itself in the usual manner (see n. 20 *infra*).

7. Examination of the State of the Society

(From the Minutes, Acta 2, 3, 8, 11, 15)

Before going on to recount the history of the individual position papers prepared by the commissions, in the order in which the decrees are here published, something should be said about the examination of the state of the Society. The Congregation placed great importance on this examination. It wanted consideration to be given both to the positive elements of recent change which ought to be favored, those elements, that is, which would give promise of great future results, and to the negative elements for which a remedy ought to be supplied.

The discussions began in the small language groups (December 6 and 9). After that, the principal points which were therein proposed were put in order and a preliminary report was distributed (December 16). The Assistancy groups and individual members of the Congregation then had time to hand in their comments. The remarks received were put together and distributed on December 22. At that, the deputation set to work at its own specific task and prepared a report which put together both the negative and the positive elements with which at least the majority of the deputation agreed (December 30).

On January 2 there was an explanatory session in the Aula. On that day Father General presented to the delegates his own opinion on the state of the Society, and at the same time he provided information on relations with the Supreme Pontiff and with the Holy See. Whatever questions the members of the Congregation wished to ask about all these matters Father General freely and fully answered.

As can be seen further on in this history, many of the topics which arose in this examination of the state of the Society were later brought up and treated as the documents of the Congregation were prepared and as several of the documents became decrees, for example in the introductory decree (Decree 1), in the decree on fidelity to the magisterium and the Supreme Pontiff (Decree 3), in the decrees on the formation of Jesuits, on the union of minds and hearts, on poverty . . . (Decrees 6, 11, 12).

8.   The Introductory Decree

(From the Minutes, Acta 61, 64, 70, 71, 72, 79, 81, 82, 83)

The introductory decree (Decree 1) had its origin in the work of the committee (see n. 6 above) set up toward the end of February, 1975, to compare the texts still in process with the letters which had been received from the Supreme Pontiff and with the address he had given on December 3. After careful consideration the committee judged that almost all the points indicated by the Supreme Pontiff were to be found in the documents being prepared by the commissions, even though those documents were still in rather different stages of being worked out. They thought this all the more the case if, as was proper, these decrees in preparation were taken together with the decrees of the 31st General Congregation, to which the present assembly often referred with the intention of explicitly confirming them. The members of this committee also judged that it would be opportune for the documents of the present Congregation to be preceded by a prefatory decree which would contain three points: (1) a confirmation of the 31st General Congregation; (2) a reaffirmation of the principal essential points about the Society which had been emphasized by the Supreme Pontiff; (3) an introduction to the decrees of the present Congregation which looked to implementation. They prepared a text as an example; it was discussed in the Assistancy meetings and in the Aula. Not a few amendments were suggested.

So a second report was prepared, which took into account the previous discussions and which contained in a shorter form the same three points, but especially with an alternative version of the second point. With this in front of them, the members of the Congregation voted on March 5 that there was to be an introductory decree. They decided that the text of the second report was to be used as a basis for that decree, but was to be again revised and put in finished form through amendments. The revised text, along with the amendments, was proposed for a final vote on March 7, and the present decree was definitively passed in the second session on that day.

In its final form the introductory decree confirms the 31st General Congregation, gives thanks to God for the progress which the Society has made, and expresses sorrow at the resistance on the part of some to a desirable renewal and also at the exaggerations on the part of some others. It sincerely recognizes the defects pointed out by the Holy Father and reaffirms in accord with his mind that the Society is a priestly, apostolic, and religious body bound to the Supreme Pontiff by a special vow regarding missions. It seeks a deeper renewal and a closer unity among ourselves and with the Supreme Pontiff. Finally, it introduces the other decrees and stresses the need for their spiritual assimilation and practical implementation.

9.   The Declaration "Jesuits Today"

(From the Minutes, Acta 10, 47, 48, 65, 66, 73, 81)

This document (Decree 2) is the fruit of the last phase of the Congregation's work. It was not until the end of December, 1974, that the previously announced inter-commission (see n. 6) on identity and charisma was set up. Its first task was to gather together from the work of the various commissions the principal points which might be especially significant in delineating our charism for today. Then it had to put them together in a single document which might furnish a description of the identity of a Jesuit as it would emerge from the present Congregation.

As the work of many of the commissions went forward, it became possible for the inter-commission to give to the Congregation on February 12 a first report. It provided as examples seven different possible formats for setting forth our identity today (a declaration, confession, profession of faith, offering or oblation, contemporary reading of the *Formula of the Institute* . . .). After the question was considered in the language groups and in the Aula, the Congregation first decided that some document on identity should be developed. Then it selected from among the various possibilities the format of a declaration which would express in a rather new way "what it meant today to be a Jesuit."

After almost one hundred suggestions had been considered, a definite text was prepared. The editors then accepted informal "friendly amendments" to it. Some formal amendments were also proposed, but the Congregation accepted only a few of these. Finally on March 1 the Declaration passed almost unanimously. However, it had to be modified in one particular. A formal "intercession" took place; the Congregation agreed to it, and so the words "human liberation" were changed in n. 11 to the present text, "the total and integral liberation of man, leading to participation in the life of God himself."

Another "intercession" was approved. Previously, the Congregation had decided that the English text was to be regarded as the official version. Now on March 6 it decided that the Latin text would be the official one, and that the English text would be the original to which reference was to be made in preparing translations.

10. Fidelity to the Magisterium and the Supreme Pontiff

(*From the Minutes,* Acta 42, 43, 44, 76, 79–83)

At the beginning of the Congregation, Commission V received the postulata which dealt both with the meaning and significance of the fourth vow and with the three points of fidelity to the magisterium, the way of acting by Jesuits in doctrinal matters and censures. All of these topics had obvious multiple interconnections. Since the question of the meaning and significance of the fourth vow was among those topics listed as priority items the Commission presented a first report in which as far as possible it dealt separately with the fourth vow, on one hand, and, on the other, with the other questions for which it had responsibility.

When the part of the report which dealt with the significance of the fourth vow was discussed, it became rather evident that the attention of many of the members was on the implications which followed from our relation to the magisterium and to the hierarchy especially in doctrinal matters. This was all the more the case in that the report on the state of the Society had acknowledged many defects in this regard. On the other hand, a great number thought that questions of doctrine and of doctrinal fidelity should not be treated together with the questions of the fourth vow but rather separately and in their own right. After this discussion, the Commission tried to prepare a new report on the fourth vow which would be more satisfactory in the light of the questions raised in the Aula.

Meanwhile, the Supreme Pontiff again in February, 1975, asked that the Congregation give greater care to this fidelity and to the correcting of errors and defects which had crept into the Society in this matter. He had already earlier, in his letter of September 15, 1973, and in his address of December 3, 1974, publicly treated of doctrinal and disciplinary fidelity toward the magisterium and the hierarchy. On February 21, 1975, under the pressure of time, Father General, as presiding officer of the Congregation and with advice and counsel of the General Assistants and the Council of the President, had to present a new schedule of the more urgent business yet to be dealt with by the Congregation. He did not therefore include in that schedule of business a separate document on the fourth vow itself, although its reaffirmation should easily be found in certain of the documents (e.g., the documents on identity and on our mission today). He did, however, take care that an explicit treatment of our fidelity to the magisterium and the Supreme Pontiff would not be neglected.

In order to make progress in treating this matter, Father General asked five of the members of the Congregation each to write a brief document on "thinking with the Church," having before their eyes also the previous work done on this topic by Commission V. From these five texts a single new version was developed and presented to the Congregation. After deliberations in Assistancy meetings and in plenary sessions, the Congregation decided that this question—not yet formally introduced in accord with the Additions to the procedural regulations—should be introduced and dealt with and that it should be done in the form of a brief separate decree. There was an opportunity to offer amendments. Finally voting took place on a revised text and on several formal amendments. The decree thus put together was approved on March 7, 1975. It stressed our obligation of reverence and fidelity and our responsibility toward the Church. It confirms our tradition of service to the Church by explaining, propagating, and defending the faith. It deplores shortcomings in recent years in these matters, and it recommends a vigilance at once fatherly and firm in preventing and correcting failings which tarnish our fidelity to the magisterium and service to the faith and the Church (Decree 3).

11. Our Mission Today: The Service of Faith and the Promotion of Justice

(*From the Minutes,* Acta 9, 10, 12–14, 16, 26–28, 33, 46, 63, 74–76)

The document on our mission today (Decree 4) is one of the principal results of this Congregation, and the work on the complex problems involved in it went on all the way through the Congregation.

Many postulata were received on the fundamental criteria of the apostolate of the Society; even more were received on the promotion of justice as an essential dimension of our apostolate as well as of our whole lives. The importance of these problems became evident right in the opening discussions to decide on the topics which were to have priority in treatment. Among the six topics which received a majority of votes were "The criteria of our apostolic service today" (first place) and "The promotion of justice" (fourth place). When the Congregation came to deciding on a "first priority" some proposed that we should take these two topics together, and that is what the Congregation did (cf. n. 5 *supra*).

If, in addition, one notes that the topic "Our mission as drawn from the apostolic character and purpose of the Society" had taken second place in the voting on priorities and was later added by the Congregation to the two topics above, it is easy to understand the general importance which problems of the apostolate held in this Congregation.

However, differing perspectives were at work which only little by little came together in a single document. The postulata on the criteria of our apostolic service today looked especially to the particular characteristics of our apostolate as a priestly work and to the significance in today's circumstances of the ministries set down in the *Formula of the Institute.* Those postulata dealt with the place to be given (and under what conditions) to professional work, the response of the Society to the apostolic needs which arise from atheism or religious indifference, the apostolic meaning of our educational endeavors, the ecumenical dimension of our apostolates, etc. The postulata commission dealt rather with the essential reality of mission (being sent) in the life of each individual Jesuit as something constitutive of our vocation, with all its consequences in the area of apostolic obedience and of the corporate body of the Society. Serious problems, ones also considered in the examination of the state of the Society, for example, apostolic dispersal or even as it were disintegration, individualism, independence in selecting apostolic activities . . . all urged that there be a strengthening of the awareness of an apostolic body, of an apostolic community, of obedience for a mission, and that the function of the superior in individual and community apostolic discernment be reinvigorated. Finally, the postulata on the promotion of justice, although in a different way and with a different insistence, tended to give more importance to this latter aspect of the apostolate today.

In the initial phase (when treating of the first priority), there was an attempt to join the two topics, "the criteria of our apostolic service" and "the promotion of justice." See, for example, the first report, "The mission of the Society and justice in the world," distributed to the Congregation on December 14, 1974. There was no lack of tension between the differing perspectives during the discussions on this report. Commissions I and IV, to whom belonged the responsibility for these two topics, began to work collaboratively. They soon saw the need for unifying in one document those matters which the Congregation might decide on with regard to the promotion of justice and those detailed explanations which it might make about the fundamental criteria of our apostolate. On the other hand, it rather quickly became evident that the Congregation ought not descend into a minutely drawn out consideration of particular areas of the apostolate, but rather that it ought to be concerned with the criteria, the style, the manner, the form of our apostolic involvement.

In the next phase of the work, in January, at the suggestion of several members, Father General, as presiding officer of the Congregation, asked not only that Commissions I and IV should try to combine their work, but also that Commission II should join them, since the topic of "mission" was itself obviously of great importance for a correct understanding and decision on our apostolic criteria today. So the editorial committees of the three commissions, I, II, and IV, worked at the same time at the preparation of a second and unified report, "On the mission of the Society with regard to the service of faith and the promotion of justice." This was approved by the vote of each of the three commissions (January 24, 1975). The report then came up for discussion, carried on at length through several sessions. On February 1 the Congregation decided by several straw votes or indicative ballots that the text should be shortened, that the experience of and proclamation of the Faith ought to have greater emphasis, that the mission of the Society with regard to atheism should be more prominently put, and finally that a few carefully worked out criteria on participation in politics should be proposed.

A new text was prepared in French and presented at the same time to the Congregation in English and Spanish versions also (third report). There was an opportunity to propose amendments in all three of these languages as well as in Latin.

Once again the text had to be thoroughly revised due to a huge mass of suggestions which came in. So a new version, a fourth report, came before the Congregation on February 21.

This time, too, there was no scarcity of amendments. A vote was taken on them and on the body of the text (in its original French version) on March 1 and 3. Here again amendments were proposed and passed which put the text more in conformity with the wishes of the Congregation. Among those amendments it seems good to point out especially those which again introduced several points which had been left out in the fourth report as originally presented. They came from the early work of Commission II, and they dealt with the community as apostolic, the function of the Superior, obedience in its mission aspect, and the awareness of the Society as a corporate body.

If one compares the earlier versions of "Our mission today" with the version of the decree as it was finally passed, one will probably find that the special and most important note of the last version is that it gives pride of place to the notion of the service of the faith as primary to the whole apostolate of the Society, while it presents the promotion of justice as an absolute requirement of such service, especially in today's circumstances. The decree also stressed, but this time in the same manner as in earlier versions, the necessity for a deeper knowledge of men and women, of their aspirations and of their way of thinking and feeling, as well as a real involvement among them, especially among those who lead a modest, indeed a poor, life and who personally suffer injustice. All Jesuits are invited to a serious examination of their relationships, their style of life, their ability to communicate their deepest convictions with those who do not share our faith, and to a thoroughgoing conversion of mind and heart. This examination is to be furthered for the whole Society under the inspiration of Father General by a systematic, well-established program in all the provinces.

12. The Work of Inculturation of the Faith and the Promotion of Christian Life
(*From the Minutes,* Acta 69, 70, 80)

The question of "inculturation" has relationship to problems of the apostolate, and as a matter of fact it is rather broadly treated in the document "Our mission today." It is a matter especially of inculturation of the faith and of Christian life in those areas of the world where Christianity is now growing among peoples of non-Western culture. The topic, however, and the recommendations reach out more broadly to those regions which were once Christian but which today are distinguished by the rapid process of secularization and by almost new cultures. Nor should we omit the obvious service which the Society can render to the Church for the inculturation of the Gospel in the context of the more universal values which are coming into being all over the world through the multiple relationships among nations (Decree 4, nn. 36 and 53–56). There are similar indications in the decree on the formation of Jesuits (Decree 6, nn. 27, 29, and *passim*).

But the Congregation wanted to pass a particular decree prepared by the commission on this "work of inculturation of the faith and the promotion of Christian life," especially in the cultures of the non-Western world, Africa, Asia, and many of the areas of Latin America. This was something new. Even though the Society in its traditions and its practices had often taken account of a needed inculturation, none at least of the more recent General Congregations had passed a specific decree on this subject.

Given its convocation toward the end of 1974, the General Congregation could hardly fail to follow in the footsteps of the recently held Synod of Bishops "on evangelization." But, in addition, it had also received many postulata on inculturation. Besides, the more numerous membership in the Congregation of Jesuits who were born in East Asia, India, and Africa was a new and very important fact.

The commission which was going to deal with this topic was first entitled *"on indigenization";* later, and more correctly it seems, it took the name "on inculturation." After the commission presented proposals in two reports, the Congregation by an almost unanimous vote decided on a brief but explicit decree on the participation of the Society in this work, and at the same time it recommended that Father General take further measures in the matter (Decree 5).

13. The Formation of Jesuits, Especially with Regard to the Apostolate and Studies
(*From the Minutes,* Acta 48, 49, 51, 52, 53, 67, 75, 77, 81)

An international commission on studies functioned as a preparatory committee for this Congregation in accord with decree 38, n. 7, of the 31st General Congregation. Already in September, 1974, it had a rather fully worked-out study of the postulata on the formation of Jesuits. Commission VII started off from this study and took into account the many elements both positive and negative in Jesuit formation as they became clear in the examination of the state of the Society. The commission judged that a very large number of the items asked for had already been satisfactorily taken care of in the eighth and ninth decrees of the 31st General Congregation, as well as in the *General Norms for Studies* which had been promulgated on October 10, 1967, as the outline of a new *Ratio* for studies in the Society[14] and just as well in Father General's Instruction on the spiritual formation of Jesuits, promulgated on December 15, 1967.[15] What was obviously needed was especially a more accurate and more thorough putting into practice of these documents.

However, supported by comments from individual members as well as from Assistancy meetings, the commission judged that some matters ought to be insisted upon. These matters had recently attained new importance and were related to some of the other decrees of the present Congregation (for example, on our mission today). They were: the apostolic integration of Jesuit formation and, in particular, the integration of studies into the apostolic life, the integration of younger members into the body of the Society, personal integration in the formation of each of us, and the continued formation of all Jesuits as necessary for the renewal of the whole apostolic body of the Society. The following recommendations were also made: the commission thought that the responsibility for formation incumbent on the provincial and the responsibility of all those engaged in formation work, including professors of Jesuits, ought to be highlighted. Care should be taken that the younger Jesuits gain familiarity with the sources of the spirituality of the Church and of the Society. So, too, should there be a care for the connection between special studies, undertaken for apostolic purposes, and philosophical and theological studies as well as spiritual formation, both personal and communitarian. The more widespread modern languages are to be learned, since they make it possible to enter into communication with other cultures and with the universal Society. Philosophical and theological studies are to be strengthened, adapted, of course, to the diversity of cultures and regions of the world. In general, the quality of studies in the Society must by every possible exertion be maintained or raised. On all of these matters the Congregation put its stamp of approval by means of the guidelines and regulations of its sixth decree. At the same time the Congregation somewhat changed the examination ad *gradum* for the profession of the four vows. This examination is to be taken by all those who have not acquired in ecclesiastical studies at least the academic degree

---

[14] *ActRSJ*, XV, 238–268.

[15] *ActRSJ*, XV, 103–133.

of the licentiate. The essential prescriptions of the Constitutions which deal with this examination are to be observed, but particular details are now left to regional regulations on studies. The provincials are to take care that in accord with the new decree all should generally acquire the licentiate in philosophy or in theology. Finally, the Congregation definitively abrogated all the decrees of previous General Congregations which are in opposition to the ninth decree of the 31st General Congregation, the sixth decree of this Congregation, and the *General Norms for Studies.*

14   The Time of Last Vows and Tertianship
(*From the Minutes,* Acta 37, 38, 39, 43)

In recent years it became evident throughout the Society that last vows were being pronounced later than before, partly because of our legislation, whether traditional or more recent (see decree 11 of the 31st General Congregation), and partly because of the abnormal delay, at least in certain provinces, in entering tertianship. Many postulata requested that last vows be able to be taken much more quickly, always supposing the necessary spiritual preparation which takes place through tertianship. Other postulata, though fewer of them, insisted on the rather profound connection which seems to exist between the decision by which the Society presents one of its members for Holy Orders and the final incorporation into the body of the Society by final vows. Mention was made that aptitude for the ministries of the Society can now better than previously be known before the end of studies, since scholastics engage in far more types of apostolic works in the course of their formation.

Commission X, whose responsibility this matter was, sought information from the provincials on the number of those who even several years after completing studies had not begun tertianship and on the reasons for this delay. The commission also heard from the several tertian instructors who were members of the Congregation about the positive results obtained from recent experiments as well as about their shortcomings.

On a great number of points there was large agreement, even if not all of those points were later retained as part of the Congregation's decree:

a. The advantage of not putting off final incorporation into the Society as had been done in these last years. Hence, there was a revision of the eleventh decree of the 31st Congregation; now the requirements consist only of ten years completed in the Society, the tertianship, and, for scholastics, priestly ordination (Decree 10).

b. The importance of tertianship according to the norms set down in the Constitutions and the necessity that those who have not yet begun it after several years since the completion of studies do so soon. As for the Brothers, it was judged good, in accord with the practice of recent years, to reaffirm that they prepare themselves for final vows by a period of more intense spiritual life which in the decree is called "tertianship" and which thus can more easily be made together with the Fathers if the provincial so judges (Decree 7).

c. A strong insistence at the present time on solid spiritual preparation before one receives Holy Orders.

d. The importance of apostolic experiments and of the study of the Institute not only during tertianship but also throughout the whole course of formation.

e. The significance of last vows as an act of definitive incorporation by which the Society sees fully ratified the total consecration which had already been expressed in first vows. This presupposes a long and serious probation throughout the whole period of formation.

f. The usefulness of providing for everyone, even after tertianship, the benefit of some period of time for spiritual renewal (see decree 6, n. 36).

g. The need to prepare tertian instructors who are capable of exercising toward their brethren the Society's care, and the appropriateness of setting up a team of instructors who work together, who mutually complement each other and who give witness to union among themselves as they help those who are making tertianship.

In order to attain the goals of tertianship, it seemed to the Congregation that two different procedures (A and B) could be used, according to provinces or regions, with the approval of Father General. In *Formula A* tertianship is made rather soon after the completion of studies, and ordination to the priesthood takes place during it, keeping of course the condition of full liberty of spirit in taking on Holy Orders. *Formula B* is similar to the experiment of recent years in many provinces, carried out in the ways approved by Father General in 1970.[16]

As for the days on which last vows are pronounced, the Congregation wanted to permit greater flexibility, which circumstances of the apostolate or of the community today demand. When it came to changing the rite used at last vows, on the contrary, the Congregation did not wish to act, since according to expert studies there seems to be no obstacle to retaining even today the usage of the Society which goes back in origin to the very rite used for the vows of our founder.

Finally it is to be noted that as far as first incorporation into the Society goes, and specifically with reference to the vows taken after the noviceship, the Congregation made no changes. Neither a consultation made throughout the Society, nor the opinions received from the provincial congregations, nor the

---

[16] *ActRSJ,* XV, 557.

mind of by far most of the members of the Congregation favored any change in this matter. There was, however, clearly a desire that the novices know still better the import of the promise contained in the first vows, namely, the promise of entering the Society and of striving with all their strength to become truly apt for this.

15. Formed Members, or Grades in the Society of Jesus

(From the Minutes, Acta 20, 21, 22, 23, 24, 25, 26, 29, 30, 53, 54, 68)

Very many postulata were sent on the subject of formed members or grades. Fifty-eight of them came from provincial congregations. A special commission had worked through 1967–1969 and in accord with the mandate of the 31st General Congregation had investigated "the whole problem of distinction of grades." The International Congress of Brothers (Villa Cavalletti, 1970) and four task forces which met in 1972 then completed this work.

Thirty-seven provincial congregations, as well as the four task forces and the Congress of Brothers asked that all Jesuits, including those who were not priests, might be admitted to the four solemn vows. On the other hand, through a letter from the Secretary of State on December 3, 1974, the Supreme Pontiff said that the extension to all, even non-priests, of the fourth vow with regard to missions seemed to present serious difficulties which would impede the approval necessary on the part of the Holy See.

In these circumstances, the Congregation by vote (228 positive and 8 negative) decided that the question of grades should be treated, thinking that there was still place for a "representation." It wanted to start a discernment in depth on the whole matter, both in order to determine the mind of the Congregation and in order, if it so turned out, to be able to present its reasons in a spirit of obedience and filial reverence to the Supreme Pontiff for his consideration.

The question was broadly discussed in the language groups and afterwards in many plenary sessions. To one of the sessions ten Brothers came, chosen from among those whose names already before the Congregation had been proposed by the members. Two of these Brothers, designated by the others, presented their opinions to the Congregation. Towards the end of these deliberations, on January 22, 1975, from an indicative or straw vote of the members it became clear that the Congregation really was tending to "represent" to the Supreme Pontiff, in the Ignatian sense of "representation," the opinion which favored the suppression of grades so that all Jesuits would pronounce the same four vows "in the conviction that thus the priestly character of the Society can and must be preserved."

This result, even though it was still only an indication of opinions, was communicated to the Supreme Pontiff in accord with the procedures of constant information employed all during the Congregation.

The Holy Father informed the Congregation that this had been done contrary to his will; he asked that the Congregation take no further action on this matter, and that it send to him a report of the reasons which had led the members of the Congregation to choose that line which had found expression in the indicative or straw vote. After he received that report, he confirmed in an autograph letter that as supreme guarantor of the essentials of the Society which were contained in the *Formula of the Institute* he could in no way grant a change in this matter.

The Congregation soon concluded the whole affair, deciding by vote that in the historical preface to the Acts of the Congregation the following paragraphs should be inserted, by which in the name of the whole Society it would declare its spirit of faithful acceptance:

"*The 32nd General Congregation, keeping in mind both Decree 5 of the 31st General Congregation and the discussion that took place in the Congregation of Procurators in 1970, subjected to careful examination those postulates dealing with the question of grades in the Society, which had been submitted by a number of provincial congregations. The Congregation presented the whole question, together with the reasons, to the Holy See.*

"*Since, however, His Holiness, Pope Paul VI, after carefully considering the matter, expressed his will and confirmed that the fourth vow of special obedience to the Holy Father regarding missions should remain reserved, according to the Institute, to those priests of the Society who successfully complete the required spiritual and doctrinal preparation, the General Congregation, in the name of the whole Society, accepted the decision of His Holiness obediently and faithfully.*

"*The Congregation, however, wanted by means of the present decree to have us continue to strengthen the unity of vocation of all of our members of whatever grade and to encourage the fuller execution both of Decree 7 of the 31st General Congregation concerning temporal coadjutors and of the norms given by that same Congregation as regards the promotion of priests to the profession of four vows.*"

16. The Permanent Diaconate

(*From the Minutes,* Acta 40, 42, 68)

Once the Second Vatican Council had restored the permanent diaconate, the 31st General Congregation removed the obstacles to the possibility of permanent deacons in the Society (Decree 6). However, "as for the religious vows to be pronounced by such deacons, whether in the future they will be the vows of temporal coadjutors or spiritual coadjutors, the Congregation abstained from passing a decree, because their functions are not yet clearly defined in the documents of the Church, and the Holy See will give further precisions on this for all religious."[17] Since these determinations have now been given, and since the Holy See is asking that the general chapters of religious institutes of men clearly determine the juridical status of their permanent deacons, the 32nd General Congregation, in order that such deacons can be an ordinary part of our institute, first of all in a more positive manner gave permission that some of the members of the Society become permanent deacons when the good of souls was seen to demand it. Then it decided that these deacons should stay in the religious state which they already had in the Society. This, however, was to be such that if they were approved temporal coadjutors (Brothers without last vows) they could be promoted to the grade of formed temporal coadjutors (Brothers with last vows); and if they were scholastics who for just causes could not be ordained priests (for example because of being completely worn out from studies), they could, in due accord with law and by way of exception, be promoted to the grade of spiritual coadjutor. As for other precisions, such as the necessary time in the Society or proper preparation for diaconate ordination, the Congregation thought they ought to be left to general or particular regulations from Father General in accord with the norms both of the Holy See and of conferences of bishops (Decree 9).

17. The Union of Minds and Hearts in the Society

(*From the Minutes,* Acta 40, 41, 59, 63, 75, 77, 78, 32)

The Congregation received a rather large number of postulata on the spiritual life, especially on prayer and on obedience and community life in the Society, as well as on spiritual discernment in common and the proper role of superiors in it. There was also no dearth of postulata on union in the Society; and in the examination of the state of the Society which the Congregation made, it did not fail to take into account the defects in our union which over the last years had shown up among us.

It seemed to the Congregation that both series of problems ought to be approached simultaneously, the personal and communitarian spiritual life and union in the Society. It also seemed that the problems of such union should not be dealt with separately in a decree which was exhortatory and perhaps abstract, but rather that it ought to make an effort to strengthen the union among ourselves through those means which the eighth part of the Constitutions points out as capable of bringing this about. As a matter of fact, the Congregation thought that the needed orientations ought to be arranged in sections bearing titles which more or less corresponded to the principal means set down in that part of the

---

[17] Historical preface to the decrees of GC XXXI, *ActRSJ,* XIV, 823.

Constitutions' first chapter ("Aids toward the union of hearts"), namely, "love of God and of our Lord Jesus Christ," relationships among the brethren, and obedience. This, then, is the origin of the decree "On union of minds and hearts," which at one and the same time treats of union with God in Christ, brotherly communion, and obedience as the bond of union (Decree 11).

Under each of these headings the Congregation put together those points which at present seem more needed. For example, with respect to personal prayer, it looked into present day difficulties, recommended mutual help, consultation with one's spiritual director, openness with superiors, shared prayer with one's brethren. To questions on community spiritual discernment it also responded, and it acted similarly in treating of the various types of fraternal communication and relationship which should flourish among us. While the 31st General Congregation pointed out the importance of community life for the Jesuit as such, now its apostolic dimensions were more forcefully recommended. The same was done vigorously with regard to the apostolic dimension of chastity. In general, the mutually necessary relationships between the religious vows and community life were highlighted. Obedience finally was considered in the context of its present circumstances which, perhaps more than those described in the Constitutions, impede union in the Society.

The Congregation then wished to commend the position of the local superior. In that same context, it dealt with the partly new question of the extent of religious authority in at least some of the directors of apostolic works and of the relationships between their positions and the responsibilities of religious superiors.

Some had sought a clarification on how to apply number 10 of the seventeenth decree of the 31st General Congregation, dealing with a possible case of conflict between the order of a superior and a member of the Society who believed in conscience that he could not obey it. The commission and the Congregation, too, at first doubted the usefulness of adding anything to the determinations set down by the 31st General Congregation other than to point out the internal dispositions needed in the persons who were involved. The question was however brought up again by means of a rather long amendment at the time when the decree was being voted on. Discussion took place on March 4; many, though not denying the usefulness of some further explanation, still thought it would be enough to have Father General give such an explanation. But at the wish of Father General himself and of some of the provincials, the discussion started up again on March 6, and the conclusion was that the Congregation itself would produce a brief explanatory statement. This statement was voted on on that same day (to be found at the end of Decree 11).

To the "orientations" on union of minds and hearts the Congregation wished to add certain "guidelines" which flowed from the former and which were to be proposed for all the members of the Society. Once this was done, the Congregation simply abrogated the Common Rules, which the 31st General Congregation had earlier dealt with in recommending to Father General that they be revised, a task which up to the present Congregation could not be done. It also recommended to Father General that, besides the "guidelines" produced by the Congregation, he put together a kind of summary and index of the cardinal points of our religious life, drawn from the decrees of the 31st and 32nd General Congregations and from the letters that he had sent to the whole Society.

18. Poverty

(From the Minutes, Acta 18, 19, 33–36, 38, 57–59, 68, 69)

The new statutes on poverty, prepared by order of the 31st General Congregation, were promulgated by Father General on September 15, 1967.[18] They were, however, only to be used experimentally, until the next General Congregation.[19] Already in 1970 Father General set up a committee of expert consultants who could give their advice for applying the statutes and for revising them in the future. This committee later evolved into the subcommission for revising the statutes on poverty when preparations began for the 32nd General Congregation. In the following years, the subcommission published three reports (July, 1972; December, 1972; July, 1973), taken for this purpose, from the hundreds of letters and comments from major superiors and local superiors and treasurers and expert consultants from all over the Society. In addition, it published two booklets (*CPCG Documenta Complementaria 8A* [116 pages] and *8B* [172 pages]) in order to encourage reflection during the preparatory phase of the Congregation on the problems connected with poverty.

After about 250 postulata on poverty came from the provincial congregations, a preparatory committee was set up to examine them, according to the norms of General Congregation XXXI, decree 38, n. 7. After a meeting at the end of July, 1974, it published *Documentum ad Congregandos* n. 12 for the members coming to the Congregation. At one and the same time, the booklet furnished a history of the work done on poverty from the 31st to the 32nd General Congregation, an analytic summary of the postulata, and the main lines of the proposals to be considered by the Congregation.

At the Congregation itself it soon became clear that it would be necessary to prepare a draft document which would have two distinct parts, one more spiritual and ascetic (which would also look to the apostolic characteristics of poverty) and the other more juridical, even though the earlier material had concerned itself almost only with institutional poverty or poverty in its juridical aspects. In

---

[18] *ActRSJ,* XV, 60 ff.

[19] GG 31, D. 18, n. 20; *ActRSJ,* XIV, 917.

this second, or juridical section, rather profound changes were proposed. For example, in place of the distinction between professed houses and colleges, the distinction would be between all the religious communities and any apostolic institute [or institutionalized apostolic work]. Or, to all the communities would be applied the regimen of poverty of the professed houses as that has been adapted by the 31st General Congregation to current economic circumstances; or, again, from the apostolic institutes no goods could be transferred to the religious communities except for a suitable remuneration for the work done by Jesuits in those institutions; or, finally, that every community was to prepare a budget to be approved by the provincial and was to distribute whatever money was left after the expenses of the year so that no surplus would be accumulated.

Because of the importance of the subject, an indicative or straw vote was first taken on these more juridical elements. In that way, the Congregation expressed its mind, for example, on not normally allowing stable revenues for the communities.

A revised draft, together with a draft of the more spiritual-ascetical part, was submitted for a vote. There was still some doubt, before the vote, whether a particularly central part of the decree, by which communities or houses could have the simple ownership of the apostolic institutes (Section B, v, 1), would contradict the *Formula of the Institute* and the Constitutions. Although the Congregation was aware that it had the power to resolve such a doubt by an authoritative declaration on its own part, it abstained from doing this and decided rather that a qualified majority (two-thirds) would be required in the voting, according to norm n. 118 of the *Formula of a General Congregation,* and that if the decree obtained this majority it would be submitted to the Holy See for confirmation.

The proposal in question passed by a vote of 191 for it and 23 against it. The decree as a whole was approved by an almost unanimous vote.[20]

It is useful to add here that it did not seem opportune to the Definitors chosen by the 31st General Congregation to ask the Holy See for the faculty of setting up non-collegial foundations which would enjoy exemption from the local Ordinary as the Congregation had recommended because this kind of privilege seemed little in accord with current tendencies in church law. Hence, other adaptations of our law of poverty had to be found by the Definitors. To this end, after a historical study, and with the deliberative vote of those Fathers of the General's curia who had an *ex officio* right to attend a General Congregation, Father General by his own authority promulgated statutes nn. 52 and 83 (on the capacity of the Society as a whole and of the provinces to possess goods). By this, decree 197, n. 1, of the *Collectio Decretorum* (Epitome 522, §1) was abrogated. Since the

---

[20] See the confirmation given by the Holy See for experimental implementation; letter of the Cardinal Secretary of State, May 2, 1975: here, pp. 396–397.

incapacity in that earlier decree was proved to take its force neither from the *Formula of the Institute* nor from the Constitutions, Father General indubitably had such a right, in the light of the Apostolic Letter *Ecclesiae Sanctae* II, nn. 6 and 7, as well as decree 18, n. 20, and decree 56, n. 1, of the 31st General Congregation.[21] Those statutes, that is, nn. 52 and 83 mentioned above, were submitted to the examination of this present Congregation, which authoritatively confirmed them and made them part of its own decree on poverty (Section C).

The other more particular dispositions of the new decree the reader can easily understand (Sections D, E, F). The general tenor and meaning of the new regulations on material goods in the Society are set forth in the first part of the decree in A, IV, nn. 11-12.

19. The General Congregation and Congregations of Procurators and Provincials

(From the Minutes, Acta 45–46, 56, 69, 79, 83*)*

Much was done about questions dealing with the General Congregation itself in the preparatory studies (especially *CPCG Documentum* 8 and *Documenta Complementaria,* n. 7), and on those same questions there were many postulata.

In the Congregation itself the following topics were the ones which were especially brought up: the periodicity and the length of a General Congregation, reduction in the number of its members, more equitable representation for independent vice-provinces, participation by members of the Society who are not professed of the four vows, the possibility of two types of General Congregations with a corresponding difference in the number of participants (one type, that is, for the election of a General and the other, with fewer participants, for business matters alone), the rights of Procurators *"ad negotia"* in a General Congregation, a more official and complete preparation before the Congregation, and a more expeditious set of procedures in the Congregation itself.

Among all these topics, the one on reducing the number of participants was discussed at the greatest length. In an indicative or straw vote, there was a majority, even though slender, in favor of a reduction. Afterwards, however, the discussion got down to methods to bring this about, and they were not fully satisfactory. So finally the Congregation decided that it did not itself want to deal further with this matter. It recommended to Father General that he establish a commission which would investigate the situation more deeply with a view to treating it and acting on it in the next Congregation, especially in relation to stabilizing or even reducing the number of members, and in relation to setting not only quantitative but also qualitative criteria in the distribution of members.

---

[21] *ActRSJ]*, XIV, 917; 994.

As to periodicity and length of General Congregations, this Congregation did not wish to make any changes. On the other hand, by a decree in the final session on March 7 it ordered that in the future the preparation for a General Congregation be more complete and official, that is, that it go up to and include the preparation of the *relationes praeviae* or first official reports (similar to those which are at present provided for in n. 119, §3 of the *Formula of a General Congregation*). It also decided that Procurators *"ad negotia"* could be elected as Secretary or Vice-Secretary of the Congregation, as members of the deputations on the state of the Society and on the screening of postulates and also as definitors. In addition, it asked that in the light of the experience of this present Congregation, the *Formula of the General Congregation* be thoroughly revised, both as to the procedural rule and the rules for dealing with substantive matters (cf. Decree 13).

As to congregations of procurators and provincials, the 32nd General Congregation made clear in an indicative vote that it was not of a mind to abolish the congregation of provincials, and so no more was done on that matter. But on the other hand, the Congregation did not act on certain postulata which tended to remove the limitation imposed by the last General Congregation by which a provincial cannot change the decision *de cogenda* taken by the congregation of his own province. It did decide to broaden the power of the congregations, both of procurators and provincials, such that both of them could in case of necessity suspend a decree of a previous general congregation until the next general congregation, and both could publish for the whole Society a report on the state of the Society (also in Decree 13).

Lastly, the Congregation commissioned Father General to apply these decisions and to insert them in the *Formulae* of the various congregations. It also commissioned him to revise the *Formula of the General Congregation,* spoken of earlier, with the help of a commission appointed by him and with the deliberative vote of those members of the General's curia who have an *ex officio* right to be members of a general congregation.

20. Provincial Congregations

(From the Minutes, Acta 33, 40, 60, 62–64, 71, 77, 80, 83)

Many postulata were received which dealt with the provincial congregation and its *Formula.* Fifty-eight such postulata spoke of enlarging participation in the election to its membership. On February 5 the General Congregation decided to reserve to itself the question of active and passive voice (voting and being voted for) in the election to a provincial congregation. The other points to be dealt with it confided to five definitors of the second type who would make decisions on them, keeping intact however the non-legislative character of a provincial congregation.

The General Congregation asked Father General, after consulting the council of the presidency and the editorial committee of the ninth commission, to propose five names before the Congregation itself elected the definitors. Father General proposed Fathers Bruce Biever (Wisconsin), Tarcisio Botturi (Bahia), Eugeen De Cooman (North Belgium), Casimir Gnanadickam (Madurai), and Mariano Madurga (Aragon). They were all elected by the Congregation on a single ballot despite the provision of n. 126, §2, of the *Formula of the General Congregation,* after a decision had been made to do it thus following upon a brief discussion.

Meanwhile, with the help of the editorial committee of Commission IX, the Congregation itself took action on the question of active and passive voice in elections to the provincial congregation. The matter, however, could only be decided late in the Congregation because it was dependent on other questions about grades, about final incorporation into the Society, and about the General Congregation. After an indicative vote on February 24 and after a decision not to change the required proportion of professed fathers in the provincial congregation, the commission prepared a greatly shortened text for a definitive vote on February 28. At that vote, the Congregation decided that the not-yet-formed members of the Society would have the same active and passive voice in a single election to a provincial congregation as other members of the Society enjoyed. However it was conditioned as follows: active voice (the right to vote) would be given five years after entrance into the Society; passive voice (the right to be voted for) after eight years; the not-yet-formed members could not be more than five in number in the congregation of a province and not more than three in the congregation of a vice-province. In addition, there would have to be at least one non-formed Jesuit as a member.

The Congregation did not assent to the proposal that in certain provinces the non-formed could make up a voting group distinct from the rest of the province.

As to the other details of the *Formula of a Provincial Congregation,* not a few changes were introduced by the decisions of the definitors, approved on March 5, 1975, by the Congregation itself. One can easily see them in the text of Decree 14. It is useful in addition to mention some things which the Congregation did not wish to change, despite postulata on these matters. They deal especially with the following: the participation of Jesuits who are bishops, extension of the limits of the powers of a provincial congregation, a variety of proposals offered with respect to the election to a provincial congregation (for example, that the election be by age groups, that one indicate an order of preference among those voted for, that a specified "substantial" number of votes be needed for a person to be elected, that from the list of the eligibles for a provincial congregation be removed those who upon being asked declare that they would be impeded from participating in a provincial congregation, that the numerical results of the election to a provincial congregation be made public). Other items that the Congregation did not wish to act on were: the introduction of multiple preferential voting for the persons to be members of a provincial congregation and the suppression of the double vote which a provincial has.

To Father General was given the commission, with the deliberative vote of the members of the curia who have a right *ex officio* to be present at a general congregation, to revise the *Formula of the Provincial Congregation* in accord with the decisions taken. To him, also, were left the decisions, with the deliberative vote of the same persons, on other minor points contained in postulatum n. 947.

21.   Government, Especially Central Government

(From the Minutes, Acta 30–32, 44, 56)

By order of the 31st General Congregation, its forty-fourth decree which dealt with the assistants and counsellors of Father General was to be reviewed by the present Congregation. The question was given careful examination already during the preparatory phase of the Congregation (cf. *CPCG Documentum* 9 and *Documenta Complementaria,* n. 7). The topics most discussed were the following: the appropriateness or inappropriateness of the distinction between the general assistants *ad providentiam* and the general counsellors; the need for the general counsellors, to make up a true council for Father General in order to enter into discernment on more difficult and more serious matters; as a consequence, the usefulness of having more general counsellors. It was also suggested that each general counsellor have a special responsibility, either sectional or regional, and that some limit of time be set for the office of counsellor. The request was also made that all the general counsellors, or at least some of them, be elected by the General Congregation.

In the Congregation itself, Commission IX not only examined the earlier studies and the postulata, but also it heard almost all the assistants, counsellors, and major officials of the curia, as well as Father General himself. It soon turned out to be clear that before anything else there was need for a more structured coordination among the various counsellors and officials. It was likewise seen that the general assistants elected *ad providentiam* ought to be *ipso facto* general counsellors. The other main provisions of Decree 44 of the 31st General Congregation could remain in place. The commission also thought that it ought to recommend a very careful inquiry by experts after the Congregation into the whole organization of the curia.

Discussions took place in the Assistancy meetings and on January 31, 1975, in the Aula. Father General himself made known his views and then left the Aula so that matters which dealt with him rather personally might be treated with full freedom. Questions were asked of the assistants and counsellors of various kinds and of the officials, some of whom also gave their own opinions. After an indicative vote, a definitive report was prepared which also served as the document to be voted on. On February 10 a decree was passed which followed the general lines set out above, and it was promulgated on the same day (Decree 15).

Certain other requests came up in some postulata. For example: that at least in some parts of the Society regional superiors should take the place of regional assistants; that a permanent vicar-general should be established to help Father General in day by day business; that the length of office of the General should be limited; that the Secretary of the Society should be one of the general counsellors. On these neither the commission nor the Congregation thought it opportune to take action. However, the Congregation did deal with and voted affirmatively for a postulatum on reorganizing the international secretariats of the Society. It gave Father General the powers necessary to bring this about.

There were also postulata on provincial and local government, and Commission IX acted on them in two reports. The questions dealt mainly with general principles of good government in the Society today (participation, implementation, timely evaluation), with the choice and preparation of superiors, with the distinction and interrelationship between religious government and the government of apostolic works (or between the superior of a community and the director of an apostolate). On all of these the Congregation passed no specific decree, but with at least some of them it dealt either in the decree "On the mission of the Society today" or in "Union of minds and hearts." Others it thought more opportune to leave to the ordinary government of Father General.

22. Election of the General Assistants and Appointment of Some of the New Regional Assistants

(From the Minutes, Acta 50, 51, 52, 83)

Once the revised decree on the general assistants and the general counsellors had been passed and promulgated, the Congregation acceded to the request presented by the four general assistants then in office that during this Congregation a new election for general assistants take place, according to the norms of Decree 44, n. 4, of the 31st General Congregation. After four days of gathering and exchanging information, the Congregation proceeded to the election in three sessions and in separate ballots on January14 and 15, 1975. The following in alphabetical order were elected: Father Jean Calvez from the Province of Atlantic France, already General Assistant (fourth ballot); Father Parmananda Divarkar from the Province of Bombay (fourth ballot); Father Cecil McGarry from the Province of Ireland (third ballot); Father Vincent O'Keefe from the Province of New York, already General Assistant (second ballot).

After the election, Father General expressed special thanks to Father Paolo Dezza and Father Horacio de la Costa for the extraordinarily helpful collaboration they had given to the whole Society in their capacity of general assistants and to Father General in their capacity as general counsellors.

On the last day of the Congregation, Father General announced that after consulting the provincials and the other members of the Congregation from those respective regions he had appointed three new Regional Assistants: Father Petar Galauner (Croatia) for the Slavic Assistancy, Father Casimir Gnanadickam (Madurai) for the Indian Assistancy, and Father Gerald Sheahan (Missouri) for the American Assistancy.

23. Members to Whom Permission Was Granted to Leave the Congregation before Its Conclusion

(From the Minutes, Acta 27, 32, 33, 49, 64, 73, 82*)*

Because the work of the Congregation went on beyond the time which many had foreseen, it had, before its termination, to grant permission to thirty-one members to leave on account of urgent business. Thus, five Fathers took final leave in the last days of January: Noël Barré (Atlantic France), Edouard Boné (Southern Belgium), Heinrich Krauss (Upper Germany), Stefan Miecznikowski (Greater Poland), Ladislas Orsy (New York). Then, up to February 13, two others: Josip Ćurić (Croatia) and Peter Huizing (Netherlands). Between February 14 and 24, seven members: Miljenko Belić (Croatia), Guy Bourgeault (French Canada), Joseph Knecht (Patna), Francis Prucha (Wisconsin), Alberto Sily (Argentina), Roger Troisfontaines (Southern Belgium), and Edmond Vandermeersch (Paris). Later, up to March 1, ten members: Thomas Clancy (New Orleans), Thomas Clarke (New York), Roman Darowski (Lesser Poland), Julien Harvey (French Canada), Gediminas Kijauskas (Lithuania), Herbert Roth (East Germany), Antonius Soenarja (Indonesia), Alain de Survilliers (Atlantic France), Louis de Vaucelles (Paris), and Quirino Weber (Southern Brazil). Then, after March 2, another seven: Luk De Hovre (Northern Belgium), Enrique Fabbri (Argentina), Paolo Molinari (Turin), John O'Malley (Detroit), Pasupasu (Central Africa), William Ryan (Upper Canada), and John Sheets (Wisconsin).

At the beginning, the members of the Congregation numbered 236; on February 1, 232; on February 13, 229; on February 24, 222; on March 1, 212; on March 7, the last day, 205.

To some Fathers, the Congregation gave permission to be away for a few days. Permission to be absent insofar as it was necessary from one or another session could be gotten from Father General as presiding officer, without a vote of the Congregation, in accord with the usage already in force in the 31st General Congregation.

24. The End of the Congregation

(*From the Minutes,* Acta 41, 42, 66, 82, 83)

On February 7, at the proposal of the deputation for the screening of postulata, a final date, February 9, was set for the reception of new postulata. Then on February 25 the Congregation set March 8 as the date beyond which it would not continue in session.

On March 6, as the end of the work of the Congregation drew near, all the members took part in a penance service for the Holy Year and in a concelebrated Eucharist at the altar of the Chair of St. Peter in St. Peter's Basilica. At that liturgy, Father General gave a homily in which he summed up the spiritual journey of St. Ignatius from Manresa to Rome.

On the morning of March 7, Father General and the four general assistants left the plenary session to go to an audience with the Supreme Pontiff. At that audience, the Pontiff gave a farewell address which Father General read to the Congregation immediately upon his return to the plenary session.[22]

On this same day, late in the afternoon, once the business at hand was completed, the General Congregation, in almost the same way as the 31st General Congregation (Decree 56), gave to Father General certain special faculties. They included: to finish the legislative work of the Congregation insofar as it was necessary, to dissolve colleges and professed houses until the next General Congregation, to give approval to the minutes of the last sessions, as well as to make whatever corrections might be necessary and to do stylistic emendations in preparing the decrees of the Congregation for publication (Decree 16).

Father General then spoke for the last time to the members assembled, and the 32nd General Congregation adjourned. The members recited the hymn, *Te Deum.* Before they left the Aula, Father General invited in as many as could be present of those Fathers and Brothers who had helped the Congregation in every way; and in the name of of the Congregation, he thanked all for such great assistance. After supper that evening there was an informal recreation period during which many of the members of the Congregation from a variety of cultural backgrounds put on a display of their artistic and humorous talents.

The Congregation lasted 96 days. There were 83 plenary sessions in the Aula (14 in December, 18 in January, 40 in February, 11 in March). In 26 smaller meeting rooms there were many sessions of the council of the presidency, of the deputations on the state of the Society and for screening postulata, of other commissions, of 18 language groups (the membership of which, after an initial grouping, was regrouped once again) and of the 12 Assistancy groups.

---

[22] This address of the Holy Father can be found on pp. 394–395.

B

DECREES

OF THE

32nd GENERAL CONGREGATION

I

Introductory Decree

I

1/ 1. The past decade in the life of the Society has been an effort under the leadership of Father General to implement the decrees of the 31st General Congregation, which aimed at adapting our life to the directives of the Second Vatican Council. The success of this effort has been significant in our apostolic work as a community, in our prayer and our faith. This is clearly a gift of God's generosity, though not realized without a painful struggle for sincere renewal.

2/ 2. The 32nd General Congregation makes its own and confirms all of the declarations and dispositions of the 31st General Congregation unless they are explicitly changed in the present decrees. The documents of the preceding Congregation accurately and faithfully express the genuine spirit and tradition of the Society. Therefore, the whole Society is urged to reflect thoughtfully and sincerely upon those documents once again, and superiors are directed to see to their ever fuller implementation.

II

3/ 3. One reason for this directive is that the progress mentioned above has not been uniform. Some Jesuits have resisted renewal and have even criticized the 31st General Congregation publicly, as though it were somehow a departure from the genuine Ignatian spirit. Others, at times, have carried new orientations to excess in their impatience to accommodate themselves and their work to the needs of the world. Out of their desire to overcome a distorted emphasis upon the transcendence of the Christian religion—one which would divorce it from experience of the world—they have fallen into a type of "immanentism" which runs counter to the Gospel message.

4/ 4. These two exaggerations, each tending in an opposite direction, have threatened unity within the Society and have given non-Jesuits cause for concern and wonder. Some among them fear that the Society may have lost the forcefulness and precision with which it once exercised its priestly and apostolic mission of service to the faith. Others, when they read publications in which Jesuits unsympathetically criticize one another, their own Father General, the magisterium of the Church, and even the Holy Father, ask whether Jesuits have lost their traditional loyalty, obedience, and devotion to the Society and the Church. Sometimes they wonder, too, and not without reason, about the depth and sincerity of faith in those Jesuits who live independent lives, unmarked by poverty, and comfortably accommodated to the world.

5/ 5. Out of his deep affection and concern for the Society, the Holy Father brought these points to the attention of the Congregation in his allocution of December 3, 1974.[1] He took that occasion to request that the 32nd General Congregation preserve and reaffirm the Society as a priestly, apostolic, and religious body, bound to the Holy Father by a special vow regarding missions. It was to a balanced renewal of religious life and a discerning rededication to apostolic service that the Holy Father clearly wished to call us. In his various letters to the whole Society, Father General has expressed the same desire.

6/ 6. The whole Society ought to take the firm and paternal words of the Holy Father gratefully and humbly to heart. We sincerely acknowledge our failings and seek, with God's grace, a more radical renewal and closer unity, both among ourselves and with the Holy Father.

III.

7/ 7. Mindful that for the majority of Jesuits the years since the 31st General Congregation have been a time of grace and spiritual and apostolic growth, the 32nd General Congregation has formulated these decrees as an invitation to even greater progress in the way of the Lord. We offer them now to our fellow Jesuits in a spirit of humility and hope—not forgetful of past shortcomings, but, with God's help, looking confidently to the future.

8/ 8. The following documents treat of challenges and opportunities arising out of our life and work; of our identity as companions of Jesus in today's world; of the Society's apostolic mission as the service of faith and the promotion of justice; of prayer and obedience, and of discernment of spirits in common, nourished by and further strengthening our union together; of a more authentic poverty and of the formation of young Jesuits.

9/ 9. These documents are commended to personal reading and community dialog in a spirit of prayer and discernment. They look far beyond words and verbal analysis. They are offered as a stimulus for conversion of heart and apostolic renewal.

10/ 10. These decrees, then, are meant for practical implementation. Only the cooperation of all Jesuits under the leadership of their superiors can achieve this goal.

---

[1] See pp. 379–390 below.

I

THE SOCIETY'S RESPONSE TO THE CHALLENGES OF OUR AGE

DECREE 2

Jesuits Today

*A response of the 32nd General Congregation to requests for a
description of Jesuit identity in our time.*

11/ 1.   What is it to be a Jesuit? It is to know that one is a sinner, yet called to
be a companion of Jesus as Ignatius was: Ignatius, who begged the Blessed Virgin
to "place him with her Son,"[1] and who then saw the Father himself ask Jesus, carrying his Cross, to take this pilgrim into his company.[2]

12/ 2.   What is it to be a companion of Jesus today? It is to engage, under
the standard of the Cross, in the crucial struggle of our time: the struggle for faith
and that struggle for justice which it includes.

13/ 3.   The Society of Jesus, gathered together in its 32nd General Congregation, considering the end for which it was founded, namely, the greater glory of
God and the service of men,[3] acknowledging with repentance its own failures in
keeping faith and upholding justice, and asking itself before Christ crucified what
it has done for him, what it is doing for him, and what it is going to do for him,[4]
chooses participation in this struggle as the focus that identifies in our time what
Jesuits are and do.[5]

A. Whence This Decision

14/ 4.   We arrive at this decisive choice from several different points of departure. The postulata received from the provinces, the panorama of the state of
the Society presented at the Congregation, and the instructions given us by the
Pope, all direct our attention to the vast expanse and circuit of this globe and the
great multitude and diversity of peoples therein.[6]

15/ 5.   Two-thirds of mankind have not yet had God's salvation in Jesus
Christ proclaimed to them in a manner that wins belief, while in societies an-

---

[1] Ignatius Loyola, MI, **Fontes Narrativi** I, "Autobiografia," n. 96.

[2] Loyola, "Autobiografia," II, 133.

[3] *FI* [3] (1); *Cons.* 136, 156, 307, 603, 813.

[4] *SpEx,* 53.

[5] GG 32, "Our Mission Today."

[6] *SpEx,* 103.

ciently Christian a dominant secularism is closing men's minds and hearts to the divine dimensions of all reality, blinding them to the fact that while all things on the face of the earth are, indeed, created for man's sake, it is only that he might attain to the end for which he himself was created: the praise, reverence, and service of God.[7]

16/ 6. Ignorance of the Gospel on the part of some, and rejection of it by others, are intimately related to the many grave injustices prevalent in the world today. Yet it is in the light of the Gospel that men will most clearly see that injustice springs from sin, personal and collective, and that it is made all the more oppressive by being built into economic, social, political, and cultural institutions of worldwide scope and overwhelming power.[8]

17/ 7. Conversely, the prevalence of injustice in a world where the very survival of the human race depends on men caring for and sharing with one another is one of the principal obstacles to belief: belief in a God who is justice because he is love.

18/ 8. Thus, the way to faith and the way to justice are inseparable ways. It is up this undivided road, this steep road, that the pilgrim Church must travel and toil. Faith and justice are undivided in the Gospel which teaches that "faith makes its power felt through love."[9] They cannot therefore be divided in our purpose, our action, our life.[10]

19/ 9. Moreover, the service of faith and the promotion of justice cannot be for us simply one ministry among others. It must be the integrating factor of all our ministries; and not only of our ministries but of our inner life as individuals, as communities, and as a worldwide brotherhood. This is what our Congregation means by a decisive choice. It is the choice that underlies and determines all the other choices embodied in its declarations and directives.

B. Original Inspiration of the Society

20 10. We are confirmed in this basic choice by being led to it from another point of departure, namely, the original inspiration of the Society as set forth in the *Formula of the Institute* and the Constitutions.

21/ 11. Our Society was founded principally for the defense and propagation of the faith and for the rendering of any service in the Church that may be for the

---

[7] *SpEx,* 23.

[8] GS, 10, 13, 22, 23, 37; Pope Paul VI, "Populorum progressio," 21, 56 ff.; "Octogesima adveniens," 45.

[9] Gal. 5.6.

[10] Synod of Bishops (1971), "Justice in the World," Introduction.

glory of God and the common good.[11] In fact, the grace of Christ that enables and impels us to seek "the salvation and perfection of souls"—or what might be called, in contemporary terms, the total and integral liberation of man, leading to participation in the life of God himself—is the same grace by which we are enabled and impelled to seek "our own salvation and perfection."[12]

22/ 12. Not only does the insight of Ignatius justify our basic choice, it specifies it. It enables us to determine what must be our specifically Jesuit contribution to the defense and propagation of the faith and the promotion of justice in charity.

23/ 13. At the very center of that insight is the sense of mission. No sooner was our companionship born than it placed itself at the disposal of "the Roman Pontiff, Christ's Vicar on earth,"[13] to be sent wherever there is hope of God's greater glory and the service of men.

24/ 14. A Jesuit, therefore, is essentially a man on a mission: a mission which he receives immediately from the Holy Father and from his own religious superiors, but ultimately from Christ himself, the one sent by the Father.[14] It is by being sent that the Jesuit becomes a companion of Jesus.

25/ 15. Moreover, it is in companionship that the Jesuit fulfills his mission. He belongs to a community of friends in the Lord who, like him, have asked to be received under the standard of Christ the King.[15]

C. Fulfillment in Companionship

26/ 16. This community is the entire body of the Society itself, no matter how widely dispersed over the face of the earth. The particular local community to which he may belong at any given moment is, for him, simply a concrete—if, here and now, a privileged—expression of this worldwide brotherhood.

27/ 17. The local Jesuit community is thus an apostolic community, not inward but outward looking, the focus of its concern being the service it is called upon to give men. It is contemplative but not monastic, for it is a communitas *ad dispersionem.* It is a community of men ready to go wherever they are sent.

28/ 18. A *communitas ad dispersionem,* but also a *koinonia,* a sharing of goods and life, with the Eucharist at its center: the sacrifice and sacrament of the Deed of Jesus, who loved his own to the end.[16] And each member of every Jesuit com-

---

[11] *FI,* [3] (1)

[12] *Cons,* General Examen [3] -2.

[13] *FI,* [3] (1)

[14] John 17.18.

[15] *SpEx,* 147.

[16] John 13.1.

munity is ever mindful of what St. Ignatius says about love, that it consists in sharing what one has, what one is, with those one loves.[17] When we speak of having all things in common, that is what we mean.

29/ 19. The Jesuit community is also a community of discernment. The missions on which Jesuits are sent, whether corporately or individually, do not exempt us from the need of discerning together in what manner and by what means such missions are to be accomplished. That is why we open our minds and hearts to our superiors and our superiors, in turn, take part in the discernment of our communities, always on the shared understanding that final decisions belong to those who have the burden of authority.

D. Distinguishing Mark of the Society

30/ 20. Not only our community life, but our religious vows are apostolic. If we commit ourselves until death to the evangelical counsels of poverty, chastity, and obedience, it is that we may be totally united to Christ and share his own freedom to be at the service of all who need us. In binding us, the vows set us free:

—free, by our vow of poverty, to share the life of the poor and to use whatever resources we may have not for our own security and comfort, but for service;

—free, by our vow of chastity, to be men for others, in friendship and communion with all, but especially with those who share our mission of service;

—free, by our vow of obedience, to respond to the call of Christ as made known to us by him whom the Spirit has placed over the Church, and to follow the lead of our superiors, especially our Father General, who has all authority over us *ad aedificationem.*

31/ 21. In our Society, the call to the apostolate is one, though shared in manifold ways. We are many members, but one body, each member contributing what in him lies to the common task of continuing Christ's saving work in the world, which is to reconcile men to God, and men among themselves, so that by the gift of his love and grace they may build a peace based on justice.

32/ 22. Because this is its common task, the Society of Jesus is, in its entirety, a sacerdotal society. But it is sacerdotal not merely in the sense of the priesthood of all the faithful. For the Society began as, and continues to be, a band of ordained ministers of the Gospel which comprises in the self-same company both those willing to share the presbyteral function of being coadjutors of the episcopal order and those willing to give themselves to those aspects of our apostolic mission for which priestly orders are not required.

---

[17] *SpEx,* 231.

33/ 23. Moreover, following Ignatius, we have asked Christ our Lord to let us render this service in a manner that gives us a personality of our own. We have chosen to give it in the form of a consecrated life according to the evangelical counsels, and we have placed ourselves at the service not only of the local churches but of the universal Church, by a special vow of obedience to him who presides over the universal Church, namely, the Successor of Peter.

34/ 24. This, then, is the distinguishing mark of our Society: it is a companionship that is, at one and the same time, "religious, apostolic, sacerdotal, and bound to the Roman Pontiff by a special bond of love and service."[18]

E. What Our Mission Demands of Us

35/ 25. Because the missions on which the Holy Father and our superiors are likely to send us will demand well trained minds and dedicated spirits, we test the vocation of those whom we admit to our ranks in various ways over an extended period of time, and we try to give them, to the best of our ability, a spiritual and intellectual formation more than ordinarily exacting. But even during their period of training these young men are already our companions, in virtue of the perpetual vows they take after the noviceship.

36/ 26. Coming from many different countries, cultures, and social backgrounds, but banded together in this way, we try to focus all our efforts on the common task of radiating faith and witnessing to justice. We are deeply conscious of how often and how grievously we ourselves have sinned against the Gospel; yet it remains our ambition to proclaim it worthily: that is, in love, in poverty, and in humility.

37/ 27. In *love:* a personal love for the Person of Jesus Christ, for an ever more inward knowledge of whom we daily ask, that we may the better love him and follow him;[19] Jesus, whom we seek, as St. Ignatius sought, to experience; Jesus, Son of God, sent to serve, sent to set free, put to death, and risen from the dead. This love is the deepest wellspring of our action and our life. It was this personal love that engendered in Ignatius that divine discontent which kept urging him to the *magis*—the ever more and more giving—the ever greater glory of God.

38/ 28. *In poverty:* relying more on God's providence than on human resources; safeguarding the freedom of the apostle by detachment from avarice and the bondage imposed by it; following in the footsteps of Christ, who preached good news to the poor by being poor himself.

---

[18] Pope Paul VI, "Address to the Members of the 32nd General Congregation," December 3, 1974, on pp. 379–390 below.

[19] *SpEx,* 104.

39/ 29. *In humility:* realizing that there are many enterprises of great worth and moment in the Church and in the world which we, as priests and religious inspired by one particular charism, are not in a position to undertake. And even in those enterprises which we can and should undertake, we realize that we must be willing to work with others: with Christians, men of other religious faiths, and all men of good will; willing to play a subordinate, supporting, anonymous role; and willing to learn how to serve from those we seek to serve.

40/ 30. This availability for the meanest tasks, or at least the desire to be thus available, is part of the identity of the Jesuit. When he offers to distinguish himself in the service of the Eternal King,[20] when he asks to be received under his standard,[21] when he glories with Ignatius in being placed by the Father "with the Son,"[22] he does so not in any spirit of prideful privilege, but in the spirit of him who "emptied himself to assume the condition of a slave, even to accepting death, death on a cross."[23]

F. Conclusion: A Jesuit Today

41/ 31/ Thus, whether we consider the needs and aspirations of the men of our time, or reflect on the particular charism that founded our Society, or seek to learn what Jesus has in his heart for each and all of us, we are led to the identical conclusion that today the Jesuit is a man whose mission is to dedicate himself entirely to the service of faith and the promotion of justice, in a communion of life and work and sacrifice with the companions who have rallied round the same standard of the Cross and in fidelity to the Vicar of Christ, for the building up of a world at once more human and more divine.

42/ 32. Deeply conscious of our utter unworthiness for so great a mission, relying only on God's love and grace, we offer together the prayer of Ignatius:[24]

> Take, O Lord, and receive
> all my liberty,
> my memory, my understanding, and my entire will.
>
> Whatever I have or hold,
> You have given to me;

---

[20] *SpEx,* 97.

[21] *SpEx,* 147.

[22] Ignatius Loyola, MI, *Fontes Narrativi* I, "Diario espiritual," n. 67.

[23] Phil. 2. 7-8.

[24] *SpEx,* 234.

> I restore it all to You
> and surrender it wholly
> to be governed by your will.
>
> Give me only your love and your grace,
> and I am rich enough
> and ask for nothing more.

DECREE 3

FIDELITY OF THE SOCIETY TO THE MAGISTERIUM AND THE SUPREME PONTIFF

43/   1.   In considering the reverence and fidelity which all Jesuits should have toward the magisterium of the Church and in a special way toward the Supreme Pontiff, the 32nd General Congregation makes the following declaration:

44/   2.   The Congregation acknowledges the obligation of this reverence and fidelity as well as our proper responsibility to the Church.

45/   3.   Mindful of the long and venerable tradition in the Society of serving the Church by explaining, propagating, and defending the Faith, the Congregation supports our Jesuits who are working in scholarly research, in publishing, or in other forms of the apostolate, and urges all of them to continue to remain faithful to this tradition. At the same time, the Congregation regrets particular failings in this matter on the part of some members of the Society in recent years. This behavior can undermine our apostolic effectiveness and firm commitment to serving the Church.

46/   4.   The Congregation recommends to all superiors that they apply the norms of the Church and the Society in a firm and fatherly way. Freedom should be intelligently encouraged, but care should be taken to prevent and correct the failings which weaken fidelity to the magisterium and service to the faith and the Church, virtues in which the Society has always striven to be outstanding.

DECREE 4

Our Mission Today: The Service of Faith and the Promotion of Justice

Introduction and Summary

47/ 1.   To the many requests received from all parts of the Society for clear decisions and definite guidelines concerning our mission today, the 32nd General Congregation responds as follows.

48/ 2.   The mission of the Society of Jesus today is the service of faith, of which the promotion of justice is an absolute requirement. For reconciliation with God demands the reconciliation of people with one another.

49/ 3.   In one form or another, this has always been the mission of the Society;[1] but it gains new meaning and urgency in the light of the needs and aspirations of the men and women of our time, and it is in that light that we examine it anew. We are confronted today, in fact, by a whole series of new challenges.

50/ 4.   There is a new challenge to our apostolic mission in a fact without precedent in the history of mankind: today, more than two billion human beings have no knowledge of God the Father and His Son, Jesus Christ, whom He has sent,[2] yet feel an increasing hunger for the God they already adore in the depths of their hearts without knowing Him explicitly.

51/ 5.   There is a new challenge to our apostolic mission in that many of our contemporaries, dazzled and even dominated by the achievements of the human mind, forgetting or rejecting the mystery of man's ultimate meaning, have thus lost the sense of God.

52/ 6.   There is a new challenge to our apostolic mission in a world increasingly interdependent but, for all that, divided by injustice: injustice not only personal but institutionalized: built into economic, social, and political structures that dominate the life of nations and the international community.

53/ 7.   Our response to these new challenges will be unavailing unless it is total, corporate, rooted in faith and experience, and multiform.

---

[1] See *FI,* especially [3] (1). The *Formula* was approved by Popes Paul III and Julius III.

[2] See *SpEx.* 102.

—*total:* While relying on prayer, and acting on the conviction that God alone can change the human heart, we must throw into this enterprise all that we are and have, our whole persons, our communities, institutions, ministries, resources.

54/ —*corporate:* Each one of us must contribute to the total mission according to his talents and functions which, in collaboration with the efforts of others, give life to the whole body. This collaborative mission is exercised under the leadership of Peter's Successor who presides over the universal Church and over all those whom the Spirit of God has appointed Pastors over the churches.[3]

55/ —*rooted in faith and experience:* It is from faith and experience combined that we will learn how to respond most appropriately to new needs arising from new situations.

56/ —*multiform:* Since these situations are different in different parts of the world, we must cultivate a great adaptability and flexibility within the single, steady aim of the service of faith and the promotion of justice.

57/ 8. While offering new challenges to our apostolic mission, the modern world provides new tools as well: new and more effective ways of understanding man, nature, and society; of communicating thought, image, and feeling; of organizing action. These we must learn to use in the service of evangelization and human development.

58/ 9. Consequently we must undertake a thoroughgoing reassessment of our traditional apostolic methods, attitudes and institutions with a view to adapting them to the new needs of the times and to a world in process of rapid change.

59/ 10. All this demands that we practice discernment, that spiritual discernment which St. Ignatius teaches us in the Exercises. Moreover discernment will yield a deeper grasp of the movements, aspirations, and struggles in the hearts of our contemporaries, as well as those in the heart of mankind itself.

60/ 11. In short, our mission today is to preach Jesus Christ and to make Him known in such a way that all men and women are able to recognize Him whose delight, from the beginning, has been to be with the sons of men and to take an active part in their history.[4]

61/ 12. In carrying out this mission, we should be convinced, today more than ever, that "the means which unite the human instrument with God and so dispose it that it may be wielded dexterously by His divine hand are more effective than those which equip it in relation to men."[5]

---

[3] See LG, 22.

[4] See Prov. 8. 22–31; Col. 1. 15–20.

[5] *Cons.* [13].

A.

Our Mission Yesterday and Today

The Charism of the Society

62/ 13. The mission we are called to share is the mission of the Church itself, to make known to men and women the love of God our Father, a love whose promise is eternal life. It is from the loving regard of God upon the world that the mission of Jesus takes its rise, Jesus who was sent "not to be served but to serve, and to give His life as a ransom for many."[6] The mission of Christ, in turn, gives rise to the mission shared by all Christians as members of the Church sent to bring all men and women the Good News of their salvation and that "they may have life and have it to the full."[7]

63/ 14. St. Ignatius and his first companions, in the spiritual experience of the Exercises, were moved to a searching consideration of the world of their own time in order to discover its needs. They contemplated "how the Three Divine Persons look down upon the whole expanse or circuit of all the earth, filled with human beings" and decide "that the Second Person should become man to save the human race." Then they turned their eyes to where God's gaze was fixed, and saw for themselves the men and women of their time, one after another, "with such great diversity in dress and in manners of acting. Some are white, some black; some at peace, and some at war; some weeping, some laughing; some well, some sick; some coming into the world, some dying, etc."[8] That was how they learned to respond to the call of Christ and to work for the establishment of His Kingdom."[9]

64/ 15. United in a single vision of faith, strong in a common hope and rooted in the same love of Christ whose companions they wished to be, Ignatius and his first band of apostles believed that the service they could give to the people of their time would be more effective if they were more closely bound to one another as members of a single body, at once religious, apostolic, and priestly, and united to the Successor of Peter by a special bond of love and service reflecting their total availability for mission in the universal Church.

65/ 16. It is in this light that we are asked to renew our dedication to the properly apostolic dimension of our religious life. Our consecration to God is really a prophetic rejection of those idols which the world is always tempted to adore, wealth, pleasure, prestige, power. Hence our poverty, chastity, and obedi-

---

[6] Matt. 20:28.

[7] John 10.10. See Matt. 9.36, 10.1–42; John 6.

[8] *SpEx,* 102, 106 (Contemplation on the Incarnation).

[9] *SpEx,* 91–100 (Contemplation of the "Kingdom").

ence ought visibly to bear witness to this. Despite the inadequacy of any attempt to anticipate the Kingdom which is to come, our vows ought to show how by God's grace there can be, as the Gospel proclaims, a community among human beings which is based on sharing rather than on greed; on willing openness to all persons rather than on seeking after the privileges of caste or class or race; on service rather than on domination and exploitation. The men and women of our time need a hope which is eschatological, but they also need to have some signs that its realization has already begun.

66/ 17. Finally, the Apostolic Letters of Paul III (1540) and Julius III (1550) recognize that the Society of Jesus was founded "chiefly for this purpose: to strive especially for the defense and propagation of the faith, and for the progress of souls in Christian life and doctrine, by means of public preaching, lectures, and any other ministrations whatsoever of the word of God, and further, by means of the Spiritual Exercises, the education of children and unlettered persons in Christianity, and the spiritual consolation of Christ's faithful through hearing confessions and administering the other sacraments," as well as "in reconciling the estranged, in holily assisting and serving those who are found in prisons and hospitals, and indeed in performing any other works of charity, according to what will seem expedient for the glory of God and the common good."[10] This primordial statement remains for us a normative one.

67/ 18. The mission of the Society today is the priestly service of the faith, an apostolate whose aim is to help people become more open toward God and more willing to live according to the demands of the Gospel. The Gospel demands a life freed from egoism and self-seeking, from all attempts to seek one's own advantage and from every form of exploitation of one's neighbor. It demands a life in which the justice of the Gospel shines out in a willingness not only to recognize and respect the rights of all, especially the poor and the powerless, but also to work actively to secure those rights. It demands an openness and generosity to anyone in need, even a stranger or an enemy. It demands towards those who have injured us, pardon; toward those with whom we are at odds, a spirit of reconciliation. We do not acquire this attitude of mind by our own efforts alone. It is the fruit of the Spirit who transforms our hearts and fills them with the power of God's mercy, that mercy whereby he most fully shows forth His justice by drawing us, unjust though we are, to His friendship.[11] It is by this that we know that the promotion of justice is an integral part of the priestly service of the faith.

---

[10] *FI*, [3] (1), approved by Julius III.

[11] See Rom. 5:89.

68/ 19. In his address of December 3, 1974,[12] Pope Paul VI confirmed "as a modern expression of your vow of obedience to the Pope" that we offer resistance to the many forms of contemporary atheism. This was the mission he entrusted to us at the time of the 31st General Congregation, and in recalling it he commended the way in which the Society down the years has been present at the heart of ideological battles and social conflicts, wherever the crying needs of mankind encountered the perennial message of the Gospel. Thus if we wish to continue to be faithful to this special character of our vocation and to the mission we have received from the Pope, we must "contemplate" our world as Ignatius did his, that we may hear anew the call of Christ dying and rising in the anguish and aspirations of men and women.

69/ 20. There are millions of men and women in our world, specific people with names and faces, who are suffering from poverty and hunger, from the unjust distribution of wealth and resources and from the consequences of racial, social, and political discrimination. Not only the quality of life but human life itself is under constant threat. It is becoming more and more clear that despite the opportunities offered by an ever more serviceable technology, we are simply not willing to pay the price of a more just and more humane society.[13]

70/ 21. At the same time, people today are somehow aware that their problems are not just social and technological, but personal and spiritual. They have a feeling that what is at stake here is the very meaning of man: his future and his destiny. People are hungry: hungry not just for bread, but for the Word of God. (Deut. 8.3; Mt. 4.4). For this reason the Gospel should be preached with a fresh vigor, for it is in a position once again to make itself heard. At first sight God seems to have no place in public life, nor even in private awareness. Yet everywhere, if we only knew how to look, we can see that people are groping towards an experience of Christ and waiting in hope for His Kingdom of love, of justice, and of peace.

71/ 22. Of these expectations and converging desires the last two Synods of Bishops have reminded us in their reflections on *Justice in the World* and *Evangelization in the Modern World*. They point to concrete forms which our witness and our mission must take today.

72/ 23. The expectations of our contemporaries—and their problems—are ours as well. We ourselves share in the blindness and injustice of our age. We our-

---

[12] Pope Paul VI, "Address to the Members of the 32nd General Congregation," December 3, 1974, pp. 519–536.

[13] We find a Gospel echo, a truly apostolic echo of the anguish and questioning of our times, in *Gaudium et Spes, Mater et Magistra, Pacem in Terris, Populorum Progressio, Octogesima Adveniens.* In these documents of the church's magisterium the needs of our world touch us and break in upon us both on the level of our personal lives and of our apostolic service.

selves stand in need of being evangelized. We ourselves need to know how to meet Christ as He works in the world through the power of His Spirit. And it is to this world, our world, that we are sent. Its needs and aspirations are an appeal to the Gospel which it is our mission to proclaim.

B.

The Challenges We Face

New Demands, New Hopes

73/ 24. The first thing that must be said about the world which it is our mission to evangelize is this: everywhere, but in very different situations, we have to preach Jesus Christ to men and women who have never really heard of Him, or who do not yet know of Him sufficiently.

a. In what were once called "mission lands" our predecessors endeavored by their preaching of the Gospel to set up and foster new Christian communities. This task of direct evangelization by the preaching of Jesus Christ remains essential today, and must be continued, since never before have there been so many people who have never heard the Word of Christ the Savior. At the same time dialog with the believers of other religions is becoming for us an ever more important apostolate.

b. In the traditionally Christian countries, the works we established, the movements we fostered, the institutions—retreat houses, schools, universities—we set up, are still necessary for the service of faith. But there are many in these countries who can no longer be reached by the ministries exercised through these works and institutions. The so-called "Christian" countries have themselves become "mission lands."

74/ 25. The second decisive factor for our preaching of Jesus Christ and his Gospel is this: the new opportunities—and problems—disclosed in our time by the discoveries of technology and the human sciences. They have introduced a relativism, often of a very radical kind, into the picture of man and the world to which we were accustomed, with the result that traditional perspectives have altered almost beyond recognition. Changes of this kind in the mind-sets and structures of society inevitably produce strong repercussions in our lives as individuals and as members of society. As a result, there has been gradual erosion of traditional values, and gradual diminution of reliance on the power of traditional symbols. Simultaneously, new aspirations arise which seek to express themselves in the planning and implementation of practical programs.

75/ 26. The secularization of man and the world takes different forms in different groups, classes, ages and parts of the world, and in all its forms offers challenges to the preaching of the Gospel to which there is no ready-made answer.

a. On the one hand, certain false images of God which prop up and give an aura of legitimacy to unjust social structures are no longer acceptable. Neither can we admit those more ambiguous images of God which appear to release man from his inalienable responsibilities. We feel this just as much as our contemporaries do; even more, perhaps, given our commitment to proclaim the God who has revealed himself in Christ. For our own sake, just as much as for the sake of our contemporaries, we must find a new language, a new set of symbols, that will enable us to leave our fallen idols behind us and rediscover the true God: the God who, in Jesus Christ, chose to share our human pilgrimage and make our human destiny irrevocably his own. To live our lives "in memory of Him" requires of us this creative effort of faith.

b. On the other hand, part of the framework within which we have preached the Gospel is now perceived as being inextricably linked to an unacceptable social order, and for that reason is being called into question. Our apostolic institutions, along with many of those of the Church herself, are involved in the same crisis that social institutions in general are presently undergoing. Here again is an experience we share with our contemporaries, and in a particularly painful way. The relevance of our work as religious, priests and apostles is often enough not evident to the men and women around us. Not only that; despite the firmness of our faith and our convictions the relevance of what we do may not be clear, sometimes, even to ourselves. This unsettles us, and in our insecurity we tend to respond to questioning with silence and to shy away from confrontation. Yet there are signs of a contemporary religious revival which should encourage us to reaffirm our commitment with courage, and not only to welcome but to seek new opportunities for evangelization.

76/ 27. Finally, a third characteristic of our world particularly significant to our mission of evangelization is this: It is now within human power to make the world more just—but we do not really want to. Our new mastery over nature and man himself is used, often enough, to exploit individuals, groups, and peoples rather than to distribute the resources of the planet more equitably. It has led, it is leading, to division rather than union, to alienation rather than communication, to oppression and domination rather than to a greater respect for the rights of individuals or of groups, and a more real brotherhood among men. We can no longer pretend that the inequalities and injustices of our world must be borne as part of the inevitable order of things. It is now quite apparent that they are the result of what man himself, man in his selfishness, has done. Hence there can be no promotion of justice in the full and Christian sense unless we also preach Jesus

Christ and the mystery of reconciliation He brings. It is Christ who, in the last analysis, opens the way to the complete and definitive liberation of mankind for which we long from the bottom of our hearts. Conversely, it will not be possible to bring Christ to people or to proclaim His Gospel effectively unless a firm decision is taken to devote ourselves to the promotion of justice.

77/ 28. From all over the world where Jesuits are working, very similar and very insistent requests have been made that, by a clear decision on the part of the General Congregation, the Society should commit itself to work for the promotion of justice. Our apostolate today urgently requires that we take this decision. As apostles we are bearers of the Christian message. And at the heart of the Christian message is God revealing Himself in Christ as the Father of us all whom through the Spirit He calls to conversion. In its integrity, then, conversion means accepting that we are at one and the same time children of the Father and brothers and sisters of each other. There is no genuine conversion to the love of God without conversion to the love of neighbor and, therefore, to the demands of justice. Hence, fidelity to our apostolic mission requires that we propose the whole of Christian salvation and lead others to embrace it. Christian salvation consists in an undivided love of the Father and of the neighbor and of justice. Since evangelization is proclamation of that faith which is made operative in love of others,[14] the promotion of justice is indispensable to it.

78/ 29. What is at stake here is the fruitfulness of all our apostolic endeavors, and notably of any coherent attempt to combat atheism. The injustice that racks our world in so many forms is, in fact, a denial of God in practice, for it denies the dignity of the human person, the image of God, the brother or sister of Christ.[15] The cult of money, progress, prestige and power has as its fruit the sin of institutionalized injustice condemned by the Synod of 1971, and it leads to the enslavement not only of the oppressed, but of the oppressor as well—and to death.

79/ 30. At a time when so many people are sparing no effort to put the world to rights without reference to God, our endeavor should be to show as clearly as we can that our Christian hope is not a dull opiate, but a firm and realistic commitment to make our world other than it is, to make it the visible sign of another world, the sign—and pledge—of "a new heaven and a new earth."[16] The last Synod vigorously recalled this for us: "The Gospel entrusted to us is the good news of salvation for man and the whole of society, which must begin here and now to manifest itself on earth even if mankind's liberation in all its fullness will

---

[14] See Gal. 5.6; Eph. 4.15.

[15] On the dignity of man, image of God and brother of Christ see: LG, 42; GS, 22, 24, 29, 38, 93; *Nuntium Councilii Vaticani II ad omnes homines,* December 20, 1962; Declarations of the Synods of Bishops of 1971, 1974; Addresses of Pope Paul VI.

[16] Apoc. 21.1.

be achieved only beyond the frontiers of this life."[17] The promotion of justice is, therefore, an integral part of evangelization.

80/ 31. We are witnesses of a Gospel which links the love of God to the service of man, and that inseparably. In a world where the power of economic, social, and political structures is now appreciated and the mechanisms and laws governing them are now understood, service according to the Gospel cannot dispense with a carefully planned effort to exert influence on those structures.

81/ 32. We must bear in mind, however, that our efforts to promote justice and human freedom on the social and structural level, necessary though they are, are not sufficient of themselves. Injustice must be attacked at its roots which are in the human heart by transforming those attitudes and habits which beget injustice and foster the structures of oppression.

82/ 33. Finally, if the promotion of justice is to attain its ultimate end, it should be carried out in such a way as to bring men and women to desire and to welcome the eschatological freedom and salvation offered to us by God in Christ. The methods we employ and the activities we undertake should express the spirit of the Beatitudes and bring people to a real reconciliation. In this way our commitment to justice will simultaneously show forth the spirit and the power of God. It will respond to humanity's deepest yearnings, not just for bread and freedom, but for God and His friendship—a longing to be sons and daughters in His sight.

83/ 34. The initiatives required to respond to the challenges of our world thoroughly surpass our capabilities. Nonetheless we must set ourselves to the task with all the resourcefulness we have. By God's grace, a new apostolic awareness does seem to be taking shape gradually in the Society as a whole. There is evidence of a widespread desire, and often of a whole-hearted effort, to renew and adapt our traditional apostolates and to embark on new ones. The guidelines that follow are meant to confirm or focus decisions and to urge us to more definite programs of action.

84/ 35. *Our involvement with the world.* Too often we are insulated from any real contact with unbelief and with the hard, everyday consequences of injustice and oppression. As a result we run the risk of not being able to hear the cry for the Gospel as it is addressed to us by the men and women of our time. A deeper involvement with others in the world will therefore be a decisive test of our faith, of our hope, and of our apostolic charity. Are we ready, with discernment and with reliance on a community which is alive and apostolic, to bear witness to the Gospel in the painful situations where our faith and our hope are tested by unbelief and injustice? Are we ready to give ourselves to the demanding and serious study

---

[17] Final Declaration of the Synod of Bishops of 1974, n. 12; see also the address of Pope Paul VI at the closing session of the Synod.

of theology, philosophy, and the human sciences, which are ever more necessary if we are to understand and try to resolve the problems of the world? To be involved in the world in this way is essential if we are to share our faith and our hope, and thus preach a Gospel that will respond to the needs and aspirations of our contemporaries.

85/   36. New forms of apostolic involvement, adapted to different places, have already been developed. The success of these initiatives, whatever form they take, requires of us a solid formation, intense solidarity in community, and a vivid awareness of our identity. Wherever we serve we must be attentive to "inculturation"; that is, we must take pains to adapt our preaching of the Gospel to the culture of the place so that men and women may receive Christ according to the distinctive character of each country, class, or group and environment.

86/   37. *Our collaboration with others.* The involvement we desire will be apostolic to the extent that it leads us to a closer collaboration with other members of the local churches, Christians of other denominations, believers of other religions, and all who hunger and thirst after justice; in short, with all who strive to make a world fit for men and women to live in, a world where brotherhood opens the way for the recognition and acceptance of Christ our Brother and God our Father. Ecumenism will then become not just a particular ministry but an attitude of mind and a way of life. Today it is essential for the preaching and acceptance of the Gospel that this spirit of ecumenism embrace the whole of mankind, taking into account the cultural differences and the traditional spiritual values and hopes of all groups and peoples.

87/   38. *The wellspring of our apostolate.* We are also led back again to our experience of the Spiritual Exercises. In them we are able continually to renew our faith and apostolic hope by experiencing again the love of God in Christ Jesus. We strengthen our commitment to be companions of Jesus in His mission, to labor like Him in solidarity with the poor and with Him for the establishment of the Kingdom. This same spiritual experience will teach us how to maintain the objectivity needed for a continuing review of our commitments. Thereby we gradually make our own that apostolic pedagogy of St. Ignatius which should characterize our every action.

C.

Apostolic Decisions for Today

People and Structures

88/   39. For the greater glory of God and salvation of men, Ignatius desired that his companions go wherever there was hope of the more universal good; go to those who have been abandoned; go to those who are in greatest need. But where is the greatest need today? Where are we to locate this hope for the more universal good?

89/ 40. It is becoming more and more evident that the structures of society are among the principal formative influences in our world, shaping people's ideas and feelings, shaping their most intimate desires and aspirations; in a word, shaping mankind itself. The struggle to transform these structures in the interest of the spiritual and material liberation of fellow human beings is intimately connected to the work of evangelization. This is not to say, of course, that we can ever afford to neglect the direct apostolate to individuals, to those who are the victims of the injustice of social structures as well as to those who bear some responsibility or influence over them.

90/ 41. From this point of view of desire for the more universal good is perfectly compatible with the determination to serve the most afflicted for the sake of the Gospel. Our preaching will be heard to the extent that witness accompanies it, the witness of commitment to the promotion of justice as an anticipation of the Kingdom which is to come.

Social Involvement

91/ 42. Our faith in Christ Jesus and our mission to proclaim the Gospel demand of us a commitment to promote justice and to enter into solidarity with the voiceless and the powerless. This commitment will move us seriously to verse ourselves in the complex problems which they face in their lives, then to identify and assume our own responsibilities to society.

92/ 43. Our Jesuit communities have to help each of us overcome the reluctance, fear, and apathy which block us from truly comprehending the social, economic, and political problems which exist in our city or region or country, as well as on the international scene. Becoming really aware of and understanding these problems will help us see how to preach the Gospel better and how to work better with others in our own particular way without seeking to duplicate or compete with their strengths in the struggle to promote justice.

93/ 44. We cannot be excused from making the most rigorous possible political and social analysis of our situation. This will require the utilization of the various sciences, sacred and profane, and of the various disciplines, speculative and practical, and all of this demands intense and specialized studies. Nothing should excuse us, either, from undertaking a searching discernment into our situation from the pastoral and apostolic point of view. From analysis and discernment will come committed action; from the experience of action will come insight into how to proceed further.

94/ 45. In the discernment mentioned above, the local superior, and at times the provincial as well, will take part. This will help to overcome the tensions that arise and to maintain union of minds and hearts. The superior will enable the members of the community not only to understand and appreciate the particular—and possibly unusual—apostolates undertaken by their companions under obedience, but also to take joint responsibility for them. And if contradictions arise as a result of a particular course of action, the community will be better prepared to "suffer persecution for justice's sake" if the decision to take that course has been prepared for by a discernment in which it had taken part or was at least represented by its superior.[18]

95/ 46. Any effort to promote justice will cost us something. Our cheerful readiness to pay the price will make our preaching of the Gospel more meaningful and its acceptance easier.

Solidarity with the Poor

96/ 47. A decision in this direction will inevitably bring us to ask ourselves with whom we are identified and what our apostolic preferences are. For us, the promotion of justice is not one apostolic area among others, the "social apostolate"; rather, it should be the concern of our whole life and a dimension of all our apostolic endeavors.

97/ 48. Similarly, solidarity with men and women who live a life of hardship and who are victims of oppression cannot be the choice of a few Jesuits only. It should be a characteristic of the life of all of us as individuals and a characteristic of our communities and institutions as well. Alterations are called for in our manner and style of living so that the poverty to which we are vowed may identify us with the poor Christ, who identified Himself with the deprived.[19] The same questions need to be asked in a review of our institutions and apostolic works, and for the same reasons.

98/ 49. The personal backgrounds of most of us, the studies we make, and the circles in which we move often insulate us from poverty, and even from the simple life and its day-to-day concerns. We have access to skills and power which most people do not have. It will therefore be necessary for a larger number of us to share more closely the lot of families who are of modest means, who make up the majority of every country, and who are often poor and oppressed. Relying on the unity we enjoy with one another in the Society and our opportunity to share in one another's experience, we must all acquire deeper sensitivity from those Jesuits who have chosen lives of closer approximation to the problems and aspirations of the deprived. Then we will learn to make our own their concerns as well

---

[18] See Matt. 5.10.

[19] See SpEx, 90, 147, 167; Matt. 25.35–45; also the decisions of the present General Congregation on poverty.

as their preoccupations and their hopes. Only in this way will our solidarity with the poor gradually become a reality.

99/ 50. If we have the patience and the humility and the courage to walk with the poor, we will learn from what they have to teach us what we can do to help them. Without this arduous journey, our efforts for the poor will have an effect just the opposite from what we intend, we will only hinder them from getting a hearing for their real wants and from acquiring the means of taking charge of their own destiny, personal and collective. Through such humble service, we will have the opportunity to help them find, at the heart of their problems and their struggles, Jesus Christ living and acting through the power of the Spirit. Thus can we speak to them of God our Father who brings to Himself the human race in a communion of true brotherhood.

The Service of Faith

100/ 51. The life we lead, the faith-understanding we have of it and the personal relationship to Christ which should be at the heart of all we do are not three separate realities to which correspond three separate apostolates. To promote justice, to proclaim the faith and to lead others to a personal encounter with Christ are the three inseparable elements that make up the whole of our apostolate.

101/ 52. We must therefore review not only our commitment to justice but our effectiveness in communicating the truths which give it meaning and in bringing men to find Christ in their daily lives. We must attentively examine our efforts to strengthen the faith of those who already believe in Christ, taking into account the formidable forces that in our time tend to undermine that faith. We must subject to a similarly searching examination our efforts to bring the Gospel to unbelievers (according to Decree 3 of the 31st General Congregation, especially n. 11).

102/ 53. In recent years the Church has been anxious to give fuller expression to her catholicity by paying more attention to the differences among her various members. More, perhaps, than in the past, she tries to take on the identity of nations and peoples, to align herself with their aspirations, both toward a socioeconomic development and an understanding of the Christian mystery, in accord with their own history and traditions.

103/ 54. The incarnation of the Gospel in the life of the Church implies that the way in which Christ is preached and encountered will be different in different countries, different for people with different backgrounds. For some Christian communities, especially those in Asia and Africa, this "economy of the Incarnation" calls for a more intensive dialog with the heirs of the great non-Christian traditions. Jesuits working in these countries will have to take account of this. In some Western countries which can hardly be called Christian any longer, the language of theology and of prayer will also have to be suitably adapted. In those countries dominated by explicitly atheist ideologies, a renewed preaching of the Gospel demands not merely that our lives be, and be seen to be, in conformity with the commitment to justice Christ demands of us, but also that the structures of theological reflection, catechesis, liturgy, and pastoral ministry be adapted to needs perceived through a real experience of the situation.

104/ 55. We are members of a Society with a universal vocation and a missionary tradition. We therefore have a special responsibility in this regard. We have a duty to ensure that our ministry is directed toward incarnating the faith and life of the Church in the culture and traditions of the people among whom and with whom we work and, at the same time, toward communion with all who share the same Christian faith.

105/ 56. Moreover, the Church is aware that today the problematic of inculturation must take into account not only the cultural values proper to each nation but also the new, more universal values emerging from the closer and more continuous interchange among nations in our time. Here, too, our Society is called upon to serve the Church; take part in her task of *aggiornamento,* of "bringing-up-to-date"; that is, of incarnating the Gospel in these values as well, these new values that are becoming increasingly planetary in scope.

The Spiritual Exercises

106/ 57. The ministry of the Spiritual Exercises is of particular importance in this regard. A key element in the pedagogy of the Exercises is that its aim is to remove the barriers between God and man so that the Spirit speaks directly with man. Inherent in this Ignatian practice of spiritual direction is a deep respect for the exercitant as he is and for the culture, background, and tradition that have gone into making him what he is. Moreover, the pedagogy of the Exercises is a pedagogy of discernment. It teaches a man to discover for himself where God is calling him, what God wants him to do, as he is, where he is, among his own people.

107/ 58. The Exercises also help to form Christians who, having personally experienced God as Savior, are able to stand back from the spurious absolutes of competing ideologies, and because of this detachment can play a constructive part in the reform of social and cultural structures. Thus, the ministry of the Spiritual Exercises is one of the most important we can undertake today. We should by all means encourage studies, research, and experiment directed toward helping our contemporaries experience the vitality of the Exercises as adapted to the new needs which are theirs. Moreover the spirit of the Exercises should pervade every other ministry of the Word that we undertake.

Guidelines for Concerted Action

108/ 59. In presenting this review of our apostolate in its various dimensions, the General Congregation wishes to continue along the lines given by Father General to the Congregation of Procurators of 1970 [See the Yearbook of the Society of Jesus, 1971–1972.] and to emphasize once more the importance of theological reflection, social action, education, and the mass media as means of making our preaching of the Gospel more effective. The importance of these means rests in the fact that, in touching its most profound needs, they permit a more universal service to humankind.

109/ 60. In the concrete:

—We must be more aware of the need for research and for theological reflection, carried on in a context which is both interdisciplinary and genuinely integrated with the culture in which it is done and with its traditions. Only thus can it throw light on the main problems which the Church and humanity ought to be coming to grips with today.

—Greater emphasis should be placed on the conscientization according to the Gospel of those who have the power to bring about social change, and a special place given to service of the poor and oppressed.

—We should pursue and intensify the work of formation in every sphere of education, while subjecting it at the same time to continual scrutiny. We must help prepare both young people and adults to live and labor for others and with others to build a more just world. Especially we should help form our Christian students in such a way that animated by a mature faith and personally devoted to Jesus Christ, they can find Him in others and having recognized Him there, they will serve Him in their neighbor. In this way we shall contribute to the formation of those who by a kind of multiplier-effect will share in the process of educating the world itself.

—We have to take a critical look at our ability to communicate our heartfelt convictions not only to persons we deal with directly, but also with those we cannot meet individually, and whom we can only help to the extent that we succeed in humanizing the social climate—attitudes and behavior—where we are engaged. In this regard the communications media would seem to play a role of great importance.

110/ 61. We should pursue these objectives not separately, in isolation, but as complementary factors of a single apostolic thrust toward the development of the whole person and of every person.

D.

A Missionary Body

111/ 62. The dispersal imposed on us today by our vocation as Jesuits makes it imperative that we strengthen and renew the ties that bind us together as members of the same Society.

112/ 63. That is why it is so important that our communities be apostolic communities, and it is the primary responsibility of the local superior to see to it that his community approach this ideal as closely as possible. Each one of us should be able to find in his community—in shared prayer, in converse with his brethren, in the celebration of the Eucharist—the spiritual resources he needs for the apostolate. The community should also be able to provide him with a context favorable to apostolic discernment.

113/ 64. It is this stress on the apostolic dimension of our communities that this 32nd General Congregation wishes to add to what the 31st General Congregation has already set forth in detail regarding the requirements of community life in the Society.[20] Our communities, even those whose members are engaged in different ministries, must have for their principle of unity the apostolic spirit.[21]

114/ 65. It is important that whether a Jesuit works in a team or whether he works alone, he must be, and must feel himself to be, sent. It is the responsibility of the superior, after he has shared with the individual Jesuit in his discernment, to see to it that the apostolic work of each is properly integrated into the global mission of the Society. The individual Jesuit normally receives his mission from his provincial superior; but it belongs to the local superior to adapt that mission to local circumstances and to promote the sense of solidarity of the members of the community with each other and with the whole body of the Society to which they belong.

115/ 66. This solidarity with the Society is primary. It ought to take precedence over loyalties to any other sort of institution, Jesuit or non-Jesuit. It ought to stamp any other commitment which is thereby transformed into "mission." The "mission" as such is bestowed by the Society and is subject to her review. She can confirm or modify it as the greater service of God may require.

116/ 67. This kind of responsibility on the part of the superior cannot be exercised without the living practice of the account of conscience, by which the

---

[20] GC 31, D. 19.

[21] See the directives of the present General Congregation in the document "The Union of Minds and Hearts," especially those regarding spiritual and community life.

superior is made capable of taking part in the discernment done by each of the members and can help him therein.[22] It presupposes that, with the help of his companions, he engage in a continual, communitarian reflection upon fresh needs of the apostolate and upon the ways and means by which they can best be met. And it asks the superior to encourage the shy and the hesitant and to see to it that each individual finds a place in the community and a place in the apostolate which will bring out the best in him and enable him to cope with the hardships and risks he may encounter in God's service.

117/ 68. The apostolic body of the Society to which we belong should not be thought of just in terms of the local community. We belong to a province, which should itself constitute an apostolic community in which discernment and co-ordination of the apostolate on a larger scale than at the local level can and should take place. Moreover, the province is part of the whole Society, which also forms one single apostolic body and community. It is at this level that the over-all apostolic decisions and guidelines must be made and worked out, decisions and guidelines for which we should all feel jointly responsible.

118/ 69. This demands of all of us a high degree of availability and a real apostolic mobility in the service of the universal Church. Father General, with the help of his advisers, has the task of inspiring the Society as a whole to serve the cause of the Gospel and its justice. But we ask all our brothers, especially the provincials, to give Father General all the support, all the ideas and assistance which they can, as he tries to carry out this task of inspiring and coordinating, even if this should shake up our settled habits or stretch horizons sometimes all too limited. The extent to which our contemporaries depend on one another in their outlook, aspirations and religious concepts, to say nothing of structural connections that span our planet, makes this over-all coordination of our efforts indispensable if we are to remain faithful to our mission of evangelization.

E.

Practical Dispositions

119/ 70. The decisions and guidelines about our apostolic mission set forth above have certain practical consequences which we now propose to detail in some points.

A Program for Deepening Awareness
and for Apostolic Discernment

120/ 71. Considering the variety of situations in which Jesuits are working, the General Congregation cannot provide the programs each region will need to

---

[22] "Union of Minds and Hearts."

reflect upon and implement the decisions and guidelines presented there. Each province or group of provinces must undertake a program of reflection and a review of our apostolates to discover what action is appropriate in each particular context.

121/ 72. What is required is not so much a research program as a process of reflection and evaluation inspired by the Ignatian tradition of spiritual discernment, in which the primary stress is on prayer and the effort to attain "indifference," that is, an apostolic readiness for anything.

122/ 73. The general method to be followed to produce this awareness and to engage in this discernment may be described (see *Octogesima Adveniens,* n. 4) as a constant interplay between experience, reflection, decision and action, in line with the Jesuit ideal of being "contemplative in action." The aim is to insure a change in our habitual patterns of thought, a conversion of heart as well as of spirit. The result will be effective apostolic decisions.

123/ 74. The process of evaluation and discernment must be brought to bear principally on the following: the identification and analysis of the problems involved in the service of faith and the promotion of justice and the review and renewal of our apostolic commitments. Where do we live? Where do we work? How? With whom? What really is our involvement with, dependence on, or commitment to ideologies and power centers? Is it only to the converted that we know how to preach Jesus Christ? These are some of the questions we should raise with reference to our membership individually, as well as to our communities and institutions.

Continuing Evaluation of Our Apostolic Work

124/ 75. With regard to the choice of ministries and the setting up of priorities and programs, the General Congregation asks that the following guidelines be taken into account.

125/ 76. The review of our ministries and the deployment of our available manpower and resources must pay great attention to the role in the service of faith and the promotion of justice which can be played by our educational institutions, periodicals, parishes, retreat houses, and the other apostolic works for which we are responsible. Not only should our structured activities undergo this review, so should our individual apostolates.

126/ 77. In each province or region, or at least at the Assistancy level, there should be a definite mechanism for the review of our ministries.[23] Now is a good time to examine critically how these arrangements are working and, if need be, to replace them by others which are more effective and allow for a wider participation

---

[23] See GC 31, D. 22.

in the process of communal discernment. The appropriate major superior should make an annual report to Father General on what has been accomplished here.

Some Special Cases

127/ 78. The General Congregation recognizes how important it is that we should be present and work with others in different areas of human activity, especially in those parts of the world which are most secularized. It also recognizes the real opportunities for apostolic work afforded, in some cases, by the practice of a profession or by taking a job not directly related to the strictly presbyteral function.[24]

128/ 79. The General Congregation considers that such commitments can be a part of the Society's mission, provided they meet the following conditions: They must be undertaken as a mission from our superiors. Their aim must be clearly apostolic. Preference should be given to work in an area which is de-Christianized or underprivileged. The activity must be in harmony with the priestly character of the Society as a whole. It must be compatible with the essential demands of the religious life—an interior life of prayer, a relationship with a Jesuit superior and a Jesuit community, poverty, apostolic availability.

129/ 80. Any realistic plan to engage in the promotion of justice will mean some kind of involvement in civic activity. Exceptional forms of involvement must conform to the general practice of the Church[25] and the norms laid down by Father General.[26] If, in certain countries, it seems necessary to adopt more detailed norms and directives, this must be seen to by provincials—as far as possible in regional conferences. These norms and directives should be submitted to Father General for approval. It will then be for the provincial—with the agreement, where the case demands it, of the local bishop or the bishops' conference—to give or refuse the permission that may be required.

International Cooperation

130/ 81. All the major problems of our time have an international dimension. A real availability and openness to change will thus be necessary to foster the growth of cooperation and coordination throughout the whole Society. All Jesuits, but especially those who belong to the affluent world, should endeavor to work with those who form public opinion, as well as with international organizations, to promote justice among all peoples. To this end, the General Congregation asks Father General to make one or other of his advisers specifically responsible for the necessary organization of international cooperation within the Society, as required by our service of faith and promotion of justice.

---

[24] See GC 31, D. 23, n. 12.

[25] See Synod of Bishops, 1971.

[26] *ActRSJ*, XV, 942.

DECREE 5

THE WORK OF INCULTURATION OF THE FAITH AND PROMOTION OF CHRISTIAN LIFE

131/ 1. In furthering the mission of evangelization and the building up of Christ's Church, the 32nd General Congregation is aware of the great importance that must be given today to the work involving inculturation of both faith and Christian life in all the continents of the world, but especially in the regions of Asia and Africa[1] and in some countries of Latin America. Mindful that from its very beginning the Society has had a long and venerable missionary tradition of promoting inculturation, the Congregation judges that this work must be pursued with even greater determination in our own day and that it deserves the progressively greater concern and attention of the whole Society. Therefore, the Congregation urgently requests all Jesuits to promote this effort according to the mind and authentic teaching of the Church[2] in order to provide greater help and service not only to the local Churches but especially to the universal Church under the Vicar of Christ on earth, to the end that all peoples and nations may be restored to unity in Christ Jesus, Our Lord.

132/ 2. The Congregation entrusts to Father General the further development and promotion of this work throughout the Society. In the first place, it recommends that, after he has considered the whole question with the help of expert assistance, Father General write a letter or instruction to the entire Society, in order to further this work in and by the Society. His purpose in writing will be to clarify for all of Ours the true meaning and theological understanding of the task and process of inculturation as well as its importance for the apostolic mission of the Society today. The Congregation also recommends to Father General that he

---

[1] See GC 32, "Our Mission Today: The Service of Faith and the Promotion of Justice," nn. 53–56, and "The Formation of Jesuits," nn. 27–29 and passim.

[2] E.g., LG, 13, 17; AG, 16–18, 22, 26; GS, 53–58. Pope Paul VI, *Populorum Progressio,* n. 65; *Insegnamenti di Paolo VI,* V/1967, 576–600, 635; VII/1969, 528–31, 542, 548–49, 609–13;VIII/1970, 1215–16, 1249; *AAS,* LXVI (1974), 625–29, 631–39. Statement of the First Plenary Assembly of the Federation of Asian Bishops' Conferences (FABC), April 27, 1974; Statement of African Bishops (AMECEA/SECAM) present at the 4th Synod of Bishops, Rome, October 20, 1974.

further this effort in any other ways which seem to him more conducive to God's greater glory.[3]

---

[3] For example, by establishing a commission to promote the work of inculturation in the Society. The members of this commission could be chosen principally from the three Assistancies of Africa, East Asia, and India, as seems best to Father General. In addition, by recommending strongly to other institutions and centers of the Society, e.g., those engaged in theological studies, the renewal of pastoral works, the publication of magazines and periodicals, the preparation of audio-visual materials, etc., studies and projects which would promote inculturation.

II

DEVELOPING THE APOSTOLIC BODY OF THE SOCIETY

DECREE 6

THE FORMATION OF JESUITS

Especially with Regard to the Apostolate and Studies

133/ 1. Since the 31st General Congregation the many changes in the world at large have brought influences to bear on the training of our scholastics and brothers. Among these changes we might mention: the development of new structures, institutions, and mentalities in many nations; a deeper appreciation of the identity and autonomy of different cultures; the profound renewal of the Church in recent years; new arrangements in many provinces for the education of our men, which is often pursued in institutions not belonging to the Society or in circumstances where the academic program is distinct from religious formation; a restructuring of community life located now in urban centers; new cultural values which often have an influence on our young men; new aspirations of young Jesuits: their sensitivity to the world of today and the problems of society, their desire to be more closely associated with their peers; the difficulty—affecting most young people today—of remaining for a long time in the status of students while desirous of taking a genuine role in the active life of the Society; their regret oftentimes at what appears an isolated existence; their desire, finally, that the Society embrace an apostolic perspective more suited to the growth of their own vocations.

134/ 2. In this context, an adequate evaluation of the present formation of Jesuits—which has not yet been done sufficiently—seems all the more necessary because, in continually changing times, constant adaptation is required in order to be sure of achieving the essential purpose of our formation. Moreover, certain defects which are apparent both in formation generally and in the organization of studies sometimes stem from a failure to fulfill the prescribed norms, as found in the following documents: Decrees 8 and 9 of the 31st General Congregation, *An Instruction of Father General on the Spiritual Training of Jesuits,* and the *General Norms for Studies* (1968).[1]

135/ 3. Therefore, the 32nd General Congregation proposes some practical norms for the evaluation of various features of formation and their execution. At the same time, it provides, in declarative form, some preliminary reflections which may help to give both young Jesuits and those who in various ways help to educate them, and indeed all of our men, a perspective on formation adapted to our times. Within this perspective the above-mentioned documents can be

---

[1] *ActRSJ,* XV, 105–33.

reread and explained. Little is said, however, about spiritual formation, because in this area the General Congregation confirms and stresses what has been prescribed in the eighth decree of the 31st General Congregation.

136/ 4. The present document, then, although dealing principally with the formation of young Jesuits, looks, in a certain sense, to all our members since all are involved in formation as that task is presented here. All of us, after all, constitute an apostolic body into which the younger members are gradually integrated. Moreover, older Jesuits themselves need a permanent and continuing formation, which our formal training must have in view from the start. Our apostolic calling requires personal and ever-deepening study not only on the part of the young but on the part of all Jesuits.

A. The Integrated Character of Apostolic Formation

137/ 5. The decision made by the 32nd General Congregation concerning the mission of the Society in today's world[2] calls us to give renewed emphasis to the apostolic character of our formation process. This was already clearly affirmed by the 31st General Congregation.[3] Moreover, the total formation of Jesuits, both scholastics and brothers, must be equal to the demands of evangelization in a world deeply troubled by atheism and social injustice.

138/ 6. It is with this world in view that our formation must prepare witnesses and ministers of the faith who, as members of the Society, are ready to be sent for the greater service of the Church into situations which are characterized by uncertainty. Their formation must make our men capable of dialogue with others, capable of confronting the cultural problems of our day. For these are the circumstances under which they must labor to promote the spiritual growth of mankind according to the tradition of the Society.

139/ 7. To respond to this apostolic vision, the whole formation of our members must be understood and promoted as a process of integration into the apostolic body of the Society.

140/ 8. This notion of integration expresses, in a synthetic way, a most important aspect of contemporary Jesuit formation which is used in this document in two different senses: as meaning both personal integration and integration into the apostolic body of the Society. These aspects should not be separated. Integration among disciplines and structures of the formation process will be treated later.

---

[2] See above, nos. 47–130, pp. 294–312

[3] GC 31, D. 8, n. 4 and D. 9, n. 1; *ActRSJ,* XIV, 872, 877.

a. Personal Integration

141/ 9. First of all, it might be good to recall some of the elements by which an apostolic personality is formed:

a. The process of apostolic formation must favor the personal assimilation of Christian experience. This demands a deep knowledge of revelation based on Sacred Scripture and on the living tradition of the Church and the ability, in the light of this knowledge, to reflect in a discerning way on the apostolate as it is concretely experienced.

b. In an apostolic formation an important place must be given to spiritual experience which is personal, vital, rooted in faith, nourished by daily prayer and the Eucharist: an experience that makes us capable of witnessing to the gift of faith before nonbelievers and of cooperating with God for the spiritual growth of those who do believe.

c. Our style of life and its attendant circumstances, both personal and communitarian, ought to favor apostolic formation. It should have the young Jesuits live in real conditions and come to know themselves, where responsibilities prevent a lapse into carelessness and individualism. This should mean that young Jesuits should not, during their time of formation, be oblivious to the actual living conditions of the people of the regions in which they live. Their style of life therefore must help them to know and understand what the people around them seek, what they suffer, what they lack.

142/ 10. Accordingly, an experience of living with the poor for at least a certain period of time will be necessary for all, so that they may be helped to overcome the limitations of their own social background. For this reason, the conditions of such an experience must be thought out carefully, so that it will be genuine, free of illusions, and productive of an inner conversion. And it must be added that our whole personal and community life ought to be characterized by the radical standard of the Gospel, in the sense that our fidelity to the evangelical choice we have made by our vows must lead us to a critical vision of ourselves, of the world, and of society. This radical standard must be appropriate to a personal insertion into the human culture of the region where the apostolate is carried out, so that one's own faith may be intelligible to other people and influence their life and culture.

143/ 11. In the whole course of formation, these diverse elements, necessary for an apostolic and priestly mission in today's world, must be harmoniously united. We should conceive and plan for the total formation of our men as a process of progressive integration of the spiritual life, of the apostolate, and of studies in such a way that the richness of the spiritual life should be the source of the apostolate, and the apostolate, in turn, the motive for study and for a more profound spiritual life.

144/ 12. This process of integration begins in the novitiate, which may be common for both scholastics and brothers, and whose purposes are formation and probation. Right from the novitiate members of the Society are to be carefully instructed in spiritual discernment. This Ignatian discernment is an essential ingredient of our apostolic formation. Indeed, today's conditions demand that a member of the Society during the whole course of formation should practice spiritual discernment about the concrete choices which, stage by stage, the service of Christ and the Church require of him. It is through this discernment that a sense of personal responsibility and true freedom will be achieved.

b. Integration into the Apostolic Body of the Society

145/ 13. The whole process of formation, through its various stages from novitiate to tertianship, should favor this integration. It should prepare our young men to be eager to fulfill the missions and perform the ministries which the Society may wish to assign to them.

146/ 14. To achieve this, the provincial must follow the entire course of development of each individual; he must take care that each understand the purpose of the stage of formation in which he is involved and profit from it according to the measure of grace granted to him. Moreover, through the whole course of this development, each young man should also be assisted by his local superior, the spiritual father, the director or prefect of studies, and his teachers to integrate intellectual reflection with apostolic experience—both personal and communitarian—in order to prepare his own apostolic orientation. Those who direct the young must therefore challenge them to develop a sense of personal responsibility. Ultimately, all who work in formation must try to become so filled with God's own wisdom that they teach and form our young as much by the lively sharing of their personal knowledge of God and man as by the communication of academic learning.

147/ 15. This integration, moreover, is to be aided by the continual experience of participating in the life of the Society as an apostolic body. On the one hand, such experience is fostered in houses of formation by a community, which the young constitute among themselves and with other Jesuits, in which there is real communication and a sharing of life, even on the spiritual level, as well as cooperation and mutual responsibility in studies and in apostolic works. If, indeed, young Jesuits live at times in apostolic communities, care must be taken that: *(a)* the communities are such as can willingly assume the responsibility of formation, along with those who have special charge of formation in the province; and *(b)* a priest, designated by the provincial, be responsible for helping them to pursue serious studies and carry on their apostolic work while still maintaining close ties with their companions.

148/ 16. On the other hand, this experience supposes a formation that is closely bound up with the activities of the province or region; those in charge of formation therefore must be men who are capable both of assisting other Jesuits and of receiving help from others. Contact, information, and cooperation with other communities and works, especially with those in the same province, should help young Jesuits to experience the whole province, indeed the whole Society, as an apostolic body united in one spirit. To achieve this, the provincial, or someone designated by him, should see that the young are given this apostolic orientation in progressive stages and by a variety of experiences, according to the talents of each and with a view to the apostolic works of the province and the Society.

149/ 17. The goal of the whole process of integration should be to assist each one, with the help of spiritual discernment, to learn not to indulge his own aspirations in an individualistic way, but to come to understand that he is a member of the body of the whole Society and shares its apostolic mission.

>   *c. Continued Formation as the Renewal of the Whole Apostolic*
>   *Body of the Society*

150/ 18. Especially in our times, when everything is subject to such rapid change and evolution, and when new questions and new knowledge, both in theology and in other branches of learning, are constantly developing, a truly contemporary apostolate demands of us a process of permanent and continuing formation. Thus formation is never ended, and our "first" formation must be seen as the beginning of this continuing process.

151/ 19. Continuing formation is achieved especially through a constant evaluation of and reflection on one's apostolate, in the light of faith and with the help of one's apostolic community. It also needs the cooperation of our professors and experts, whose theory can shed light on our praxis, even while they themselves are led to more profound reflection by the apostolic experience of their fellow Jesuits. This kind of communication will also assist the integration of the young into the apostolic life of the province, and the contact between formation and the apostolate will profit the whole Society.

152/ 20. This continuing formation demands that definite periods of time be given to formal courses or simply to private study, whether in theology or other disciplines, as required for one's apostolate.

B.   Integration of Studies into the Apostolic Life

153/ 21. Since our mission today is the proclamation of our faith in Jesus Christ, which itself involves the promotion of justice, our studies must be directed toward this mission and derive their motivation from it. In a world where faith is fostered only with great difficulty and in which justice is so broadly violated, our wish is to help others arrive at a knowledge and love of God and a truly fraternal love of men, to help them lead lives according to the Good News of Christ and to renew the structures of human society in justice. Ministers of the Word of God can bring such help to others only if they have themselves acquired a profound vision of reality, from personal reflection on the experience of man in the world and on his transcendent finality in God. They must make their own God's revelation of Himself in Jesus Christ, as it is contained in Sacred Scripture and expressed in the life of the Church and in the teaching of the Magisterium. Such personal and accurate assimilation cannot be obtained without continued discipline and the labor of tireless and patient study.

154/ 22. Thus the Society has opted anew for a profound academic formation of its future priests—theological as well as philosophical, humane, and scientific—in the persuasion that, presupposing the testimony of one's own life, there is no more apt way to exercise our mission. Such study is itself an apostolic work which makes us present to men to the degree that we come to know all the more profoundly their possibilities, their needs, their cultural milieu. Our studies should foster and stimulate those very qualities which today are often suffocated by our contemporary style of living and thinking: a spirit of reflection and an awareness of the deeper, transcendent values. For this reason, our young men should be reminded that their special mission and apostolate during the time of study is to study. Thus, the desire for a more active service, which the young feel so deeply, ought to be itself the animating force which penetrates all their studies.

155/ 23. The brothers also who participate in the apostolic activity of the Society according to Decrees 7 and 8 of the 31st General Congregation,[4] should receive appropriate theological instruction and a better formation in what concerns their work, according to the measure of the gifts they have received from God.

156/ 24. From different parts of the Society it has been reported that our philosophical studies in recent years have, for various reasons, suffered deterioration. The General Congregation urges both superiors and professors to take the necessary means to strengthen the philosophical training of our men. Sufficient time must be given to it, and it must be done in a mature, unified, and coherent fashion, reaching a serious level of academic quality. The Society expects for its scholastics the kind of long-term philosophical training which is in touch with the radical problems of human existence and which is a mature reflection on the different intellectual traditions of mankind, in such a way that it can be integrated with subsequent or concomitant theological reflection.

---

[4] *ActRSJ,* XIV, 861, 871; see also *ActRSJ,* XV, 567–570.

157/ 25. The numerous points of contact between philosophy and other fields of learning, contact with contemporary problems and with the present and future lives of students, ought to be pointed out. Because of today's diversity of cultures, sciences, ideologies, and social movements, priests in the Society ought to be men who possess balance and depth in their thinking and who can communicate to others with credibility their own convictions regarding meaning and values.

158/ 26. Theological training should be well integrated, sufficiently systematic, adapted to the exigencies of our mission, and conducted according to the norms of the Church. The whole of this training supposes above all a personal experience of the faith which must be developed and explained by a knowledge of Sacred Scripture, Christian doctrine, and moral theology. Students should be encouraged to establish a critical dialogue between theology and human culture, between faith and the real questions and problems which occupy the minds of the people among whom we exercise our apostolate. This reflection cannot be effective today except through an integration of the human sciences with philosophy and theology, both in teaching and in learning. Cooperation and communication among professors can be a great help towards this.

159/ 27. In accord with the norm of Decree 9, n. 18, of the 31st General Congregation,[5] those studies should be fostered that readily help our young men attain a harmonious, balanced human and religious maturity; studies leading not only to a living knowledge of man and his modern world, but also suited to expressing ourselves to the people of our times. Also, our formation must be such that the Jesuit can be one with the people to whom he is sent, capable of communicating with them. He must be able to share their convictions and values, their history, their experience and aspirations; at the same time, he must be open to the convictions and values of other peoples, traditions, and cutures. Hence training in the sciences, in languages, in literature, in the classic "liberal arts," in modern media of communication, and in the cultural traditions of the nation, must be undertaken with much greater care.[6]

160/ 28. Moreover, the apostolic activities of the scholastics and brothers, accepted as a genuine mission from superiors, must be so directed and so subjected to evaluation that a real connection will be possible between apostolic activities and studies. Such activities are a part of apostolic formation for everyone, and part of the strictly priestly formation for those who are called to the ministerial priesthood: they ought to be integrated into the curriculum of studies as a basis for further reflection. For studies can be so tied in with these

---

[5] *ActRSJ*, XIV, 880.

[6] See *NG* 85–95; *ActRSJ*, XV, 258–260.

different experiences that by the experiences, the studies themselves can be appreciated in a new light.[7]

161/ 29. In the whole course of formation, especially during philosophical and theological studies, a deep and authentic involvement with the local culture should be fostered, according to regional differences; yet care should also be taken to promote unity of minds and hearts in the Society. To foster this union, all the young members of the Society must cultivate Ignatian spirituality and be taught a theology which is grounded in the tradition and official teaching of the Church, though adapted to the needs of the times and of local cultures. For this purpose, meetings of those responsible for formation and professors of Ours in the various regions and in the whole Society can be very helpful. The young men themselves, by communication among the various provinces and regions, should acquire better knowledge of the unity and diversity of the Society, which will lead them to a true sense of its universality.

162/ 30. Those who teach our men ought to manifest by their labor and living example this integration of the intellectual, spiritual, and apostolic life. To them is committed a prime role in the intellectual apostolate of the Society. They teach in the name and by the mandate of theChurch.[8] By their scholarship and with openness of mind, they seek out ways to develop a more profound understanding of the faith and to make it known to men, taking into account the questions and the needs of our times and of their own nations. They are called by the Society not only to teach their disciplines and to carry on scholarly research, but are also responsible for fostering each in his own way, the integral formation of our men— intellectual and spiritual, priestly and apostolic—in the spirit of the Society.

C. Norms

163/ 31. The provincial is responsible for all aspects of the formation of those who belong to his province. He is responsible for both the persons and the institutions of the Society charged with formation. However, it is appropriate that there be a delegate who should have the immediate care for the various aspects of formation of each young Jesuit in the province (or in the region, where circumstances so dictate).

a. There should be regional or provincial commissions to advise superiors in the direction of formation in accord with local conditions.[9]

b. These commissions should be made up both of those who are in charge of formation and also of some who are working in various apostolic min-

---

[7] See *NG* 116–117; *ActRSJ,* XV, 263–264.

[8] GC 31, D. 9, n. 43.

[9] See GC 31, D. 9, n. 16; *ActRSJ,* XIV, 819 and NG 10; *ActRSJ,* XV, 241.

istries. They should evaluate the status of formation in the province or region on a regular basis.

164/ 32. The General Congregation suggests to Father General that one of the general counsellors should have special concern for the integral formation of Jesuits throughout the Society. He ought also to help Father General in insisting on the execution of the decrees of this Congregation on formation, in adapting the *General Norms for Studies* and in evaluating experiments relative to formation.

165/ 33. Those who are in charge of formation should take care that our scholastics and brothers, especially in the period immediately after the novitiate, become familiar with the sources of the spirituality of the Church and the Society and with its history and traditions and that they study them with a view toward their own progress and the progress of others.

166/ 34. Provincials should be mindful of poverty in the matter of expenses for new arrangements of formation communities and institutions and in the pursuit of special studies.

167/ 35. In accord with the resources and the apostolic needs of the different regions or provinces, provincials should provide for the spiritual, intellectual, and apostolic renewal of all our men. At determined times, all should be given sufficient opportunity for study and for reflection about their apostolic life. This program should be carried out with serious application according to a plan approved by the provincial.

168/ 36. It is suggested that, more or less ten years after completing tertianship, Jesuits who have had experience in apostolic ministries and offices be given the opportunity for intensive spiritual renewal during two or three months.

169/ 37. Studies in the Society are governed by the common law of the Church and by Decree 9 of the 31st General Congregation unless this present decree in a particular case provides otherwise. All the decrees of previous General Congregations which are contrary either to this decree or to Decree 9 of the 31st General Congregation or to the *General Norms for Studies* are definitively abrogated. These *General Norms* which Father General promulgated in place of the previous *Ratio Studiorum* are to be continually revised and adapted to new needs.[10]

170/ 38. Because of the importance of philosophical and theological studies in the tradition and apostolic life of the Society, provincials should see to it that in general all acquire the licentiate in either theology or philosophy and that those who manifest greater interest and talent should continue further studies in order to acquire higher degrees. What is said in Decree 9, nn. 33–40, of the 31st General Congregation concerning special studies should also be implemented.

---

[10] See GC 31, D. 9, n. 15; *ActRSJ,* XIV, 879.

171/ 39. In faculties or institutions where the curriculum in philosophy and theology is flexible, the superior of the scholastics or the prefect of studies, according to the determination of the provincial, is responsible for arranging the curriculum of each scholastic according to his ability and his future apostolic work.

172/ 40. The studies of brothers should be in accord with the needs of the province as well as their ability, interest, and future apostolic work. Their education in religious studies should be commensurate with their ability and adapted to their other studies.

173/ 41. Scholastics are to devote at least two years to the study of philosophy.[11] But when these studies are combined with other subjects or with the study of theology, they must be pursued in such a way that the equivalent of two years is devoted to them.

174/ 42. *a.* The four year study of theology, prescribed by the Church for all who are preparing for the priesthood, is to be observed. But when the regular curriculum of theology is completed in three years, a fourth year is to be added which should be dedicated either to preparation for a degree in theology or, in an approved program, to the integration of theological studies into one's formation, especially one's pastoral formation.

175/ *b.* If, however, there is an introductory course in theology, under the direction of a faculty of theology, beginning in the novitiate and continued through the period of philosophical studies, a careful evaluation should be made to determine whether the quality of this program is such that it might be equivalent to the first year of the theological curriculum.

176/ 43. Special studies, understood according to their apostolic character, should be earnestly fostered by superiors. Those who undertake such studies, especially in secular universities, should be assisted to understand and personally to assimilate the interrelationship between these studies and their philosophy and theology. They should have special spiritual assistance and should be integrated into the life of a community of the Society.

177/ 44. A solid education should also be fostered in literature, the arts, sciences, history, and the various aspects of the culture of the region where the apostolate will be carried on. The study of modern means of social communication should also be encouraged. An academic degree should be required as the usual means to evaluate our education in these fields in order to make our apostolic service more effective.

---

[11] GC 31, D. 9, n. 22.

178/ 45. Besides their own language, our young men should learn one or other of the more common modern languages which would facilitate communication with other cultures and with the universal Society.

179/ 46. Although the curriculum of studies for the scholastics may be arranged in a number of ways, such unity ought to be observed in the regional programs as to make it possible for the scholastics, without extreme difficulty, to take part of their training in another province or region.

180/ 47. Formation in apostolic activities ought to be carried on in a progressive fashion under the direction of a competent coordinator who should direct the young Jesuits in their activities, bring them to examine the activities critically, and help them to carry them out. Such activities, which are to be undertaken as a mission from superiors, should be so arranged that they lead to a deeper level of spiritual and intellectual reflection. For this purpose, it will be especially helpful, according to the mind of the Constitutions, for the scholastics to become accustomed to directing others in the Spiritual Exercises under the supervision of an experienced director.[12] Moreover, these apostolic experiences should be an integral part of the curriculum of studies.

181/ 48. In institutions where scholastics are taught by Jesuits, these Jesuit professors should remember that the mission which they have received from the provincial extends also to the formation of scholastics. Therefore, a team of professors should be chosen which has the aptitude for carrying on scholarly work, for teaching, and for cooperating in the integral formation of the scholastics. With regard to this point, professors should be conscious of their responsibility toward the Society.

182/ 49. *a.* In provinces where scholastics study in faculties or institutions which do not belong to the Society, superiors should see to it that the formation proper to the Society is provided with all the necessary means, for example, by complementing the curriculum with special courses.

183/ *b.* Where, however, the faculty or institution is directed by the Society but the academic direction is separate from the religious direction (of the community), superiors are responsible for promoting mutual cooperation in order to achieve the integral formation of our men.

184/ 50. The *Regional Orders of Studies* are to be sufficiently revised so that they will truly correspond to the requirements of this decree. Such revisions are, in good time, to be submitted to Father General for approval.

185/ 51. To establish the level of learning required of those who may be admitted to the profession of four vows, of all those who have not acquired a higher

---

[12] *Cons.* [408–409].

degree, at least a licentiate, in sacrcd studies[13] an *examen ad gradum* is required according to the Constitutions.[14] It must be an oral examination in philosophy and theology, before four examiners. Decree 9, n. 29, of the 31st General Congregation is abrogated. Everything else dealing with the length of the examination, its program, and the way of giving the grades for the examination is to be determined in the Regional Orders of Studies approved by Father General.

186/ 52. In each province there should be a serious consideration of how this decree is to be implemented. A report on this matter is to be sent to Father General.

---

[13] See GC 31, D. 11, n. 3 (1 and 2); *ActRSJ,* XIV, 887.

[14] *Cons.* [518].

DECREE 7

TERTIANSHIP

187/ 1.   Just as the 31st General Congregation, so also the 32nd General Congregation holds the institution of tertianship in high regard.[1] Therefore, provincials should urge priests and coadjutor brothers who have not yet made their tertianship to do so as soon as possible.

188/ 2.   The tertianship of the coadjutor brothers enjoined by the 30th General Congregation[2] is to be observed faithfully, for it has contributed much to the spiritual advancement of the brothers. When it is judged opportune, and the provincial permits, this period of formation may be made together with our priests or candidates for the priesthood.

189/ 3.   The 32nd General Congregation approves two tertianship plans, A and B, understanding that, with Father General's approval, they may be adopted in different provinces and regions:

Plan A: After completing the Society's required studies of theology, the candidate will enter his third probation. The experiment of the month-long Spiritual Exercises is to be made within the first months of the tertianship. Then, allowing for a suitable interval after the retreat, ordinations to the diaconate and priesthood will take place. During the course of the tertianship, a solid knowledge of the Institute and a deeper understanding of the spirit of the Society are to be fostered; but a notable part of the time after priestly ordination is to be devoted to ministries, primarily pastoral, under competent supervision. At the end of this tertianship year, the priests can be promoted to final vows. In individual cases, and for a just cause, the provincial is authorized to postpone a scholastic's entry into tertianship; but if this is done, priestly ordination and final vows will likewise be postponed.

190/   *Plan B:* When the third year of theology is completed and an appropriate spiritual preparation has been made, the scholastic can receive ordination to the priesthood. After ordination, and some time after the course of studies is finished, tertianship is to be made; this should be done not later than three years after priestly ordination, except for a just cause, with the provincial's approval.

It is better that the tertian have an assignment and work in an apostolic community, provided that, in the judgment of the Instructor, this assignment and

---

[1] GC 31, D. 10, n. 1; *ActRSJ,* XIV, 885.

[2] GC30, D. 42; *ActRSJ,* XIII, 333; (CD, 387).

work are compatible with the experiments and duration of residence required in the forms of tertianship approved by Father General,[3] so that while in an active life, the tertian may be formed to be a Jesuit contemplative in action.

DECREE 8

Grades in the Society of Jesus

191/ 1. The 32nd General Congregation again lays very great stress on promoting the unity of vocation of the entire body of the Society, as enshrined in our Constitutions. It asks each and every member to make this unity shine forth in the life, work, and apostolate of all communities; to ensure that grades be not a source of division, let there rather be, by means of the day-to-day efforts of everyone, a complete union of the one religious, priestly, and apostolic body in the love of Christ the Lord and the service of the Church.

192/ 2. Furthermore, the Congregation commends and urges:

a. that the participation of the temporal coadjutors in the life and apostolic activity of the Society be further promoted, fulfilling the recommendations of the 31st General Congregation completely;[4]

b. that the norms for the promotion of priests to the profession of four vows, better adapted by the 31st General Congregation to today's circumstances, be put into practice both for those who are at present spiritual coadjutors and for approved scholastics. Candidates, however, are to be selected in such a way as in fact to meet the demands of those criteria of selection.

---

[3] *ActRSJ,* XV, 557, letter of April 15, 1970.

[4] GC 31, D. 7, nn. 2, 3, 4; *ActRSJ,* XIV, 862.

DECREE 9

THE PERMANENT DIACONATE

The 32nd General Congregation amends Decree 6 of the 31st General Congregation[1] as follows:

193/ 1. In willing compliance with the desire of the Church, which commends the restoration of the permanent diaconate in the Eastern Churches, where the custom was discontinued,[2] and also in the Western Church, where in the judgment of the bishops and with the approval of the Holy See such renewal may lead to the spiritual progress of the faithful,[3] the General Congregation declares that our Society can be helped by having some members who are permanently engaged in the service of the Church by means of the holy order of the diaconate.

194/ 2. Those members who for good reasons approved by Father General are ordained permanent deacons will retain the grade that they already have in the Society; if they are approved coadjutors, they are to be advanced to the grade of formed temporal coadjutors, all requisites having been observed; if they are scholastics, they can be admitted by Father General to the grade of spiritual coadjutors, by way of exception, once all requisites have been observed, but they cannot be made superiors in the strict sense.

195/ 3. It is entrusted to Father General to obtain the necessary faculties from the Holy See so that there can be permanent deacons in the Society; and also to establish, whenever he judges it opportune, general or particular norms concerning the permanent diaconate in the Society.

---

[1] *ActRSJ,* XIV, 861.

[2] See OE, 17.

[3] See LG, 29; AG, 16.

DECREE 10

Time of Last Vows

196/ 1.   As to decree 11, of the 31st General Congregation:[1]

a. n. 2, 6°, is abrogated.

b. n. 2, 7°, shall be revised to read: "At least ten full years in the Society, including the years spent in initial studies of philosophy and theology in the Society."

c. n. 2, 8°, is abrogated.

d. n. 6, 3°, shall be revised to read: "If they are temporal coadjutors, they have completed ten years of religious life and have made the tertianship required by Decree 42 of the 30th General Congregation;[2] if they are approved scholastics, they have completed the length of time in the Society prescribed in n. I.b above."

197/ 2.   In the case of scholastics, ordination to the priesthood (which, generally, is not to be deferred more than three years after studies of theology are completed) and the tertianship prescribed in the Constitutions must precede final vows.

198/ 3.   The 9th Decree of the 12th General Congregation[3] is abrogated; but the days on which final vows have traditionally been pronounced in the Society are commended anew.

---

[1] *ActRSJ,* XIV, 887, 888.

[2] CollDecr 387.

[3] CollDecr 167.

III

WITNESS TO THE GOSPEL IN TODAY'S CIRCUMSTANCES

DECREE 11

The Union of Minds and Hearts

Orientations and Guidelines for Our Spiritual Life and Our Life in Community

199/ 1.　The 32nd General Congregation confirms and commends the declarations and directives of the 31st General Congregation on the religious life contained in its Decrees 13–17 and 19.[1] We believe them to be as helpful today in promoting our continual progress in spirit as when they were formulated, and hence they are implicitly assumed throughout the following statement.

200/ 2.　It must, however, be added that our experience during the last ten years of trying to live up to those declarations and directives, and the choices we have now made regarding our mission today, seem to call upon us, as well as to enable us, to give a sharper focus to our religious life as Jesuits. We believe that focus is the *union of minds and hearts [unio animorum] in the Society*. It is toward preserving and strengthening that union of minds and hearts under present-day conditions that the following orientations and practical norms are directed.

201/ 3.　We see our mission today as this: with renewed vigor to bear witness to the Gospel and, by the ministry of the Word, made operative in Christian charity, to help bring about in our world the reign of Christ in justice, love, and peace.[2] For just as Christ by his words and deeds, by his death and resurrection, made God's justice the world's salvation, and by so doing gave all men hope of becoming truly and wholly free, so we, his followers, are called upon to bear the witness of word and life to God's salvific love of the world in which we live.[3]

202/ 4.　The carrying out of this mission demands a very wide dispersion both of men and of ministries, given the great social and cultural diversity of our world. Hence, what St. Ignatius says about the need for union of minds and hearts among us was never more true than now: "The more difficult it is for members of this congregation to be united with their head and among themselves, since they are so scattered among the faithful and among unbelievers in diverse regions of the world, the more ought means to be sought for that union.

---

[1] *ActRSJ,* XIV, 889–926. D. 18, on Poverty, of the 31st GC, has been revised by the present GC.

[2] See GC 32, D. 4. "Our Mission Today: The Service of Faith and the Promotion of Justice."

[3] See Luke 4. 18–19, 6. 20–21; Matt. 11. 5, 12. 18–21; Gal. 2. 10; James 2. 1–18.

For the Society cannot be preserved, or governed, or, consequently, attain the end it seeks for the greater glory of God, unless its members are united among themselves and with their head."[4]

203/ 5.   Moreover, that very union of minds and hearts which participation in Christ's mission requires will at the same time be a powerful aid to that mission, since it will be a visible sign of the love of the Father for all men. In the following orientations, therefore, we treat of our *union with God in Christ,* from which flows our *brotherly communion with one another,* a communion strengthened and made apostolically efficacious by the *bond of obedience.*

A. Union with God in Christ

204/ 6.   Where, then, do we begin? We begin with the Ignatian insight that the unity of an apostolic body such as ours must be based on the union of each and all with God in Christ.[5] For if we have come together as a companionship, it is because we have, each of us, responded to the call of the Eternal King.[6]

205/ 7.   In seeking this union with God in Christ, we experience a *difficulty peculiar to our times,* and we must be prepared to meet it. The material conditions of our world—a world of sharply contrasted affluence and misery—and the spiritual climate engendered by them, tend to produce in our contemporaries an inner emptiness, a sense of the absence of God. The expressions, signs, and symbols of God's presence which reassured men in the past do not seem to be able to fill the present emptiness. We are still groping for the new expressions, signs, and symbols that can do so. In the meantime, we ourselves are sometimes plunged in this climate of emptiness; and so it is crucial for us somehow to regain that continual *familiarity* with God in both prayer and action which St. Ignatius considered absolutely essential to the very existence of our companionship.

206/ 8.   We are thus led, inevitably, to the absolute necessity of *personal prayer,* both as a value in itself and as a source of energy for apostolic action. "The charity of Christ urges us to personal prayer and no human person can dispense us from that urgency."[7] We need it for the familiarity with God which consists in finding him in all things, and all things in him. Christ himself gave us an example of this. St. Ignatius urges it in both the Exercises and the Constitutions. Our own personal experience confirms it. For while it is "in action" that we are called to be contemplative, this cannot obscure the fact that we *are* called to be "contemplative."

---

[4] *Cons.* [655].

[5] *Cons.* [671],

[6] *SpEx* 98.

[7] GC 31, D. 14, n. 7; *ActRSJ,* XIV, 893.

207/ 9.   And yet, many of us are troubled because, although we want to pray, we cannot pray as we would like and as our apostolic commitments demand we should. In the midst of our individual, isolated efforts to pray as we should, perhaps we should listen to Christ's reminder that "where two or three are gathered in my name, there am I in their midst."[8] Does this not suggest that if we need assistance it is in our companionship that we must seek it: in dialogue with the spiritual counsellor, in openness to the superior, in shared prayer with our brothers?

208/ 10.   Moreover, let us not forget that while our world poses obstacles in the way of our search for union with God in Christ, it also offers suggestions for surmounting those obstacles, which we should submit to an Ignatian discernment of spirits in order to determine where in them the Spirit of God is moving us. There is, for instance, the contemporary stress on spontaneous prayer, with a minimum of formalism. There is the interest in, and understanding of, the different approaches to union with God developed by the non-Christian religions. There are the various forms of prayer in community which lead to a mutually enriching exchange of faith experiences. There is, finally, the remarkable renewal taking place today in the giving and the making of the Spiritual Exercises, whose vivifying influence extends beyond the limits of the formal retreat into the daily life of prayer.[9]

209/ 11.   Not only that; fidelity to the Exercises energizes our apostolic action. It enlarges our inner freedom to respond readily to the demands which the service of faith may make of us. It deepens in us the self-abnegation that unites us to Christ crucified,[10] and thus to the poverty, humiliations, and sufferings by which he saved the world.[11] And, not least, it fills us with joy: the joy of service which, more than anything else, will attract others to join our companionship; the abiding joy of men whom nothing can separate from the love of God which is in Christ Jesus our Lord.[12] Thus, the Spiritual Exercises, in which as Jesuits we especially experience Christ and respond to his call, lie at the heart of our Jesuit voca-

---

[8] Matt. 18. 20.

[9] There is steady growth in the practice of shared prayer which can greatly help our awareness of both God and our fellow men. Schools of prayer and houses of prayer have also developed. Different kinds of community prayer are facilitating the sharing of faith and spiritual experiences with others in the community. Eucharistic concelebrations, meetings on spiritual topics, spiritual conversations, reading of Sacred Scripture or part of the liturgical hours in common, the review of life in community: all these practices can strengthen our fraternal union as members of an apostolic community as well as our personal relationship with Christ.

[10] Phil. 2. 5–8.

[11] *SpEx* 167.

[12] Rom. 8. 39.

tion. Returning every year to the Exercises, each Jesuit renews in them his dedication to Christ.

210/ 12. Our union with God in Christ is furthered not only by formal prayer, personal and communitarian, but also by the offering of Christ's sacrifice and the reception of his sacraments. Every Jesuit community is a faith community, and it is in the Eucharist that those who believe in Christ come together to celebrate their common faith. Our participation at the same table in the Body and Blood of Christ, more than anything else, makes us one companionship totally dedicated to Christ's mission in the world.

211/ 13. Inwardly strengthened and renewed by prayer and the sacraments, we are able to make apostolic action itself a form of union with God. Our service of the faith *[diakonia fidei]* and our service of men then become, not an interruption of that union but a continuation of it, a joining of our action with Christ's salvific action in history. Thus contemplation flows into action regularly, and we realize to some extent our ideal of being contemplatives "in action."

B. Brotherly Communion

212/ 14. From union with God in Christ flows, of necessity, brotherly love. Love of the neighbor, which union with Christ and with God in Christ implies and includes,[13] has for its privileged object in our case, the companions of Jesus who compose our Society.[14] They are our companions; and it is our community ideal that we should be companions not only in the sense of fellow workers in the apostolate, but truly brothers and friends in the Lord.

213/ 15.   *a.* By forming in this way a community of brothers, we bear witness to the presence of God among men: God who, as Trinity, is, beyond all imagining, a community of Love; God who, made Man, established with men an everlasting covenant.[15] Even our interpersonal relationship within the community, then, has an apostolic dimension, in that it must set the tone of our relationship with those outside the community who serve in the apostolate with us, and, indeed, with all men of good will who work for justice or sincerely seek the real meaning of human life. Not only that; it must set the tone of our relationship with those we seek to serve: with those who are our neighbors not simply by local propinquity, but by a sharing of concerns and aspirations.

214/ 16. But let us realistically face the facts that make community building difficult today. More so today than in the past, our membership is drawn from very different social and cultural backgrounds. Moreover, the modern world plac-

---

[13] 1 John 3. 14–15; 4. 7–8, 16; 5. 1.

[14] *Cons.* [671].

[15] John 13.34 sq.

es a much heavier stress on individual freedom than on the subordination of the individual to the group. Our response to these realities will be to transform them from obstacles to aids in community building. Our basic attitude toward cultural differences will be that they can enrich our union rather than threaten it. Our basic altitude toward personal freedom will be that freedom is fulfilled in the active service of love.

215/ 17. Not that we should adopt an attitude of indiscriminate tolerance, a weary attitude of "peace at any price." Our attitude should be, rather, that of the Contemplation for Obtaining Love: "to consider how all blessings and gifts descend from above, such as my limited power from the supreme and limitless power on high, and so with justice, goodness, piety, mercy; as rays from the sun, as water from the spring."[16] We come to the Society from many lands, many ways of thought and life, each one of which has received a particular grace from God's infinite bounty. As companions of Jesus and each other, we wish to share with one another what we have and are, for the building up of communities dedicated to the apostolate of reconciliation.

216/ 18. *b.* Hence the need of opening up and maintaining clear channels of communication within our communities and among them, a need which St. Ignatius foresaw when, in terms of the communication facilities of his time, he called for regular and frequent letter writing back and forth between communities and individuals, and between head and members.[17] In any case, it is clear that our communities should not be self-enclosed but most open; they are *communities for mission.* They receive their mission from authority; but authority itself expects the community to discern, in union with its superior and in conformity with his final decision, the concrete ways whereby that mission is to be accomplished and the procedure by which it is to be evaluated and revised in the light of actual performance. In other words, it is with the community as with the individual: it is from the inner life of grace and virtue that force flows outward to the works proposed to us.[18] Hence the need to structure in our communities, flexibly, to be sure, but firmly, a way of life that favors personal and community prayer, provides for the relaxation of tensions and the celebration of life, and establishes a climate in which men dedicated to apostolic service can—as the apostles of Jesus did—gradually grow to the height of their vocation.[19]

217/ 19. Fraternal communication within the community can take many forms according to different needs and circumstances. But its basic presup-

---

[16] *SpEx* 237.

[17] *Cons.* [673, 821].

[18] *Cons.* [813].

[19] Mark 6. 30–31.

position is, at the human level, sincerity and mutual trust[20] and, at the level of grace, those gifts of God with which our companionship began and by which it is maintained.[21]

218/ 20. Certain features of our Ignatian heritage can be given a communitarian dimension; provided, of course, the personal practice for which they were originally intended is not abandoned. For instance, the examination of conscience could, at times, be made a shared reflection on the community's fidelity to its apostolic mission. Similarly, fraternal correction and personal dialogue with the superior can usefully become a community review of community life style.

219/ 21. *c.* We can go further and say that community spiritual interchange can, under certain conditions, become *communitarian discernment.* This is something quite distinct from the usual community dialogue. It is "a corporate search for the will of God by means of a shared reflection on the signs which point where the Spirit of Christ is leading,"[22] and the method to follow in such communitarian discernment is analogous to that which St. Ignatius teaches for the making of a personal decision on a matter of importance.[23]

220/ 22. There are prerequisites for a valid communitarian discernment. On the part of the individual member of the community, a certain familiarity with the Ignatian rules for the discernment of spirits, derived from actual use;[24] a determined resolution to find the will of God for the community whatever it may cost; and, in general, the dispositions of mind and heart called for and cultivated in the First and Second Weeks of the Exercises. On the part of the community as such, a clear definition of the matter to be discerned, sufficient information regarding it, and "a capacity to convey to one another what each one really thinks and feels."[25]

221/ 23. Clearly, the requisite dispositions for true communitarian discernment are such that they will not be verified as often as those for ordinary community dialogue. Nevertheless, every community should seek to acquire them, so that when need arises it can enter into this special way of seeking the will of God. Indeed, inasmuch as it should be characteristic of a Jesuit to be in familiar contact with God and to seek his will constantly in a spirit of true Ignatian indifference, even ordinary community meetings and house consultations can incorporate ele-

---

[20] *SpEx* 22.

[21] *Cons.* [134, 812].

[22] R.P. Arrupe, "De Nostrorum in spiritu institutione," *ActRSJ*, XV (1967), 123–4.

[23] *SpEx* 169–89.

[24] *SpEx* 313–36.

[25] R.P. Arrupe, "De spirituali discretione," *ActRSJ*, XV (1971), 767–73.

ments of true communitarian discernment, provided we seriously seek God's will concerning the life and work of the community.

222/ 24. What is the role of the superior in communitarian discernment? It is, first, to develop, as far as he can, the requisite disposition for it; second, to decide when to convoke the community for it, and clearly to define its object; third, to take active part in it as the bond of union within the community and as the link between the community and the Society as a whole; and, finally, to make the final decision in the light of the discernment, but freely, as the one to whom both the grace and the burden of authority are given. For in our Society the discerning community is not a deliberative or capitular body but a consultative one, whose object, clearly understood and fully accepted, is to assist the superior to determine what course of action is for God's greater glory and the service of men.

223/ 25. *d.* Times of stress and trial that might threaten our fraternal communion from time to time can become moments of grace, which confirm our dedication to Christ and make that dedication credible. For, obviously, there is a reciprocal relationship between the religious vows and community life.[26] The living of the vows promotes and strengthens community life; community life, in turn, if truly fraternal, helps us to be faithful to our vows.

224/ 26. The orientations of this 32nd General Congregation regarding the *vow of poverty* are to be found in a separate declaration.

225/ Our vow of *chastity* consecrates a celibacy freely chosen for the sake of the Kingdom of God. By it, we offer an undivided heart to God, a heart capable of a self-giving in service approaching the freedom from self-interest with which God himself loves all his creatures. This is the witness we are called upon to give to a world which calls the value of celibacy into question; and the 32nd General Congregation simply and wholly confirms what the 31st General Congregation declared regarding the apostolic value of the vow of chastity.[27] We might simply add that celibacy for the sake of the Kingdom has a special apostolic value in our time, when men tend to put whole classes of their fellow human beings beyond the margins of their concern, while at the same time identifying love with eroticism. In such a time, the self-denying love which is warmly human, yet freely given in service to all, can be a powerful sign leading men to Christ who came to show us what love really is: that God is love.

---

[26] See GC 31. D. 19, n. 4; *ActRSJ*, XIV, 919.

[27] GC 31, D. 16; *ActRSJ*, XIV, 898 sq.

C. Obedience: The Bond of Union

226/ 27. "This union is produced, in great part, by the bond of obedience."[28] And precisely because it is our bond of union, it is the guarantee of our apostolic efficacy. Today, especially, given the wide dispersion of our apostolic enterprises, the need for us to acquire highly specialized skills in highly specialized works, and the consequent need, in many places, to make a distinction between our apostolic institutes and our religious communities, the preservation of unity of purpose and direction becomes a prime necessity.

227/ 28. In this task of unification the role of the major superior has been well defined by the 31st General Congregation.[29] What this 32nd General Congregation would like to stress is the equally important *role of the local or community superior.* Given the conditions alluded to above, even if the local superior does not have the direction of the apostolic work owing to the appointment of a director of the apostolate, he nevertheless retains the responsibility to confirm his brethren in their apostolic mission and to see to it that their religious and community life is such as to enable them to fulfill that mission with God's grace. Moreover, the task of the superior is not only to support the mission of the members of his community, but at times to determine it more precisely, "in such wise that the individuals dwelling in some house or college have recourse to their local superior or rector and are governed by him in every respect."[30]

228/ 29. His part is to stimulate as well as to moderate the apostolic initiatives of the members of his community. But, above all, the preservation of the community as a fraternal union depends on him. Whatever the kind of community over which he presides—and our mission today demands an astonishing variety of them—his task is to keep it together in love and obedience by that spiritual mode of governance "in all modesty and charity in the Lord" recommended and exemplified by St. Ignatius.[31]

229/ In addition to superiors, there are also *directors of works.* Where fitting, and in accord with norms that must be approved by Father General, the director of a work can have true religious authority in directing the efforts of those who have been assigned to work in that apostolate so that everything may be directed to the greater glory of God and the progress of others in Christian life and teaching. In carrying out his office, the director of the work should be alert to the advice and suggestions of his brother Jesuits and ready to receive their help. If any difficulties arise in reconciling the duties of the superior or superiors of commu-

---

[28] *Cons.* [659; see 662, 664, 666].

[29] GC 31, D. 46; *ActRSJ,* XIV, 978 sq., cf. D. 22; *ActRSJ,* XIV, 931.

[30] *Cons.* [662].

[31] *Cons.* [667].

nities and the director of the work, they should be resolved in statutes drawn up for this purpose.

230/ 30. Today, more than ever before, that spiritual mode of governance is needed. The contemporary stress on individual initiative mentioned earlier, combined with the wide range of opportunities open to that initiative, tends to obscure the sense of mission essential to Ignatian obedience and may dislodge it altogether, unless we make fuller use of the special instrument for spiritual governance bequeathed to us by St. Ignatius: the *account of conscience.*

231/ 31. Vowed obedience, whether in humdrum or in heroic matters, is always an act of faith and freedom whereby the religious recognizes and embraces the will of God manifested to him by one who has authority to send him in the name of Christ. He does not necessarily have to understand why he is being sent. But both the superior who sends and the companion who is sent gain assurance that the mission is really God's will if it is preceded by the dialogue that is the account of conscience. For by it the superior acquires an inner knowledge of those subject to his authority: what they can and what they cannot do, and what help they need by way of counsel or resource to do what they can. The companion, in turn, learns what the mission on which he is being sent involves and what, concretely, he must do to discharge his responsibility.

232/ 32. The more the account of conscience is genuinely practiced, the more authentic will our discernment be of God's purpose in our regard and the more perfect that union of minds and hearts from which our apostolate derives its dynamism. A community from which sincerity and openness in mutual relationships are absent soon becomes immobilized in purely formal structures which no longer respond to the needs and aspirations of the men of our time, or else it disintegrates altogether.

233/ 33. Beyond the limits of the strict matter of our vow of obedience extends our duty of *thinking with the Church.* Our being united among ourselves depends, in the last analysis, on our being united in both mind and heart to the Church that Christ founded. The historical context in which St. Ignatius wrote his Rules for Thinking with the Church is, of course, different from ours. But there remains for us the one pillar and ground of truth, the Church of the living God,[32] in which we are united by one faith and one baptism to the one Lord and to the Father.[33] It behooves us, then, to keep undimmed the spirit of the Ignatian rules and apply them with vigor to the changed conditions of our times.

234/ 34. Clearly, the union of minds and hearts of which we speak is difficult of achievement. Equally clearly, it is demanded by our apostolic mission. Our wit-

---

[32] 1 Tim. 3. 15.

[33] Eph. 4. 5.

ness to the Gospel would not be credible without it. The sincere acceptance and willing execution of these orientations and norms set forth by this present Congregation will help toward that union. But human means fall short. It is the Spirit of God, the Spirit of love, that must fill the Society. For this we humbly pray.

D. Guidelines

235/ 35. Because "the work of our redemption is constantly carried on in the mystery of the Eucharistic Sacrifice,"[34] all of our members should consider daily celebration of the Eucharist as the center of their religious and apostolic life.[35] Concelebrations are encouraged, especially on days when the community can more easily gather together.

236/ 36. In order to respond to the interior need for familiarity with God, we should all spend some time each day in personal prayer. Therefore, for those still in formation, "the Society retains the practice of an hour and a half as the time for prayer, Mass, and thanksgiving. Each man should be guided by his spiritual father as he seeks that form of prayer in which he can best advance in the Lord. The judgment of superiors is normative for each."[36]

For others, "our rule of an hour's prayer is to be adapted so that each Jesuit, guided by his superiors, takes into account his particular circumstances and needs, in the light of a discerning love."[37]

237/ 37. The time order of the community should include some brief daily common prayer and at times, in a way that is appropriate for each apostolic community, a longer period for prayer and prayerful discussion. Shared prayer, days of recollection, and the Spiritual Exercises in common are recognized as fruitful means for increasing union, since they provide the opportunity for reflecting before God on the mission of the community and, at the same time, express the apostolic character of our prayer.

238/ 38. Our entire apostolic life should be examined with the spiritual discernment proper to the Exercises, so that we might increasingly put into practice what God expects of us and purify the motivation of our lives. One means available to us is the daily examination of conscience, which was recommended by St. Ignatius so that we might be continually guided by the practice of spiritual discernment.

---

[34] GC 31, D. 14, n. 10; *ActRSJ*, XIV, 894. [The official Latin text at his point begins a newly numbered set of reference notes for the "Guidelines" in this decree. However, to avoid confusion, we will continue with the same sequence until the end of this section.]

[35] R.P. Arrupe, "De Nostrorum in spiritu institutione," *ActRSJ*, XV, 121 sq.

[36] GC 31, D. 14, n. 12, 2°; *ActRSJ*, XIV, 895.

[37] GC 31, D. 14, n. 11; *ActRSJ*, XIV, 895.

239/ 39. Since we need the grace of continual conversion of heart "to the love of the Father of mercies"[38] that the purity and freedom of our lives in God's service might increase, all should frequent the Sacrament of Reconciliation.[39] We should also willingly participate in communal penitential services and strive to promote the spirit of reconciliation in our communities.

240/ 40. Dialogue with a spiritual director on a regular basis is a great help for growing in spiritual insight and learning discernment. Every Jesuit, especially during formation but also when he is engaged in an active apostolate, should make every effort to have a spiritual director with whom he can speak frequently and openly. The provincials should endeavor to identify and prepare spiritual fathers who are experienced in personal prayer and who have good judgment. This is especially true for the formation communities.

241/ 41. The local superior is also responsible for the spiritual vitality of the community. He should take care that the community is a true faith community precisely because he is concerned with its apostolic mission. For this reason, he should consider it part of his job to provide the conditions that foster personal and community prayer, the sacramental life, and communication on a spiritual level. He should also take care that every Jesuit be able to find in the organization of community life whatever is necessary for recollection and for a suitable balance between work and rest.

242/ 42. The Spiritual Exercises are a privileged means for achieving renovation and union in the Society and for revitalizing our apostolic mission. They are a school of prayer and a time when a man has the spiritual experience of personally encountering Christ.

243/ For this reason, the 32nd General Congregation confirms n. 16 of Decree 14 of the 31st General Congregation.[40] In addition, it recommends:

a. That, especially at the time of the annual visitation, the provincials inquire about the way our members are making the Spiritual Exercises;

b. That, especially during this period of renovation in the Society, those who are already formed be encouraged to make the full Exercises extended over a month. This can be an effective means of implementing the conclusions of the 32nd General Congregation;

c. That, in the provinces, the greatest care be given to the formation of those who have the talent to direct the Exercises;

---

[38] PO, 186.

[39] Sacred Congregation for Religious: "Circa usum et Administrationem Sacramenti Paenitentiae et circa idoneitatem ad Professionem Religiosam," n. 3; Dec. 8, 1970.

[40] GC 31, D. 14, n. 16; *ActRSJ,* XIV, 896.

d. That those already formed should at times make the annual retreat under the personal direction of a skilled director.

244/ 43. The 32nd General Congregation confirms and recommends all that is contained in the decrees of the 31st General Congregation concerning devotion to the Sacred Heart and Our Lady, as they pertain to both the spiritual life of Ours and the apostolate. In the promotion of these devotions, account should be taken of the differences which exist in various parts of the world.[41]

245/ 44. All Jesuits, even those who must live apart because of the demands of their apostolate or for other justifiable reasons, should take an active part in the life of some community. To the extent that the bond with a community and its superior is more than merely juridical, that union of minds and hearts which is so desirable will be kept intact.

246/ 45. Every community of the Society should have its own superior.

247/ 46. The account of conscience is of great importance for the spiritual governance of the Society, and its practice is to be esteemed and cultivated. Therefore, all should give an account of conscience to their superiors, according to the norms and spirit of the Society.[42] In addition, the relationships between superiors and their brethren in the Society should be such as to encourage the account of conscience and conversation about spiritual matters.

248/ 47. Taking into account the mission it has been given, every community should after mature deliberation establish a time order for community life. This time order should be approved by the major superior and periodically revised.

249/ 48. Since our communities are apostolic, they should be oriented toward the service of others, particularly the poor, and to cooperation with those who are seeking God or working for greater justice in the world. For this reason, under the leadership of superiors, communities should periodically examine whether their way of living sufficiently supports their apostolic mission and encourages hospitality. They should also consider whether their style of life testifies to simplicity, justice, and poverty.

250/ 49. Communities will not be able to witness to Christian love unless each member contributes to community life and gives sufficient time and effort to the task. Only in this way can an atmosphere be created which makes communication possible and in which no one goes unnoticed or is neglected.[43]

---

[41] GC 31, D. 15; *ActRSJ,* XIV, 897; and D. 16, n. 7e; *ActRSJ,* XIV, 901.

[42] GC 31, D. 17, n. 8; *ActRSJ,* XIV, 908.

[43] *SpEx* 22, "It is necessary to suppose that every good Christian is more ready to put a good interpretation on another's statement than to condemn it as false."

251/ 50. To the extent possible, superiors should strive to build an Ignatian apostolic community in which many forms of open and friendly communication on a spiritual level are possible. Since it is a privileged way to find God's will, the use of communal spiritual discernment is encouraged if the question at issue is of some importance and the necessary preconditions have been verified.

252/ 51. Solidarity among communities in a province as well as fraternal charity require that communities be open to men of different ages, talent, and work.

253/ 52. The dwelling and arrangement of the community should be such that it allows for needed privacy and encourages the spiritual, intellectual, and cultural development of community members. These are necessary conditions for the fulfillment of our apostolic mission.

254/ 53. Within limits imposed by our profession of poverty, communication and union among members of the Society should be strengthened in the following ways:

a. gatherings of communities in the same city or regions should be encouraged;

b. workshops and task forces should be established for each area of the apostolate;

c. regular meetings should be held of the superiors of each province and the provincials of each assistancy or major region.

E. The Common Rules

255/ 54. The Common Rules approved by the 4th General Congregation and revised by the 27th General Congregation are abrogated. Number 14 of Decree 19 of the 31st General Congregation is also abrogated.[44]

a. This Congregation recommends to Father General that at his discretion he publish a *summary* of the decrees of the 31st and 32nd General Congregations, together with a summary of the letters he has written to the Society since the 31st General Congregation. This summary can serve as an index of principal features of our religious life.

b. It is left to provincials, with the approval of Father General, to determine for each province or group of provinces more particular norms which shall be adapted to local circumstances.

---

[44] See *ActRSJ,* XIV, 925.

F. Declaration concerning Decree 17, Number 10 of the 31st General Congregation[45]

256/ 5. What is contained in Decree 17, n. 10, should be understood in the following way:

a. The ordinary means of dealing with a conflict of this type is through sincere dialogue, according to the Ignatian principle of representation and following upon prayer and appropriate consultation.

b. A Jesuit is always free to approach a higher superior.

c. If the conflict cannot be resolved either through dialogue or recourse to a higher superior, other persons—some of whom may be from outside the Society—may be called by mutual consent to assist in forming one's conscience more clearly. This should be done privately and without publicity.

d. The procedure cannot be imposed on either the superior or the Jesuit involved. It is entirely voluntary and unofficial. It is nothing more than a new effort to find the divine will.

e. The opinion of those consulted has no juridical effect on the authority of the superior. It is merely advisory.

f. If, after this procedure, a Jesuit still feels he cannot obey in good conscience, the superior should determine what should be done. "But a man who, time after time, is unable to obey with a good conscience, should take thought regarding some other path of life in which he can serve God with greater tranquility."[46]

---

[45] See *ActRSJ,* XIV, 909. [See p. 120 in this volume.]

[46] GC 31, D. 17, n. 10; *ActRSJ,* XIV, 910.

DECREE 12

POVERTY

For a More Authentic Poverty

257/ 1.   In recent times and especially since the Second Vatican Council, the Church, her families of religious, indeed the whole Christian world have been striving for a deeper understanding and new experiential knowledge of evangelical poverty. This Congregation, like its predecessor, has tried earnestly to enter into this movement and to discern its implications for our Society.

258/ 2.   Voluntary poverty in imitation of Christ is a sharing in that mystery revealed in the self-emptying of the very Son of God in the Incarnation. The Jesuit vocation to poverty draws its inspiration from the experience of St. Ignatius and the Spiritual Exercises and is specified by the *Formula of the Institute* and by the Constitutions.[1] It is the charism of the Society to serve Christ poor and humble. The principle and foundation of our poverty, therefore, is found in a love of the Word made Flesh and crucified.

A.   Signs of the Times

259/ 3.   Reflection on the Gospel in the light of the signs of our times has illumined new aspects of this religious poverty. Contemporary man has become very aware of massive, dehumanizing poverty, not only material but spiritual as well. Everywhere there are to be found men of good will working for a social order of greater justice and the abolition of oppressive structures. At the same time, the appetite for enjoyment and consumption of material goods spreads everywhere and verges on a practical atheism. The rich, individuals and nations, are thereby hardened in their readiness to oppress others, and all, rich and poor, are duped into placing man's whole happiness in such consumption. Still, there are those who react against this materialism and seek a new liberty and another happiness in a simpler way of life and in the pursuit of higher values. On all sides there is felt a desire to discover new communities which favor a more intimate interpersonal communication, communities of true sharing and communion, concerned for the integral human development of their members. Our lives, our communities, our very poverty can and should have a meaning and a message for such a world.

260/ 4.   These common experiences of contemporary man are signs of the times which prompt us to seek a deeper insight into the mystery of Christ. Re-

---

[1] *SpEx* 98, 147, 167; *ConsMHSJ* I, "Deliberatio de Paupertate," pp. 78 sq.; "Deliberatio de Paupertate," "Ephemeris S.P.N. Ignatii," p. 86 sq.; *Cons.* [553 sq.].

ligious poverty still calls to the following of Christ poor, but also to a following of Christ at work in Nazareth, identifying with the needy in his public life, the Christ of heartfelt compassion, responding to their needs, eager to serve them.[2] For centuries, the perfection of religious poverty was found in mendicancy. He was counted poor who lived on alms, placing all his hopes in the providence of God operative through benefactors. With growing clarity the Church invites religious to submit to the common law of labor.[3] "Earning your own living and that of your brothers or sisters, helping the poor by your work—these are duties incumbent upon you."[4] Indeed the Church encourages religious "to join the poor in their situation and to share their bitter cares."[5] Response to such invitations is presented as an expression of vowed poverty suited to our times. Calling all the faithful more urgently than ever to spend themselves in the promotion of social justice, the Church shows that she places high hopes in the efforts of those who have consecrated themselves and all they have to Christ by the vow of poverty.[6] Something of an evolution seems to have taken place: today the primary import of religious poverty is found not only in an ascetic-moral perfection through the imitation of Christ poor, but also, and more in the apostolic value of imitating Christ, forgetful of self in his generous and ready service of all the abandoned.

261/ 5.   The Society cannot meet the demands of today's apostolate without reform of its practice of poverty. Jesuits will be unable to hear the "cry of the poor"[7] unless they have greater personal experience of the miseries and distress of the poor. It will be difficult for the Society everywhere to forward effectively the cause of justice and human dignity if the greater part of her ministry identifies her with the rich and powerful, or is based on the "security of possession, knowledge, and power."[8] Our life will be no "witness to a new and eternal life won by Christ's redemption or to a resurrected state and the glory of the heavenly kingdom,[9] "if individually or corporately, Jesuits are seen to be attached to earthly things, even apostolic institutions, and to be dependent on them. Our communities will have no meaning or sign value for our times, unless by their sharing of themselves and

---

[2] Pope Paul VI, Adhortatio Apostolica, "Evangelica Testificatio," June 29, 1971; *AAS* (1971), p. 497 sq., 17.

[3] PC, 13; see ET, 20.

[4] ET, 20.

[5] ET, 18.

[6] ET, 17.

[7] Ps. 9.13; Job 34.28; Prov. 21. 13; ET, 17.

[8] ET, 19.

[9] LG, 44.

all they possess, they are clearly seen to be communities of charity and of concern for each other and all others.

B. Our Response

262/ 6. That the Society has long been uneasy about the practice of poverty by individuals, communities, and apostolic institutes is evidenced by hundreds of postulates from all parts of the world. The Congregation, mindful of its duty, has tried to answer this call of the Society, not so much by words and exhortation as by new structures of temporal administration. The single intent is to strengthen and confirm the practice of poverty.

263/ 7. The first aim of the reform to be outlined below is finally to "answer the demands of this real and not pretended poverty."[10] In a world of mass starvation, no one can lightly call himself poor. It is perhaps regrettable that we have no other word to designate this note of religious life, since poverty means very different things to different people. At the very least, religious poverty should try hard to limit rather than to expand consumption. It is not possible to love poverty or experience its mysterious consolations, without some knowledge of its actuality. The standard of living of our houses should not be higher than that of a family of slender means whose providers must work hard for its support. The concrete exigencies of such a standard are to be discerned by individuals and communities in sincere deliberation with their superiors. It should look to food and drink, lodging and clothing, but also and perhaps especially to travel, recreation, use of automobiles, and of villas, vacations, etc. Some should scrutinize their leisure, sometimes such as hardly the rich enjoy. The need for reform is so frequently evident and demanded by so many Provincial Congregations that no person or community may decline this examination.

264/ 8. The grace of our vocation demands loyal and generous effort to live that poverty required by the Society's spirit and law. The frequent engagement of Ours in professions and salaried offices is not without dangers, not only for the spirit of gratuity, but even for the observance of common life itself. Such work is to be chosen only as a more effective means to the communication of the faith or to spiritual advancement, without thought of remuneration or of the privileges attached to an office. Independence from the community in acquisition or expenditure, a vice with manifold disguises, cannot be tolerated. Every Jesuit must contribute to the community everything he receives by way of remuneration, stipend, alms, gift, or in any other way. He receives from the community alone everything he needs. In the same way, by cheerfully and gratefully accepting the community's standard of living, each undertakes to support his brothers in their efforts to live and to love pov-

---

[10] GC 31, D. 18, n. 7; *ActRSJ,* XIV, 913.

erty. Those who are unwilling to observe this double law of common life, separate themselves from the fraternity of the Society in spirit if not in law.

265/ 9. The voluntary poverty of religious is the attempt of fallen men to achieve that liberty from inordinate attachment, which is the condition of any great and ready love of God and man. In the Society this very liberty to love is in the service of the apostolate. Every Jesuit, no matter what his ministry, is called "to preach in poverty,"[11] according to the *sacra doctrina* of the Two Standards,[12] and this poverty has a spiritual power not to be measured in human terms. Apostolic efficiency and apostolic poverty are two values to be held in an on-going tension, and this is a rule for apostolic institutes as well as for individuals. The expedience of retaining rich and powerful institutions, requiring great capital outlay, is to be weighed prudently and spiritually. Since these institutions are but means, the attitude of the Society should be that of the Third Class of Men, and according to the rule of *tantum-quantum,* fully as ready to abandon as to retain, to the greater service of God. The faithful practice of religious poverty is apostolic, too, in its contempt of personal gain, which commends the Gospel and frees the apostle to preach it in all its integrity. It is apostolic, finally, in that communities which are really poor, by their simplicity and fraternal union, proclaim the beatitudes, "manifesting to all believers the presence of heavenly goods already possessed here below."[13]

266/ 10. This Congregation has spoken elsewhere of the necessity of commitment to the cause of justice and to the service of the poor. The Church regards such ministry as integral to the contemporary practice of poverty.[14] Such commitment is everywhere needed, but in many places it is a very condition of credibility for the Society and for the Church. The insertion of communities among the poor so that Jesuits may work for them and with them, or at least may acquire some experience of their condition, is a testimony of love of the poor and of poverty to which the Church encourages religious.[15] Implementation of this proposal will have to be different in our widely differing circumstances. Unless there be evident reason to the contrary, however, provincials should encourage those communities which, in union and charity with the rest of the province, choose to practice a stricter poverty, or to live among the poor, serving them and sharing something of their experience.[16]

---

[11] *MHSJ,* MI "S. Ignatii . . . Epistolae et Instructiones," I, 96.

[12] *SpEx,* 147.

[13] LG, 44; GS, 72; GC 31, D. 18, nn. 4, 7, 16a; D. 19, 7 sq.; AA, 4.

[14] ET, 18, 20.

[15] ET, 18, 20.

[16] *Cons.* [580]; *Examen Generale* 81.

C. New Structures

267/ 11. The better to meet the new demands of our poverty, the Congregation has undertaken a reform of the structures of temporal administration. The keystone of this reform is the distinction between apostolic institutes and the communities which serve them. The former are governed by the present law of the "colleges" [technically so called in the law of the Society], and so may possess endowments and needful revenue. Communities, however, are assimilated to "professed house" [also technically so called], and may have no stable revenues from capital.

268/ 12. With the recognition of remuneration for work as a legitimate source of support, there is less emphasis on alms as the only legitimate source of income for a community.[17] On the other hand, there is greater stress on the apostolic use of all revenues. Communities must live a simple and frugal life within an approved budget. They may not accumulate capital but must dispose of any annual surplus, according to a provincial plan which will look to the needs of communities, of apostolates, and of the poor. As far as possible, apostolic institutes, too, are bound by this law of fraternity and solidarity towards other ministries. Neither the capital nor the revenues of our institutes may profit our communities, except for approved remuneration for services rendered. If an institute is suppressed, its assets are reserved for use in other apostolic enterprises.

D. Conclusion

269/ 13. It is clear that admission of sin and true conversion of heart will help more toward a lived poverty than any revision of law. For that favor we must pray God earnestly as part of the grace of our vocation, to which we must remain open. While law can support spirit, no legal reform will profit anything unless all our members elect evangelical poverty with courage at the invitation of the Eternal King, Christ Our Lord. Let all superiors in meditation and prayer become deeply conscious of their responsibility to forward this renovation of poverty. Each member should recall that this reformed poverty will never be realized unless all unitedly and generously support superiors in this task.

270/ 14. This is the desire of the Congregation, this its prayer to God for the Society, a poverty profoundly renewed,

> —simple in community expression and joyous in the following of Christ;
>
> —happy to share with each other and with all;
>
> —apostolic in its active indifference and readiness for any service;

---

[17] GC 31, D. 18, n. 15; *ActRSJ,* XIV, 915.

—inspiring our selection of ministries and turning us to those most in need;

—spiritually effective, proclaiming Jesus Christ in our way of life and in all we do.

The authenticity of our poverty after all does not consist so much in the lack of temporal goods, as in the fact that we live, and are seen to live, from God and for God, sincerely striving for the perfection of that ideal which is the goal of the spiritual journey of the Exercises: "Give me only your love and your grace, and I am rich enough, and ask for nothing more."[18]

272/ 15. The following norms are the principles for the revision of the statutes on poverty. It will take time to reduce them to familiar practice. It is the internal law of charity and love which will be their best interpreter, that law which leads all of us to "love poverty as a mother, and . . . when occasions arise, feel some effects of it."[19] The Congregation earnestly commends this decree to the faithful observance of all.

E. Norms

Terminology

273/ 16. In this decree by *community* is understood any group of Jesuits legitimately constituted under the authority of a local superior.

274/ 17. *Apostolic institutes* are those institutions or works belonging to the Society which have a certain permanent unity and organization for apostolic purposes, such as universities, colleges, retreat houses, reviews, and other such in which our members carry on their apostolic work.

All communities can have apostolic institutes

275/ 18. All communities can have attached to them one or more apostolic institutes in which the whole community or some of its members exercise their apostolate.

The separation to be put into effect

276/ 19 By the law of the Society, there is to be established a distinction between communities and apostolic institutes, at least with regard to the destination and usufruct of their goods and between the financial accounts of each.

277/ 20. A distinction of moral persons, canonical or civil, is also recommended, where this can be effected without great inconvenience, preserving al-

---

[18] *SpEx,* 234.
[19] *Cons* [287].

ways the apostolic finality of the institutes and the authority of the Society to direct them to such ends.

The resources of institutes may not be diverted to the use of the communities

278/ 21. The goods of apostolic institutes of the Society may not be diverted to the use or profit of our members, except for a suitable remuneration, to be approved by the provincial, for work in such institutes or for services rendered to the same.

Poverty of communities

279/ 22. All communities dedicated to pastoral work or to any other apostolic functions are equated to professed houses in what pertains to poverty.[20] However, all may be the juridical subject of all rights, including ownership, pertaining to the apostolic institutes attached to such communities.

280/ 23. Seminaries for our members[21] retain their own regime of poverty. Houses or infirmaries for our aged or sick are equated to the former.

Annual community budgets

281/ 24. In each community the responsible administrators will draft each year at the appointed times and according to the norms established by the provincial, a projected budget as well as a statement of revenues and expenses. These will be communicated to the community as soon as convenient and are to be approved by the provincial.

Disposition of surplus

282/ 25. That the life of our communities may be "removed as far as possible from all infection of avarice and as like as possible to evangelical poverty,"[22] the surplus of each community will be distributed yearly according to the provision of nn. 27–31 except for a moderate sum to be approved by the provincial for unforeseen expenses. This sum is never to exceed the ordinary expenses of one year.

283/ 26. The first beneficiary of such surplus in each community will be the apostolic institute or institutes attached to the same if these stand in need, unless the provincial with his consultors should decide otherwise.

Sharing resources

284/ 27. According to the norms to be established by the provincial and approved by Father General, there is to be provision for the distribution of the com-

---

[20] See GC 31, D. 27, n. 7; *ActRSJ,* XIV, 948.

[21] See *Epitome Instituti Societatis Jesu,* n. 29.

[22] FI, n. 7.

munities' surplus mentioned in n. 25, for the benefit of those communities or works of the province which are in greater need.

285/ 28. In this sharing of resources, the needs of other provinces, of the whole Society, and of non-Jesuits will be considered.[23]

286/ 29. Major superiors can require that individual communities, according to their capacities, contribute a certain sum of money to the relief of the needs of other communities or apostolic institutes of the province or of other provinces, even if this should require some reduction in their standard of living, which in any case must always be frugal.[24]

287/ 30. Provinces are permitted to provide insurance for old age and for sickness, either through their own "Arca," or with other provinces, or by participation in governmental or in private plans.

288/ 31. A Charitable and Apostolic Fund of the Society is to be established for the benefit of communities and works of the Society, and, should need arise, for externs as well. It is not to be permanently invested but what it receives is to be distributed.

Father General is to determine the sources of this fund, its administration and manner of distributing benefits, with the assistance of advisers from different parts of the Society.

Poverty of apostolic institutes

289/ 32. Apostolic institutes, churches excepted, can have revenue-bearing capital and stable revenues, adequate to their purposes, if such seem necessary to the provincial.

290/ 33. Superiors and directors, mindful that we are sent to preach in poverty, will take great care that our apostolic institutes avoid every manner of extravagance and limit themselves strictly to the functional, attentive to the standards of similar institutes or works of their region and to the apostolic finality of our institutes. It is the responsibility of the provincial to determine what is required so that the apostolic institutes belonging to the Society manifest this character and mark of apostolic evangelical poverty.

291/ 34. With due respect for the needs of apostolic institutes and, if this applies, for the statutes of the institute and the will of benefactors, provincials, with the approval of the General, will provide for a more equitable and apostolically effective sharing of resources among the apostolic institutes of the province, looking always to God's greater service.

---

[23] See GC 31, D. 48, n. 4; *ActRSJ,* XIV, 981.

[24] See GC 31, D. 18, n. 9; *ActRSJ,* XIV, 914.

292/ 35. Those responsible for the administration of apostolic institutes will present to the provincial at the appointed times, the annual budget of the institute, a statement of the year's revenues and expenses, and, if required, a balance sheet.

293/ 36. If an apostolic, institute be suppressed, the superiors, according to their respective competence, will take care that its assets be devoted to another apostolic work or placed in the fund for apostolic works of the province or of the Society, respecting always, if this applies, the statutes of the institute and the will of benefactors. Such assets may never be destined to the use or benefit of a community, of a province, or of the Society.

Norms of transition

294/ 37. The Statutes on Poverty, promulgated by Father General on September 15, 1967, continue in force with the same authority as at promulgation, except for those norms which are contrary to the provisions of this decree.

295/ 38. The General Congregation charges Father General, with the help of a commission to be constituted by himself, to have the Statutes revised according to the principles, prescriptions, and recommendations of this decree and to promulgate them as soon as possible on his own authority.

Recommendations to the commission for the revision of the statutes
on poverty

296/ 39. The General Congregation recommends the following to the commission for the revision of the statutes on poverty:

a. The statutes should prescribe that in temporal administration and especially in investments of the Society, of provinces, or communities and apostolic institutes, care be had for the observance and due promotion of social justice.

b. In editing the revised statutes, the provisions which look to the personal and community practice of poverty should be so published in a compendium as to serve in the best manner possible for reflection and spiritual discernment, while those matters which have little to do with the daily practice of poverty of our members should be relegated to an appendix or to an Instruction on Temporal Administration.

c. The commission should give serious study to many well considered postulates, either of provincial congregations or of individuals, to the end that according to the diligent prudence of the commission,

—provision may be made in the Statutes for those matters which do not exceed the competence of Father General;

—those which exceed his authority may be thoroughly investigated so that clear proposals in their regard can be made to the 33rd General Congregation.

F. Capacity of the Society and of Provinces to Possess Temporal Goods

297/ 40. The General Congregation, confirming the provisions of the statutes on poverty promulgated September 15, 1967, concerning the capacity of the Society and of provinces to possess temporal goods,[25] decrees the following:

1. The Society, provinces, vice-provinces, and missions dependent and independent, as distinguished from communities and apostolic institutes, are capable of possessing even revenue-bearing capital and of enjoying fixed and stable revenues, within the limits here defined, provided always that such goods and revenues are not applied to the support of the professed or formed coadjutors, except as permitted below, 3*a* and *b*.

298/ 2. The Society may possess such revenue-bearing capital and fixed and stable revenues only to promote certain apostolic works of a more universal kind or to relieve the needs of missions and provinces.

The Society is owner of the Charitable and Apostolic Fund mentioned above in n. 31.

299/ 3. Provinces, vice-provinces, and missions dependent and independent, can possess revenue-bearing capital and can enjoy fixed and stable revenues, only for the following purposes:

a. For the support and education of those in probation or engaged in studies *(Arca Seminarii);*

b. For the support of the aged and the sick;

c. To set up or develop houses or foundations, whether these have already been established or are yet to be established, according as necessity or opportunity may indicate *(Arca Fundationum);*

d. To promote certain works, such as retreat houses, especially for non-Jesuits, centers for the social apostolate or for the diffusion of Catholic teaching by means of the media of social communication, for charitable enterprises both in and outside the Society, and for other apostolates which otherwise would lack sufficient resources *(Arca Operum Apostolicorum).*

---

[25] See Statutes on Poverty, nn. 52, 83; *ActRSJ,* XV, 81, 88.

G. Definition of Revenues Prohibited to Communities

300/ 41. The 32nd General Congregation authentically declares that the fixed and stable revenues prohibited to our communities are completely defined to be those revenues from property, moveable or immoveable, either belonging to the Society or so invested in foundations, which the Society can claim in law.

H. Amendment of Decree 18 of General Congregation XXXI

301/ 42. In Decree 18, n. 16, d, of the 31st General Congregation[26] after the words "may be accepted;" the following is to be added: "so also the remuneration attached to certain stable ministries, such as those of hospital chaplains, catechists, and the like."

I. A Faculty of Dispensation to Be Asked of the Holy See

302/ 43. The General Congregation charges Father General to request of the Holy See, at least as a precaution, the faculty to dispense in individual cases, both communities and churches of Jesuits from the prohibition of having stable revenues, in the case of revenues not deriving from investment with the intention of gain, and which are judged necessary or very useful.[27]

---

[26] See *ActRSJ*, XIV, 916.

[27] See the letter from Jean Cardinal Villot, Secretary of State, May 2, 1975, p. 546, by which this faculty has been granted under certain conditions, and also by which the Holy See has confirmed as experimental the Norms under E, as well as the declaration under H.

IV

CONGREGATIONS AND GOVERNMENT

DECREE 13

The General Congregation and Congregations of Procurators and Provincials

303/ 1. The 32nd General Congregation confirms Decree 38 of the 31st General Congregation on the preparation for a general congregation.[1] It further defines this decree in the following ways:

a. The preparation for a general congregation should be complete, in the sense that it should include the drafting of the preliminary reports which are now described in the first sentence of n. 119, No. 3, of the *Formula of the General Congregation.* In as far as possible, these reports should be prepared for all the topics which the coming general congregation will be likely to treat.

b. The preparation for a general congregation should also be authoritative, in the sense that the preliminary reports and studies described in *(a)* above, to the extent that they are produced or approved by the official preparatory committee described in *(c)* below, should be recognized by the general congregation as part of its official work, although the congregation retains the power to complete this preparatory work itself.

c. If it seems useful, the preliminary committees foreseen in n. 7 of Decrce 38 of the 31st General Congregation may be set up, but, in any case, an official preparatory committee should be established in due time. Its members are to be chosen by the General or the Vicar General, acting with his council, from among those who will attend the coming congregation. This committee should meet early enough to complete the preparations described in *(a)* and *(b)* above.

306/ 2. The *Formula of the General Congregation* should be revised with regard to both its procedure and its method of handling business from the calling of the congregation until its closing.

307/ 3. The additional procedural norms adopted by the32nd General Congregation for its own use should also be reviewed.

308/ 4. In the future, those who attend the congregation only *"ad negotia"* (according to the norm contained in n. 7, of the *Formula of the General Congregation*) may be elected secretary or assistant secretary of the congregation and members of the committee on the state of the Society and the committee for screening postulates. They may also be elected *"Definitores."*

---

[1] GC 31, D. 38; *ActRSJ,* XIV, 970.

309/ 5.   In addition to what is contained in n. 3 of Decree 39 of the 31st General Congregation,[2] the power of both the congregation of procurators and the congregation of provincials is augmented so that they may:

1° prepare and present to the Society a report on the state of the Society;

2° suspend decrees of previous general congregations until the next general congregation, if this seems necessary.

310/ 6.   The 32nd General Congregation gives the following commission and authority to Father General: That, with the help of a commission and with the deliberative vote of those fathers of the General Curia who have a right by reason of their office to attend a general congregation, he should:

a. revise the *Formula of the General Congregation* as well as the additional procedural norms, as described in nn. 2 and 3 above, in light of the experience of this general congregation;

b. introduce into the *Formula of the General Congregation* the changes mentioned in nn. 1 and 4 above and determine the particulars which may be required to carry out the decisions of this General Congregation regarding these changes.

c. as far as necessary, adapt and change the *Formula of the General Congregation* to accomplish the above;

d. make any decisions, of a more particular nature, which may be required to implement n. 5 above. As far as necessary, he may also change the *Formulas* of both the congregation of procurators and the congregation of provincials to include the new decisions which pertain to those congregations.

311/ 7.   The 32nd General Congregation recommends to Father General that he establish a commission to examine the following questions in more detail in preparation for their consideration and decision by the next general congregation :

—stabilizing the number of those who attend a general congregation;

—apportioning the members of the general congregation according to criteria which are not only quantitative but also qualitative;

—reducing the numbers of those who attend a general congregation.

---

[2] *ActRSJ*, XIV, 971.

DECREE 14

THE PROVINCIAL CONGREGATION

The 32nd General Congregation has decided the following about the provincial congregation.

A. The Congregation in General

312/ 1. The power of the provincial congregation is not to be increased. However, before the provincial congregations meet, Father General may send to the delegates questions about the state of the province so that on these questions action might be taken in the provincial congregation.

313/ 2. In the *Formula of the Provincial Congregation:*

—n. 6; the clause is omitted: "The day of arrival of the delegates be so set that the next day is the first day of the congregation."

—n. 32, §1, is to begin: "The members legitimately begin the congregation immediately, and at the appointed time . . ."

—n. 49 is thus corrected: "From the beginning of the congregation there be posted . . ."

—n. 50 is thus corrected: "At the time established by the provincial for the first session, whoever are present. . ."

—n. 58 is thus corrected: "Ninth, unless the congregation should prefer to make the choice in the following session, it should determine the day after which it will not be allowed to present any other postulatum, which should be the second day or at most the fourth day after the day on which the first session was held."

314/ 3. In the *Formula,* n. 95, the following fourth paragraph is to be added: "In cases of provinces which have been dispersed both within and outside their native country because of religious persecution or other adverse conditions and in which the group existing outside the province constitutes a quasi-province, even if the provincial himself or a delegate elected according to the norm of n. 10 can come from the province to the general congregation, the General or Vicar-General, having consulted and received the approval of the general assistants, can name as a full delegate one of the professed of four vows from among those working outside the territory of their native country."

315/ 4. The minor questions treated in Postulatum 947[1] are to be left to the decision of Father General with a deliberative vote of those fathers of the General's Curia who have a right *ex officio* to attend a general congregation.

3161/ 5. With reference to the *Formula of the Provincial Congregation,* the General Congregation directs and empowers Father General, with a deliberative vote of those fathers of the General's Curia who have a right, *ex officio,* to attend a general congregation, to bring that *Formula* up to date and, where necessary, change it and introduce those points on which the General Congregation gave an affirmative vote.

B. Participation in the Congregation

317/ 6. As to the number of delegates to be elected to a provincial congregation, Father General has the power to allow Vice-provinces which have a large number of members to use the norms of provinces for that number, without increasing the number of delegates whom they may send to the general congregation.

318/ 7. The number of those who attend the provincial congregation *ex officio* should be in some way decreased.

    a. To be retained *ex officio* are those superiors ordinarily named by Father General. But at this time it is recommended that Father General review the list of superiors whom he names in each province and use criteria based on the importance of different offices and even the separation of office of superior from that of director of the apostolic work so that he move toward reducing the number of superiors named by himself.

    b. The consultors of the province do not attend the provincial congregation *ex officio*; the treasurer of the province, however, does.

319/ 8. In the *Formula of the Provincial Congregation:*—n. 19, §1, 2° is changed to read as follows: "That there be included in the congregation and computed within the forty members of the congregation (twenty in a vice-province) two or more persons from this territory to be determined by the General or Vicar-General according to the number of Jesuits within the territory and its distance from the province. The General or Vicar-General will designate one of these because of the office he holds. The others will be elected from the list of those who have passive voice by those who have active voice in the territory. The election will be conducted by the superior of the territory. This election process will take place and the results will be reviewed by the superior with his consultors before the rest of the province proceeds to vote on naming the other delegates to the congregation. In the case of such a special election, the members of that territory lose active and passive voice in the election of delegates from the rest of the province."

---

[1] See the postulata sent to the 31st General Congregation.

320/ 9. To n. 21, §1, 1°, the following is to be added; "It is recommended, however, that as far as possible, they choose delegates from different apostolic works and houses." In his letter convoking the congregation, the provincial should make the same recommendation.

321/ 10. To n. 21, §1, 4°, in place of "It is permitted to seek in confidence information from one or another prudent man," the following is to be substituted: "It is permitted, with discretion and charity, to seek information from other persons."

322/ 11. To Jesuits without final vows, participation in the provincial congregation is granted under the following conditions:

a. All scholastics and brothers without final vows have active voice five years after their entrance into the Society; they have passive voice eight years after their entrance into the Society. With regard to the number of those without final vows in the provincial congregation: there should be at least one; there may not be more than five in the provinces, nor more than three in the vice-provinces.

b. More specific norms concerning this participation should be determined by Father General with the deliberative vote of those fathers of the General Curia who have the right, *ex officio,* to attend a general congregation. This should be done in a flexible way but within the norms given above.

c. These norms and determinations should be reviewed by the next general congregation.

323/ 12. In the *Formula of the Provincial Congregation,* n.29, §3, the first words are to be changed to read as follows: "Those who according to the judgment of the committee of assessors mentioned in paragraph 2 or the preparatory committee . . . etc." In n. 13 the following words are to be added: "5th—Those exclaustrated according to the Code of Canon Law, n. 639; 6th—Those who have sought a change to the lay state or to be dismissed from the Society. If the petition is still secret and the person seeking a change to the lay state or dismissal wishes his name to remain on the list of those having passive voice so that his petition remain secret, his name can be kept on the list. But if it happens that he is elected, he must, *ipso facto,* be considered ineligible by the committee of assessors."

C. Actions within the Congregation

324/ 13. In the *Formula of the Provincial Congregation,* n.26 is to be changed to read as follows: "Before the beginning of the congregation, let two lists be prepared and sent in due time to the delegates to the provincial congregation . . . etc."

325/ 14. The *Formula of the Provincial Congregation* is so to be changed as to meet the concerns expressed below without imposing on all provinces the obligation of following this method of procedure:

a. Setting a deadline beyond which postulata may not be sent for consideration by the congregation, without however limiting the right of delegates to submit postulata during the course of the congregation;

b. Sending the postulata to the delegates to the provincial congregation early enough to permit them to study them and to propose amendments before the congregation;

c. Establishing small committees to arrange the postulata in order, and to develop further the topics proposed;

d. All the above should be done in such a way that the anonymity of the authors of the postulata is preserved. It should also be done in a way that preserves the obligation of secrecy and without prejudice to any decision which the committee for screening postulata may wish to make.

326/ 15. The *Formula of the Provincial Congregation* is to be changed to meet the concerns expressed below without however ordering that this method be followed. In this revision, provision should be made for harmonizing these changes with the power of the committee for screening postulata.

a. That there be committees to study the postulata;

b. That the conclusions of these committees be explained to the congregation by a reporter;

c. That after receiving suggestions, the committee can again study or reshape the postulata;

d. That all the above be carried out according to the regulations of the *Formula of the Provincial Congregation* concerning the method of voting.

327/ 16. The *Formula,* n. 44, §2, is to read as follows: "In public votes different methods can be used at the discretion of the provincial according to the importance of the different subjects involved, but the directive in n. 83, §1, must be maintained.'"

328/ 17. In the election of the committee for screening postulata, if it seems fitting to the provincial congregation, a prior indicative vote can be taken.

329/ 18. In the *Formula,* n. 73, §2, is to be changed so that the phrase "immediately before the election of all substitutes" replaces the phrase "immediately after the election of all substitutes."

DECREE 15

Central Government of the Society

A. Assistants and Counsellors of Father General

330/ 1. Decree 44 of the 31st General Congregation, in force experimentally until now,[1] is definitively confirmed by the 32nd General Congregation, with however the following modifications:

a. At the end of I, 1, should be added: "who will also be general counsellors."

b. I, 4, now reads as follows: "Even a general congregation called for business should proceed to a new election of general assistants. Former assistants may be reelected to the same office."

c. At the end of II, 7, should be added: "At least the general counsellors will normally give their advice gathered together in council."

d. At the end of II, 8, is added: "In addition to the four general counsellors elected by the general congregation as general assistants, Father General should name at least two more general counsellors, having first consulted the regional assistants and obtained the deliberative vote of the general assistants."

331/ 2. All the contrary dispositions of previous general congregations, which were suspended by the 31st GeneralCongregation[2] (cf. I, 6; II, 9), are now definitively abrogated.

B. Recommendations Made to Father General

332/ 3. The General Congregation recommends to Father General the following:

a. The general counsellors should form a council which in its manner of working goes beyond the consultation of the individual counsellors. It will be a regular and stable working group to collaborate organically with Father General in the formation of policy, in decision-making, and in planning execution. It will not only take up problems proposed to it but also propose matters to be considered. Its members should examine together what matters ought to be treated, especially in the light of the varied perspectives of the different members. Finally, it will promote discernment regarding serious and universal matters.

---

[1] *ActRSJ,* XIV, 976–978.

[2] GC 31, D. 44, I-6 and II-9; *ActRSJ,* XIV, 977.

b. Father General should give the care of some sector of the life of the Society or of some geographical region, or even of both, to each of the general counsellors.

c. A general assistant or general counsellor should not ordinarily remain in office for more than about eight years, nor should all of them be changed at the same time.

d. The regional assistants should be brought together as a group once a month for discussion of business.

e. A review should be undertaken of the organization and coordination of the administration of the General Curia by people expert in this matter. In this review, the possibility of lessening the number of Jesuits engaged in the central administration should be considered.

Meanwhile, every effort should be made to coordinate as much as possible the work of the different counselors and officials of the Curia; some form of structural intercommunication and collaboration should be encouraged. Father General should commit the special care of this matter to the Secretary of the Society.

C. Reviewing the System of World Secretariats

333/ 4. The 32nd General Congregation gives the General the mandate and the authority to review the system of world secretariats of the Society, suspending contrary decrees of previous general congregations until the next general congregation. In this review of the secretariats, however, the purposes intended by the previous general congregations should be kept in mind.

DECREE 16

Powers Granted to Father General

334/ 1.   For the proper completion of the legislative work of the 32nd General Congregation, Father General is empowered, after obtaining the deliberative vote of those fathers of the General Curia who have a right ex officio to attend a general congregation, and without prejudice to the powers given him in other decrees, to abrogate or modify decrees of past general congregations that seem not to be in accord with the decrees of this 32nd General Congregation.

335/ 2.   Moreover, the 32nd General Congregation grants to Father General the following:

1 ° That he himself, if it should be a matter of necessity, can suppress colleges and professed houses, with the deliberative votes, however, of the general counsellors and of the provincial of the province in whose territory the house to be suppressed is located and after consulting the regional assistant.

2° That the minutes of some sessions that could not be distributed to the fathers of the Congregation should be approved by Father General and the general assistants.

3° That with respect to decrees that must be promulgated after the close of the Congregation, it should be permitted to Father General:

a. to make whatever corrections seem obviously needed;

b. to reconcile contradictions, if any are detected, according to the mind of the Congregation, but after having ascertained the deliberative vote of those fathers of the General Curia who have a right *ex officio* to attend a general congregation;

c. to edit the decrees with regard to style;

d. where necessary, to combine different decrees into one, while preserving the meaning and intent of each;

e. to fix a *vacatio legis* or delay with respect to enforcement, in the light of circumstances, when promulgating the decrees.

C

DOCUMENTS OF THE HOLY SEE WHICH PERTAIN TO THE CONGREGATION

I. Address of Pope Paul VI to the Members of the 32nd General Congregation

December 3, 1974

Esteemed and beloved Fathers of the Society of Jesus,

As we receive you today, there is renewed for us the joy and trepidation of May 7, 1965, when the Thirty-first General Congregation of your Society began, and that of November 15 of the following year, at its conclusion. We have great joy because of the outpouring of sincere paternal love which every meeting between the Pope and the sons of St. Ignatius cannot but stir up. This is especially true because we see the witness of Christian apostolate and of fidelity which you give us and in which we rejoice. But there is also trepidation for the reasons of which we shall presently speak to you. The inauguration of the 32nd General Congregation is a special event, and it is usual for us to have such a meeting on an occasion like this; but this meeting has a far wider and more historic significance. It is the whole Ignatian Society that has gathered at Rome before the Pope after a journey of more than four hundred years, and is reflecting, perhaps, on the prophetic words that were heard in the vision of La Storta: "I will be favorable to you in Rome" (P. Tacchi-Venturi, SI, *Storia della Compagnia di Gesù in Italia narrata col sussidio di fonti inedite,* Vol. II, part 1, Rome, 1950, 2nd ed., p. 4, n. 2; P. Ribadeneira, *Vita Ignatii,* Chapter IX: *Acta Sanctorum Julii,* t. VII, Antwerp, 1731, p. 683).

There is in you and there is in us the sense of a moment of destiny for your Society, which in our hearts concentrates memories, sentiments, and the presages of your role in the life of the Church. Seeing you here as representatives of all your provinces throughout the world, our glance embraces the whole Ignatian family, some thirty thousand men, working on behalf of the Kingdom of God and making a contribution of great value to the apostolic and missionary works of the Church—religious men who are dedicated to the care of souls, often passing their whole lives in hiddenness and obscurity. Certainly each one of your confreres sends forth from his heart towards this Congregation profound desires, many of which are expressed in the postulata, and which therefore require from you, the delegates, a careful understanding and a great respect. But more than the number, it seems to us that there must be taken into account the quality of such wishes, whether they be expressed or silent, which certainly embrace conformity to the vocation and charism proper to Jesuits—transmitted by an uninterrupted tradition—conformity to the will of God, humbly sought in prayer, and conformity to the will of the Church in the tradition of the great spiritual impulse that has sustained the Society in the past, sustains it now, and will always sustain it in the future.

We realize the special seriousness of the present moment. It demands of you more than a routine performance of your function: it demands an examination of the present state of your Society, one that will be a careful synthesis, free and complete, to see how it stands with regard to the difficulties and problems that beset it today. It is an act that must be accomplished with extreme lucidity and with a supernatural spirit—to compare your identity with what is happening in the world and in the Society itself—listening exclusively, under the guidance and illumination of the magisterium, to the voice of the Holy Spirit, and consequently with a disposition of humility, of courage, and of resoluteness to decide on the course of action to be adopted, lest there be prolonged a state of uncertainty that would become dangerous. All this with great confidence.

And we give you the confirmation of our confidence: we love you sincerely, and we judge that you are able to effect that renewal and new balance which we all desire.

This is the meaning of today's meeting, and we want you to reflect on it. We already made known our thought in this regard through the letters that the Cardinal Secretary of State sent in our name on March 26, 1970, and on February 15, 1973, and with that letter of September 13, 1973, *In Paschae Sollemnitate,* which we sent to the General and through him to all the members of the Society.

Continuing along the line of thought of the last-mentioned document, which we hope has been meditated and reflected upon by you, as was our wish, we speak to you today with special affection and a particular urgency. We speak to you in the name of Christ and—as you like to consider us—as the highest Superior of the Society, by reason of the special bond which from the time of its foundation links the Society itself to the Roman Pontiff. The Popes have always placed special hope in the Society of Jesus.

On the occasion of the previous Congregation, we entrusted to you, as a modern expression of your vow of obedience to the Pope (*AAS* 57 (1965), p. 514; 58 (1966), p. 1177), the task of confronting atheism. And today we are turning to you, at the beginning of your work to which the entire Church is looking, to strengthen and stimulate your reflections. We observe you in your totality as a great religious family, which has paused for an instant and is deliberating about the road to be followed.

And it seems to us, as we listen in this hour of anxious expectation and of intense attention "to what the Spirit is saying" to you and to us (see Rev. 2:7 ff.), that there arise in our heart three questions which we feel bound to answer: "Where do you come from?" "Who are you?" "Where are you going?"

So we stand here before you, like a milestone, to measure in one sweeping glance, the journey you have already made.

I. Hence, *where do you come from?* Our thought goes back to that complex sixteenth century, when the foundations of modern civilization and culture were being laid, and the Church, threatened by schism, began a new era of religious and social renewal founded on prayer and on the love of God and the brethren, that is, on the search for genuine holiness. It was a moment bound up with a new concept of man of the world, which often—although this was not the most genuine humanism—attempted to relegate God to a place outside the course of life and history. It was a world which took on new dimensions from recent geographical discoveries, and hence in very many of its aspects—upheavals, rethinking, analyses, reconstructions, impulses, aspirations, etc.—was not unlike our own.

Placed against this stormy and splendid background is the figure of St. Ignatius. Yes, where do you come from? And we seem to hear a united cry—a "voice like the sound of the ocean" (Rev 1:15)—resounding from the depths of the centuries from all your confreres: We come from Ignatius Loyola, our Founder—we come from him who has made an indelible imprint not only on the Order but also on the spirituality and the apostolate of the Church.

With him, we come from Manresa, from the mystical cave which witnessed the successive ascents of his great spirit: from the serene peace of the beginner to the purifications of the dark night of the soul, and finally to the great mystical graces of the visions of the Trinity (cf. Hugo Rahner, *Ignatius von Loyola u. das geschichtliche Werdenseiner Frommigkeil,* Graz, 1947, Chapter III).

There began at that time the first outlines of the Spiritual Exercises, that work which over the centuries has formed souls, orienting them to God, and which, among other things, teaches the lesson of treating "the Creator and Lord with great openheartedness and generosity, offering him all one's will and liberty, so that his divine Majesty may avail himself, in accordance with his most holy will, of the person and of all that he has" (*Annotaciones,* 5: *Monumenta Ignatiana,* second series, *Exercitia Spiritualia S. Ignatii de Loyola et eorum Directoria,* new edition, t. I, *Exerc. Spir.:* MHSI, Vol. 100, Rome, 1969, p. 146).

With St. Ignatius—you answer us again—we come from Montmartre, where our Founder on August 15, 1534, after the Mass celebrated by Peter Faber, pronounced with him, with Francis Xavier, whose feast we celebrate today, with Salmeron and Lainez and Rodrigues and Bobadilla, the vows which were to mark as it were the springtime bud from which in Rome the Society would flower (See P. Tacchi-Venturi, op. cit., Vol. II, part I, p. 63 ff.).

And with St. Ignatius—you continue—we are in Rome, whence we departed fortified by the blessing of the Successor of Peter, from the time when Paul III, responding to the ardent appeal of Cardinal Gaspare Contarini in September, 1539, gave the first verbal approval—the prelude to that Bull *Regimini Ecclesiae*

Militantis of September 27, 1540, which sanctioned with the supreme authority of the Church the existence of the new Society of Priests. It seems to us that its originality consisted in having grasped that the times required people who were completely available, capable of detaching themselves from everything and of following any mission that might be indicated by the Pope and called for, in his judgment, by the good of the Church, putting always in first place the glory of God: *ad maiorem Dei gloriam.* But St. Ignatius also looked beyond those times, as he wrote at the end of the *Quinque Capitula* or *First Sketch of the Institute of the Society of Jesus:* "These are the matters which we were able to explain about our profession in a kind of sketch. We now complete this explanation in order to give brief information both to those who ask us about our plan of life and also to those who will later follow us if, God willing, we shall ever have imitators along this path" (P. Tacchi-Venturi, op. cit., Vol. I, part II, Rome, 2nd ed., 1931, p. 189).

This is what your predecessors wanted of you, this is how you came to be: it can be said that these facts give the definition of the Society. This definition is extracted from the origins of the Society; it indicates the Society's constitutional lines and imprints upon it the dynamism which has supported it throughout the centuries.

II. We know then who you are. As we summarized in our Letter, *In Paschae Sollemnitate,* you are members of an Order that is religious, apostolic, priestly, and united with the Roman Pontiff by a special bond of love and service, in the manner described in the *Formula Instituti.*

You are *religious,* and therefore men of prayer, of the evangelical imitation of Christ, and endowed with a supernatural spirit, guaranteed and protected by the religious vows of poverty, chastity, and obedience. These vows are not an obstacle to the freedom of the person, as though they were a relic of periods that have sociologically been superseded, but rather a witness to the clear desire for freedom in the spirit of the Sermon on the Mount. By means of these commitments, the one who is called as Vatican II has emphasized—"in order to derive more abundant fruit from the grace of Baptism . . . intends to be freed from the obstacles which might draw him away from the fervor of charity and the perfection of divine worship and consecrates himself to the service of God" (*Lumen Gentium,* 44; See *Perfectae Caritatis,* 12–14). As religious you are men given to austerity of life in order to imitate the Son of God, who "emptied himself to assume the condition of a slave" (Phil 2:7) and who "was rich but became poor for your sake, to make you rich out of his poverty" (2 Cor 8:9). As religious you must flee—as we wrote in the above-mentioned Letter—"from those facile compromises with a desacralized mentality, which is evidenced in so many aspects of modern behavior," and you must likewise recognize and live—courageously and in an exemplary way—"the ascetical and formative value of the common life," guarding it intact against the tendencies of individualism and singularity.

You are, moreover, *apostles,* that is, preachers of the Gospel, sent in every direction in accordance with the most authentic and genuine character of the Society. You are men whom Christ himself sends into the whole world to spread his holy doctrine among the people of every state and condition (See Spiritual Exercises, n. 145: See MHSI, Vol. 100, Rome, 1969, p. 246). This is a fundamental and irreplaceable characteristic of the true Jesuit, who indeed finds in the Exercises, as in the Constitutions, continuous inducements to practice the virtues proper to him, those virtues indicated by St. Ignatius, and this practice even more strongly, with greater striving, in a continual search for the better, for the *"magis,"* for the greater (See the *criteria* of the Constitutions). The very diversity of ministries to which the Society dedicates itself takes from these sources its most profound motive of that apostolic life which must be lived *pleno sensu.*

You are likewise *priests:* this, too, is an essential character of the Society, without forgetting the ancient and established tradition of enlisting the help of Brothers who are not in Sacred Orders and who have always had an honored and effective role in the Society. Priesthood was formally required by the Founder for all professed religious, and this with good reason, because the priesthood is necessary for the Order he instituted with the special purpose of the sanctification of men through the Word and the sacraments. Effectively, the sacerdotal character is required by your dedication to the active life—we repeat—*pleno sensu.* It is from the charism of the Order of priesthood, which conforms a man to Christ sent by the Father, that there principally springs the apostolic character of the mission to which, as Jesuits, you are deputed. You are therefore priests, trained for that *familiaritas cum Deo* on which St. Ignatius wished to base the Society; priests who teach, endowed with the *sermonis gratia* (See *Monumenta Ignatiana, Sancti Ignatii de Loyola Constitutiones Societatis Iesu,* t. Ill, textus latinus, p. 1, c. 2, 9 (59–60); MHSI, Vol. 65, Rome, 1938, p. 49); oriented to see "that the Lord's message may spread quickly and be received with honor" (2 Thess 3:1). You are priests who serve or minister the grace of God through the sacraments; priests who receive the power and have the duty to share organically in the apostolic work of sustaining and uniting the Christian community, especially with the celebration of the Eucharist; priests who are therefore aware, as we mentioned in one of our talks in 1963, of "the antecedent and consequent relationship [of the priesthood] with the Eucharist, through which the priest is the minister of so great a sacrament and then its first adorer, wise teacher, and tireless distributor" (Address to the Italian clergy at the Thirteenth National Week of Pastoral Renewal, September 6, 1963: *AAS* 55 (1963), p. 754).

And finally you are *united with the Pope* by a special vow: since this union with the Successor of Peter, which is the principal bond of the members of the Society, has always given the assurance—indeed it is the visible sign—of your communion with Christ, the first and supreme head of the Society which by its very name is his—the Society of Jesus. And it is union with the Pope that has always rendered the members of the Society truly free, that is, placed under the direction of the Spirit, fit for all missions—even the most arduous and most distant ones— not hemmed in by the narrow conditions of time and place, and endowed with truly Catholic and universal energy.

In the combination of this fourfold note we see displayed all the wonderful richness and adaptability which has characterized the Society during the centuries as the Society of those "sent" by the Church. Hence there have come theological research and teaching, hence the apostolate of preaching, of spiritual assistance, of publications and writings, of the direction of groups, and of formation by means of the Word of God and the Sacrament of Reconciliation in accordance with the special and characteristic duty committed to you by your holy Founder. Hence there have come the social apostolate and intellectual and cultural activity which extends from schools for the solid and complete education of youth all the way to all the levels of advanced university studies and scholarly research. Hence the *puerorum ac rudium in christianismo institutio,* which St. Ignatius gives to his sons, from the very first moment of his *Quinque Capitula,* or *First Sketch,* as one of their specific aims (See P. Tacchi-Venturi, op. cit., Vol. I, part II, p. 183). Hence the missions, a concrete and moving testimony of the "mission" of the Society. Hence the solicitude for the poor, for the sick, for those on the margins of society. Wherever in the Church, even in the most difficult and extreme fields, in the crossroads of ideologies, in the front line of social conflict, there has been and there is confrontation between the deepest desires of man and the perennial message of the Gospel, there also there have been, and there are, Jesuits. Your Society is in accord with and blends with the society of the Church in the multiple works which you direct, also taking account of the necessity that all should be unified by a single aim, that of God's glory and the sanctification of men, without dissipating its energies in the pursuit of lesser goals.

And why then do you doubt? You have a spirituality strongly traced out, an unequivocal identity and a centuries-old confirmation which was based on the validity of methods, which, having passed through the crucible of history, still bear the imprint of the strong spirit of St. Ignatius. Hence there is absolutely no need to place in doubt the fact that a more profound commitment to the way up till now followed—to the special charism—will be the source of spiritual and apostolic fruitfulness. It is true that there is today widespread in the Church the temptation characteristic of our time: systematic doubt, uncertainty about one's identity, desire for change, independence, and individualism. The difficulties that you have noticed are those that today seize Christians in general in the face of the profound cultural change which strikes at one's very sense of God. Yours are the difficulties of all today's apostles, those who experience the longing to proclaim the Gospel and the difficulty of translating it into a language accessible to modern man; they are the difficulties of other religious orders. We understand the doubts and the true and serious difficulties that some of you are undergoing. You are at the head of that interior renewal which the Church is facing in this secularized world, especially after the Second Vatican Council. Your Society is, we say, the test of the vitality of the Church throughout the centuries; it is perhaps one of the most meaningful crucibles in which are encountered the difficulties, the temptations, the efforts, the perpetuity and the successes of the whole Church.

Certainly it is a crisis of suffering, and perhaps of growth, as has been said many times. But we, in our capacity as Vicar of Christ, who must confirm the brethren in faith (See Lk 22:32), and likewise you, who have the heavy responsibility of consciously representing the aspirations of your confreres—all of us must be vigilant so that the necessary adaptation will not be accomplished to the detriment of the fundamental identity or essential character of the role of the Jesuit as is described in the *Formula Instituti*, as the history and particular spirituality of the Order propose it, and as the authentic interpretation of the very needs of the times seem still today to require it. This image must not be altered; it must not be distorted.

One must not call apostolic necessity what would not be other than spiritual decadence. Just as St. Ignatius is said to have clearly advised, any confrere sent on mission must by all means take care not to forget his own salvation in order to attend to that of others. Not only was it wrong to commit even the slightest sin for the greatest possible spiritual gain; it was not even right to put himself in danger of sinning. (See *Monumenta Ignatiana,* first series, *Sancti Ignatii de Loyola Epistolae et Instructiones,* t. XII, fasc. II: MHSI, Annus 19, fasc. 217, January, 1912, Madrid, pp. 251–52.) If your Society puts itself at risk, if it enters onto paths full of danger which are not its own, there suffer also thereby all those who, in one way or another, owe to the Jesuits so very much of their Christian formation.

You are as well aware as we are that today there appears within certain sectors of your ranks a strong state of uncertainty, indeed a certain fundamental questioning of your very identity. The figure of the Jesuit, as we have traced it out in its principal aspects, is essentially that of a spiritual leader, an educator of his contemporaries in Catholic life, within, as we have said, his proper role, as a priest and as an apostle. But we are asking, and you are asking yourselves, as a conscientious verification and as a reassuring confirmation, what is the present state of the life of prayer, of contemplation, of simplicity of life, of poverty, of the use of supernatural means? What is the state of acceptance and loyal witness in regard to the fundamental points of Catholic faith and moral teaching as set forth by the ecclesiastical magisterium? The will to collaborate with full trust in the work of the Pope? Have not the "clouds on the horizon" which we saw in 1966, although "in a great measure dispersed" by the Thirty-first General Congregation (*AAS* 58 [1966], p. 1174), unfortunately continued to cast a certain shadow on the Society? Certain regrettable actions, which would make one doubt whether the man were still a member of the Society, have happened much too frequently and are pointed out to us from many sides, especially from bishops of dioceses; and they exercise a sad influence on the clergy, on other religious, and on the Catholic laity. These facts require from us and from you an expression of sorrow, certainly not for the sake of dwelling on them, but for seeking together the remedies, so that the Society will remain, or return to being, what is needed, what it must be in order to respond to the intention of the Founder and to the expectations of the Church today. There is needed an intelligent study of what the Society is, an experience of situations and of people. But there is also needed—and it is as well to insist on this—a spiritual sense, a judgment of faith on the things we must do and on the way that lies ahead of us, taking into account God's will, which demands an unconditioned availability.

III. Therefore, *where are you going?* The question cannot remain unanswered. You have, in fact been asking it for some time, asking it with lucidity, perhaps with risk.

The goal to which you are tending, and of which this General Congregation is the opportune sign of the times, is and must be without doubt the pursuit of a healthy, balanced, and suitable *aggiornamento* to the right desires of our day in essential fidelity to the specific character of the Society and in respect for the charism of your Founder. This was the desire of the Second Vatican Council, with the Decree *Perfectae Caritatis* which hoped for "the continued return to the sources of every Christian life and to the original spirit of institutes, and the adaptation of the institutes themselves to the changed conditions of the times" (op. cit., 2). We would like to inspire you with full confidence and encourage you to keep pace with the attitudes of the world of today, recalling to you, nevertheless, as we did in a general way in the Apostolic Exhortation *Evangelica Testificatio,* that such necessary renewal would not be effective if it departed from the particular identity of your religious family which is so clearly described in your fundamental rule or *Formula Instituti.* As we said: "For a living being, adaptation to its surroundings does not consist in abandoning its true identity, but rather in asserting itself in the vitality that is its own. Deep understanding of present tendencies and of the needs of the modern world should cause your own sources of energy to spring up with renewed vigor and freshness. It is a sublime task in the measure that it is a difficult one" (op. cit., 5: *AAS* 63 [1971], p. 523).

Hence we encourage you with all our heart to pursue the *aggiornamento* willed so clearly and authoritatively by the Church. But at the same time, we are all aware of both its importance and its innate risk. The world in which we live places in crisis our religious outlook and sometimes even our option of faith: we live in a dazzling perspective of worldly humanism, bound up with a rationalistic and irreligious attitude with which man wants to complete his personal and social perfection exclusively by his own efforts. On the other hand for us, who are men of God, it is a question of the divinization of man in Christ, through the choice of the Cross and of the struggle against evil and sin. Do you remember the "*sub crucis vexillo Deo militare et soli Domino atque Romano Pontifici . . . servire?*" (Bull *Regimini Militantis Ecclesiae,* in P. Tacchi-Venturi, op. cit., Vol. I, part II, *Documenti,* Rome, 1931, pp. 182–83).

The century of Ignatius underwent a humanistic transformation equally powerful even though not as turbulent as that of the succeeding centuries which have seen in action the teachers of systematic doubt, of radical negation, of the idealistic Utopia of an exclusively temporal kingdom on earth, closed to every possibility of true transcendence. But "where is the master of worldly argument? Has not God turned the wisdom of this world into folly? Since in God's wisdom the world did not come to know him through 'wisdom,' it pleased God to save those who believe through the absurdity of the preaching of the Gospel" (1 Cor 1:20–21). We are the heralds of this paradoxical wisdom, this proclamation. But as we recalled to our brethren in the Episcopate at the end of the Synod, so we also repeat to you, that, notwithstanding the difficulties: "Christ is with us, he is in us, he speaks in us and by means of us and will not let us lack the necessary help" (*L'Osservatore Romano,* October 27, 1974, p. 2) in order that we may pass on the Christian message and wisdom to our contemporaries.

A realistic glance at this world makes us alert to another danger: the phenomenon of novelty for its own sake—novelty which questions everything. Novelty is the stimulus for human and spiritual progress. This is true only when it is willing to be anchored to fidelity to him who makes all things new (Rev. 21:5), in the ever self-renewing mystery of his death and resurrection, to which he assimilates us in the sacraments of his Church. This is not true when novelty becomes a relativism that destroys today what it built up yesterday. It is not difficult to see what you should use to combat these temptations, and these same means will keep you moving forward yourselves—they are faith and love.

Hence, in the road that opens before you in this remaining part of the century, marked by the Holy Year as a hopeful presage for a radical conversion to God, we propose to you the double charism of the apostle—the charism which must guarantee your identity and constantly illumine your teaching, your centers of study, your periodical publications. On the one hand, *fidelity*—not sterile and static, but living and fruitful—to the faith and to the institution of your Founder, in order that you may remain the salt of the earth and the light of the world (see Mt 5:13, 14). Guard what has been entrusted to you (see 1 Tim 6:20; 2 Tim 1:14). "Put on the armor of God so that you may be able to stand firm against the tactics of the devil. Our battle is not against human forces but against the principalities and powers, the rulers of this world of darkness . . . You must put on the armor of

God if you are to resist on the evil day; do all that your duty requires, and hold your ground" (Eph 6:11–13).

On the other hand, there is the charism of love, that is of generous *service* to all men, our brethren traveling with us towards the future. It is that anxiety of Paul which every true apostle feels burning within him: "I made myself all things to all men in order to save some at any cost. . . . I try to be helpful to everyone at all times, not anxious for my own advantage but for the advantage of everybody else, so that they may be saved" (1 Cor 9:22; 10:33).

Perfection lies in the simultaneous presence of two charisms—fidelity and service—without letting one have the advantage over the other. This is something that is certainly difficult, but it is possible. Today the attraction of the second charism is very strong: the precedence of action over being, of activity over contemplation, of concrete existence over theoretical speculation, which has led from a deductive theology to an inductive one; and all this could cause one to think that the two aspects of fidelity and love are mutually opposed. But such is not the case, as you know. Both proceed from the Holy Spirit, who is love. People are never loved too much, provided they are loved only in the love and with the love of Christ. "The Church endeavors to show in every argument that revealed doctrine, to the extent that it is Catholic—embraces and completes all the right thoughts of men, which in themselves always have something of the fragmentary and paltry" (H. deLubac, *Catholicisme,* Paris, 1952, Chapter 9, p. 248). But if this is not the case, readiness to serve can degenerate into relativism, into conversion to the world and its immanentist mentality, into assimilation with the world that one wanted to save, into secularism and into fusion with the profane. We exhort you not to be seized by the *spiritus vertiginis* (Is 19:14).

For this purpose, we wish to indicate to you some further orientations which you can develop in your reflections:

A. *Discernment,* for which Ignatian spirituality especially trains you, must always sustain you in the difficult quest for the synthesis of the two charisms, the two poles of your life. You will have to be able always to distinguish with absolutely lucid clarity between the demands of the world and those of the Gospel, of its paradox of death and life, of Cross and Resurrection, of folly and wisdom. Take your direction from the judgment of St. Paul: "But because of Christ, I have come to consider all these advantages that I had as disadvantages. Not only that, but I believe nothing can happen that will outweigh the supreme advantage of knowing Christ and the power of his resurrection and to share his sufferings by reproducing the pattern of his death. That is the way I can hope to take my place in the resurrection of the dead" (Phil. 3:7–8, 10–11). We recall always that a supreme criterion is the one given by Our Lord: "You will be able to tell them by their fruits" (Mt. 7:16); and the effort which must guide your discernment will be that of being docile to the voice of the Spirit in order to produce the fruit of the Spirit, which is "love, joy, peace, patience, kindness, goodness, trustfulness, gentleness and self-control" (Gal 5:22).

B. It will also be opportune to remember the need to make a proper *basic choice* among the many appeals that come to you from the apostolate in the modern world. Today—it is a fact—one notes the difficulty of making properly thought-out and decisive choices; perhaps there is a fear that full self-realization will not be achieved. Hence there is the desire to be everything, the desire to do everything and to follow indiscriminately all the human and Christian vocations—those of the priest and the lay person, those of the Religious Institutes and of the Secular Institutes—applying oneself to spheres that are not one's own. Hence then arise lack of satisfaction, improvisation, and discouragement. But you have a precise vocation, that which we have just recalled, and an unmistakably specific character in your spirituality and in your apostolic vocation. And this is what you must profoundly study in its main guidelines.

C. Finally, we once more remind you of *availability of obedience.* This, we would say, is the characteristic feature of the Society: "In other Orders," St. Ignatius wrote in his famous letter of March 26, 1553, "one can find advantages in fastings, vigils, and other austerities . . .; but I greatly desire, beloved brothers, that those who serve our Lord God in this Society may be marked by the purity and perfection of obedience, with true renunciation of our wills and the abnegation of our judgments" (*Monumenta Ignatiana,* first series, *Sancti Ignatii de Loyola Societatis Iesu Fundatoris Epistolae et Instructiones,* t. IV, fasc. V: MHSI, Annus 13, fasc. 153, September, 1906, Madrid, p. 671).

In obedience there is the very essence of the imitation of Christ, "who redeemed by obedience the world lost by its lack, *factus obediens usque ad mortem, mortem autem crucis*" (ibid.). In obedience lies the secret of apostolic fruitfulness. The more you do the works of pioneers, the more you need to be closely united with him who sends you: "All apostolic boldness is possible, when the apostles' obedience is certain" (Loew, *Journal d'une mission ouvrière,* p. 452). We are certainly aware that if obedience demands much from those who obey, it demands even more of those who exercise authority. The latter are required to listen without partiality to the voices of all of their sons, to surround themselves with prudent counsellors in order to evaluate situations sincerely, to choose before God what best corresponds to his will and to intervene with firmness whenever there is departure from that will. In fact, every son of the Church is well aware that obedience is the proof and foundation of his fidelity: "the Catholic knows that the Church only commands because of the fact that she first obeys God. He wants to be a 'free man,' but recoils from being among those 'who make use of freedom as a pretext for evil' (1 Peter 2:16). Obedience is for him the price of freedom, just as it is the condition for unity" (H .de Lubac, *Meditation sur l'Eglise,* p. 224, cf. pp. 222–30).

Beloved sons!

At the end of this encounter we believe that we have given you some indications concerning the path which you must take in today's world; and we have also wanted to indicate to you the path which you must take in the world of the future. Know it, approach it, serve it, love it—this world; and in Christ it will be yours. Look at it with the same eyes as St. Ignatius did; note the same spiritual requirements; use the same weapons: prayer, a choice for the side of God, of his glory, the practice of asceticism, absolute availability. We think that we are not asking you too much when we express the desire that the Congregation should profoundly study and restate the essential elements *(essentialia)* of the Jesuit vocation in such a way that all your confreres will be able to recognize themselves, to strengthen their commitment, to rediscover their identity, to experience again their particular vocation, and to recast their proper community union. The moment requires it, the Society expects a decisive voice. Do not let that voice be lacking!

We are following with the most lively interest this work of yours, work which ought to have a great influence upon your holiness, your apostolate, and your fidelity to your charism and to the Church. We accompany your work especially with our prayer that the light of the Holy Spirit, the Spirit of the Father and of the Son, may illumine you, strengthen you, guide you, rouse you, and give you the incentive to follow ever more closely Christ crucified. So let us now together turn to Jesus in prayer, in the very words of St. Ignatius:

"Receive, Lord, my entire liberty. Take my memory, my intellect, and my whole will. Whatever I have or possess you gave to me. I give it all back to you, Lord. Dispose of it according to your will. All that I ask and desire is your holy will; give me your love and your grace. That is enough for me, and I ask for nothing: more" (*Spiritual Exercises ,* n. 234, op. cit., MHSI, Vol. 100, Rome," 1969, pp. 308–09).

This is the way, this is the way, brothers and sons. Forward, *in Nomine Domini.* Let us walk together, free, obedient, united to each other in the love of Christ, for the greater glory of God. Amen.

II. Letter of the Cardinal Secretary of State to Father General

December 3, 1974

Secretariat of State

The Vatican, December 3, 1974

Most Reverend Father:

His Holiness has given me the responsibility to convey to you and to the members of the Society his sincere satisfaction with the meeting held this morning, the feast of St. Francis Xavier, with those that are to take part in the 32nd General Congregation.

In the address which the Holy Father gave to those present, he certainly indicated his lively concern—expressed also in the letter which he sent to you on September 15, 1973—that the Society itself, in its praiseworthy and responsible attempt at *"aggiornamento"* in accord with the needs of the times, would remain faithful in its essential characteristics set down in the fundamental rule of the Order, that is, in the *Formula of the Institute.*

To this end the Supreme Pontiff did not fail to consider the possibility which might be proposed and which you yourself brought up in the recent audience with him on November 21st; that is, the proposal to extend to all the religious of the Society of Jesus, even those who were not priests, the fourth vow of special obedience to the Supreme Pontiff "with regard to missions"—reserved according to the Institute to those religious who are priests and who have satisfactorily completed the required spiritual and doctrinal preparation. He desires to let you know that such a change in the light of more careful examination seems to present grave difficulties which would impede the approval necessary on the part of the Holy See.

I am sending this communication to you so that you may have it before you as the work of the General Congregation develops.

I am happy to take the occasion of professing myself with religious respect,

Most devotedly yours,

Jean Cardinal Villot

III. Autograph Letter of His Holiness Paul VI
to Father General

February 15, 1975

To his beloved son, Pedro Arrupe, S.J.,

General of the Society of Jesus

We have received the letter which you sent to us and the account which we requested of the reasons which moved the General Congregation in its voting on the problem of grades and the fourth vow. We have not failed duly to consider it.

As regards more recent events, we confirm what our Cardinal Secretary of State wrote to you at our request on December 3 last. Again we repeat with all regard for you and for the Fathers of the Congregation: no change can be introduced related to the fourth vow.

As the supreme guarantor of the *Formula of the Institute,* and as universal pastor of the Church, we cannot allow this point in any way to be infringed upon, since it constitutes one of the pivotal points of the Society of Jesus. In excluding the extension of the fourth vow what moves us is not some less important feeling or an anguish-free knowledge of the problems. Rather it is that profound respect and deep love which we have for the Society as well as the persuasion of the great good which the Society in the future is called upon to provide for the ever more difficult work of the Church, if it is kept what its founder wished it to be—obviously with opportune adaptations which do not go beyond the limits of its basic identity.

Precisely in this view of things we want to express to you a doubt which arises in us from certain orientations and dispositions which are emerging from the work of the General Congregation: Is the Church able to have faith in you here and now, the kind of faith it has always had? What will the relationship of the ecclesiastical hierarchy toward the Society be? How will the hierarchy itself in a spirit free from fear be able to trust the Society to carry on works of such moment and of such a nature? The Society now enjoys a prosperity and an almost universal extension which as it were set it apart and which are in proportion to the trust which was always placed in it. It has a spirituality and doctrine and discipline and obedience and service and an example which it is bound to maintain and to witness to. Therefore we repeat confidently the question which we asked in our address on the 3rd of December at the beginning of the Congregation "Where are you going?"

In the days which you still have left to you for your common work, we ardently exhort you, my dear son, you and your brethren, to a yet deeper reflection on your responsibilities, and on your great potentialities as well as on the dangers which threaten the future of that farsighted and deserving "Society of Priests" founded by St. Ignatius.

As we wrote to you on September 15, 1973, this is a decisive hour "for the Society of Jesus, for its future and also for all religious congregations." Let us think of the innumerable repercussions that a line of action which—God forbid—was contrary to what we set out above could have on the Society and even on the Church. For this reason we "most insistently" ask you to consider seriously before the Lord the decisions to be made. It is the Pope who humbly but with an intense and sincere affection for you repeats with fatherly alarm and utter seriousness: Think well, my dear sons, on what you are doing.

For this reason we request that you send to us before their publication the decisions already made or soon to be made by the General Congregation.

In this serious hour we pray intensely for our beloved Society of Jesus while with a full heart we impart to you and to all its members all over the world, in the name of the Lord our apostolic benediction.

From the Vatican, February 15, 1975, the twelfth year of our Pontificate.

Paul VI

IV. Address of Pope Paul VI in the Presence of Father General and the General Assistants

March 7, 1975

Beloved Members of the Society of Jesus:

Almost three months ago, on the third of last December, it was a consolation for Us to receive in audience all the Fathers of the Society of Jesus who are members of the 32nd General Congregation just when they were undertaking their work. We were happy to indicate to them, the representatives before our eyes of the entire Ignatian family, our esteem for all the members "who labor for the Kingdom of God and carry on very valuable work for the apostolic and missionary endeavors of the Church" (*AAS* 66; 1974; p. 712). We now have, therefore, a great occasion for rejoicing since we have yet another opportunity of once again giving evidence of our great, paternal, and sincere good will for this religious order that is so clearly joined with Us and is certainly very dear to Us.

For our part, We admit that We were impelled by the very spirit of love, by which We embrace all of you, to interpose our authority with the superiors of your Society—as you well know—in rather recent circumstances. We thought that this action had to be taken because of our consciousness that We are the supreme protector and guardian of the *Formula of the Institute,* as well as the Shepherd of the Universal Church. Actually, at that time We were not a little pleased by the fact that the members of the General Congregation favorably understood the force and meaning of our recommendations and showed that they received them with a willingness to carry them out. Now We wish once again to cite the words of the Apostle Paul: "I wrote [what] I did ... [confident that] you all know that I could never be happy, unless you were. When I wrote to you, in deep distress and anguish of mind, and in tears, it was not to make you feel hurt but to let you know how much love I have for you" (2 Cor. 2:3–4).

Some of you, perhaps in order to inject new vigor into the life of your Society, thought that it would be necessary to introduce substantially new elements into the *Formula of the Institute,* that is, into its primary norms or into its adaptation to the present social milieu. For our part, We cannot allow changes based on such reasoning to enter into your religious institute, which is of its very nature so special and so fully approved, not only by historical experience but also by hardly doubtful indications of divine protection. We feel that the Society must indeed be adapted and adjusted to this age of ours and must be enriched with new vitality, but always in accord with the principles of the Gospel and the Institute. It must not be transformed or deformed.

In view of this persuasion and our abundant love, We shall continue to take a solicitous part in all your affairs as often as the good of the Society or the Church seems to demand such involvement.

At the close of this Congregation, We gladly take advantage of the occasion to give this reminder to each and every son of St. Ignatius, scattered as they are throughout the world: Be loyal! This loyalty, which is freely and effectively shown to the *Formula of the Institute,* will safeguard the original and true form of the companions of Ignatius and strengthen the fruitfulness of their apostolate. This same loyalty must be considered a condition that is absolutely necessary to every type of ministry to which you are called, so that the name of Jesus may be spread and glorified throughout the world in the many and diverse areas of endeavor where you labor as members of a priestly and apostolic religious order that is united to the Supreme Pontiff by a special vow.

When We consider the great quantity of works which have been entrusted to you and which demand minds of proven maturity of judgment and firm wills outstanding in humility and generosity, it is our wish that all the members of the Society of Jesus be supported by supernatural helps and that they always rely on them! For no salvation can be brought to the world except through the selfless outpouring of the cross of Jesus Christ (see Phil. 2:7–8) and "the foolishness of the message that we preach" (1 Cor. 1:21).

Therefore We exhort all the companions of Ignatius to continue with renewed zeal to carry out all the works and endeavors upon which they have so eagerly embarked in the service of the Church and that they be aware of the importance of their tasks while at the same time they rely on the help and assistance of God who alone suffices just as he alone was always sufficient for Ignatius and Francis Xavier in the midst of the great needs which they experienced. You should be aware of the fact that not only the eyes of contemporary men in general but also and especially those of so many members of other religious orders and congregations and even those of the universal Church are turned toward you. May such grandly conceived hopes, then, not be frustrated! Go, therefore, and proceed in the name of the Lord. As sons and brethren, go forth always and only in the name of the Lord.

With our Apostolic Blessing, We wish to confirm this desire of our heart.

V. Letter of the Cardinal of State to Father General

May 2, 1975

The Secretary of State

N. 281428

Vatican City, May 2, 1975

Very Reverend Father,

In fulfillment of my office, I submitted to the Holy Father for his consideration the decrees of the 32nd General Congregation of the Society of Jesus which the Congregation presented to him in accord with the desire he expressed to you in a letter dated the 15th of last February.

The Holy Father carefully examined these texts which represent the culmination of the work of the General Congregation, whose progress he followed with keen, loving, and personal concern. He has commissioned me to return these decrees to you, together with the following observations.

From an examination of the decrees, it appears that well-known circumstances prevented the General Congregation from achieving all that His Holiness had expected from this important event, and for which, at different times and in various ways, he gave some paternal suggestions, especially in his allocution of the 3rd of December, 1974, when he indicated his hopes for the Congregation. In any case, he has directed that the decrees be returned to you so that they can be put into effect according to the needs of the Society, with the hope that your worthy Jesuit brothers may draw strength from these decrees as they continue their progress in genuine fidelity to the charism of St. Ignatius and the *Formula of the Institute.*

However, while some statements in the decrees merit total acceptance, others are somewhat confusing and could, because of the way they are expressed, give grounds for misinterpretation. Therefore, the Holy Father desires that some particular recommendations pertaining to certain decrees be sent to you and to your companions. You will find them appended to this letter, and I would ask that you regard them in that spirit of obedience which has always characterized the Society,

Finally, with reference to the decree, "On Poverty," which you presented to him in your filial letter of the 14th of last March, His Holiness could not help but notice how thoroughly you undertook the complicated task of adapting the Society's legislation in this area to contemporary needs in accord with the norms

I conveyed in my letter of February 26, 1973. Because of the sensitive nature of this subject, however, and because of the character of the innovations introduced, it would be well if this decree were implemented "experimentally," in such a way that the next general congregation can reexamine the whole question in depth against the background of experience gained in the years ahead. As to the faculty for dispensing from the vow of poverty which you requested in your letter, I am to inform you that the Vicar of Christ grants you this in the individual cases where, with the deliberative vote of your council, it seems necessary.

Questions may arise about the interpretation of the decrees as a whole. In this event, the Holy Father sincerely desires that reference always be made to the norms and directives contained either in his address to you on the 3rd of December or in other documents of the Holy See pertaining to the Congregation.

The Holy Father hopes that these remarks will be taken as the context within which the decrees of the 32nd General Congregation are accurately understood and correctly implemented. For this reason, it seems most appropriate that this letter and the added reflections be published along with the decrees and thus be available to those responsible for reading and applying these decrees.

The Holy Father follows the work of the Society with special and fervent prayer to the Lord that it always remain true—as he said in his final talk of March 7th last—to itself and to its mission in the bosom of the Church. It is also his prayer that the Society continue to perform those ministries of apostolic service and evangelical witness, in the name of Jesus, which are expected of it today. These desires the Holy Father confirms with his special blessing.

Devotedly yours,

J. Cardinal Villot

Appendix

Particular Observations about Certain Decrees

The decree *Our Mission Today:*
Diakonia Fidei and the Promotion of Justice,
and the declaration *Jesuits Today*

The promotion of justice is unquestionably connected with evangelization, but—as the Holy Father said in his closing remarks to the last Synod of Bishops in October of 1974—"Human development and social progress in the temporal order should not be extolled in such exaggerated terms as to obscure the essential significance which the Church attributes to evangelization and the proclamation of the full Gospel" (*AAS* 66, 1974, 637).

This applies to the Society of Jesus in a special way, founded as it was for a particularly spiritual and supernatural end. Every other undertaking should be subordinated to this end and carried out in a way appropriate for an Institute which is religious, not secular, and priestly. Moreover, we must not forget that the priest should inspire lay Catholics, since in the promotion of justice theirs is the more demanding role. The tasks proper to each should not be confused.

It is also helpful to recall that work for the promotion of justice should be undertaken in accord with directives drawn up by the local hierarchy and in consideration of the conditions peculiar to each region

The decree *On Fidelity to the Magisterium and the Roman Pontiff*

It is most opportune that the General Congregation has confirmed the traditional fidelity of the Society to the magisterium and the Holy Father. However, the expression, "Freedom should be intelligently encouraged," should not be allowed to provide grounds for disregarding the rules for "Thinking with the Church," which are proper to the Society.

The decree *Concerning the Formation of Jesuits*

There is laudable insistence upon solid philosophical and theological education. However, in keeping with the Conciliar Decree *Optatam Totius,* those engaged in philosophical instruction should bear in mind that organized body of solid doctrine gathered—as a patrimony—by the Church.

Moreover, in theological studies, after a careful investigation of the sources, "by way of making the mysteries of salvation known as thoroughly as they can be, students should learn to penetrate them more deeply with the help of speculative reason exercised under the tutelage of St. Thomas, and they should learn, too, how these mysteries are interconnected" (#16).

The decree *On Poverty*

Superiors should take very seriously their responsibility to see that the distinction between the apostolic institute and the religious community is properly observed so that ways of acting which are contrary to the genuine Ignatian poverty may be avoided. Furthermore, the performance of ministries which, by tradition, are undertaken gratuitously should not be lightly abandoned.

The decree *Concerning the Province Congregation*

The extension of active and passive voice to nonformed members significantly expands the process of election to a provincial congregation. However, since the decree itself stipulates that the norms therein contained should be reviewed by the next general congregation, timely and serious study should be given to this whole question, so that it can be resolved in a way which is both more equitable and more in keeping with the spirit of the Society.

D

MEMBERS OF THE 32nd
GENERAL CONGREGATION

(In Alphabetical Order

President: VERY REVEREND FATHER PEDRO ARRUPE
Elected General on May 22, 1965

Last Name, First Name, and Province

Abellán, Pedro	Toledo	Bamberger, Stefan	Switzerland
Acévez, Manuel,	Mexico	Baragli, Enrico	Rome
Achaerandio, Luis	Central America	Barré, Noël	Western France
Adám, John	Hungary	Begley, John	Australia
Adami, Leopoldo	Southern Brazil	Belic, Miljenko	Croatia
Agúndez, Melecio	Castile	Berden, Pavel	Slovenia
Aizpún, José	Gujarat	Bergoglio, Jorge	Argentina
Aldecoa, José Antonio	Loyola	Besanceney, Paul	Detroit
Alfaro, Juan	Loyola	Biever, Bruce	Wisconsin
Alvarez-Bolado, Alfonso	Castile	Blanco, Benito	Antilles
Amet, Henri	Western France	Boné, Edouard	Southern Belgium
Antunes,Manuel	Portugal	Bortolotti, Roberto	Rome
Arango, Gerardo	Colombia	Botturi, Tarcisio	Bahia
Arevalo, Catalino	Philippines	Bourgeault, Guy	French Canada
Arroyo, José	Toledo	Brenninkmeyer, Bernward	East Germany
Arrupe, Pedro	Japan	Browne, Joseph	New York
Arvesú, Federico	Antilles	Buckley, Michael	California
Athazhapadam, Thomas	Patna		

Cachat, Leo	Patna
Calvez, Jean-Yves	Western France
Casassa, Charles	California
Chabert, Henrí	Southern France
Chu, Bernard	China
Clancy, Thomas	New Orleans
Clarke, Thomas	New York
Cleary, Richard	New England
de Colnet, Yves	Northern France
Connery, John	Chicago
Connor, James	Maryland
Coreth, Emerich	Australia
Correia-Afonso, John	Bombay
Costa, de la Horacio	Philippines
Costes André	Southern France
Counihan, John	Zambia
Cruz, Luís A	Ecuador
Ćurić, Josip	Croatia
Cuyás, Manuel	Tarragona
Daniel, William	Australia
Dargan, Herbert	Hong-Kong
Dargan, Joseph	Ireland
Darowski, Roman	Lesser Poland
Decloux, Simon	Southern Belgium
De Cooman, Eugeen	Northern Belgium
Deenen van, Jan	Netherlands
De Hovre, Luk	Northern Belgium
De Mello, Anthony	Bombay
Dezza, Paolo	Venice-Milan
Díaz Bertrana, Marcos	Baetica
Días de Moura, Laercio	East-Central Brazil
Divarkar, Parmananda	Bombay

D'Mello, Ambrose	Kanara
Domínguez, Héctor	Baetica
Dortel-Claudot, Michel	Northern France
D'Souza, Noel	Calcutta
D'Souza, Romuald	Goa-Poona
Dullard, Maurice	Ranchi
Echeverría, José Luis	Venezuela
Egaña, Francisco	Loyola
Ekka, Philip	Ranchi
Ekwa bis Isal	Central Africa
Fabbri, Enrique	Argentina
Fang, Chih-Jung Marc	China
Farrell, Walter	Detroit
Fernández, Avelino	León
Fernández-Castañeda, José Luis	Peru
Flaherty, Daniel	Chicago
Fragata, Julio	Portugal
Galauner, Petar	Croatia
Galbraith, Kenneth	Oregon
Ganzi, Igino	Turin
Gerhartz, Johannes Günter	Lower Germany
Giorgianni, Giovanni	Sicily
Gnanadickam, Casimir	Madurai
Gordon, Douglas	Madurai
Grez, Ignacio	Chile
Guidera, John	Jamshedpur
Guindon, William	New England
Gutiérrez, Enrique	Mexico
Gutiérrez Semprún	Castile
Hall, Bernard	England
Hannan, Michael	Salisbury

Hardawirjana, Robert	Indonesia	van Leeuwen, Hans	Netherlands
Harvanek, Robert	Chicago	Leite, Antonio	Portugal
Harvey, Julien	French Canada	Lesage, Jacques	Paris
Hayashi, Shogo	Japan	Londoño, Fernando	Colombia
Hebga, Meinrod	West Africa	Lucey, Paul	New England
Hillengass, Eugen	Upper Germany	Macchi, Angelo	Venice-Milan
Hoël, Marc	Northern France	Mac Gregor, Felipe	Peru
Hoffmann, Georg	East Germany	Madurga, Mariano	Aragon
Hortal, Jesús	Southern Brazil	Mahoney, Martin	New York
Huarte, Ignacio	Venezuela	Malone, Patrick	Upper Canada
Huber, Eduard	Upper Germany	Marranzini, Alfredo	Naples
Hughes, Gerard J.	England	Martini, Carlo	Turin
Huizing, Peter	Netherlands	Mayo, Benigno	Philippines
Iglesias, Ignacio	León	McCarthy, Charles	China
Jiménez, Gustavo	Colombia	McGarry, Cecil	Ireland
Kaufmann, Leo	Oregon	McPolin, James	Ireland
Kern, Walter	Austria	Meharuj, Carlos	Uruguay
Kijauskas, Gediminas	Lithuania	Menacho, Antonio	Bolivia
Knecht, Joseph	Patna	Mendes de Almeida, Luciano	East-Central Brazil
Koczwara, Tadeusz	Greater Poland	Mendizábal, Miguel	Japan
Kolacek, Josef	Bohemia	Mertens, Victor	Central Africa
Kolvenbach, Peter-Hans	Near East	Miecznikowski, Stefan	Greater Poland
Krauss, Heinrich	Upper Germany	Mitchell, Robert	New York
Kullu, Patrick	Ranchi	Molinari, Paolo	Turin
Kunz, Erhard	Lower Germany	Montes, Fernando	Chile
Kyne, Michael	England	Moragues, Ignacio	Aragon
		Moreland, Gordon	Oregon
Lambert, Louis	New Orleans	Moysa-Rosochacki, Stefan	Lesser Poland
Lapize de Salée, Bernard	Southern France	Mruk, Anton	Lesser Poland
Lariviere, Florian	French Canada	Muguiro, Ignacio	Peru
Laurendeau, Louis	French Canada	Navarrete, Urbano	Aragon
Leäo, Joaquim	Mozambique		

Ochagavía, Juan	Chile	Segura, Manuel	Baetica
O'Keefe, Vincent	New York	Seibel, Vitus	Upper Germany
O'Malley, John	Detroit	Sencik, Stefan	Slovakia
Orsy, Ladislas	New York	Sheahan, Gerald	Missouri
O'Sullivan	Australia	Sheets, John	Wisconsin
Padberg, John	Missouri	Sheridan, Edward	Upper Canada
Panuska, Joseph	Maryland	Sily, Alberto	Argentina
Pasupasu	Central Africa	Small, Harold	Oregon
Pelenda, Bikakala	Central Africa	Soenarja, Antonius	Indonesia
Pereira, Joaquim	East-Central Brazil	Soltero, Carlos	Mexico
Pérez-Lerena Francisco	Antilles	Sorge, Bartolomeo	Venice-Milan
Perniola, Vito	Ceylon	Sucre, Gustavo	Venezuela
Perz, Zygmunt	Greater Poland	Suradibrata, Paul	Indonesia
Petrucelli, Donato	Naples	de Survilliers, Alain	Western France
Philipps, Bertram	Bombay	Tabao, Fr.ançois-Xavier	Madagascar
Pilz, Johann Chr.	Austria	Taylor, Eamon	New York
Piña, Joaquin	Paraguay	Tejerina, Angel	León
Popiel, Jan	Lesser Poland	Tomé, Mariano	Cuba
Prucha, Paul	Wisconsin	Torres Gasset, Juan	Tarragona
Rakotonirina, Charles-Remy	Madagascar	Troisfontaines, Roger	Southern Belgium
Randriambololona, Philibert	Madagascar	Tucci, Roberto	Naples
Rendina, Sergio	Venice-Milan	Vadakel, Paul	Kerala
Roth, Herbert	East Germany	Valero, Urbano	Castile
Russell, John	Hong-Kong	Van Bladel, Louis	Northern Belgium
Russo, Biagio	Sicily	Vandermeersch, Edmond	Paris
Ryan, William	Upper Canada	Vanni, Ugo	Rome
San Juan, Vicente	Philippines	Varaprasadam, Arul Maria	Madurai
Santana, Hindenburg	Northern Brazil	de Varine-Bohan, Jean	Paris
Sanz, Criado Luis M.	Toledo	de Vaucelles, Louis	Paris
Scaduto, Mario	Sicily	Vaughan, Richard	California
Schasching, Johann	Austria	Vela, Luis	León
Scheifler, Xavier	Mexico	Vella, Arthur	Malta

Vergnano, Carlo	Turin	Weber, Quirino	Southern Brazil
Viard, Claude	Southern France	Whelan, Joseph	Maryland
Vives, José	Tarragona	Wulf, Friedrich	Lower Germany
Walsh, Maurice	Jamaica	Yamauchi, James	New Orleans
Walsh, Terence	Upper Canada	Yanase, Mutsuo	Japan
Weber, Leo	Missouri	Zamarriego, Tomás	Toledo

THE 33rd GENERAL CONGREGATION
OF THE
SOCIETY OF JESUS

September 1, 1983—October 25, 1983

LETTER OF PROMULGATION FROM FATHER GENERAL

To the Whole Society

Reverend fathers and dear brothers in Christ,

Pax Christi!

By this letter I communicate to all the provinces, vice-provinces, missions and regions of the Society the decrees of the 33rd General Congregation, in the name of this same Congregation, so that they may be published in our houses and communities.

Decree 2 "On Poverty," which needed approval by the Holy See in a special manner and which was submitted to the Holy Father on October 29, was definitively approved and confirmed by him, as the Cardinal Secretary of State reported in a letter of November 3.

All of these decrees enter into force as of the date of this letter.

While I give thanks to the Lord for the successful outcome of the General Congregation, I strongly commend to your Sacrifices and prayers the study and implementation of the decrees set down by the Congregation and now promulgated to the greater glory and service of our Lord and God.

The servant of all of you in Christ,

Peter-Hans Kolvenbach, S.J.

General of the Society of Jesus

Rome, November 20, 1983
Solemnity of the Feast of Christ the King

A

HISTORICAL PREFACE
TO THE DECREES
OF THE 33rd GENERAL CONGREGATION

Excerpted from the Official Minutes of the Congregation

A

HISTORICAL PREFACE TO THE DECREES
OF THE 33RD GENERAL CONGREGATION

Excerpted from the Official Minutes of the Congregation

1. Prior to Convocation

As far back as 1980 Very Reverend Father General Pedro Arrupe had in mind the summoning of a general congregation to which, after the votes of the provincials had been secured, he would submit his resignation from the office of Superior General. The Supreme Pontiff John Paul II, however, asked Father General to postpone this step so that the Society might prepare itself more profoundly for a congregation.[1] The following year, after a grave illness unexpectedly befell Father General on August 7,[2] the Supreme Pontiff in a letter dated October 5[3] named Father Paolo Dezza (Italy) as his Delegate in charge of seeing to the preparation of the Society for the general congregation and the temporary government of the Society. He also named Father Giuseppe Pittau (Japan) to be the Delegate's Coadjutor.

On February 27, 1982, the Supreme Pontiff addressed the provincials of the Society, who had met together with Father Delegate in Villa Cavalletti, concerning his desires with respect to the Society and to the preparation of the congregation, and at the same time expressed his confidence that the convocation itself could occur before the year's end.[4] This, in fact, came about when, on December 8, 1982, Father Delegate, with the permission of the Supreme Pontiff, summoned the General Congregation for September 1, 1983. "The task of General Congregation XXXXIII will be first of all to deal with the resignation of Father General and the election of a new General; then it will be to treat of those matters which are to be reviewed in accord with the will of the Holy See (cf. Cardinal Villot's letter of May 2, 1975, pp. 396–397 above) and of General Congrega-

---

[1] AR XVIII, 225 (Letter of July 3, 1980).

[2] AR XVIII, 608 ff.

[3] AR XVIII, 401.

[4] AR XVIII, 721–734.

tion XXXXII; and finally, as the General Congregation itself judges best, it will treat the postulates sent to the General Congregation."[5] Father Delegate asked that the province congregations be completed by April 10, 1983.

2. The Official Preparatory Committee Is Established

After the province congregations were completed, Father Delegate promptly established the "Official Preparatory Committee" (in accordance with the *Formula of the General Congregation,* 12, #1), which was being put to use for the first time. Those named to this committee from each of the Assistancies were: Fathers Albert Beaudry (English), Michel Chu (East Asian), James A. Devereux (American), Julian Fernandes (Indian), Claude Flipo (French), Johannes G. Gerhartz (German), Joao MacDowell (Southern Latin American), Daniel Pasupasu (African), Zygmunt Perz (Slavic), Roberto Tucci (Italian), Urbano Valero (Spanish), and Jesus Vergara (Northern Latin American). It was the task of the Official Preparatory Committee, according to the norms of the *Formula of the General Congregation,* "to complete the proximate preparation" (12, #1), and to do that in an "authoritative" manner in the sense that the studies and reports produced or approved by it "should be regarded as part of the official work of the Congregation and acknowledged by the Congregation itself" (10, #2, 2°).

3. The Work of the Official Preparatory Committee

The Preparatory Committee convened in Rome at the General Curia on June 1, 1983, and carried on its efforts up to the end of the month. It undertook first, in accordance with the norm of the *Formula* of the General Congregation 13, its duty of screening the postulates and in doing so examined all those sent by the province congregations and those that individuals had sent within the prescribed time. It drew up a report on the postulates admitted for handling in the General Congregation or given to Father General or rejected.

Next it prepared necessary preliminary reports. Three of these dealt with points that a future Congregation would have to handle by wish of the Holy See (cf. letter of Cardinal Villot, May 2, 1975) and of the 32nd General Congregation, namely, the question of confirmation of Decree 12 of the 32nd General Congregation with respect to poverty, and certain questions about participation in a province congregation and about the makeup of a general congregation.

The other preliminary reports prepared by the Official Preparatory Committee had to do with our apostolic mission (with questions about the confirmation and clarification of Decree 4 of the 32nd General Congregation, and about some of its applications, especially concerning the promotion of peace and international order, about collaboration with lay persons, about the apostolate of edu-

---

[5] AR XVIII, 856–858.

cation, and about some other types of apostolate), with the coadjutor brothers, with religious life, with the formation of Jesuits, with the relationship of the Society to the hierarchical Church. On all these topics, moreover, drafts of statements that might be useful for discussion in the General Congregation were prepared.

At the conclusion of these efforts, in early July, Father Delegate sent an announcement to all those who were to attend the Congregation in order to inform them about the main points handled by the Preparatory Committee. The preliminary reports themselves, along with the postulates assembled by categories and a report on the postulates, were handed to all who were to attend the Congregation the day they reached Rome for the General Congregation. They were able to apply themselves to the study of these materials from the start of the Congregation, that is, even before the election of the Superior General.

4.   The Members of the Congregation Convene

On the prescribed day almost all those who were to participate in the Congregation were on hand in Rome at the General Curia and the adjoining House of Writers. Still, a few were missing. Because of circumstances a province congregation could not be held in Bohemia, Hungary, Lithuania, Romania, and Slovakia. From Hungary only the provincial came, but he was joined by another member of the same province (but living outside its territory) who was named by Father Delegate in accordance with the norm of the *Formula of the Province Congregation,* 95, #4. For Bohemia, Lithuania, and Slovakia, Father Delegate, in accordance with the norm of the *Formula of the Province Congregation,* 95, #3, named as members three Jesuits living outside their native countries. But no one came on behalf of Romania. During the first days of the Congregation, Father Joseph Labaj (Provincial of Wisconsin) was absent because of illness. He came afterwards and took part in the election of Father General and of the General Assistants. On September 23, however, he had to take permanent leave of the Congregation.

5.   Concelebration with Pope John Paul II

On the first day of the Congregation, September 2, which was the first Friday of the month, the Supreme Pontiff John Paul II wished to come from Castel Gandolfo to our Curia in order that he might concelebrate the Eucharistic liturgy with the members of the Congregation and address them in a homily. After the liturgy was concluded, in a further demonstration of exceptional good will, of his own accord he also stayed on to visit with the members of the Congregation and to speak familiarly with each of them.

6. First Session of the Congregation

(From the Minutes, Acta 1)

In the afternoon of the same day, the first session was held. After the singing of the hymn *Veni Creator Spiritus* and a brief greeting delivered to the members by Father Delegate, the Congregation was declared to be fully and legitimately in session. Then the Congregation had put before it the case of the four electors from France and the five from Italy, called on behalf of each of the vice-provinces that exist in these large provinces, in accordance with the statutes set down by Father General (AR XVI, 749 and AR XVII, 359). When this decision was ratified, the nine electors were summoned to the Aula. The Congregation also decreed the admission, as observers in these first sessions, but excluding the session of the election, those members who had the right to participate only in matters of business and likewise Father Donald Campion (New York), the director of the Information Office.

Next, approval was given to the "Additions" on procedure proposed by Father Delegate, as well as norms on information that he presented. Approval was given likewise to the creation, proposed by Father Delegate, of a committee to supervise the communication of information. This committee was made up of Fathers Marcello Azevedo (Central East Brazil), Joaquin G. Bernas (Philippines), Andre Costes (France), Federico Lombardi (Italy), Fernando Montes (Chile), Stanislaw Opiela (Greater Poland), Vitus Seibel (Upper Germany), and Urbano Valero (Castille).

7. Acceptance of Very Reverend Father Arrupe's Resignation

(From the Minutes, Acta 2, 3)

On September 3, after the election of Father M. Azevedo (Central East Brazil) as Secretary of the Congregation for the election and of Father J. G. Gerhartz (Northern Germany) as his Assistant, the Congregation dealt with the question of accepting or not accepting the resignation of Very Reverend Father Pedro Arrupe. After a brief discussion this resignation was accepted by a secret vote. A special solemn session, at which were present also members of the Curia community and all the other Jesuit houses in Rome, was held in the afternoon of the same day, in order to manifest the Society's gratitude to Very Reverend Father Arrupe, just as different postulates from province congregations expressly requested. Father Delegate delivered an address in which he recalled the examples given us all by Father Arrupe, his total dedication to his office and his ardent love for the Society and every one of its members, and the unflagging inspiration he gave to the Society in its effort to adapt itself according to its own spirit to new circumstances and needs. Finally, Father Delegate stressed the new model of abnegation set before all by Father Arrupe in these last years, namely, when he wanted to put into action the procedure authorized by the 31st General Congregation for resigning from his office, but had to postpone his resignation and was subsequently struck by illness.

After thunderously protracted applause, Father Ignacio Iglesias (Leon), a member of the Congregation, read the text of a message to the Society drafted by Father Arrupe with the help of the General Assistants. This memorable session was brought to a close with a reception in the Curia garden. On the next day, which was a Sunday, a Eucharistic liturgy was concelebrated in the cathedral at La Storta with Father Arrupe, who also visited the nearby chapel that had recently been restored in accordance with his wish. A homily prepared by Father Arrupe was read by Father Juan Luis Fernandez-Castaneda (Peru) and the consecration of the Society to the Sacred Heart of Jesus was renewed according to a text edited by Father Arrupe some years ago.

8. Election of the Deputation on the State of the Society

(From the Minutes, Acta 4)

On the morning of September 4 those fathers were elected who would form the deputation on the state of the Society together with Father Delegate and his Coadjutor and the four General Assistants (Jean-Yves Calvez, Parmananda Divarkar, Cecil McGarry, Vincent O'Keefe): Philibert Randriambololona (for the African Assistancy), John O'Callaghan (American Assistancy), Juan Ochagavia (Southern Latin American), Carlos Soltero (Northern Latin American), Michael Campbell-Johnston (English), Robert Rush (East Asian), Denis Delobre (French), Eugen Hillengass (German), Ignacio Iglesias (Spanish), Michael Amaladoss (Indian), Bruno Bois (Italian), Zygmunt Perz (Slavic). When Fathers Amaladoss, O'Callaghan, and Ochagavia subsequently were elected General Assistants, the Congregation elected three others as their substitutes: Fathers Parmananda Divarkar, Joseph O'Hare, and Manuel Guttierrez Semprun, in accordance with the norms of the *Formula of the General Congregation,* 100, #2.

After the election of the deputies it was announced that the time set for presenting information to the deputation was a period of two days, i.e., up to and including September 6. Information was given also about the list of judges concerning "ambition" in accordance with the norm of the *Formula of the General Congregation,* 54.

9. Report of Father Delegate and the Four Days for Gathering Information

(From the Minutes, Acta 5, 8)

On September 5, Father Delegate made a report, in accordance with the spirit of the *Formula of the General Congregation,* 37, on those things he had done from October 5, 1981, when the government of the Society was entrusted to him. On the following day, he replied to the written observations and questions that had been handed in by members of the Congregation. On September 8, 1983, the report on the state of the Society drafted by the deputation was distributed. The Congregation decreed that the quatriduum for gathering information in preparation for the election of the Superior General should begin on September 9. On the following day, Father Delegate reminded all of the special duty of recollection and he also stressed the importance of our rules for the giving and receiving of information on an individual basis, which forbid everything that could have even the appearance of any kind of propaganda. In fact, an atmosphere of deep recollection, prayer, and spiritual discernment flourished during these four days, an experience that was praised by all the electors.

10. Election of the Superior General

(From the Minutes, Acta 9)

After the completion of the quatriduum, on the morning of September 13, all the members of the Congregation, with Father Delegate as presiding celebrant, concelebrated the Mass of the Holy Spirit. At the conclusion of the sacred liturgy, the electors went immediately to the Aula of the Congregation where, in accordance with the *Formula,* they were enclosed. When the hymn *Veni Creator* was said, Father Edward Sheridan (Upper Canada), the speaker duly designated for the occasion, gave a 15-minute exhortation to the electors, in accordance with the prescription of the *Formula of the General Congregation,* 75, #1 "for the election of a Superior who would be best suited for the greater service of God." After that, all prayed for the rest of the hour.

Then, after all the prescriptions of the *Formula* were fulfilled, by majority vote on the first ballot Father Peter-Hans Kolvenbach of the vice-province of the Near East, was elected Superior General of the Society. He had been formerly provincial of this vice-province and for almost two years was serving as rector of the Pontifical Oriental Institute in Rome. The formal certification of this election was drawn up immediately and signed by Father Delegate. The news was sent to the Supreme Pontiff, who was in Austria engaged in an apostolic journey.

In remarks he delivered immediately after the election, the new Superior General made plain again the Society's enormous gratitude toward Father Arrupe, and expressed the fullest thanks to Father Paolo Dezza for his work as the Pope's Delegate as well as to Father Giuseppe Pittau for the staunch assistance he rendered, and to the entire Curia, but especially to the General Assistants for the way in which they helped the entire Society in the last years.

Then Father Pedro Arrupe came into the Aula and greeted with heartfelt warmth his successor as Superior General of the Society. All then moved on to the Curia chapel to give thanks to God with a *Te Deum*.

11. Election of the Secretary and Sub-Secretaries and Likewise of the Deputation for Handling Substantive Matters

(From the Minutes, Acta 10)

After the election of the Superior General, on September 15 Father Johannes Gunter Gerhartz (Northern Germany) was elected Secretary for the further work of the Congregation, i.e., for substantive matters. Fathers Simon Decloux (Southern Belgium) and Jean-Yves Calvez (France) were elected as Sub-Secretaries. The deputation for handling substantive matters was also established immediately and the following were elected to it: Fathers Daniel Pasupasu (for the African Assistancy), Vincent O'Keefe (American), Joao MacDowell (Southern Latin American), Cesar Jerez (Northern Latin American), Cecil McGarry (English), Giuseppe Pittau (East Asian), Henri Madelin (French), Hans van Leeuwen (Netherlands), Urbano Valero (Spanish), Abraham Puthumana (Indian), Roberto Tucci (Italian), and Petar Galauner (Slavic).

A small committee within this deputation was elected to assist in handling the daily problems concerning the order of treatment of topics (cf. *Formula of the General Congregation,* 101, #6). The members of this committee were Fathers Henri Madelin, Vincent O'Keefe, and Roberto Tucci. The latter two along with Father Simon Decloux were named by Father General as Moderators of the various sessions (in accordance with the norm of the *Formula of the General Congregation,* 101, #7).

12. Reports on the Work Rendered by the Preparatory Committee. Setting Up of Commissions

(From the Minutes, Acta 11, 12, 13, 14)

In accordance with a decision made on September 16, the quatriduum prior to the election of the General Assistants began on the following day, i.e., September 17. During the period of the quatriduum, however, the first steps were taken with respect to handling substantive matters. On the one hand, preliminary reports of the Official Preparatory Committee on the province congregation and on coadjutor brothers were presented in the Aula. On the other hand, the Congregation entrusted the setting up of commissions on handling substantive matters to Father General together with the deputation on handling substantive matters. Eight commissions were immediately set up: On Poverty (Moderator: Father Eugen Hillengass); On the Province Congregation (Moderator: Father Stefan Bamberger); On the General Congregation (Moderator: Father Jean-Yves Calvez); On Our Mission (Moderator: Father Juan Ochagavia, who was replaced by Father William Ryan when he was later elected a General Assistant); On the Relationship of the Society to the Church and Its Hierarchy (Moderator: Father Theodor Beirle); On Coadjutor Brothers (Moderator: Father Claude Flipo); On Religious Life (Moderator: Father Rex Pai); On Jesuit Formation (Moderator: Father Michael Amaladoss). Each commission had twelve members, one from each Assistancy, except, however, for the Commission on Our Mission, which had two members from each Assistancy.

After a few days a judicial committee was established, made up of three members, namely, Fathers Antonio Arza (Loyola), Francisco Egana (Loyola) and Ladislas Orsy (New York). In the final days of the Congregation, a small special commission was set up to handle a certain postulate concerning the law of the Society on parishes.

13. Election of General Assistants and Admonitor and Appointment of General Counsellors and Certain Regional Assistants

(From the Minutes, Acta 15, 16, 17, 20)

The election of the general assistants was held, in accordance with the norm of the *Formula of the General Congregation,* 136, #2, in three different sessions. In the first, on September 21, two were elected; in the second, in the afternoon of the same day, one; in the third, on September 22, one. Those elected were: Father Michael Amaladoss, from the Province of Madurai; Father Simon Decloux, from the Province of Southern Belgium; Father John J. O'Callaghan, from the Province of Chicago; Father Juan Ochagavia, from the Province of Chile.

By the fact of their election the four General Assistants became also General Counsellors. Father General afterwards, with a deliberative vote of the General Assistants, named two other General Counsellors: Fathers Giuseppe Pittau (Japan) who most recently functioned as Coadjutor to the Pope's Delegate, and Urbano Valero (Castille) who hitherto was rector of the Pontifical University of Comillas. Father Simon Decloux (Southern Belgium) was elected Admonitor of the Superior General on September 24.

During the course of the Congregation, some Regional Assistants also were appointed: for the American Assistancy, Father Joseph Whelan, hitherto provincial of the province of Maryland; for the East Asian Assistancy and at the same time for the Italian Assistancy, Father Giuseppe Pittau, already appointed as a General Counsellor; for the French Assistancy, Father Simon Decloux, already elected as General Assistant, General Counsellor and Admonitor; for the Spanish Assistancy, Father Urbano Valero, already appointed as General Counsellor; for the Indian Assistancy, Father Noel D'Souza (Calcutta), hitherto rector of the Jesuit theologate in Pune; for the Slavic Assistancy, Father Andrzej Koprowski (Greater Poland), hitherto rector of the Jesuit theologate in Warsaw.

14. Method of Handling Substantive Matters

(From the Minutes, Acta 27, 30)

The process followed in handling substantive matters in this Congregation was most frequently the same: an oral presentation of a preliminary report *(relatio praevia)* drafted by the Official Preparatory Committee; meetings of Assistancy groups for the purpose of preparing written comments; a revised report *(relatio secunda)* prepared by a commission (with a presentation of the comments received, a judgment of the commission and a draft of a decree or declaration to be issued by the Congregation); a brief oral presentation of the revised report with an opportunity to pose questions for the sake of clarification and the debate itself in the Aula (without any previous consideration in small groups); presentation of amendments and a final vote on them and on the body of the text. In certain cases, however, the text, after the debate in the Aula, would have to be rewritten by the commission again and an opportunity found for a new presentation and debate.

Still, it soon became evident that a wish existed in the Congregation to have all those elements that could be said to be rather orientative and inspirational in nature woven together and unified in a single document that would reveal to all the members of the Society the Congregation's own thinking on both our mission and our life. Nevertheless, it seemed good not to make a decision in this matter too quickly in order to avoid hindering the work of the individual commissions and the serious treatment of each theme.

After a discussion on the matter in a plenary session on October 6, the Congregation determined to attempt the drafting of one document that would bring together the texts prepared by individual commissions, after they were debated in the Aula but prior to the final process of amendments. Amendments, therefore, properly speaking, were made with respect to a document already unified by a certain editorial committee. This committee was empowered to eliminate repetitions and as far as possible unify the style. The editorial committee set up on October 11 included Fathers Albert Beaudry (French Canada), Ignacio Igiesias (Leon), and Joseph O'Hare (New York).

This is the genesis of the document "Companions of Jesus Sent into To-day's World."[6] It was brought into the Aula on October 18. At that time the first part, and later the second, was submitted for study to the Assistancy groups, in which the majority of the amendments were prepared that were later brought forward in the Aula. Voting on all amendments and on the entire document took place on October 24.

Beyond the single document there remained questions having to do with the province congregation and the general congregation as well as the confirmation, in the proper sense of the word, of Decree 12 of the 32nd General Congregation concerning poverty.[7]

In the sections that follow, these three latter points are treated first, and then those contained in the "unique document" (Decree 1) in the order in which they are found in the document itself.

15. On the Province Congregation

(From the Minutes, Acta 13, 25)

The 31st General Congregation instituted representation in the province congregation through a preliminary election, in which also spiritual coadjutors and coadjutor brothers, within certain limits, could be elected. The 33rd General Congregation, however, decreed some measure of participation also for those not yet with final vows,[8] but wished that the provisions thus set down should be reviewed by the next General Congregation. In addition, the Secretary of State, in a letter of May 2, 1975, asked for a review of the entire question by a future General Congregation.[9]

The 33rd General Congregation was obliged, therefore, to examine the matter. A broad body of information was gathered from the provinces both through postulates and through replies to a document sent out by Father Delegate along with a letter of December 31, 1982.[10] After considering this information, the Preparatory Committee prepared a preliminary report which examined the whole issue, including the question of a preliminary election itself.

Then the commission and the Congregation itself devoted like attention to all aspects of the question, including the problem of whether the limitation on

---

[6] D. 1, see n. 41 ff. below.

[7] D. 2–6, see pp. 456–461 below.

[8] GC 32, D. 14, n. 11.

[9] AR XVI, 461.

[10] AR XVIII, 909 ff.

the number of coadjutor brothers who are admitted to a province congregation should perhaps be lifted.

After study and debate, it was concluded, first, that the system of a preliminary election for forming a province congregation should be retained; but, second, that the norms set by the 32nd General Congregation on the participation of members without final vows should remain in force but should be reviewed again by the next General Congregation. For it was seen, on the one hand, that the harmful effects which were feared had not arisen in the province congregations of 1978 and 1983, but rather that beneficial results with respect to union and integration have appeared and gravely harmful effects certainly are not to be expected prior to the next general congregation. On the other hand, it was seen that the time for experimentation has not yet been sufficiently lengthy to permit a definitive judgment in the matter.[11]

With this conclusion reached, the Congregation did not wish to decree anything about other points (e.g., concerning the limit on the participation of coadjutor brothers with final vows). For some of these points require deeper study, that must be made prior to the next Congregation, on account of the connection with the priestly nature of the Society.

16. On the Composition of the General Congregation

(From the Minutes, Acta 19, 26, 28, 35)

With respect to the general congregation, the outstanding question concerned the composition and number of its members. The 31st and 32nd General Congregations already had considered the problem but could not decide on a solution.[12] The 32nd Congregation, however, in its Decree 13, n. 7, recommended to the Superior General that he should set up a commission "to examine the following questions in more detail in preparat15.

ion for their consideration and decision by the next general congregation:

— stabilizing the number of those who attend a general congregation;

— apportioning the members of the general congregation according to criteria which are not only quantitative but also qualitative;

— reducing the numbers of those who attend a general congregation."

The commission was already set up in 1975. It included Fathers Johannes G. Gerhartz (Northern Germany) as chairman, and Jean-Yves Calvez (France),

---

[11] See D. 5, p. 459 below.

[12] Cf. Historical Preface to the Decrees of GC 31, n. 31 (AR XIV 836–837); Historical Preface to the Decrees of GC 32, n. 19 (AR XVI, 301–302).

Paolo Dezza (Italy), Casimir Gnanadickam (Madurai), and William G. Guindon (New England). The commission conducted widespread consultations and presented three successive reports between 1976 and 1982. The third of these reports was sent to the province congregations prior to the 33rd General Congregation. After an analysis both of the unequal situations arising from the traditional system of representation in a general congregation and of difficulties coming from the great number of members of a congregation, the report proposed several solutions. All of them offered the possibility of greater proportionality, to the extent that small units (having their own characteristic experience) would send at least one elector and thus account would be taken of qualitative representation. Different solutions, however, offered different degrees of reduction of numbers (or at least numerical stabilization).

If any of the solutions offered were to gain the consensus of the Congregation, it would be possible to abolish the title of independent vice-province. The name province would be employed in future also for what are currently independent vice-provinces. For the sole difference with respect to an independent vice-province concerned participation in a general congregation.

All these proposals were endorsed by the Official Preparatory Committee, which introduced slight changes with regard both to restoring a slightly higher proportion of those sent by the provinces through election, and to a slightly greater favoring of the larger provinces. These changes were subsequently lessened by the Commission in accordance with comments received.

A concern about the representation of different cultures and experiences, which had been manifested back in the 32nd General Congregation, surfaced again in this Congregation. For the most part, however, it seemed that the proposed solutions answered this concern to a sufficient degree.

In another area, some difficulty seemed to be present in the fact that, according to the proposed solutions, not all provincials would enter a general congregation *ex officio*. Still, it did not seem possible to reduce the number of members of a congregation if every single one of the provincials should have to enter *ex officio*, or else the proportion of those sent by the provinces through election would be too greatly reduced with respect to the total number of members. The matter, as was well known, has importance, not only in itself, but also because it is a question of change in the *Constitutions*, n. 682 ("To give some method of procedure . . . three will come from each province: the provincial and two othes chosen by the other participants in the province congregation").

For this reason, in the end, a. solution was approved that stabilizes the number of members in a Congregation (about 200) and reduces it slightly (by comparison with the actual number, which has been more or less 230, for a Congregation to handle substantial matters) and at the same time excludes very few provincials of provinces (a smaller number than those who are currently provincials of independent vice-provinces) from participation by virtue of office.[13]

As far as those members of the General Curia are concerned who participate in a general congregation by virtue of office, the Congregation wished to have also the general counsellors who are not general assistants and the regional assistants enter as electors *ex officio,* and did not wish that a limit should be imposed by law on the number of members of the Curia who enter *ex officio* as electors.

The Congregation also took up certain other points of the *Formula of the General Congregation.*[14] Moreover, it empowered Father General to change some parts of the Formula that have to do with the handling of substantive issues, in virtue of the authority of the 33rd General Congregation if necessary, in the preparation of efficient methods and procedure for a future general congregation.[15]

17. On Poverty

(From the Minutes, Acta 23, 29, 36, 38)

At the time the 32nd General Congregation was updating the norms of our poverty by its Decree 12, it wished that the text should be submitted *ad cautelam* to the Holy See on certain points (especially that communities could be the juridical subjects of apostolic institutes attached to them) that touch the *Formula of the Institute* in some manner. The Holy See replied, however, that the Decree could take effect "experimentally," "so that the next General Congregation may examine the question completely in the light of experience that will be had in the years ahead."[16] The 33rd General Congregation, therefore, had to treat the matter once again.

Father Delegate sent questions on Decree 12 of the 32nd General Congregation to the province congregations on December 31. The Preparatory Committee examined the replies received from practically every province. It concluded that from the experience in hand it would seem that the Decree should be confirmed without change. A special committee composed of Fathers Adolfo Bachelet (Italy), Francisco Egaña (Loyola), Johannes G. Gerhartz (Northern Germany),

---

[13] See D. 3, pp. 456–457 below.

[14] D. 4, see p. 458 below.

[15] Ibid.

[16] Cf. Letter of the Cardinal Secretary of State to Father General, May 2, 1975 (AR XVI, 459). Cf. the letter of Father Arrupe to Pope Paul VI concerning the Decree on Poverty from GC 32 (AR XVI, 711–719).

Eugen Hillengass (Upper Germany), and Urbano Navarrete (Aragon) reached the same conclusion.

Once again the commission set up in the Congregation examined the replies and all the postulates. It seemed clear to it that the norms introduced by the 32nd General Congregation should be confirmed, even though some doubted the experience in hand was sufficiently protracted. The matter was discussed in plenary session and the Congregation decreed that the confirmation should possess a definitive character, so long as the Holy See itself confirmed it.[17]

At the same time, it seemed necessary to recall to the minds of all Jesuits the first part of Decree 12 of the 32nd Congregation concerning the spirit of our poverty and its other practical aspects. However, some wished that many points of this sort should be treated once more, others that only a small number should be stressed. When an indicative vote had been taken, paragraphs on "life in poverty" were drafted that succeeded in gaining their own place, finally, in the document "Companions of Jesus Sent into Today's World" (nn. 23-27). They insist on a deeper assimilation of evangelical poverty and on its application. Mention is made also of the spirit of gratuity that is proper to our Institute, a matter that must always be kept in mind, in accordance with the wishes of the Holy See, in choosing ministries.

18. On the Attitude of the Society toward the Church and Its Hierarchy

(From the Minutes, Acta 20, 34, 38)

A statement on the attitude of our Society toward the Church and its hierarchy holds first place in the "unique document."

The Congregation was led to make this statement on several counts. More than once in recent years the Popes have addressed the Society on this matter and commended to us full fidelity. The Congregation itself was conscious both of defects which have come about in certain circumstances in recent years as well as of the great, even heroic, fidelity of so many Jesuits toward the Church and the Roman Pontiff. Finally, there were quite a few postulates urging the Congregation to treat this topic.

At the same time, however, the Congregation understood that it could not handle, by itself, all the special questions or difficulties and tensions that today's apostolate in this field commonly carries with it. Therefore, it wished to entrust to Father General the task of making further determinations insofar as it will be necessary to do so, and to commend to him special attention with regard

---

[17] D. 2, see p. 456 below.

to this aspect of our life and activity. In general, the Congregation desired to express forthrightly the Society's full insertion in the Church and its wish to serve the Church according to the words of the Second Vatican Council "in its doctrine, life and cult."

19.   On Our "Life in the Spirit"

(From the Minutes, Acta 17, 30, 38)

Several postulates were received from the provinces concerning spiritual life in the Society. The Sovereign Pontiff, moreover, strongly recommended to us a deep life in the Spirit. The Congregation, therefore, judged it opportune to undertake an evaluation of recent advances as well as deficiencies in attending to the spiritual life. It seemed to the Congregation that a renewal is under way and also that this is on account of an impulse given to many Jesuits by recent apostolic orientations ("option for faith and justice, service of the poor, participation in their life").

This renewal, nevertheless, must be pursued with all vigor. In the first place, therefore, the Congregation wished, rather than undertaking a new treatment of the whole of our spiritual life, to insist again on integration of spiritual life and apostolate, which without doubt demands a regular practice of personal prayer. Then it underscored regular recourse to spiritual discernment, and finally all-out abnegation that should reveal itself in very concrete aspects of our life (in availability, in a definite regularity of life, in transcending individualism).

At the end of its statements on "Life in the Spirit," the Congregation made special recommendation of the summary "On Religious Life in the Society of Jesus" edited by Father Arrupe in 1975 at the request of the 32nd General Congregation.[18]

20.   On the Coadjutor Brothers

(From the Minutes, Acta 14, 24, 32, 35, 36)

The Congregation received from the Official Preparatory Committee a rather full draft document on the brothers that endeavored to respond to a variety of petitions (e.g., on the specific identity of the vocation, on the lack of vocations) contained in the postulates. Still, both the commission and the Congregation itself experienced some difficulty in handling these questions. It seemed best that it should not attempt to enter into overly specialized theological questions about which a great difference of opinions and formulations is evident. On the contrary,

---

[18] AR XVI, 632 ff; paragraphs on "Life in the Spirit" can be found below under nn. 9–14 of Decree 1, pp. 441–442 below.

the Congregation experienced no hesitancy on essential points, especially on the very great importance of both the religious life and the work of the brothers in our Society, on continuing efforts toward fraternal equality among all members, on improving still more the formation of brothers, on expanding still more their participation in the apostolate.

The Congregation wished, therefore, to set these matters before the whole Society in a spirit of candor and trust. The sentence that expressed fully the decisive conviction of the Congregation, in a direct line with Father Arrupe's addresses, is this: "The Society needs the brothers, first of all for themselves and then for their labors, for the sake of both its community life and its apostolate." At the same time the Congregation underscored the complementarity of the work of the brothers to those tasks that are properly the work of priests.[19]

Some consideration was given to the question of whether or not the three essential vows of religion, aside from the fourth vow, might become the same for all members, including the brothers.

In the end, the Congregation did not wish to debate the question of whether Father General should be directed to begin a study of this matter with a view to a declaration in a future Congregation. But Father General himself stated that among the topics concerning the life and vocation of the brothers that he would have to submit to a more profound study, there would have to be included the question of the comparability of the three vows so as to see whether and in what way a change on that point could help in the solution of the general problem (cf. Minutes 36/5).

21. On the Formation of Jesuits

(From the Minutes, Acta 19, 31, 36, 38)

The Official Preparatory Committee was in favor of a very brief statement about formation within the Society. In the end the General Congregation issued an even shorter text. It did so, however, only after careful consideration of the situation with the help of a commission and on its own, and having taken account of the Supreme Pontiff's insistence on solid spiritual and intellectual formation.

It was seen that real progress had been brought about in this respect within the Society in recent years. Moreover, Father General had recently promulgated new General Norms of Studies, and new regional orders of studies had been approved for almost all regions. These would seem to be sufficient to enable us to meet the formation needs for our mission. It seemed opportune, therefore, to in-

---

[19] D. 1, n. 17 ("Life in Communion with the Coadjutor Brothers," nn. 15–19), see p. 443 below.

sist on their execution rather than to add new norms. The heart of the statement[20] is found in these words: "We need solid religious training, serious studies and genuine integration into the apostolic body of the Society."

Although it wished to make no mention of this point in its statement, the Congregation did treat also of the possibility of some directory on other aspects of formation beside the program of studies. It was anxious to insist on the integration needed between the spiritual, communitarian, and apostolic aspects of formation, and also on the need to promote continuing formation. It concluded by inviting Father General to examine, in dialogue with the Assistants, the possibility and opportuneness of editing some kind of "Directory of Formation" which would gather together principles of the Society's tradition with regard to aspects of formation that are not treated in the General Norms of Studies, and with regard to the integration of its various dimensions and different stages.

22. On Our Mission

(From the Minutes, Acta 18, 22, 33)

From the very beginning of the Congregation, it was foreseen that the question of apostolic mission would hold a central place in the deliberations. This stems certainly from the very nature of our Society which is established on mission. Moreover, recent circumstances made some sort of evaluation of our apostolate even more necessary at the time of this Congregation.

The orientations given by the 32nd General Congregation in its Decree 4, "On Our Mission Today: the Service of Faith and the Promotion of Justice" (along with Decree 2, "Jesuits Today"), have had an exceedingly deep influence. The idea of the promotion of justice as "an absolute exigency" of the service of faith, in which the mission of the Society consists, had an especially great impact.[21] In general, these thrusts were positive both in our universal apostolate as well as in our spiritual life. At the same time, however, unilateral tendencies occasionally revealed themselves in the application of Decree 4 of the 32nd General Congregation. John Paul II had several times lately referred to this in remarks he addressed to us.[22] As far back as 1975, the Secretary of State had sent us some

---

[20] D. 1, nn. 20–22; see pp. 444 below.

[21] GC 32, D. 4, n. 2.

[22] "Allocution to the Fathers Provincials," Feb. 27, 1982, n. 8 (AR XVIII, 728–729); "Homily to the Members of the 33rd General Congregation," September 2, 1983 (see pp. 464–465 below, n. 7). Cf. also the Directives given by Father Delegate, March 25, 1982; "I. The Apostolate of the Society" (AR XVII, 791–793).

special words of exhortation on the proper application of Decrees 2 and 4 of the 32nd General Congregation.

In these circumstances it is not surprising that the greater number of all the postulates sent to the General Congregation called for both the confirmation of the apostolic orientations given by the last General Congregation and also the clarification of certain points (e.g., on the relationship between faith and justice, on the sense of justice that we ought to foster, on the activities proper to Jesuits as priests and religious or, on the contrary, less proper, and so forth).

At the same time, a good many were asking that, in the field of the promotion of justice, the General Congregation should draw the Society's attention to many very grave problems of the present moment in the area of the preservation of human rights and the fostering of international peace.

At the same time, there were expectations of a clear confirmation of the importance of the educational and intellectual apostolates as well as research. Some felt that in certain sectors of the Society these had enjoyed less esteem after the 32nd Congregation. There was also a wish for an intensification of collaboration with the laity and the confirmation and renewal of different traditional apostolates of the Society.

Both the Preparatory Committee and the commission in the Congregation worked hard at examining and discussing all these matters. One thing emerged in the course of these efforts and received confirmation by an indicative vote on October 1: a wish for a quite brief statement that would contain directive guidelines, criteria, and a listing of new fields of apostolate, and, under another aspect, that would take off from a consideration of the wishes of the Supreme Pontiff concerning the Society's apostolate.

In that same indicative vote the Congregation expressed a wish for some evaluation, but of a general nature, regarding the application of Decree 4 of the 32nd General Congregation. It also called for sobriety in setting forth theological and spiritual guidelines. Finally it wished that the remaining matters (e.g., new fields of the apostolate or the confirmation of traditional ministries) should be treated very briefly, i.e., by way of enumeration, with an exception made for the apostolate of education and research.

All this explains the nature of the statement—contained in the second part of the "unique document"—that the Congregation offers to the Society for the direction of our general activities in the years immediately ahead. There is first an evaluation of past experience (nn. 31–33). After that comes the consideration of pressing needs stemming from the condition of the world (nn. 34–36). Then the Congregation recalls the appeals and wishes of the Supreme Pontiff; it accepts them in the name of the Society with a grateful heart and shows itself ready to carry out their full execution (nn. 37–38). At the same time it confirms the apostolic orientations set down by the last two Congregations, especially, however, by the 32nd General Congregation in its Decree 4 (n. 38). It insists then on certain essential aspects of our way of proceeding (nn. 39–42), on some applications (nn. 43–46), and on some dispositions required for the credibility of our mission (nn. 47–49). The conclusion lays strong stress on the centrality of faith in Christ. The statement is a confirmation of orientations already received, but its primary concern is the "future" (n. 50).

23. On the Closing of the Congregation

(From the Minutes, Acta 34, 40, 42, 43, 44)

Father Joseph Labaj, as has already been mentioned, had to leave the Congregation because of increasingly serious illness after the election of the Superior General and General Assistants. Three other members, Fathers Michael Buckley (California), Andre Costes (France) and Enrico Mariotti (Italy), received permission to be absent for several days. In the same way Fathers Luis Alvarez-Ossorio (Baetica) and Edmundo Rodriguez (New Orleans) were absent for several days, each in order to attend the funeral of his father. Similarly, Father Jesus Montero Tirado (Paraguay) was absent for a few days in order to attend the funeral of his mother. Two others had to be given permission to depart before the conclusion, but this took place only on October 23, very shortly before the end. On the one hand, the permission that Father Janos Tamas (Hungary) had for visiting outside his native land could not be prolonged; on the other hand, Father Urbano Valero (Castile) had to be present in Madrid to open the academic year. Since Father Bruno Bois (Italy) also had to be absent during the last days because of fatigue and Father Dionisio Sciuchetti (Bahia) had to be absent because of the death of a relative, the members of the Congregation, who had numbered 220 at the beginning, totaled 215 toward the end. Father Arrupe, who is counted among those members, could not take an active part in the sessions of the Congregation because of the state of his health.

As the end of its labors neared, on October 13 the Congregation set October 16 as the last date for introducing new postulates. It did not wish, on the contrary, to settle on the last day of the Congregation as early as October 13, even though a determination of this sort had been requested by a motion of order. The Congregation decided, however, that the final sessions should be expedited by a change in the practice with regard to time allowed for speaking. Thus anyone who asked permission to speak in writing had it for five minutes (instead of seven), and those who asked by flicking on their red light could speak only for three minutes (instead of five).

On October 21 the Congregation empowered Father General to see to the proper completion of the legislative work of the Congregation insofar as necessary. It also empowered him to suppress colleges and professed houses until the next General Congregation and to approve the Acta of the last sessions as well as to make necessary corrections and polish up the style before promulgating the decrees of the Congregation. Additional powers were granted him that seem to be required at this time on account of the new codification of canon law to ensure the possibility either of requesting certain dispensations from the Holy See or of adopting or filling out our law in accord with the demands of the new Code.[23]

All voting on the document "Companions of Jesus Sent into Today's World" was completed on October 24. The Congregation wished, however, that time be left, should it be needed, for presenting intercessions. The last session, therefore, of the Congregation took place on October 25 in the afternoon. It was in this session that the 33rd General Congregation declared itself ended. The hymn *Te Deum* was chanted in the Aula and immediately after this session a Eucharistic concelebration was held in the Curia chapel. Father General announced that this concelebration would be in thanksgiving most especially for Father Paolo Dezza, as well as for Father Giuseppe Pittau and the former General Assistants. He added that the General Congregation had reaped the fruits that Father Dezza had sowed by insisting chiefly on the union of our whole Society. Before the Communion, all renewed the consecration of the Society to the Sacred Heart of Jesus according to a formula introduced by Father Arrupe.

Finally, after supper, there was a social gathering in which many artistic and comic talents were put on display. In both the last session of the Congregation and the final Eucharistic concelebration, as well as in that recreation after supper, Father General had occasion to express thanks to all whose assistance had been a big aid to the Congregation.

24. Some Other Points to Be Noted

On three occasions all the members of the Congregation concelebrated a Eucharistic liturgy under the presidency of Father General: September 16, i.e., three days after his election; October 15 in the Basilica of St. Peter's as pilgrims of the Holy Year of Redemption; and finally the last day, as just mentioned. On other days different groups celebrated the Eucharist in different languages in several chapels of the Curia and of the House of Writers.

---

[23] D. 6, see pp. 460–461 below.

Before each plenary session of the Congregation there was a fifteen-minute period of prayer under the leadership of one of the Congregation's members.

Just as the Supreme Pontiff, John Paul II, had done at the beginning, so too afterwards, on October 17, the Prefect of the Sacred Congregation for Religious, Cardinal Eduardo Pironio, visited the Congregation and spoke to the members both about the Synod of Bishops and religious life at the present moment as well as about what the Church expects of our Society.

The Congregation lasted for 54 days. There were 43 plenary sessions held in the Aula. The Congregation frequently made use of Assistancy groups, but did not have recourse to another type of small meetings, namely, language groups.

B

DECREES OF THE
33rd GENERAL CONGREGATION

DECREE 1

COMPANIONS OF JESUS SENT INTO TODAY'S WORLD

INTRODUCTION (1–5)

PART I: COMPANIONS OF JESUS

A. Life in the Church (6–8)

B. Life in the Spirit (9–14)

C. Life in Communion with the Coadjutor Brothers (15–19)

D. Training for Ministry (20–22)

E. Life in Poverty (23–27)

PART II: SENT INTO TODAY'S WORLD

Introduction (28–30)

A. Our Experience (31–33)

B. Challenging Context (34–36)

C. Papal Calls (37)

D. Confirmation (38)

E. Our Way of Proceeding (39–42)

F. Some Applications (43–46)

G. Prerequisites for Credibility (47–49)

Conclusion (50)

DECREE 1

INTRODUCTION

1/ 1. In accepting the voluntary resignation of Father Pedro Arrupe, who spent himself tirelessly for 18 years shaping the Society's apostolate and inspiring its spiritual life, the 33rd General Congregation was conscious of living through a time of special grace and importance in our history. His moving decision followed by the joyful election of Father Peter-Hans Kolvenbach encouraged us from the outset to embark on our work with firm convictions of hope and continuity. **2/** 2. We have borne in mind the significant events that have marked the life of the Church and the Society in the years following the Second Vatican Council. In the light of the Church's teaching and the exhortations addressed to us by recent Popes, considering the needs of our times and the postulates sent by our fellow Jesuits, we have wished to verify, specify more accurately, and confirm the orientations given by General Congregations 31 and 32.

3/ 3. While examining the state of the Society and refleting more deeply on our experience, the limitations and constraints of our religious life and apostolic labors became evident. Returning to our Ignatian sources, the desire to offer ourselves to the greater service of Christ our Lord grew within us. And in our docility to the action of the Spirit, we have wanted to share with the whole Society the results of our deliberations.

4/ 4. We believe there is more need at the moment to put into practice what has already been asked of us than to produce extensive declarations or new decrees. For "love shows itself in deeds rather than in words."[1] Accordingly General Congregation 33 wanted to take up only those questions that seemed more urgent, together with some specific matters entrusted to it.

5/ 5. As it began its deliberations, the Congregation took note of the need for greater unity among us, the unity which comes from the Spirit of Jesus and which should express itself in brotherly love and a vision shared by all Jesuits of the Society's mission today for the glory of the Father

---

[1] SpEx, 230

Part I

Companions of Jesus

A. Life in the Church

6/   6. Seeking to lead a life worthy of the vocation to which we have been called,[1] the Society commits itself again to serving the Church in her teaching, life, and worship, and helping here to offer to the world "all that she herself is, all that she believes."[2] In the spirit of St. Ignatius, we wish to show our commitment "not less but rather more in good works than in words,"[3] for the edification of those with whom we work, so that we may become more generous servants of the people God has gathered for the world's salvation.[4]

7/   7. The General Congregation therefore recalls with gratitude that from its very beginning the Society has existed "to serve the Lord alone and the Church, His spouse, under the Roman Pontiff."[5] Now, in a spirit of faith, our Society confirms again the traditional bond of love and service which united it with the Roman Pontiff. We wish to respond to his desires expressed on various occasions and to carry out his missions. At the same time we intend to cooperate with the College of Bishops in its service of the Gospel.

8/   8. So many Jesuits in our day are bearing witness to this fidelity toward the Church and the Roman Pontiff; in all parts of the world they are fulfilling with constancy the missions entrusted to them, and some indeed are suffering persecution, even in prisons or internment camps. We are not unaware that recently our fidelity under certain circumstances has not been perfect and has caused concern to those who exercise pastoral office. Accordingly, we seriously urge all members of the Society, for the good of the whole Church, to consider how we may grow in that obedience which is profoundly rooted in both truth and love.[6] Looking to our future life and apostolate, we wish to encourage all to foster a truly Ignatian readiness for active collaboration with the Supreme

---

[1] Eph. 4, 1.

[2] DV, 8.

[3] *Cons.* 637.

[4] LG, 9, 48.

[5] FI, 1.

[6] Fr. Arrupe, *The Local Superior: His Apostolic Mission,* 18-21 (AR XVIII, 565–567).

all to foster a truly Ignatian readiness for active collaboration with the Supreme Pontiff and all who share pastoral office with him. The General Congregation is conscious of the difficulties and tensions which often accompany the apostolate in today's world. Accordingly, to find solutions in so serious a matter, it asks Father General to promote further studies enabling him to help and guide Jesuits in teaching doctrine and in their pastoral activity. He should also provide that, in a way suited to our times, the "Rules for Thinking with the Church"[7] be applied in the light of the Second Vatican Council. Finally, let the entire Society seek to incorporate itself more and more vigorously and creatively in the life of the Church so that we may experience and live its mystery within ourselves.[8] Thus we may be indeed for the people of God servants of the joy of the Lord.[9]

B.   Life in the Spirit

9/ 9. We will be better able to serve the Church, the better we learn through experience to hear the Holy Spirit, since "we believe that the same Holy Spirit present in Christ our Lord and in the Church instructs and guides us in the salvation of our souls."[10]

10/ 10. In recent years a renewed consciousness concerning our religious life has been felt throughout the Society. The decrees of GC 31 (8, 13–17, 19) and GC 32 (2, 4, 11) as well as the writings of Father Arrupe have developed a spiritual doctrine at once profoundly rooted in the Gospel and our tradition and yet one which responds to the challenges of our times. This renewal manifests itself especially in the new impetus given to the Spiritual Exercises and to apostolic discernment. The commitment to faith and to justice, the service to the poor, and especially the willingness to share their life, have been an invitation to the whole Society to embrace a more evangelical way of life.

11/ We also recognize deficiencies in the way we have lived our commitment. These difficulties are frequently due to overwork, to a kind of monotony in our religious life, to a lack of spiritual vitality within our communities—all of which empoverish our encounter with God. This means we must continually renew our efforts if we are to enter more deeply into the meaning of our life as Jesuits: men totally committed to the glory of God and the service of others.[11]

12/ 11. As a consequence, the General Congregation invites all Jesuits to strive, personally and communally, toward an even greater integration of our

---

[7] SpEx, 352–370.

[8] SpEx, 104.

[9] 2 Cor. 1, 24.

[10] SpEx, 365.

[11] FI, 1.

spiritual life and apostolate. Following the example of St. Ignatius, a Jesuit's life is rooted in the experience of God who, through Jesus Christ and in the Church, calls us, unites us to one another, and sends us forth. The Eucharist is the privileged place where we celebrate this reality. Only to the extent that he is united to God so that he be "led gladly by the divine hand,"[12] is a Jesuit "a man on a mission." In this way, he will learn to find God in all things, the God who is present in this world and its struggle between good and evil, between faith and unbelief, between the yearning for justice and peace and the growing reality of injustice and strife. But we cannot achieve this familiarity with God unless we set aside a regular time for personal prayer.

13/   12.   If we are to hear and respond to the call of God in this kind of world, then we must have a discerning attitude. For us Jesuits the way of discernment involves: the examination of conscience, prayer and brotherly dialogue within our communities, and the openness to superiors that faciliates obedience.

14/   13.   We cannot attain this discerning attitude without self-abnegation. Sign of our joy at the approach of the Kingdom[13] and result of a progressive identification with Christ, who "emptied himself being born in the likeness of man,"[14] this abnegation is required by the Spiritual Exercises: to divest ourselves of "self-love, self-will, and self-interest."[15] It is only through detachment from all we have and are, that we can receive all from God in faith and give ourselves wholly to others in love. Without such an attitude we cannot present ourselves as interiorly free enough for the authentic service of Him who calls us.

15/   Today our interior liberty will show itself in:

  – a greater availability on the part of the whole Society as well as the individual Jesuit which will enable us to respond, in obedience, to the cultural differences and changes in our modern world;

  – a rhythm of life which allows us to maintain our commitment to the world and still gives us space for solitude and silence, as well as for necessary relaxation and joyous celebration within our communities;

  – a self-transcendence rejecting that individualism which inhibits integration into community life, necessary both for the expression and support of our faith.

16/   14.   The Society possesses a spirituality which gives us the way to live day by day as companions of Jesus. That way has been clearly spelled out in the book-

---

[12] *Cons.* 813.

[13] Mt. 13, 44.

[14] Phil. 2, 7.

[15] SpEx, 189.

lets *Readings from the Constitutions of the Society of Jesus* and *Jesuit Religious Life.*[16] The 33rd General Congregation is convinced that the reading and practical application of these excerpts will greatly help toward the renewal we seek and give us that "hope which does not deceive" as we face the demands of our time.

C.　Life in Common with the Coadjutor Brothers

17/　15.　We do not serve the Lord and the Church as isolated individuals but rather as men who have offered their lives to follow Christ "by living and dying in the Lord with and in this Society"[17] as its members. The kind of body St. Ignatius envisioned can hardly exist if all of its members do not share fully in its life.

18/　16.　With regard to the brothers, we wish to remind everyone that throughout the Society's history they have provided a witness to the gospel in their religious lives and made a great contribution to its apostolate through their hard work. In recent times the lives of the brothers have become more adapted to modern conditions: more appropriate formation has been arranged, the range of apostolates has been widened, and the equality of all companions as brothers together is better lived.

19/　17.　For its part the Congregation, while sharing the concern expressed in many parts of the world, once again proclaims and affirms the incalculable value of the brothers' vocation, through which the Society develops its mission to the full. The Society needs the brothers, first of all for themselves and then for their labors, for the sake of both its communities and its apostolates. They share in the same religious commitment and take on work that is complementary to that characteristic of priests, thus effectively helping the Society to achieve its one and only goal.[18] Being all members of the same body,[19] we complete and enrich one another so that we can imitate the way of life offered by the Son of God to the disciples who followed him.[20] This is why the Congregation considers that the absence of brothers is a serious defect and that we cannot remain satisfied with the present situation.[21]

---

[16] AR XVII, 625–626. [Editor's note: These booklets are now available in the one booklet, *Jesuit Religious Life Today* (St. Louis: The Institute of Jesuit Sources), 1977.]

[17] *Cons.* 51.

[18] FI, 1: "according to the grace which the Holy Spirit has given to him and according to the particular grade of his own vocation"; *Cons.* 522.

[19] *Cons.* 511;　MI, Epp. XI, 438.

[20] LG, 44.

[21] Fr. Arrupe, *Report of Father General on the State of the Society,* Sept. 27, 1978 (AR XVII, 451): *Meeting with Brothers* (AR XVII, 379 ff.).

20/ 18. We are aware of the difficulties that prevent the Society from receiving fresh vocations and that arise in part from present-day social and cultural conditions. While acknowledging the seriousness of these problems, we nevertheless believe they can be overcome provided that all of us—scholastics, brothers and priests—set about the implementation of the decrees of the last two General Congregations and take seriously their practical implications. Consequently the 33rd General Congregation directs that:

– Provincials, with the help of the brothers, should examine the situation in their provinces and take all possible steps to promote brothers' vocations. Everyone should take an active interest in this work.

– Apostolic communities with brothers, according to the directives of Decree 11 of GC 32, should be fostered as the most effective means of strengthening the sense of being part of one mission and of increasing the high regard we have for one another.

– Particular care should be taken with the spiritual, doctrinal, technical, and personal formation of the brothers in accordance with the directives of Decree 7, n. 7 of GC 31 and other norms of the Society.[22]

21/ 19. Finally the Congregation openly declares that we must change our attitudes[23] so that our behavior toward one another in the Society is not ruled by human standards prevailing outside,[24] but by the example of Christ who came not to be served, but to serve.[25] Then we shall be able to welcome brothers into the Society, for they are indeed given to us by God.

D. Training for Mission

22/ 20. The very great difficulty and demands of our enterprise oblige us to give careful attention to questions of formation. In recent years formation has received a new thrust from the decrees of General Congregations 31 and 32, and from Father Arrupe's direction. The best way of maintaining progress along these lines will be the Society's resolute implementation and more thorough appropriation of the directives received, keeping in mind the Church's recommendations.[26] There should be faithful adherence to the General Norms for Jesuit studies and the Regional Orders which apply them; particular care should be taken to assure

---

[22] Cf. also *Normae Generales de Studiis NN,* 1980, n. 58–65.

[23] GC 31, D. 7, n. 1.

[24] 1 Cor. 2, 23–25, 30; *Examen,* 101.

[25] Mk. 10, 45.

[26] John Paul II, *Allocution to the Fathers Provincial* (AR XVIII, 721 ff.) and *Homily to the Members of the 33rd General Congregation* (see pp. 465–470 below).

the integration of the spiritual, communitarian, intellectual and apostolic aspects of formation.

23/ 21. To be credible witnesses to the Gospel today and servants of the Church faithful to St. Ignatius's spirit, we need solid religious training, serious studies, and genuine integration into the apostolic body of the Society. Moreover the demands of our mission today touch not only the young men in formation, but all Jesuits, even the formed, who have to look for ways to meet these demands by pursuing their own "continuing formation."[27]

24/ 22. The 33rd General Congregation asks Father General to continue to promote the quality of our formation, for both brothers and scholastics, particularly by giving help and encouragement to the *formatores* and by fostering widespread collaboration and the exchange of experiences in this area. It also earnestly invites all Jesuits to take to heart the task of attracting vocations to the Society, especially by prayer and the example of their lives as individuals and in community.

E.   Life in Poverty

25/ 23. The Spirit of the Lord has called us to be free,[28] so that we can enter into full communion with our brothers and sisters and dedicate ourselves totally to the integral service of the human family. Such freedom, however, as we learn in the Spiritual Exercises, cannot be separated from poverty.[29] In fact, without poverty, such freedom cannot exist.

26/ 24. One of the decisions that this Congregation was obliged to make concerned the confirmation of Decree 12 of the 32nd General Congregation. The Congregation urges all superiors to promote both the spirit and the execution of this Decree, as well as Decree 18 of GC 31.

27/ 25. Changes in our administrative structures have helped us greatly in recent years to live a more authentic Ignatian poverty. In many instances, a greater equality among our communities in their manner of life has resulted, along with a more ready desire to share our material goods and to experience more fully the actual living conditions of the poor. Still we recognize we have not yet fully assimilated into our lives the profound implications of those decrees, nor have we always been led, under their inspiration, to the transformation of our personal and community lives, as well as of our apostolic activity, that they propose. We must therefore strive with new heart to become truly poor with Christ poor so that we can really be said "to preach in poverty."

---

[27] Fr. Delegate, *On Continuing Formation* (AR XVIII, 661 ff.).

[28] Rom. 8, 15.

[29] SpEx, 136–147.

28/ 26. The situation of the poor, who live today in a world where unjust structures force the greater part of the human family to exist in dehumanizing conditions, should be a constant reminder to us that God takes the part of the poor, according to that salvific design revealed in Jesus Christ who "came to proclaim the Good News to the poor."[30] In recent years, the Church has summoned us to a greater solidarity with the poor and to more effective attempts to attack the very causes of mass poverty.

29/ 27. For these reasons, we urge every Jesuit to make these decrees part of his life by faithful observance of the norms they propose for our personal and communal lives which, in their modesty and even frugality, should offer a striking contrast to the spirit of "consumerism" that pervades so many societies. In sharing our goods with the poor, we should look first to those whose needs are greatest so that we do not remain untouched by their hardships and anxieties. In our apostolic works, we should try to combine a desire for evangelical simplicity with the necessary concern for efficiency. In our choice of ministries, the spirit of gratuity proper to our Institute should be carefully kept in mind so that "the exercise of those ministries which, according to our tradition, were provided gratuitously should not be abandoned too easily."[31]

---

[30] Lk. 4, 18.

[31] *Letter of the Cardinal Secretary of State to Father General,* May 2, 1975, pp. 396–397 above (AR XVI, 461).

PART II

Sent into Today's World

Introduction

30/ 28. The way of life we have described above is an essential condition, particularly today, if we are to identify ourselves with and follow the One who has been sent.[1] It is also an essential requirement if we are to work effectively for the fulfillment of His mission.[2]

31/ The General Congregation, recognizing that every Jesuit is identified as one who has been "sent" and at the same time wishing to respond to concerns expressed by the universal Society, has paid particular attention to the meaning of our mission today. We do not pretend to present a definitive exposition of this issue. Still, we have tried to reach a better understanding of what the Lord, through the mediation of the Church, has asked of us that we might give ourselves to this work without reserve and "that we might hear anew the call of Christ dying and rising in the anguish and aspirations of men and women."[3]

32/ 29. The experience of the Society's apostolic efforts in recent years, expressed in reports and postulates that have come to us from around the world, enables the 33rd General Congregation to address with both confidence and humility the topic of our mission today. We speak with confidence because we believe the options made by the 31st and 32nd General Congregations have been in conformity with the renewal inspired by the Second Vatican Council, the Synods of Bishops, and the teachings of recent Popes. We speak with humility because we recognize the difficulties of the task and our own failures to respond wholeheartedly as religious priests and brothers to the challenge of integral evangelization in our modern world.

33/ 30. First we review briefly how we have carried out our mission as expressed by the 32nd General Congregation: "to engage, under the standard of the Cross, in the crucial struggle of our times: the struggle for faith and that struggle for justice which it includes."[4] We then look at the challenge of the modern world in the light of the calls addressed to the Society by recent Popes which help us to

---

[1] Fr. Arrupe, *Letter on Apostolic Availability* (AR XVII, 140).

[2] GC 32, D. 4, n. 13.

[3] GC 32, D. 4, n. 19.

[4] GC 32, D. 2, n. 2.

focus our mission. Finally, looking to the future, we attempt to discern how we might best fulfill this mission in some of its specific implications.

A. Our Experience

34/ 31. In keeping with the requests of the Popes and the mind of the Society itself, the 33rd General Congregation continued the review of our mission, especially with regard to papal concern for integral evangelization and the proper role of a priestly order.[5] We have found these years an experience of grace and conversion for us as individuals and as a body. We have made serious efforts to address realistically the issues of atheism and indifference in our secularized world. Our religious life has been enriched by the opportunity to "labor with"[6] Jesus in the greater service of the Kingdom. This closeness to the Christ of the Exercises has brought us closer to the poor with whom he identified himself.[7] At times it has also brought us the persecution for his sake that he promised his followers. [8] Our service of faith and promotion of justice has made the Society confront the mystery of the Cross: some Jesuits have been exiled, imprisoned, or put to death in their work of evangelization. Some have been prevented from attending this Congregation.

35/ 32. But we who engage in this mission are sinners. Our reading of Decree 4 of GC 32 has at times been "incomplete, slanted and unbalanced."[9] We have not always recognized that the social justice we are called to is part of that justice of the Gospel which is the embodiment of God's love and saving mercy.[10] We have not learned to enter fully into a mission which is not simply one ministry among others, but "the integrating factor of all our ministries."[11] We have found it difficult to understand the Church's recent emphasis on changing the structures

---

[5] *Letter of the Cardinal Secretary of State to Father General,* May 2, 1975 (AR XVI, 456–461); John Paul I, *Alloc, ad Cong. Proc.* (AR XVII, 212–217); Fr. Arrupe, *Final Address of Father General to the Congregation of Procurators* (AR XVII, 540–558); John Paul II, *Allocution to the Presidents of Provincial Conferences* (AR XVII, 639–641); Fr. Arrupe, *Letter to all Major Superiors* (AR XVII, 823–827); John Paul II, *Allocution to the Fathers Provincial* (AR XVIII, 721–734); John Paul II, *Homily to the Members of the 33rd General Congregation,* n. 7 (see pp. 465–466 below).

[6] SpEx, 93.

[7] Mt. 25, 34–46; Ignatius Loyola, *Letter to the Fathers and Brothers of Padua,* August 7, 1547: "Friendship with the poor makes us friends of the eternal King."

[8] Jn. 15, 20.

[9] Fr. Arrupe, *Rooted and Grounded in Love,* 67 (AR XVIII, 500).

[10] GC 32, D. 4, n. 18.

[11] GC 32, D. 2, n. 9.

of society,[12] and what our proper role should be in collaborating with the laity in this process of transformation.

36/ 33. In all honesty, we must also acknowledge that this new understanding of our mission can lead to tensions both in the Society and outside it. Some have at times emphasized in a unilateral fashion one aspect of this mission to the detriment of the other. Yet neither a disincarnate spiritualism nor a merely secular activism truly serves the integral Gospel message.[13] Our experiences of recent years have made us increasingly aware that the more a Jesuit is exposed to situations and structures alien to the faith, the more he must strengthen his own religious identity and his union with the whole body of the Society as represented by the local community to which he belongs.

B. Challenging Context

37/ 34. As we implement our mission, the Exercises invite us to contemplate the world of today with the loving gaze of the Three Divine Persons, that we may be drawn to understand its needs as God does and offer ourselves to share in His work of its salvation. As expressed in the Institute, the mission of the Society consists in the integral salvation in Jesus Christ of all women and men, a salvation begun in the present life and brought to its fulfillment in the life to come. In this mission, the promotion of justice is today a matter of growing urgency in the Church's work of evangelization; this dimension of our apostolate must therefore be fostered with particular care.[14]

38/ 35. Our contemplation of the world reveals a situation frequently hostile to the spreading of the Kingdom. The dominant ideologies and systems— political, economic, social, and cultural—often prevent an adequate response to the most elementary aspirations of the human family at both national and international levels. A pervasive materialism and the worship of human autonony obscure or obliterate concern for the things of God, leaving the minds and hearts of many of our contemporaries cold and empty. This both reveals and causes a profound crisis of faith that expresses itself in an atheism at once theoretical, practical, and institutional. Lack of respect for a loving Creator leads to a denial of the dignity of the human person and the wanton destruction of the environment. Massive poverty and hunger, brutal oppression and discrimination, a frightening arms race and the nuclear threat: all offer evidence of sin in human hearts and in the core of contemporary society.

---

[12] Paul VI, *Octogesima Adveniens,* 43–45; Synod of Bishops 1971, *Justitia in Mundo;* John Paul II, *Redemptor Hominis,* 14–16.

[13] *Evangelii Nuntiandi,* 26–38.

[14] FI, 1; *Cons.* 3; John Paul II, *Allocution to the Fathers Provincial,* 8 (AR XVIII, 728).

39/ 36. Yet even as we consider these things, we observe other signs of the times that encourage us and give us hope. There is throughout the world a heightened sense of the solidarity of the human family and a rising consciousness, especially among the young, that conditions of misery and oppression cannot be tolerated. The Church, enlivened by the Second Vatican Council and expressing itself in new forms of community and parish life, is more and more engaged in works of peace and justice. Many of the world's religions and cultures are experiencing a new vitality; and there are indications of a growing search for meaning, sometimes expressed in more profound reflection and in prayer.

C.   Papal Calls

40/ 37. It is in this context that we Jesuits hear the calls that have come to us from recent Popes. Their calls give apostolic orientations to our mission today, and must illumine, enrich, and specify the options before us. As we opened the 33rd General Congregation, we heard Pope John Paul II tell us: "The Church today expects the Society to contribute effectively to the implementation of the Second Vatican Council."[15] Moreover he repeated the mandate to confront the problem of atheism and cooperate in that profound renewal needed by the Church in a secularized world. He invited us to adapt our traditional apostolates to the different spiritual necessities of today, singling out the renewal of Christian life, the education of youth, the formation of the clergy, the study of philosophy and theology, research into humanistic and scientific cultures, and missionary activity. He encourged us to pay particular attention to ecumenism, relations with other world religions, and the task of authentic inculturation. Finally the Pope, speaking of our apostolate, again drew our attention to the need to promote, within the Church's evangelizing action and in conformity with our priestly and religious Institute, "the justice, connected with world peace, which is an aspiration of all peoples."[16]

D.   Confirmation

41/ 38. In the light, therefore, of requests coming from the whole Society, the needs of the world, and the Church's teaching, the 33rd General Congregation readily receives the calls which the Pope has made to the Society, and commits itself to a full and prompt response. At the same time, we confirm the Society's mission expressed by the 31st and 32nd General Congregations, particularly in the latter's Decrees 2 and 4, which are the application today of the *Formula of*

---

[15] John Paul II, *Homily to the Members of the 33rd General Congregation,* 6 (see pp. 465–470 below).

[16] John Paul II, ibid, 7.

the Institute and of our Ignatian charism.[17] They express our mission today in profound terms offering insights which serve as guidelines for our future responses:

  – the integration of the service of faith and the promotion of justice in one single mission;[18]

  – the universality of this mission in the various ministries in which we engage;[19]

  – the discernment needed to implement this mission;[20]

  – the corporate nature of this mission.[21]

E. Our Way of Proceeding

42/ 39. If we are to fulfill our mission, we must be faithful to that practice of communal apostolic discernment so central to "our way of proceeding," a practice rooted in the Exercises and Constitutions.[22] This way of proceeding calls for a review of all our ministries, both traditional and new.

43/ 40. Such a review includes: an attentiveness to the Word of God; an examen and reflection inspired by the Ignatian tradition; a personal and communitarian conversion necessary in order to become "contemplatives in action"; an effort to live an indifference and availability that will enable us to find God in all things; and a transformation of our habitual patterns of thought through a constant interplay of experience, reflection, and action. We must also always apply those criteria for action found in the 7th part of the Constitutions as well as recent and more specific instructions concerning choice of ministries[23] and occupations or tasks to be avoided.[24] This process, undertaken in the local community, province, or region, leads to apostolic decisions made by superiors, after normal consultation and with accountability to Father General.

---

[17] GC 32, D. 4, n. 2.

[18] GC 32, D. 2, n. 8.

[19] GC 32, D. 2, n. 9.

[20] GC 32, D. 4. n. 10.

[21] GC 32, D. 4. n. 62–69.

[22] Fr. Arrupe, *Our Way of Proceeding* (AR XVII, 691–722); Fr. Arrupe, *Litt. ad univ. Soc. "De spirituale discretione,"* Dec. 25, 1971 (AR XV, 767–773); Fr. Arrupe, *The Local Superior: His Apostolic Mission* (AR XVIII, 571–572, n. 33–36).

[23] GC 31, D. 21–32; GC 32, D. 4, n. 60.

[24] GC 32, D. 4, n. 80; CollDecr, 239.

44/ 41. But such an effort runs the risk of failure unless we attend to the practical conditions required for its serious application.[25] These conditions, to be given special attention both in initial and ongoing formation, include: deeper involvement in the lives of the people around us in order to hear "the joys and the hopes, the griefs and the anxieties of the people of this age, especially those who are poor or in any way afflicted";[26] a regular exposure to new situations of life and thought which oblige us to question our way of seeing and judging; a gradual assimilation of that apostolic pedagogy of St. Ignatius; a well-informed use of social and cultural analysis; and an inculturation which opens us to the newness of Jesus the Saviour in the evolution of every people, and thereby prevents us from absolutizing our perceptions and actions.

45/ 42. Definitions alone cannot clarify the apostolic directions of our mission. Such clarity can only come when we are faithful to the process and conditions of communal discernment and to the lived experience of religious men striving to labor with Christ in serving the Kingdom. For we will then understand better how the service of faith and the promotion of justice are not two juxtaposed, much less conflicting, goals but a single commitment which finds its coherence and deepest expression in that love of God and love of neighbor to which God calls us in the One Great Commandment.[27] One cannot act justly without love. Even when we resist injustice we cannot prescind from love, since the universality of love is, by the express desire of Christ, a commandment that admits of no exceptions."[28] To attain this universal love, we must continually learn how to seek God in faith, both for his own sake and as the abiding source of all justice and love. Striving for God's reign here on earth with works of justice, love, and peace, we also know we are foreshadowing the new age which is to come.

F. Some Applications

46/ 43. As we continue to respond to our mission, as described in paragraph 38, traditional apostolates take on fresh importance, while new needs and situations make new demands on us. The essential ministries of preaching the Gospel, fostering sacramental life, giving the Exercises, teaching, formation of the clergy, the work of catechetics, the promotion of Christian communities, and evangelizing those who have not yet heard of Christ — all should contribute to strengthening the faith that does justice.[29]

---

[25] GC 32, D. 4, n. 35–38.

[26] GS, 1.

[27] Jn. 15, 9–16; 1 Jn. 4, 7–20; Mt. 22, 34–40; Mk. 12, 28–34; Lk, 10, 25–37.

[28] Fr. Arrupe, *Rooted and Grounded in Love,* 56 (AR XVIII, 495).

[29] John Paul II, *Allocution to the Fathers Provincial,* 8 (AR XVIII, 728).

47/   44. Of great importance among the ministries of the Society are the educational and intellectual apostolates. Jesuits who work in schools of whatever kind or level or who are engaged in non-formal or popular education can exercise a deep and lasting influence on individuals and on society. When carried out in the light of our mission today, their efforts contribute vitally to "the total and integral liberation of the human person leading to participation in the life of God himself."[30] Research in theology and philosophy, in the other sciences and in every branch of human culture is likewise essential if Jesuits are to help the Church understand the contemporary world and speak to it the Word of Salvation. The opportunities and responsibilities of these apostolates require a change of heart and an openness to human needs around us; they also demand a solid intellectual formation. Jesuits in these fields and our men in more direct social and pastoral ministries should cooperate and benefit from one another's expertise and experience. Finally, the Society should promote the apostolate of the social communications media which, like education and intellectual work, reaches large numbers of people and so permits "a more universal service to humankind."[31]

48/   45. Among new needs and situations we list, without any attempt to be exhaustive, certain problems that call for our special concern since they have been mentioned frequently in the postulates. While a number of Jesuits have already been working for years in these areas, the General Congregation now wishes to bring them to the attention of the whole Society:

—   the spiritual hunger of so many, particularly the young, who search for meaning and values in a technological culture;

—   attacks by governments on human rights through assassination, imprisonment, torture, the denial of religious freedom and political expression: all of which cause so many to suffer, some of them fellow Jesuits;

—   the sad plight of millions of refugees searching for a permanent home, a situation brought to our special attention by Father Arrupe;

—   discrimination against whole categories of human beings, such as migrants and racial or religious minorities;

—   the unjust treatment and exploitation of women;

—   public policies and social attitudes which threaten human life for the unborn, the handicapped, and the aged;

—   economic oppression and spiritual needs of the unemployed, of poor and landless peasants, and of workers, with whom many Jesuits, like our worker priests, have identified themselves in order to bring them the Good News.

---

[30] GC32, D. 2, n. 11.

[31] GC 32, D. 4, n. 59.

49/ 46. As an international body, the Society of Jesus commits itself to that work which is the promotion of a more just world order, greater solidarity of rich countries with poor, and a lasting peace based on human rights and freedom. At this critical moment for the future of humanity, many Jesuits are cooperating more directly in the work for peace as intellectuals, organizers, and spiritual leaders, and by their witness of non-violence. Following the example of recent Popes, we must strive for international justice and an end to an arms race that deprives the poor and threatens to destroy civilization. The evangelical call to be genuine peacemakers cautions us to avoid both naiveté and fatalism.

G.   Prerequisites for Credibility

50/ 47. The full realization of the Church's mission after the Second Vatican Council calls us to sincere collaboration with the bishops, with other religious, with the diocesan clergy, and with other Christians as well as with people of other religious faiths.

51/ In particular, we must work more closely with lay men and women, respecting and supporting their distinct responsibility and vocation in the Church and in the world. Recent experience teaches us we can make a real contribution to forming a truly apostolic laity as well as receive from them great strength in our own vocation and for our mission. The renewal of Ignatian spirituality in certain fields (Exercises, Christian Life Communities, etc.) can help deepen this mutual collaboration.[32]

52/ 48. The validity of our mission will also depend to a large extent on our solidarity with the poor. For though obedience sends us, it is poverty that makes us believable. So, together with many other religious congregations, we wish to make our own the Church's preferential option for the poor.[33] This option is a decision to love the poor preferentially because there is a desire to heal the whole human family. Such love, like Christ's own, excludes no one but neither does it excuse anyone from its demands. Directly or indirectly, this option should find some concrete expression in every Jesuit's life, in the orientation of our existing apostolic works, and in our choice of new ministries. "Only when we come to live out our consecration to the Kingdom in a communion that is for the poor, with

---

[32] Fr. Arrupe, *Epist. de Congregationibus Marianis seu Communitatibus Vitae Christianae* (AR XV, 321–327); Fr. Arrupe, *Our Secondary Schools: Today and Tomorrow,* 20–21 (AR XVIII, 268–270).

[33] scris, *Religiosi et Promotio Humana,* n. 4 and 6, note 25; ET, 17–18; John Paul II, *Laborem Exercens,* 8; John Paul II, *Dives in Misericordia,* 3; Fr. Arrupe, *Rooted and Grounded in Love,* 61 (AR XVIII, 497).

the poor and against all forms of human poverty, material and spiritual, only then will the poor see that the gates of the Kingdom are open to them."[34]

53/   49.   Finally, in all our ministries, our work will only be credible if the practice of justice is evident in our personal lives, our communities, and our institutions. In this way we can contribute to promoting that justice in the Church which is a necessary condition for evangelization.[35]

Conclusion

54/   50.   In the task of announcing the Gospel, faith in Jesus Christ is first and last. It is a faith which comes alive only in works of love and justice. Our mission as Jesuits has, from the outset, been to seek the greater glory of God and the salvation of souls. Confirming "the service of faith of which the promotion of justice is an absolute requirement"[36] as the contemporary expression of that mission, we look to the future and renew again our commitment in "a communion of life and work and sacrifice with the companions who have rallied round the same standard of the Cross and in fidelity to the Vicar of Christ, for the building up of a world at once more human and more divine."[37]

55/   We confidently call upon the intercession of the Queen and Mother of our Society for the complete fulfillment of this mission, imploring her with our Holy Father Saint Ignatius to "intercede for us sinners with her Son and Lord and to obtain for us the grace so that, in conjunction with our own efforts, we may change from weak and sad individuals to strong and happy ones for the glory of God."[38]

---

[34] Fr. Kolvenbach, *Homily in St. Peter's Basilica,* Oct. 15, 1983 (see pp. 483–484 below).

[35] Synod of Bishops 1971, *Justitia in Mundo.*

[36] GC 32, D. 4, n. 2.

[37] GC 32, D. 2, n. 31.

[38] St. Ignatius Loyola, *Obras Completas,* B.A.C., Madrid, 4th ed., p. 647.

DECREE 2

On Poverty

56/ 1. The 33rd General Congregation, having taken into consideration the replies from the province congregations concerning the experience of the decree, closely examined in its entirety Decree 12 of the 32nd General Congregation, which had been approved "experimentally" by the Holy See.

57/ 2. Having carefully considered all these matters, the General Congregation definitively confirms Decree 12 of the 32nd General Congregation and asks, according to the mind of the 32nd General Congregation, the confirmation of the Holy See with regard to nn. 22 and 42 of Decree 12.

58/ 3. The Congregation affirms that Decrees 18 and 12, of the 31st and 32nd General Congregations respectively, fully respond to the demands of the poverty of our Institute in today's circumstances.

59/ 4. With the promulgation of the new Statutes on Poverty (Sept. 8, 1976, AR XVI, 911 ff.), nn. 37-39 of Decree 12 of the 32nd General Congregation ("Norms of Transition" and "Recommendations to the Commission for the Revision of the Statutes on Poverty") cease to have effect. The statutes, as such, possess the authority of ordinations of Father General and in future may be reviewed when and insofar as may be opportune.

DECREE 3

On the Composition of the General Congregation

60/ 1. #1. *Formula of the General Congregation* 6, 3°–4° is changed in this way:

61/ 1° From provinces where the number of members remains less than 0.5% of the total membership of the Society of Jesus, one elector will be sent to the general congregation who is a professed of four vows elected by the province congregation.

62/ 2° From provinces where the number of members is at least 0.5% but remains less than 1.4% of the total membership of the Society, two electors will be sent to the general congregation: the provincial ex officio and another professed of four vows elected by the province congregation.

63/   3° From provinces where the number of members is at least 1.4% but remains less than 2.4% of the total membership of the Society, three electors will be sent to the general congregation: the provincial and two other professed of four vows elected by the province congregation.

64/   4° From provinces where the number of members is at least 2.4% but remains less than 3.2% of the total membership of the Society, four electors will be sent to the general congregation: the provincial and three other professed of four vows elected by the province congregation.

65/   5° From provinces where the number of members is at least 3.2% but remains less than 4% of the total membership of the Society, five electors will be sent to the general congregation: the provincial and four other professed of four vows elected by the province congregation.

66/   6° From provinces where the number of members is at least 4% but remains less than 4.8% of the total membership of the Society, six electors will be sent to the general congregation: the provincial and five other professed of four vows elected by the province congregation.

67/   7° In a province where the number of members is at least 4.8% of the total membership of the Society, seven electors will be sent to the general congregation: the provincial and six other professed elected by the province congregation.

68/   #2. The distinction between an independent vice-province and a province is no longer held and those independent vice-provinces currently existing by this decree become provinces.

69/   #3. For the purpose of calculating the number of members in each province in #1, those who are applied *(applicati)* are counted as members of the province to which they are applied.

70/   2. *Formula of the General Congregation* 6, 2° is changed to include among the electors both general counsellors who are not general assistants and regional assistants.

71/   3.   Other special norms which may be necessary both in the *Formula of the General Congregation* and in the *Formula of the Province Congregation* in order to render nn. 1 and 2 properly effective will be set down by the Superior General with the deliberative vote of those members of the General Curia who have the right to attend the general congregation by virtue of office at least *ad negotia.*

72/   4.   Those points set down in nn. 1 and 2 will be submitted to a new examination in the next upcoming general congregation. They remain in force, however, until they are legitimately changed.

DECREE 4

ON THE FORMULA OF THE GENERAL CONGREGATION

73/ 1. In the *Formula of the General Congregation,* n. 12, #1:

74/ The second sentence is to be changed in this way:

"Its members, to be drawn as far as possible from among those to participate in the congregation from each of the assistancies, will be named by the superior (or vicar) general with his council and after the respective regional assistants have been heard."

75/ In the same paragraph a third sentence is to be added:

"It is permissible for the electors to indicate to the superior (or vicar) general some names from their own assistancy suited for this committee."

76/ 2. In the *Formula of the General Congregation,* n. 42, #4:

At the end of the paragraph, after "applied," these words are to be added:

"or region to which he is assigned."

77/ 3. In the *Formula of the General Congregation,* n. 130, #2:

After the words "for peace and union," these words are to be added:

"best equipped to proffer counsel on behalf of the entire Society."

78/ 4. In preparing methods and a process for handling substantive matters, in anticipation of the 34th General Congregation, Father General is empowered to change some parts of the *Formula of the General Congregation* that have to do with the handling of substantive matters insofar as needed and he may do so with the authority of the 33rd General Congregation, after obtaining the deliberative vote of those members of the General Curia who have a right by reason of their office to attend a general congregation.

DECREE 5

On the Province Congregation

79/ The 33rd General Congregation, in fulfillment of a mandate from the preceding General Congregation and as a response to the recommendation of the Cardinal Secretary of State in an appendix to a letter sent to Father General (May 2, 1975) with regard to the decree of that General Congregation "On the Province Congregation," after having carried out a diligent review of the norms and determinations in n. 11 of that decree, made this determination:

80/ 1° Since the application of the norms of the 32nd General Congregation concerning the participation of members not yet in final vows in the province congregation occurred only twice and indeed within a brief span of time, and yet no grave harm in fact arose from that experience, but on the contrary an impetus to union and integration of all the members in the life of the Society emerged, and since new harm is not to be expected from the application of these norms over not too extended a time and with proper attention, the norms and determinations in Decree 14, n. 11, of the 32nd General Congregation should continue in force and will be reviewed by the next General Congregation.

81/ 2° In order that this review may proceed in the proper way, Father General should see that the necessary studies are conducted in due time. With the help of these studies, other questions which touch on participation in the province congregation and which were proposed by the province congregations recently conducted, especially that concerning the abrogation of a limit on the participation of formed coadjutor brothers in a province congregation as it is connected with the priestly character of the Society, will have more light shed on them and can be properly solved.

DECREE 6

On Powers Granted by the General Congregation to the Superior General

I. Powers Which Were Granted to the Superior General at the End of the General Congregation

82/ The 33rd General Congregation grants to the Superior General:

1° That he is empowered, after obtaining the deliberative vote of those fathers of the General Curia who have a right *ex officio* to attend a General Congregation, and without predjudice to the powers given him in other decrees, to abrogate or modify decrees of past General Congregations that seem not to be in accord with the decrees of this 33rd General Congregation.

83/ 2° That he is empowered, after obtaining the deliberative vote of those fathers of the General Curia who have a right *ex officio* to attend a General Congregation, to abrogate or modify regulations of the *Formulas* of the General Congregation, the Province Congregation, the Congregation of Procurators, and the Congregation of Provincials that seem not to be in accord with the decrees of this 33rd General Congregation.

84/ 3° That he himself, for a just reason, can suppress colleges and professed houses, with the deliberative votes of the general counsellors and the provincial of that province in which a college or house to be suppressed is located, and after consulting the regional assistant.

85/ 4° That he may approve of the minutes which could not be communicated with the fathers of the Congregation in accordance with the norm of the *Formula of the General Congregation,* n. 142, #4, 1°.

86/ 5° That in accordance with the norm of the same *Formula of the General Congregation,* n. 142, #4, 2°, in the decrees of this General Congregation he can:

87/ *a.* make corrections that seem obviously needed, and reconcile contradictions, if any are detected (according to the mind of the Congregation and, after having ascertained the deliberative vote of those fathers of the General Curia who have a right *ex officio* to attend a General Congregation).

88/ *b.* to edit the decrees with regard to style.

II. Special Powers That Are Granted to the Superior General in View of the Early Entrance into Effect of the New Code of Canon Law

89/ 1. The 33rd General Congregation empowers the Superior General, after he shall have listened to the advice of experts and obtained the deliberative vote of the general counsellors:

90/ 1° If need be, to seek dispensations of the Holy See from laws of the new Code of Canon Law soon to take effect, in order to preserve the substantials of our institute.

91/ 2° In so far as it may be necessary, to compose decrees by which those elements that the new Code of Canon Law demands should be contained in Constitutions (cf. canon 587, #1) may be inserted in our legislation and that are not found in these or in decrees of general congregations that are still in effect. These decrees will be submitted to examination by the next General Congregation.

92/ 3° Insofar as is fitting for the good government of the Society, to adapt our law to the demands of the new Code. These regulations are to be submitted to examination by the next General Congregation.

93/ 2. The Superior General is given the mandate to prepare by suitable studies for a review of our own law and of our privileges, to be completed by the next General Congregation.

C

DOCUMENTS RELATING TO THE 33rd GENERAL CONGREGATION

Homily of the Holy Father to the Members of the 33rd General Congregation in the Chapel of the General Curia

September 2, 1983

"I implore you therefore to lead a life worthy of your vocation. . . .
Do all you can to preserve the unity of the Spirit by the peace that
binds you together." (Ephesians, 4, 1–3)

My very dear brothers:

1. I am happy to find myself in your midst, as you have wished, to concelebrate the Eucharistic Sacrifice and in this way to beg for an outpouring of the Holy Spirit's gifts on the General Congregation that you are opening. In this occasion, the words of Paul to the Ephesians, that you heard in the first reading, take on a prophetic meaning. And it is with these same words that I address myself to you with heartfelt emotion. Just as the Apostle did, so I too exhort you to conduct yourselves in a manner worthy of the vocation you have received, to preserve attentively unity of spirit by the peace that binds you together.

In greeting you I greet all the Jesuits of the world, engaged on every frontier in the life of the Church: indeed this is a great family, called by a special vocation to serve the Name of Christ, with a total availability for all the concerns of this Kingdom. At this moment, I feel it is present right here, united by the same calling of the Spirit, that Christ spills out from his breast upon you, as on all the Church: "From his breast shall flow fountains of living water."

In this spirit of an outpouring of hearts, in an attentiveness to the divine activity, today the General Congregation begins. It is an official action in the life of your religious family, an important moment to live in unity of spirit. This is a unity of "ecclesial spirit" because you are rooted vitally in the Church, one, holy, catholic, and apostolic, that you have pledged yourselves to serve with total fidelity, with an awareness that it is a universal sacrament of salvation through the riches of truth and divine life that it imparts to mankind. A unity of the "Ignatian Spirit," because that special charism, one that makes the Society a privileged instrument of the Church's action at all levels, is the all embracing and distinctive element that the Founder himself wanted for your activity and your mission.

And this unity is born out of one faith, one baptism, one Christian and religious vocation, that is its logical and austere flowering. It is nourished by the trinitarian, theological reality, that is, by the life of the one Father, the one Lord, the one Spirit. And today, we are experiencing that in a special way: "One body, one Spirit, just as you were all called into one and the same hope when you were called."

Here you have the theological and spiritual roots of today's events. For having offered me the consolation of experiencing them together with you I give you my heartfelt thanks, my very dear brethren.

2. This General Congregation takes on, then, a special importance by reason of its twofold objective. In the first place, it must provide a successor to the revered Father Arrupe. I am delighted to greet him here in person and to express to him the gratitude of all for having continued to sustain the Society by his example, by his prayer, and by his sufferings.

Your Congregation has, in addition, the task of setting the orientations, of spelling out the guidelines in the years immediately ahead so that there may be an ever better realization, in the special circumstances of the present moment, of the ideal of the Society as it is set forth in the formula of your Institute: "To serve as a soldier of God beneath the banner of the Cross . . . and to serve the Lord alone and the Church, his spouse, under the Roman Pontiff, the vicar of Christ on earth" (Apostolic Letter *Exposcit debitum,* July 21, 1550).

Such a twofold task is certainly weighty; and it is important that you should keep in mind the orientations and recommendations that my revered predecessors, Paul VI and John Paul I, communicated to you on the occasion of your most recent Congregations, and that I myself expressed to you on the occasion of the meeting of your Provincials in February of last year. They are orientations and recommendations that retain their full weight and that you should have in mind in the work of the Congregation in order to guarantee the happy outcome on which the vitality and development of your Institute depends. Hence the need to call on the Holy Spirit: "Come, Holy Spirit, and fill the hearts of your faithful."

3. Your General Congregation is an event that is destined also to have some important repercussions in the life of the Church. This is why I take an active interest in it. The Society of Jesus is still the most numerous religious order; it is spread out to every part of the world; it is engaged, for the glory of God and the sanctification of men and women, even in the most difficult fields and in key ministries that are of great benefit to the service of the Church. On that account, very many keep their eyes on you, whether they be priests or lay persons, religious men or religious women; and what you do often has some reverberations that you do not suspect.

Thus my predecessors have many times underlined the vast influence that the Society's actions exercise in the Church. In particular, Paul VI, of revered memory, did not hesitate to state that "a very special bond links your society to the Catholic Church; your fortune in a certain measure, has an impact on the fortune of the entire Catholic family" (April 21, 1969; cf. AAS 61, 1969, p. 317). If this responsibility weighs on all the members of the Society of Jesus, it weighs today in a special fashion on you who have been chosen as members of this General Congregation. This is why the Pope in this moment is especially close to you in prayer with his best wishes and his fatherly encouragement. And he repeats this with the words of the Letter to Ephesians: "I implore you . . . therefore to lead a life worthy of your vocation. Bear with one another charitably, in complete selflessness, gentleness and patience. . . . Do all you can to preserve the unity of the Spirit by the peace that binds you together."

4. To this end, I am certain that you will keep well in mind the providential nature and the specific purpose of the Society. As I have said, it is engaged in a wide range of difficult ministries. In the course of the meeting with the Provincials in February of last year, I had rapidly sketched out a picture of the activities that you have been called to exercise: involvement in the renewal of Christian life, in the spread of authentic Catholic doctrine, in the education of young people, in the formation of the clergy, in deepening of research in the sacred sciences and in general even of secular culture, especially in the literary and scientific fields, in missionary evangelization (cf. *AAS* 74, 1982, pp. 551–565).

For this array of such differing apostolic tasks, in forms that are both traditional as well as new, in response to the needs of the times that have been underlined by the Second Vatican Council, I address once again to you my words of encouragement, with full confidence, "just as you were all called into one and the same hope when you were called." The Pope counts on you, he expects so much of you.

5. On that account, the very special link that the Society maintains with the Pope, who is responsible for the unity of the Church in its entirety, assures to the Society itself an effectiveness and certainty when it expends itself, with full availability and complete fidelity, in the struggle on all these fronts of ecclesial action, today as in the days of its origin.

At that moment, your Founder, desirous of dedicating himself totally to the service of Christ the Lord, at the same time as his first companions, under the mysterious guidance of Providence made his way to Rome, in the days of Pope Paul III, in order to place himself completely at the disposition and to accomplish the missions that the Pope would point out to him, and to do that in the place that he would determine; you know how Paul III accorded a very willing reception to this proposal, while seeing in it a special sign of divine action.

In this perspective, the "fourth vow" takes on a special meaning. It certainly does not tend to put a check on generosity, but only to assure a sphere of activity that is deeper and broader, in the certainty that the most inward and most secret motivation for this religious obedience, of this bond with the Pope, is that of being able to respond in the most incisive way and with a much greater dedication, "immediately, without delay without any manner of excuse," to the needs of the Church, in apostolic fields both old and new.

While expressing to you my thankfulness for all that the Society has accomplished during more than four centuries of fruitful activity, I am sure that I can continue still in the future to rely on the Society for support in the exercise of my apostolic ministry and to count always on your faithful collaboration for the good of the entire People of God. You know that the Pope is with you and prays for you so that, in constant fidelity to the voice of the Spirit, the Society of Jesus may continue to draw from God's grace the strength and drive to carry on its vast and varied apostolate.

6.   The Church has always considered your Society as a group of religious, prepared spiritually and doctrinally, who are ready to do what is asked of them in the context of the Church's universal mission of evangelization.

The Supreme Pontiffs throughout the centuries have not failed to entrust these missions to you, looking at the most urgent needs of the Church and trusting in your generous availability. To limit myself to the most recent times, I wish to recall the mission that my venerable predecessor Paul VI committed to you on May 7, 1965, "to resist atheism vigorously with united forces," a mission which 1 urgently repropose to you, for as long as this "tremendous danger that hangs over humanity" continues (*AAS* 57, 1965, p. 514).

In November 1966, after the Second Vatican Council which had just ended, the same Pope asked you to cooperate in that deep renewal which the Church is facing in this secularized world. And I myself, in the above-mentioned discourse to your Provincials, confirmed that "the Church today expects the Society to contribute effectively to the implementation of the Second Vatican Council, just as, at the time of Saint Ignatius and also afterwards, it strove with every means to make known and to apply the Council of Trent and to help in a special way the Roman Pontiffs in the exercise of their supreme Magisterium" (*AAS*, 74, 1982, p. 557). To this end I invited you, and today I renew this invitation, to adapt to the different spiritual necessities of the present day "the various forms of the traditional apostolate that even today retain all of their value" and to pay ever greater attention to "the initiatives which the Second Vatican Council especially encouraged," like ecumenism, the deeper study of the relations with non-Christian religions, and the dialogue of the Church with cultures. In this regard, I am acquainted with and approve your commitment to inculturation, so important for evangelization, provided that it is joined to an equal commitment to preserving Catholic doctrine pure and intact.

7.   Speaking of your apostolate I did not fail at that time to call to your attention the necessity that is found within the evangelizing action of the Church to promote the justice, connected with world peace, which is an aspiration of

all peoples. But this action must be exercised in conformity with your vocation as religious and priests, without confusing the tasks proper to priests with those that are proper to lay people, and without giving in to the "temptation to reduce the mission of the Church to the dimensions of a simply temporal project . . . (to reduce) the salvation of which she is the messenger . . . to material well-being" (*Evangelii Nuntiandi,* 32). This is the magnificent field of an apostolate open before you, to work with renewed zeal, faithful to the mandate received from the Pope, under the leadership of the new Superior General, and in close collaboration among yourselves.

The generous realization of this ideal will increase ever more your apostolic thrust; it will help you to overcome the difficulties that in the mysterious plan of Providence are usually connected with the works of the Lord; and it will raise up numerous vocations of generous young men who, listening to the voice of the Holy Spirit, desire also today to consecrate their own lives for an ideal which deserves to be lived and thus to cooperate actively in the divine work of the redemption of the world.

8. The redemption of the world! Indeed, it is here that your General Congregation is being held by coincidence with the extraordinary Holy Year during which the Church tries to live more intensively the mystery of Redemption; your vocation consists precisely in seeking to follow Christ, Redeemer of the world, by being his collaborators in the redemption of the entire world; consequently you should excel in the service of the divine King, as stated in the offering that concludes the Contemplation on the Kingdom of Christ in the *Spiritual Exercises* of Saint Ignatius.

My very dear brothers! May this be, for you, the special fruit of the Jubilee Year: a renewed drive in your vocation, that invites you above all to a personal conversion: "Open wide the doors to the Redeemer," to allow penetration by the love of Christ and by his Spirit, bringing to pass what is said in the petition that Saint Ignatius recommends in the second week of the *Exercises:* "to know the Lord intimately in order to love Him and to follow Him evermore closely." Intimate knowledge, strong love, and the closer following of the Lord are the soul of your vocation. In other words, you ought to be a Society of contemplatives in action who strive in every way to see, to know and to experience Christ, to love Him and to make Him loved, to serve Him in every way and in all things and to follow Him even up to the Cross.

On the other hand, one does not know the Lord—and you who are masters of the spiritual life teach that to others—without at the same time placing oneself, with total docility and abandonment, under the influence of the Holy Spirit, whom Christ has poured out over humanity as a majestic and ever flowing river. As we have heard in the Gospel of Saint John, Christ calls us to come to Him and drink: "If anyone thirst, let him come to me and drink." This thirst should impel us to enter into intimate contact with Christ in order to contemplate with Him the Heavenly Father and thereby to draw strength, light, perseverance, fidelity in exterior action.

In order to reach this state of contemplation, Saint Ignatius demands of you that you be men of prayer, in order to be also teachers of prayer; at the same time he expects you to be men of mortification, in order to be visible signs of Gospel values. The austerity of a simple and poor life should be a sign that Christ is your sole treasure. The renunciation, with joyful fidelity, of ties of family affection should be a further sign of your universal love which opens your hearts in purity of spirit to Christ and to the brethren. Obedience on the grounds of faith should be a sign of your close imitation of Christ who was obedient even to death on the Cross. Union of minds and hearts in a fraternal community life that overcomes any possible differences or conflicts should be an example in the Church, in this year when we celebrate not only the Jubilee of Redemption, but also the Synod of Reconciliation.

I also ask you that the young men who are recruited to your Society be formed from the novitiate on in this renewed spirit of commitment to exemplary religious life.

9. That, my very dear brothers, is what the events of today suggest to us for common reflection. I hope that in this General Congregation, which is taking place in the Jubilee Year of Redemption, you may truly follow the voice of the Holy Spirit that calls you to "do all you can to preserve the unity of the Spirit by the peace that binds you together."

Together with this fidelity may generosity in the service of Christ the Lord and of the Church, his spouse, in union with his vicar on earth, be the characteristic of every true Jesuit. May it be the impetus to the works of the General Congregation that starts today. May it be the commitment of the government of the new General you are about to elect. All this the Church expects from you. The same expectation is shared by the Pope who participates in this solemn ritual, who unites himself with you in fervent prayer and who blesses you by imploring with you:

"Come, Holy Spirit, fill the hearts of your faithful,
and enkindle in them the fire of your love."

2. Address of Homage of Fr. Paolo Dezza to Pope John Paul II

September 2, 1983

Most Holy Father,

As we begin this solemn celebration, may I express to Your Holiness, in the name of all here present, our heartfelt thanks!

Thanks for allowing us to meet you on the very first day of our General Congregation.

Thanks too for inviting us to join you in this Eucharistic Sacrifice, at which we invoke the blessings of the Holy Spirit on our work in the days to come.

Thanks moreover for coming all the way from Castel Gandolfo to our own Headquarters, which will be the scene of our labors.

We are deeply moved by this gesture of great good will. Rejoicing with us are all the members of the Society of Jesus: the men who are serving in every part of the world, and—I may add—those that have attained the bliss of heaven; chief among them, our Father Saint Ignatius, who will see in this great event a further confirmation of that special bond that commits the Society to the Vicar of Christ, and which he regarded as the "principle and chief foundation" of our order.

When Ignatius and his first companions came to Rome, their hearts were ablaze with a twofold love: love for Christ, the eternal and universal King, whom alone they wanted to serve; and love for all humanity, to whom they wished to bring the Good News and the grace of Christ. Not knowing where they might best achieve their purpose, they approached the universal Pastor of the Church, and from him received instructions and a mission.

We too, in our day, come as their successors, our hearts ablaze with a twofold love: love for Christ the Lord, to whom we have consecrated—and would consecrate ever more fully—our lives; and love for the people all around us, who are in the grip of such dire need, both spiritual and material, and to whom we want to bring the Good News of Jesus Christ, his grace, and perfect wholeness. Having in mind our special vow of obedience to the Supreme Pontiff with regard to missions, we approach Your Holiness for instructions and a mission.

Our General Congregation has in view: first, to elect a Superior General who will receive from the Pope the missions that he can in his turn entrust to members of the Society, while he watches over their faithful accomplishment; second, to enact decrees that can help in the carrying out of missions: by promoting the renewal of our interior life from which flows the effectiveness of external activity, and by wisely planning our apostolic efforts.

We do realize, Holy Father, and we readily admit our limitations and shortcomings. But there is in all of us a solid and sincere will to be faithful to our vocation.

The best witnesses to this are the great number of our brothers who in every quarter of the globe and in every field of apostolate are toiling strenuously for the cause of Christ.

There is witness too from those who, while subject to unfriendly governments and deprived of religious liberty, strive by all means to exercise their ministry, though faced with the gravest difficulties, such as have prevented some from being present on this occasion, like the Provincials of Bohemia, Slovakia, Lithuania and Romania. A very special witness is borne by those dearly loved brothers who are suffering persecution for the sake of Christ, like those in China and Vietnam who have recently been condemned to prison or the concentration camp, because of their loyalty to Christ and to his Vicar on earth.

To call them to mind on this solemn occasion is for us both a duty and a grace. To have before us their example will be an inspiration to imitate their steadfastness in faith and in love. To offer up their sacrifice in union with the Eucharistic Sacrifice which we are about to celebrate around this altar, is to reinforce our plea for an abundance of heavenly graces—as a pledge of which, Most Holy Father, we have your presence in our midst today and the apostolic blessing which we humbly request.

Translation of a transcription of the address delivered by Father
Delegate at the opening of an official session of the 33rd General
Congregation, in the presence of representatives of the Jesuit com-
munities of Rome.

September 3, 1983

First of all, I want to welcome all of you and to thank those who have accepted our invitation to join us for this truly extraordinary session of the General Congregation. Yesterday with great joy the General Congregation began its work with the Mass of the Holy Spirit concelebrated with the Holy Father who so kindly wanted to be with us and to meet each delegate personally. This morning, however, with no joy we gathered to accomplish another task, that of accepting the request of our beloved and revered Father General concerning his resignation from office. It was the intention of the General Congregation, which we now fulfill, to hold this special official session in order to offer Father General the homage of our profound gratitude for and recognition of all that he has accomplished during his eighteen years as General. In taking this action the Congregation is sure that it is expressing the desires and sentiments of Jesuits everywhere and in particular that it is responding to the request of many postulates from Province Congregations which asked that, on the occasion of this resignation from office, there be an official and public expression of the Society's esteem, affection, and gratitude to Father Arrupe. For this reason we have wished to lend greater solemnity to this function by inviting others to be present, first of all the members of the General Curia who throughout these years have been firsthand witnesses of the untiring activity of Father General, then representatives of the Roman houses that constitute a part of the Society which lives and works close to Father General and, by their international character, represent the whole Society in a special way.

There are so many reasons for gratitude toward Father General. Gratitude in the first place for the example that he has always given us of religious virtue. He is a man of God, of prayer and of mortification—a model of those virtues which are proper to every Jesuit and which ought to characterize the General as he is described by St. Ignatius in Part Eight of the Constitutions. Another motive for thanks is the fact that in these eighteen years he has dedicated himself totally to his office without letting anything else occupy and scatter his energies. He has been animated by an ardent love for the Society that he has been able to inspire in others. And it is this total dedication to his office, this intense love for the Society, that prompted him to visit every part of the world in order to become personally acquainted with individual Jesuits and apostolates, in order to see concrete situations and difficulties, in order to encourage, to comfort, to inspire. Parenthetically, I would like to mention the letter which the fathers of the Vice-Province of Slovakia sent to me and from which I read only a sentence yesterday. There is another passage of the letter in which they dwell at length on the visit that Father General paid them some fifteen years ago and that has left in them such a deep impression and a stimulus for generous loyalty to their vocation in spite of the difficult conditions in which they live. And it was precisely at the end of one of these long and tiring journeys on which he spent himself without reserve for the Society that he was struck by the illness from which he is still suffering.

But it is not only the prodigious amount of work he has done that is the reason for our gratitude, but also the spirit that has given life to all this labor. Father Arrupe's election as General coincided more or less with the close of the Second Vatican Council and his term of office covered the difficult postconciliar period. During this time the Church undertook the task of self-renewal and updating in all sectors of its corporate life, one of the most important of which is religious life. Already before the Council, in the immediate postwar period, there was a widespread perception of the need of such updating. I remember the well-attended special Congress of 1950, called by the Holy See to promote appropriate modernization of religious life. I recall the various papal documents that appeared in the years following the Council and the decree, *Perfectae Caritatis.* Father General was in full agreement with the line indicated by the Council, precisely in the challenging effort to reconcile what is enduring, and therefore unchangeable, in the charism of the Society with the demands of the current situation in the life of the Church and of the world. This is a difficult and delicate task and it is no wonder that in so many areas there was a difference of opinion. Nor is it surprising that many concrete directives were criticized, especially when false interpretations or exaggerated applications of some directives led to abuses that Father General himself often deplored. But no one has ever criticized—or could ever criticize—the generous dedication that animated his work of adapting the life and apostolate of the Society to the demands of today's world.

The very request to resign his office, which Father General had already offered three years ago, is a confirmation of his commitment to renewal. Those who were in the 31st General Congregation will remember the lively debate about the life term of the General. On one side were the reasons set down in the Constitutions in favor of a generalate for life. On the other, were the difficulties arising from contemporary developments in the modern world that make a life term of office much more burdensome. These considerations have led the Church to set limits on the office of bishops, who are invited to resign at a certain age. The question naturally arose about what we should do.

And from that long and profound discussion came the solution of retaining the generalate for life but providing the possibility of resignation when age, health, or special circumstances indicate that it would be suitable for the General to leave office. It was a solution which appeared to be the best one theoretically, but I remember someone asking: But can it ever be put into practice? Father General wanted to demonstrate that this solution could indeed be put into practice, and he courageously wanted to set the example. While still in good health despite his advanced years, he took the decision to offer his resignation. Even if Father Arrupe's desire could not be satisfied at the time—and then the painful stroke came which brought on his present infirmity—along with his example of generous detachment, he wanted also to give us, as he continues to give us, his example of inner resignation. This truly edifying example has merited the praise of the Holy Father in his allocution of February of last year to the Provincials and again yesterday in his homily and has won the admiration and respect of the whole Society. Not only will Father General continue to help the Society through his prayer, his example and his sufferings, but also, even in his present state of enforced inactivity—I might almost say of enforced silence—he continues to speak, to act, to animate, to encourage. He does this through his writings, his books, and other publications which make his thoughts live in our midst, not only in the Society, but also outside the Society where especially some of his letters have been particularly effective for good.

It gives me pleasure to recall here a personal episode. On the day after the death of Pope Paul VI in 1978, his private secretary, wishing to give me some memento of the Pope, presented me with the Holy Father's copy of the *Ordo Paenitentiae* which served as a reminder of our weekly meetings for confession. After the Council, new liturgical formulas were approved for the various sacraments and a new *Ordo Paenitentiae* was published in Latin. It was permitted to use this after publication, even though not obligatory, until the date set by each Episcopal Conference after the appearance of translations in various languages. Now, I was accustomed to use the Latin form of absolution, so one Saturday evening just after the Latin text of the *Ordo Paenitentiae* appeared, I pronounced the formula of absolution according to the new form. The Pope looked at me; he had not expected this. On the following Saturday he showed up for confession with his own copy of the new *Ordo Paenitentiae* so that he could read for himself the act of contrition which was not obligatory but suggested in the new Ordo. And from that day until the last confession a few days before his death, he always came with this *Ordo Paenitentiae*. It was a precious memorial for me especially when, on leafing through the volume, I found so many interesting letters and notes of the Holy Father. And there I found a copy of Father General's letter on the integration of the spiritual life and the apostolate, which Father General had published just about a year previously. The Pope had obviously kept it at hand. He liked it and put it in this book which was one he also used for prayer and meditation, showing this way that he had read and reflected and meditated on that letter of Father Arrupe, so giving us the consolation of knowing the influence of the wise words of Father Arrupe that were helpful even to the Pope himself.

On this occasion of our public expression of gratitude and homage we wanted to offer something that Father General could have close to hand and that would be a perpetual reminder of this occasion and of the filial affection of all those present. But after some discreet enquiries as to what might please Father General, I discovered that anything he was given would very likely be passed on within a few days as a gift to someone else. However, there was one thing which would really please him: an autographed message from the Holy Father that he could keep as a constant reminder. The Holy Father granted our request and just yesterday signed this photograph, endorsing in his own hand the words he used when speaking of Father General in his homily yesterday morning, so that Father General can preserve this personal message from the Pope which confirms the close union and affection between them.

Tomorrow we shall conclude this act of gratitude and homage to Father General in the cathedral near the Chapel of La Storta, so dear to Father General because of the well known vision of St. Ignatius, which Father General had restored with the help of the whole Society. There we shall concelebrate Mass with him, praying that the Lord will reward him abundantly for all the good he has accomplished on our behalf and that He will console and support him in his painful illness.

4. Message of Fr. Pedro Arrupe to the Society

September 3, 1983

Dear Fathers:

How I wish I were in a better condition for this meeting with you! As you see, I cannot even address you directly. But my General Assistants have grasped what I want to say to everyone.

More than ever, I now find myself in the hands of God. This is what I have wanted all my life, from my youth. And this is still the one thing I want. But now there is a difference: the initiative is entirely with God. It is indeed a profound spiritual experience to know and feel myself so totally in his hands.

At the end of eighteen years as General of the Society, I want first of all, and above all, to give thanks to the Lord. His generosity toward me has been boundless. For my part, I have tried to respond, well knowing that all his gifts were for the Society, to be shared with each and every Jesuit. This has been my persistent effort.

In these eighteen years my one ideal was to serve the Lord and his Church—with all my heart—from the beginning to end. I thank the Lord for the great progress which I have witnessed in the Society. Obviously, there would be defects too—my own, to begin with—but it remains a fact that there was great progress, in personal conversion, in the apostolate, in concern for the poor, for refugees. And special mention must be made of the attitude of loyalty and filial obedience shown toward the Church and the Holy Father, particularly in these last years. For all of this, thanks be to God.

I am especially grateful to my closest collaborators, the General Assistants and Counsellors—and to Father O'Keefe in the first place—to the Regional Assistants, the whole Curia, and the Provincials. And I heartily thank Father Dezza and Father Pittau for their loving response to the Church and to the Society, on being entrusted with so exceptional a task by the Holy Father. But above all it is to the Society at large, and to each of my brother Jesuits, that I want to express my gratitude. Had they not been obedient in faith to this poor Superior General, nothing would have been accomplished.

My call to you today is that you be available to the Lord. Let us put God at the center, ever attentive to his voice, ever asking what we can do for his more effective service, and doing it to the best of our ability, with love and perfect detachment. Let us cultivate a very personal awareness of the reality of God.

To each one of you in particular I would love to say—"tantas cosas": so much, really.

From our young people I ask that they live in the presence of God and grow in holiness, as the best preparation for the future. Let them surrender to the will of God, at once so awesome and so familiar.

With those who are at the peak of their apostolic activity, I plead that they do not burn themselves out. Let them find a proper balance by centering their lives on God, not on their work—with an eye to the needs of the world, and a thought for the millions that do not know God or behave as if they did not. All are called to know and serve God. What a wonderful mission has been entrusted to us: to bring all to the knowledge and love of Christ!

On those of my age I urge openness: let us learn what must be done now, and do it with a will.

To our dear brothers too, I would like to say "tantas cosas"—so much, and with such affection. I want to remind the whole Society of the importance of the brothers; they help us to center our vocation on God.

I am full of hope, seeing the Society at the service of the one Lord and of the Church, under the Roman Pontiff, the vicar of Christ on earth. May she keep going along this path, and may God bless us with many good vocations of priests and brothers: for this I offer to the Lord what is left of my life, my prayers, and the sufferings imposed by my ailments. For myself, all I want is to repeat from the depths of my heart:

> Take, O Lord, and receive: all my liberty, my memory, my understanding and my whole will. All I have and all I possess—it is all yours, Lord: you gave it to me; I make it over to you: dispose of it entirely according to your will. Give me your love and your grace, and I want no more.

5. Homily of Fr. Pedro Arrupe at La Storta

September 4, 1983

It is in many ways fitting that at the conclusion of my ministry as Superior General of the Society of Jesus, I should come here to La Storta to sing my "Nunc Dimittis"—even though it be in the silence imposed by my present condition.

The veteran Simeon, at the close of a long life of service, and in the magnificent splendor of the Temple of Jerusalem, attained his ardent desire when he received the child Jesus in his arms and drew him to his heart. In the very modest chapel of La Storta, Ignatius of Loyola, when about to begin a new life of service as Founder and first General of our Society, felt himself drawn to the Heart of Christ: "God the Father placed him with Christ his Son," according to his own earnest prayer to the Virgin Mary.

I would not dare compare myself to these two outstanding servants of the Lord. But I can affirm that I have always had a great devotion to the experience of Ignatius at La Storta, and that I am immensely consoled at finding myself in this hallowed place to give thanks to God on arriving at journey's end. "For my eyes have seen your salvation." How often in these eighteen years I have had proof of God's faithfulness to his promise: "I will be favorable to you in Rome."

A profound experience of the loving protection of divine providence has been my strength in bearing the burden of my responsibilities and facing the challenges of our day. True, I have had my difficulties, both big and small; but never has God failed to stand by me. And now more than ever I find myself in the hands of this God who has taken hold of me.

The liturgy of this Sunday seems just made to express my sentiments on this occasion. Like St. Paul I can say that I am "an old man, and now also a prisoner of Christ Jesus." I had planned things differently; but it is God who disposes, and his designs are a mystery: "Who can divine the will of the Lord?" But we do know the will of the Father, that we become true images of the Son; and the Son tells us clearly in the Gospel: "Anyone who does not carry his cross and come after me cannot be my disciple."

Father Lainez, from whom we have the words of the promise: "I will be favorable," proceeds to explain that Ignatius never understood them to mean that he and his companions would be free of suffering. On the contrary, he was convinced that they were called to serve Christ carrying his cross: "He felt he saw Christ, with the cross on his back, and the eternal Father by his side, saying to him: 'I want that you take this man as your servant.' And so Jesus took him, saying: 'I want that you serve us.' Because of this, conceiving great devotion to this most holy Name, he wished to call our fellowship: the Society of Jesus.''

This name had already been chosen by the companions before they came to Rome to offer their services to the Pope. But it received a very special confirmation from the experience at La Storta. One can notice a close relationship between the phrases employed by Lainez and those of the *Formula of the Institute* approved by Julius III: "Whoever wishes to enlist under the standard of the Cross as a soldier of God in our Society, which we desire to be distinguished by the name of Jesus, and to serve the Lord alone and the Church his Spouse, under the Roman Pontiff, the vicar of Christ on earth."

What was for Ignatius the culmination and summing up of so many special graces received since his conversion, was for the Society a pledge that it would share in the graces of the Founder in the measure in which it remained faithful to the inspiration that gave it birth. I pray that this celebration, that is for me a farewell and a conclusion, be for you and for the whole Society represented here, the beginning of a new period of service, with fresh enthusiasm.

May the collaboration of the whole Society in the renovation of the chapel of La Storta be an abiding symbol and an unfailing inspiration for a united effort at spiritual renewal, trusting in the graces whose memory is enshrined in La Storta. I shall remain at your side with my prayers.

Like St. Ignatius, I implore the Virgin Mary that we may all be placed with her Son; and that as Queen and Mother of the Society she be with you in all the labors of the General Congregation, and especially in the election of the new General.

6. LETTER OF FATHER GENERAL TO THE WHOLE SOCIETY

September 14, 1983

Dear Fathers and Brothers,   P.C.

On the day after my election as General, I wish to take this opportunity for a first contact with the whole Society.

Because I have been involved particularly with service of the Eastern Churches and in working above all in Lebanon, in a deeply troubled corner of the world, I have had only infrequent occasion to meet with Jesuits other than those in the Middle East and at the Oriental Institute in Rome. I have to get to know the Society. Still I feel united to all of you, having fundamentally the same single vocation, the same apostolic mission, based on the Exercises and the Constitutions of Saint Ignatius, clarified for us by the discernments in the Spirit of the General Congregations and enriched in our own days by the whole spiritual and apostolic drive that the Lord has given us through the person of Father Pedro Arrupe.

It is with a great faith in the Society that I have taken up this task. The Lord wishes to make use of our Society to announce to the men and women of today's world—with a pastoral preference for those who suffer injustices in this world—the Good News of the Kingdom in a way that speaks to their culture and condition of life. He wants us in this way to serve His Church and the vicar of Christ, Pope John Paul II.

I ask your prayers and your availability as I assure you of mine so that the Society, with an unceasingly renewed effort, may hear what the Spirit is saying today to the Church.

Peter-Hans Kolvenbach, S.J.
Superior General of the Society of Jesus

7. HOMILY OF FATHER GENERAL

September 16, 1983

As we take up again the work of the General Congregation, the Lord invites us this morning to lose our life for His sake and take up the cross, our own cross, and follow Him. This word of the Lord should in no way call forth in us somber reflections on our weaknesses and shortcomings, our limitations and failures, even if these are, in fact, our cross.

The Gospel serves to remind the General Congregation that the great majority of Jesuits are men who, following the example of St. Ignatius, desire to lose their life in order that their brothers and sisters—all men and women—may live by the true life, the life of God. Without doubt the General Congregation must pass laws and decrees, but this legislative labor has only one purpose: to liberate the energies of love for Christ, that are alive in the Society, so that they may bear abundant fruit. Through all the deliberations and decisions of the General Congregation there should be always present among us the Jesuit who is willing to lose his life so that Christ may live in his brothers and sisters. It is this Jesuit whom we represent and it is for him that we labor in the General Congregation so that he be able to fulfill the Ignatian ideal of his life.

Finally, the Lord invites the General Congregation to carry its own cross and lose its life in order to follow the lamb wherever He goes. What St. Ignatius presupposes in the meditation on the Kingdom is still fully true today: so many Jesuits are ready to work and watch. But the *magis* of the Kingdom consists in working and watching as it pleases the divine Majesty, working and watching only when the Lord deigns to choose and admit me to such a state and way of life. The postulates that the Society has entrusted to the discernment of the General Congregation reveal the intense desire of Jesuits to live the Paschal Mystery today so that others may come alive. The General Congregation is called to lose its life in desiring for the Society—through its decrees, initiatives, and projects—only that which pleases "the divine Majesty."

Through the intercession of St. Ignatius we offer this Eucharistic prayer, beseeching for the General Congregation the blessing of God the Father, through his Son Jesus Christ, in the Holy Spirit. Amen.

8.   Homily of Faher General in St. Peter's Basilica

October 15, 1983

During this Eucharist which the General Congregation is celebrating for the reconciliation of all men and women in Christ, the Lord speaks to us through his Beatitudes. As if alone containing the key to all Jesus said and did, the Beatitudes are the only example of our Lord's teaching among the mysteries of his life that St. Ignatius invites us to meditate and contemplate (SpEx, 278). Following in the steps of St. Ignatius, the last General Congregation asked the Society to make sure that all its service of faith as well as its promotion of justice was carried out in the spirit of the Beatitudes (GC 32, D. 4, n. 33). Under the guidance of the Exercises we want to spend a few minutes turning the Lord's Beatitudes into prayer.

To be genuine this prayer on the Beatitudes needs to follow the Lord's example and be based on a communion in life and death with the poor and those who weep, with the hungry and those who suffer in war, with the persecuted and those who are victims of injustice. The man who absorbs the Beatitudes in prayer is never just an observer. Nor does he merely share in the suffering he observes; he finds that he is responsible for it. All his sinful cooperation—in thought, action and omission—shows he is in partnership with the people described in the Exercises, in words only too appropriate today, as blind creatures who die and go down to the hell which man in his hatred makes for himself (SpEx, 106). With great clarity the last General Congregation summed up the responsibility we all share: today we can make the world a more just place, but we do not really want to do so (SpEx, 76). And Father Arrupe added: we can no longer regard inequality and injustice as the inevitable hazards of nature; they are the results of our own selfishness (*L'esperance ne trompe pas,* p. 56; cf. also S.J. Documentation n. 38, Dec. 20, 1978). Only by confessing our fault, only by acknowledging our wickedness in changing the life-giving force of the Beatitudes, locked in the heart of every person, into a death sentence; only then will the Beatitudes become part of our flesh for the reconciliation of all men and women.

This true communion with the deeper history of humanity is also the source of our confidence that we can "save souls" by unveiling to them the true face of God in Christ on the Cross. This Epiphany of the Lord, who is meek and the maker of peace, poor in the depths of his being and merciful to the very end, persecuted and crucified, shows us just how far God will go to remain faithful to his Beatitudes of love and to what horrible lengths man will go in his curse of hatred. "Raising my eyes to Christ nailed to the Cross, I shall ponder within myself" (SpEx, 53). Underneath all forms of wretchedness and injustice we always find the blood-stained face of Christ crucified, but—mystery of faith—his embodiment of the Beatitudes also enables us unfailingly to find the seeds of reconciliation. "When I am lifted up from the earth, I shall draw all to myself" (Jn. 12, 32).

And this is the call of the Eternal King, our one Beatitude (SpEx, 91). The Lord wanted to need us to reconcile men in his Name. The Exercises ask us as disciples to follow the Master in the greatest poverty (SpEx, 98), but they do not cast us in one mold nor do they exclude any way of life or type of work in order that we may be truly poor, makers of peace, persecuted for the justice of the Kingdom. The Eternal King makes us the keepers of the Beatitudes today, ministers of reconciliation (2 Cor. 5, 1), so that we can change the curses of the first Adam into the blessings of the new city of God where men and women are reconciled with God and enjoy his gifts and pardon. Only when we come to live out our consecration to the Kingdom in a communion that is for the poor, with the poor, and against all forms of human poverty, material and spiritual, only then will the poor see that the gates of the Kingdom are open to them. The poor are certainly not happy in their deprivation any more than the persecuted are happy in their oppression. The Beatitudes do not license us to make misfortune sacred or to adopt a resigned attitude in the face of human suffering. Today more than ever the Beatitudes can only be proclaimed and their message of universal reconciliation only heard if they become a vital force in everyday life and action, as they were for the Lord. They must be seen to be at the service of men and women, all brothers and sisters of the Lord, in the very places where life, death, and hope in the future are at stake, hope for peace through the blood of his Cross (Col. 1, 20).

So our Eucharist becomes an election of love in the Ignatian sense. We come together round the Lord's table (1 Cor. 11, 20) which no one leaves hungry after receiving the Bread of Life (Jn. 6) like the bread we need each day (Lk. 11, 3). In our communion at this Mass we consecrate ourselves to the Paschal Mystery which is lived by the poor of the Lord; the peacemakers, the merciful, the meek of heart, the persecuted, the oppressed for his Name, until he comes to reconcile a new earth and a new heaven in his lasting Beatitude.

9. STATEMENT OF FATHER GENERAL ON THE BROTHERS

During the 36th Session of the 33rd General Congregation

October 15, 1983

By this morning's voting, the General Congregation has chosen not to open up in this Congregation a discussion on the opportuneness of extending to the brothers, as to all members of the Society, the same vows of poverty, chastity, and obedience in order the better to integrate them in the body of the Society.

Considering the importance of the questions that have to do with our brothers and the fact that half of the Congregation would have wished up to now to treat of this question, I think that Father General, while studying the general problem of the brothers, cannot neglect the problem of the three vows in order to see if and how it could help toward the solution of the general problem.

Naturally, no decision can be made before another General Congregation because you are dealing with a question that touches the *Formula of our Institute*. To be able, however, to present to the next General Congregation the results of a careful study of the problem and of its implications will certainly help to the best solution of the problem of the brothers, one that is a heartfelt concern of the entire Society.

10. HOMILY OF FATHER GENERAL AT THE CLOSE OF THE 33RD GENERAL CONGREGATION

October 25, 1983

The gospel of this final Eucharistic liturgy (Mk. 10, 17–22) of the General Congregation is not only the central point of all Christian action, but—especially after Anthony the Copt—it is a word of life that every religious vocation seeks to fulfill, radically and existentially. It is no wonder that this dialogue between the Master and the man on his knees (10: 17) contains the salient features of this intensive period with the Lord that the General Congregation has been living for 54 days.

"Master, what must I do?" Each delegate recognizes himself in this prayer. Each one has been willing to spend his own precious time in praying, speaking, and listening in order to insert the work of the Society in the eternal project of the Master who alone grants a share in life (10:17). To spend our own time, in order to question the Wholly-Other and to address questions to so many others who speak to us—more than we believe—in the name of the Lord.

Listening to the teaching imparted to us by John Paul II in this chapel at the beginning of the General Congregation, and listening to so many words and so many silences which echoed the experiences of the whole Society, each delegate has shared in the Ignatian discernment with the best that is in him. In this Eucharist let us pray to the Master that the General Congregation may continue in the whole Society, thanks above all to listening to our witness and to meditating on its documents, and that our hearts may continue to be restless until His divine Majesty may be served (SpEx, 135).

In answer to our prayer: "Master, what must I do?" the Lord has replied: "You know the commandments" (10: 19). This 33rd General Congregation is intensely characterized by that which we already know and by that which the Society has observed from its earliest days (10: 20). Hence the confirmation of the decisions of the preceding General Congregations, the promulgation of the laws that are indispensable for the government of the Society, the specification of the preferential options of our apostolic activity and of the foundations of our religious life. By calling the commandments of our religious consecration by their proper name, this General Congregation has recalled beyond all ambiguity or compromise the ministry of the Jesuit priest and the great vocation of the Jesuit brother, devotion to the Church in its apostolic visibility and constructive fidelity to the magisterium, poverty dedicated to the service of the Lord's poor, and the urgency of real apostolic needs to which every Jesuit should respond. Let us pray to the Lord in this Eucharist that by repeating in the commandments all the love of the Society for its Lord (Jn. 15, 9), it may attain a fresh gospel transparency and clarity in its religious commitment with an undivided heart (1 Cor. 7, 35).

However, despite all this legislation, "There is one thing you lack" (10:21): the Lord asks us to forsake material security by selling our own goods and giving ourselves to his poor (10: 22), and to forsake all legal assurance (10: 20) in order to focus our whole existence, in the insecurity of the paschal ways, on this man of Nazareth who is the Word of God. A unique document of the General Congregation to express this unique word of love (SpEx, 230). It is aware, in accord with the warning of Father Pedro Arrupe, "that in our day words do not gain credibility, and thus we must incarnate them and live them." This document thus says everything, free of any inflexibility or narrowness, by entrusting the authenticity of the mission we are to accomplish and the integrity of our religious consecration to the impulsion of the Spirit who will help our fellow Jesuits to incarnate and live these words in very diverse situations, often painful and complex, where his divine Majesty has wished to place us.

Let us pray to the Lord in this Eucharist that he not let us go away sad like the man of the gospel (10: 22), but with the paschal joy that no man can take away (Jn. 16, 21–22), because by means of this 33rd General Congregation the Lord has given to the Society a new life and because he who alone is good (10:18) has been good to us in Rome.

11. Letter of the Cardinal Secretary of State on the Definitive Confirmation of the Decree on Poverty

Secretariat of State

N.120.380

The Vatican

November 3, 1983

Very Reverend Father:

On October 29 you sent to the Supreme Pontiff a detailed report concerning the work and conclusions of the 33rd General Congregation about the Decree on Poverty which had been enacted by the 32nd General Congregation and approved "experimentally" by Pope Paul VI of venerated memory.

I am happy to let you know that the Supreme Pontiff, after studying all the documents you have sent, has definitively confirmed this decree.

While I inform you of the pleasure with which the Holy Father received your expressions of deep devotion, I add that he invokes an abundant measure of heavenly graces on you as well as on your entire Congregation, and bestows the benevolent apostolic blessing that you seek.

I take the opportunity to renew the expression of my own regard.

Devotedly in the Lord,

A. Cardinal Casaroli

Very Reverend Peter-Hans Kolvenbach, S.J.

Superior General of the Society of Jesus

Rome

D

MEMBERS OF THE 33rd GENERAL CONGREGATION

(In Alphabetical Order)

President: VERY REVEREND FATHER PEDRO ARRUPE

Elected General on May 22, 1965

Rev. Fr. PAOLO DEZZA

Delegate of the Holy Father from October 5, 1981

Rev. Fr. GIUSEPPE PITTAU

Coadjutor of the Delegate of the Holy Father

Last Name, First Name, and Province

Acevedo, Marcello de C.	East-Central Brazil	Bamberger, Stefan	Switzerland
Adami, Leopoldo	Southern Brazil	Barre, Noël	France
Agius, Alfred	Malta	Beaudry, Albert	French Canada
Almeida, Leslie	Goa-Puna	van Beeck, Frans	Netherlands
Alvarez-Ossorio, Luis M.	Baetica	Beirle, Theodor	Upper Germany
Amaladoss, Michael	Madurai	Bergoglio, Jorge	Mario Argentina
Antolović, Josip	Croatia	Bernas, Joaquin G.	Philippines
Araujo, José	Equador	Bertolusso, Vincenzo	Italy
Arnaiz, José	Antilles	Bianchini, Sergio	Italy
Arroyo, José	Toledo	Bois, Bruno	Italy
Arrupe, Pedro	Japan	Brassil, J. Paul	Zambia
Arteaga, José	Chile	Brenninkmeijer, Gregory	Netherlands
Arza, Antonio	Loyola	Browne, Joseph T.	New York
Awamoto, Paulus Teruo	Japan	Buckley, Michael J.	California

Burns, Patrick J.	Wisconsin	Dullard, Maurice	Ranchi
Byrne, Brendan	Australia	Durack, Jerome F.	Patna
Calvez, Jean-Yves	France	Earle, George	England
Campbell-Johnston, Michael	England	Egan, Liam A.	Macau–Hong-Kong
Cardo, Franco Carlos	Peru	Egaña, Francisco J.	Loyola
Carlson, Gregory I.	Wisconsin	Ellacuría, Ignacio	Central America
Carriere, Bernard French	Canada	Fang Chih-jung, Mark	China
Case, Francis E.	Oregon	Fernandes, Julian	Karnataca
Chang Ch'un-shen, Aloysius Berchmans	China	Fernandes, Stanislaus	Gujurat
Chu Li-Teh, Michel	China	Fernandez, Avelino	León
Chu Meng-Chuan, Bernard	China	Fernandez-Castaneda, Jose Luis	Peru
Clark, John W.	California	Fleming, David L.	Missouri
Cooke, Vincent M.	New York	Flipo, Claude	France
Corella, Jesús	Castile	Fonseca, Michael	Ranchi
Costes, André	France	Galauner, Petar	Croatia
Czerwinski, Josef	Austria	Galli, Agide	Western Africa
Damiani, Antonio	Italy	Garcia, Nelson	Antilles
Danuwinata, Francis X.	Indonesia	Garcia Gomez, Matias	Baetica
Dargan, Joseph	Ireland	Garcia Hernandez, Ros Ramon	Peru
Darminta, Joseph	Indonesia	Garcia Rodriguez, Jose Antonio	Castile
Decloux, Simon	Southern Belgium	Gellard, Jacques	France
De la Marche, Marc	Northern Belgium	Gerhartz, Johannes Gunter	Northern Germany
Delobre, Denis	France	Gnanadickam, Casimir	Madurai
de Mello, Anthony	Bombay	Gonzalez Faus, José Ignacio	Aragon
Devereux, James A.	Maryland	Gray, Howard J.	Detroit
Dezza, Paolo	Italy	Grzebien, Ludwik	Southern Poland
de Diego, Luis	Venezuela	Guindon, William G.	New England
Divarkar, Parmananda	Bombay	Gutiérrez Semprún, Manuel	Uruguay
D'Mello, John F	Patna	Hall, Bernard	England
Doyle, Patrick	Ireland	Harnett, Philip	Ireland
D'Souza, Alphonse	Calcutta	Harrington, Daniel J.	New England
D'Souza, Noel	Calcutta	Harvanek, Robert F.	Chicago
Duffy, Paul	Australia	Hegyi, Janos	Hungary

Hennaux, Jean-Marie	Southern Belgium	McGarry, Cecil	Ireland
Henriot, Peter J.	Oregon	McGarry, William J.	New York
Hillengass, Eugen	Northern Germany	Menendez, Valentin	Central America
Hughes, Kenneth J.	Jamaica	Menendez Urena, Enrique	León
Iglesias, Ignacio	Spain	Miyares, José Manuel	Antilles
Jacqmotte, Guy	Northern Belgium	Montero Tirado, Jesús	Paraguay
Javorka, Jozef	Slovakia	Montes, Fernando	Chile
Jerez, Cesar	Central America	Moragues, Ignacio J.	Aragon
Jeyaraj, Michael	Madurai	Morujao, Manuel	Portugal
Karekezi, Augustin	Central Africa	Munzihirwa Mwene, Ngabo	Central Africa
Kavanaugh, John F.	Missouri	Nakai, Makoto	Japan
de Kergaradec, Yves	France	Nebres, Bienvenido F.	Philippines
Klein, Alfons	Upper Germany	O'Callaghan, John J.	Chicago
Klein, J. Leo	Chicago	Ochagavía, Juan	Chile
Kokalj, Joze	Slovenia	O'Donovan, Leo	Maryland
Kolvenbach, Peter-Hans	Near East	O'Flaherty, Edward M.	New England
Kunz, Erhard	Northern Germany	O'Hare, Joseph A.	New York
Kuriakose, Joseph	Madurai	O'Keefe, Vincent T.	New York
Kyne, Michael	England	O'Malley, John W.	Detroit
Labaj, Joseph J.	Wisconsin	O'Neill, Charles E.	New Orleans
Lambino, Antonio B.	Philippines	Opieła, Stanisław	Greater Poland
Laurendeau, Louis	French Canada	Orsy, Ladislas	New York
Lavelle, Michael J.	Detroit	O'Sullivan, Patrick	Australia
van Leeuwen, Hans	Netherlands	Ozog, Eugeniusz	Southern Poland
Lombardi, Federico	Italy	Pai, Rex A. Prov.	India
Londono, Fernando	Colombia	Pasupasu, Daniel	Central Africa
Lopez Rosas, Ernesto	Argentina	Pelka, Florian	Greater Poland
Luhmer, Klaus	Japan	Pereira, Joaquim	East-Central Brazil
Mac Dowell, João	East-Central Brazil	Perz, Zygmunt	Greater Poland
Madelin, Henri	France	Pfahl, Rolf -Dietrich	Northern Germany
Mahan, Terrance L.	California	Pittau, Giuseppe Coad.	Japan
Mariotti, Enrico	Italy	Plamondon, Louis	East Africa
Matić, Marko	Croatia	Platzgummer, Helmut	Austria

Plazaola, Juan	Loyola	Seron, Eduardo	Aragon
Prabhu, John C.	Jamshedpur	Servais, Emmanuel	Southern Belgium
Prendergast, Terrence	Upper Canada	Sheahan, Gerald R.	Missouri
Puca, Pasquale	Italy	Sheridan, Edward F.	Upper Canada
Pullattu, Mathew	Kerala	Soares-Prabhu, George	Bombay
Puthumana, Abraham	Patna	Soenarja, Antonius	Indonesia
Rambla, Josep Maria	Tarragona	Soltero, Carlos	Mexico
Randriambololona, Philibert	Madagascar	Sosa, Arturo	Venezuela
Rasolo, Louis	Madagascar	Spence, Kenneth	Zimbabwe
Rasquinha, Edwin	Bombay	Spidlik, Tomas	Bohemia
Razafintsalama, Adolphe	Madagascar	Stahel, Thomas H.	New Orleans
Remolina, Gerardo	Colombia	Steczek, Boguslaw	Southern Belgium
Restrepo, Alvaro	Colombia	Stellini, Emmanuel	Calcutta
Riedlsperger, Alois	Austria	Swinnen, Andres Maria	Argentina
Rocha e Melo, Luis	Portugal	Tamas, Janos	Hungary
Rodriguez, Edmundo	New Orleans	Tejerina, Angel	León
Roeffaers, Hugo	Northern Belgium	Topno, Pascal	Ranchi
Royce, Thomas R.	Oregon	Trias Bertran, Jorge	Bolivia
Royon, Elias	Toledo	Tucci, Roberto	Italy
Rush, Robert T.	Japan	Ugalde, Luis	Venezuela
Ryan, William F.	Upper Canada	Valero, Urbano	Castile
Sagi, Janko	Croatia	Vaz Pato, Manuel	Portugal
Salvat, Ignasi	Tarragona	Vergara, Jesus	Mexico
Samarasinghe, Ashley	Sri Lanka	Vigil Avalos, Carlos	Mexico
Sanchez del Rio, Luis T.	Toledo	Vives, Josep	Tarragona
Santana, Hindenburg	Northern Belgium	Weber, Ivo P.	Southern Brazil
Saulaitis, Antanas	Lithuania	Weber, Joao Quirino	Southern Brazil
Sciuchetti, Dionisio	Bahia	Weber, Leo F.	Missouri
Segura, Manuel	Baetica	Whelan, Joseph P.	Maryland
Seibel, Vitus	Upper Germany	Wood, William T.	New York

THE 34th GENERAL CONGREGATION OF THE SOCIETY OF JESUS

January 5, 1995—March 22, 1995

LETTER OF PROMULGATION

To the Whole Society

Dear Brothers,

The Peace of Christ

All of the responsibilities for action on its decrees entrusted to me by General Congregation 34—held at Rome from 5 January to 22 March 1995—have now been completed. Therefore, in the name of that same congregation, I hereby promulgate to the provinces and regions the decrees which it passed and all the legislative work it accomplished. This is being done so that they may be distributed to all the houses (Coll. d., 3, §4) and be faithfully and everywhere observed by all (Const. [718]).

With the exception of Decrees 21, 22, and Decree 23, letters A, B, C, and D, the decrees of General Congregation 34 take effect as of today. Letter E of Decree 23, "Father General's Assistants and Counselors," actually took effect immediately after its approval in the congregation itself. In order that it be better known and understood before being put into practice, the remaining legislative work of the congregation—the Constitutions as annotated by the congregation and their "Complementary Norms"—will take effect as of 1 January 1996, the Solemnity of the Blessed Virgin Mary Mother of God and the Giving of the Name of Jesus, the titular feast of the Society. Decrees 21, 22, and Decree 23, letters A, B, C, and D, will take effect on that same day. Until then, the current law of the Society remains in force and is applicable in all circumstances. On this occasion of the promulgation of the entire work of General Congregation 34, I invite the entire Society to give thanks to God

> *for his Spirit's gift of discernment, with which our gathering was especially marked*

> *for the gift of an inspiring diversity in the delegates, which enriched our common path to God*

> *for the gift of union in our apostolic body, which was strongly expressed in the renewal of the Constitutions*

> *for the gift of courage by which, through its decrees, the Society responded to all that was ambiguous or erroneous in our way of praying, working, and living in our Society*

for the gift of energy, with which on the threshold of the third millennium the Society has affirmed and renewed its vocation of serving the mission of Christ

This act of giving thanks must include all those who by their prayer or work, by their abilities or availability, proved to be the hand of God at work in the general congregation. First among these is His Holiness John Paul II, who followed the preparation for and work during the congregation with great solicitude and goodwill. In the letter included with this document, he gives new proof of the trust he places in the Society of Jesus.

May the Lord, who has clearly blessed this beginning, bring to completion with his power and light the implementation of this new and demanding mission.

Yours fraternally in Christ,

Peter-Hans Kolvenbach, S.J.
Superior General

Rome, 27 September 1995

On the 455th anniversary of the pontifical approbation of the Society of Jesus

Enclosure: Letter of His Holiness John Paul II [See pp. 693–694]

HISTORICAL PREFACE
TO THE DECREES OF THE 34th
GENERAL CONGREGATION

Historical Preface

1. Antecedents

On 12 February 1992 Father General Peter-Hans Kolvenbach wrote to all major superiors and moderators of provincial conferences "to inform you of a process I have set in motion for the preparation of our next general congregation." He was entrusting this preparation to three of his general counselors, Fathers Michael Amaladoss (themes), Urbano Valero (updating our law), and John J. O'Callaghan (general coordination). He wrote again on 8 September, describing "the progress made in the remote preparations for General Congregation 34, which could be convoked in the latter half of 1993 so as to begin its work in the first half of 1995." In the meantime the synod of bishops, on consecrated life, would take place and the Society itself would hold a symposium on the vocation and mission of the Jesuit brother.

A few days later, 27 September 1992, the anniversary of the confirmation of the Society, in a letter now addressed "To the Whole Society," Father General gave the exact dates for the official convocation and the beginning of the general congregation, as well as the deadline for holding the preceding province congregations.

At the Curia in Rome, the preparatory work progressed steadily. In January 1993 came the second edition of the two booklets dealing with the revision of our law, which had originally been presented at the congregation of provincials at Loyola in 1990. On 15 May 1993æ the secretary of the Society sent out abundant literature relating to the "preparation of the province congregations." In May and August of that year, two "tabloids" were circulated, highlighting the problems that were regarded as most pressing; their content was spelled out in longer and more detailed essays. The whole Society now began to work in a great variety of ways, inspired by a further exhortation of Father General, dated Easter 1993, urging that the general congregation be "a moment of real discernment."

On 8 September 1993, as planned, Father General issued the official convocation of the general congregation, fixing its first plenary session for 5 January 1995. Together with the letter were some brief notes on who would participate, and seven "proposals of Father General for examination and discussion at General Congregation 34."

The province congregations were held within the prescribed time limit: they formulated their postulates, elected their delegates, and studied the proposals of Father General. When all had been completed, on 15 February 1994 Father General announced the setting up of the *Cœtus prævius officialis*, the commission charged with the immediate preparation of the general congregation (cf. FGC 12, §1), made up of Father General himself and "members of the congregation from each of the individual Assistancies": the three above mentioned general counselors and Fathers Carlos Cardó (ALM), Lisbert D'Souza (ASM), Jean Ilboudo (AFR), Gerwin Komma (ECE), Adolfo Nicolás (ASO), Vincent O'Keefe (USA), Salvatore Pandolfo (ITA), Valentin Pozaić (EOR), Gerardo Remolina (ALS), Guillermo Rodríguez-Izquierdo (HIS), and Mark Rotsaert (EOC).

On that same day Father General convoked the symposium that had been announced on the vocation and mission of the Jesuit brother: it was to be held at Loyola from 12 to 24 June, with the participation of thirty brothers, nineteen priests and one scholastic, representing the eleven assistancies of the Society.

The *Cœtus prævius* held its first session in Rome, 13 to 21 April. The members "succeeded in familiarizing themselves with the postulates which had come thus far and identifying the major areas needing further preparation." Father General wrote again to the major superiors, with details about this meeting and other work being done. The letter bore the date 12 June, which he deliberately chose "to coincide with the opening session of the Symposium on the Vocation and Mission of the Jesuit Brother." The entire Society was asked to join in thanksgiving to the Lord for the "rich presence" among us of brothers. He also reported on the reply of the Holy See (28 March 1994) to his request for permission to discuss in the general congregation the possibility that in the future all formed Jesuits would be incorporated into the Society by the same solemn vows of poverty, chastity, and obedience: "His Holiness judges that the matter . . . should not be treated in the next general congregation."

The Symposium on the Vocation and Mission of the Jesuit Brother produced a total of twenty-seven propositions on "identity–mission–communion–formation," which Father General accepted both for his own governance and for transmission to the *Cœtus prævius*. This he said in yet another letter, of 15 July 1994, where he also gave the names of the seven brothers being called to the general congregation as *procuratores ad negotia*, according to FGC 7: Brothers Bernard Coumau (EOC), Ian Cribb (ASO), Conrad Fonseca (ASM), Manuel Ibáñez Castillo (HIS), Charles J. Jackson (USA), Muwawa Ndolo (AFR), and Affonso Wobeto (ALM).

In the meantime the secretary of the Society, Father Hans Zwiefelhofer, undertook the task of putting together and systematically arranging the 637 postulates coming from the province congregations and the 142 sent so far by individuals. Each one was given a code name in Latin and placed in one of the fourteen categories that had previously been determined. The resulting "dossier" would facilitate the further work of the *Cœtus prævius*.

This *Cœtus prævius* was very busy from 4 to 25 July, handicapped by the heat of a Roman summer but assisted by a team of experts (Fathers José Javier Aizpún (GUJ), Michael Czerny (CSU), Vincent J. Duminuco (NYK), João Mac Dowell (BRC), Alois Riedlsperger (ASR), Elías Royón (TOL), and James W. Sauvé (WIS), with Isidro María Sans (LOY) assisting as secretary. The result was an updated list of postulates, which were now presented, first in order of arrival, and then in a new arrangement which indicated the provisional judgment about them: those to be put before the general congregation, others to be taken up by the ordinary (or extraordinary) administration of Father General, and finally some that were rejected. The vast majority obviously figured in the first group. The most important fruit of their efforts was the drafting of seventeen *relationes præviæ*, corresponding to as many areas of concern. In each there was an account of the postulates involved and their overall content, with an assessment of the proposals they made and a suggested response. The last two of these *relationes*, dealing with the proposals of Father General and the way in which the revision of our law would be studied and voted on during the congregation, were prepared by a parallel commission meeting during those same days, chaired by Father Urbano Valero (CAS) and made up of experts in the Society's Institute: Fathers Norbert Brieskorn (GSU), Gianfranco Ghirlanda (ITA), Richard A. Hill (CFN), José Roque Junges (BRM), Geoffrey King (ASL), Zygmunt Perz (PMA), and Anthony Roberts (JAM), with secretarial assistance from Fathers José Antonio Artigas (TOL) and Estanislao Olivares (BET). The *relationes* developed by this second commission were expressly approved by the *Cœtus prævius* itself.

These *relationes præviæ* were translated into the three official languages of the congregation (English, French, and Spanish) and sent to all the delegates in September, as matter for reflection at the meetings that they would hold by assistancies during the following months. For all this material there is an authoritative, detailed, and grateful record in a letter sent by Father General on 30 August 1994 "To all the Delegates to the General Congregation."

In addition to the letter on the work of the *Cœtus prævius*, Father General informed "All Major Superiors" on 19 July 1994 of his decision to set a deadline for sending private postulates: "I would ask you to please notify the members of your province or region that all individual postulates must arrive in Rome on or before 1 October 1994."

A further communication of Father General, dated 20 October 1994, with information about the immediate preparations for GC 34, said: "Preparations for the congregation are moving ahead well. By now many of the assistancies have held meetings of all their delegates, finding them good occasions to begin to become familiar with each other as persons and to go over together the work of the *Cœtus prævius*. In Rome, the Interim Steering Committee is working to make concrete the process endorsed in principle by the *Cœtus*, to be proposed for the approval of the Congregation. As a way to introduce that process . . . I will ask you to start our work together with three days of prayer and reflection, individually and in small groups."

The time came, finally, to ensure that a support system was in place, with its innumerable practical details, prepared to function behind the scenes to facilitate the activity of the congregation, beginning with the arrival of the many delegates. A team was set up for this, charged with planning and executing all that concerned reception, accommodation in the Curia and the Domus Pacis, transport between the two, arrangements for printing, communicating, translating, informing, photocopying, obtaining documentation, celebrating the liturgy— even for taking care of the laundry.

2. Inauguration

Except for the few that came early, delegates arrived in Rome by various means on 3 and 4 January 1995; on the eve of the date fixed for the first session only three of the 223 members still had not arrived. The multiplicity of languages, facial features, and complexions left no doubt that the totality represented a truly universal Society. As for age, the range extended from the American Father Maurice Walsh (NEN) with a full seventy-eight years behind him to Father Simon P. Metena (ACE) from Zaire, who had just recently celebrated his thirty-seventh birthday.

At 8:30 on the morning of Thursday, 5 January 1995, in the Church of the Holy Spirit next to the Curia, the inaugural concelebration was presided over by Cardinal Martínez Somalo, prefect of the Congregation for Institutes of Consecrated Life and Societies of Apostolic Life. In his homily he commented on the Gospel of the day (John 1:25–43), which recounts the call of the first disciples of the Lord. This served as basis for his words of encouragement, before the final invocation to our Lady of the Way, "the support, guide and lodestar" of the Society in its evangelizing ventures:

> Christ himself will call to you once again: Follow me! He will grant you the abundant light of his Spirit that you might grasp what his call demands and what the Society must keep giving to the Church, in line with the service that St. Ignatius constantly urged, *ad majorem Dei gloriam*!

There was a brief session in the congregation aula, for instructions of a practical and technical nature, especially the use of the electronic equipment, which was subsequently employed nearly a thousand times, under the supervision of Father Sauvé. Then all moved to the *Sala Clementina* in the Vatican, where at 12 noon His Holiness Pope John Paul II received them in audience, with a warm message (cf. Appendix I) and "his blessing for the business which is to be handled in the congregation" (FGC 110).

At 5:30 P.M. of that same day the first official plenary session of GC 34 was held, chaired by Father General himself. After the recitation of the hymn *Veni Creator*, the name of each of the members was called (FGC 104). Father General explained the absence of three, as mentioned above, and the reason for the presence of some others. So too, he introduced the personnel that would help in the proper functioning of the activity of the congregation: translators, secretaries for minutes, press officers, technicians. Finally he put the two traditional questions required at the beginning of every congregation: "Num congregatio sit censenda plena et legitima [FGC 105]; num suppleri debeant omnes defectus, si qui forte acciderint, tam in congregationibus provincialibus quam alii quicumque" (FGC 107). The hearty "yes" to both questions was uttered in silence, thanks to the marvels of modern electronics that can begin the proceedings with just the touch of a button.

In the shade of a statue of St. Ignatius, donated by the Province of Upper Canada and placed beside the presidential table, the congregation was now launched on its course, committed to discern in the light of "the Supreme Wisdom" what must today "be determined for the greater glory of God."

There followed the announced triduum of "prayer and reflection," which occupied the weekend. Father General directed it himself, with three addresses which provided matter for personal meditation, to be followed by dialogue in small linguistic groups (Appendix II): "On the Call or Vocation of This Congregation" (in English); "On the Mission and Body of the Society" (in Spanish); "On Our Law and Our Life" (in French). The triduum reached its climax on Sunday the eighth, Feast of the Baptism of the Lord, with a solemn Eucharist at 6:00 P.M. in the auditorium of Domus Pacis, concelebrated by all the delegates and presided over by Father Nguyen Cong Doan, representing the Society in Vietnam.

In the course of the triduum, three general introductions were briefly presented: Father O'Callaghan recalled the purpose of the tabloids, the work of the *Cœtus prævius*, the meetings by assistancies, and the activity of the preparatory committee; he also explained the alternatives envisaged by FGC 103, §1, for setting up the necessary commissions which would have to study the concrete themes, and suggested a possible timetable for this process. Father Czerny presented the booklet that had been distributed, "A Proposal for the Way of Proceeding of General Congregation 34." Father Valero introduced the "final scheme" (third edition, August 1994) for the revision of our law, and explained the plan proposed for discussing and voting on the material.

3. Organization

Setting up the organizational structure of the congregation took some time; but it had to be done with quiet patience precisely to ensure that it would subsequently function with smooth efficiency. The initial steps were the simplest: to elect, first of all, the secretary of the congregation and his two assistants (FGC 109), the members of the *"Deputatio de statu Societatis"* (FGC 111), and of the *"Deputatio ad negotia, sive de tractatione negotiorum"* (FGC 112), which was thenceforth to be called the Coordinating Committee.

These elections were carefully prepared, in line with FGC 42, §5, in meetings by assistancies, chaired by the respective regional assistants: the first meeting (on the evening of Sunday the eighth) was spent in reflection within the assistancy; the second (on Monday the ninth in the morning) in comparing one's conclusions with those of other assistancies—-thanks to the information that was collected and made available to the assistants between the two sessions.

Then came the successive elections, with secret balloting and with the following results. Secretary: the Provincial of Japan, Father Adolfo Nicolás; assistant secretaries: Fathers Pierre Belanger (GLC) and Jaime Oraá (LOY). *Deputatio de statu Societatis*: Fathers Jean Ilboudo (AFR), Carlos Cardó (ALM), Alvaro Restrepo (ALS), Varkey Perekkatt (ASM), Paul Tan Chee Ing (ASO), Steven van der Grinten (ECE), Henri Madelin (EOC), Lojze Bratina (EOR), Elías Royón (HIS), Gian Giacomo Rotelli (ITA), and Howard J. Gray (USA). Coordinating Committee *(ad negotia)*: Fathers Valerian Shirima (AFR), Francisco Ivern (ALM), José Morales Orozco (ALS), Lisbert D'Souza (ASM), Joaquin G. Bernas (ASO), Franz Meures (ECE), Michael Czerny (EOC), Valentin Pozaić (EOR), José Fernández-Martos (HIS), Federico Lombardi (ITA), and Joseph P. Daoust (USA). This committee, at its first meeting that same Monday, the ninth in the evening, chose three moderators who would chair the plenary sessions of the congregation in turns: Fathers Ivern, Rotsaert, and Shirima.

Once the basic organizational structure was in place, the procedure had to be determined as definitely as possible. The congregation would have to accept and approve, with whatever improvements were deemed desirable, the scheme presented on Friday the sixth. It was studied in assistancy meetings, which produced suggestions and amendments. The main ones were voted on in the plenary session of Wednesday the eleventh. Worthy of note are the restriction of speaking time, so that discussions might not be unduly prolonged, and provision for a periodic evaluation of the procedure now adopted, to allow for changes if experience should call for them. In this way the delegates had at their service an arrangement that was fairly clear and precise, and geared to the specific needs of this particular general congregation.

On Thursday the twelfth came the time to set up the commissions envisaged in FGC 113 (cf. 103). First of all it was decided to adopt the second alternative proposed in FGC 103, §1: to entrust the task to "the General together with the *Deputatio de tractatione negotiorum.*" This group proposed three successive steps: (1) the whole congregation chooses the themes to be discussed, (2) the Coordinating Committee assigns the chosen themes to the commissions that may be judged opportune, (3) the same committee appoints every delegate to a commission, taking account of the preferences expressed by the assistancies.

For the first step, a preliminary list was prepared, with forty-six themes: sixteen had been selected by the *Cœtus prævius* in its original *Relationes præviæ*, twenty-nine came from delegates gathered by assistancies, and one was proposed orally by an individual in his own name. A second list had twenty-nine topics relating to the revision of our law which the congregation might take up for particular study and discussion: thirteen had already been judged deserving of special attention by the preparatory technical commission in its seventeenth *Relatio prævia*, and sixteen came from assistancies. The rest of the project for revision would be submitted to the congregation for a more global approval. The assistancies through their spokesmen could urge their preferences and proposals. On Friday the thirteenth an indicative vote was taken to determine the themes and questions to be given priority, at least at the beginning. The result was a total of twenty-two themes and twelve questions.

With this in hand as the fruit of the first step, the committee moved to the second and third. It decided to start with sixteen commissions and to postpone until later the study of the particular themes "Our Mission Today" and "The Identity of the Jesuit." It assigned to each commission some twelve to fifteen members, chosen in terms of competence, preference, and diversity, with a provisional coordinator named until each one could elect a president and secretary. It also circulated "a proposal for getting started." Likewise it undertook to screen the private postulates that had come in after the summer meeting of the *Cœtus prævius,* or had been presented by delegates. Those accepted were transmitted to the relevant commissions. These were the topics allotted to the sixteen commissions:

1: Formation; a strong appeal for excellence in studies

2: Promoting vocations to the Society

3: Cooperation with laity and others in mission

4: The revision of our law

5: The intellectual apostolate; theological reflection; the place and importance of theology; universities

6: Evangelization and interreligious dialogue

7: Evangelization and culture/cultures: inculturation

8: Means of communication

9: Our religious and community life

10: Proposals of Father General; interprovince cooperation; the international Roman institutions

11: *Sentire cum/in Ecclesia;* signs of the times; ecumenism

12: Leadership in the Society and in institutions; implementation of recent directives; planning

13: Characteristics of Jesuit ministry; our way of proceeding; discernment

14: The Jesuit brother

15: Promotion of justice; the position of women; the marginalizing of Africa

16: The priestly character of the Society: its meaning

4. Documents

On Monday, 16 January, the commissions chose their presidents and secretaries and immediately began their work: prayer, reflection, discernment, drafting, comparing results. A week later each one presented a progress report to the congregation. In the meantime, thanks to suggestions from the assistancies, the Coordinating Committee revised the "way of proceeding," and the *Deputatio de statu* continued to refine its report.

Tuesday the twenty-fourth was graced with a brief visit from Cardinal Paolo Dezza, who was welcomed with affection and enthusiastic applause, and listened to with close attention and gratitude as he recalled memories of previous general congregations held in that very hall.

On 3 February the *Deputatio de statu* presented its revised report, which was received with applause and discussed for most of four subsequent plenary sessions. To reflect the content of these discussions, the *Deputatio* drew up a complementary report qualifying some elements of the original. In a subsequent note the Coordinating Committee called to mind the character and finality of this report: not being addressed to the whole Society, it does not require approbation, much less promulgation. The report is in fact confidential and has never been published by previous congregations. It is nevertheless a very useful document for the ordinary government and a point of reference for other documents drawn up by the congregation; moreover, it could provide material for the delegates, but only for statements made in their own name.

From 30 January on, the various commissions began to present their first drafts to the assembly, after obtaining the necessary clearance from the Coordinating Committee, which was always responsible for the progress of the proceedings. In this early phase, the whole congregation collaborated in the improvement of the first drafts for each of the commissions, while the assistancies and individuals also made comments and suggestions. With this in hand, each commission could redo its work in the next phase. The revised document was again presented at a plenary session, and subjected to debate, followed by an indicative vote to see if it was worth retaining. If it cleared this hurdle, it came to the final phase: further polishing in the light of the debate, one more presentation, precise amendments, and a final vote on these and then on the definitive text.

The first document to enter the second phase was on ecumenism. But the first to reach the finish line was on assistants and general counselors, in response to Proposal VI of Father General. This decree modified decrees of GCs 31 and 32, eliminating the distinction between "general assistants and counselors" and "regional assistants": all regional assistants would automatically be members of Father General's council. In accordance with what had been determined, Father General proceeded on February the twenty-eighth to the naming of ten counselors (and regional assistants): Fathers Marcel Matungulu Otene (AFR), João Mac Dowell (ALM), Valentín Menéndez (ALS), Julian Fernandes (ASM), Paul Tan Chee Ing (ASO), Wendelin Köster (ECE), Elías Royón (EMR), Jacques Gellard (EOC), Bogusław Steczek (EOR), and Francis E. Case (USA). The congregation then elected four assistants *ad providentiam* (FGC 130–37) and an admonitor (FGC 138–41). In these elections, the four assistants *ad providentiam* were chosen from among the ten appointed counselors: Fathers Case, Fernandes, Gellard, and Menéndez; the same was true of the admonitor elected, Father Gellard.

Just about this time a general disquiet began to be noticed, a sort of crisis: time was running out, the documents seemed too many and not equally relevant, or were merely repeating what earlier congregations had said. So the Coordinating Committee decided to propose a "way out" to be followed in the third and last remaining month: to set up three teams that would trim the material produced, so as to arrive at briefer statements, though this might require a painful pruning of what was already in bloom.

One team was to work on an inspiring introduction to the whole body of decrees and juridical norms; another would put together all that referred to evangelization; and the last had to select from, and if necessary revise, the rest of the texts. The congregation approved this plan by a large majority.

The result is seen in the thematic index contained in the table of contents at the beginning of this volume: a comprehensive introduction, "United with Christ in Mission"; then a first unit on "Our Mission" with its own introduction and three specific documents on justice, culture, and interreligious dialogue; a second unit treating of some "Aspects of Jesuit Life for Mission": priests and brothers, chastity and poverty, vocations; a third concerned with the context of Jesuit mission "In the Church," beginning with our fundamental *sentire cum Ecclesia* and going on to speak of some of our companions on pilgrimage: other Christian churches (ecumenism), the laity, and women; a fourth dealing in particular with the theme "Dimensions and Particular Sectors of Our Mission": communication media, intellectual work, educational institutions, parish ministry, and ecology; yet a fifth on the topic "Structures of Government"; finally a conclusion stressing the authentic and basic "Characteristics of Our Way of Proceeding." The final voting was concluded on 20 March with the approval of the last eight of the proposed documents.

5. Law

The revision of the law proper to the Society was from the beginning regarded as the central concern of GC 34; this had been already envisaged in GC 33. That could be why Father General devoted his third introductory talk to the topic "Our Law and Our Life." He recalled that St. Ignatius did not want to bequeath to us the constitutions as a finished product, and that his companion and successor, Father Laínez,

> saw in this unfinished work of Ignatius a summons to a creative fidelity, the Society's responsibility, when gathered in general congregation, to renew, enrich, and clarify with new apostolic experiences, demands, and urgencies, the way pointed out to us by the pilgrim Ignatius.

An extensive and meticulous work of preparation had been going on for several years. The congregation must now add the finishing touches, with the help of Commission 4, which had been entrusted with this topic, without forgetting that according to "the way of proceeding" that had been approved, an effort had to be made to "integrate the study and treatment of the project for the revision of our law with the discussion of themes pertaining to our life and mission."

At the planning stage, the congregation reserved to itself the handling of twelve questions on law. Commission 4 now had to work on them in collaboration with other commissions which might be concerned with a particular question. In addition, it must further revise the project that had been presented to the congregation in its third edition (August 1994). This double task was attended to alongside the work of the other commissions, as reported in the previous section. The second presentation of each part of the Complementary Norms, as improved with some amendments, was begun on 23 February, with a general introduction by the president of Commission 4, Father King, and a special word about Parts I and II on the following day. At the opening prayer of the plenary session that morning, Father General contributed a reminder on the special importance of the subject, and a petition borrowed from St. Ignatius, that the Blessed Trinity deign to "confirm" the fruit of "our reflection and our voting" (Appendix III).

On Saturday, 18 March, with the approval of Part IX (Part X had been approved earlier together with Part V), the work of the congregation on this material having to do with our law was concluded. The event was celebrated with an enthusiastic burst of prolonged applause for Father Valero and his wholehearted and efficient dedication to this mission entrusted to him by the Society—clearly, with the assistance of many others. In token of gratitude he was given ten roses, one for each part of the Constitutions and their respective Complementary Norms. He placed the flowers at the feet of the statue of St. Ignatius, founder and first lawgiver of the Society.

6.   Conclusion

On Wednesday the twenty-second came the approval of the faculties granted to Father General for the promulgation of the authorized text of the decrees passed by the general congregation, once such corrections as might be deemed necessary had been made and the revision of the law completed by taking account of what might have to be added to the Complementary Norms because of the decrees of this very congregation. Besides, the finishing touches had to be given to the authoritative text of the Complementary Norms and the Notes to the Constitutions, in order to publish in a single volume the Constitutions, the Notes, and the Complementary Norms. Father General and four elected delegates (Fathers Johannes Günter Gerhartz, Federico Lombardi, John O'Callaghan, and Mark Rotsaert) are to ensure that any additions, corrections, editing, and translation of the latter will be done according to the mind of the general congregation.

During the time prescribed by FGC 128 for the presentation of, discussion of, and voting on possible "intercessions," the members engaged in a sincere and fruitful exchange of their personal experiences in the course of the past three months.

On 22 March at 2:55 P.M. the closure of the congregation was decreed (FGC 143) and celebrated with a grateful *Te Deum Laudamus* (FGC 145). Immediately, Father General dispatched a telegram to His Holiness John Paul II, in his own name and that of all the delegates, thanking him for his paternal regard, reaffirming the unreserved loyalty of the Society to the Vicar of Christ, and seeking his apostolic benediction on the results of the general congregation. A cordial reply was received a few days later, forwarded by Msgr... Giovanni Battista Re, *sostituto* in the Secretariat of State (Appendix V).

That same evening, delegates and support staff gathered at the Church of the Gesù for a final concelebrated Eucharist. In a brief homily (Appendix IV) Father General expressed "in the spirit of the Gospel of today" what all might expect as the fruit of this GC 34.

DECREES OF THE

34th GENERAL CONGREGATION

I

INTRODUCTION

1. United with Christ on Mission

DECREE 1

United with Christ on Mission

1/ 1. **The Work of General Congregation 34.** The major work of GC 34 has been the revision of our law and the orientation of our mission for today. The first project had two goals: to provide an annotated text of the *Constitutions* capable of influencing the present-day life of the Society and to make available a set of *Complementary Norms to the Constitutions*, derived for the most part from general congregations, to enable Jesuits to put the character and mission of the Society into daily practice. The orientation of our mission for today appears particularly in the decree "Servants of Christ's Mission" and its three companion decrees: "Our Mission and Justice," "Our Mission and Culture," and "Our Mission and Interreligious Dialogue."

2/ 2. While focusing on these two tasks, this general congregation also treated a number of important areas of Jesuit life and mission which are included as decrees or recommendations. Other important areas of Jesuit life—spiritual life, formation, obedience, community life, the local superior—which have been treated by recent general congregations and are incorporated into the Complementary Norms, are recommended to the ordinary government of the Society.

3/ 3. **Servants of Christ's Mission.** In its work, GC 34 stands in continuity with the spirit and emphases of GCs 31, 32, and 33. Like these congregations, GC 34 asks the Society to sustain both its spiritual and community renewal and its efforts to meet the challenges and opportunities of the modern world. In our review of the state of the Society, we faced our limitations and weaknesses, our lights and shadows, our sinfulness. But we also found much that was wise and good, especially the powerful and pervasive effort to pursue the service of faith and that struggle for justice which it includes. In the review of our graces over these years, we found again "the omnipotent hand of Christ, God and our Lord."[1] In gratitude for so much good accomplished and for so much forgiven, we follow this Christ, the Crucified and Risen Lord, in pilgrimage and labor. We see our renewal of the law and our review of our life and apostolic labor as one reality, the confirmation of our union as servants of Christ's mission.

4/ 4. **Pilgrimage and Labor.** The congregation invites the entire Society to read and pray over this updating of our law and orientation of our mission for

---

[1] *Const.* [812].

today. One way of doing this would be in the light of the Ignatian images of pilgrimage and labor.

5/ 5. Just as the pilgrim Ignatius found that "God treated him . . . as a schoolmaster treats a child whom he is teaching,"[2] so Ignatius, as general and master of the spiritual life, continued his journey into the more profound discovery of God. The pilgrim search of Ignatius united him to Christ, led him to choose poverty with Christ poor, and to enter more deeply into the mystery of Christ's passion and resurrection. Out of his incessant search for God's presence and will, Ignatius developed a way of proceeding. This way of proceeding is found in the pilgrimage of the Spiritual Exercises from sinner beloved and forgiven to disciple called to labor in the vineyard and to suffer with Christ; it is in the pilgrimage of the Constitutions from the first inquiry about the Society in the General Examen to the mature acceptance of responsibility for the Society in Parts V–X; it is in the personal examen of his own life where each Jesuit finds his own pathway to God, and in the communal narrative of these past thirty years of renewal and reorientation. Like that of Ignatius, our way of proceeding is both a pilgrimage and a labor in Christ: in his compassion, in his ceaseless desire to bring men and women to the Father's reconciliation and the Spirit's love, and in his committed care for the poor, the marginalized, and the abandoned.

6/ 6. The *Autobiography* narrates the evolving power of grace which molded Ignatius into a man who opened himself to the needs of others. This simple reality, to help others, spurred Ignatius to study and training, to the gathering of companions, and, eventually, to the founding of the Society. That same simple reality, to help others, continues to inspire our Society today. The updating of our law and the decrees and recommendations of this congregation are animated by the desire to help people as Jesus Christ helped people. The documents of this congregation specify particular groups—the poor, lay men and women, persons of other religions—and focus on particular works from schools to parishes to research centers; the overarching motive is the simple Ignatian desire to help people in Christ. But the documents of this congregation also call us to learn how to be helped by people: how to be poor, how to see the Church as enriched by lay leadership, how to listen to the experience of women today, how to find God in the religious traditions of people from other beliefs, how to engage in respectful dialogue, how to become involved in the new cultural world of communication, and how to let the young give us hope and dreams for the future.

7/ 7. Ignatius presents a Christ who is on the move, traveling through villages and visiting synagogues to preach the Kingdom, going where people dwell and work. This contemplative identification of Jesus on mission is linked to the Election of the Exercises. In their own communal apostolic discernment, which

---

[2] *Autobiography* [27].

led to the founding of the Society, Ignatius and his companions saw this as their unique call, their charism: to choose to be with Christ as servants of his mission, to be with people where they dwell and work and struggle, to bring the Gospel into their lives and labors.[3]

8/   8.   As pilgrims on Christ's mission, we are ready to be dispersed to any part of Christ's vineyard, to labor in those parts of it and in those works which have been entrusted to us.[4] This congregation is aware of the varied cultural and apostolic situations of the Society worldwide. In some parts of the Society we are becoming fewer and older. In other parts of the Society we are young, part of an emerging national consciousness, and are beginning to have a new influence within the Society itself. Some of us live in countries only nominally Christian and increasingly secular. Others of us live in countries deeply religious but with few Christians. Others still work in countries where the Christian faith remains alive among the majority, especially among the poor, but where it nevertheless faces the challenges of injustice and secularism. Some of us are emerging from years under totalitarian government and are redeveloping Jesuit life and work. Yet all of us are called to be servants of Christ's universal mission in the Church and the world of today, to adapt the Society's apostolic priorities to our cultural situations and to our way of proceeding.

9/   9.   In Jesus Christ, we can accept the magnitude of this challenge—to work at the integration of faith and justice, to strive to understand how the Gospel is to be inculturated, to embark with new zeal on the task of interreligious dialogue, to continue to join our professional and pastoral skills to the Ignatian way of proceeding. The Crucified Jesus reminds us that in weakness and vulnerability God's love can shine forth mightily. The Risen Jesus reminds us that our hope rests in his power over death and his continued identification with those who bear his name.

10/   10.   **Friends in the Lord.** A number of postulates asked for some further directions in the areas of spiritual and community life. Our efforts to meet these concerns brought us back repeatedly to Decree 11 of GC 32, "The Union of Minds and Hearts in the Society of Jesus." That decree is a classic statement. As such, it represents one more instance of the need for the Society to continue to implement the decrees we already possess.

11/   11.   Moreover, beneath the renewal of our law is a reverence for persons, an effort to make law serve the lived experience of Jesuits, to help the community of the Society become more united in its witness to the Gospel and in its labor. Other documents, on chastity, poverty, and vocations, underscore the opportu-

---

[3] Deliberation of 1539, MHSI, Ignatiana s. III, pp. 1-7.

[4] *Const.* [603].

nity we have in community life to bear witness that living in Christ can make men happy and wholesome, maturely capable of living and expressing their faith, willing to offer one another care, support, and challenge. Again, there is need for Jesuits themselves to be in dialogue with one another, to create an atmosphere of discerning listening and exchange. The decree on cooperation with laity summons us to an attitude of listening and exchange with those who are vital partners in our service of Jesus Christ and his Church. While the term was rarely used, GC 34 was touching upon the Christian virtue of hospitality, of making the Society a symbol of welcome—to the poor, to lay people, to those searching for meaning, to those who want to talk seriously about religious issues. No community life is possible, however, and no renewal can be truly fruitful unless each Jesuit "keep before his eyes God, and the nature of this Institute which he has embraced and which is, so to speak, a pathway to God."[5] His vocation summons each Jesuit to find privileged time and space to pray with Christ, as friend to friend, learning from this encounter how to be a servant of his mission. This personal friendship in Christ, sustained by our Eucharistic fellowship, liberates us for the union of minds and hearts envisioned in Part VIII of our *Constitutions*.

12/ 12. **Conclusion.** In his address to the delegates, Pope John Paul II called the Society to discern its particular contribution "to the new evangelization on the brink of the third millennium."[6] As we present the renewal of our law and our orientation of the mission of the Society for today, this congregation is, first of all, filled with gratitude for all those Jesuits who have striven to make the Ignatian ideals of love and service their own in an eminent way. They include men who lived quietly and unknown; men who were renowned scholars, preachers, and teachers; men who laid down their lives for the Gospel, for the Church, and for the poor; men who lived simply and faithfully in a world that never understood their poverty, chastity, or obedience; men who brought our Society to this moment. We give thanks to God for them.

13/ 13. Second, we are heartened by our younger brothers who will assume the leadership of our ministries in the years to come. For their dedication to Ignatian values, for their abilities in a variety of ministries, for their readiness for apostolic responsibility, we give thanks. We ask them to see their formation as guided radically by the updating of our law, so that they, along with the entire Society, can come to a re-cognition of—a renewed affection for—the Constitutions as the Society's privileged expression of its charism and spirituality: in a word, as the identity of the Jesuit.

---

[5] *Formula* [3].

[6] John Paul II, Allocution to General Congregation 34, 5 January 1995, n. 2; see p. 663 below.

14/   14.   Ultimately, the Society of Jesus is the mysterious work of God, calling us to live and labor in the vineyard of Christ our Lord. We can and should be good instruments revitalizing our lives and renewing our ministries.[7] But, finally, we must stand in surrender to the hope with which Ignatius ends the Constitutions, trusting that God will sustain this Society which bears the name of his Beloved Son.[8] We praise this God of our Lord Jesus Christ, asking his Spirit to be our guide as we live out what we have written here and journey with confidence and humility as servants of Christ's mission.

---

[7] Cf. *Const.* [813].

[8] Cf. *Const.* [812].

II

OUR MISSION

DECREE 2

SERVANTS OF CHRIST'S MISSION

15/ 1. As the Society of Jesus, we are servants of Christ's mission. In the thirty years since General Congregation 31, and particularly in the twenty years since GC 32, the Society has felt both the strength of the Crucified and Risen Christ and its own weakness: this has been a time of testing for us, but also a time of great grace. Our many faults we know and confess; our graces are more important because they come from Christ. Some have left us to serve the Lord in other ways of life; others, shaken by the events of this period, have a weakened confidence in the quality of our vocation. But we have also become, in a resilient way, a community of "friends in the Lord," supporting one another in the freedom which Christian love brings, deeply affected by the deaths of our Jesuit martyrs in this period. In these years, throughout the Society, we have been purified in the faith by which we live, and have grown in our understanding of our central mission. Our service, especially among the poor, has deepened our life of faith, both individually and as a body: our faith has become more paschal, more compassionate, more tender, more evangelical in its simplicity.

16/ 2. The Society has also become a body more diverse than ever before, engaged in a variety of ministries at the crossroads of cultural conflict, social and economic struggles, religious revivalism, and new opportunities for bringing the Good News to peoples all over the world.

17/ • Jesuits in Africa are engaged in the challenge of building up a young and vibrant African Church, rooted in the richness of different cultures, creating new bonds of solidarity among their peoples, and struggling to overcome the global forces that tend to marginalize the whole continent.

18/ • Jesuits in Asia and Oceania are engaged in the struggles of the poor and the indigenous peoples for justice; especially in Asian countries where Christians are a small minority, they dialogue with other cultural and religious traditions in an effort to put the Gospel in touch with Asian life and to bring the richness of Asian culture to the living of the Gospel.

19/ • Jesuits in Latin America, confronted by societies in which there are huge disparities between the lives of rich and poor, continue to stand with the poor as they work for the justice of the Kingdom. They also enable the voices of the poor to teach the Church about the Gospel, drawing upon the rich faith of the people and of indigenous cultures.

20/ • Jesuits in former Communist countries, after long years of harassment and imprisonment for their faith, are helping their people in their search for an authentic way of living in a regained freedom.

21/ • Jesuits in Western Europe, through a range of educational, spiritual, and pastoral ministries, are helping to maintain the vitality of faith and of Christian communities in the face of religious indifference. They also strive in a variety of ways to accompany and help those who are at the margins of society.

22/ • Jesuits in North America are dealing with the challenges of new forms of cultural and economic deprivation. They work in close cooperation with many others in trying to influence the complex structures of society where decisions are made and values are shaped.

23/ All of us are engaged in the Society's mission in ways appropriate to the varied contexts in which we work. For we have one mission, shared by priests and brothers, and many ministries which we undertake as a service of Jesus Christ and his work of reconciling the world to God.

24/ 3. The Church, whose mission we share, exists not for itself but for humanity, bearing the proclamation of God's love and casting light on the inner gift of that love. Its aim is the realization of the Kingdom of God in the whole of human society, not only in the life to come but also in this life. We exercise our Jesuit mission within the total evangelizing mission of the Church.[1] This mission is "a single but complex reality which develops in a variety of ways": through the integral dimensions of life witness, proclamation, conversion, inculturation, the genesis of local churches, dialogue and the promotion of the justice willed by God.[2] Within this framework, in accordance with our charism, our tradition, and the approval and encouragement of popes through the years, the contemporary Jesuit mission is the service of faith and the promotion in society of "that justice of the Gospel which is the embodiment of God's love and saving mercy."[3]

25/ 4. When Ignatius was confirmed in his mission at La Storta, the Eternal Father said to Christ, "I want you to take this man as your servant": it was at the will of the Father that Jesus Christ, carrying his Cross as a standard of victory, took Ignatius as servant of his mission, to labor with him under that same Cross until his work is accomplished. It is a vision which confirms the call which Christ, the Eternal King, extends in the *Spiritual Exercises:*

---

[1] Cf. John Paul II, Allocution to General Congregation 34, 5 January 1995, nn. 2 and 9; see pp. 663, 667–668 below..

[2] John Paul II, Encyclical letter *Redemptoris Missio*, n. 41.

[3] GC 33, D 1, n. 32. In other places in this present decree, this justice is also described as "the justice willed by God," "the justice of God's Kingdom," and God's "justice in the world."

Whoever wishes to come with me has to be content with the same food
I eat, and the drink, and the clothing which I wear, and so forth. So too
each one must labor with me during the day, and keep watch in the night,
and so on, so that later each one may have a part with me in the victory,
just as each has shared in the toil.[4]

26/ Ignatius, and all those called to this service, are taught to be companions in hardship with Christ in his ministry. In the Spiritual Exercises, we contemplate the mission of Christ as a response of the Blessed Trinity to the sins which afflict the world. We contemplate the Incarnate Son born in poverty, laboring to bring the Kingdom through word and deed, and finally suffering and dying out of love for all men and women. In the pedagogy of the Exercises, Jesus invites us to see in his earthly life the pattern of the mission of the Society: to preach in poverty, to be free from family ties, to be obedient to the will of God, to enter his struggle against sin with complete generosity of heart. As the Risen Lord, he is now present in all who suffer, all who are oppressed, all whose lives are broken by sin. As he is present, so we too want to be present, in solidarity and compassion, where the human family is most damaged. The Jesuit mission, as a service of the Crucified and Risen Lord, is always an entry into the saving work of the Cross in a world still marked by brutality and evil. Because we are companions of Jesus, our identity is inseparable from our mission. Nadal makes it clear that, for Ignatius, although the Risen Christ is now in glory, through the Cross he is present in the suffering which continues in the world for which he died: "Christ, having risen from the dead, and dying now no more (Rom. 6:9), still suffers in his members, and constantly carries his Cross so that he said to Paul, 'Why do you persecute me?'"[5]

27/ 5. St. Ignatius was clear that, as the Society was not instituted by human means, so its ministries are preserved and fostered only by the all-powerful hand of Christ.[6] Thus, as we receive our mission from Christ, whatever fruitfulness it bears is entirely dependent on his grace. And it is the Risen Christ who calls and empowers us for his service under the banner of the Cross:

28/ • The Risen Christ, far from being absent from the world's history, has begun a new presence to the world in the Spirit. He is now present to all men and women and draws them into his Paschal Mystery. He continues to mediate God's work of bringing salvation, justice, and reconciliation to a world that is still broken by its sins.

---

[4] *SpEx* [93].

[5] MHSI, Ignatiana s. IV, p. 314.

[6] *Const.* [812].

29/ • The Risen Christ who calls us is the firstborn from the dead, the first of many brothers and sisters who, through his love, will enter God's embrace. He is the loving and healing presence among us, ensuring that the scars of brutality and death will not always disfigure our human history. His death on the tree of the Cross bears fruit that continues to be "for the healing of the nations" (Rev. 22:2).

30/ • The Risen Christ fulfills God's promises to the Jewish people and continues to bring all peoples together with them, to create one new humanity in the Spirit, uniting them in one living body (Eph. 2:15f.). In him, all human hostilities are healed.

31/ 6. The mission of the Society derives from our continuing experience of the Crucified and Risen Christ who invites us to join him in preparing the world to become the completed Kingdom of God. The focus of Christ's mission is the prophetic proclamation of the Gospel that challenges people in the name of the Kingdom of his Father; we are to preach that Kingdom in poverty. He calls us to be at the very heart of the world's experience as it receives this promise of the Kingdom and is brought to receive God's gift in its fullness. It is still an experience of the Cross, in all its anguish and with all its power, because the enigmas of sin and death are still part of the reality of the world. He calls us "to help men and women disengage themselves from the tarnished and confused image that they have of themselves in order to discover that they are, in God's light, completely like Christ."[7] And so we undertake all our ministries with a confidence that the Lord takes us, as he did Ignatius, as his servants— not because we are strong, but because he says to us, as he said to St. Paul, "My grace is suficient for you, for my power is made perfect in weakness" (2 Cor. 12:9).

The Graces Christ Gives

32/ 7. The Risen Christ's call to us to join him in laboring for the Kingdom is always accompanied by his power. A particular grace was given to the Society when GC 32 spoke of our mission today as "the service of faith, of which the promotion of justice is an absolute requirement."[8] This description of the main focus of our work and spirituality and its integrating principle is grounded in the Formula of the Institute, which, after speaking of the purpose of the Society—"to strive especially for the defense and propagation of the faith and for the progress of souls in Christian life and doctrine"—identifies a range of activities which mediate this goal: ministries of the Word and ministries of interiority, ministries of sacramental service, teaching catechism to children and the unlettered. Finally,

---

[7] Peter-Hans Kolvenbach, Discourse to General Congregation 34, 6 January 1995; see pp. 265–275 below.

[8] GC 32, D 4, n. 2.

pointing to the centrality of the works of mercy in Christian life, it opens up a horizon of social ministries to be exercised by a Jesuit on behalf of those in need:

> Moreover, he should show himself no less useful in reconciling the estranged, in holily assisting and serving those who are found in prisons and hospitals, and indeed in performing other works of charity, according to what will seem expedient for the glory of God and the common good.[9]

33/ 8. The commitment of the Society to a radical life of faith that finds expression in the promotion of justice for all derives its inspiration from this foundational declaration in the apostolic letter of Pope Julius III. We have recovered, for our contemporary mission, the centrality of working in solidarity with the poor in accord with our Ignatian charism. As though with new eyes, we read, as a prophetic text for our time, what Polanco under Ignatius's guidance wrote to the community at Padua in 1547:

> So great are the poor in the sight of God that it was especially for them that Jesus Christ was sent into the world: "By reason of the misery of the needy and the groans of the poor, now will I arise, says the Lord" (Ps. 11:6). And elsewhere, "He has anointed me to preach the Gospel to the poor" (Luke 4:18), a word which our Lord recalls when he tells them to give an answer to St. John, "The poor have the Gospel preached to them" (Matt. 11:5). Our Lord so preferred the poor to the rich that he chose the entire college of his apostles from among the poor, to live and associate with them, to make them princes of his Church and set them up as judges of the twelve tribes of Israel—that is, of all the faithful—and the poor will be his counselors. To such a degree has he exalted the state of poverty! Friendship with the poor makes us friends of the eternal King.[10]

34/ 9. Being "friends of the Lord," then, means being "friends with the poor," and we cannot turn aside when our friends are in need. We are a community in solidarity with them because of Christ's preferential love for them. We understand more clearly that the sinfulness of the world, which Christ came to heal, reaches in our time a pitch of intensity through social structures which exclude the poor—the majority of the world's population—from participation in the blessings of God's creation. We see that oppressive poverty breeds a systemic violence against the dignity of men, women, children, and the unborn which cannot be tolerated in the Kingdom willed by God. These are the signs of the times

---

[9] *Formula* [3].

[10] MHSI, I, 572-77, Letter 186, 7 August 1547. English translation in *Letters of St. Ignatius of Loyola*, ed. W. J. Young (Loyola University Press, 1959), p. 148.

which call us to realize that "God has always been the God of the poor because the poor are the visible proof of a failure in the work of creation."[11]

35/ 10. Pope John Paul II speaks of the pervading "structures of sin," particularly characterized by "the all-consuming desire for profit and the thirst for power" in all cultures. Because the life of the spirit is inseparable from social relations, he calls on people of all faiths and none to become aware of "the urgent need to change the spiritual attitudes which define each individual's relationship with self, with neighbor, with even the remotest human communities, and with nature itself."[12] It is a summons which we, as Jesuits committed to the action of the Holy Spirit both in the human heart and in the world, cannot refuse; consequently, in the conduct of our personal and community lives and in whatever ministries we undertake—whether works of pastoral service, academic scholarship, spiritual ministry, or education—we will live in ways which look to the fullness of the Kingdom in which justice, and not human sin, will hold sway. In the words of Pope John Paul II,

> Working for the Kingdom means acknowledging and promoting God's activity, which is present in human history and transforms it. Building the Kingdom means working for liberation from evil in all its forms. In a word, the Kingdom of God is the manifestation and realization of God's plan of salvation in all its fullness.[13]

36/ 11. Ours is a service of faith and of the radical implications of faith in a world where it is becoming easier to settle for something less than faith and less than justice. We recognize, along with many of our contemporaries, that without faith, without the eye of love, the human world seems too evil for God to be good, for a good God to exist. But faith recognizes that God is acting, through Christ's love and the power of the Holy Spirit, to destroy the structures of sin which afflict the bodies and hearts of his children. Our Jesuit mission touches something fundamental in the human heart: the desire to find God in a world scarred by sin, and then to live by his Gospel in all its implications. This, the instinct to live fully in God's love and thereby to promote a shared, lasting human good, is what we address by our vocation to serve faith and promote the justice of God's Kingdom. Jesus Christ invites us, and through us the people we serve, to move, in conversion of heart, "from solidarity with sin to solidarity with him for humanity," and to promote the Kingdom in all its aspects.[14]

---

[11] Peter-Hans Kolvenbach, "Our Mission Today and Tomorrow," *Faith Doing Justice: Promoting Solidarity in Jesuit Ministries* (1991), pp. 48f.

[12] John Paul II, Encyclical letter *Sollicitudo Rei Socialis*, nn. 36-38.

[13] John Paul II, Encyclical letter *Redemptoris Missio*, n. 15.

[14] Peter-Hans Kolvenbach, "Our Mission Today and Tomorrow," op. cit., p. 49.

37/   12.   This faith in God is inescapably social in its implications, because it is directed towards how people relate to one another and how society should be ordered. In many parts of the world, we see social and moral disintegration. When a society has no moral and spiritual basis, the result is conflicting ideologies of hatreds which provoke nationalistic, racial, economic, and sexual violence. This in turn multiplies the abuses that breed resentment and conflict, and locks groups into an aggressive fundamentalism which can tear the fabric of society apart from within. Society then falls prey to the powerful and the manipulative, the demagogue and the liar; it becomes the center of social and moral corruption.

38/   13.   But a faith that looks to the Kingdom generates communities which counter social conflict and disintegration. From faith comes the justice willed by God, the entry of the human family into peace with God and with one another. It is not exploitative propaganda but religious faith, as the inspiration of the human and social good found in God's Kingdom, that alone can take the human family beyond decline and destructive conflict. If wrongs are to be acknowledged and resolved, then possessiveness, chauvinism, and the manipulation of power have to be challenged by communities grounded in religious charity, the charity of the Suffering Servant, the self-sacrificing love shown by the Savior. The community which Christ creates by his death challenges the world to believe, to act justly, to speak respectfully to one another of serious things, to transform its systems of relations, to take Christ's commandments as the basis of its life.

The Dimensions of Our Mission

39/   14.   We reaffirm what is said in Decree 4 of GC 32: "The service of faith and the promotion of justice cannot be for us simply one ministry among others. It must be the integrating factor of all our ministries; and not only of our ministries but also of our inner life as individuals, as communities, and as a worldwide brotherhood."[15] The aim of our mission received from Christ, as presented in the Formula of the Institute, is the service of faith.[16] The integrating principle of our mission is the inseparable link between faith and the promotion of the justice of the Kingdom. In this present congregation we want to deepen and extend, in a more explicit way, the Society's awareness of those integral dimensions of our mission to which Decree 4 drew attention and which are now reaching maturity in our experience and in our present ministries. We have found that whenever our ministries are conducted most fruitfully, these elements are present.

---

[15] GC 32, D 2, n. 9.

[16] "[F]ounded chiefly for this purpose: to strive especially for the defense and propagation of the faith and for the progress of souls in Christian life and doctrine" (Formula [3]).

40/ 15. Decree 4, having made its central affirmation about the inseparability of the service of faith and the promotion of justice, then speaks of "our mission to evangelize," particularly through dialogue with members of other religious traditions and through the engagement with culture which is essential for an effective presentation of the Gospel.[17] Thus the aim of our mission (the service of faith) and its integrating principle (faith directed towards the justice of the Kingdom) are dynamically related to the inculturated proclamation of the Gospel and dialogue with other religious traditions as integral dimensions of evangelization. The integrating principle extends its influence into these dimensions which, like branches growing from the one tree, form a matrix of integral features within our one mission of the service of faith and the promotion of justice.

41/ 16. In our experience since GC 32, we have come to see that our service of faith, directed towards the justice of God's Kingdom, cannot avoid these other dimensions of dialogue and presence within cultures. The proclamation of the Gospel in a particular context ought always to address its cultural, religious, and structural features, not as a message that comes from outside, but as a principle that, from within, "animates, directs and unifies the culture, transforming and remaking it so as to bring about 'a new creation.'"[18]

42/ 17. In our positive approach to religions and cultures, we recognize that all of them—including the "Christian West" throughout its history—have also found ways of being closed to the true freedom offered by God. Justice can truly flourish only when it involves the transformation of culture, since the roots of injustice are embedded in cultural attitudes as well as in economic structures. The dialogue between the Gospel and culture has to take place within the heart of the culture. It should be conducted among people who regard each other with respect, and who look together towards a shared human and social freedom. In this way, too, the Gospel comes to be seen in a new light; its meaning is enriched, renewed, even transformed. Through dialogue the Gospel itself, the Word ever ancient and ever new, enters the minds and hearts of the human family.

43/ 18. There cannot, in short, be an effective proclamation of the Kingdom unless the Gospel, having been brought to the very center of a society, touches its structural, cultural, and religious aspects with its light.

44/ • There is effective dialogue with members of other traditions when there is a shared commitment to a transformation of the cultural and social life within which people live.

---

[17] GC 32, D 4, n. 24.

[18] Pedro Arrupe, Letter to the Whole Society on Inculturation, *AR* 17 (1978): p. 257.

45/ • The transformation of human cultures requires a dialogue with the religions that inspire them and a corresponding engagement with the social conditions that structure them.

46/ • If our faith is directed towards God and his justice in the world, this justice cannot be achieved without, at the same time, attending to the cultural dimensions of social life and the way in which a particular culture defines itself with regard to religious transcendence.

47/ 19. Today we realize clearly:

> No service of faith without
> > promotion of justice
> > entry into cultures
> > openness to other religious experiences

> No promotion of justice without
> > communicating faith
> > transforming cultures
> > collaboration with other traditions

> No inculturation without
> > communicating faith with others
> > dialogue with other traditions
> > commitment to justice

> No dialogue without
> > sharing faith with others
> > evaluating cultures
> > concern for justice

48/ 20. In the light of Decree 4 and our present experience, we can now say explicitly that our mission of the service of faith and the promotion of justice must be broadened to include, as integral dimensions, proclamation of the Gospel, dialogue, and the evangelization of culture. They belong together within our service of faith—they are "without confusion, without separation"—because they arise out of an obedient attentiveness to what the Risen Christ is doing as he leads the world to the fullness of God's Kingdom. These dimensions within our unified mission develop the insights offered by our most recent congregations and the Society's apostolic experience in many parts of the world. Here, there is a profound, and Spirit-inspired, instance of *sentire cum ecclesia in missione*, appropriate to the ways in which our charism enriches the Church's evangelizing mission.

49/ 21. In the light of these reflections, we can now say of our contemporary mission that the faith that does justice is, inseparably, the faith that engages other traditions in dialogue, and the faith that evangelizes culture

DECREE 3

Our Mission and Justice

50/ 1. In response to the Second Vatican Council, we, the Society of Jesus, set out on a journey of faith as we committed ourselves to the promotion of justice as an integral part of our mission. That commitment was a wonderful gift of God to us, for it put us into such good company—the Lord's surely, but also that of so many friends of his among the poor and those committed to justice. As fellow pilgrims with them towards the Kingdom, we have often been touched by their faith, renewed by their hope, transformed by their love. As servants of Christ's mission, we have been greatly enriched by opening our hearts and our very lives to "the joys and the hopes, the griefs and the anxieties of the men and women of this age, especially those who are poor or in any way afflicted."[1]

51/ 2. And we have done so in many ways. The promotion of justice has been integrated into traditional ministries and new ones, in pastoral work and social centers, in educating "men and women for others," in direct ministry with the poor. We also acknowledge our failures on the journey. The promotion of justice has sometimes been separated from its wellspring of faith. Dogmatism or ideology sometimes led us to treat each other more as adversaries than as companions. We can be timid in challenging ourselves and our institutional apostolates with the fullness of our mission of faith seeking justice.

52/ 3. Therefore we want to renew our commitment to the promotion of justice as an integral part of our mission, as this has been extensively developed in General Congregations 32 and 33. Our experience has shown us that our promotion of justice both flows from faith and brings us back to an ever deeper faith. So we intend to journey on towards ever fuller integration of the promotion of justice into our lives of faith, in the company of the poor and many others who live and work for the coming of God's Kingdom.

53/ 4. For the vision of justice which guides us is intimately linked with our faith. It is deeply rooted in the Scriptures, Church tradition, and our Ignatian heritage. It transcends notions of justice derived from ideology, philosophy, or particular political movements, which can never be an adequate expression of the justice of the Kingdom for which we are called to struggle at the side of our Companion and King.[2]

---

[1] Vatican Council II, *Gaudium et Spes*, n. 1. Cf. GC 33, D 1, n. 41.

[2] Cf. John Paul II, Encyclical letter *Centesimus Annus*, n. 25.

New Dimensions of Justice

54/ 5. The struggle for justice has a progressive and gradually unfolding historic character, as it confronts the changing needs of specific peoples, cultures, and times. Previous congregations have called attention to the need to work for structural changes in the socioeconomic and political orders as an important dimension of the promotion of justice.[3] They also urged working for peace and reconciliation through nonviolence; working to end discrimination against people based on race, religion, gender, ethnic background, or social class; working to counter growing poverty and hunger while material prosperity becomes ever more concentrated.[4] Each of us may focus our efforts in only one or other of these dimensions, but all of them are of continuing importance in the Society's overall mission of the promotion of justice.

55/ 6. More recently we have become increasingly aware of other dimensions of this struggle for justice.[5] Respect for the dignity of the human person created in the image of God underlies the growing international consciousness of the full range of *human rights*. These include economic and social rights to the basic necessities of life and well-being; personal rights such as freedom of conscience and expression and the right to practice and share one's faith; civil and political rights to participate fully and freely in the processes of society; and rights such as development, peace, and a healthy environment. Since persons and communities are intertwined, there are important analogies between the rights of persons and what are sometimes called the "rights of peoples," such as cultural integrity and preservation, and control of their own destiny and resources.[6] The Society, as an international apostolic body, must work with communities of solidarity in supporting these rights.[7]

56/ 7. In our times there is a growing consciousness of the *interdependence* of all peoples in one common heritage. The globalization of the world economy and society proceeds at a rapid pace, fed by developments in technology, communicaion, and business. While this phenomenon can produce many benefits, it can also result in injustices on a massive scale: economic adjustment programs and market forces unfettered by concern for their social impact, especially on the poor; the homogeneous "modernization" of cultures in ways that destroy traditional cultures and values; a growing inequality among nations and—within nations—between rich and poor, between the powerful and the marginalized. In

---

[3] Cf. GC 32, D 4, nn. 20, 40; GC 33, D 1, nn. 32, 46.

[4] Cf. GC 32, D 4, n. 20; GC 33, D 1, nn. 45f.

[5] Cf. John Paul II, Encyclical letter *Sollicitudo Rei Socialis,* n. 26.

[6] Cf. John Paul II, Encyclical letters *Redemptor Hominis,* n. 14; *Sollicitudo Rei Socialis,* n. 29.

[7] Cf. number 10, below.

justice, we must counter this by working to build up a world order of genuine solidarity, where all can have a rightful place at the banquet of the Kingdom.[8]

57/ 8. *Human life*, a gift of God, has to be respected from its beginning to its natural end. Yet we are increasingly being faced with a "culture of death" which encourages abortion, suicide, and euthanasia; war, terrorism, violence, and capital punishment as ways of resolving issues; the consumption of drugs; turning away from the human drama of hunger, AIDS, and poverty. We need to encourage a "culture of life." Measures to do this would include the promotion of realistic and morally acceptable alternatives to abortion and euthanasia; the careful development of the ethical context for medical experimentation and genetic engineering; working to divert resources from war and the international traffic in arms towards providing for the needs of the poor; creating possibilities for lives of meaning and commitment instead of anomie and despair.

58/ 9. Preserving the integrity of creation underlies growing concern for the *environment*.[9] Ecological equilibrium and a sustainable, equitable use of the world's resources are important elements of justice towards all the communities in our present "global village"; they are also matters of justice towards future generations who will inherit whatever we leave them. Unscrupulous exploitation of natural resources and the environment degrades the quality of life; it destroys cultures and sinks the poor in misery. We need to promote attitudes and policies which will create responsible relationships to the environment of our shared world, of which we are only the stewards.

59/ 10. Our experience in recent decades has demonstrated that social change does not consist only in the transformation of economic and political structures, for these structures are themselves rooted in sociocultural values and attitudes. Full human liberation, for the poor and for us all, lies in the development of *communities of solidarity* at the grass-roots and nongovernmental as well as the political level, where we can all work together towards total human development.[10] And all of this must be done in the context of a sustainable, respectful interrelation between diverse peoples, cultures, the environment, and the living God in our midst.

Urgent Situations

60/ 11. As a congregation gathered from all over the world, we have become aware of critical situations affecting hundreds of millions of people which call for

---

[8] "But when you give a banquet, invite the poor, the crippled, the lame, and the blind" (Luke 14:13; cf. Luke 16:19-31). Cf. John Paul II, Encyclical letter *Sollicitudo Rei Socialis,* n. 33.

[9] Cf. John Paul II, Encyclical letter *Centesimus Annus,* n. 37.

[10] Cf. John Paul II, Encyclical letters *Sollicitudo Rei Socialis,* nn. 27 ff.; *Centesimus Annus,* n. 49.

special concern in the Society. We do not mean to present an exhaustive list or to divert our efforts from unjust situations closer to each one of us. But the following are especially relevant to the Society as an international apostolic body and cry out for our urgent attention.

61/   12.   The *marginalization of Africa* in the "new world order" renders an entire continent paradigmatic of all the marginalized of the world. Thirty of the world's poorest countries are African. Two thirds of the world's refugees are African. Slavery, colonial and neocolonial subjugation, internal problems of ethnic rivalry and corruption have all created an "ocean of misfortunes" there. Yet there is also much life and great courage in the African people as they struggle together to build a future for those who will come after them. The general congregation asks the universal Society to do whatever it can to change international attitudes and behavior towards Africa.

62/   13.   The recent collapse of totalitarian systems in *Eastern Europe* has left behind devastation in all areas of human and social life. The people there are grappling with the difficult task of reconstructing a social order through which all can live in authentic community, working for the common good, responsible for their own destinies. In years past, many people, including Jesuits, gave magnificent witness to solidarity, fidelity, and resistance. Now they need the cooperation and familial assistance of the international community in their struggle for a secure and peaceful future. The Society must do everything possible to stand by them.

63/   14.   *Indigenous peoples* in many parts of the world, isolated and relegated to marginal social roles, see their identity, cultural legacy, and natural world threatened. Other social groups—an example would be the *Dalits*, considered "untouchables" in some parts of South Asia—suffer severe social discrimination in civil and even ecclesial society. The general congregation calls on the whole Society to renew its long-standing commitment to such peoples.

64/   15.   In many parts of the world, even in the most developed countries, economic and social forces are *excluding* millions of people from the benefits of society. The long-term unemployed, young people without any possibility of employment, exploited and abandoned children of the streets, the aged who live alone without social protection, ex-convicts, victims of drug abuse and those afflicted with AIDS—all these are condemned to lives of dire poverty, social marginalization and precarious cultural existence. They require of us the attention which our biblical tradition demands for "the orphans, widows, and strangers in your midst."

65/   16.   There are over forty-five million *refugees and displaced persons* in today's world, 80 percent of whom are women and children. Often lodged in the poorest of countries, they face growing impoverishment, loss of a sense of life and culture, with consequent hopelessness and despair. The Jesuit Refugee Service accompanies many of these brothers and sisters of ours, serving them as companions, advocating their cause in an uncaring world. The general congregation appeals to all provinces to support the Jesuit Refugee Service in every way possible. And we call on the international Society to join efforts with other international institutions and organizations to combat the injustices which uproot peoples from their land and families.

Implementation

66/ 17. The promotion of justice requires, before all else, our own continuing personal conversion—finding Jesus Christ in the brokenness of our world, living in solidarity with the poor and outcast, so that we can take up their cause under the standard of the Cross. Our sensitivity for such a mission will be most affected by frequent direct contact with these "friends of the Lord," from whom we can often learn about faith. Some insertion into the world of the poor should therefore be part of the life of every Jesuit. And our communities should be located among ordinary people wherever possible.

67/ 18. During their formation, young Jesuits should be in contact with the poor, not just occasionally, but in a more sustained manner. These experiences must be accompanied by careful reflection as part of the academic and spiritual formation and should be integrated into training in sociocultural analysis. Living contact with other cultures and a style of life in which "at times they feel some effects of poverty" will help them grow in solidarity with the poor and with the "other" in our richly diverse world.[11] Continuing formation of older Jesuits should also foster such experiences of different social and cultural realities.

68/ 19. In each of our different apostolates, we must create communities of solidarity in seeking justice. Working together with our colleagues, every Jesuit in his ministry can and should promote justice in one or more of the following ways: *(a)* direct service and accompaniment of the poor, *(b)* developing awareness of the demands of justice joined to the social responsibility to achieve it, *(c)* participating in social mobilization for the creation of a more just social order.

69/ 20. Forming "men and women for others" is appropriate not only in our educational institutions but in ministries of the Word and the Spiritual Exercises, in pastoral apostolates and communication. Social centers and direct social action for and with the poor will be more effective in promoting justice to the extent that they integrate faith into all dimensions of their work. Thus each Jesuit ministry should work to deepen its particular implementation of our full mission of faith and justice, which cannot but be enriched by efforts towards a more effective dialogue and inculturation.

70/ 21. Jesuit institutions can use the following means to help in implementing our mission: institutional evaluation of the role they play in society, examination of whether the institution's own internal structures and policies reflect

---

[11] *Const.* [287].

our mission, collaboration and exchange with similar institutions in diverse social and cultural contexts, continuing formation of personnel regarding mission.

71/ 22. Each province should evaluate its apostolic planning using the Ignatian criteria found in the Constitutions, read in the light of our mission today.[12] When understood in the light of the faith which seeks justice, the criterion of "greater need" points towards places or situations of serious injustice; the criterion of "more fruitful," towards ministry which can be more effective in creating communities of solidarity; the criterion of "more universal," towards action which contributes to structural change to create a society more based on shared responsibility. After decisions are made, it is of crucial importance to evaluate the process of implementation. Annual review of the accomplishment of objectives during the year can help determine objectives for the coming year. Serious and regular review of effectiveness in carrying out our mission will give credibility and realism to our province and institutional planning.

72/ 23. At the interprovincial and international levels, the Society must continue to find ways to collaborate with other national and international groups or organizations, both nongovernmental and official, for a part of our responsibility as an international apostolic body is to work with others at the regional and global level for a more just international order. The Society must therefore examine its resources and try to assist in the formation of an effective international network so that, also at this level, our mission can be carried out.

73/ 24. Above all, we need to continue with great hope on our journey towards the Kingdom. As "servants of Christ's Mission," we base our hope ultimately in Jesus Christ, crucified and risen, to preserve, direct, and carry us forward in our service of faith and promotion of justice.[13] And we can thus keep seeking justice insistently.

> The Society continues to insist on the promotion of justice. Why? Because it corresponds to our very spirituality. . . . The promotion of justice signifies a call for the Society to insert ourselves even more profoundly in the concrete lives of peoples and nations—as they actually are and not as we think they ought to be.[14]

74/ Thus our pilgrimage will lead us again to sharing more and more deeply in the joys and the hopes, the griefs and the anxieties of all God's people

---

[12] Cf. *Const.* [622f.].

[13] *Const.* [134], [812].

[14] Peter-Hans Kolvenbach, "Our Mission Today and Tomorrow," op. cit., p. 49.

DECREE 4

OUR MISSION AND CULTURE

75/ 1. General Congregation 34 has brought together Jesuits from the cultures of Asia, the former Communist countries of Eastern Europe, the European Community, Africa, North America, Australia, and Latin America; this composition has heightened our awareness of the diversity of cultures in both the world and the Society, and of the need to address the importance for our mission of the *Gospel and culture*.[1]

76/ 2. In recent years, the Church has made this theme one of its central points of reflection. Pope Paul VI wrote that "the split between the Gospel and culture is without a doubt *the tragedy of our time*."[2] More recently, Pope John Paul II has presented inculturation as one of the fundamental aspects of the Church's total evangelizing mission, and points to the *mutuality* between the Gospel and the cultures it engages. The Christian message is to be open to all cultures, bound to no single culture and made accessible to every human person through a process of inculturation, by which the Gospel introduces something new into the culture and the culture brings something new to the richness of the Gospel:

> Through inculturation the Church makes the Gospel incarnate in different cultures and at the same time introduces people, together with their cultures, into her own community. She transmits to them her own values, at the same time taking the good elements that already exist in them and renewing them from within.[3]

77/ 3. The process of inculturating the Gospel of Jesus Christ within human culture is a form of *incarnation* of the Word of God in all the diversity of human experience, in which the Word of God comes to take up a dwelling place in the human family (cf. John 1:14). When the Word of God becomes embedded in the heart of a culture, it is like a buried seed which draws its nourishment from the earth around it and grows to maturity. Inculturation can also be related to the *Paschal Mystery*: cultures, under the impact of the liberating power of the Gospel, rid themselves of their negative features and enter the freedom of God's Kingdom. The Gospel brings a prophetic challenge to every culture to remove all

---

[1] "Culture" means the way in which a group of people live, think, feel, organize themselves, celebrate, and share life. In every culture, there are underlying systems of values, meanings, and views of the world, which are expressed, visibly, in language, gestures, symbols, rituals, and styles.

[2] Paul VI, Apostolic exhortation *Evangelii Nuntiandi*, n. 20.

[3] John Paul II, Encyclical letter *Redemptoris Missio*, n. 52.

those things which inhibit the justice of the Kingdom. Inculturating the Gospel means allowing the Word of God to exercise a power within the lives of the people, without at the same time imposing alien cultural factors which would make it difficult for them truly to receive that Word. "Evangelization is not possible without inculturation. Inculturation is the existential dialogue between a living people and the living Gospel."[4]

78/ 4. This process has always been a part of the life of the Church: in the early Christian centuries, the Church, while proclaiming its faith in ways that a Hellenistic culture could receive, was at the same time shaped by that culture. Insights which first originated outside the Jewish and Christian context came to find a place within the very heart of Christianity. A similar process is going on today in many parts of the world, as representatives of indigenous cultures, the great religious traditions, and critical modernity bring insights which the Church must consider as part of the dialogue between Christian experience and the diversity of other experiences. In this way, the Church is recovering, in our times, the creativity shown in the early centuries and in the best of its evangelizing work.

79/ 5. Particular challenges must be faced today in order to enable an existential dialogue of this kind to take place amid the wide variety of cultures in which the Church is present:

80/ 5, 1. Contemporary secular culture, which has developed partly in opposition to the Church, often excludes religious faith from among its accepted values. Consequently, some cultures which were once shaped by Christian faith have, in differing degrees, turned away from Christianity towards a form of life in which the values of the Gospel are marginal. Religious belief is often dismissed as a disruptive source of social divisions which the human family has outgrown; in the eyes of many of our contemporaries, the Church has no credibility as a commentator on human affairs.

81/ 5, 2. The great cultures of Asia, in spite of centuries of missionary activity, still do not regard Christian faith as a living presence at the heart of the Asian experience. In general, it is inseparably linked with a Western culture which they distrust. Many committed Christians in Asia feel a split between their Asian cultural experience and the still-Western character of what they experience in the Church.

82/ 5, 3. All over the world, the increasing pace of urbanization leads to impoverished millions in the great cities. These people are struggling with an agonizing cultural transition as they emigrate from rural areas and are forced to leave behind their traditional cultures. At the same time, this transition is producing

---

[4] Peter-Hans Kolvenbach, "Living People, Living Gospel," Address to the International Workshop on Native Ministry, Anishinabe, Canada, 12 October 1993.

a new cultural synthesis in which elements of traditional wisdom are woven into new forms of popular organization and celebration.

83/   5, 4.   Among indigenous people there has been a resurgence of consciousness of their distinctive cultures, and they must be supported with the liberating power of the Gospel.

84/   5, 5.   In Africa, there is a great desire to create a truly African Christianity, in which the Church and African cultures form an inseparable union. There is also a desire to free the Gospel from a colonial legacy which undervalued the quality of indigenous African cultural values, and to bring it into a more profound contact with African life.

Jesuit Mission and Culture

85/   6.   As Jesuits we live a faith directed towards the Kingdom, through which justice becomes a shaping reality in the world; we therefore bring the particular quality of that faith into dialogue with members of the religions and cultures of our contemporary world. We have said in the decree "Servants of Christ's Mission" that "our mission of the service of faith and the promotion of justice must be broadened to include, as integral dimensions, proclamation of the Gospel, dialogue, and the evangelization of culture"; we have insisted on the inseparability of *justice, dialogue, and the evangelization of culture.*[5]

86/   7.   This is not just a pragmatic apostolic strategy; it is rooted in the mysticism flowing from the experience of Ignatius, which directs us simultaneously towards the mystery of God and the activity of God in his creation. Both in our personal lives of faith and in our ministries, it is never a question of choosing either God *or* the world; rather, it is always God *in* the world, laboring to bring it to perfection so that the world comes, finally, to be fully *in* God:[6]

> Ignatius proclaims that for human beings there is no authentic search for God without an insertion into the life of the creation, and that, on the other hand, all solidarity with human beings and every engagement with the created world cannot be authentic without a discovery of God.[7]

87/   8.   The mission of the Society, in service to the Crucified and Risen Christ, is directed to the ways in which he makes his presence felt in the diversity of human cultural experiences, in order that we may present the Gospel as Christ's explicitly liberating presence. Ours must be a dialogue, born of respect for people, especially the poor, in which we share their cultural and spiritual val-

---

[5] GC 34, D 2, n. 20.

[6] *SpEx* [235–37].

[7] Peter-Hans Kolvenbach, Discourse to General Congregation 34, 6 January 1995; see pp. 676–683 below.

ues and offer our own cultural and spiritual treasures, in order to build up a communion of peoples instructed by God's Word and enlivened by the Spirit as at Pentecost. Our service of the Christian faith must never disrupt the best impulses of the culture in which we work, nor can it be an alien imposition from outside. It is directed towards working in such a way that the line of development springing from the heart of a culture leads it to the Kingdom.

88/ 9. In the exercise of our mission, we bring a simple criterion from our Ignatian tradition: in our personal lives of faith, we learn that we are in *consolation* when we are fully in touch with what God is doing in our hearts, and we are in *desolation* when our lives are in conflict with his action. So, too, our ministry of evangelizing culture will be a ministry of consolation when it is guided by ways that bring to light the character of God's activity in those cultures and that strengthen our sense of the divine mystery. But our efforts will be misguided, and even destructive, when our activity runs contrary to the grain of his presence in the cultures which the Church addresses, or when we claim to exercise sole proprietorial rights over the affairs of God.

89/ 10. This intuition is what has led Jesuits to adopt such a positive approach to the religions and cultures in which they work. The early Jesuits, in their schools, linked Christian catechesis to an education in classical humanism, art, and theater, in order to make their students versed both in faith and in European culture. It is also what prompted Jesuits outside Europe to express a profound respect for indigenous cultures and to compose dictionaries and grammars of local languages, and pioneering studies of the people among whom they worked and whom they tried to understand.

90/ 11. Particularly at the present time, when the sensitive quality of so many indigenous cultures is threatened by powerful, but less benign, pressures, we want to recover a reverence for culture as exemplified by the best of our predecessors. Throughout the world, Jesuits are working with great numbers of ethnic groups, tribes, and countries with traditional cultures. Theirs is a wonderful patrimony of culture, religion, and ancient wisdom that has molded their peoples' identities. These peoples are now struggling to affirm their cultural identity by incorporating elements of modern and global culture. We must do what we can to keep this relation between traditional cultures and modernity from becoming an imposition and try to make it a genuine intercultural dialogue. This would be a sign of liberation for both sides. Our intuition is that the Gospel resonates with what is good in each culture.

91/ 12. At the same time, we acknowledge that we have not always followed this intuition. We have not always recognized that aggression and coercion have no place in the preaching of the Gospel of freedom, especially in cultures which are vulnerable to manipulation by more powerful forces. In particular, we recognize that

92/   • we have often contributed to the alienation of the very people we wanted to serve;

93/   • Jesuit evangelizers have often failed to insert themselves into the heart of a culture, but instead have remained a foreign presence;

94/   • in our mission, we have failed to discover the treasures of humanity: the values, depth, and transcendence of other cultures, which manifest the action of the Spirit;

95/   • we have sometimes sided with the "high culture" of the elite in a particular setting: disregarding the cultures of the poor and sometimes, by our passivity, allowing indigenous cultures or communities to be destroyed.

96/   We acknowledge these mistakes and now seek to profit from the cultural diversity and complexity within the apostolic body of the Society today. We realize that the process of inculturation is difficult yet progressive.

97/   13. As the greater part of our men work within their own cultures, they will, in the service of faith, enter into dialogue with their own cultural world, witness to the creative and prophetic Spirit, and thus enable the Gospel to enrich these various cultures—and, in turn, be enriched by its inculturated presence in different contexts. We try to understand the reality of people's experience, because only then can the proclamation of the Gospel relate to their lives. We bring the Gospel into an open dialogue with the positive and negative elements that these cultures present. In this way, the Gospel comes to be seen in a new light: its meaning is enriched, renewed, even transformed by what these cultures bring to it. Father Pedro Arrupe drew attention to the importance of inculturation for the contemporary Jesuit mission:

> Inculturation is the incarnation of Christian life and of the Christian message in a particular cultural context, in such a way that this experience not only finds expression through elements proper to the culture in question, but becomes a principle that animates, directs and unifies the culture, transforming it and remaking it so as to bring about a "new creation."[8]

God's Dialogue with the World

98/   14. The Gospel, God's prophetic word, continues the dialogue which God has begun with all men and women, who already share in *the mystery of uni-*

---

[8] Pedro Arrupe, Letter to the Whole Society on Inculturation, *AR* 17 (1978): p. 230.

ty begun in creation.[9] It brings them explicitly into contact with his *mystery of salvation.* God opens their hearts to the *mystery of fullness,* "through the invisible action of the Spirit of Christ," which awaits the human family as its destiny.[10]

99/ 15. As disciples of the Risen Lord, we believe that his Paschal Mystery radiates throughout the whole of human history, touching every religion, every culture, and every person, including those who do not know him and those who, in conscience, cannot bring themselves to have faith in him. The centrality of the Paschal Mystery, *Gaudium et Spes* declares,

> applies not only to Christians but to all people of good will in whose hearts grace is secretly at work. Since Christ died for everyone, and since the ultimate calling of each of us comes from God and is therefore a universal one, we are obliged to hold that the Holy Spirit offers everyone the possibility of sharing in this Paschal Mystery in a manner known to God.[11]

100/ 16. How everyone shares in the Paschal Mystery is known to God; that they share in it is what the Church is led by God to believe. It is the Risen Christ who is constantly active in all dimensions of the world's growth, in its diversity of cultures and its varied spiritual experience. As there is a unified goodness in God's work of creation, so in Christ's redemptive work, the fragmentation caused by sin is being healed by a single thread of grace throughout the restored creation.

101/ 17. One way of serving God's mystery of salvation is through dialogue, a spiritual conversation of equal partners, that opens human beings to the core of their identity. In such a dialogue, we come into contact with the activity of God in the lives of other men and women, and deepen our sense of this divine action: "By dialogue, we let God be present in our midst; for as we open ourselves in dialogue to one another, we also open ourselves to God."[12] We try to enable people to become aware of God's presence in their culture and to help them evangelize others in their turn. The ministry of dialogue is conducted with a sense that God's action is antecedent to ours. We do not plant the seed of his presence, for he has already done that in the culture; he is already bringing it to fruitfulness, embracing all the diversity of creation, and our role is to cooperate with this divine activity.

102/ 18. The work of God in the diversity of human history is seen in the long process of enlightened human growth—still incomplete!—as expressed in reli-

---

[9] John Paul II, *Address on the Day of World Prayer at Assisi,* 27 October 1986, *AAS* 79 (1987): pp. 865-71.

[10] Pontifical Council for Interreligious Dialogue and Congregation for the Evangelization of Peoples, *Dialogue and Proclamation: Reflections and Orientations on Interreligious Dialogue and the Proclamation of the Gospel of Jesus Christ* (1991), n. 29.

[11] Vatican Council II, *Gaudium et Spes,* n. 22.

[12] John Paul II, "Address to the Leaders of Non-Christian Religions" (Madras, 5 February 1986), *AAS* 78 (1986): pp. 769 ff.

gious, social, moral, and cultural forms which bear the mark of the silent work of the Spirit. In the conceptions of the mind, in the habits of the heart, in the root metaphors and values of all cultures—even, we might say, in the very process by which our physical bodies become capable of intense spiritual experience—God is preparing the conditions in his creatures for the loving acknowledgement of his truth, making them ready for the transformation promised in Christ. "All are called to a common destiny, the fullness of life in God."[13]

Our Mission and Critical Postmodern Culture

103/ 19. This is true even of those cultures where there is a difficult dialogue with men and women who think they have gone beyond Christianity or any religious commitment. We need to pay particular attention to them because of their influence throughout the world. Some cultures today are inclined so to restrict religious faith to the realm of the private and the personal, even regarding it as a strange eccentricity, that it is difficult for the Gospel to "animate, direct, and unify" contemporary secular culture.[14] We recognize that many of our contemporaries judge that neither Christian faith nor any religious belief is good for humanity.

104/ 20. The problems of working in these contexts need no elaboration here, because the boundary line between the Gospel and the modern and postmodern culture passes through the heart of each of us. Each Jesuit encounters the impulse to unbelief first of all in himself; it is only when we deal with that dimension in ourselves that we can speak to others of the reality of God. In addition, we cannot speak to others if the religious language we use is completely foreign to them: the theology we use in our ministry cannot ignore the vista of modern critical questions within which we too live. Only when we make sense of our own experience and understanding of God can we say things which make sense to contemporary agnosticism.

105/ 21. This is a ministry which should not ignore the Christian mystical tradition that repeatedly treats of the wordless and imageless experience of God which surpasses human concepts: "Si comprehendis, non est Deus," said Augustine.[15] The experience of a silence surrounding the nature of God may be the starting point for many of our contemporaries, but it is also found within the depths of Christian experience and faith. There is a fragmentation of Christian faith in God in postmodern culture, in which human spirituality becomes detached from an explicitly religious expression. People's spiritual lives have not died; they

---

[13] Dialogue and Proclamation, op. cit., n. 27.

[14] Pedro Arrupe, Letter to the Whole Society on Inculturation, *AR* 17 (1978): 256-81.

[15] St. Augustine, *Sermo* 117, *PL* 38, 663.

are simply taking place outside the Church. "Post-Christian culture" witnesses, strangely and implicitly, to a reverence for the God who cannot be imaged by human beings without destroying the divine mystery: this is related to what Christians mean by "the Father." It also tries to find meaning within the very structure of human, embodied experience: this is related to the Christian belief that the "meaning" of the world (the "Logos") is made known to us in the humanity of Jesus. And there is a deep desire, expressed through a concern for the environment, to revere the natural order as a place where there is an immanent, but transcendent presence: this connects with what Christians call the "Spirit."

106/ 22. The aim of an inculturated evangelization in post-Christian contexts is not to secularize or dilute the Gospel by accommodating it to the horizon of modernity, but to introduce the possibility and reality of God through practical witness and dialogue. We have to recognize that today humanity can find many answers in science which earlier generations could derive only from religion. In a predominantly secular context, our faith and our understanding of faith are often freed from contingent cultural complications and, as a result, purified and deepened.

107/ 23. A genuine attempt to work from within the shared experience of Christians and unbelievers in a secular and critical culture, built upon respect and friendship, is the only successful starting point. Our ministry towards atheists and agnostics will either be a meeting of equal partners in dialogue, addressing common questions, or it will be hollow. This dialogue will be based upon a sharing of life, a shared commitment to action for human development and liberation, a sharing of values and a sharing of human experience.[16] Through dialogue, modern and postmodern cultures may be challenged to become more open to approaches and experiences which, though rooted in human history, are new to them. At the same time theology, when developed with an eye to contemporary critical culture, may help people discover the limits of immanence and the human necessity of transcendence.

108/ 24. We need to recognize that the Gospel of Christ will always provoke resistance; it challenges men and women and requires of them a conversion of mind, heart, and behavior. It is not difficult to see that a modernist, scientific-technological culture, too often one-sidedly rationalistic and secular in tone, can be destructive of human and spiritual values. As Ignatius makes clear in the Meditation on Two Standards, the call of Christ is always radically opposed to values which refuse spiritual transcendence and promote a pattern of selfish life. Sin is social in its expression, as is the counterwitness offered by grace: unless a Christian life distinctly differs from the values of secular modernity, it will have nothing special to offer. One of the most important contributions we can make to crit-

---

[16] Dialogue and Proclamation, op. cit., n. 42.

ical contemporary culture is to show that the structural injustice in the world is rooted in value systems promoted by a powerful modern culture which is becoming global in its impact.

Change and Hope

109/ 25. It is part of our Jesuit tradition to be involved in the transformation of every human culture, as human beings begin to reshape their patterns of social relations, their cultural inheritance, their intellectual projects, their critical perspectives on religion, truth, and morality, their whole scientific and technological understanding of themselves and the world in which they live. We commit ourselves to accompany people, in different contexts, as they and their culture make difficult transitions. We commit ourselves to develop the dimension of an inculturated evangelization within our mission of the service of faith and the promotion of justice.

110/ 26. "Ignatius loved the great cities"; they were where this transformation of the human community was taking place, and he wanted Jesuits to be involved in the process. The "city" can be for us the symbol of our current efforts to bring fulfillment to human culture. That the project, in its present form, is seriously flawed no one doubts; that we are more skeptical now than we were even thirty years ago is true; that there have been massive dislocations and inequalities is clear to all; that the totalitarian experiments of this century have been brutal and almost demonic in intensity none will dispute; that it seems sometimes to resemble the Babel and Babylon of the Bible is all too evident. But our aim is the confused but inescapable attempt to cooperate in the creation of that community which, according to the Book of Revelation, God will bring about—and God *will* bring it about—in the form of the holy city, the radiant New Jerusalem: "By its light shall the nations walk; and the kings of the earth shall bring their glory into it, and its gates shall never be shut by day—and there shall be no night there. They shall bring into it the glory and the honor of the nations" (Rev. 21:24-26). Until that day arrives, our vocation is to work generously with the Risen Christ in the all-too-human city where there is poverty of body and spirit, domination and control, manipulation of mind and heart; and to serve the Lord there until he returns to bring to perfection the world in which he died.

Perspectives

111/ 27, 1. We must recognize the complexities of achieving a fully inculturated evangelization within the life of a people; while all our ministries have to be conducted with an awareness of their cultural dimension, the inculturation of the Gospel may be slow simply because cultural changes are slow.

112/ 27, 2. We must recognize that our world is increasingly aware of the rights as well as the diversity of cultures, and that each cultural group is properly asserting the qualities of its heritage. We need to respect these diverse cultures in their self-affirmation and to work along with them creatively.

1ƒ   27, 3.   In every ministry, we must recognize that the salvific work of God's revelation is already present in every culture and that God will bring it to completion.

114/   27, 4.   We must remember that we do not directly "evangelize cultures"; we evangelize people in their culture. Whether we are working in our own culture or in another, as servants of the Gospel we must not impose our own cultural structures, but witness to the creativity of the Spirit which is also at work in others. Ultimately, the people of a culture are the ones who root the Church and the Gospel in their lives.

115/   27, 5.   All of us need to recognize that every large culture contains within it a range of ethnic cultures and new subcultures which are often ignored.

116/   27, 6.   The call to inculturated evangelization is not simply for those working in a land other than their own. All of our works take place in a particular cultural setting with positive and negative features which the Gospel must touch.

117/   27, 7.   We need to listen carefully when people say that the Gospel does not speak to them, and begin to understand the cultural experience behind this statement. Does what we say, and what we do, correspond to the real and urgent needs of the people around us in their relationship to God and to others? If the answer is negative, then perhaps we are not fully engaged in the lives of the people we serve.

Guidelines

118/   28.   To further the Society's ability to promote inculturation, we offer the following guidelines:

119/   28, 1.   Our option for the poor should reach out also to their cultures and values, often based on a rich and fruitful tradition. This will permit a creative and mutual respect within societies, and the promotion of a more fertile cultural and religious atmosphere.

120/   28, 2.   The lifestyle of Jesuit communities should bear credible witness to the countercultural values of the Gospel, so that our service of faith can effectively transform the patterns of local culture.

121/   28, 3.   Our commitment to social justice and ongoing human development must focus on transforming the cultural values which sustain an unjust and oppressive social order.

122/ 28, 4. Each stage of our formation programs should root us in the cultures of the people we serve. They should focus on sharing the life and experience of those people and on trying to understand the culture from within.

123/ 28, 5. There must be an integration of the dynamic of inculturation and the apostolic renewal both of Jesuits and of those who work with us. This is essential for our own conversion of heart and for a rediscovery of the freshness of the Gospel through its dialogue with culture.

124/ 28, 6. An experience of a culture other than our own will help us grow into a vision more open to what is universal and more objective about our own native cultures.

125/ 28, 7. Our educational institutions, in particular, have a crucial role to play in linking Christian faith to the core elements in contemporary and traditional cultures.

126/ 28, 8. We commit ourselves to the creation of genuinely "local churches" which can contribute to the richness of the universal communion of the Church of Christ. We will also look for ways of creating indigenous theology, liturgy, and spirituality, and of promoting the right and freedom of peoples to encounter the Gospel without being alienated from their culture.

127/ 28, 9. As an international apostolic body, the Society is uniquely able to draw upon a range of cultural experience in its ministries and to promote an intercultural dialogue, contributing in this way to the Church's mission, at the service of God's plan to bring together all peoples into the communion of his Kingdom (Eph 1:10; 2 Cr. 5:19).

DECREE 5

Our Mission and Interreligious Dialogue

Introduction

128/ 1. If we imagine ourselves with the Trinity, in the spirit of Ignatius, looking down on the earth as the third millennium of Christianity is about to unfold, what do we see? More than five billion human beings—some male, some female; some rich, many more poor; some yellow, some brown, some black, some white; some at peace, some at war; some Christian (1.95 billion), some Muslim (1 billion), some Hindu (777 million), some Buddhist (341 million), some of new religious movements (128 million), some of indigenous religions (99 million), some Jewish (14 million), some of no religion at all (1.1 billion).[1] What meaning and what opportunity does this rich ethnic, cultural, and religious pluralism that characterizes God's world today have for our lives and for our mission of evangelization? And how do we respond to the racism, cultural prejudice, religious fundamentalism, and intolerance that mark so much of today's world?

129/ 2. General Congregation 34 encourages all Jesuits to move beyond prejudice and bias, be it historical, cultural, social, or theological, in order to cooperate wholeheartedly with all men and women of goodwill in promoting peace, justice, harmony, human rights, and respect for all of God's creation. This is to be done especially through dialogue with those who are inspired by religious commitment, or who share a sense of transcendence that opens them to universal values.

The Church and Interreligious Dialogue

130/ 3. Vatican II has exhorted all Catholics to a dialogue which will "acknowledge, preserve, and promote the spiritual and moral goods found in other religions, and the values in their society and culture" in order to "join hands with them to work towards a world of peace, liberty, social justice, and moral values."[2] The Holy Father has repeatedly asked Jesuits to make interreligious dialogue an

---

[1] *International Bulletin of Missionary Research*, 19, No. 1 (January 1995): p. 25. According to the editor, these statistics are taken from the *World Christian Encyclopedia*, updated and projected using a new demographic analysis provided by researchers at the United Nations. As with all statistics, they must be used with care.

[2] Vatican Council II, *Nostra Aetate* nn. 2, 3.

apostolic priority for the third millennium.[3] In a world where Christians comprise less than 20 percent of the population, it is imperative that we collaborate with others to achieve common goals. In the context of the divisive, exploitative, and conflictual roles that religions, including Christianity, have played in history, dialogue seeks to develop the unifying and liberating potential of all religions, thus showing the relevance of religion for human well-being, justice, and world peace. Above all we need to relate positively to believers of other religions because they are our neighbors; the common elements of our religious heritages and our human concerns force us to establish ever closer ties based on universally accepted ethical values. Dialogue is "an activity with its own guiding principles, requirements, and dignity"[4] and it should "never be made a strategy to elicit conversions."[5] To be religious today is to be interreligious in the sense that a positive relationship with believers of other faiths is a requirement in a world of religious pluralism.

131/ 4. The Society must foster the *fourfold dialogue* recommended by the Church:

> *a.* The *dialogue of life*, where people strive to live in an open and neighborly spirit, sharing their joys and sorrows, their human problems and preoccupations

> *b.* The *dialogue of action*, in which Christians and others collaborate for the integral development and liberation of people

> *c.* The *dialogue of religious experience*, where persons, rooted in their own religious traditions, share their spiritual riches, for instance, with regard to prayer and contemplation, faith and ways of searching for God or the Absolute

> *d.* The *dialogue of theological exchange*, where specialists seek to deepen their understanding of their respective religious heritages, and to appreciate each other's spiritual values[6]

132/ This dialogue of theological exchange can more easily be carried on with religions which have a written tradition. However, the dialogue with indigenous religions is equally important. These religions express a sense of the divine

---

[3] John Paul II, "Ad quosdam Societatis Iesu Sodales," 27 February 1992, *AR* 18 (1982): p. 728; Homily at General Congregation 33, 2 September 1983, *AR* 18 (1983): p. 1093; Allocution to General Congregation 34, 5 January 1995, n. 6; see pp. 666 below.

[4] John Paul II, Encyclical letter *Redemptoris Missio*, n. 56.

[5] Federation of Asian Bishops' Conferences (FABC), published in G. Rosales and C. G. Arévalo, eds., *For All the Peoples of Asia* (New York: Orbis, 1992), p. 167.

[6] Pontifical Council for Interreligious Dialogue and Congregation for the Evangelization of Peoples, *Dialogue and Proclamation: Reflections and Orientations on Interreligious Dialogue and the Proclamation of the Gospel of Jesus Christ* (1991), n. 42.

and the transcendent which must be "approached with great sensitivity, on account of the spiritual and human values enshrined in them."[7] They play an important role in creating ecological harmony and human equality and have developed a great variety of expression and ways of communicating religious experience through devotional practices, ritual, dance, and song, which are a true source of blessings.

The Society and Interreligious Dialogue

133/ 5. Our experience in the service of faith and promotion of justice over the last twenty years has brought many of us into closer contact with believers of other religions. They have helped us to respect the plurality of religions as the human response to God's salvific work in peoples and cultures. We realize that God, who wants all people to be saved, leads believers of all religions to the harmony of the Reign of God in ways known only to him.[8] God's Spirit is in continuous dialogue with them. "Interreligious dialogue at its deepest level is always a dialogue of salvation, because it seeks to discover, clarify, and understand better the signs of the age-long dialogue which God maintains with humanity."[9] An open and sincere interreligious dialogue is our cooperation with God's ongoing dialogue with humanity. "By dialogue we let God be present in our midst, for as we open ourselves to one another, we open ourselves to God."[10] Interreligious dialogue is therefore "a work desired by God," "an integral element of the Church's evangelizing mission," which finds expression in the service of faith and the promotion of justice.[11]

134/ 6. Our *service of faith* takes place today in a world that is becoming increasingly conscious of the plurality of spiritual experiences in diverse religions. Dialogue helps us to recognize that these religions are graced with an authentic experience of the self-communication of the divine Word and of the saving presence of the divine Spirit.[12] In ecclesial communion we experience in Jesus

---

[7] Pontifical Council for Interreligious Dialogue and Congregation for the Evangelization of Peoples, *Dialogue and Proclamation: Reflections and Orientations on Interreligious Dialogue and the Proclamation of the Gospel of Jesus Christ* (1991), n. 14.

[8] Cf. Federation of Asian Bishops' Conferences, Statement of 20 November 1979, in Rosales and Arévalo, op. cit., p. 115.

[9] John Paul II, "Address to the Pontifical Council for Interreligious Dialogue," 13 November 1992. Cf. *Bulletin* of the Council, n. 82 (1993), p. 6.

[10] John Paul II, "Address to the Leaders of non-Christian Religions," Madras, 5 February 1986, *AAS* 78 (1986): p. 769f.

[11] John Paul II, "Address to the Pontifical Secretariat for Non-Christians," 28 April 1987. (Cf. *Bulletin* of the Secretariat no. 66 [1987], p. 224; Dialogue and Proclamation, op. cit., n. 38).

[12] Cf. FABC statement of November 1986, in Rosales and Arévalo, op. cit., p. 259.

Christ the uniquely concrete revelation of the divine Word and the universally significant outpouring of the divine Spirit. With love and conviction we share this experience with our sisters and brothers of other religions, for "we are all pilgrims setting out to find God in human hearts."[13]

135/ 7.   Interreligious dialogue and *proclamation* of the Gospel are not contrary ministries, as if one could replace the other. Both are aspects of the one evangelizing mission of the Church.[14] "These two elements must maintain both their intimate connection and their distinctiveness; therefore they should not be confused, manipulated, or regarded as identical, as though they were interchangeable."[15] Dialogue reaches out to the mystery of God active in others. Proclamation witnesses to and makes known God's mystery as it has been manifested to us in Christ. Our spiritual encounter with believers of other religions helps us to discover deeper dimensions of our Christian faith and wider horizons of God's salvific presence in the world. "Dialogue is a new way of being Church."[16] Through proclamation others encounter the compassionate God in the life, death, and resurrection of Jesus Christ, whose Spirit brings about a new creation in all realms of life. Without in any way relativizing our faith in Jesus Christ or dispensing with a critical evaluation of religious experiences, we are called upon to grasp the deeper truth and meaning of the mystery of Christ in relation to the universal history of God's self-revelation. "It is the same Spirit, who has been active in the incarnation, life, death, and resurrection of Jesus and in the Church, who was active amongst all peoples before the Incarnation and is active amongst the nations, religions, and peoples today."[17]

136/ 8.   Our involvement in the promotion of justice takes place in a world in which the problems of injustice, exploitation, and destruction of the environment have taken on global dimensions. Religions have also been responsible for these sinful elements. Hence our commitment to justice and peace, human rights, and the protection of the environment has to be made in collaboration with believers of other religions. We believe that religions contain a liberating potential

---

[13] Paul VI, "Address at the Eucharistic Congress," Bombay, 12 March 1964, *AAS* 57 (1965): pp. 124-26.

[14] "*Evangelizing mission,* or more simply *evangelization,* refers to the mission of the Church in its totality.... Proclamation ... occupies such an important place in evangelization that it has often become synonymous with it and yet it is only one aspect of evangelization.... Dialogue means all positive and constructive interreligious relations with individuals and communities of other faiths which are directed at mutual understanding and enrichment" (*Dialogue and Proclamation,* op. cit., nn. 8f.).

[15] John Paul II, Encyclical letter *Redemptoris Missio,* n. 55.

[16] Paul VI, Encyclical letter *Ecclesiam Suam,* n. 63.

[17] FABC statement of November 1986, in Rosales and Arévalo, op. cit., p. 259.

which, through interreligious collaboration, could create a more humane world.[18] Through this process the Holy Spirit overcomes the structures of sin and creates anew the face of the world until God will be all in all. Jesus always focused on the human person as the center of religious beliefs and practices. Hence commitment to integral human liberation, especially of the poor, becomes the meeting point of religions. "Christians will join hands with all men and women of goodwill and work together in order to bring about a more just and peaceful society in which the poor will be the first to be served."[19]

Guidelines

137/ 9. Though interreligious dialogue is an integral element of Jesuit mission, the forms of its practice depend on the concrete situations of our life and work. Indigenous religions and the great world religions, the new religious movements and the fundamentalist groups invite us to a dialogue that is proper to the perspective and challenge of each. Hence no universally valid guidelines can be given for the dialogue itself. What is important is that we grow in openness to the divine Spirit to be able to walk with others on a "fraternal journey in which we accompany one another towards the goal which God sets for us."[20] The following guidelines offer an orientation for developing a culture of dialogue in our life and ministry.

138/ 9, 1. Our spirituality should be characterized by a "deep respect for everything that has been brought about in human beings by the Spirit who blows where he wills."[21] Consequently, we must be alert to the global quest for a contemplative experience of the Divine, and compassionate towards the poor who seek justice and freedom. We will seek to be enriched by the spiritual experiences and ethical values, theological perspectives, and symbolic expressions of other religions.

139/ 9, 2. Genuine dialogue with believers of other religions requires that we deepen our own Christian faith and commitment, since real dialogue takes place only between those rooted in their own identity. For this reason, we need a solid foundation in philosophy and theology, with a special focus on the person and mystery of Jesus Christ. GC 34 urges all Jesuits to study carefully the decrees of Vatican II, the papal documents, and the statements of episcopal conferences on the value and necessity of interreligious dialogue.

---

[18] John Paul II, "Address to the Leaders of non-Christian Religions," Madras, 5 February 1986, *AAS* 78 (1986): p. 768.

[19] John Paul II, Message to the People of Asia, Manila, 2 March 1981. See *Bulletin* of the Secretariat for Non-Christians 46 (1981), p. 14.

[20] John Paul II, Allocution at the Day of Prayer for World Peace, Assisi, 27 October 1986, *AAS* 79 (1987): p. 868.

[21] John Paul II, Encyclical letter *Redemptoris Missio*, n. 56.

140/ 9, 3. In our formation a closer acquaintance with the beliefs and practices of other religions must be given through special courses and actual involvement in a pluralistic milieu. Since the core of all true religion consists in its capacity to lead people to an authentic and deeper spiritual experience, it is important that we strengthen in our formation the mystical dimension of Christian faith and Jesuit spirituality in encounter with the spiritual traditions of others.

141/ 9, 4. Our proclamation of the Gospel must be sensitive to the religious and cultural background of those to whom it is addressed, and "attentive to the signs of the times through which the Spirit of God is speaking, teaching, and guiding all men and women."[22]

142/ 9, 5. Theological reflection must dwell on "the significance in God's plan of the different religious traditions and the experiences of those who find in them their spiritual nourishment."[23] It has to explore the meaning of the Christ-event in the context of the spiritual evolution of humanity articulated in the history of religions.

143/ 9, 6. Our commitment to justice demands that we share in the life and the struggles of the poor and work with believers of other religions in creating basic human communities founded on truth and love.[24] In social action we willingly collaborate with them in the prophetic denunciation of the structures of injustice and in the creation of a world of justice, peace, and harmony.

144/ 9, 7. Our *social and cultural centers* will identify and promote the liberating dynamics of the local religions and cultures, and initiate common projects for the building of a just social order.

145/ 9, 8. Our educational institutions will conscientize their students on the value of interreligious collaboration and instill in them a basic understanding of and respect for the faith vision of the members of the diverse local religious communities, while deepening their own faith response to God.

146/ 9, 9. Pastoral service will prepare our Christian communities for dialogue. We must be concerned with people beyond the limits of the Christian community and help them experience God's compassionate love in their lives. "We are all children of God and we must all work together in harmony for the mutual benefit

---

[22] *Dialogue and Proclamation*, op. cit., n. 78.

[23] *Dialogue and Proclamation*, op. cit.,. n. 78.

[24] FABC statement of November 1985, in Rosales and Arévalo, op. cit., p. 254.

of all."[25] The Church is a "community in pilgrimage journeying with peoples of other faiths towards the Kingdom that is to come."[26] In this process she is called to be the voice of the voiceless, in particular of the young, women, and the poor.

147/ 10. Some Jesuits have already been trained for the fourth aspect and are actively engaged in conversations among experts in religious traditions. Their experience has been rewarding and fruitful. Their own faith has been deepened and shared with others, and their respect for the spirituality of other religions has grown. But given the task ahead, their number is inadequate.

148/ 11. GC 34 encourages each assistancy to prepare Jesuits able to become experts in the fourth aspect of interreligious dialogue. Since this dialogue is becoming a global concern, such planning should include interprovincial and international exchange of persons and be done in collaboration with other groups. Jesuits involved in this aspect of interreligious dialogue have a two-directional responsibility: (1) to engage in honest, respectful dialogue with experts in the other religious traditions, and (2) to communicate the fruits of this dialogue to those of the Society engaged in the first three aspects of dialogue, in order to help them understand and appreciate its urgency. Since this is a new and uncharted frontier, there will certainly be misunderstandings and misconceptions. We are once again invited to make ours the presupposition of St. Ignatius: "to be more eager to put a good interpretation on a neighbor's statement than to condemn it."[27]

Concrete Responses

149/ 12. Dialogue with the *Jewish* people holds a unique place. The first covenant, which is theirs and which Jesus the Messiah came to fulfill, "has never been revoked."[28] A shared history both unites us with and divides us from our elder brothers and sisters, the Jewish people, in whom and through whom God continues to act for the salvation of the world. Dialogue with the Jewish people enables us to become more fully aware of our identity as Christians. Since the publication of *Nostra Aetate* in 1965, the Catholic Church has radically renewed the Jewish-Christian dialogue after centuries of polemics and contempt in which our Society shared.[29] To enter into a sincere and respectful relationship with the Jewish people is one aspect of our efforts to "think with and in the Church."

---

[25] Paul VI, "Address to Non-Christians," Rome, 5 March 1967. See *Bulletin* of the Secretariat for Non-Christians 5 (1968): p. 65.

[26] FABC statement of August 1987, in Rosales and Arévalo, op. cit., p. 300.

[27] *SpEx* [22].

[28] John Paul II, Allocution to the Jewish Community, Mainz, 17 November 1980, *AAS* 73 (1981): p. 80. (Cf. Rom. 11:29).

[29] Cf. Vatican Council II, *Nostra Aetate*, n. 4.

150/ 13. The emergence of *Islam* as a religious, political, and economic force is a fact of our world even in Western Christian countries; it has truly become a global religion. Although rivalry, conflict, and even war in previous centuries have made dialogue in recent times more difficult, both the Church and the Society have striven to build bridges of mutual understanding between Christians and Muslims. In Vatican II the Church expressed her esteem for Muslims, recognizing the positive values in Islam and pointing to the close bond Muslims have with the Church.[30] The relations of the Society of Jesus with Muslims go back to St. Ignatius himself, from the time he discerned his vocation at Manresa as the call to go to Jerusalem and remain there among Muslims. The experience of Jesuits who have approached Muslims with preparation, knowledge, and respect has often shown that a fruitful dialogue is indeed possible. However, in some places Jesuits have found it difficult to dialogue with Muslims, especially in states based on Islamic law. In such situations they feel apprehensive about possible violations of religious rights and even of basic human rights. To face such situations, Jesuits need great faith, courage, and the support of the rest of the Society.

151/ 14. *Hindus* in general welcome the Christian initiatives of dialogue. Their threefold way of spiritual growth through ardent devotion, profound meditation, and action for the welfare of all offers an integrated vision and way of life. Their profound philosophical enquiries and mystical perceptions, their noble ethical values, "ashram" heritage, and rich symbolism of popular religious practices—all open broad avenues for fruitful dialogue. In the context of social discrimination and revivalist movements, partly the result of religious ideologies, Jesuit involvement in dialogue between Hindus and Christians becomes a great imperative.

152/ 15. *Buddhism,* in its many forms, is a major religion influencing the lives of millions of people around the world. The Four Noble Truths and the Eightfold Path of the Buddha propose a view of this world based on its essential inadequacy and a way of life which, through the practice of ethical discipline, wisdom, and meditation, leads to a state of inner liberation and spiritual enlightenment. Buddhism calls its followers to a selfless universal compassion for all living creatures; it has a special appeal for contemporary men and women seeking a true, personal spiritual experience. Dialogue with Buddhists enables Christians to join hands with them to face the basic frustration so many feel today and to address together problems of justice, development, and peace; in addition, it invites Christians to rediscover the contemplative riches within their own tradition.

153/ 16. The phenomenon of religious *fundamentalism,* which is found in all religions, including Christianity, poses serious difficulties. A passionate concern to return to the foundations of each religion combined with a reaction to the onslaught of modern secular culture has given great impetus to the growth

---

[30] Vatican Council II, *Nostra Aetate*, n. 3; *Lumen Gentium*. n. 16.

of revivalist movements. The history of oppression of one religion by a more dominant one has produced animosities and prejudices which add fuel to such movements. Often religious feelings and structures are manipulated by political, economic, cultural, or ethnic power groups in order to safeguard their vested interests. All this results in fundamentalist ideologies and movements within religious communities. Our Jesuit responsibility is "to understand why the members of a revivalist movement have taken their particular stance, and to discover in an unprejudiced manner their legitimate intentions and hurt feelings."[31] This can pave the way for dialogue and reconciliation, which would demand from us the willingness to acknowledge our past intolerant attitudes and injustices towards others.[32] Apostolic discernment should be used to determine what can be done in such situations.

Conclusion

154/ 17. As companions of Jesus sent into today's world, a world characterized by religious pluralism, we have a special responsibility to promote interreligious dialogue. The Ignatian vision of reality provides the spiritual inspiration and ministerial grounding for this urgent task. It opens our eyes to the incomprehensible mystery of God's salvific presence *(Deus semper major)* in the world. It makes us sensitive to the sacred space of God's direct dealing with human persons in history. The contemplation of God laboring in all things helps us to discern the divine spirit in religions and cultures. The Kingdom meditation enables us to understand history as God's history with us. The Jesuit heritage of creative response to the call of the Spirit in concrete situations of life is an incentive to develop a culture of dialogue in our approach to believers of other religions. This culture of dialogue should become a distinctive characteristic of our Society, sent into the whole world to labor for the greater glory of God and the help of human persons.

Recommendations to Father General

155/ 18. GC 34 asks Father General to explore the feasibility of setting up a secretariat for interreligious dialogue to promote and coordinate Jesuit initiatives in this area. The secretary could help to ensure that training programs for Jesuits are organized in view of a wider involvement in dialogue. He could publish a bulletin for the exchange of Jesuit experiences and theological reflections in the area of dialogue.

---

[31] FABC statement of 3 November 1988, in Rosales and Arévalo, op. cit., p. 309.

[32] Secretariat for Non-Christians, *Guidelines for a Dialogue between Muslims and Christians* (Ancora Press, 1971), pp. 74-77.

156/ 19. The general congregation asks Father General to explore the possibility of establishing a department for the study of religions at the Gregorian University. This department could offer academic courses on Judaism, Islam, Hinduism, Buddhism, and other religions, as well as on the theology of religions. It could establish academic rapport with other universities and centers for religious studies in various parts of the world.

157/ 20. The general congregation asks Father General to explore the possibility of expanding the scope of the apostolate of the Jesuit community of the Pontifical Biblical Institute in Jerusalem, so that, in dialogue and in concert with other Christian centers in Jerusalem, the Jesuits there might explore programs in interreligious dialogue among Jews, Christians, and Muslims, along with their continuing work of biblical and spiritual renewal of Jesuits from various provinces.

III

ASPECTS OF JESUIT LIFE
FOR MISSION

DECREE 6

The Jesuit Priest: Ministerial Priesthood and Jesuit Identity

Introduction

158/ 1. Dynamic movements in Church and society suggest that we undertake a specific consideration of the priestly dimension of Jesuit life more complete than the last three congregations were able to offer. We present, not an elaborated theology of priesthood, but only a way of considering the priestly dimension of Jesuit identity and mission in the light of our founding inspiration. We have in mind several concrete issues that affect the life of the Society in many parts of the world. Since Vatican II, the Church has undergone many changes which have also been felt within the Society. From different parts of the Society, Jesuits have requested a greater clarity and confidence about the nature of the priestly vocation as this is lived out in a Jesuit context. Younger Jesuits in particular, as they move towards priestly ordination, desire a deeper understanding of this aspect of our vocation.

159/ 2. In many countries, Vatican II has generated a powerful impulse among lay men and women to share more profoundly in the Church's ministries. But it remains important that Jesuits continue to have confidence in the value of the apostolic service that they offer precisely as priests.

160/ 3. Since the council, priests in religious orders have been called to a deeper relationship with diocesan bishops. While recognizing our clear duty to cooperate with bishops in and through the Church for the coming of God's Kingdom, we see a need to express the particular quality of apostolic *religious* priesthood as part of our Jesuit contribution to the Church's reflection and mission.

161/ 4. We are aware of the different experiences of priesthood in our various cultural contexts. Because the Society has never been more culturally diverse than it is today and because a full engagement with human culture has been part of the Society's charism, we wish to recognize these differences, while being at the same time confident of the fundamental common features of Jesuit ministerial priesthood.

162/ 5. Finally, we are conscious that Jesuit priests share a common apostolic calling with Jesuit brothers. Within this foundational union, the qualities of both vocations are an enrichment of the Society's total identity and mission, and we have tried to describe the features of Jesuit ministerial priesthood with full respect for the quality of the brothers' charism.

Our Common Mission

163/ 6. The Epistle to the Hebrews says that Christ is "a merciful and faithful high priest in the service of God" who makes "a sacrifice of atonement for the sins of the people" (2:17). Through their baptism, Christians participate in Christ's priestly work of reconciling the world to God and are called to mediate this reconciliation in their lives. As Jesuit religious, we give a particular expression to this dignity through our consecration and our apostolic mission in the Society: ours is a "ministry of reconciliation" (2 Cor. 5:18) in the service of Christ. We are deeply conscious that the Society of Jesus is made up of priests and brothers: we are a community of "friends in the Lord," sent in mission by Christ, and together we form "a complex apostolic body, wherein each companion shares in and contributes to a single apostolic vocation, respecting the personal call of the Spirit."[1] Each Jesuit enriches the Society's mission and contributes to what St. Paul calls "the priestly service of the Gospel of God" (Rom. 15:16).

Priesthood at the Service of the Church

164/ 7. By their ordination, Jesuit priests also share in the ministerial priesthood by which Christ, through the gifts of the Spirit, unceasingly builds up his Church, guides his people through the pastoral office, and leads them into the Kingdom of his Father.[2] The companions of Jesus who offer themselves to the Church for priestly ministry do so because they discern this as the will of the Lord, which the Church confirms by ordaining and commissioning them for ministerial service in its name. In this way, the Society relates its apostolic charism to the dynamic of the Church's ordained ministry; the Church, in turn, accepts this apostolic service offered by the Society and recognizes what Jesuits bring as an enrichment of the priestly office exercised in the Church.

165/ 8. At the time of its founding and throughout its history, the exercise of ministerial priesthood has been regarded as central to the Society's identity and apostolic mission.[3] For this reason, when he addressed General Congregation 32, Pope Paul VI declared ministerial priesthood to be an "essential character" of the Society:[4] it is directed towards and necessary for the Society's apostolic mission

---

1 Peter-Hans Kolvenbach, Address to the First Congregation of Provincials (26 September 1990) 9, *AR* 20 (1990): p. 494.

2 *Catechism of the Catholic Church*, n. 1547. "Only Christ is the true priest, the others being only his ministers" (Thomas Aquinas, *Heb.* 7.4).

3 *Formula* [6].

4 Paul VI, Allocution to General Congregation 32, 3 December 1974, n. 2; see p. 379 above.

to carry out whatever tasks the Church may ask of it. Jesuit priests receive ordination so that, by this commission, the Society can fully exercise the specifically Jesuit apostolic mission of "serving the Lord alone and the Church, his spouse, under the Roman Pontiff, the Vicar of Christ on earth."[5]

166/ 9. Jesuit priesthood, therefore, is a gift from God for universal mission. By putting themselves directly at the service of the pope, the first Jesuits expressed their readiness to be sent wherever there was hope of the greater glory of God and the help of souls. Ignatius and his first companions, therefore, placed their priestly ministry, not at the service of a bishop's pastoral care for a particular diocese, but at the service of the Sovereign Pontiff for the service of the universal Church. Since the Society conducts its ministries with a constant readiness for new service, the scope of Jesuit priestly service is universal; its aim is apostolic and it is exercised under the pope's universal solicitude for the needs of the Church and the world.

Characteristic Activities

167/ 10. Inspired by Christ, "the first Evangelizer," and by the example of Ignatius and his first companions, Jesuit priestly service is exercised through a wide range of ministries.[6] The apostolic letters of Paul III (1540) and Julius III (1550) approve a whole series of activities proper to Jesuit priests: ministries of the Word and ministries of interiority, ministries of reconciliation and teaching, ministries of sacramental service, teaching catechism to children and the unlettered, ministries of social concern. These characteristic activities of the first companions are the archetypes of Jesuit priestly service as exercised on behalf of the Church's mission, and they continue to inspire the Society today to undertake a program of "integral evangelization" concerned with the good of the whole human person. The Church asks the Society to engage in whatever "will seem expedient for the glory of God and the common good"; this is our "pathway to God."[7]

168/ 11. Since the foundation of the Society, Jesuits have exercised their ministry most particularly where the needs are greatest, where there are not others to minister to these needs, and where the more universal good may be found.[8] Jerome Nadal expressed this central aspect of our charism: "The Society cares for

---

5 *Formula* [3].

6 John Paul II, Allocution to General Congregation 34, 5 January 1995, n. 7; see pp. 663–668 below.

7 *Formula* [3].

8 *Const.* [622].

those persons who are either totally neglected or inadequately attended to. This is the basic reason for the founding of the Society, this is its power, this is what makes it distinctive in the Church."[9]

169/ 12. This spirit continues to shape what Jesuits do as priests: their ministry is particularly directed towards those who have not heard the Gospel, those who are at the margins of the Church or of society, those who have been denied their dignity, those who are voiceless and powerless, those weak in faith or alienated from it, those whose values are undermined by contemporary culture, those whose needs are greater than they can bear.[10] For the Jesuit priest, the world is where he is to be most active, in the name of Christ the healer and reconciler. Pope Paul VI pointed to our presence at the boundaries between human culture and the Gospel:

> Wherever in the Church, even in the most difficult and extreme fields, in the crossroads of ideologies, in the front line of social conflict, there has been and there is confrontation between the deepest desires of the human person and the perennial message of the Gospel, there also there have been, and there are, Jesuits.[11]

Present Tasks

170/ 13. Within the varied contexts in which the Society's contemporary mission is conducted, common tasks are to be found: how to find words that speak to the men and women of our time who are no longer moved by the Christian message, how to be faithful to the tradition of the Church and at the same time interpret it in secularized cultures, how to minister effectively to both the poor and the rich, how to integrate our spiritual ministries with our social ministries, how best to serve in a Church in which there are tensions, how to make evangelical poverty part of our contemporary witness, how to mediate between different cultures and groups within the same country, how to enable the Church to be truly Catholic in the comprehensiveness and cultural variety of its practice and faith; finally, how to enable the world to become, in all aspects of its life, the Kingdom that Christ proclaimed.

171/ 14. A specific challenge today is to embody Christ's ministry of healing and reconciliation in a world increasingly divided by economic and social status, race and ethnicity, violence and war, cultural and religious pluralism. These divisions must be a focus of Jesuit priestly ministry because Christ's work of reconciliation breaks down the walls of division among peoples "in order to create in him-

---

9 Nadal, MHSI, vol 90a, *Orationis Observationes,* "Societas curam habet earum animarum de quibus vel nullus est qui curet vel, si quis curet, is negligenter curat. Haec est ratio institutionis Societatis, haec virtus, haec dignitas in Ecclesia" ([316] [p. 126]).

10 GC 32, D 4, n. 42.

11 Paul VI, Allocution to General Congregation 32, op. cit., n. 2, pp. 663–664 below.

self one new humanity" (cf. Eph. 2:14f.). We live in a broken world where men and women are in need of integral healing, the power for which comes ultimately from God. Therefore, Jesuit priestly mission is directed, inseparably, towards justice for the poor and the reconciliation of the world to God through the preaching of the Gospel.

172/ 15. In the light of our tradition, we can say that no ministry which prepares the way for the Kingdom or which helps to arouse faith in the Gospel is outside the scope of Jesuit priests. In recent years we have come to recognize that "it is for the priest, as sign and minister of the Lord's active presence, to be present in or to collaborate with all human efforts which help in establishing the Kingdom."[12] We have also described the Jesuit mission as engaging "under the standard of the Cross, in the crucial struggle of our time: the struggle for faith and that struggle for justice which it includes."[13] The ways in which this is implemented must always be appropriate to the milieus in which Jesuit ministry is conducted: this will take different forms in different contexts, according to circumstances. Many have asked if this is appropriate for Jesuit priests: do not some activities lie outside the range legitimate for priests? We answer that the Society's commitment to this mission is prompted, neither by a facile optimism about the progress of world history nor by a specific social program, but by a humble desire to share in the work of Christ who reconciled the world to God through his priestly death. Our Jesuit martyrs, who have died for their faith and their people in many parts of the world, show that Jesuits live under the banner of the Cross. And the Cross is the sign that, as followers of Christ, we will be spared nothing: our Jesuit mission is conducted with faith in the Resurrection, since only God resolves the enigmas of suffering and death in this present age.

Drawing on Our Tradition

173/ 16. The way in which Jesuits exercise their ministerial priesthood takes its character from our apostolic mission to labor with Christ in proclaiming the Kingdom.[14] Our first companions envisaged a universal, itinerant ministry of evangelization, teaching, works of charity, and poverty of life: an evangelical *imitatio apostolorum*, a radical pattern of apostolic discipleship, was to be the wellspring for what they did as priests. "It is the primary vocation to be like the apostles which marks henceforth the way of being 'priest' in the Society of Jesus."[15] Under the inspiration of the Spiritual Exercises, they wanted to be like Christ in giving freely of themselves to anyone in need; they wanted to live like him who came not to be served but to serve; they wanted to act like him in preaching to the

---

[12] GC 31, D 23, n. 7.

[13] GC 32, D 2, n. 2.

[14] *SpEx* [95].

[15] Peter-Hans Kolvenbach, op. cit., n. 7, *AR* 20 (1990): p. 493.

crowds; they wanted to share his concern for the needs of the poor and the sick. We recall that the Jesuit theologians at the Council of Trent were instructed by Ignatius to spend part of their time visiting hospitals and instructing small children; their public work of lecturing at the council was to be balanced by acts of mercy which went unnoticed except by the poor who received them.[16]

174/ 17. In the conduct of their ministries, Ignatius wanted Jesuit priests to avoid ways of proceeding which the Spiritual Exercises present as contrary to the Gospel: riches and success, honors and recognition, power, pride, and prestige. He insisted that Jesuit priests should not accept appointment to bishoprics or to other ecclesiastical dignities, offices, and benefices, but should have the poverty and freedom necessary for mission. Ignatius wanted them to ask for the grace to be truly poor in companionship with Christ, to be obedient in their mission, to be held in low esteem if God would be thus served, and to live as "priests of Christ freely poor."[17] Jesuit priests today are to be like them in doing what they judge to be the most urgent and fruitful apostolic tasks, in an apostolic horizon unrestricted by divisions of class or culture, and with no regard for their personal gratification.

175/ 18. Wherever they are, Jesuit priests make their apostolic contribution to the life of the local church, while at the same time being faithful to their charism and keeping their freedom for mission. At any given moment, the Jesuit priest lives in a particular local church, and willingly cooperates with the local bishop in the Church's mission.[18] But he recognizes that, in every local Church, it is the particular charism of the *diocesan* clergy to be the primary agents of the bishop's pastoral care; because he is not a diocesan priest, he recognizes that he exercises his ministry in complementary ways. As such, a Jesuit tries to direct what he does as a priest towards those who are not easily reached by the Church's ordinary ministry.

176/ 19. Just as Jesuit priests form a common apostolic body with brothers, so it is also necessary that they promote and enhance the ecclesial service offered by religious in other communities and by lay men and women who want to share more profoundly in the Church's ministry. The recent growth of lay ministries in the Church, far from being a threat to what is offered by Jesuits in their priestly ministry, corresponds to one of the fundamental charisms of our Ignatian tradition. Through the Spiritual Exercises, Jesuits are particularly concerned with helping others enter more into their baptismal dignity as servants of Christ. Our Jesuit tradition recognizes that God deals with individuals, always to deepen in them

---

16 "To the Fathers Sent to Trent" (1546), MHSI, vol. 22, MI, Series Prima (T. I., Madrid, 1903): pp. 386–89.

17 Peter-Hans Kolvenbach, op. cit. n. 13, *AR* 20 (1990): p. 495.

18 Vatican Council II, *Lumen Gentium*, n. 28.

the life of grace and always through them to strengthen the life of the Church; this is in perfect agreement with the perspective offered by the *Catechism of the Catholic Church* on the character of ministerial priesthood in the Church:

> While the common priesthood of the faithful is exercised by the unfolding of baptismal grace—a life of faith, hope, and charity, a life according to the Spirit— the ministerial priesthood is at the service of the common priesthood. It is directed at the unfolding of the baptismal grace of all Christians. The ministerial priesthood is a *means* by which Christ unceasingly builds up and leads his Church.[19]

177/ 20. From their Ignatian tradition, Jesuits bring to their ministerial priesthood a profound respect for the ways in which God is already at work in the lives of all men and women. God's action does not begin with what we do; already, in the blessings of creation, God has laid the foundation for what he will accomplish through the graces of redemption. Consequently, in the exercise of their ministerial priesthood, Jesuits try to see what God has already done in the lives of individuals, societies, and cultures, and to discern how God will continue that work. By drawing attention to the graced character of all human life, this insight influences the way in which Jesuit ministerial priesthood is exercised in different areas:

178/ 20, 1. It is always aimed at building up the human person in the individual character of each one's life of grace;

179/ 20, 2. It encourages us to become involved in disciplines which, although they may have no explicitly Christian perspective, are nevertheless central to the way in which human beings understand themselves and the world around them;

180/ 20, 3. It makes us take a positive attitude towards dialogue with the range of human cultures and the traditions of religious belief, morality, and spirituality found in our world;

181/ 20, 4. It opens the way to a positive ecumenical commitment, since it values the diversity and mutuality of charisms found in the different Christian traditions.

182/ 20, 5. It directs our attention towards those who, though they are excluded from power and wealth, are already rich in grace.

183/ 21. The ministries of the Word—the ministries named before all others in the Formula of our Institute—have always been of primary importance for Jesuit priestly ministry.[20] These ministries, which take as many forms as our mission demands, require for their effectiveness profound and dedicated study, especially a thorough knowledge of Scripture and tradition, skill in preaching, and a human maturity and cultural breadth. The tradition of learned priestly

---

[19] *Catechism of the Catholic Church*, n. 1547.

[20] *Formula* [1]; cf. Vatican Council II, *Lumen Gentium*, n. 28; *Presbyterorum Ordinis*, n. 2.

ministry and intellectual excellence is deeply embedded in our way of proceeding. In the exercise of Jesuit ministerial priesthood, knowledge is not power but service of the Kingdom.

184/ 22. Christ's own ministry of words and deeds reached its consummation in the saving mystery of his death and resurrection: so Jesuit priests join the many forms of their ministry of the Word to the Church's celebration of the Eucharist, by which Christ draws people into his Paschal Mystery. The Word of God is proclaimed in different ways, so that all may find their place at the Eucharistic and Heavenly Banquet through the mercy of God. "God desires everyone to be saved and to come to the knowledge of the truth" (1 Tim. 2:4): this is the core of the Society's apostolic preaching and the reality which the Church proclaims at the Eucharist. Here the Risen Lord bestows life and enables the Church to become what it is, the body of Christ. Here, too, this least Society of Jesus is constantly re-created by our reception of the Word of Truth and the Bread of Life.

The Stages of Ministry

185/ 23. Each stage in the preparation for and exercise of priestly ministry introduces a new element which modifies and strengthens a man's identity as a Jesuit: he moves, first of all, from the life of a scholastic to accepting the Church's call to ordination. Then, working through the challenges of being a young priest, he will undertake active ministries, eventually passing to the priestly apostolic life exercised in old age. Each of these stages—linked to the natural life cycle—marks, not a diminution, but a deeper entry into the experience of Jesuit priestly life: what begins as a joyful act of trust in the call of the Lord and is then lived out with generous self-giving in ministry reaches its culmination when, in old age and perhaps great weakness, the Jesuit priest fully enters Christ's Paschal Mystery. The way in which this occurs will, of course, differ for each one according to the way God leads him, but usually there are significant moments in the process.

186/ 24. As he moves closer to priestly ordination, a scholastic may be anxious about his worthiness and suitability as a minister of Word and Sacrament: this may be the call of Christ, but has he the personal strength to accept it and live it? He may feel uneasy about the public role in the Church which ordination will bring: in some countries where public criticism of the Church is strong, there may even be external pressure on him not to identify himself with the hierarchical Church in this way. In other situations, a scholastic may be tempted to see priesthood as a way of entering a world of clerical privilege, rather than as a path of humble service. In a very personal way, he will face the fact that priestly ministry is always exercised in the context of ordinary human weakness and the complex historical development of the Church's life. Various factors can make a scholastic question the rightness of applying for ordination, and the Society must listen very carefully to his fears and help him choose priesthood freely as the way in which his Jesuit identity is to be placed at the service of God's Kingdom and

Church. This is an important moment in a scholastic's discernment of the Ignatian tradition of *sentire cum ecclesia,* which is always prompted by a deeper *sentire cum Christo*—a desire to work with Christ in preparing the way for the Kingdom and, in this way, to serve the Church that is his Body. We should remember that Ignatius made a bold act of trust in Christ's Lordship of the Church when he placed the Society at the service of the sixteenth-century papacy: it was a dramatic gesture showing that, in the Ignatian tradition, humble service of Christ is inseparable from a loving service of the Church.

187/ 25. The first few years after ordination present a new set of challenges: priestly ministry is itself something new; only time, pastoral experience, reflection, and help from others—both from fellow Jesuits and from the people he is called to serve—will allow the full development of confidence, wisdom, and compassion in this vocation. He is simultaneously engaged in the task of integrating himself on a permanent basis into the apostolic body of the Society; it is a time when he is particularly in need of the support of superiors and the friendship of his fellow Jesuits. There is a certain ordinariness to his life: he no longer finds himself moving through the various stages of formation and receiving, at each juncture, formal approval from superiors.

188/ 26. In his work as a priest, as well as in encountering the diverse and sometimes conflicting expectations of the people he seeks to serve, he will also receive the warmth of their appreciation as someone who is compassionate and is trying hard to be of service. Lay people have an important role in building up his confidence in his ministry. The young priest will surely recognize that ordination has not taken away his human weakness. Sometimes these first few years can be a time when things go wrong, and the young priest may be confronted by an unexpected lack of coherence in his life: he may realize that the peace he is ordained to give to others is not completely filling his own heart. If he comes through this— and every Jesuit, in some cases dramatically, has a strong experience of his sinfulness—it can be a profound moment of grace as he confronts the frailty within which his ministry is exercised. In the words of St. Paul, who himself had to come to this understanding, "We have this treasure in earthen vessels to show that the transcendent power belongs to God and not to us" (2 Cor. 4:7).

189/ 27. In the years after final vows, the ordained Jesuit experiences all the pressures and complexities of priestly ministry in the Society: he will probably be engaged in a ministry which makes constant and exhausting demands on him; in addition he may be asked to undertake other responsibilities in the Society. He may find that much of his time is taken up with work that is directly neither pastoral nor sacramental, but is a response to the demands of our corporate mission and the broad range of activities proper to our Jesuit vocation. These are not peripheral to Jesuit priesthood, but are the acts of service by which we address the apostolic needs of our world.

190/ 28. Like every Jesuit, he holds himself in readiness to move at the request of superiors in the service of the Gospel—a readiness that does not become easier as he gets older. These are the years when only deepening love of Christ can balance the pressures of work. The task for the Jesuit priest, in the midst of these multiple demands, is to continue a life of faith and a generous and humble service of Christ. Even if he is not primarily involved in direct pastoral service of others, it will help him to keep his priestly identity alive if he is able to minister regularly to a sacramental community; lay people, especially the poor, build the personal faith of those who serve them.

191/ 29. Although the typical Jesuit priest continues to be engaged in apostolic work well beyond "retirement age," there generally comes a time when such external work must cease. When this happens, he can be tempted to think that his life has lost its primary purpose; he needs to learn from the Lord that, on the contrary, he is being offered a new way of carrying out his Jesuit apostolic mission. Old age in no way diminishes his priesthood and true apostolic vitality. Even if he can only attend the Eucharist and pray privately for the Lord's blessing on the work of the Church and his fellow Jesuits, it is precisely in this that he continues to be a valued apostle and worker. Here, perhaps most of all, he is called to live a life of priestly prayer for others, in union with Christ the High Priest who has gone before us as the pioneer of our faith (Heb. 12:2). In his address to the Society towards the end of his life, when he was very frail, Father Arrupe depicted the experience of many older Jesuits:

> More than ever, I now find myself in the hands of God. This is what I wanted all my life from my youth. And this is still the one thing I want. But now there is a difference: the initiative is entirely with God. It is indeed a profound spiritual experience to know and feel myself so totally in his hands.[21]

192/ 30. Finally, we ask all Jesuit priests to have confidence in the charisms of their ministry, and we also ask all brothers and scholastics to have confidence in the charisms which they receive: these are complementary gifts of the Spirit by which the Society is able to serve in the name of Christ. We ask for God's blessing on all that we do.

Recommendation to Father General

193/ 31. GC 34, while in full accord with the Society's charism and its desire to be available for mission, nevertheless firmly restates the Society's tradition to

---

[21] Pedro Arrupe, Message to the Society, 3 September 1983, *AR* 18 (1983): p. 987.

resist, insofar as is compatible with obedience, nominations to the episcopacy. For St. Ignatius this principle was vital for the mission and well-being of "this least Society" and was not contradictory to his desire to be available for mission. Jesuits were to serve the Church and the Supreme Pontiff, but not as bishops.[22] To clarify this issue, the general congregation urges Father General to continue in dialogue with the Holy See on this matter and, if it would be ueful, to issue as a result further clear norms to be followed by any Jesut informed that he is being considerd as a candidate for the epscopacy.

---

22 *Const.* [817f.].

DECREE 7

The Jesuit Brother

Introduction

194/ 1. The "Proposals" of the Loyola Symposium[1] together with a substantial number of postulates from provinces have manifested the Society's desire to probe more deeply into the meaning and import of statements of recent general congregations which describe the vocation and mission of the brother within the body of the Society.[2]

195/ Responding to this desire, General Congregation 34 wishes to depict the role of the brother in a way that is more in accord with present reality, but always consistent with the description of the identity of a Jesuit given by Decree 2 of GC 32. In this way we intend to join fidelity to our origins with a renewal appropriate to the present moment.[3]

Identity

196/ 2. The Jesuit brother is a man who has accepted the call of the Father to be a "companion of Jesus." By his vows he consecrates his life freely to help the mission common to the apostolic, religious, and priestly body of the Society: "the service of the faith of which the promotion of justice is an absolute requirement."[4]

197/ 3. From the very beginning of his conversion, Ignatius felt called to "help others," to give himself entirely to the service of "the Eternal King and Lord of all."[5] The group of companions, "friends in the Lord," were to find in their discernment how they were to live their apostolic vocation in the Church: by founding a religious order.

198/ At that decisive moment, the apostolic experience of Ignatius and his companions was already linked to the exercise of priestly ministry. Their experience was articulated in the Formula of the Institute, which enumerates the minis-

---

[1] June 12–24, 1994; cf. *AR* 21 (1994): pp. 54–59.

[2] GC 32, D 7; GC 32, D 8; GC 33, D 1, nn. 72–76.

[3] Cf. Vatican Council II, *Perfectae Caritatis*, n. 2; Congregation for Religious and Secular Institutes and Congregation for Bishops, *Mutuae Relationes*, n. 11, *AAS* 70 (1978): p. 480.

[4] GC 32, D 4, n. 2.

[5] Cf. *SpEx* [95].

tries they would perform to fulfill the specific purpose of the new order: "to serve the Lord alone and the Church, his Spouse, under the Roman Pontiff, the Vicar of Christ on earth."[6]

199/   But the mobility which apostolic universality demanded, the multiplicity of pastoral ministries, and especially the need for help in carrying out the mission led Ignatius to accept into the body of the Society a diversity of members, priests and brothers, all of whom would share the same vocation and contribute to the one mission.

200/ 4.   From its beginnings the Society has conceived of itself as a universal "body." This Pauline metaphor (cf. 1 Cor. 12: 12 ff.), much loved by St. Ignatius and used frequently in the Constitutions to refer to the entire Society, expresses his idea of our vocation as both one and diverse.

201/   All members of the Society, in a variety of social and cultural situations, have been graced with the same call to follow Jesus poor and humble. We have all heard the same invitation to serve him in his Church; we have all been sent on the same mission.

202/   At the same time, Ignatius, "rejecting all egalitarianism and all uniformity . . . believed deeply in the diversity of vocations, which is based on the fact that God calls each one by name. It is only in this spirit of openness and acceptance that the various gifts which together make up the Society can blossom."[7] For this reason Ignatius considered grades in the Society as different ways of being incorporated into the one body and fulfilling one and the same mission, without implying in any way differences of perfection or merit in the divine service.[8] So "the apostolic body of the Society is modeled, like that of the apostles, on union in diversity . . . , a diversity united by the bond of charity."[9]

203/ 5.   Recent general congregations, in affirming the unity of vocation in the Society, have reminded us of the need to examine our attitudes so that diversity is not an obstacle to being truly "united, heart and soul" (Acts 4:32). This congregation repeats that call to make the integration of all Jesuits into the one body of the Society more complete and more effective everywhere. We must exert ourselves to discover the ways in which our communities and our apostolic activities, the places we live and work as priests and brothers, can express simply and transparently the oneness of vocation and mission in the Society.

---

6 *Formula* [3].

7 Peter-Hans Kolvenbach, Address to the First Congregation of Provincials, *AR* 20 [1990]: p. 486.

8 Cf. *Examen* [13].

9 Peter-Hans Kolvenbach, S.J., "The Vocation and Mission of the Jesuit Brother," Loyola Symposium, *CIS*, n. 78 (1995), p. 12, citing *Const.* [624].

204/ 6. Brothers, in the same way as priests, are integrated into the Society by reason of the one common call of the Lord to follow him in living out the evangelical radicality of religious life. But a vocation to religious life is distinct from a vocation to priesthood. "In some ways the religious brother embodies religious life in its essence, and so is able to illustrate that life with particular clarity."[10]

205/ Therefore, the first and most important contribution of a brother is the gift of his own self, offered freely in service to the Lord.[11] As a consequence, through a life that is manifestly religious, he offers a prophetic witness, in the Church and in the Society, to the world of today.

Mission

206/ 7. The brother lives his religious vocation as one "sent." He is essentially a man with a mission which he receives ultimately from Christ himself, through his superiors.[12] He carries out this mission as a member of an apostolic body completely dedicated "with God's grace not only to the salvation and perfection of the members' own souls, but also with that same grace to labor strenuously in giving aid towards the salvation and perfection of the souls of others."[13]

207/ As members of the same body, brothers share in and contribute to the one apostolic vocation through the personal call of the Spirit, and enrich the mission of the Society by their participation in what St. Paul called "the priestly service of the Gospel of God" (Rom. 15:16).

208/ The specific missions which brothers can be given include many of the functions and ministries which the Formula of the Institute enumerates as proper to the Society.

209/ These activities carried out by the first companions continue to inspire the Society today as well. GC 31 already affirmed that the apostolic activity of brothers is defined by those same principles which define the apostolate of the whole Society: attention to the greater service of God and the universal good.[14]

210/ Today the Society describes our Jesuit identity in terms of the need "to engage, under the standard of the Cross, in the crucial struggle of our time: the struggle for faith and that struggle for justice which it includes."[15] Brothers, then, are intimately involved in every apostolic task of the Society through which

---

[10] Kolvenbach, "The Vocation and Mission, Preface, p. 3.

[11] Cf. Pedro Arrupe, "Contribution of Jesuit Brothers to the Apostolic Community of the Society," *AR* 27 (1978): p. 381.

[12] Cf. GC 32, D 2, n. 14.

[13] *Examen* [3].

[14] Cf. GC 31, D 7, n. 2.

[15] GC 32, D 2, n. 2.

this mission is carried out; they contribute to every kind of material and technical work at the service of the apostolate and of the body of the Society, and to the explicit proclamation of Jesus through spiritual help and conversation, the Spiritual Exercises, catechesis, and teaching. They make themselves available to be sent to those who experience discrimination, to those deprived of dignity, to those without voice or power, to those searching for the meaning of their existence, to those whose faith is failing, to those who want to be told the Good News of Jesus, as well as to the communities and works which need their help in order to carry out the mission of the Society.

211/ 8. The rich history of brother saints and blessed and the multiplicity of tasks and ministries in which brothers have been and are engaged throughout the world clearly show the variety and complementarity which characterize the apostolic mission of the brother in the Society.

212/ It is appropriate that, along with the figure of brothers like Alphonsus Rodríguez and Francisco Gárate, who achieved sanctity in domestic tasks, we make known the lives of others like James Kisai, Dominic Collins, and Nicholas Owen, who labored with dedication and generosity in the external ministries of the Society even to the surrender of their very lives. This will contribute to a more comprehensive image of the brother's vocation and can attract new vocations.

Communion

213/ 9. There have been significant advances since GC 31 in the integration and participation of brothers in the life and apostolic mission of the Society. Their formation has improved, they have been given responsibilities in important works and apostolic activities, they have been appointed to positions such as community and province consultors. Based on the positive results of these experiences, GC 34 encourages the whole Society to continue to move in the same direction: it is the best way to express the unity of vocation and mission in the body of the Society.

214/ 10. In some places the full realization of this integration still meets with resistance. Attitudes persist among us which call for conversion, and there is need for a greater esteem and appreciation of the brother's vocation; attitudes and sociocultural prejudices alien to the Gospel must not color mutual relations within the Society.

215/ 11. If everyone—priests, brothers, and scholastics—shares in all aspects of community life, including faith, domestic tasks, relaxation, prayer, apostolic discernment, the Eucharist, and the Spiritual Exercises, we will truly become "friends in the Lord." This sharing of life will help to build up communities of shared responsibility in our common following of Jesus, and complementarity in the one mission. To make this sharing a reality among us, we need human and spiritual maturity and a better formation in interpersonal communication.

216/ 12. Since the term "temporal coadjutor" is no longer in common use among us, GC 34 directs that in the future, in our official or other texts, only the term "brother" or "Jesuit brother" should be used, and not the term "temporal coadjutor."

217/ 13. The congregation asks Father General, if he judges it helpful, to set up an office (secretariat) or appoint a priest or brother (counselor) to be in charge of all matters related to brothers, for a more effective implementation of what is prescribed in this decree and in those of previous general congregations.

Formation

218/ 14. A reduced number of vocations ought not to result in lowered standards for admission to the novitiate. Those admitted to be brothers must be men of faith, committed to service, sufciently mature, suited to life in community, and capable of being integrated into the body and mission of the Society.

219/ Where it is deemed necessary, prenovitiate programs are to be established which can help candidates achieve the level necessary to enter the novitiate.

220/ 15. GC 34 believes it may be helpful that provinces sometimes admit candidates to the grade of *Indifferent* so that, in the course of the novitiate, they can better discern their vocation to priesthood or brotherhood.

221/ 16. Those responsible for the formation of brothers should help them to focus their deepest desires, and to fix firmly in their hearts an appreciation of their vocation, a will to serve, and an enthusiasm for the mission of the Society.

222/ 17. Well-structured formation programs are to be established for Jesuit brothers, in order to prepare them adequately for life, service, and social integration within the Society. Such programs are to include the human, communitarian, spiritual, theological, pastoral, and professional dimensions. Some of those with the requisite qualities are to be prepared to work as province vocation promoters and *formatores*. When possible, for the sake of greater integration, brothers in formation are to live in the same communities as scholastics. Provincials are to follow the development of formation programs closely, applying these norms with suitable flexibility.

223/ 18. Where a single province cannot manage such a program either because of a lack of resources or a reduced number of brothers, interprovincial or even interassistancy collaboration is recommended.

224/ 19. Brothers must have the opportunity to learn a foreign language, in accord with the recommendations of this general congregation found in the decree "Interprovincial and Supraprovincial Cooperation."[16] This will enable better communication with companions from other regions and allow greater availability for certain international missions.

---

16 GC 34, D 21, n. 10.

225/ 20. To be effective in mission, all Jesuits need to be well informed in all that pertains to their apostolic work; they also need to be supported in their faith life. Consequently, formed brothers are encouraged to attend programs of ongoing formation in spiritual and psychological renewal and in pastoral and professional development.

Conclusion

226/ 21. GC 34 has introduced important changes in our law to achieve more effectively the integration and participation of brothers in the common vocation and mission of the Society. Among these changes, we note the following:

- a normative formulation of one specific vocation and mission: NC 6, §1, 1°-3°;

- eliminating the title "temporal coadjutor" in everyday language and in future official documents: NC 326, §4;

- special preparation for entrance into the novitiate, when this is necessary: NC 25, §2a;

- ordinarily, novitiate in common with scholastics: NC 43, §1;

- common formation in the novitiate for those aspects of our vocation which are common; separate formation for those which are distinct: NC 48, §§2f.;

- abolishing the rule that forbids additional education after entrance into the Society, and new rules about studies: *Examen* [117]; NC 81, §3; 83, §3; 98; 243, §2f.;

- modification of those passages in the Examen and the Constitutions that refer to tertianship only for scholastics: *Examen* [119], *Const.* [514, 516];

- encouraging communities that include priests, brothers, and scholastics in order to promote fraternal union and union in the apostolic mission: NC 326, §§ 3, 4c;

- granting passive voice for election as electors in a general congregation: GC 34, Decree 23, A. n. 2; this will be included in the revision of the Formulas for General and Province Congregations;

- abolishing the limitation on the number of brothers with final vows who can take part in a province congregation: implicitly in GC 34, D 23, D, n. 4; this will be included in the revision of the Formula for a Province Congregation.

227/ 22. At the same time we wish to recall that if true *communion* is to be fostered among all members of the Society, the first and most necessary requirement is an attitude of mind and heart which esteems and welcomes each Jesuit as a brother and friend in the Lord: "What helps most . . . towards this end must be, more than any exterior constitution, the interior law of love and charity which the Holy Spirit writes and engraves in our hearts."[17]

DECREE 8

Chastity in the Society of Jesus

Introduction

228/ 1. In the course of the present century, in many parts of the world, the meaning of sexuality within human relationships has undergone significant change. Increasingly, men and women experience their sexuality as a gift which enables them to express intimate love and commitment. For many of them, sexuality is understood as part of the "sacrament of marriage" by which the love of God is experienced within their marital love for one another. At the same time, these decades have brought awarenes s of structural injustices imposed on women, as well as some of the distortions, exploitations, and abuses that have accompanied changing gender roles and expressions of sexuality. Moreover, contemporary advertising and entertainment have given sexual expression an unprecedented centrality within various cultures. These last few decades have been labeled "the sexual revolution."

229/ 2. During this same time period, celibacy has come under heavy criticism from within as well as from outside the Church. Thousands have left religious life or active priestly ministry to enter into marriage. The media have carried sensational stories of infidelity and abuse. From all over the world, questions and doubts are posed about the meaning and the value of priestly or religious chastity.

230/ 3. General Congregation 34 wishes to address these questions, to say something directly and honestly about the meaning of chastity in Jesuit life and our resolve to continue to support it. We do not publish this decree because we judge that infidelity in chastity is widespread within the Society of Jesus. On the contrary, we are convinced that, despite the challenges and testing of these years, fidelity in chastity characterizes the life of the Society today as it has characterized it in the past, by the gracious goodness of God. This conviction is grounded on the extensive knowledge of their companions possessed by members assembled here from each province of the Society, confirmed by the congregation's lengthy examination of the present state of the Society. It is this graced fidelity that we hope to strengthen and confirm in the face of so many cultural forces that contradict it.

---

[17] *Const.* [134].

231/ 4.   The purpose of this decree, then, is to give an authoritative answer to the following question: What is the chastity that a Jesuit vows and how can the Society of Jesus continue to foster it in its integrity?

The Call to Chastity

232/ 5.   Ignatius understood the Society of Jesus to be rooted in a fundamental detachment and a determination to serve God totally.[1] The Society was to be one realization of the apostolic life: "Lord, we have left all things and have followed you" (cf. Luke 18:28). This renunciation for the Jesuit comprises "home or wife or brothers or parents or children for the sake of the Kingdom of heaven" (Luke 18:29). A deeply personal love makes it possible to follow Christ in this way, a love that chooses him in place of all that is renounced.[2] When a Jesuit speaks of this, he is speaking of his vow of chastity—a chastity that grace has made possible and that has been chosen, as was that of Jesus, to serve in mission the Kingdom of heaven.

233/ 6.   To the ridicule of some and the puzzlement of many, Ignatius maintained that a Jesuit is to strive to imitate in his chastity the purity of the angels.[3] But this does not mean that he is to act as if he regretted his body. He is rather called to embody in his life that singleness of vision and readiness for mission which is the Ignatian understanding of the angels. They were for Ignatius "the ministering spirits sent to serve." They lived in immediate familiarity with God, and they served as God's ministers in drawing human beings to himself.[4] In his chastity a Jesuit endeavors to realize in his actions and in his thoughts an analogous, undeflected union with God in prayer and ministry.

---

1 *Examen* [53]: "Those founders' mind was that those received into [this Society] should be persons already detached from the world and determined to serve God totally."

2 The Ignatian commentary upon Matt. 19:29 and Luke 18:30 is very strong, describing the Jesuit as "one who is dead to the world and to self-love and who lives only for Christ our Lord, having Him in place of *[en lugar de]* fathers or brothers or of all things" (*Examen* [61]).

3 *Const.* [547].

4 *SpEx* [329, 331, 335]; cf. *SpEx* [60]; OC [681], [683f.]: *Const.* [813]. This interpretation of the Ignatian understanding of the imitation of "angelic purity" in a chastity that unites singleness of heart in prayer and ministry is confirmed by the remarkable statement of Peter Ribadeneira: "Oyle dezir que quería haverse con los próximos como los ángeles para con nosotros, en dos cosas: una, en no faltar de su parte, dando las ayudas possibles, por quitarles de todo mal, etiam espiritual; 2o, en no se pertubar de cosa alguna por lo que les acaesciesse (como los ángeles no dexan de ver y gozar a Dios), ni contristarse en manera que perdiesse nada de su devoción. Dezía también que, aunque Dios destruyese toda la Compañía, él no pensava contristarse se en modo que perdiesse nada de sudevoción para con Dios" (Peter Ribadeneira, "Dichos y Hechos de N. P. Ignacio," MHSI, vol. 73, MI, *FontNarr,* II, 476). For the tradition behind this interpretation of "angelic purity," see the Carthusian Ludolph of Saxony, *Vita Jesu Christi,* ed. Rigollot (Paris, 1878), Pars I, caput xxii, sectio 6, and II, vi. Cited and translated by Joseph F. Conwell, S.J., "Living and Dying in the Society of Jesus or Endeavoring to Imitate Angelic Purity," *Studies in the Spirituality of Jesuits* 12, n. 3 (May 1980): pp. 7f.

234/ 7. By the vow of chastity, then, a Jesuit is consecrated and united to God precisely as God is "laboring in all things" for the salvation of human beings.[5] Chastity is first of all his gracious gift, calling the Jesuit to a discipleship and renunciation that can free his heart from the natural concern for an exclusive relationship and draw it into the universal charity of God towards all men and women.[6] It is a gift to be, in this way, configured to Christ.

The Apostolic Character of Chastity

235/ 8. This life of chastity consecrated to God offers a living witness that Christ can engage human beings in so comprehensive a love and a prophetic reminder that we were created finally for that future life with God in which the children of the resurrection "will neither marry nor give in marriage" (Luke 20:34–36). In this way, living unmarried for the sake of the Kingdom of heaven preaches the Gospel in deeds rather than words. It can disclose that God and the Kingdom of God—both as the passion and the hope of a person's life—can be absolute, prevailing in attraction over all other human values. For this reason, such a life has been seen in the Church throughout its history as a most suitable means "for religious to spend themselves readily in God's service and in works of the apostolate."[7]

236/ 9. Accordingly, in our Society not only poverty and obedience but also chastity is essentially apostolic. It is not understood by Jesuits as directed exclusively to their personal sanctification, but as calling them to be one with Christ in labor for the salvation of the human race.[8] According to the whole intent of our Institute, we embrace apostolic chastity as a special source of spiritual fruitfulness in the world, as a means for a more prompt love and a more total apostolic availability towards all men and women.[9] That is why the chastity of Jesuits does not compete with marriage, but rather reinforces its value. Both point to a love and a fidelity which is deeper than sexual expression and of which Christian marriage and religious chastity are divergent and sacred realizations. Few are called to the

---

[5] *SpEx* [236].

[6] Cf. GC 31, D 16, n. 3; *SpEx* [236]. The vow of chastity as understood here corresponds to the way it was expressed in the *Quinque Capitula* of 1539 and the Formula of the Institute of 1540—as the total giving of oneself to God's call. Only in the later version of the Formula, that of 1550, were the other vows added to the initial sentence. See Antonio M. de Aldama, S.J., *The Formula of the Institute: Notes for a Commentary*, trans. Ignacio Echániz (Rome: CIS, 1990), pp. 2f., 41. The phrase "exclusive human relationships" denotes those relationships that are so centered in themselves that they exclude or impede a sharing of this love with others.

[7] Vatican Council II, *Perfectae Caritatis,* n. 12. Cf. *Presbyterorum Ordinis,* n. 16 and GC 31, D 16, nn. 3, 4.

[8] For this conjunction between the commitment to the apostolic life and to personal sanctification in "the same [grace]," cf. *Examen* [3]. The vows are then introduced as means to that end [4].

[9] GC 31, D 16, n. 4.

life of a Jesuit, but for the man who is called, chastity only makes sense as a means to a greater love, to a more authentic apostolic charity.

237/ 10. This may be especially relevant today, when so many tend to put whole classes of human beings beyond the horizons of their concerns, while at the same time identifying love with eroticism and hedonism and exploiting such an identification to fuel financial gain and human degradation. A love that is warmly human yet freely offered to all, especially to the poor and the marginalized, can be a powerful sign leading people to Christ, who came to show us what love really is, that God is love.[10]

238/ 11. Because of his chastity, a Jesuit can live in radical apostolic availability. His assignments always have something of the provisional about them; he must remain open to the summons of obedience to another place, to another task. This detachment from *stabilitas,* from the definition of himself within a single family or extended set of relatives or even a particular church, culture, and place, characterizes a Jesuit. It is constitutive of his obedience, and it is his remaining celibate for the Kingdom of God that makes such obedience for mission possible. If this apostolic availability is not to cripple his affectivity, it is only because his chastity embodies a contemplative love that includes all human beings and makes the Jesuit open and able to find God everywhere.

239/ 12. To God, then, and to his world, Jesuits have chosen to offer in union with Christ the sincere, simple, and demanding life of consecrated chastity.[11]

The Matter and Meaning of the Vow of Chastity

240/ 13. Because of the confusion in current times, we must be as clear as possible about the meaning of this vow if we are to observe it as part of the shared meaning of our lives. It arises from and is based upon a conscious and free decision under grace.[12] By his vow of chastity, a Jesuit devotes himself to the Lord and to his service in such a unique love that it excludes marriage and any other exclusive human relationship, as well as the genital expression and gratification of his sexuality. Thus the vow entails the obligation of complete continence in celibacy for the sake of the Kingdom of heaven.[13] Following the evangelical counsel of chastity, the Jesuit aspires to deepen his familiarity with God, his configuration to Christ, his companionship with his brother Jesuits, his service to others, and at the same time to grow in his personal maturity and capacity to love. The witness of many Jesuits confirms that there is a deep happiness in such a life of personal love and service.

---

[10] GC 32, D 2, n. 26.

[11] GC 31, D 16, n. 2.

[12] GC 31, D 16, n. 6.

[13] CIC 599.

The Cost of This Discipleship

241/ 14. A Jesuit should not deceive himself about the cost of such a decision. It involves renunciation of conjugal intimacy, denial of the very human desire for his own children, and turning away from a unique affective bonding that is one of life's richest experiences and a normal condition for human growth. He surrenders the joys of belonging to and living within his own family. If he did not sometimes feel the painful loss of some of humanity's most lovely and most tender joys, he would be less than human. Other joys, even deeper joys, will enter his life, but they cannot remove all sense of void.

242/ 15. Through his chastity, then, the Jesuit lives in some solitude—not loneliness, but solitude. There will be times when this solitude will become a desert, as he experiences little or no satisfaction or support in what is around him; at other times, it may even become the cross, the experience of futility, anguish and death.[14]

243/ 16. Throughout his life a Jesuit will give his time and his talents to others without thought of recompense. He does not build his own business or his own career, because he does not build his own home and family. His chastity has made it possible for him to grow in his poverty. At the end of his life, through his vow of chastity, he will have become poor in a way that his previous talents and education and energies made impossible. Now all of these belong to yesterday; they have been spent for others. He has finally become poor as did Christ, who, "although he was rich, made himself poor for our sakes" (2 Cor. 8:9).[15] He has become a man who possesses neither family nor property, has built up nothing for himself, and looks to God for the definition of his life. This poverty that flows from his chastity is not the destruction of his Jesuit life; in many ways it is its completion and fulfillment.[16] But he should not disguise the cost of such a life.

Normative Principles and Guidelines

244/ 17. **Prenote:** While many of the constitutive elements of being a Jesuit have been treated elsewhere, they give indispensable support to a life of chastity and will be included here so that Jesuit life and its requirements can be seen as an organic unity.

---

[14] GC 31, D 16, n. 5.

[15] Ignatius alludes to this text in his letter to Peter Contarini (August 1537), OC [631f.].

[16] Jesuits have found an eloquent expression of this in the farewell message of Father Pedro Arrupe to the Society: "How I wish I were in a better condition for this meeting with you. As you see, I cannot even address you directly. But my general assistants have grasped what I want to say to each one. More than ever, I now find myself in the hands of God. This is what I have wanted all my life, from my youth. And this is still the one thing I want. But now there is a difference: the initiative is entirely with God. It is indeed a profound spiritual experience to know and feel myself so totally in his hands" (*AR* 18 [1983]: pp. 986f.).

245/ 18. I. The *familiarity with God* and the friendship with Christ that lie at the origins of his vocation sustain a Jesuit in his fidelity. It was this love that first drew him to such a life; the commitments of chastity cannot continue or flourish without its continual growth. This conscious, loving union with God is prayer, whether at formal moments of explicit focus or as the atmosphere that permeates each day.

Guidelines

246/ 19.   [1] This should be a principal concern of all Jesuits: to seek the conscious presence of the Lord in such private prayer as meditation, contemplation, and the examination of conscience and in such community prayer as the Liturgy of the Hours, communal discernment, and group spontaneous prayer. In their manifold occupations, Jesuits can learn to reverence the divine presence as the horizon in which they live, to apprehend the immanent providence of God that draws them into its own working for the salvation of human beings, and to hold on to God as the purpose that energizes their work—learning thus to find God in all things. The celebration of the Eucharist—frequently together as a community—ought to be central to such a life, and the sacrament of reconciliation ought to exercise a significant influence over it. Annually they are to commit themselves conscientiously to making the Spiritual Exercises. All of these components of Jesuit life flow from the fundamental directive of the Formula of the Institute: Let the one who wishes to live our life "take care, as long as he lives, first of all, to keep before his eyes God."[17]

247/ 20.   [2] From experience, the Society has learned that pivotal to its fidelity in chastity has been the strong though humble and simple devotion to the Blessed Virgin that has flourished among us since the time of St. Ignatius.[18]

248/ 21. II. *Community life* figures importantly here. It is not that the community compensates for a wife and children, but rather that it can and does support a life that is lived in their denial. Through the many forms of their mutual presence to one another and their investment of themselves in one another's lives, Jesuits mediate to each other the presence of that Lord to whom they have offered themselves through their vow of chastity. It is this mediation, this interchange that makes their community religious. The continual and vital commitment of Jesuits to one another is a condition for a concomitant growth in chastity.[19]

249/   Thus the apostolic chastity of a Jesuit cannot be lived in an aloof withdrawal from others. As a true "gift from above," apostolic chastity should lead to communion both with one's brother Jesuits and with the people we serve. It is

---

17 *Formula* [3].

18 For the radical foundation of this experience of the Society in the prior experience of Ignatius himself, see *Autobiography* [10].

19 GC 32, D 16, n. 7b.

sad if chastity is so corrupted that it leads only to a self-enclosed bachelorhood.[20] Community life, then, must be not only a support but also the privileged context for living a wholesome and humane chastity. When community life is strong in its support and truthful in its challenge, then Jesuits are inspired through their chastity to make visible the God who labors to help others. It is important both to appreciate and to develop the strong bond between apostolic chastity and apostolic community.

Guidelines

250/ 22.   [3] Our houses are to be communities where the life of prayer and the interchange with one another of religious values habitually characterize daily life. There should be periods of the day and of the week in which the members of the community meet for prayer, recreation, and meals. It is also important that there should be longer periods of recollection and prayer during the year in which Jesuits in the community share with one another the religious realities and mission by which they live. In a manner appropriate to the Society, liturgy ought to mark the rhythm of the Jesuit community, as it is to characterize any vital Christian community. Each of its members is called by the Society today to take the responsibility to foster such a community.[21]

251/ 23.   [4] These communities should embody a deeply Christian hospitality "according to the custom of different places" so that we share what we have and what we are with men and women to whom we are related in friendship or committed in our apostolate. On the other hand, Jesuits need a certain privacy in special parts of the house. Since the customs of various cultures differ so radically, it is left to province government to determine what is appropriate in this matter. In general, it can be said that these arrangements are to be such as to obviate any ambiguity that could occasion misinterpretations.[22]

252/ 24. III.   The *life of ministry* also strengthens that attachment to the Lord which is the source of chastity. There is a consciousness of Christ in ministry that is not available to the Jesuit outside this apostolic experience, the Christ to whom he is united as the instrument wielded by the divine hand.[23] It is also the same grace by which Jesuits move in fidelity and growth towards God as that by which "they labor in giving aid towards the salvation and perfection of the souls of their fellow men and women."[24] Furthermore, chastity belongs essentially to our chosen way of relating to others. The sense of meaning and the joy that come from

---

[20] *SpEx* [184].

[21] For a full description of the Jesuit community as well as a description of the process by which one is built, cf. GC 32, D 11.

[22] CIC 667, 1.

[23] *Const.* [813].

[24] *Const.* [3].

apostolic experience in turn sustain the significance of the chastity that made this apostolic life possible. This can be especially true when ministry is realized within the world of the oppressed and of the poor. But in every case, this mutual support between Jesuit chastity and ministerial commitments is only possible if Jesuits minister gratuitously and without orienting this pastoral work to their own enhancement.

Guidelines

253/ 25.   [5] The Society expects from every Jesuit not only fidelity to his vows but the normal public signs of this fidelity. Jesuits should embody in their ministry and in their lives an unequivocal "professional" conduct *(modestia)* that manifests their commitments as priests and as religious.[25] Their manner of proceeding—both as a community and as individuals—ought to preclude any ambiguity about their lives, enabling those to whom they minister to rely instinctively upon their disinterestedness and fidelity.

254/ 26.   [6] It is especially important that those in ministries like spiritual direction, counseling, or therapy keep appropriate "professional" boundaries, aware of the possibility of affective transference and countertransference, and resistant to confusing such ministerial relationships with those of intimate friendship.[26]

255/ 27.   [7] The differences among particular cultures and attitudes require that Jesuits be especially sensitive in this area. Those traveling abroad are to attend carefully to the local feelings and attitudes concerning the relations between women and men. It would be unreasonable for traveling Jesuits to expect local people to view their conduct as it would be understood in their own native land. Failure to take this into account can result in a witness contrary to the very gospel values they have given their lives to proclaim.

256/ 28.   IV. *Discernment and self-discipline* are imperative for fidelity in chastity. Contemporary popular culture is heavily influenced by commercial propaganda, advertising, and the lucrative exploitation of sexual sensibilities for financial gain. Excessive passive entertainment can become addictive and debilitating. In

---

25 A "professional" relationship implies much more than a merely contractual or even business relationship in that, unlike these latter, it is conducted not between equals but between two unequal parties, one of whom (the professional) has expertise and experience in the relevant area, while the other (the client) is ignorant in this area and requires access to professional skills and acumen. The professional to this degree is, quite legitimately, in a position of power and authority. To act "professionally" involves not only making one's expertise available but also not abusing the power relationship to manipulate the client. It requires objectivity, impartiality, sensitivity, and delicacy both in making the expertise available and in empowering the client to pursue his or her interest, rather than inducing in the client a dependence on the professional.

26 Cf. Pedro Arrupe, "Our Way of Proceeding," *AR* 17 (1979): pp. 718 ff. Father Arrupe recalled that the first Jesuits seem to have showed in their ministry a special delicacy in the matter of chastity; their circumspection and their prudence in this area became proverbial.

this area, a Jesuit must be critically aware. The directions of Ignatius and the experience of the Society over the past centuries emphasize that a certain sober realism, discernment, and abnegation are necessary to deal with the many influences that enter into a Jesuit's life. This need for discipline of the body and of the mind has for millennia been recognized in many spiritual traditions, and Jesuits can learn much from these spiritual masters to discipline and integrate the body and the mind into a life of prayer and service.

Guidelines

257/ 29.　　[8] Religious discretion is appropriately brought to bear on every element in Jesuit life, and this entails the practice of the examination of conscience, mortification, and custody of the senses. Concretely, a Jesuit ought to weigh the influences he admits into his life through entertainment, television, videos, reading, recreation, and travel as well as through personal relationships. To live an integral life, one must ask realistically whether this or that particular influence or practice strengthens or weakens a life of fidelity in chastity and its public witness.[27] Furthermore, a Jesuit should not be ashamed to honestly notice the temptations and desires that would prompt him to behavior incongruent with his commitments. Instead, he ought to seek help in dealing with these desires and inclinations.

258/ 30.　　[9] Everyone should be aware that any failure in living faithfully the vow of chastity or any ambiguous relationships can afflict others cruelly, both spiritually and psychologically. Besides the issue of serious sin, such behavior can compromise the credibility of the Society within a culture that is skeptical about any fidelity in chastity and seriously injure its apostolic effectiveness.

259/ 31.　V. *Affective Maturation:* Since grace presupposes nature, spiritual maturation goes hand in hand with an adequate affective maturation. Affective maturation means the development and the integration of all the forces and emotions of the human personality; it embraces more than just the sexual, but it presents a special challenge to a life with the renunciations that our chastity involves. The process of affective maturation for the individual Jesuit takes place within the context of his human relationships. It occurs in and through all phases of life, but especially at moments of crisis.

---

[27] Certain directions from the Spiritual Exercises could profitably be adapted and brought to bear to aid a decision to put order into the manifold cultural influences that surround a Jesuit if and when those influences become disordered. For example, the "Rules for Ordering Oneself in the Matter of Eating" [210–17], which Ignatius places within the Third Week, and "The First Method of Prayer" as this relates to the "five senses of the body" [238–48].

Guidelines

260/ 32.   [10] The individual Jesuit must recognize, first of all, that under grace he bears the responsibility for his own human growth. It is he above all who must see that his life is characterized by that equilibrium which empowers him to remain conscious of his feelings and in contact with the deepest stirrings of his motivations and human powers. With discernment he must learn to differentiate among the "motions" within his life, to follow in the direction of those that move him towards God and to deny satisfaction to those that do not.[28] Second, he should not attempt to isolate himself from the challenges and crises of life, but to deal with these with such honesty that he finds his relationship with God and his own self-acceptance deepened.[29] Third, he ought to see to it that he can give both his feelings and his creativity appropriate expression, and he is to develop an educated sensibility for the humane achievements of life that are found in the arts, literature, music, and so forth. Fourth, he must avoid a style of life and of work that puts him under excessive affective stress or that necessitates a continual suppression of his own feelings and leads eventually to affective regression, "burnout," or some kind of psychic disturbance. Last and most important, friendships should be very much part of his life. The ability to form mature friendships with other Jesuits and with women and men who are not Jesuits, as well as the capacity to collaborate in equality with others, is a sign of affective maturity. Friendships can not only support a life of dedicated chastity but can also deepen the affective relationship with God that chastity embodies.

261/ 33.   [11] Spiritual direction is an indispensable aid towards spiritual and affective maturation. Spiritual directors can help those being directed to bring affective experiences into these conversations for an appreciation and discernment of their meaning. But a spiritual director must not confuse the ministry of spiritual direction with psychological counseling or therapy. If psychological problems emerge, the directee is to be recommended to a counselor, psychologist, or psychiatrist.

262/ 34.   [12] Superiors can contribute significantly to the affective growth of those whom they serve. They can further in their communities an atmosphere of understanding and of friendship among its members. On the other hand, they should not shrink from the more unpleasant responsibilities of their office: to set boundaries, to challenge their brothers to a more integral Jesuit life, and to insist that the community give unequivocal witness to its vowed life. As a matter of fact,

---

28 *Const.* [260]; *SpEx* [331–36].

29 See, for example, the petition for grace in the First Week of the Exercises, in which the exercitants pray for the understanding of their own internal disorder [63], and also the directions for the repetition, that one returns in prayer to those areas in which one has found the greatest desolation as well as the greatest consolation [62].

maturation is often furthered more by this kind of challenge than by a permissiveness that looks for peace at all costs.

263/ 35. VI. The *Account of Conscience* and *Spiritual Direction* have been stressed in recent documents of the Society as critical for our religious life. They take on additional importance precisely in their contribution to the growth of Jesuits in chastity.

Guidelines

264/ 36.   [13] Superiors should recognize as a principal task the fostering of mutual confidence and openness between their companions in the Society and themselves. This contributes wonderfully to the honesty and vitality of the account of conscience, the frankness of its interchange and the help that it can offer every Jesuit.

265/ 37.   [14] It is very important that spiritual directors are given appropriate training, especially those that are *formatores*. This is additionally necessary today because of contemporary influences and issues regarding affective maturity and sexuality.

266/ 38.   [15] Every Jesuit must realistically recognize that he will be as effective in helping others to lead a chaste life as he himself is faithful in leading such a life with integrity and is aware of his own inner inclinations, passions, anxieties, and emotions. Further, chastity is a shared responsibility of all Jesuits to safeguard seriously and to further through their mutual fraternal support and friendships as well as through the aid they offer superiors in their care for their companions and for the Society.

267/ 39. VII.   *Admission and Dismissal.* Before admission into the novitiate—as later during the years of formation—the Society should attempt to examine realistically whether the candidate has the charism and character for this kind of life with its demands for celibate chastity. An affective maturation in the Society is only possible when a man possesses an adequate basic disposition, both spiritual and affective. While superiors carry grave responsibilities before God for the internal life of the Society and its public credibility, as well as for those who will be affected by the pastoral ministry of its members, their ability to carry out these responsibilities depends upon the willingness of both candidates and their fellow Jesuits to be open with them about whatever difficulties they have. While their responsibilities call them to accompany their fellow Jesuits in their spiritual journey with kindness blended with firmness, superiors can only make their best efforts, and these in the light of the knowledge they possess.

268/ 40. But superiors can find decisions about admission and dismissal deeply troubling, especially if they are unaware of the norms of the Society or if the rules given for their application are ambiguous and they feel alone in their difficult decision. To formulate such norms remains the office of the ordinary government of the Society, and their prudent application will "depend upon many particular circumstances of persons, times, and places," as Ignatius insisted.[30] In general, however, the long experience of the Society together with its fundamental documents indicates the following guidelines, while the norms for their application are to be set by the general.

Guidelines

269/ 41.   [16] Superiors—with compassion and understanding—should try to probe issues of emotional strain and inner distress that each candidate carries from his history, attempting to deal honestly with such questions as those of affective maturity, of genuine capacities for sexual abstinence, especially if the candidate has had a previous history of intimate sexual relations and other experiences of this nature. The Society and the candidate need to have as clear an appreciation of these factors as possible in order to make a sound judgment about the ability of the candidate to live our life.

270/ 42.   [17] When someone cannot live the vow of chastity with integrity, inner freedom, and joy, that is, when he cannot find God in his life of chastity, in conscience he ought not to proceed to vows or to major orders but should leave the Society and find another way of life where he can serve God in peace and fidelity.[31]

271/ 43.   [18] With deep sorrow, it must be acknowledged that for the good of the Society and those affected by its pastoral mission, they should not remain in the Society, whatever their grade, whose repeated acts with another against chastity show them in all likelihood unable to live their public profession of chastity with integrity, even after appropriate therapeutic rehabilitation.[32]

272/ 44.   [19] According to his best knowledge and judgment, the superior should also challenge with fraternal concern and kindness those involved in inappropriate relationships or exclusive friendships that can compromise dedicated chastity, cause scandal, or wound the union of minds and hearts that is to characterize Jesuit life.

Recommendation to Father General

273/ 45.   Since a general congregation has neither the time nor the resources to treat this entire matter in all of its dimensions, GC 34 asks Father General to establish a commission of experts who can examine thoroughly the issues atten-

---

30 *Const.* [211].

31 *Const.* [204f.], [819]. For the manner of "dismissal," cf. *Const.* [223–27].

32 For the norms alluded to in this text and the discretion ["discrete zeal"] with which they are to be applied, cf. *Const.* [208], [210f.], [819]. Cf. also [212], [215]. For the usage in the early Society, see Jerome Nadal, MHSI, vol. 90, *Commentarii de Instituto Societatis Iesu,* bk. 5, "In Examen Annotationes," [75] (p. 160).

dant on the fidelity and credibility of chastity in the Society and on a sound affective formation of young Jesuits and those who are already formed. Further, we recommend that each conference of provincials work out the cultural adaptation of these guidelines, study the issues connected with affective formation, and outline the appropriate pedagogies for this development among Jesuits. The results of this study should be submitted to Father General for his approval.

DECREE 9

POVERTY

Introduction

274/ 1.   In response to the powerful calls of recent general congregations, Jesuits have made noticeable efforts to live a more authentic poverty, both personally and in communities.[1] Work with and for the poor has been promoted; the generosity and hospitality of our houses has increased; separation of community from work has brought greater clarity regarding expenses; there are more financial cooperation and a sharper sensitivity to justice. All in all, we have advanced in detachment, simplicity of life, solidarity, and fraternal sharing—attitudes which mark the evangelical poverty we promised.[2] For all of this, we must be grateful to God.

275/ 2.   At the same time, despite this progress, we must admit that we have not yet reached the deeper renewal that General Congregation 32 in its Decree 12 asks of us in this regard. The postulates sent to this congregation show dissatisfaction with our comfortable style of life; they call on us to consider whether our way of life bears credible witness to the vow of evangelical poverty.

276/ 3.   This is not a marginal concern. We know well that, for St. Ignatius, poverty is "a safeguard of religious life," whose lack "weakens, wears out, and ruins" our way of being.[3] Moved by the Spirit of Jesus, Ignatius and his first compan-

---

[1] GC 31, D 18; GC 32, D 12; D 2, nn. 20, 28; D 4, n. 49; GC 33, D 1, nn. 23-27; D 2.

[2] GC 32 already expressed the "analogic" character of the religious poverty (D 12, n. 7): "In a world of mass starvation, no one can lightly call himself poor. It is perhaps regrettable that we have no other word to designate this note of religious life, since poverty means very different things to different people. At the very least, religious poverty would try hard to limit rather than to expand consumption."

[3] Cf. *Const.* [553], [816]. Cf. also Letter to the Fathers and Brothers at Padua, 7 August 1547, MHSI, *Epp.S.Ign.,* I, 572–77. Although written by Polanco at the request of St. Ignatius, it contains the attitude of the founder regarding poverty understood as a gift of God which draws Jesuits to the poor, "the friends of the [Eternal] King."

ions felt called to "preach in poverty."[1] The authenticity of our poverty is the test of our being or not being Jesuits manifestly following Christ "poor and humble," as we learned in the Spiritual Exercises.[2]

The Apostolic and Prophetic Dimension of Our Poverty

277/ 4.   Our poverty is apostolic because it witnesses to God as the one Lord of our lives and the only Absolute; it distances us from material goods and frees us from all attachment so that we can be fully available to serve the Gospel and dedicate ourselves to the most needy. In this way poverty is itself a mission and a proclamation of the Beatitudes of the Kingdom.

278/ 5.   Our poverty is also prophetic. In recent decades the cry of the poor has become more piercing. But the gap between rich and poor is being reinforced rather than diminishing. Unbridled capitalism produces disproportionate growth for some economic sectors, exclusion and marginalization for many others. Contemporary society is infected by consumerism, hedonism, and lack of responsibility. The values considered important today are personal fulfillment, competition, efficiency, and success at any cost. In view of this panorama of contrasts, our personal and community poverty becomes a sign and message of a different logic, that of evangelical solidarity.

279/ 6.   Poverty is the unequivocal condition of our credibility.[3] In the face of the attitudes and values that dominate the mentality of the world today, the radical exercise of evangelical poverty becomes a countercultural witness to the value of gratuity which St. Ignatius praised so much.[4] By this gratuity we profess the boundless and freely bestowed love of God who gave his Son for us in the total emptying of the Incarnation and the Cross. By our poverty we also show that we as persons and as "body" consider ourselves the "least Company," which lives from God and for God rather than putting its trust in material goods, since the powerful love of the Lord acts through our littleness.

Guidelines and Helps

280/ 7.   In order to renew our apostolic poverty, GC 34 wishes to insist again on some of the more pressing recommendations given us by recent general congregations.

281/ 8.   1.   Our *manner of life* personally and in communities has to be simple, hospitable, and open. There are certainly Jesuits and communities which live

---

[1] To Jaime Cassador, 12 February 1536, S. Ign., *Epp. et instruct.*, MHSI I, 96. Cf. *Spiritual Diary* (MHSI, *Const.* I, 86–158, n. 15); *Deliberation on poverty* (MHSI, *Const.* I, 78–83).

[2] Cf. *SpEx* [116].

[3] Cf. GC 33, D 1, n. 48.

[4] Cf. *Examen* [4]; *Formula* [4]; *Const.* [398], [565], [816].

an exemplary, austere life. However, we must admit that in some instances the style of our life is far from that lived by modest families of the locale. We must sincerely examine whether in certain spheres (travel, personal cars, private use of television, meals in expensive restaurants, vacations, the number of domestic employees, and so forth) we live according to the requirements of our poverty; we must also ask whether we truly earn our livelihood by our labor.[5] A community life of shared poverty is a source of joy, and unity of hearts is strengthened by sharing of goods.[6] The testimony of simplicity and sobriety of life can also be a means for awakening in some who visit us the desire to become companions of Jesus. We firmly believe that a separation of living quarters from workplace, as recommended by GC 31, helps to strengthen the simplicity and intimacy of our community life.[7]

282/ 9. 2. *Economic openness* and dependence on the community for income and expenses are indispensable for a life of fraternal poverty. From the community we receive what we need; to the community we give everything that comes to us—as remuneration for our work, stipends, alms, gifts, or in any other way.[8] This desire to share with one's brothers without holding back anything as one's own must remain characteristic of a Jesuit who desires radically to follow Jesus. Since the use of modern conveniences such as credit cards and personal bank accounts may bring one to live financially on the margins of the community, all should be fully honest with the superior regarding the use of money. Those who have influential and well-salaried positions must be especially alert; even though the acceptance of these positions must be discerned with the superior and the gain coming from them can never be a determining factor in choosing them, they carry within themselves the temptation to live a more comfortable lifestyle.[9] In the same way clarity and austerity of life are not helped by appropriating for personal use the economic or material means pertaining to one's apostolic work.

283/ 10. 3. *Spiritual discernment* will make us "vigilant servants" regarding the evangelical quality of our lives.

284/ 11.   *a.* The personal discernment so recommended by St. Ignatius can be practiced in prayer and the examen. Only the intimate knowledge of the Lord who has given up all for our sake will enable us to love him more deeply and follow him more closely in his detachment. The examen will help us to notice God's footprints in our lives, the God who calls us daily to dedicate ourselves "more" freely, since he himself desires to give himself "more," "to give himself to us as

---

5 Cf. GC 32, D 12, n. 7.

6 Cf. GC 31, D 18, n. 13.

7 Cf. GC 31, D 19, n.7.

8 GC 32, D 12, n. 8.

9 GC 32, D 12, n. 8.

much as possible."[10] An aid here is spiritual direction which can make our personal discernment more sound and safe from any self-deception. A frank and trusting relationship between the members of the community and the superior is also desirable, so that he is not limited to giving permissions, but can really help each one to observe poverty in its purity and to overcome its difficulties.

285/ 12.   *b.* An important topic for *community* discernment should be our lifestyle. What is required is that the community make a common plan that reflects its desire to live simply and in solidarity, a plan which can be easily evaluated at regular intervals. It must include the concrete means to attain simplicity and the manner in which the spirit of gratuity is manifested by the community; furthermore, it must specify how goods will be shared among the companions and with the poor. The time prior to the annual visitation of the provincial can be a suitable occasion for evaluation. Drawing up an annual budget, with careful and complete presentation to the community and not merely as a routine, has been found helpful as a means to evaluate lifestyle to see if it is comparable to "modest families of the region." Effort is needed to keep within the budget, and the community must be informed about how well this is being accomplished.[11] When these helps are neglected, "private incomes" can easily appear in the life of Jesuits and money can easily be spent on superfluities.

286/ 13.   4. The changes in our administrative structures introduced by GC 32 are intended to enable communities to live more modestly and with a greater sense of shared responsibility. For this reason the *sharing of goods* has been established, so that community surplus is annually distributed to the apostolic work dependent on it, to other communities or works that are needy whether within the province or outside it, and to the poor.[12] As far as possible, apostolic institutions are also subject to the same fraternal law regarding other apostolic works in need of help.[13] The reform which separates the economic structures of community from those of the work has generally resulted in positive steps towards a greater solidarity of sharing and the greater economic openness so necessary in our communities and institutions. However, the desired results have not been achieved everywhere; at times there is simply a separation of administration and accounting, without having any effect on the economic standards of community life.[14] GC 34 asks that these reforms be carried out with sincerity; when observed carefully, they can transform both our personal and community life and our apostolic activity.

---

[10] *SpEx* [234].

[11] Cf. GC 32, D 12, n. 24.

[12] Cf. GC 32, D 12, nn. 25–29; GC 31, D 19, n. 6b.

[13] Cf. GC 32, D 12, nn. 12, 34.

[14] Cf. GC 33, D 1, n. 25.

287/ 14. 5. In order to "feel" *[sentir]* the anxieties and aspirations of the dispossessed in an Ignatian way, we need *direct personal experience.*[15] Profound experience is what changes us. We can break out of our habitual way of living and thinking only through physical and emotional proximity to the way of living and thinking of the poor and marginalized.

288/ 15.   *a.* The *lived experience* of poverty and marginalization should accompany each Jesuit during his life, even when his main occupation will not be work with the neediest. It is the desire "when occasions arise, [to] feel some effects of [poverty]" that has to motivate our finding time for such experiences.[16] They can be occasions for radical conversion. It was among the poor of the hospitals and slums of Venice and Rome that the first members of the Society "experienced privation and need," but they also came to know that "a life removed as far as possible from all infection of avarice and as like as possible to evangelical poverty is more gratifying, more undefiled, and more suitable for the edification of others."[17] Therefore their desire for each one who would come after them was that "his food, drink, clothing, shoes, and lodging will be what is characteristic of the poor," and that these followers would seek "to reach the same point as the [first members] or to go further in our Lord."[18] From the witness of many companions who live with the poor, we know that, along with the hard lessons of poverty, such experiences bring the evangelical values of celebration, simplicity, and hospitality which so often characterize the life of the poor. Superiors should facilitate such experiences and allow the required time to those who want them.

289/ 16.   *b.* Solidarity with the poor cannot be the concern only of some Jesuits; it has to typify our life and our ministry. So whatever the mission given us may be, we have to work within it *for* the benefit of the poor and for a more just and fraternal world. Moreover, the insertion of communities in areas of poverty and marginalization is a special witness to love for the poor and for the poverty of Christ.[19] Fortunately the number of these communities has grown; in them Jesuits serve selflessly, working *with* the poor and living *as* they do. Provincials must continue to promote such communities so that, while maintaining a strong sense of belonging to the body of the province, they are a visible application of our preferential option for the poor and contribute by means of fraternal exchange to increasing the social sensibility of the province.

290/ 17. 6. We frequently make use of means and institutions in our apostolates which in themselves are not poor (since they must in fact always be suitable

---

¹⁵ Cf. GC 32, D 12, n. 5.

¹⁶ *Const.* [287].

¹⁷ *Formula* [5].

¹⁸ *Examen* [81].

¹⁹ GC 32, D 12, n. 10; D 4, nn. 35f., 49f.

to their apostolic purpose). Here it is fitting to recall that effectiveness and apostolic poverty are two values which must be kept in ongoing tension; this should be the rule for each individual as much as for communities and works.[20] Maintaining this difficult equilibrium requires constant discernment and a readiness to abandon such institutions and means when they no longer result in the "greater service" of God.

Poverty as Grace

291/ 18. For St. Ignatius the material poverty of a Jesuit was a grace; he asked that "it be loved as a mother," called it a "jewel" and "beloved of God."[21] Grace always brings joy and peace, and we must appreciate poverty and desire it as a grace. However, for many of us this has not always been the case; we live it incoherently and, often, as an imposition. Let us decide "with great spirit and freedom," putting aside our fears, so that we may come closer to him who "makes all things new," to ask him, personally and in community, for the grace of poverty and the wisdom to live it as a gift. Renewed poverty will have the simultaneous effect of evangelical renewal in the quality of life of the Society. To live poverty as a grace in an egotistic world lacking a sense of responsibility for others will place us joyfully with the Son and with those among whom the Son wants to be, the poor and neglected of the earth.

---

[20] Cf. GC 32, D 12, n. 9; GC 31, D 18, n. 4.

[21] *SpEx* [147]; *Const.* [287] "Letter to the Fathers and Brothers at Padua," op. cit., n. 2.

DECREE 10

The Promotion of Vocations

292/ 1.   The Society of Jesus cannot fulfill its mission without further vocations. General Congregation 34 therefore calls on all our companions to work vigorously for vocations. Clearly, a vocation is a gift from God, and no human effort can replace the action of the Spirit. Nonetheless, God uses human instruments. Each Jesuit and each Jesuit community must take responsibility for ensuring that we can carry out our mission in the years to come.

293/ 2.   Our mission and spiritual heritage make us all promoters of vocations; vocation promotion simply means helping young people hear and respond to the stirrings of the Spirit in their hearts. Naturally, vocation promotion does not necessarily produce a vocation to the Society of Jesus. It leads to various types of a Christian response, and we must carefully respect the particular way in which the Spirit calls each person. At the same time, young people can only choose what they know and love. Every Jesuit and every Jesuit community must do everything possible actively to present the Society of Jesus to others in such a way that those whom God calls will know and appreciate who and what we are.

294/ 3.   The quality of our lives as Jesuits gives a human image to God's call. If we really expect vocations, we must examine whether our relationship with God, our communities, and our apostolates are what we profess them to be. Destructive criticism, bitterness, and even contempt for our way of life and the vows are devastating for those who might be considering a Jesuit vocation. Fortunately, most Jesuits are positive and lead lives of great fidelity. Even so, many of us are too hesitant and too timid in offering what we have to others.

295/   Does our prayer remain a secret except to ourselves, or do we talk about our experience of God, including its dificulties, with others and with our brother Jesuits? Do our communities remain mysterious to all except Jesuits, or are they open and welcoming to those who seek us? Do young people see us working together, sometimes struggling but still supporting one another, praying together? Does our apostolic zeal communicate itself to others, so that they, too, will want to commit themselves to God's service?

296/ 4. We must promote vocations as widely as possible, so that we might reflect the culture and experience of those we seek to serve. With special sensitivity and encouragement, we need to seek possible vocations among minority cultures, immigrants, and indigenous people.

297/ We recommend that Father General, after studying the experience of vocation promotion in the whole Society, write a letter on the practical aspects of promoting vocations to the Society.

IV

IN THE CHURCH

DECREE 11

On Having a Proper Attitude of Service in the Church

Introduction

298/ 1. When General Congregation 33 spoke of our "Life in the Church,"[1] it committed the Society once again to "serving the Church in her teaching, life, and worship."[2] In his final address to the congregation of procurators,[3] Fr. General Peter-Hans Kolvenbach reiterated this commitment. GC 34 reaffirms this long and permanent tradition of service proper to the Society, one to which we dedicate ourselves not only as religious but also, and especially, in virtue of the fourth vow of obedience to the pope in regard to missions.

299/ 2. This service is exercised in myriad humble, sometimes hidden, ways by Jesuit priests and brothers missioned to the labors of parish and mission station, pulpit and confessional, workshop and printing press, classroom and laboratory.

300/ 3. Equally humble and hidden is the service exercised by Jesuit theologians, by consultors of the dicasteries of the Holy See, by consultants and resource persons for episcopal conferences and individual diocesan bishops. Along with the more public service of scholarly research, teaching, speaking, and writing, these are intellectual tasks that require freedom, openness, and courage in the objective service of truth.

301/ 4. Our Jesuit service can also be the dangerous commitment of witness and struggle against the forces of injustice and persecution, both social and religious, a witness that has been once again sealed by the blood of martyrs. In recent decades, as throughout our history, the heroism of our many brothers who have suffered and died for their fidelity to the Church bears clear and irrefutable witness that the Society's foundational commitment is truly "to serve the Lord alone and the Church, his spouse, under the Roman Pontiff."[4]

---

[1] GC 33, D 1, nn. 6–8.

[2] *Ibid*, n. 6.

[3] Peter-Hans Kolvenbach, Final Address to the Congregation of Procurators 67, 8 September 1987, nn. 8f., *AR* 19 (1987): pp. 1081–84.

[4] *Formula* [3].

Church and World: The New Context

302/ 5.   Jesuits today exercise this service in a world gripped by strong sociopolitical and technological changes, often of a revolutionary character, fueled by the struggle for justice, modernization, and development. This dialectic of change produces multiple problems from which the Society cannot be immune.

303/ 6.   Since the Second Vatican Council, the Church has been engaged in its own dialectic of *traditio et progressio*. New strains and conflicts have arisen as it seeks to respond to the call for an evangelization that is ever old yet ever new. These tensions affect several aspects of the Church's life: liturgy, doctrine, ethics, discipline, pastoral ministry, and the inculturation of each of these.

304/ 7.   Vatican II was a prophetic event, producing a momentous renewal within Catholicism not witnessed since the Council of Trent. This dynamic ecclesial creativity reveals a People of God on pilgrimage, striving, under the guidance of the Holy Spirit, to live a recovered ecclesiology of collegial (or "synodal" for the Eastern churches) coresponsibility. Those disoriented by the inevitable conflicts that result from such an invigorating new vision should recall that most major ecumenical councils have set in motion a very lengthy process of reform and renewal which did not reach a lived consensus for centuries.

305/ 8.   The ecclesiological renewal of Vatican II has helped us rediscover the Universal Church as a *koinōnia* of local churches under the entire college of bishops, of which the bishop of Rome is the head. This, in turn, has renewed our consciousness of the distinctive and inalienable ecclesial role of the laity in the life of the Church. Can we be surprised that this deepened sense of the coresponsibility of all God's people for the whole life of the Church has led to more voices speaking, and that they are not all saying the same thing? This is a source of vitality—as well as of creative tensions.

Challenges of the Times

306/ 9.   Attentive to this summons to work with the People of God in the spirit of Vatican II and GCs 32 and 33, and invited by the Pope to help in the implementation of the same council, the Society renews its fidelity to the teaching of the Church as it discerns and confronts the signs of the times. For among those signs are contemporary developments that can pose intellectual, cultural, and pastoral challenges to that fidelity.

307/ 10.   Hunger, religious and racial persecution, disordered economic and cultural development, the lack of political freedom and social justice; widespread socioeconomic discrimination, exploitation, and sexual abuse, especially of women and children; callous disregard for the precious gift of life; pastoral challenges of secularity; social anonymity and the alienation of modern urbanization; the dissolution of the family: all these confront, often massively, the Church—and therefore ourselves—and demand our response.

308/ 11. Even positive developments are not without their ambiguities: remarkable advances in the life sciences and the accompanying new problems of bioethics, the need to nuance cherished theological theories in the light of contemporary hermeneutics and historiography, the new culture created by the explosion of mass media, internal problems of liturgical discipline and sacramental life provoked by modernization and inculturation. These are among the "new situations being presented to the Society, demanding, in full fidelity to the Magisterium of the Church, valid responses to so many healthy questions from the People of God" to which Father General alludes in his final address to the congregation of procurators.[5] This fidelity will adhere to the accepted norms of assent and to Catholic teaching on the hierarchy of truths and the development of Church doctrine, as contained in the official documents of the Magisterium and in the common teaching of proven Catholic theologians.[6]

309/ 12. A Jesuit, especially the scholar or theologian engaged in research and the molding of informed public opinion, will see these challenges as occasions for service. His mission must ensure that the Christian tradition maintains its respectability as a coherent and valid world view in dialogue with the realm of secular scholarship and science. Only through the exacting labor of the scholarly enterprise, carried out with faith and in an atmosphere of freedom and mutual trust, can the Church remain an active force for good in the contemporary world of intellectual and cultural discourse. GC 34 expresses its deep appreciation to, solidarity with, and support for the Jesuits engaged in this crucial service to the Church today.

310/ 13. Such service requires courage and integrity; it can also involve pain. As Father General said, aware of "strong tensions within the Church from which the Society may not stand aloof, and through their very apostolic responsibility, Jesuits are inevitably dragged into conflictual, even explosive ecclesiastical situations."[7] Our response to such situations can give rise to tensions with some Church authorities. Despite—indeed, because of—our sincere desire to live in fidelity to the Magisterium and the hierarchy, there may be times when we feel justified, even obliged, to speak out in a way that may not always win us general approval and could even lead to sanctions painful to the Society and constituting an impediment to our work.

311/ 14. To do so does not put the Jesuit in a stance of disobedience or revolt. Ignatian obedience, in accord with the tradition of Catholic theology, has always

---

[5] Peter-Hans Kolvenbach, op. cit., n. 7, *AR* 19 (1987): p. 1081.

[6] Cf. Vatican Council II, *Unitatis Redintegratio*, n. 11; Congregation for the Doctrine of the Faith, *Mysterium Ecclesiae*, 24 June 1973, nn. 4f., CIC 750–54; CCEO 598–600; *Catechism of the Catholic Church*, nn. 85 ff.

[7] Peter-Hans Kolvenbach, op. cit., n. 4, *AR* 19 (1987): p. 1079.

recognized that our first fidelity must be to God, to the truth, and to a well-formed conscience. Obedience, then, cannot exclude our prayerful discernment of the course of action to be followed, one that may in some circumstances differ from the one suggested by our religious and Church superiors. Such discernment, and its respectful representation to superiors, is an authentic element of our Ignatian tradition confirmed in GC 31[8] and clarified in GC 32.[9]

312/ 15. At the same time, Ignatian obedience is one of concrete fidelity to the real, visible, hierarchical Church, not to some abstract ideal. This Church is not something distinct from us: it is the community of believers to which we belong and whose virtues and defects, triumphs and tragedies, we share. Once the discernment is accomplished and the representations made, the Jesuit attitude will ultimately be one modeled on the "Rules in Order to Have the Proper Attitude of Mind in the Church Militant" of St. Ignatius.[10]

313/ 16. In saying this we are well aware that the context in which Ignatius wrote these rules is very different from that of today. But Ignatian service in the Church is not a history lesson. It is a profound mystical bond that transcends the particularities of its historical origins in the sixteenth-century Church. Rooted in faith that the Holy Spirit is guiding the Church, it drives us to seek the *magis,* serenely confident that "to them that love God, all things work together unto good" (Rom. 8:28).

314/ 17. Therefore, if there is a time for speaking out, there may also be a time for silence, chosen by discernment or even imposed by obedience. If there is a time for representation, there is also a time for the abnegation of our intellect and will, which becomes for us a new way of seeing through the clouds of suffering and uncertainty to a higher truth and wisdom, that of the Cross.

The Jesuit Response: A Contemporary Perspective

315/ 18. A contemporary Ignatian response to these problems is given in the address of Father General to the congregation of procurators to which we have already referred.[11] It is not meant to provide an updated version of the "Rules in Order to Have the Proper Attitude of Mind in the Church Militant";[12] still less does it pretend to give an exhaustive treatment of the theme or of its history and interpretation.[13] We find instead a profound reflection on the foundational

---

[8] GC 31, D 17, n. 10.

[9] GC 32, D 11, n. 55.

[10] *SpEx* [352–70].

[11] Peter-Hans Kolvenbach, op. cit. nn. 8f., *AR* (1987): pp. 1081–84.

[12] Kolvenbach, op. cit., n. 8; the updating was mandated by GC 33, D 1, n. 8.

[13] Kolvenbach, op. cit., n. 9.

inspiration that motivated the Society to integrate itself more fully into a living experience of the mystery of the Church, in the spirit of the fourth vow in regard to missions that so distinctively unites us with the Holy Father.

316/ 19. This congregation makes its own the teaching of Father General's address and recommends it to the whole Society for attentive study in an atmosphere of prayer, examen, and individual and communal reflection and discernment. In accord with GC 33, Father General affirms that the Society must "seek to incorporate itself more and more vigorously and creatively into the life of the Church,"[14] and "learn in the Church, with the Church, and for the Church how to live our faith as adults in the conditions, cultures, and languages of this end of the century."[15]

317/ 20. If our love of Christ, inseparable from our love for his spouse the Church, impels us to seek the will of God in each situation, it can also oblige us to engage in constructive criticism based on a prayerful discernment. But it cannot justify a lack of solidarity with the Church, from which we are never in any way distinct or apart. In the elaboration and expression of our theological views and in our choice of pastoral options, we must always actively seek to understand the mind of the hierarchical Church, having as our goal the end of the Society to help souls. At the same time, we must try to articulate the *sensus fidelium* and help the Magisterium discern in it the movements of the Spirit in accord with the teaching of Vatican II.[16] Formed by the experience of the Spiritual Exercises and desirous of being faithful to this Ignatian vision, we pray God to instill in us the spirit that animates these Ignatian rules.

318/ 21. Even when it is not possible to refrain from all critical observations in the objective evaluation of certain situations in the life of the Church, or even of the comportment of persons holding responsible positions in its service, we will always seek to do so in this spirit. As men of integrity, we must of course be true to our consciences. But we will speak (or keep silent) in prudence and humility, and with a sense of genuine respect and affection for the pastors of the Church, both local and universal.[17] We will strive for the honesty to gratefully acknowledge the grace of their guidance as a needed corrective to whatever may be tainted by narrowness or the limitations of what is personal and subjective. We will be aware that as members of the Society we are bound to them in a special way, and that our prime concern is to cooperate with them in building up and, where necessary, healing both the universal and local churches.

---

[14] GC 33, D 1, n. 4.

[15] Peter-Hans Kolvenbach, op. cit. n. 17, *AR* 19 (1987): p. 1089.

[16] Cf. Vatican Council II, *Lumen Gentium*, nn. 12, 35.

[17] Cf. *SpEx* [353].

319/ 22. We will be conscious, too, that the Church cannot be explained in purely sociopolitical terms, but is animated by a transcendent Spirit that guides and authenticates the Christian community through the collegial action of the Pope and bishops,[18] and is affirmed by the *sensus fidelium*.[19]

The Jesuit Response: Concrete Modalities

320/ 23. We will recognize that, particularly in sensitive doctrinal and moral questions, it is often difficult for magisterial statements to explicitate exhaustively all aspects of an issue. Rather than indulging in selective and superficial criticism, we will look for the central message and, through discerning theological reflection, attempt to understand it in depth and explain it positively, respectfully, and clearly.

321/ 24. We will keep difficulties in perspective and not isolate them from their context. We will not underestimate the possibility of giving scandal, nor forget that between the extremes of premature, ill-considered public criticism and servile silence there exists the alternative of moderate and respectful expression of our views.[20] We will avoid particular interests and bear in mind the greater good of the whole Church. When possible, we will seek recourse through official channels;[21] we will remain in active dialogue and discernment with our own superiors in the Society, and conduct consultation and dialogue with other competent Church authorities in a spirit of mutual respect and understanding. To this end, wherever possible we will show ourselves ready to foster informal personal contacts of cordial friendliness with the local bishops in areas where we exercise our mission, and seek to contain and defuse possible sources of conflict before they develop.

322/ 25. If the Church appears to be attacked or defamed in the media, we cannot limit ourselves to a dismissive condemnation of such abuses. We must enter the world of communication and defend the truth, while at the same time honestly acknowledging conflicts and polarities within the Church. Though we will do so without sharpening tensions or weakening authority, we cannot avoid issues which, as news, the media will present in any event.

323/ 26. We must cooperate with the media so that the Church's true face can appear and the Gospel be inculturated in this new mass culture as well. We will strive to see that issues conducive to good receive effective media attention. Though we remain always loyal to the truth, our Ignatian sense of *sentire cum*

---

[18] Cf. *SpEx* [365].

[19] Cf. Vatican Council II, *Lumen Gentium*, nn. 12, 35.

[20] Cf. John Paul II, Allocution to General Congregation 34, 5 January 1995, n. 6; see pp. 663–668 below.

[21] Cf. *SpEx* [362].

ecclesia will lead us to present what is praiseworthy in the Church, revealing the bonds of affection that make us love the Church and cleave to it as a source of life, solace, and healing, as an internal authority for genuine religious experience, as a nurturing matrix of our deepest values.[22]

Conclusion: Fidelity to Our Jesuit Charism to Serve

324/ 27. If in today's world the Society is to be engaged "in the most difficult and extreme fields, in the crossroads of ideologies, in the front line of social conflict," as the Holy Father said in his address at the beginning of this congregation,[23] repeating the words of Pope Paul VI at the opening of GC 32,[24] we are there as "men whom Christ himself sends into the world to spread his holy doctrine among people of every state and condition."[25]

325/ 28. In that same spirit, on this eve of the third millennium we pledge ourselves once again to generous service of all our brothers and sisters. This service will be Christian only if anchored by fidelity to him who makes all things new. It will be Jesuit only if it is in union with the successor of Peter. For this union has always given us the assurance—indeed, it is the visible sign—"of our communion with Christ, the first and supreme head of the Society which by its very name is his: the Society of Jesus."[26]

---

[22] Cf. *SpEx* [353–63].

[23] John Paul II, Allocution to General Congregation 34, 5 January 1995, n. 8; see pp. 663–668 below.

[24] Paul VI, Allocution to General Congregation 32, 3 December 1974, n. 2; cf. Documents of General Congregation 32, p. 380 above.

[25] Paul VI, Allocution to General Congregation 32; cf. *SpEx* [145].

[26] Paul VI, Allocution to General Congregation 32.

DECREE 12

Ecumenism

326/ 1. The signs of the times give stark proof of the fact that a faith doing justice must necessarily lead to ecumenical and interreligious dialogue and cooperation. In many parts of the world, it is precisely religious divisions that are a force contributing to injustice, violence, and even warfare. In situations of conflict, often fueled by historic confessional hostilities, ecumenism calls us to pardon and to love as essential co`mponents of a Gospel-inspired struggle for justice and reconciliation. As peoples move towards ever closer political, economic, social, and cultural unity, and as nations once divided by centuries of hatred and conflict form new supranational economic and political structures, the historic divisions of Christianity represent a flagrant counter witness to the Gospel message "ut omnes unum sint" (John 17:21).

327/ 2. Therefore General Congregation 34 reaffirms the Society's commitment to ecumenism in the most vigorous and explicit terms; it is an apostolate not only in need of revitalization in its present moment of crisis but one for which the Society is suited by its global outreach and numerous institutions dedicated to formation in the Christian spirit.

328/ 3. Ecumenism is not only a specific work for which some Jesuits must be trained and missioned; it is a new way of being a Christian. It tries to be more than just honest and truthful and fair; it attempts to work disinterestedly in service of the truth. It seeks to see things from the other's point of view and to take seriously the other's critique of one's own communion and its historic errors and failings. Like Ignatius's preamble to the Spiritual Exercises,[1] it seeks to put the best interpretation on what the other says and does. In a word, ecumenism seeks what unites rather than what divides; seeks understanding rather than confrontation; seeks to know, understand, and love others as they wish to be known and understood, with full respect for their distinctiveness, through the dialogue of truth, justice, and love.[2]

329/ 4. In choosing the path of ecumenism, the Society is responding not only to its discernment of the signs of the times but to the repeated calls of the

---

[1] Cf. *SpEx* [22].

[2] Cf. GC 32, D 4, n. 37.

Church[3] and preceding general congregations.[4] It is also responding, with even greater urgency today, to the exigencies of the ministry of faith and justice. The need, therefore, is not for new legislation, but for a more effective implementation of existing legislation.

330/ 5.   Consequently, the general congregation

a. recommends greater attention to initial and ongoing ecumenical formation in the Society, in accordance with the norms of GC 31, Decree 26, nn. 4–8, and The 1993 Directory on Ecumenism, Section II, nn. 55–91, especially 79[5]

b. draws attention to the recent norms of the Congregation for Catholic Education for courses in ecumenism and Eastern Christian studies[6]

c. recommends an attentive fostering of ecumenical sensitivity in all our ministries

d. reaffirms the concrete proposals of GC 31, Decree 26, nn. 9–14 concerning the practice of ecumenism

---

[3] Cf. especially (1) Vatican Council II, *Unitatis Redintegratio, Lumen Gentium, Orientalium Ecclesiarum,* and *Dignitatis Humanae.;* (2) John Paul II, Apostolic letter *Tertio Millennio Adveniente,* n. 16; also his allocutions at GC 33, 2 September 1983, n. 6, and at GC 34, 5 January 1995, n. 5; (3*) The 1993 Directory on Ecumenism* of the Pontifical Council for Promoting Christian Unity.

[4] GC 31, D 26; GC 33, D 1, n. 37; *Complementary Norms,* 253, 4° and 269, §§2f.

[5] One could also usefully consult the document of 20 May 1993, *Ecumenical Formation: Ecumenical Reflections and Suggestions: A Study Document of the Joint Working Groups between the Roman Catholic Church and the World Council of Churches* (Vatican Press, 1993).

[6] Congregation for Catholic Education, Letter of 6 January 1987, Prot. N. 340/86.

DECREE 13

COOPERATION WITH THE LAITY IN MISSION

331/ 1. A reading of the signs of the times since the Second Vatican Council shows unmistakably that the Church of the next millennium will be called the "Church of the Laity." During the past thirty years increasing numbers of lay people have responded to the call to ministry flowing from the grace received in baptism.[1] The actualization of their vocation in so many and such varied situations has become the predominant way by which the People of God minister to the world in promotion of the Kingdom. This growth of lay ministry will surely continue to expand during the next millennium. The Society of Jesus acknowledges as a grace of our day and a hope for the future that laity "take an active, conscientious, and responsible part in the mission of the Church in this great moment of history."[2] We seek to respond to this grace by offering ourselves in service to the full realization of this mission of the laity, and we commit ourselves to that end by cooperating with them in their mission.[3]

332/ 2. We discover a similar grace if we read the signs of the times in the apostolic work of the Society of Jesus over the past thirty years. Spurred by the council, General Congregation 31 urged us to "foster the cooperation of the laity in our own apostolic works."[4] Since that time a growing cooperation with the laity has expanded our mission and transformed the ways in which we carry it out in partnership with others. It has enriched what we do and how we understand our role in that mission. Jesuit works in some areas of the world depend primarily upon lay persons for the carrying out of the mission of the Society. We foresee the expansion of lay apostolic leadership in Jesuit works in years to come and pledge ourselves to assist this development.

333/ 3. We also cooperate with many others: priests, men and women religious, with their distinct charisms, as well as people of all faiths and beliefs who seek to build a world of truth, justice, freedom, peace, and love. We are grateful for this cooperation and are enriched by it.

---

[1] Vatican Council II, *Lumen Gentium*, n. 31.

[2] John Paul II, Apostolic Exhortation *Christifideles Laici*, n. 3.

[3] GC 31, D 33, n. 34; Peter-Hans Kolvenbach, Address to the Congregation of Provincials 1 "*De Statu Societatis*," n. 19, *AR* 20 (1990): p. 451; Peter-Hans Kolvenbach, "To Friends and Colleagues of the Society of Jesus," *AR* 20 (1990): pp. 601–7.

[4] GC 31, D 33, n 6.

334/ 4. Jesuits are both "men for others"[5] and "men with others."[6] This basic characteristic of our way of proceeding calls for an attitude and readiness to cooperate, to listen and to learn from others, to share our spiritual and apostolic inheritance. To be "men with others" is a central aspect of our charism and deepens our identity.

335/ 5. Because of the experiences of the recent past, many Jesuit provinces as well as many lay persons have urged this general congregation to take new steps forward in cooperation. In response to these requests we offer recommendations concerning *(a)* the Society's service to the laity in their ministry, *(b)* formation of both laity and Jesuits for this cooperation, *(c)* Jesuit cooperation with laity in works of the Society, other works, and associations, and *(d)* opportunities for the future.

A. Service to the Laity in Their Ministry

336/ 6. The expansion and variety of lay apostolic service in our day has remarkable dimensions. Many lay persons recognize their activity as Christian ministry and seek to be trained for and commissioned to this service. Others engage in apostolic service in a more informal and implicit manner. Still others participate in lay associations for varied apostolic purposes. In all these ways many lay men and women give witness to the Gospel. Where they live, worship, and work, laity are taking on greater responsibility for the ministry of the Church. Called to be holy and concerned for faith, justice, and the poor, they evangelize the structures of society.

337/ 7. The Society of Jesus places itself at the service of this mission of the laity by offering what we are and have received: our spiritual and apostolic inheritance, our educational resources, and our friendship. We offer Ignatian spirituality as a specific gift to animate the ministry of the laity. This apostolic spirituality respects the unique spirituality of the individual and adapts itself to present needs; it helps persons to discern their call and "in all things to love and serve the Divine Majesty."[7] We offer to laity the practical wisdom we have learned from more than four centuries of apostolic experience. Through our schools, universities, and other educational programs we make pastoral and theological training available. Perhaps most important, we join with them in companionship: serving together, learning from and responding to each other's concerns and initiatives, dialoguing with one other on apostolic objectives.

---

[5] Pedro Arrupe, "Men for Others," Address to the Tenth International Congress of Former Jesuit Students of Europe, 1973. English text printed by the Jesuit Secondary Education Association, U.S.A.

[6] Peter-Hans Kolvenbach, "To Friends and Colleagues of the Society of Jesus," *AR* 20 (1990): p. 602.

[7] *SpEx* [233].

B. Formation of Laity and Jesuits

338/ 8. Putting ourselves at the service of the apostolate of the laity challenges us. We need to respond to their desire for formation so that they are able to minister as fully as possible according to their call and gifts. This formation should draw on the abundant resources and experiences of the Society. We should not hesitate to offer, when requested, the experience of the Spiritual Exercises and our spiritual direction. We can encourage them towards the apostolic priority of the service of faith and the promotion of justice with a preferential love of the poor. By responding in this way we offer who we are. As persons whose lives are centered on loving and serving God in all things, we should help others recognize and discern the apostolic possibilities of their lives and work. Laity who collaborate in Jesuit apostolates can expect from us a specific formation in Ignatian values, help in discernment of apostolic priorities and objectives, and practical strategies for their realization.

339/ 9. Cooperation with laity in mission requires the formation and renewal of all Jesuits. Initial formation must develop our capacity for collaboration with both laity and fellow Jesuits by means of education and experiences of ministerial cooperation with others. Ongoing formation in apostolic situations—if we listen to others, learn from their spirituality, and face together the difficulties of genuine cooperation—will deepen this capacity. Both in our initial and ongoing formation, lay people can help us understand and respect their distinct vocation as well as appreciate our own.

C. Jesuit Cooperation with Laity

340/ 10. Recent experience enables us to see three dimensions of our cooperation with others in mission: (i) lay collaboration in Jesuit apostolic works, (ii) the cooperation of Jesuits in the works of others, and (iii) our support of and contribution to lay apostolic associations related to the Society and its mission.

i. Collaboration in Works of the Society

341/ 11. We collaborate with the laity in works of the Society. A work of the Society substantially contributes to realizing the mission of the Society, manifests Ignatian values, and bears the name "Jesuit" with the Society's approval. The Society takes "ultimate responsibility" for this work.[8] Examples are Jesuit educational institutions, parishes, social centers, retreat houses, and the Jesuit Refugee Service.

342/ 12. Each such work must be guided by a clear mission statement which outlines the purposes of the work and forms the basis for collaboration in it. This mission statement should be presented and clearly explained to those with whom

---

[8] GC 31, D 33, n 6. Civil laws, which vary from country to country, affect the way in which the Society exercises its responsibility and must be respected.

we cooperate. Programs are to be provided and supported (even financially) to enable lay people to acquire a greater knowledge of the Ignatian tradition and spirituality and to grow in each one's personal vocation.

343/ 13. All those engaged in the work should exercise coresponsibility and be engaged in discernment and participative decision making where it is appropriate. Lay persons must have access to and be trained for positions of responsibility according to their qualifications and commitment. A lay person can be the director of a Jesuit work.[9] When this is the case, Jesuits receive from the provincial their mission to work in the institution, and they carry out this mission under the direction of the lay director.[10] In institutions where Jesuits are a small minority, special attention should be given both to the leadership role of lay colleagues and to appropriate means for the Society to assure the Jesuit identity of the work.

ii. Cooperation in Non-Jesuit Works

344/ 14. Our mission today also calls us to cooperate more closely with institutions, organizations, and activities which are not sponsored by the Society.[11] Among these are social development and welfare centers, educational and research institutions, seminaries and religious institutes, international organizations, labor unions, ecclesial base communities and grass-roots movements. This cooperation is a way of witnessing to the Gospel and to Ignatian spirituality. It allows us to enter into milieus where the Curch wishes to be present. Our cooperation there can express solidarity with others while learning from them in a way which enriches the Society and the Church.

345/ 15. Cooperation in these works should be in accord with the Society's criteria for the choice of ministries, especially service of the faith and promotion of justice. The Jesuit should be missioned with clear apostolic objectives and remain in continuous discernment with his superior and apostolic community.

iii. Cooperation with Associations

346/ 16. Many lay persons desire to be united with us through participation in apostolic associations of Ignatian inspiration.[12] The Society views positively this growth of lay associations. They give witness to the Ignatian charism in the world,

---

[9] Peter-Hans Kolvenbach, Final Address to the Congregation of Provincials 1, *AR* 20 (1990): pp. 508f.

[10] This direction is the authority over the institution and its mission rather than the religious authority which is the subject matter of our vows.

[11] GC 31, D 33, n. 3.

[12] Peter-Hans Kolvenbach, "To Friends and Colleagues of the Society of Jesus," op. cit.

enable us to undertake with them works of greater dimensions, and help their members to live the faith more fully. Jesuits are encouraged to study these various associations, to know them through personal contact, and to develop a genuine interest in them.

347/ 17. Among the privileged means both for the Christian formation of lay people in Ignatian spirituality and for partnership in a common mission, the Society actively promotes several different associations.[13]

348/ • Christian Life Communities address people who, being formed in the Spiritual Exercises, hear a call to follow Jesus Christ more closely and to make a life commitment to work with others through apostolic witness and service. The community dimension supports this apostolic commitment. We pledge ourselves to share Ignatian spirituality with them and to accompany them in their mission.

349/ • Jesuit Volunteer programs offer service marked especially by concern for the poor and work for justice, community living, simple lifestyle, and Ignatian spirituality. Provinces are encouraged to support these volunteer associations, to develop better national and international networks among them, and to recognize them as a work of the Society where desired and appropriate.

350/ • Jesuit Past-Student Associations enable those who once attended our schools to better carry out their responsibility to "make fruitful in their lives and in the world the formation they have received."[14] Qualified Jesuits should be assigned to help them in ongoing spiritual, ethical, and social formation, as well as in identifying apostolic needs.

351/ • The Apostleship of Prayer seeks to form Christians shaped by the Eucharist, devoted to the Heart of Christ through the daily offering and prayer for the intentions of the Church, and committed to apostolic service. The Society supports and promotes this pastoral service entrusted to it by the Holy Father, as well as the Eucharistic Youth Movement.

D. Opportunities for the Future

352/ 18. The present moment is a moment of grace. As lay people continue to grow in their service to the world, the Society of Jesus will find opportunities for cooperation with them reaching far beyond our present experience. We will be stretched in our creativity and energy to serve them in their ministry. We will be called upon to take a supportive role as they become more responsible for our

---

[13] This list does not in any way mean to exclude other communities or movements with which the Society has very privileged and fruitful links in various countries.

[14] Peter-Hans Kolvenbach, Address to the Third World Congress of Former Jesuit Students, Versailles 1986, *AR* 19 (1986): pp. 621–29.

own apostolates. We will be challenged to live out more fully our identity as "men for and with others." As we look to this future, we suggest some possibilities for our response to this opportunity and grace.

i. Empowering the "Church of the Laity"

353/ 19. Lay men and women will assume more and more responsibility for the ministries of the Church in parishes, diocesan structures, schools, theological institutions, missions, and works of justice and charity. We can expect a flourishing of specialized ministries, ecclesial movements, and lay apostolic associations of more varied purpose and inspiration. With our charism and experience we will make a specific and needed contribution to these apostolic endeavors. For this we must increasingly shift the focus of our attention from the exercise of our own direct ministry to the strengthening of laity in their mission. To do so will require of us an ability to draw out their gifts and to animate and inspire them. Our willingness to accept this challenge will depend on the strength of our Jesuit companionship and on a renewal of our response to the call of Christ to serve his mission.

ii. Lay Leadership in Works of the Society

354/ 20. The emerging "Church of the Laity" will also have an impact on our own Jesuit apostolic works. This transformation can enrich these works and expand their Ignatian character if we know how to cooperate with the grace of the emergence of the laity. When we speak of "our apostolates," we will mean something different by "our." It will signify a genuine Ignatian partnership of laity and Jesuits, each of us acting according to our proper vocation. Lay persons will rightly take on a greater role of responsibility and leadership within these works. Jesuits will be called on to support them in their initiative by Ignatian formation, the witness of our priestly and religious lives, and promotion of Jesuit apostolic values. If our service will be more humble, it will also be more challenging and creative, more in accord with the graces we have received. This actualization of the lay vocation can show more clearly the grace of our vocation.

iii. Developing an Ignatian Apostolic Network

355/ 21. A challenge for future cooperation with the laity in mission can be found in the number of individuals, co-workers, former Jesuits, associations, and communities both lay and religious who find a common spirituality and apostolic motivation in the experience of the Spiritual Exercises. The existence of so many Ignatian-inspired persons testifies to the continuing vitality of the Exercises and their power for apostolic animation. The grace of the new era of the Church and the movement to solidarity impel us to work more decisively to strengthen the bonds among all these persons and groups. Thus we can develop what might be called "an Ignatian apostolic network."

356/ 22. Such a network will foster better communication and provide personal and spiritual support among these persons and groups. It will maximize the mission of Ignatian-inspired persons in their evangelization of the world. In this way the Society of Jesus can make a specific contribution to the new evangelization. The shaping of this Ignatian apostolic network will require wide consultation, careful discernment, and careful, gradually developed planning. The general congregation asks Father General, with the assistance of qualified Jesuits and others, to study this possibility.

iv. Some Joined to the Society by Closer Personal Bond

357/ 23. The possibility of joining lay persons more closely to the Society was given official recognition in GC 31. It urged Father General "to study the ways by which such bonds and a more stable and intimate collaboration" could be achieved.[15] Some experience of closer bonding has occurred since then. GC 34 views this as one among several ways of future lay cooperation. It recommends ten years of experimentation of "juridical bonding" of individual lay persons to the Society of Jesus and offers directions for experimentation, asking the next general congregation to evaluate these experiments.

358/ 24. The purpose of these experiments with closer bonding is apostolic— to extend the missioning process of the Society to lay persons, who accompany and are accompanied by Jesuits in apostolic discernment and activity. The juridical bond will be some form of contractual agreement of the Society with individual lay persons; they may or may not form an association among themselves for companionship, mutual support, and apostolic strength, but they are not admitted into the body of the Society. The distinctiveness of their lay vocation is preserved; they do not become quasi religious.

359/ 25. Elements to be considered in experimental programs include

    a. procedures for selection of associates

    b. adequate and appropriate formation

    c. terms of agreement regarding rights, responsibilities, duration, and evaluation

    d. mutual discernment with the provincial or his delegate about mission

    e. norms for the possible communal life of associates

    f. norms for informal relationships with Jesuit communities

    g preparation and assignment of Jesuits to accompany associates

    h. financial and other practical arrangements

---

[15] GC 31, D 34.

A Call to Renewal

360/ 26. Cooperation with the laity is both a constitutive element of our way of proceeding and a grace calling for individual, communal, and institutional renewal. It invites us to service of the ministry of lay people, partnership with them in mission, and openness to creative ways of future cooperation. The Spirit is calling us as "men for and with others" to share with lay men and women what we believe, who we are, and what we have, in creative companionship, for "the help of souls and the greater glory of God."

DECREE 14

Jesuits and the Situation of Women in Church And Civil Society

Introduction

361/ 1. General Congregation 33 made a brief mention of the "unjust treatment and exploitation of women."[1] It was part of a list of injustices in a context of new needs and situations which Jesuits were called to address in the implementation of our mission. We wish to consider this question more specifically and substantially on this occasion. This is principally because, assisted by the general rise in consciousness concerning this issue, we are more aware than previously that it is indeed a central concern of any contemporary mission which seeks to integrate faith and justice. It has a universal dimension in that it involves men and women everywhere. To an increasing extent it cuts across barriers of class and culture. It is of personal concern to those who work with us in our mission, especially lay and religious women.

The Situation

362/ 2. The dominance of men in their relationship with women has found expression in many ways. It has included discrimination against women in educational opportunities, the disproportionate burden they are called upon to bear in family life, paying them a lesser wage for the same work, limiting their access to positions of influence when admitted to public life, and, sadly but only too frequently, outright violence against women themselves. In some parts of the world, this violence still includes female circumcision, dowry deaths, and the murder of unwanted infant girls. Women are commonly treated as objects in advertising and in the media. In extreme cases, for example, in promoting international sex tourism, they are regarded as commodities to be trafficked in.

363/ 3. This situation, however, has begun to change, chiefly because of the critical awakening and courageous protest of women themselves. But many

---

[1] GC 33, D 1, n. 48.

men, too, have joined women in rejecting attitudes which offend against the dignity of men and women alike. Nonetheless, we still have with us the legacy of systematic discrimination against women. It is embedded within the economic, social, political, religious, and even linguistic structures of our societies. It is often part of an even deeper cultural prejudice and stereotype. Many women, indeed, feel that men have been slow to recognize the full humanity of women. They often experience a defensive reaction from men when they draw attention to this blindness.

364/ 4. The prejudice against women, to be sure, assumes different forms in different cultures. Sensitivity is needed to avoid using any one simple measurement of what counts as discrimination. But it is nonetheless a universal reality. Further, in many parts of the world, women already cruelly disadvantaged because of war, poverty, migration, or race, often suffer a double disadvantage precisely because they are women. There is a "feminization of poverty" and a distinctive "feminine face of oppression."

The Church Addresses the Situation

365/ 5. Church social teaching, especially within the last ten years, has reacted strongly against this continuing discrimination and prejudice. Pope John Paul II in particular has called upon all men and women of goodwill, especially Catholics, to make the essential equality of women a lived reality. This is a genuine "sign of the times."[2] We need to join with interchurch and interreligious groups in order to advance this social transformation.

366/ 6. Church teaching certainly promotes the role of women within the family, but it also stresses the need for their contribution in the Church and in public life. It draws upon the text of Genesis which speaks of men and women created in the image of God (1:27) and the prophetic praxis of Jesus in his relationship with women. These sources call us to change our attitudes and work for a change of structures. The original plan of God was for a loving relationship of respect, mutuality, and equality between men and women, and we are called to fulfil this plan. The tone of this ecclesial reflection on Scripture makes it clear that there is an urgency in the challenge to translate theory into practice not only outside but also within the Church itself.

The Role and Responsibility of Jesuits

367/ 7. The Society of Jesus accepts this challenge and our responsibility for doing what we can as men and as a male religious order. We do not pretend or claim to speak for women. However, we do speak out of what we have learned from women about ourselves and our relationship with them.

---

[2] John Paul II, Apostolic letter *Mulieris Dignitatem* and apostolic exhortation *Christifideles Laici*; Message for the World Day of Peace, 1 January 1995.

368/ 8. In making this response we are being faithful, in the changed consciousness of our times, to our mission: the service of faith, of which the promotion of justice is an absolute requirement. We respond, too, out of the acknowledgement of our own limited but significant influence as Jesuits and as male religious within the Church. We are conscious of the damage to the People of God brought about in some cultures by the alienation of women who no longer feel at home in the Church and who are not able with integrity to transmit Catholic values to their families, friends, and colleagues.

Conversion

369/ 9. In response, we Jesuits first ask God for the grace of conversion. We have been part of a civil and ecclesial tradition that has offended against women. And, like many men, we have a tendency to convince ourselves that there is no problem. However unwittingly, we have often contributed to a form of clericalism which has reinforced male domination with an ostensibly divine sanction. By making this declaration we wish to react personally and collectively, and do what we can to change this regrettable situation.

Appreciation

370/ 10. We know that the nurturing of our own faith and much of our own ministry would be greatly diminished without the dedication, generosity, and joy that women bring to the schools, parishes, and other fields in which we labor together. This is particularly true of the work of lay and religious women among the urban and rural poor, often in extremely difficult and challenging situations. In addition, many religious congregations of women have adopted the Spiritual Exercises and our Jesuit Constitutions as the basis for their own spirituality and governance, becoming an extended Ignatian family. Religious and lay women have in recent years become expert in giving the Spiritual Exercises. As retreat directors, especially of the Exercises in daily life, they have enriched the Ignatian tradition and our own understanding of ourselves and of our ministry. Many women have helped to reshape our theological tradition in a way that has liberated both men and women. We wish to express our appreciation for this generous contribution of women, and hope that this mutuality in ministry might continue and flourish.

Ways Forward

371/ 11. We wish to specify more concretely at least some ways in which Jesuits may better respond to this challenge to our lives and mission. We do not presume that there is any one model of male-female relationship to be recommended, much less imposed, throughout the world or even within a given culture. Rather we note the need for a real delicacy in our response. We must be careful not to interfere in a way that alienates the culture; rather we must endeavor to facilitate a more organic process of change. We should be particularly sensitive to adopt a pedagogy that does not drive a further wedge between men and women who in certain circumstances are already under great pressure from other divisive cultural or socioeconomic forces.

372/ 12. In the first place, we invite all Jesuits to listen carefully and courageously to the experience of women. Many women feel that men simply do not listen to them. There is no substitute for such listening. More than anything else, it will bring about change. Unless we listen, any action we may take in this area, no matter how well intentioned, is likely to bypass the real concerns of women and to confirm male condescension and reinforce male dominance. Listening, in a spirit of partnership and equality, is the most practical response we can make and is the foundation for our mutual partnership to reform unjust structures.

373 13. Second, we invite all Jesuits, as individuals and through their institutions, to align themselves in solidarity with women. The practical ways of doing this will vary from place to place and from culture to culture, but many examples come readily to mind:

374/ 13, 1. explicit teaching of the essential equality of women and men in Jesuit ministries, especially in schools, colleges and universities

375/ 13, 2. support for liberation movements which oppose the exploitation of women and encourage their entry into political and social life

376/ 13, 3. specific attention to the phenomenon of violence against women

377/ 13, 4. appropriate presence of women in Jesuit ministries and institutions, not excluding the ministry of formation

378/ 13, 5. genuine involvement of women in consultation and decision making in our Jesuit ministries

379/ 13, 6. respectful cooperation with our female colleagues in shared projects

380/ 13, 7. use of appropriately inclusive language in speech and official documents

381/ 13, 8. promotion of the education of women and, in particular, the elimination of all forms of illegitimate discrimination between boys and girls in the educational process

Many of these, we are happy to say, are already being practiced in different parts of the world. We confirm their value, and recommend a more universal implementation as appropriate.

382/ 14. It would be idle to pretend that all the answers to the issues surrounding a new, more just relationship between women and men have been found or are satisfactory to all. In particular, it may be anticipated that some other questions about the role of women in civil and ecclesial society will undoubtedly mature over time. Through committed and persevering research, through exposure to different cultures, and through reflection on experience, Jesuits hope to participate in clarifying these questions and in advancing the underlying issues of justice. The change of sensibilities which this involves will inevitably have implications for Church teaching and practice. In this context we ask Jesuits to live, as always, with the tension involved in being faithful to the teachings of the Church while at the same time trying to read accurately the signs of the times.

Conclusion

383/ 15. The Society gives thanks for all that has already been achieved through the often costly struggle for a more just relationship between women and men. We thank women for the lead they have given and continue to give. In particular, we thank women religious, with whom we feel a special bond, and who have been pioneers in so many ways in their unique contribution to the mission of faith and justice. We are grateful, too, for what the Society and individual Jesuits have contributed to this new relationship, which is a source of great enrichment for both men and women.

384/ 16. Above all we want to commit the Society in a more formal and explicit way to regard this solidarity with women as integral to our mission. In this way we hope that the whole Society will regard this work for reconciliation between women and men in all its forms as integral to its interpretation of Decree 4 of GC 32 for our times. We know that a reflective and sustained commitment to bring about this respectful reconciliation can flow only from our God of love and justice, who reconciles all and promises a world in which "there is neither Jew nor Greek, there is neither slave nor free, there is neither male nor female, for you are all one in Christ Jesus" (Gal. 3:28).

V

DIMENSIONS AND PARTICULAR SECTORS OF OUR MISSION

DECREE 15

COMMUNICATION:
A NEW CULTURE

385/ 1. **A road and a call.** Our Father Ignatius identified the cultural shift of his time: the passage from the Middle Ages to the Renaissance. Recognizing the values of the emerging culture, with its concern for individuals and their spiritual growth, Ignatius oriented the Society of Jesus towards the future. He knew how to integrate gospel values and traditional cultural values with this new culture. Jesuits today are called to understand the changes that are occurring at the end of this twentieth century: the proliferation of electronic media and the so-called information revolution, as well as the new ways of learning and knowing that accompany them. This world of communication develops what is widely identified as a new culture, one that is nonlinear, image-oriented, intuitive, and affective in its understanding of the world.

386/ 2. **Ambiguity.** For all its marvels, this new world, characterized by an exponential development of the means of communication, is filled with ambiguities. Its media and language are often used in manipulative and undemocratic ways for negative and ephemeral ends. In addition, it often propagates a materialist or consumer-dominated mentality that fails to promote genuine human growth or make people receptive to the gospel message. Such false values sometimes threaten even our own Jesuit life. It is therefore necessary for us to become critical consumers and, even more, critical practitioners of social communication.

387/ 3. **Sector or dimension?** Communication in the Society has usually been considered a sector of apostolic activity, a field for some specialists who have often felt isolated or on the margin of the apostolic body. The Society must rather acknowledge that communication is not a domain restricted to a few Jesuit professionals, but a major apostolic dimension of all of our apostolates. Clearly, not all Jesuits need to be directly engaged in media. Nevertheless, every Jesuit, in order to be effective, must be aware of and well versed in the language and symbols, as well as the strengths and weaknesses, of modern communication culture. This is to create a shift in our awareness, making us realize that the new communication environment is a milieu in which large numbers of people can be reached and enriched, and where literacy, knowledge, and solidarity can be fostered.

388/ 4. **The service of faith.** The proposed cultural renewal will allow Jesuits more effectively to share the faith they are called to serve. Sometimes this will involve the direct proclamation of the Gospel and its values to large groups through mass media, or to smaller groups through group media. At other times a more indirect approach might be taken to awaken individuals to a better personal assimilation of the Christian message. In all cases this will require us to use language understood by both communication professionals and the inhabitants of the global village. Jesus, who himself communicated his Father's message through parables, miracles, and acts of compassion, must be our model.

389/ 5. **Justice in communication.** Communication is a powerful tool which must be used in the promotion of justice in our world. But we must also look critically at the authoritarian methods and unjust structures of communication and information organizations themselves. The promotion of justice within communication calls for the coordinated action of Christians and other people of goodwill in several areas. Freedom of the press and information must be promoted in countries where they are nonexistent or threatened by state control or ideological manipulation. An equitable flow of communication between industrialized and developing countries needs to be established. At present, the rich countries dominate the world with their information, films, and television programs. The voices and images of less powerful nations and cultures are largely absent from the global village. All Jesuits, especially philosophers, theologians, social scientists, those directly involved in the promotion of justice, as well as those involved in the production of creative works, should be conversant with communication ethics.

390/ 6. **Media education.** In the new media culture, it is important to educate media users to understand and make creative use of communication techniques and language, not only as individuals but also as participants in the social dialogue. Media education has as its goal a critical understanding which gives people the ability to sift out distortion, to identify hidden messages, and to make informed choices about media consumption. Such understanding returns power to the consumer and confers freedom from media manipulation and domination. Jesuit educators must be among the best "media-educated people" in order to participate in this broad educational task.

391/ 7. **People-oriented media.** The language of the new media culture can be spoken using simple and low-cost tools. Radio, especially used for popular education, is often an effective medium. More broadly, all Jesuits should learn to use alternative media such as posters, video and audio cassettes, and compact disks in their apostolic work. In some circumstances folk media, street plays, puppetry, or images in liturgy could be appropriate instruments for evangelization.

392/ 8. **A mission: Vatican Radio.** In response to the invitation from the Holy Father given at the beginning of this general congregation,[1] the Society

---

[1] John Paul II, Allocution to General Congregation 34, 5 January 1995, n. 5; see pp. 663–668 below.

commits itself to continue serving the universal Church through Vatican Radio. It is a concrete means for the Society to implement its mission to serve the faith and promote justice in the field of communication, within a framework of international collaboration.

393/ 9. **To understand and to speak the language.** We must provide well–organized communication curricula for all Jesuits in formation; we should also provide communication training as part of ongoing formation. In many places the Society has already begun to provide suitable training, integrated into the various stages of formation. These efforts must be sustained and, where lacking, adequate steps should be taken to ensure such training. Formation in communication will, among its important goals, ensure critical knowledge of the rhetoric of this new culture, foster an appreciation of its aesthetic dimension, develop the skills required for teamwork and for the effective use of media and information technology for the apostolate. Early in their formation, young Jesuits who show creative talent for communication work could be encouraged and enabled to pursue specialized training. Care should be taken to help Jesuits during their studies to integrate professional requirements and sound theological knowledge with the exigencies of religious life. The Society's Secretariat for Social Communication (JESCOM), among its other tasks, is to serve as a resource in developing communication programs for Jesuit formation.

DECREE 16

The Intellectual Dimension of Jesuit Ministries

394/ 1. Since its foundation, the Society has held intellectual labor in high esteem, as a significant contribution to the discovery of the creative work of God and to the recognition of the legitimate autonomy of human inquiry. This tradition of the Society is particularly relevant today within the context of urgent issues confronting us in our mission. For this reason General Congregation 34 strongly reaffirms the distinctive importance of the intellectual quality of each of our apostolic works. The value of this aspect of our ministry is fundamental in contemporary circumstances, characterized as they are by changes which are as rapid as they are radical.

395/ 2. Where pietism and fundamentalism join forces to disparage human abilities, *human reason* will be ignored or held of little account. Contrariwise, especially in countries where secularism holds sway or which have recently emerged from Marxist atheism, some seem to regard *faith* as little more than a "superstition" which will gradually disappear in the face of ever more rapid human progress. But freedom and the ability to reason are attributes which characterize human beings as created in the likeness of God and are closely tied to genuine faith. Therefore, everywhere and in all circumstances, an intellectual tradition continues to be of critical importance for the Church's vitality as well as for the understanding of cultures which deeply affect each person's way of thinking and living. All of us experience the need to "explain" the hope that dwells in us (cf. 1 Pet. 3:15) and the concern to acknowledge "everything that is true, everything that is honorable, everything that is upright and pure, everything that we love and admire, whatever is good and praiseworthy" (Phil. 4:8).

396/ 3. For this reason, GC 34 resolutely encourages a vigorous spiritual and intellectual formation for young Jesuits and ongoing spiritual and intellectual formation for every Jesuit. The Society, sensitive to present needs and challenges, must insist on the necessity not only for each one's ongoing acquisition of knowledge but also on the ongoing development of each one's personal capacity to analyze and evaluate, in our circumstances of rapid change, the mission which he has received. There can be no substitute for individual, painstaking, and, quite frequently, solitary work. Such capacity is indispensable if we wish to integrate the promotion of justice with the proclamation of faith, and if we hope to be effective in our work for peace, in our concern to protect life and the environment, in our defense of the rights of individual men and women and of entire peoples. Serious and active intellectual inquiry must also characterize our commitment to integral evangelization. This assumes a basic knowledge of the economic, social, and political structures in which our contemporaries find themselves immersed, and it cannot be ignorant of the development of traditional and modern cultures or of the effects of the emerging culture of communication. For evangelization to be effective, accuracy in knowledge, respect for the other in intercultural dialogue, and critical analysis are all imperative.

397/ 4. In apostolic works which are more directly intellectual, professional formation and competence are to be accompanied by that legitimate responsible autonomy and freedom which are requisites for progress in scholarly teaching and research. Furthermore, today more than ever before, it is essential that we recognize the specific characteristics of each of the various scholarly disciplines, including science and technology. We must help our contemporaries to respect this autonomy and freedom and to recognize these specific characteristics. For those with faith, to deny "the rightful autonomy of science" can lead to tragedies well known in the history of recent centuries.[1] We who have learned to pray before the "Eternal Lord of all things" must, therefore, be especially careful to avoid the same mistakes under new forms.[2]

398/ 5. The intellectual dimension of every apostolic work also supposes that each Jesuit knows how to be active in companionship with others. Those engaged in an intellectual life experience periods of exaltation and of doubt, of recognition and of being ignored, of intense satisfaction and of bitter trial. More than is the case in other areas, an intellectual mission calls for a humble ability to accept praise and also to face rejection and controversy; this mission is constantly exposed to the judgment of others in conversations, in scholarly publications, and in the media. To accept this reality simply and directly is one way of being "servants of Christ's mission"—the Christ who continues his paschal mystery through us.

399/ 6. These characteristic challenges of the intellectual apostolate require that each of us acquire the ability to live the creative tension between profound insertion into all the details of our work and an open and critical attitude towards other points of view and other cultural or confessional positions. However, acceptance of such tension must not lessen our witness of personal commitment to the service of the Church in its journey towards the Kingdom of God.

400/ 7. Among the ways of being engaged in the intellectual apostolate in the service of the Kingdom of God, theological research and reflection has a special place and merits specific mention. Father Pedro Arrupe named theological reflection as one of the four priority apostolates of the Society of Jesus.[3] Among

---

[1] Vatican Council II, *Gaudium et Spes*, n. 36.

[2] *SpEx* [98].

[3] Pedro Arrupe, Address to the Congregation of Procurators 65, 10 May 1970, *AR* 15 (1970): pp. 908 f.

the urgent contemporary issues needing theological reflection, he listed humanism, freedom, mass culture, economic development, and violence. GC 32 cited and confirmed Father Arrupe's emphasis on theological reflection and also called for a social analysis of the structural causes of contemporary injustices and for Ignatian discernment regarding the appropriate apostolic response to these injustices.[4] GC 34 reconfirms the need for this theological reflection and, to the issues it must address, adds the contemporary understanding of the promotion of justice, including inculturation and interreligious dialogue.

401/   Theological reflection, social analysis, and discernment are phases of a process which Pope John XXIII and Vatican II called "reading the signs of the times": the effort to discern the presence and activity of God in the events of contemporary history in order to decide what to do as servants of the Word.[5] This will bring the perennial sources of Catholic theology to bear upon the lived experiences, individual and communal, of the members of the faith community that is the Church, especially their experience of poverty and oppression; it relates Catholic theology to the secular disciplines, especially philosophy and the social and natural sciences, in order to discern, illuminate, and interpret the opportunities and problems of contemporary life.

402/ 8.   When theological reflection is undertaken with the seriousness of research and the creativity of imagination that it merits, within the broad spectrum of Catholic theology and in the midst of the varied circumstances in which Jesuits live and work, it can give rise to specific theologies which, in diverse times and places, incarnate the gospel message. Theological research and reflection in service of the Gospel can thus help to respond to the broadest questions of the human mind and the deepest yearnings of the human heart.

403/ 9.   Not only in our ministries, but also in our personal way of seeing and interpreting individual, social, cultural, and political situations, and even in our spiritual life, we can be guided by such reflection. It will be the more productive to the extent that it roots itself in a personal faith lived and expressed in the Christian community. It must be attentive to the questions which reality poses to believing men and women. And the Jesuit engaged in such reflection must know how to join awareness of contemporary circumstances with a careful listening to the voice of God in personal prayer.

---

[4] GC 32, D 4, nn. 59 f.; cf. nn. 44, 71–74.

[5] Cf. Vatican Council II, *Gaudium et Spes*, nn. 4, 11, 44.

DECREE 17

JESUITS AND UNIVERSITY LIFE

404/ 1.   Jesuits have been engaged in university teaching, research, and scholarly publication almost since the foundation of the Society. From astronomy to classical ballet, from the humanities to theology, Jesuits try to enter into the languages and discourses of their inherited or emerging cultures. They attempt to discover, shape, renew, or promote human wisdom, while at the same time respecting the integrity of disciplined scholarship. They also seek to accompany in faith the men and women molded by the potent cultural forces inherent in the university as an institution. St. Ignatius was aware of the wide cultural impact of universities and chose to send Jesuits there, as places where a more universal good might be achieved. Throughout our history we have continued to affirm this basic Ignatian intuition.

405/ 2.   Today, approximately three thousand Jesuits work in nearly two hundred of our own institutions of higher learning, touching the lives of more than half a million students; other Jesuits exercise this mission in other universities. This apostolic activity not only has an influence on the lives of students; it goes beyond the immediate university milieu. We recognize that universities remain crucial institutional settings in society. For the poor they serve as major channels for social advancement. In and through universities, important debates take place about ethics, future directions for economics and politics, and the very meaning of human existence, debates that shape our culture. Neither the university as an institution and as a value for humanity nor the still urgent imperative for an unflagging Jesuit commitment to our tradition of fostering university life stands in need of any fresh defense.

406/ 3.   Moreover, many excellent documents already exist which treat the role and future of Jesuit universities.[1] General Congregation 34 wishes only to

---

[1] Cf.   • GC 31, DD 28, 29, 30; GC 32, D 4; GC 33, D 1, n. 44

• Pedro Arrupe, "Discourse at the Universidad de Deusto," Bilbao, May 1970 (Rome, C.I.S. 1971, pp. 102–16); "Apostolic Priorities," Address to the Congregation of Procurators, Rome, 5 October 1978 (*AR* 17 [1980]: pp. 518–81); "The Intellectual Apostolate as a Mission of the Society Today" (*AR* 16, [1976]: p. 76)

• Peter-Hans Kolvenbach, "The Jesuit University Today," 5 November 1985, *AR* 19 (1985): pp. 394–403; "Address at the Centenary Celebration of the Universidad de Deusto," Bilbao, 5 June 1987, *Selección de escritos del Padre Peter-Hans Kolvenbach* (Provincia de España, 1992), pp. 377–84); "Address to the U. S. Jesuit Higher Education Assembly," 7 June 1989, S.J. *Documentation 64* (August 1989): pp. 1–11; "La Universidad:

encourage Jesuits engaged in this important and traditional Jesuit work and to consider two relatively fresh challenges to Jesuit universities.

A Challenge from the Structure of Universities

407/ 4. During the past thirty years, Jesuit higher education has undergone very rapid development in size, complexity, and more participative structures of government. During this same period, the number of Jesuits engaged in a university, or at least the proportion of Jesuits within the entire university community, has greatly diminished: lay and religious colleagues join with us in a common enterprise. In some places Jesuits no longer "own" our universities in any real sense. In others, government regulations create a situation in which we no longer fully "control" them. In places, some ecclesiastical superiors may be distrustful of the freedom necessary for a university truly to function in accord with its specific aims.

408/ 5. In response to this challenge, Jesuits must continue to work hard, with imagination and faith and often under very difficult circumstances, to maintain and even to strengthen the specific character of each of our institutions both as *Jesuit* and as a *university*. As we look to the future, we need consciously to be on guard that both the noun "university" and the adjective "Jesuit" always remain fully honored.

409/ 6. The noun guarantees a commitment to the fundamental autonomy, integrity, and honesty of a university precisely as a university: a place of serene and open search for and discussion of the truth. It also points to the mission proper to every university—its dedication to research, teaching, and the various forms of service that correspond to its cultural mission—as the indispensable horizon and context for a genuine preservation, renewal, and communication of knowledge and human values.[2] As Jesuits, we seek knowledge for its own sake and at the same time must regularly ask, "Knowledge for what?"

A Challenge from Faith and Justice

410/ 7. We affirm the adjective "Jesuit" no less strongly. This presupposes the authentic participation in our basic Jesuit identity and mission of any university calling itself Jesuit, or any university which operates ultimately under our responsibility. While we want to avoid any distortion of the nature of a university or any reduction of its mission to only one legitimate goal, the adjective "Jesuit" never-

---

Espacio para la unidad de las ciencias," Universidad Javeriana, Bogota, 26 February 1990; "Educación y valores: A la Universidad Iberoamericana sobre un nuevo modelo de Universidad," Mexico City, 23 August 1990; "Apostolado educativo, familia y sociedad nueva," Guadalajara, Mexico, 29 August 1990; "En el centenario de la Universidad Pontificia Comillas," October 1992

· John Paul II, Apostolic constitution *Ex Corde Ecclesiae*

[2] John Paul II, Apostolic constitution *Ex Corde Ecclesiae*, Art. 2.1.

theless requires that the university act in harmony with the demands of the service of faith and promotion of justice found in Decree 4 of GC 32. A Jesuit university can and must discover in its own proper institutional forms and authentic purposes a specific and appropriate arena for the encounter with the faith which does justice.

411/ 8. We applaud the many ways in which Jesuit universities have tried to apply this decree, both in the lives of students through outreach programs of mutual contact and service with the poor, and in the central teaching, research, and publication aims of the university. If it remains true that most Jesuit universities must, in various ways, strive to do even more in order to embody this mission of service to the faith and its concomitant promotion of justice, this only reflects the challenge all Jesuits face to find concrete and effective ways in which large and complex institutions can be guided by and to that justice which God himself so insistently calls for and enables. The task is possible; it has produced martyrs who have testified that "an institution of higher learning and research can become an instrument of justice in the name of the Gospel."[3]

412/ 9. The complexity of a Jesuit university can call for new structures of government and control on the part of the Society in order to preserve its identity and at the same time allow it to relate effectively to the academic world and the society of which it is part, including the Church and the Society of Jesus. More specifically, in order for an institution to call itself Jesuit, periodic evaluation and accountability to the Society are necessary in order to judge whether or not its dynamics are being developed in line with the Jesuit mission. The Jesuits who work in these universities, both as a community and as individuals, must actively commit themselves to the institution, assisting in its orientation, so that it can achieve the objectives desired for it by the Society.

413/ 10. Jesuit universities will promote interdisciplinary work; this implies a spirit of cooperation and dialogue among specialists within the university itself and with those of other universities. As a means toward serving the faith and promoting justice in accord with their proper nature as universities, they can discover new perspectives and new areas for research, teaching, and university extension services, by means of which they can contribute to the transformation of society towards more profound levels of justice and freedom. Thus our universities have a clear opportunity to promote interuniversity collaboration and, in particular, to undertake common projects between Jesuit universities of developed and developing countries.

---

[3] Peter-Hans Kolvenbach, Address to the Congregation of Provincials 1 (20 September 1990), *AR* 20 (1990): p. 452.

414/ 11. A Jesuit university must be outstanding in its human, social, spiritual, and moral formation, as well as for its pastoral attention to its students and to the different groups of people who work in it or are related to it.

415/ 12. Finally, we recall how crucial it is for the whole Church to continue to have dedicated Jesuits engaged in university work. They are committed, in the most profound sense, to the search for the fullness of truth. We are assured that, despite occasional appearances to the contrary, the truth we seek will ultimately be one. That truth, rooted as it is in God, will make us free. GC 34 sends a warm word of greeting and encouragement to all those Jesuits dedicated to make authentic and currently fresh this long-standing but sometimes challenged Jesuit commitment to the university apostolate.

DECREE 18

Secondary, Primary, and Nonformal Education

416/ 1. In the past twenty years, in response to General Congregations 32 and 33, significant apostolic renewal has been initiated and carried forward by the large number of Jesuits and lay people working in the apostolate of secondary education. In increasing numbers our educational institutions are accessible to students from economically disadvantaged groups. The quality of the education has improved in line with the principles enunciated in recent educational documents of the Society.[1] Jesuit-lay cooperation has developed significantly, with each party contributing in a distinctive way towards the total formation of the students. Our schools have become platforms, reaching out into the community, not only to the extended school community of parents, former students, and friends but also to the poor and the socially disadvantaged in the neighborhood. Furthermore, we have willingly shared our educational heritage with others when asked to do so.

417/ 2. GC 34 gratefully acknowledges these developments and urges that they be continued. Allowing for diverse situations throughout the world, the ideas and practices drawn from the documents mentioned above must inspire school mission statements, policies, programs and the entire school milieu. The Jesuit identity of our schools and Jesuit-lay cooperation can be ensured only by careful selection of administrators and teachers, both Jesuits and others, and—especially for those who will assume positions of major responsibility—adequate formation in the Ignatian charism and pedagogy. In some regions well-designed formation programs are already being offered to Jesuit and lay teachers and administrators; the Society's secretary for education should encourage such programs elsewhere; they can yield great dividends for the ends that we desire.[2]

418/ 3. In response to different situations and for a variety of apostolic reasons, Jesuits in many areas are engaged in the apostolate of primary and preprimary education. We confirm that such schools "are very important and not contrary to our Institute" and also declare that because they can provide a solid academic and religious foundation during the formative early years, they can be one of the most effective services we offer to people, especially the poor.[3]

---

[1] *The Characteristics of Jesuit Education* (1987) and *Ignatian Pedagogy: A Practical Approach* (1993).

[2] Cf. Pedro Arrupe, "Our Secondary Schools Today and Tomorrow," 13 September 1980, n. 21, *AR* 18 (1980): pp. 268–70.

[3] GC 31, D 28, n.16.

419/ 4. The educational apostolate of the Society has been greatly enriched by the contributions made by centers of nonformal education, established in both rural and urban areas of developing countries. These centers provide education outside the traditional school system for both youth and adults among the poor. With the help of a participative pedagogy, they organize programs to eradicate illiteracy and supply training in technical and social skills, as well as offer a religious and ethical formation geared to the analysis and transformation of the society in which the students live. They educate their students as "men and women for others" who can assume leadership roles in their own communities and organizations. The number of persons whom we serve through these centers is very large; as a means towards the promotion of justice, this ministry of nonformal education is fully in accord with our Jesuit mission. Especially in the light of the decree "Servants of Christ's Mission," GC 34 encourages Jesuits, religious, and lay persons to continue their dedicated work in this important but difficult apostolate, and recommends cooperation between Jesuit centers for nonformal education and our Jesuit schools, universities, and social centers.

DECREE 19

Parish Ministry

Parish Ministry Today

420/ 1.   Approximately 3,200 Jesuits labor in two thousand parishes throughout the world. In recognizing the important service to the Church represented by this investment of manpower, we affirm that "the parish apostolate is not contrary to our Constitutions" and add that, under certain circumstances, it is an appropriate apostolate for carrying out our mission of serving the faith and promoting justice.[1]

421/ 2.   The parish, moreover, offers a favorable context to live with the poor and to be in solidarity with them.

Goals and Characteristics of a Jesuit Parish

422/ 3.   A parish is Jesuit if, committed to the pastoral goals and policies of the local church, it also "participates in the apostolic priorities of the Society"[2] and in the mission plan of the province, according to "our way of proceeding."[3] As central to its life, the parish gathers as a community to celebrate its joys, struggles, and hopes—in the Word, in the Eucharist, and the other sacraments—in well-planned, creative, and inculturated ways. A parish becomes an evangelized and evangelizing community committed to "justice and reconciliation" and makes its popular devotions relevant to contemporary needs.[4]

423/ 4.   A Jesuit parish is energized by Ignatian spirituality, especially through the Spiritual Exercises, and by individual and communal discernment. It tries to provide well-developed programs in catechesis and formation for both individuals and families; it offers opportunities for spiritual direction and pastoral counseling. Following the model of the election in the Spiritual Exercises, it helps individuals to discern their vocation in life.

424/ 5.   The parish opens itself progressively to ecumenical and interreligious dialogue and reaches out to alienated Christians as well as to nonbelievers. It grows into a participative church through such means as basic human and ecclesial communities and promotes opportunities for lay participation and leadership.

---

[1] GC 31, D 27, n. 10.

[2] Peter-Hans Kolvenbach, "Creativity in the Pastoral Ministry," to Jesuit pastors of South Asia (JEPASA), 1993.

[3] Pedro Arrupe, "Some Guidelines for the Parish Apostolate," *AR* 17 (1979): p. 893.

[4] Cf. GC 32, D 4, nn. 17 f.

425/ 6.   In its service of the faith, a Jesuit parish is called upon to develop strategies to promote local and global justice by means of both personal conversion and structural change. Networking with other Jesuit apostolic works as well as other ecclesial and civil organizations, it opposes all forms of discrimination and contributes to a genuine culture of solidarity which transcends parish boundaries.

The Jesuit in a Parish

426/ 7.   A Jesuit is missioned to a parish, Jesuit or otherwise, in order to contribute meaningfully to its total life. He should be selected for his lived spirituality and pastoral competence. He must be able to interact positively with various age groups and should have the necessary skills for working collegially with laity and other members of the parish staff.

427/ 8.   Jesuits in parish ministry should have ongoing contact with other Jesuits, diocesan pastors, and other religious ministering in the region. They should spend time with them for collective reflection and common action.

428/ 9.   A Jesuit destined to become a pastor must have special training, especially in such skills as homiletics, liturgy, catechesis, sociocultural analysis, social communication, and conflict management. In addition, opportunities for contact with model parishes and appropriate pastoral training centers must be available to him for ongoing formation. It is also recommended that apostolic experiments in parishes be made available to Jesuits from the early stages of formation.

A Mandate to Father General

429/ 10.   We mandate Father General to evaluate and update our existing norms for accepting and withdrawing from parishes and to communicate the results to the whole Society.[5] Given the many different types of parishes in the world, provincials will need to adapt the norms to local situations

---

[5] Cf. GC 31, D 27, n. 10.

DECREE 20

Ecology

(Recommendation to Father General)

430/ 1. The contemporary debate between development and ecology is often posed as an opposition between First World desires and Third World needs; in fact the terms refer to many interrelated problems throughout the world. The Society of Jesus can contribute to overcoming some elements of the dilemma by encouraging both international awareness and local action. The many postulates received offer rich suggestions on this subject.

431/ 2. This congregation recommends to Father General that a study be made regarding the following issues:

2, 1. How our Ignatian spirituality provides us with a foundation for a universal response

2, 2. How our apostolates can contribute in their specific ways, and also can further effective collaboration, and

2, 3. How this issue affects our lifestyle and the decisions that we make in our institutions

432/ The results of this study should be communicated to the whole Society as an orientation for our way of proceeding.

VI

DECREE 21

INTERPROVINCIAL AND SUPRAPROVINCIAL COOPERATION

Our Vision

433/ 1. Ignatian heritage. The international character of our mission finds its genesis in the Trinitarian vision of Ignatius; its meaningful expression is found in our fourth vow of obedience to the Holy Father. Ignatius and his companions decided to form a single apostolic body to be placed at the disposal of the Vicar of Christ for universal mission. For Ignatius, the more universal was the service, the more was it divine. This has meant, throughout our history, that Jesuits are ready to go wherever in the world their service is most needed; availability is to be an attitude of the individual Jesuit and a characteristic of the whole Society: mobile, agile, responding to the needs of a fast-changing world.

434/ 2. The world and the Church today. Today, more than ever, the needs of the world constitute an urgent call to put our Ignatian universalism into practice. Growing consciousness of the world has given us a deeper realization that some problems are global in nature and therefore require global solutions: the division between rich and poor and the consequent need to seek an alternative socioeconomic world order, the struggle to overcome the international forces that tend to marginalize the entire continent of Africa, the need to rebuild entire societies after the collapse of totalitarian regimes, a better redistribution of the resources available for evangelization. The needs that call for common action are many; the difficult search for world unity requires the presence, witness, and involvement of the Society.

435/ 3. Living our heritage. Effective apostolic service also requires a lived awareness of the local church. We must promote inculturation in order to evangelize all peoples and all cultures. We must be apostolically rooted in a way that does not weaken the universal character of our call and service. We are to dedicate all our energies to the particular mission we have received, contributing to the dynamic life of the individual apostolic work, community, and province in which we serve, without losing our awareness of being sent into the Lord's universal vineyard. Together we form *unum corpus apostolicum*. To live this tension between the local and the universal is not easy; our universal consciousness needs to be nourished, expressed, and challenged.

What Have We Achieved?

436/ 4.   Recent general congregations have emphasized the universal dimension of our vocation and, in various ways, stressed the importance of international cooperation.[1] Provincials have been reminded that in addition to their responsibility for their own provinces, they share responsibility with Father General for the needs of the whole Society.[2] In response, many positive fruits have been produced. The awareness of being one universal body has grown. Ignatian universalism is being expressed in many distinct ways: mutual help and solidarity among different provinces and regions, sharing of information and experiences, interprovincial meetings and work groups, a variety of activities undertaken in common. In particular, conferences of major superiors have fostered better communication and attention to common problems; in some cases they have been able to establish common works.

437/ 5.   However, we agree with Father General that "we do not exploit all the possibilities given to us by being an international apostolic body."[3] A certain kind of provincialism, the immediate demands of local needs, and a lack of appropriate interrelated structures have prevented us from realizing our global potential. If we are to respond to the calls of today's world in fidelity to our universal vocation, we must move beyond current accomplishments. We must deepen a worldwide spirit and strengthen formal structures and informal ties that will better enable global and regional cooperation. In the spirit of this general congregation, a spirit of implementation, we offer the following recommendations.

Recommendations

438/ 6.   **Fostering an attitude of universalism.** In response to the grace of our Jesuit vocation, we must foster an attitude of universalism not only in the admission and formation of new members but as an interior attitude of all Jesuits, particularly those having responsibility for governance.

439/ 7.   *Candidates:* The universality of the Society is to be presented to candidates; evaluation of their suitability is to take into account their openness to and capacity for this characteristic of our vocation.

440/ 8.   *Formation:* The universality of the Society as a characteristic of our Ignatian charism is to be emphasized at each stage of formation. The appropriation of this dimension of our charism can be reinforced by experiences of the universal Society such as international meetings of those in formation and opportu-

---

[1] GC 31, D 48, n. 8; GC 32, D 4, n. 81; GC 33, D 1, n. 46.

[2] GC 30, D 49; GC 32, D 4, n. 68; *Guidelines for Provincials,* n. 58.

[3] Peter-Hans Kolvenbach, Address to the Congregation of Provincials 1, Loyola, 1990.

nities to become familiar with another culture in another part of the world. As far as possible, Jesuits should receive a part of their formation in another culture.[4]

441/ 9. *Permanent formation:* One objective of ongoing formation is to foster an attitude of universalism through experiences of the universal character of the Society: every Jesuit should have such opportunities. This will not only develop a personal sense of Ignatian universalism but also enable provinces to develop a more global perspective.

442/ 10. *Facility in languages:* In order to facilitate communication with other cultures and throughout the universal Society, all are to learn languages other than their own, and the Society as a whole should try to have a common language. To that end, Jesuits in formation will learn English; those whose mother tongue is English will learn another modern language of global significance, to be determined by the cultural context in which they live. As far as possible, Jesuits who have completed initial formation are encouraged to follow the same principle.

443/ 11. *Being sent on mission to another culture:* The ideal of Jesuit universalism is that every Jesuit should be available for assignment anywhere in the world. In practice, since the transition from one culture to another may not be easy, screening and training procedures have to be established. In addition, we need to ensure that a man being sent to a different culture or on an international mission is psychologically mature enough to live what could be a less rooted style of life. To this end, some form of *informationes* should be used.

444/ 12. *Governance:* For the effective living-out of our universality, it is essential that those responsible for governance in the Society, particularly provincials along with their consultors, have a strong sense of this charism and "possess the qualities and endowments so absolutely necessary for the establishment of true and productive cooperation among themselves. . . . Father General should, moreover, have these qualities in mind when naming provincials" and their consultors.[5] The meeting of new provincials with Father General is an appropriate time to emphasize their role in developing the universal character of the Society.

445/ 13. **Developing global and regional networking.** The official structure for the governance of the Society—Father General, his council, and major superiors throughout the world—constitutes a framework for the development of many different forms of global and regional cooperation and networking, with examples ranging from an interprovince novitiate to the Jesuit Refugee Service.

446/ 14. *Global networking:* Although numerous regional and international networks already exist, to exploit more fully the possibilities given us by being an international body, additional global and regional networks must be created.

---

[4] General Norms for Jesuit Studies, n. 46.

[5] GC 31, D 48, nn. 8, 1° b.

Such networks of persons and institutions should be capable of addressing global concerns through support, sharing of information, planning, and evaluation, or through implementation of projects that cannot easily be carried out within province structures. The potential exists for networks of specialists who differ in expertise and perspectives but who share a common concern, as well as for networks of university departments, research centers, scholarly journals, and regional advocacy groups. The potential also exists for cooperation in and through international agencies, nongovernmental organizations, and other emerging associations of women and men of goodwill. Initiative and support for these various forms of networks should come from all levels of the Society, but the secretariats of the General Curia must continue to play an important role in establishing them.

447/   In many respects, the future of international cooperation remains largely uncharted. With creative imagination, openness, and humility, we must be ready to cooperate with all those working for the integral development and liberation of people.

448/ 15. *Twinning:* Twinning, which has replaced the traditional concept of "mission regions," has become an increasingly effective instrument for mutually enriching exchanges between provinces around the globe. A thorough review of twinning is recommended in order to redefine its goals and functions, so that greater solidarity and a more effective matching of resources with needs can be achieved. Mission offices are invited to participate in this review, so that they may broaden their function to include a concern for greater cooperation and effectiveness.

449/ 16. **Conferences of Major Superiors.** General Congregation 34 reaffirms the establishment of conferences of major superiors, recommended by GC 31 as a structural means for interprovincial and supraprovincial cooperation; it strongly urges Father General to promote the development of these conferences.

450/ 17. *Variety:* It is recognized that for a number of reasons significant differences exist in the degree to which conferences have developed in the different regions of the Society. Rather than seeking uniformity, the design and the mode of operating of the various conferences of major superiors will reflect cultural and regional differences.

451/ 18. *Objectives:* In spite of their differences, for the sake of a necessary consistency among conferences it is recommended that the objectives of each include the following:

     a. to open the Society of a given region to the universal dimensions of the Society

     b. to help major superiors become more aware of their responsibility for the Society and the Church throughout the entire region

     c. to facilitate unity, communication, a common vision, and effective leadership among major superiors *d.* to set priorities, to plan for and coordinate common activities

452/ 19. *Composition:* The composition of a conference is determined by Father General after consultation and taking into account geographical and cultural factors, in order to ensure that cooperation among the provinces involved will be meaningful and fruitful. It may be necessary to restructure some existing conferences so as to increase the number of common interests among the member provinces.

453/ 20. *Conditions for effectiveness:* As conferences become more structured, true and productive interprovince and supraprovince cooperation will require the effective leadership of a moderator, along with statutes approved by Father General.

454/ 21. **Moderators of conferences of major superiors.** The moderator is to assist in the development of a common vision for the region and for the whole Society, and guide efforts towards the setting of priorities, planning, and decision making. As the executive of the conference, he carries out decisions, implements policies, and oversees common undertakings such as common works, projects, and services. He also promotes various forms of cooperation among the Jesuits in the provinces of the conference and their apostolic works.

455/ 22. *Authority of the moderator:* The moderator of a conference must have the authority needed to call its major superiors to research, planning, and setting of priorities, and then to call them to carry out the required actions both within provinces and regionally. The major superiors themselves remain jointly responsible for the implementation of actions decided upon and for the provision of the resources needed for common works. The respective authority and responsibilities of the moderator and of the major superiors of the conference, along with procedures for making decisions, are to be specified in the statutes approved by Father General.

456/ 23. *Common works:* When a common work is under the care of a conference, any division at the level of major superior between apostolic responsibility for the work and *cura personalis* of the Jesuits assigned to it on a permanent basis should be avoided as much as possible, so as to safeguard the normal conditions necessary for authentic Ignatian government.

457/ 24. *Personnel for common works:* Established rules and objective criteria will govern the assignment of personnel from the provinces and regions. When a major superior is asked to make a particular man available for a common work, he should normally give this request a priority at least equal to the needs of his own province or region.

458/ 25. *Meetings of moderators:* Moderators will be called together annually by Father General *(a)* to heighten their own sense of the universal character of the Society, *(b)* to gain a better understanding of the global priorities of the Society, and *(c)* to work with Father General in overseeing and encouraging the further development of regional and global cooperation. Stability rather than rapid turn-over of membership within the group of moderators will enable these meetings to have the desired continuity that will make them more effective.

459/ 26. *Communication:* Communication among moderators, especially when called for by further development of regional and global priorities, is to be encouraged. In addition, regular communication between the moderators and their respective regional assistant(s) will enable everyone involved to serve the Society more effectively. Regional assistants for the provinces involved will be invited to meetings of the conference.

460/ 27. *Attendance at meetings:* All moderators, including those who are not also provincials, attend general congregations and meetings of provincials *ex officio.*

461/ 28. **Priorities.** Father General, with his staff and in his regular direct contacts with provincials and with the moderators of the conferences, will discern the greater needs of the universal Church and will establish global and regional priorities. These priorities are to be taken into consideration as conferences and provinces establish their own respective priorities. Annual letters should evaluate apostolic effectiveness based on these priorities.

DECREE 22

INTERPROVINCIAL HOUSES AND WORKS IN ROME

462/ 1.   Following a tradition that originated with St. Ignatius, and in the spirit of our fourth vow, General Congregation 34[1] confirms the commitment of the Society of Jesus to the interprovincial works entrusted to us by the Holy See[2] as reaffirmed by Pope John Paul II in his opening allocution to this congregation.[3] We recognize the valuable service which these institutions offer to the universal Church in the name of the whole Society; we are grateful to the Jesuits who have sustained them; at a time when their opportunities for service to the Church are increasing in importance, we wish to ensure, and even enhance, the effectiveness of these works. We therefore call upon the whole Society, especially major superiors, who share Father General's responsibility for these institutions, to unite in a common effort to further this important service to the universal Church.

463/ 2.   In order to address certain long-standing, complex, and potentially threatening concerns in an effective way, immediate and decisive action is needed. GC 34 therefore gives the following **mandates** to Father General:

464/ 3.   Father General shall commission a thorough evaluation of the Pontifical Gregorian University, the Pontifical Biblical Institute, and the Pontifical Oriental Institute, together with the support these institutions receive from the provinces. This evaluation, while respecting the specific academic character and autonomy of these institutions, is to include academic policies and programs, faculty recruitment and development, financial management and accountability, the structures of the Jesuit communities, and the governance structures of the works and of the Delegation for the International Roman Houses. We strongly recommend that the charge to conduct this evaluation be given to a group of persons with experience, expertise, and interest in these works, including representatives from these institutions and from outside them, and involving Father General's

---

[1] Three previous general congregations have recommended to Father General and the whole Society a special concern for the Pontifical Gregorian University and its associated institutes: GC 29, D 17, n. 2; GC 30, D 18, n. 1; GC 31, D 31.

[2] The interprovincial works in Rome entrusted to the Society by the Holy See include the Pontifical Gregorian University, the Pontifical Biblical Institute, the Pontifical Oriental Institute, the Pontifical Russicum College, Vatican Radio, and the Vatican Observatory. There are also interprovincial works of the Society itself: the Historical Institute, the College of St. Robert Bellarmine, and the International College of the Gesù.

[3] Cf. John Paul II, Allocution to General Congregation 34, 5 January 1995, n. 5; see pp. 663–668 below.

delegate. Based on the recommendations of this group, Father General shall take those measures necessary to strengthen these works significantly and ensure their future.

465/ 4.   The delegate of Father General shall, with the faculties of a major superior received from him, have religious and apostolic responsibility for the interprovincial houses and works in Rome and for the Jesuits assigned to them.

466/ 5.   Father General shall establish a permanent interprovincial commission composed of representatives from the conferences of major superiors and including experienced educators and administrators, to assist him and his delegate with the ongoing governance of the interprovincial houses and works in Rome.

DECREE 23

Congregations and Governance

A. The General Congregation

467/ 1.   General Congregation 34 has examined Decree 3 of GC 33 in the light of experience and the replies of the province congregations and has established the following:

468/   1°   The rules for the composition of a general congregation introduced by GC 33, D. 3, nn. 1 and 2, are to be maintained, but still *ad experimentum*.

469/   2°   Those elected in the province congregations should constitute a majority of the members of the general congregation.

470/ 2.   In order to favor the participation of all members in the life of the Society, as recommended by Vatican Council II and prescribed in the revised Code of Canon Law,[1] GC 34 decrees that all formed coadjutors have the right to be electors in a general congregation and establishes the following with regard to their representation:

471/   1°   All formed members of the Society who do not already have the right to attend the general congregation *ex officio* have passive voice in the province congregation to be chosen as electors (and substitutes) to the general congregation.[2] During the latter, however, formed coadjutors will not have passive voice for election to an office for which the profession of four vows is required.

472/   2°   If the total number of formed coadjutors elected is more than 10 percent of the members (elected and *ex officio*) of the general congregation, the

---

[1] CIC 631 n. 1; Vatican Council II, *Perfectae Caritatis* n. 14.

[2] FPC 59, §§ 2f.

one most recently admitted to final vows will be replaced by a substitute elected from the same province who is professed of four vows.

473/ 3° In any case, Father General (or Vicar General) will provide for the participation of some brothers, at least as procurators *ad negotia*.

474/ 3. The Formula of the Province Congregation and the Formula of the General Congregation are to be revised in conformity with what has been established in this present decree.

475/ 4. GC 34 recommends that Father General establish a commission to study the possibilities and advantages of a new model for the general congregation which, while maintaining the Ignatian principles for such a congregation, would make it both more effective and more efficient. Among the areas to be studied would be a new examination of the significance and importance of the main criteria currently employed to determine the composition of a general congregation, which do not seem compatible with the goal of a notable reduction of its members. The results of these studies are to be discussed at the next general congregation.

476/ 5. Moreover, GC 34 recommends to Father General that an evaluation be done of the preparation for and the way of proceeding in this general congregation. In the light of this evaluation and in order to prepare more effective methods and dynamics for treating business in GC 35, Father General may, with the authority delegated by this general congregation, modify those prescriptions of the Formula of a General Congregation that deal with preparation and the treating of business, if he judges it opportune, with the deliberative vote of all the Fathers of the General Curia who have a right *ex officio* to attend a general congregation.

B. Congregation to Elect a Temporary Vicar General

477/ 1. Father General is to deposit in writing the name or names of the temporary vicar(s) general he wishes to appoint in case of his death[3] and in case of his incapacity.[4]

478/ 2. The congregation to elect a temporary vicar general, if held, is to be composed of the following:

479/ 1° All the Fathers of the General Curia who have a right *ex officio* to be electors in a general congregation

480/ 2° All those Fathers who have an office in the place where the congregation is to be held which gives them a right *ex officio* to attend a province congregation, and who are professed of four vows, to be called by seniority of profes-

---

[3] *Const.* [687].

[4] *Const.* [773, 786].

sion in such a way that the total number of members of the congregation shall not exceed forty

481/ 3.   The minimum number of members to begin the congregation is ten.

482/ 4.   The Formula of the Congregation to Elect a Temporary Vicar General is to be revised in conformity with what has been established in the *Complementary Norms to the Constitutions* and in the present decree.

C. Congregations of Procurators and Provincials

483/ 1.   GC 34 has examined Decree 39 of GC 31 in the light of experience and the replies of the province congregations and has established the following:

484/ 2.   The congregation of procurators will take place every four years, according to the modalities prescribed in the Formula for the Congregation of Procurators, n. 1, §1.

485/ 3.   The congregation of provincials is abolished.

486/ 4.   Approximately every six years beginning from the last general congregation, Father General shall convoke a meeting of all provincials, in order to consider the state, the problems, and the initiatives of the universal Society, as well as international and supraprovincial cooperation.

487/ 5.   Since province congregations will be convoked less frequently than in the past, it is recommended that provincials convoke other types of meetings which will promote the participation and coresponsibility of all its members in the discernment and life of the province.

488/ 6.   The Formula of the Congregation of Procurators is to be revised in conformity with what has been established in this present decree:

1°   Title: Formula of the Congregation of Procurators.

2°   N. 1, §1: "Every four years after the end of the last general congregation, counting from 26 September (unless another day of the same civil year seems more suitable to Father General), procurators from all the provinces are to convene who have been elected according to the prescriptions of the Formula of the Province Congregation."

3°   N. 1, §2: "It is not to be postponed for another four years but is to be held the following year."

4°   Title I: the title itself is to be canceled (because there is no longer a Title II).

5°   N. 2, §1, 2°: "Under the leadership of the Superior General, they are to confer on the state and more universal undertakings of the Society. For the better preparation of the members of the congregation of procurators, the Superior General should communicate to them in good time the points for consultation in the congregation."

6°   N. 2, §2: "The congregation may put together and offer to the Society a report on the state of the Society": to be canceled.

7° N. 3: "The congregation is composed of the Superior General, the vicar or the coadjutor vicar, the assistants *ad providentiam*, the general counselors, the procurators elected by the provinces or their substitutes according to the Formula of the Province Congregation, nn. 3, § 1, 2°; 61; 96. The place of the assistants *ad providentiam* can be taken by their substitutes, named by the Superior General and approved by the majority of the provincials, provided the assistants whose substitutes they are, are not present."

8° N. 6: ". . . the Superior General with the assistants *ad providentiam* is to e xamine the acts of the province congregations."

9° Nn. 17, §§1 and 2: to be canceled.

10° N. 31, §1: ". . . are to be given to the Superior General with the assistants *ad providentiam* for approval."

11° Title II (nn. 36–40): all to be canceled.

D The Province Congregation

489/ 1. GC 34, in accord with the provisions of GC 33, Decree 5, has reexamined the norms for the province congregation in the light of experience and the responses of the provinces, and has established the following:

490/ 2. With regard to the number of participants in the province congregation by reason of the prior election, the norms now in force (Formula of a Province Congregation [FCP], 15, par. 1, 2%) are to be maintained.

491/ 3. The provincial, with the deliberative vote of the *Cætus praevius*, can designate up to five members in those provinces which have at least 0.5 percent of the total membership of the Society, and three in the other provinces.

492/ 4. The participants in the province congregation must be

1° Professed of four vows: at least 50 percent

2° Formed members: at least 80 percent

493/ 5. Of the elected and *ex officio* participants in the province congregation, there must be at least

1° One formed brother

2° Two approved members, of whom at least one is not ordained

494/ 6. The socius of the provincial is to participate *ex officio* in the province congregation.

495/ 7. With regard to active and passive voice in the election prior to the province congregation, the norm currently in force is to be maintained: five years in the Society for active voice (FCP 18, 1°) and eight years in the Society for passive voice (FCP 18, 2°).

496/ 8. At the beginning of the congregation, the provincial will propose some questions on the state of the province, so that the congregation is able to have a consultation on the situation of the province, under the leadership of the provincial.

497/ 9. For a postulate to be proposed to the general congregation or to the Superior General in the name of the province congregation, it must be approved by more than half the votes of those present, nn. 44 and 45 notwithstanding.

498/ 10. The Formula for a Province Congregation is to be revised in accord with the present decree.

499/ 11. Moreover, the general congregation mandates Father General to study and, insofar as is necessary, authorizes him to modify, with the deliberative vote of the Fathers of the Curia who have the right *ex officio* to attend a general congregation, the following points of the Formula of a Province Congregation:

1° Drawing by lot the letter of the alphabet which will come first in the list for the prior election (FCP n. 20)

2° Simplification of the process of handling the ballots in the prior election (FCP nn. 22, 23, 24, 25)

3° Modification of the norm for translating into Latin the documents of the province congregation (FCP n. 90, 3, 2%)

4° Passive voice of the superiors of common houses: possibly retaining this right in one's own province (FCP n. 17, 1, 3%)

5° Passive voice of the "applied" to other provinces: retaining and using this right in one's own province, with the prior agreement of the provincials involved (FCP n. 10, 1)

6° Incompatibility of the office of Procurator, Relator, or Substitute with that of the provincial-designate, whatever the time when he is to enter into office (before or after the congregation in question) (FCP nn. 61, 3, 4; 62; 93, 2, 3)

E. Father General's Assistants and Counselors

500/ In response to Father General's invitation, GC 34 has considered various questions having to do with the central government of the Society, especially with regard to the assistants and counselors of the Superior General. It has established the following norms, which modify some norms in Decree 44 of GC 31 and Decree 15 of GC 32.

I. Father General's Council

501/ 1. Father General shall have a council composed of about twelve members.

502/ 2. The four assistants *ad providentiam* shall be general counselors.

503/ 3.   All regional assistants shall be general counselors.

504/ 4.   Thus, the general council will be composed of the four assistants *ad providentiam*, the regional assistants, and those general counselors charged with looking after important aspects of the life of the universal Society. One person can combine different functions. The secretary of the Society, as secretary, shall take part in the meetings but will not be a general counselor.

505/ 5.   The other major officials and the sectoral secretaries will participate in meetings of the general council whenever their particular competence would be helpful and in enlarged meetings which will be called periodically.

506/ 6.   If Father General constitutes a reduced group within the council to deal with administrative matters and current questions which do not require that his entire council meet together in consultation, it is recommended that

507/   •   the four assistants *ad providentiam* be part of this reduced group

508/   •   the members should have a certain stability, which means they should not be changed too often, nor should different members be changed at the same time

II. Election of the Assistants *ad Providentiam* and Appointment of the General Counselors during the General Congregation

509/ 1.   Each general congregation will proceed to elect the four assistants *ad providentiam*, and Father General will renew his council according to the following procedure. This procedure is to be reviewed by the next general congregation.

510/   1° The electors of each assistancy will propose to Father General by secret ballot the names of three candidates, normally from their own assistancy, who would be suitable to become general counselors and to be appointed as regional assistant.

511/   2° From these names, Father General will appoint a sufficient number of general counselors, at least to cover the need for regional assistants.

512/   3° The congregation will elect the four assistants *ad providentiam* according to the Formula of a General Congregation, nn. 130–37, choosing them from four different assistancies and taking account of the names of those appointed by Father General as general counselors (while retaining the freedom also to elect other persons).

513/   4° Former assistants *ad providentiam* may be reelected by the general congregation, and former general counselors may be reappointed by Father General.

514/   5° In addition to those appointed in the process described above, Father General retains the right to appoint other general counselors for the care of important sectors of the Society's life. These appointments are to be made after hearing the opinions of the other general counselors, and with the deliberative vote of the four assistants *ad providentiam.*

III. Replacement of the Four Assistants *ad Providentiam* and of the General Counselors outside a General Congregation

515/ 1. The four assistants *ad providentiam* normally remain in office until the next general congregation. For their replacement outside a general congregation, the norms presently in force are confirmed.[5]

516/ 2. It is recommended that the general counselors who are not assistants *ad providentiam* remain in office for six to eight years, and that they not all be replaced at the same time.

517/ 3. When there is to be a change of a general counselor who is not an assistant *ad providentiam* but who will have to perform the task of regional assistant, Father General will ask the provincials of the assistancy concerned to propose to him three names of possible candidates, from among whom he will name the new general counselor.

518/ 4. For the replacement of a general counselor who is not an assistant *ad providentiam* and who will not have the task of a regional assistant, Father General will name the new general counselor after hearing the opinion of the other general counselors and with the deliberative vote of the assistants *ad providentiam.*

IV. Final Provisions

519/ 1. Once approved by the general congregation, this decree will come into force immediately after the three days allowed for intercessions (FCG 128, §1) have ended.

520/ 2. This decree abrogates contrary dispositions in Decree 44 of GC 31 and Decree 15 of GC 32.

DECREE 24

The Ongoing Formation of Superiors

(Recommendation to Father General)

521/ In order to assist in the ongoing formation of superiors, General Congregation 34 recommends that Father General publish updated versions of the following documents: *Guidelines for Provincials, Guidelines for Local Superiors, Guidelines for the Distinction and Relations between the Director of a Work and the Religious Superior.*

---

[5] Cf. *Collectio Decretorum*, n. 269, §§1–6; *Normae Complementariae* n. 376, §§1–6.

DECREE 25

Powers Granted and Mandates Entrusted by the General Congregation to Father General

522/ 1.   General Congregation 34 grants to Father General the power and responsibility to establish the authoritative and definitive version of the congregation's decrees and recommendations. This work will include the following:

523/ 1, 1. To make whatever corrections are clearly needed, including the correction of discriminatory language

524/ 1, 2. To edit the decrees and recommendations with regard to style, and to reconcile contradictions if any are detected

525/ 1, 3. Thus to establish the authoritative text, based on the original language(s) in which each decree or recommendation was written

526/ 1, 4. To have the decrees and recommendations translated accurately into the three official languages of the congregation

527/ 2.   This work will be accomplished by members of the General Curia assisted, if necessary, by Jesuits from elsewhere; it will be finally approved by Father General with the deliberative vote of those Fathers of the General Curia who have a right *ex officio* to attend a general congregation.

528/ 3.   GC 34 grants Father General the power to abrogate or modify decrees of past general congregations that are not in accord with the decrees of this present general congregation, after obtaining the deliberative vote of those Fathers of the General Curia who have a right *ex officio* to attend a general congregation, and without prejudice to the powers given him in other decrees.

529/ 4.   GC 34 entrusts to Father General the power and responsibility to complete the work on the *Complementary Norms* and the *Notes to the Constitutions* according to the mind of the general congregation, with the deliberative vote of four delegates elected by the general congregation:

530/ 4, 1. To complete the definitive choice of texts from the decrees of GC 34 to be incorporated into the *Complementary Norms*, based on but not limited to the list drawn up by the commissions and collated by Commission 4 towards the end of the congregation

531/ 4, 2. To assure that discriminatory language, inconsistencies, and unnecessary repetitions are corrected

532/ 4, 3. To establish the final authoritative Latin text of the *Notes* and *Complementary Norms* and to authorize their accurate translation into the three official languages

533/ 4, 4 Thus to declare the *Constitutions*, *Notes*, and *Complementary Norms* ready for publication in one volume

534/ 5. GC 34 grants Father General the power to approve the minutes which could not be communicated to the delegates of the congregation, in accordance with the norms of the Formula of the General Congregation, n. 142, §4, 1ᵃ.

VII

CONCLUSION

26. Characteristics of Our Way
of Proceeding

DECREE 26

Conclusion: Characteristics of Our Way of Proceeding

535/ 1. Certain attitudes, values, and patterns of behavior join together to become what has been called the Jesuit way of proceeding. The characteristics of our way of proceeding were born in the life of St. Ignatius and shared by his first companions. Jerome Nadal writes that "the form of the Society is in the life of Ignatius."[1] "God set him up as a living example of our way of proceeding."[2]

536/ 2. General Congregation 34 considered which of these characteristics we need especially to draw upon today and the form they must take in the new situations and changing ministries in which we labor. We suggest that the following be included among them.

1. Deep Personal Love for Jesus Christ

537/ 3. *Here it will be to ask for an intimate knowledge of our Lord, who has become human for me, that I may love him more and follow him more closely.*[3]

538/ 4. In remorse, gratitude, and astonishment—but above all with passionate love—first Ignatius, and then every Jesuit after him, has turned prayerfully to "Christ our Lord hanging on the Cross before me" and has asked of himself, "What have I done for Christ? What am I doing for Christ? What must I do for Christ?"[4] The questions well up from a heart moved with profound gratitude and love. This is the foundational grace that binds Jesuits to Jesus and to one another. "What is it to be a Jesuit today? It is to know that one is a sinner yet called to be a companion of Jesus as Ignatius was."[5] The mission of the reconciled sinner is the mission of reconciliation: the work of faith doing justice. A Jesuit freely gives what he has freely received: the gift of Christ's redeeming love.

539/ 5. Today we bring this countercultural gift of Christ to a world beguiled by self-centered human fulfillment, extravagance, and soft living, a world that prizes prestige, power, and self-sufficiency. In such a world, to preach Christ poor

---

[1] Nadal, MHSI, vol. 90, *Commentarii de Instituto Societatis Iesu,* bk. 5, [§II] (p. 268) and [52*a] (p. 287).

[2] Nadal, MHSI, ibid, [33] (p. 262).

[3] *SpEx* [104].

[4] *SpEx* [53].

[5] GC 32, D 2, n. 1.

and humble with fidelity and courage is to expect humiliation, persecution, and even death. We have seen this happen to our brothers in recent years. Yet we move forward resolutely out of our "desire to resemble and imitate in some manner our Creator and Lord Jesus Christ . . . since he is the way which leads men to life."[6] Today, as always, it is deep, personal devotion to Jesus, himself the Way, that principally characterizes the Jesuit way of proceeding.

2. Contemplative in Action

540/ 6. *I shall not fail to recall that grace which he had in all circumstances, while at work or in conversation, of feeling the presence of God and of tasting spiritual things, of being contemplative even in the midst of action; he used to interpret this as seeking God in all things.*[7]

541/ 7. The God of Ignatius is the God who is at work in all things: laboring for the salvation of all as in the Contemplation to Attain Love; working immediately and directly with the exercitant as in Annotations 15 and 16; laboring as Christ the King for the liberation of the world; beginning, preserving, directing, and advancing the Society of Jesus as at the beginning and end of the Constitutions.

542/ 8. For a Jesuit, therefore, not just any response to the needs of the men and women of today will do. The initiative must come from the Lord laboring in events and people here and now. God invites us to join with him in his labors, on his terms, and in his way. To discover and join the Lord, laboring to bring everything to its fullness, is central to the Jesuit way of proceeding. It is the Ignatian method of prayerful discernment, which can be described as "a constant interplay between experience, reflection, decision, and action, in line with the Jesuit ideal of being 'contemplative in action.'"[8] Through individual and communal apostolic discernment, lived in obedience, Jesuits take responsibility for their apostolic choices in today's world. Such discernment reaches out, at the same time, to embrace the larger community of all those with whom we labor in mission.

3. An Apostolic Body in the Church

543/ 9. *Finally we decided in the affirmative; namely, that . . . we should not break this divinely constituted oneness and fellowship, but rather strengthen and consolidate it ever more, forming ourselves into one body.*[9]

544/ 10. Following the example of Jesus, the first Jesuits would be sent, as far as possible, in groups of at least two.[10] Even when dispersed, a bond of unity—with

---

[6] *Examen* [101].

[7] Nadal, MHSI, vol. 47, *Epistolae P. Hieronimi Nadal, 1546–1577,* bk. 4, p. 651.

[8] GC 32, D 4, n. 73.

[9] First conclusion of the Deliberations of the First Fathers in 1539, MHSI, Vol. 63, p. 3.

[10] Cf. *Const.* [624].

superiors and among themselves—remained strong through the constant communication and writing of letters that Ignatius insisted on, and especially through the account of conscience. Xavier, laboring far from Rome in the Indies, put it simply: "[T]he Society is love."[11]

545/ 11. Jesuits today join together because each of us has heard the call of Christ the King. From this union with Christ flows, of necessity, a love for one another. We are not merely fellow workers; we are friends in the Lord. The community to which we belong is the entire body of the Society itself, however dispersed over the face of the earth. Though we come from many nations and cultures and speak many languages, our union is enriched, not threatened, by diversity. In shared prayer, in conversation, and in the celebration of the Eucharist, each of us finds the spiritual resources needed for an apostolic community. And in our service of the Lord and his spouse, the Church, the People of God, we are especially united to the Roman Pontiff in order to be sent on the missions he may entrust to us.[12] As men of the Church, we cannot but think with the Church, guided by the Spirit of the Risen Lord.[13]

4. In Solidarity with Those Most in Need

546/ 12. *And what they should especially seek to accomplish for God's greater glory is to preach, hear confessions, lecture, instruct children, give good example, visit the poor in the hospitals, exhort the neighbor according to the amount of talent which each is conscious of possessing, so as to move as many as possible to prayer and devotion.*[14]

547/ 13. Ignatius and his followers began their preaching in poverty. They worked with the powerful and the powerless, with princes, kings, and bishops, but also with the women of the street and with the victims of the plague. They linked their ministry to the powerful with the needs of the powerless.

548/ 14. Today, whatever our ministry, we Jesuits enter into solidarity with the poor, the marginalized, and the voiceless, in order to enable their participation in the processes that shape the society in which we all live and work. They, in their turn, teach us about our own poverty as no document can. They help us to understand the meaning of the gratuity of our ministries, giving freely what we have freely received, giving our very lives. They show us the way to inculturate gospel values in situations where God is forgotten. Through such solidarity we become "agents of inculturation."[15]

---

[11] To Father Ignatius of Loyola, Cochín, 1 December 1549, p. 5.

[12] Cf. *Formula* [1].

[13] *SpEx* [365].

[14] Instruction of Ignatius to the Fathers at the Council of Trent, 1546.

[15] Pedro Arrupe, Letter and Document on Inculturation, *AR* 17 (1978): p. 236.

5. Partnership with Others

549/ 15. *For that same reason too, preference ought to be shown to the aid which is given to the great nations, such as the Indies, or to important cities, or to universities, which are generally attended by numerous persons who by being aided themselves can become laborers for the help of others.*[16]

550/ 16. Partnership and cooperation with others in ministry is not a pragmatic strategy resulting from diminished manpower; it is an essential dimension of the contemporary Jesuit way of proceeding, rooted in the realization that to prepare our complex and divided world for the coming of the Kingdom requires a plurality of gifts, perspectives, and experiences, both international and multicultural.

551/ 17. Jesuits, therefore, cooperate with lay women and men in the Church, with religious, priests, and bishops of the local church in which they serve, with members of other religions, and with all men and women of goodwill. To the extent that we develop a wide-ranging web of respectful and productive relationships, we fulfil Christ's priestly prayer "that they may all be one" (John 17:21).

6. Called to Learned Ministry

552/ 18. *After the pilgrim realized that it was not God's will that he remain in Jerusalem, he continually pondered within himself what he ought to do. At last he inclined more to study for some time so he would be able to help souls, and he decided to go to Barcelona.*[17]

553/ 19. Ignatius very quickly saw the need for learning in the service of the faith and the ministry of the Word. In the Formula of the Institute we read, "[T]his Institute requires men who are thoroughly humble and prudent in Christ as well as conspicuous in the integrity of Christian life and learning."[18] Therefore it is characteristic of a Jesuit that he embodies in creative tension this Ignatian requirement to use all human means, science, art, learning, natural virtue, with a total reliance on divine grace.

554/ 20. In our ministry today we respect and appreciate the good in contemporary culture and critically propose alternatives to the negative aspects of that same culture. In the context of the complex challenges and opportunities of our contemporary world, this ministry requires all the learning and intelligence, imagination and ingenuity, solid studies and rigorous analysis that we can muster. To overcome ignorance and prejudice through learning and teaching, to make the Gospel truly "Good News" in a confused and troubled world through theological reflection, is a characteristic of our Jesuit way of proceeding.

---

[16] *Const.* [622].

[17] *Autobiography* [50].

[18] *Formula* [5].

7. Men Sent, Always Available for New Missions

555/ 21. *If they were not given permission to remain in Jerusalem, they would return to Rome and present themselves to the Vicar of Christ, so that he could make use of them wherever he thought it would be to the greater glory of God and the service of souls.*[19]

556/ 22. Nadal, in promulgating the *Constitutions,* asked: Why are there Jesuits? There are diocesan priests and bishops. He answers simply that our charism, indeed our reason for existence, is that we might go where needs are not being met. Our way of proceeding encourages this mobility.[20]

557/ 23. A Jesuit is essentially a man on a mission, a mission he receives from the Holy Father and from his own religious superior, but ultimately from Jesus Christ himself, the one sent by the Father. Jesuits remain "ready at any hour to go to some or other parts of the world where they may be sent by the Sovereign Pontiff or their own superiors."[21]

558/ 24. Therefore, it is characteristic of our way of proceeding that we live with an operative freedom: open, adaptable, even eager for any mission that may be given us. Indeed, the ideal is an unconditional consecration to mission, free of any worldly interest, and free to serve all men and women. Our mission extends to the creation of this same spirit of mission in others.

8. Ever Searching for the *Magis*

559/ 25. *Those who wish to give greater proof of their love, and to distinguish themselves in whatever concerns the service of the Eternal King and the Lord of all, will not only offer themselves entirely for the work . . . but make offerings of greater value and of more importance.*[22]

560/ 26. The *magis* is not simply one among others in a list of Jesuit characteristics. It permeates them all. The entire life of Ignatius was a pilgrim search for the *magis,* the ever greater glory of God, the ever fuller service of our neighbor, the more universal good, the more effective apostolic means. "[M]ediocrity has no place in Ignatius's worldview."[23]

561/ 27. Jesuits are never content with the status quo, the known, the tried, the already existing. We are constantly driven to discover, redefine, and reach out

---

[19] *Autobiography* [85].

[20] Nadal, MHSI, vol. 90a, *Orationes Observationes,* [281] (p. 113).

[21] *Const.* [588].

[22] *SpEx* [97].

[23] Peter-Hans Kolvenbach, To the Friends and Colleagues of the Society of Jesus, *AR* 20 (1991): p. 606.

for the *magis*. For us, frontiers and boundaries are not obstacles or ends, but new challenges to be faced, new opportunities to be welcomed. Indeed, ours is a holy boldness, "a certain apostolic aggressivity," typical of our way of proceeding.[24]

Conclusion

562/ 28.   Our way of proceeding is a way of challenge. But "this way of proceeding is the reason why every son of the Society will always act and react in a consistently Jesuit and Ignatian way, even in the most unforeseen circumstances."[25]

563/ 29.   May we ever live more faithfully this way of Christ modeled for us by St. Ignatius. For this we pray in a prayer of Father Pedro Arrupe:

> Lord, meditating on "our way of proceeding," I have discovered that the ideal of *our* way of acting is *your* way of acting.
>
> Give me that *sensus Christi* that I may feel with your feelings, with the sentiments of your heart, which basically are love for your Father and love for all men and women.
>
> Teach me how to be compassionate to the suffering, to the poor, the blind, the lame, and the lepers.
>
> Teach us your way so that it becomes our way today, so that we may come closer to the great ideal of St. Ignatius: to be companions of Jesus, collaborators in the work of redemption.[26]

---

[24] Pedro Arrupe, *Our Way of Proceeding*, n. 12, *AR* 17 (1979): p 697.

[25] Arrupe, *Our Way of Proceeding*, n. 55, *AR* 17 (1979): p. 719.

[26] Arrupe, *Our Way of Proceeding*, n. 56, *AR* 17 (1979): pp. 719–22.

VIII

DOCUMENTS RELATING TO THE
34th GENERAL CONGREGATION

1. ALLOCUTION OF POPE JOHN PAUL II

5 January 1995

Dearly beloved Delegates of the Society of Jesus,

1.   With the celebration of the Eucharist, in the course of which you invoked the Holy Spirit, you began your general congregation this morning. Your work will extend over the coming weeks.

At the very beginning you also desired to meet with the Pope, in order to underline the singular charism of fidelity to the Successor of Peter which, according to St. Ignatius, should characterize the Society of Jesus. You expect to receive "missions" from the Pope, as the Constitutions of your Institute say, "that in everything God our Lord and the Apostolic See may be better served."[1] Following in the footsteps of your Founder and his first companions, with this gesture of loyalty to the ministry of the Roman Pontiff you declare that the Society is totally and without reservation of the Church, in the Church, and for the Church.

I greet you with great joy, beloved Religious, addressing my remarks first and foremost to your superior general, Father Peter-Hans Kolvenbach, thanking him for the sentiments he has just expressed in the name of all. Along with him, I greet the general council and the 223 delegates who, representing Jesuits from all over the world, give witness to the vitality and fruitfulness of the Society of Jesus, in the midst of all the various situations and problems it faces.

2.   Your general congregation certainly understands the particular importance of this present historical moment, since it is essentially dedicated to discerning the specific contribution your Institute is called to make to the *new evangelization, on the brink of the third Christian millennium,* as well as to updating the internal organization and legislation of the Society of Jesus so that it can render ever more faithful and effective service to the Church.

So that you may better undertake the task before you, I would like to propose for your reflection a few points of reference which are surely not new to you. I am certain that these will help you in defining more carefully your contribution to the evangelizing mission of the Church in our contemporary world, especially in view of the "Great Jubilee" of the year 2000, in which a "new springtime of Christian life" will be revealed, thanks to the openness of believers to the action of the Holy Spirit.[2]

---

[1] *Const.* [612].

[2] Cf. John Paul II, Apostolic constitution *Tertio Millennio Adveniente,* n. 18.

3. First of all, the Society of Jesus is called to reaffirm unequivocally and without any hesitation its specific *way to God*, which St. Ignatius sketched out in the Formula of the Institute: *loving fidelity to your charism* will be the certain source of renewed effectiveness. The Servant of God Paul VI reminded the participants of General Congregation 32 of this: "You have a spirituality strongly traced out, an unequivocal identity, and a centuries-old confirmation which was based on the validity of methods, which, having passed through the crucible of history, still bears the imprint of the strong spirit of St. Ignatius. Hence there is absolutely no need to doubt the fact that a more profound commitment to the way followed up until now—to the special charism—will be the renewed source of spiritual and apostolic fruitfulness." The late Holy Father added: "All of us must be vigilant so that the necessary adaptation will not be accomplished to the detriment of the fundamental identity or essential character of the role of the Jesuit as described in the Formula of the Institute as history and the particular spirituality of the order propose it, and as authentic interpretation of the very needs of the times seem still to require it. This image must not be altered; it must not be disfigured."[3]

Do not be afraid, then, to be ever more authentic sons of St. Ignatius, living fully your original inspiration and your charism in these last days of the century, deepening your full commitment to the Society of Jesus. Your charism calls you to be witnesses to the primacy of God and of his will. "Ad maiorem Dei gloriam": the religious life, the apostolate, commitment to the world of culture, to social work, and to care of the poor must always have as their single end the greater glory of the Lord. All this points clearly to the primacy of spirituality and of prayer: neglecting them would mean betraying the gift that you are called to be for the Church and for the world.

4. Your commitment to the new evangelization in the light of the third millennium is based on this demanding spiritual and ascetic foundation which ought to be the basis for every apostolic activity. It requires first and foremost a *renewed dedication to the actualization of the command the Lord entrusted to the Church*: "Go into all the world and proclaim the Gospel to every creature" (Mark 16:15). This command of Christ is an essential aspect of the Church's mission.

"Founded chiefly for this purpose: to strive especially for the defense and propagation of the faith,"[4] the Society of Jesus, following the example of St. Ignatius and his beloved companion St. Francis Xavier, has offered in every moment of its existence a significant contribution, including the blood of its martyrs, to the realization of the Church's missionary task throughout many parts of the world.

---

[3] *Insegnamenti di Paolo VI,* 12 (1974), pp. 1181f.

[4] *Formula* [1].

I am certain that this general congregation will not fail to pay appropriate attention to such a fundamental aspect of your apostolate. Today, as you well know, new nationalisms, radical ideologies, religious syncretism, certain theological interpretations of the mystery of Christ and his saving work, the difficulty of finding a balance between the need for the inculturation of the Gospel and the unity of the message contained in it, as well as other political, sociological, and religious circumstances, threaten to compromise the very foundations of your presence and evangelical activity in many countries. Despite these difficulties, I encourage the whole Society to persevere in its mission to proclaim the Gospel within the perspective of the Kingdom of God.

5.   The task of evangelization also requires a *more generous self-sacrifice in order to promote the full communion of all Christians.* In my recent apostolic letter *Tertio Millennio Adveniente,* I pointed out the supreme importance of the unity of all Christians: "As the new millennium approaches, among the most ardent petitions of this special moment, the Church asks the Lord that unity among all Christians of every denomination might increase, leading to the achievement of full communion."[5] In this great struggle the whole Church ought to find the Society in the vanguard. Resisting every temptation toward individualism, independence, or parallelism, the Society is called to give a stirring testimony to fraternal concord and ecclesial harmony.

The energies that the Society devotes to collaborating in every part of the Church's life are well known. In this regard, I encourage you to keep alive this fundamental note of your charism of *serving the universal Church,* overcoming every temptation of provincialism, regionalism, or isolationism that could endanger the very existence of certain international and interprovincial works of great importance for the universal Church and for the local churches. On this occasion, I want to thank the Society for the work of the Pontifical Gregorian University, the Pontifical Biblical Institute, the Pontifical Oriental Institute, and Vatican Radio. On the other hand, however, in those places where you exercise your ministries, you must respectfully cooperate with the pastoral planning of the bishops in their teaching and in their care for the local communities entrusted to them.

A similar interior attitude should inspire theological research which Jesuits, animated by the spirit of faith, undertake in humble fidelity to the teachings of the Magisterium. What is there to say about teaching that forms the younger generation? This teaching must strive to provide students with a clear, solid, and organic knowledge of Catholic doctrine, focused on knowing how to distinguish those affirmations that must be upheld from those open to free discussion and those that cannot be accepted.

---

[5] Apostolic letter *Tertio Millennio Adveniente,* n. 16.

6. With these points as your bases, what emerged in the preparation of the general congregation is an insistent priority for the Third Millennium: *missionary outreach and the promotion of a dynamic of ecclesial communion* that extends into ecumenism, directs interreligious dialogue, and inspires the service of human rights and peace as foundations of a civilization of love.

It is clear that no one can hope to heal the wounds and the divisions of the world without a total commitment of self to the service of communion in the Church. We must be very attentive, therefore, lest the faithful be confused by questionable teachings, by publications or speeches clearly at variance with the Church's teachings on faith and morals, or by any attitudes that offend communion in the Spirit. In this context I want to thank the Lord for the good that the Jesuits accomplish throughout the world spreading the Gospel of salvation through the witness of your words and your lives. I encourage you to continue on this path, dear brothers, surmounting every difficulty and relying constantly on the help of God, as well as the support of the Apostolic See, which expects much from you in this period of human history, troubled, yes, but through God's providence also rich in apostolic and missionary possibilities.

7. This is the moment of new evangelization, which demands of the Society an apostolic commitment renewed and ever more concrete "in its devotion, its methods, and its expressions."[6]

Such a commitment must be rooted first of all in faith in the Lord who can fully sustain the Society even in difficult moments like our own, so that it may never cease to work generously for the increase of the Kingdom "by means of public preaching, lectures, and any other ministry whatsoever of the Word of God, and further by means of the Spiritual Exercises, the education of children and unlettered persons in Christianity, and the spiritual consolation of Christ's faithful through hearing confessions and administering the other sacraments."[7] Indeed, this Society is of the Lord Jesus, and his is the good that it daily accomplishes in its service to culture, especially in the university world, in the formation of youth, and in the spiritual support of so many priests, religious men and women, and lay people. The fruits of divine grace are found no less in the apostolates of the parishes, in social centers, in the area of mass-media work, and in many centers for alleviating human suffering.

All this richness is part of the dynamism of the new evangelization, relying not on human calculation or refined strategies, but on a humble and confident relationship with him who is the first evangelizer, Christ: "The apostolic energy

---

[6] *Insegnamenti di Giovanni Paolo II,* 6/1 (1983), p. 698.

[7] *Formula* [1].

of the new evangelization springs from a radical communion with Christ, the first evangelizer."[8]

To achieve authentic forms for inculturation of the faith and to promote the values of justice, peace, and solidarity so needed in nations around the world as fruits of Christian life, we must focus every apostolic effort on the *proclamation of Christ, the Redeemer of humanity.*

It is certainly true that the Society is deeply committed to social work and to the service of the least of humanity. How could this not be so? How could one strive for the "greater glory of God" in all things, while forgetting that, as St. Irenaeus wrote, "the glory of God is the human person fully alive"? But such a mission should never be removed from the global service of the evangelizing mission of the Church, which is responsible for the salvation of every person and of the entire person, because of our supernatural destiny.

Dear brothers, the discernment that you are called to undertake during this general congregation must define ever more precisely your apostolate as a mission of utterly transparent evangelization, characterized by a powerful sense of God's presence, of love for the Church and for each individual as the "way of the Church," by a recognition of the gift of your vocation, and by the joy that comes from fidelity to God's mercy.

8. Forming future apostles for such ascetic and pastoral directions is a fundamental need. You should always insist on a solid and lengthy formation for the professed of the Society. Your founder explicitly insisted that no one should be admitted to profession without thorough formation.[9] Pope Paul VI recognized that "[w]herever in the Church, even in the most difficult and extreme fields, in the crossroads of ideologies, in the front line between the deepest human desires and the perennial message of the Gospel, there have been, and there are, Jesuits."[10] Because this continues to be true, you must "not accede to the easy temptation of softening this formation, which invests such importance in each of its aspects: human, spiritual, doctrinal, disciplinary, and pastoral."[11]

I am fully aware of the great effort that has been expended to respond to such expectations. In this regard, I also want to express my appreciation for how much the Society of Jesus has done to improve the formation of the brothers, who are irreplaceable members of your order's life and apostolate.

9. My dear Jesuits, the recent synod of bishops dedicated to the consecrated life and to its mission in the Church and in the world has addressed to all reli-

---

[8] Final Document of the 1992 CELAM Conference, Santo Domingo, n. 28.

[9] Cf. *Formula* [5].

[10] *Insegnamenti di Paolo VI,* 12 (1974), p. 1181.

[11] *Insegnamenti di Giovanni Paolo II,* 5/1 (1982), p. 715.

gious an urgent appeal that *they perform their prophetic mission at the service of the new evangelization*, giving visible and clear witness in their style of life, in their work and prayer, in radical imitation of our chaste, poor, and obedient Lord. May this appeal inform and accompany the labors you are about to undertake, and guide the choices you are called upon to make. Be well assured that the Church needs your able contribution to proclaim the Gospel of Christ more effectively to the people of our time.

May Holy Mary, who sustained and illumined your Founder, help you to "keep always before your eyes God and then the nature of this Institute."[12] May she guide you with maternal love.

In support of all your generous plans, I ask God for abundant heavenly gifts for each of you, and from my heart I impart on you and on all the members of the Society of Jesus a special Apostolic Blessing.

---

[12] *Formula* [1].

2. Introductory Discourses of Father General

A: On the Call or Vocation of This Congregation

5 January 1995

In the Constitutions, which will have an important place in this General Congregation 34, St. Ignatius creatively characterizes how the ordinary government must serve the whole Society. To justify the absence of a regular general congregation or of a general chapter at set periods—"for example, every three or six years, more or less" [678]—Ignatius observes that "it does not seem good in our Lord that such a congregation should be held at definite intervals or very often; for the Superior General through the communication which he has with the whole Society and through the help he gets from those near him, can spare the Society as a whole from that work and distraction as far as possible" [677].

This introduction fits into the concern to spare the members of GC 34 the effort of meticulously studying Part Eight of the *Constitutions* and of losing time on an in-depth examination. Its sole purpose is to remind us of what a general congregation meant for Master Ignatius, what he expected from it, and what the Society today, in our concrete situation at the end of the second millennium, can personally and communally expect from it.

At the beginning of the congregation, it is good to recall "in the Lord" that, despite its administrative and juridical appearances, this assembly has its source and origins in the spiritual experience of Ignatius and his first companions. Before it acquired its present structure and became the plan now outlined in the Constitutions, the general congregation was a lived event whose thrust was to prolong the deliberations and the encounter of the first Fathers as friends in the Lord. The general congregation is of course the supreme authority, the highest level of power in the Society; but for Master Ignatius the congregation was above all a "personal union" [677], an encounter of persons. Here is how he approaches the chapter in question: "Now let us come to the union of persons which takes place in congregations of the Society" [677]. If in the depths of his vocation and mission, the Jesuit is a man who is sent and if, because he is sent, he belongs to an apostolic body scattered more or less all over the world, then for Ignatius there are only two ways that a Jesuit can feel a part of the Society: (1) by the union of hearts and minds, maintained by a wide exchange of information—correspondence—and by reciprocal visits; and (2) by means of the visible and tangible union of the companions in a general congregation. A congregation is always a spiritual union in the Spirit, and sometimes a "corporal union" [677], as one secretary expressed it. It is no surprise then to see Ignatius slowly abandon the term "chapter" for his preferred term, "congregation," not only to avoid any monastic tendency in the Society but also to proclaim in the very word itself that the general congregation is the whole Society. One only has to study the text of the *Constitutions* to see that for the first Jesuits there was no difference or distinction between the Society as an apostolic body and the general congregation. When the congregation meets, then "conveniet Societas," and to convoke a general congregation is to "Societatem ... congregare."

Thus, as Ignatius himself conceived it, the general congregation is the Society itself, responsible for its whole apostolic body. While it is the supreme authority, it is not so as a body above the Society or even within the Society, but instead because it is the Society itself in the personal encounter of the companions of Jesus. In its beginnings the Society could be identified with the founding Jesuits, or a bit later with the small number of professed who made up the "Societas professa." But it is striking that Ignatius maintained, at least in principle, his perspective on the general congregation as a gathering of the whole Society which could help "toward uniting the distant members with their head and among themselves" (before [655], title of Part VIII).

As usual, apostolic work prevails in Ignatius's thought. If for the sake of mission general congregations must not be multiplied without reason, so also for the sake of the same mission those sent to Rome should be only "those who can come conveniently. Thus it is clear that those who are physically ill are not included, nor are those who are in places very distant, for example, in the Indies, nor those who have in their hands some undertakings of grave importance which cannot be omitted without great inconvenience" [682]. In four hundred and fifty years the Society has called only thirty-four general congregations, and only seven of those without an election. Thus the Society has remained faithful to Ignatius's apostolic concern.

Seeing you here today in this *aula* and knowing what most of you are involved in, I realize very well that those of you who were easily able to come are few, and those who have come from far away are many, interrupting apostolic work of great importance. This is only one more reason to ensure that, as St. Ignatius insisted, the business at hand be dealt with as soon as possible [711]. The absence of 90 percent of the Society does not matter, for Ignatius's perspective has remained unchanged: it is the entire Society which is here; and, before being delegates, participants, elected or convoked, all are first and foremost members of one and the same body of the Society. Gathered together in a general congregation, in the spirit of Ignatius we are none other than members of the universal Society, which is not a federation of provinces and regions and not a conglomeration of assistancies, but one single apostolic body. It would go against Ignatius's idea of a meeting of friends in the Lord for one to see himself as delegated or elected to defend or promote some ideology or a particular opinion of a province or region.

Furthermore, this assembly does not operate like a parliamentary system. While respecting the interaction of majority and minority votes, Ignatius introduces a non-parliamentary factor when he invites us to be more charismatic than democratic. He invites us to discover that to some of us God our Lord has given more abundant gifts to feel and express what would be conducive to God's service [686]. Thus while ensuring each participant's freedom and rights, Ignatius reminds us that a congregation is an event which goes beyond a well-run and well-managed meeting. It is a privileged moment for us as the Society of Jesus to experience intensely the responsibility of each and all of us for our common work of serving the greater glory of God.

Nevertheless the participants in a general congregation are by no means anonymous Jesuits, standardized gears of a well-oiled machine. Ignatius's goal for a general congregation is to gain the best-possible information for a discernment solidly based on experience and on reading the signs of the times, thus bringing us to the best decision in order to adjust and strengthen our missionary service [683]. The participants will be all the more valuable for this process of communal discernment the more they reflect some aspect of the mission, life, work, prayer, and cooperation of the Society in their own culture and traditions, according to their formation and experience and their theological perspectives. "For to a great extent the congregation is an aid toward settling something wisely, either through the greater information which it possesses or through some more distinguished persons who express their opinion" [679].

In this congregation as well, the Society has paid more attention to qualitative than to quantitative representation. This has been precisely to gain as universal a view as possible, without skimming over the real problems of the Society, the Church, and the world at the end of the second millennium, and without confining ourselves to the detailed and the personal, the particular and the ephemeral. Thus in this general congregation, assistancies with many Jesuits are less represented than those with fewer, precisely to permit the greatest presence of all the aspects and dimensions of the Society's life and work in the world. We must call upon the entire accumulated experience of the members of the general congregation. Chapter 7 of Part VIII of the *Constitutions* deals with how to decide in matters other than the election of a superior; in many numbers of this chapter, Ignatius describes with his usual meticulousness how all are called to give the best of themselves in their participation and sharing to arrive at the best-possible decision. With no better material means than table and paper, copies and books, Ignatius demonstrates his concern that each participant place all his personal qualities as so many gifts of God at the disposal of all. All their presentations must be submitted in writing—*verba volant, scripta manent*—and are deposited on a table placed in the midst of the general congregation. Copies are made so that nothing may be lost of someone's personal contribution made in the service of all. Even once a decision has been taken, Ignatius leaves open the possibility of returning to it [711ff. and 716], convinced that the Spirit might speak through precisely a late intervention. For Ignatius such respect for everyone's sharing and participating on the basis of his own experiences and convictions is a condition for deciding "in a manner conducive to the greater glory of God our Lord" [711], even if in the end "the side to which the majority inclines will prevail and the whole congregation will accept it as from the hand of God our Lord" [715].

By putting together each one's qualities and by a genuine exchange of gifts, the general congregation is called to a true communal discernment on questions of importance that involve the future [680], or even on some very difficult questions which concern the entire Society or its manner of proceeding, for the greater service of God our Lord [680]. Ignatius, who is always very sensitive to the tension between apostolic work and common life, hopes on the one hand that the general congregation will work on these questions expeditiously to avoid long absences from apostolic work [711]. On the other hand, proceeding expeditiously should not prevent seeking unanimity, if possible, precisely because of the need for clear and unified missionary action. Thus discernment in common is undertaken less to gain a majority vote than to work toward the consent of all to a union of action which is for the glory of God and the good of the Society.

Since the days of St. Ignatius and his first companions, one single mission has always united the Society: to serve Christ, our Lord and Savior, by continuing his work throughout the world. But this mission must be realized in very diverse ecclesial conditions, in extremely varied life contexts and work situations, and in response to very different needs. Our personal temperaments and preferences, our talents and tastes, our desires and dreams are so pronounced, especially today, that individualism seems a lesser evil: allowing a semblance of peaceful coexistence which seems, realistically speaking, to be the most one can expect for union among us.

Nevertheless, Ignatius expected that when friends in the Lord deliberate and discern in common, they would all decide along the same lines. These lines would not lead to uniformity; they would extinguish neither the rich diversity of personal and cultural gifts nor the disconcerting variety of conditions in which we must act. Rather, "along the same lines" would lead to a union of minds and hearts which would underlie and sustain any action of the apostolic body of the Society.

For a communal discernment to result in this union, it must be led by the same Spirit, as the first Jesuits often put it. Ignatius expressed it slightly differently:

> [S]ince the light to perceive what can best be decided upon must come down from the First and Supreme Wisdom, Masses and prayers will be offered in the place where the congregation is held as well as in the other regions of the Society. This should be done throughout the time the congregation lasts and the matters which should be settled within that time are being discussed, to obtain the grace to conclude them in a manner conducive to greater glory to God our Lord. [711]

In elaborating a whole program of conscientization and discernment in common, GC 32 in Decree 4 (73ff.) describes this way of proceeding as a constant interrelation between "experience, reflection, decision, action" according to the Jesuit ideal, "in actione contemplativus." According to Decree 4, the result will be a transformation of our habitual ways of thinking, a conversion of spirits as well as of hearts, and this transformation will produce apostolic decisions.

We can still turn to the first companions to learn what is a true deliberation, reflection, and discussion that leaves room for the Spirit to intervene. Thus we will be able to speak of contemplative prayer during an authentic interplay between these elements—not only before and after—an interplay in which the Spirit can break through; and we will let ourselves be seized by that same Spirit. The Spirit's intervention keeps us from hardening our opinions, from stiffening our expressions and even from absolutizing our most intimate convictions and our most valuable experiences. Would we not deprive the Spirit of all freedom to intervene if we desired to reach a decision at all costs and in feverish haste, setting by ourselves the conditions of God's response? On the contrary, does not the interrelation of "contemplation and action" in discernment mean that we do not want to enclose the Society within the false certitude of a watertight project that covers everything? Does it not mean rather that we want to leave some uncertainty that would allow the Spirit, through events and inspirations, to overturn our projects and call our plans into question?

This margin of uncertainty will not paralyze the Society's work: rather it will affirm that even a general congregation of the Society of Jesus exercises no lordship over the Lord's vine. It will free us from the paralyzing obsession of wanting to be masters of a field which we of course have to plant and water, but to which only God gives life. Moreover, if some who did not know Ignatius's life in the Spirit were to read the chapter on a general congregation called to deal with business, they would find a sober and meticulous exposition to assure good order and an effective and efficient dispatching of business, in an atmosphere which respects each one's freedom of expression, and which is clearly oriented toward taking decisions. For Ignatius, a general congregation is first of all a meeting with a particular organization and administration, with procedures and votes, which means a labor based on serious evaluation and laborious discussion, and hours of demanding work, not to mention the moments when we despair of ever reaching any decisions at all. The general congregation will never be the expression of a disincarnate spirituality.

And yet, Ignatius does not hesitate to attribute to this highly complex mechanism the most specific and the best of what the Spirit taught him so that "all may turn out as is expedient for his greater service, praise, and glory" [693]. Above all, the general congregation fits into the dynamism which pushes the Society toward its end—Glory—that is inscribed as much in the Spirit's call as in the human response to that call. While service, praise, and glory are proposed to us as the purpose of the general congregation, we are nevertheless referred back to our historical condition, to our experience and our know-how, to our enthusiasm and our patience in the concrete work which is a general congregation.

Ignatius likes to link "spirit" and "way of doing things," the famous "way of proceeding" which we will have to update in this very general congregation. Thus we are totally removed from a spirituality which is restricted to the religious domain, but also from a socioeconomic seminar to analyze the problems of our day. To be fully a general congregation in the spirit of Ignatius, the Spirit must be able to work in a certain kind of practice which we call discernment in common. It is well known that what makes the difference, what transforms this meeting into a congregation of the Society of Jesus, is finally our intention. But our intention must not remain on the abstract level of desire: to be authentic, it must be translated into our attitude here; it must be incarnated in our involvement in this meeting of the whole Society. Concretely this means taking the congregation to heart, even if none of you has sent himself to Rome: if you are here, it is because of someone else's will expressed in a nomination, a vote, or a call.

Even so, discernment in common is much more than friendly and congenial participation: it calls on our entire person to bring our contribution with all that we are as bearers of the Spirit, and it also calls on us to renounce ourselves by recognizing the Spirit speaking to us through the other. As early as their first deliberations in Rome, our companions already knew that a discernment in common could not succeed without the freedom gained by going beyond self-love, by letting go of one's particular views. Accepting this renunciation made in the Spirit in no way means bowing resignedly before the predominant majority opinion; rather, it calls one's personal certitudes into question in the conviction that by so doing the Spirit can lead us to a more intensely clear convergence and, concretely, to a more valuable service.

During this general congregation there will also be moments when we will simply have to question the Spirit together and, in the light of the Spirit, put our points of view together in order to sense bit by bit the common inclination by which the same Spirit is leading our discernment. According to the words of Decree 4 of GC 32, such an attitude will require a transformation of our entire person, of our customary schemes of thought, and a conversion of spirits as well as of hearts, from which our apostolic decisions will result (73). In their reactions to the tabloids, some Jesuits commented that the gaze on the surface of the earth, covered with people, as suggested by St. Ignatius in the contemplation on the Incarnation, can only be a valid starting point for a vision of current reality if this gaze allows itself to be illuminated by a vision of faith and an act of hope rooted in the same love of Christ (cf. GC 32, D 4, n. 15). This condition makes the difference in personal attitude between a panoramic consideration of our world in order to develop a sociopolitical, cultural, or economic policy, and a contemplation of this same reality for the purposes of a discernment which would lead to apostolic choices and decisions. Along the same lines, these reactions to the tabloids also insisted on the need to personalize this kind of analysis. Ignatius in the First Week of the Exercises tries to make us become aware of our connivance with a death-dealing history and our solidarity with perverted human society. In the same way, we must not list the miseries and pains of our age without bravely discerning our personal and communal complicity, so that the discernment might consequently lead us in the same Spirit to apostolic decisions and choices which will engage us personally and communally to proclaim the Gospel of the Lord in the years to come. Without this total availability to service, proof of the praise and glory of God, a communal discernment would not deserve the name, and neither would a general congregation of the Society of Jesus.

Master Ignatius knew that this was a question of life and death for the Society. Consequently, he did not hesitate to list all the obstacles to the gift of self in a discernment. Among them he draws attention to a "lack of judgment or a notable obstinacy in one's personal opinions" [184]. Those who have set themselves up as all-knowing can also sometimes be problematic [656ff.], or Jesuits of high prestige who are used to the favor of the great of this world [656]. But according to Ignatius the most significant obstacle to the union so necessary in Christ our Lord for the proper functioning of the Society is too great a number of insufficiently mortified Jesuits [657].

The fragility of our person comes on top of the difficulty, with which Ignatius was very familiar, of assuring union of hearts among so many Jesuits scattered among the faithful and among unbelievers in various parts of the world [655]. Here once again we feel the Spirit breaking through. In admitting that humanly speaking it is an impossible mission to get so many and such different companions to come to a decision along the same lines, Ignatius recognizes that discernment in common is less a task to be accomplished than a gift of God to be received. It is precisely because it is a gift to be received that Ignatius counts on the prayerful accompaniment of the whole Society [693 and 711]. This is the same link which joins us in the general congregation to Jesuits spread out all over the world, whom we are called to represent as a whole.

In this way, gathered together in a general congregation which is the Society of Jesus, we engage in a discernment in common which is a constant interrelation of apostolic contemplation and action under the influence of the Spirit; according to the great resources which the Lord has entrusted to us, we take on those problems of our day which the Lord wants to entrust to us here on the threshold of the third millennium:

- by taking on the joys and pains of the men and women who the Lord places on our path for us to help

- in solidarity with all those who suffer from destitution and sickness, from injustice and violence, to whom the Lord wants to send us

- in communion with the Lord's Church which must be able to count on us as men of the Church in its universal solicitudes and its pastoral concerns

- and by speaking and acting in the name of our brother Jesuits scattered throughout the earth but united with our gathering from which they hope for both old and new in order to move forward in their mission with greater clarity and stronger courage

May this mission, our mission, be constantly before us in this congregation as we contemplate the mysteries of the One who is sent, the Lord. In this way may our choices and decisions to renew our apostolic action be stamped by what the Spirit will teach us to lead us to his Truth.

B: On the Mission and Body of the Society

6 January 1995

Our confrère Pierre Teilhard de Chardin on several occasions expressed the desire to change the name of today's solemnity, or at least to change the prefix. To emphasize that we are celebrating the day on which our Lord revealed himself with full clarity as the foundation of all and of everything, beginning and end, alpha and omega, we should speak of a "dia-phany" and not of an "epi-phany." For it is less a question of a sudden bursting into history of him who is its creator and savior than of a mysterious and silent "dia-phany" by which Christ sheds light on the true foundation of all beings, by acting in them and by them to lead all towards their fulfillment, God becoming all in all. Teilhard, in his own words, did not read the story of the Magi as if it were photographic truth but a truth that provides enlightenment about him who fills the universe with his dynamic presence, about him who alone gives meaning to our history, about him who, in all and for all, is forever the all-high God.

It is this "dia-phany," this revelation of God in "all created things," which dazzled and deeply moved Ignatius. In today's mystery, the search for God takes place by means of the book and the star; likewise, when he states a "principle and foundation" for the adventure of the Spirit to which he invites us, Ignatius proclaims that for a man or woman there is no authentic search for God without insertion into the created world, and that, on the other hand, no solidarity with men and women and no engagement with the created world can ever be authentic without a discovery of God. In keeping with this vision, his Constitutions are based on this mystique of God's presence to his work, on this "dia-phanous" or quite simply "theo-phanous" design of a creation which again has to be made just and beautiful, true and peaceful, united and reconciled with God, as on the first day.

Out of this perspective the Society of Jesus was born, in the conviction that to serve God who reveals himself as God-with-us is *ayudar a las almas* (to help souls), is to help men and women disengage themselves from the tarnished and confused image that they have of themselves, in order to discover themselves, in God's light, as in complete likeness with him. It is with a similar viewpoint that Ignatius in the *Constitutions* [814] recalls that the best way to glorify God our Lord, who wishes to be glorified with what he gives as Creator (that is, nature) and with what he gives as author of grace (namely, the supernatural), is to cultivate carefully the natural means— with, however, one condition: that we are not to put our confidence in them, but that we make use of them to cooperate with divine grace.

That is "the path of divine service on which we have entered" [134]. But Ignatius would not be Ignatius if he did not consider "this road towards God" as a path which God himself in Christ, who is the "way," had revealed to him by giving the grace to "start" (*Autobiography* [11]).

But let us return to the Gospel to contemplate the Magi on their journey. Magi from the Orient! This is something quite shattering—at least unexpected. Did Matthew forget Leviticus's advice: "Do not turn to mediums, or wizards; do not seek them out, to be defiled by them: I am the Lord your God" (19:31)? Or did Matthew have the modern mentality which believes that there is nothing new to discover in the West, while a bewitching and exotic light comes from the Orient? At all events, these quite unusual Magi, great searchers of the heavens, lived with the same question which will cause the first apostles to ask, "Rabbi, where are you staying?" (John 1:38).

What leads them to ask this question is a star which acts not only as a means, but as an item of sharing, in Teilhard's expression, or an instrument of union, in the spirit of Ignatius. In today's Gospel we discover that the word of God is not only entrusted to Scripture and its exegetes, but it manifests itself also in the open book of the night, which sings the glory of God while it responds to the watchman's expectation through the light of a dawn which announces the new day (Ps. 130:6).

"We have seen his star in the East, and have come to worship the Lord." These are the Magi, prototypes of a Church which is the offspring of paganism; they force the chosen people to open their books, to discover in them that fundamentally they reveal the Christ as clearly as did the heavens, which guided those travelers by means of the star. The opening of the sacred books "that I too may come and worship him" makes clear even to the heart of the usurper the hidden desire of a kingdom of justice and truth. The Magi were able to help Herod encounter the king awaited by his people, even though the recognition implied the renunciation of his own royalty. As did the Magi, he should have taken a different route. This refusal of a different route is also the fate of the scribes who, in their pitiful blindness, did not see in the Scriptures him who came not to destroy them but rather to give them the fullness of their divine meaning.

And there is the infant with his mother. It is not the Virgin with the Infant; it is the Infant with the Virgin, acknowledging that his only glory on earth is to be fully human, by means of his mother. When Ignatius proposes this mystery of Christ's life for our contemplation, he repeats four times "to adore": to come to adore (*SpEx* [267]) before returning by a different route. This adoration is concretely expressed by the gifts: gold for the king, incense for God, myrrh for the mortal in expectation of immortality. But if the Magi gave only gifts, they would have given nothing. In adoration they gave themselves and thus made "offerings of greater value and of more importance" (*SpEx* [97]). These Magi whose profession it was to search, to discern, to see, saw only a small infant, but they recognized what went infinitely beyond their perceptions: there appeared—diaphanously—in the weakness of this infant the glory "of the eternal King and Lord of all" (*SpEx* [97]).

A star, a book, a new-born infant . . . a king, tempted by riches, as very often happens (*SpEx* [142]) under the standard of Lucifer, the mortal enemy of our human nature (*SpEx* [136]); some scribes who in their obsession to save their acquired truth do not decide to deny themselves in order to go to God, and thus remain in the second "class" of Ignatius (*SpEx* [154]); and the Magi who, by turning, chose this other road which Ignatius calls in the Constitutions "the path of Christ our Lord" [582] on which the traveling companion "accepts and desires with all possible energy whatever Christ our Lord has loved and embraced" [101].

It is the alternative road, the one among all the others that leads to God, which should guide this general congregation if it wishes to be a congregation of the Society of Jesus. Are we on this road in so obvious a way that it is clear to all? Are we dragging our feet along this road, or are we seen "to go forward in the path of the divine service" [260] and even "to run in the path of Christ our Lord"

[582]? Or have we, rather, lost our way and no longer know where we are going? As in the case of the scribes of Jerusalem, the intellectual capacity and the verbal ability of the Society are such that in the general congregation words will not be lacking to express "the path of Ignatius, the pilgrim" in decrees and words, in laws and messages; but following the Magi is a question of setting out to make choices and refusing to go astray; it is a question of getting personally involved in concrete deeds (*SpEx* [230]).

The Magi were aware that the path leading to where the infant remained went against the current. For the infant was scarcely born and already a hostile world was weaving around him, silently but effectively, a full network of alliances and plots, of accusations and enmities. The overall picture, reported by the press, sufficiently shows that our path towards God, as that of Christ, while it will certainly not be determined, will still be strongly affected by the machinations of the prince of this world and his Herods. If the path under Christ's standard, emblazoned with poverty, humiliation, and injustice (*SpEx* [147]), collides with the triad of "riches, honor, pride," it is not because there is no other solution, but because the companions of Jesus, his servants and his friends [146], are setting out to "help all" ([146]), not in a dream world or an unreal world, but in our world as it is and as it will, if left to itself, go to destruction. As a result Ignatius wished that "in the vineyard of Christ our Lord which is so extensive," the Society would be able to choose the part "which has the greater need; because of the lack of other workers or because of the misery and weakness of one's fellow men and women in it and the danger of their eternal condemnation" (*Const.* [622]). "Similarly, the Society ought to labor more intensely in those places where the enemy of Christ our Lord has sown cockle, and especially where he has spread bad opinion about the Society or stirred up ill will against it so as to impede the fruit which the Society could produce" [622].

Therefore, in a world where production and consumption, market and profit are more and more evident as an unavoidable aspect of ownership, should not our path towards God be that of the poor, as we commit ourselves with them and for them to recall to all that the human person does not live by bread alone but by this word of Christ, who demands for each one without exception the integrity of humanity and the destruction of every dehumanizing structure? In a world where religious and cultural differences so often lead to violence and war to maintain and strengthen themselves, should not our path towards God witness to a union of hearts and of spirits in which diversity is understood as mutual enrichment? In a world which is desperately seeking happiness and pleasure derived from the desire for possessions, seduction, and power while scorning the rights of others, cannot our path towards God open up others to the meaning of the beatitudes? There is no doubt that words which speak of the good have filled venerable books for centuries, but the announcement of the good news takes place not by the repetition of words, but rather by the testimony of life, by witnesses of flesh and blood who, by prophetically living Christ's Gospel, make the path towards God incarnate. If we look into ourselves and our communities, can we say, in keeping with the directives given by GC 32, that we are companions of Jesus, that we are committed under the standard of the cross, that we are taking part in the decisive struggle of our age, namely, the struggle for the faith and the struggle for the justice which that faith implies (GC 32, D 2, n. 2)? Let us go further: are we where we are expected to be in order to be living witnesses of the good news?

It will be a great grace if we leave this general congregation with a clear personal and communal answer to these questions which are fundamental to the fecundity of the tremendous work which the Society produces.

On returning to their homeland, did the Magi announce the good news? The gospel account says nothing about this. Ignatius observed: "Though this is not mentioned in the Scripture it must be considered as stated. . . . For Scripture supposes that we have understanding" (*SpEx* [299]). As a matter of fact, he knew from experience that when we meet God and have a passion for him, we can only desire this grace for others. Once we are enriched with this intimacy with the Lord, we ask only to become impoverished in order to enrich others with this abundance. This is something that the Christian Orient has grasped; and in the well-known "Akathistos Hymn," it sings of the Magi that, "having become bearers of God, they return, fulfilling your prophecy; while proclaiming you before all as the Christ, they leave Herod like a fool incapable of singing Alleluia." The meeting with the Lord changed them. God truly reveals himself only by turning our hearts inside out. In the Epiphany it is not a message that is communicated or information that is exchanged. There is a meeting of the new-born with the Magi, and this reciprocal recognition makes the Magi living witnesses of the good news. By their transformed being they become the good news and thus proclaim in this dialogue of life the Light of the nations. If it should happen that when examining our identity as Jesuits, we sense that we are no longer these living witnesses to the Gospel, the primary cause is a lack of the personal experience of God, whatever form it may take.

Four years ago Pope John Paul II, while speaking to the religious of Latin America, remarked that "it can sometimes happen that the People of God do not always encounter the hoped-for support among consecrated souls because perhaps they do not reflect in their way of living a sufficiently strong sense of the God that they should communicate." It is true that everything connected with evangelization—to continue the epiphany which has been entrusted to us as our responsibility—is in transition or crisis. The demand for evangelization now extends to every part of the globe; but its urgency is no longer felt as it was at the time of the first Jesuits. Today's Gospel proves that no one can be forced to embrace the faith against his will: and in the encounter with the Magi from a religion outside the covenant, Matthew proclaims the Epiphany to all of humanity and to each individual—without denying that this recognition should come first of all from the chosen people.

Faced with this reality, which is both old and new, our terminology has lost its certitude; and a theology which takes into account God's will to manifest himself as Savior of all, transcending the unique vocation of the irreplaceable Church and Gospel, stammers as it searches for an identity. This hesitation, or even confusion, concerning evangelization has not only left a feeling of insecurity in this whole area of the Lord's manifestation to the world; it has weakened and even stifled the missionary spirit which has always characterized the Society. Because the apostolic body of the Society has no other purpose than to be involved "especially in the concerns of the missions" (found here and there in the Constitutions), to permit this spirit to be extinguished would at the same time mean to deprive each of us of his vocation and of his mission. While making available the greatest possible diversity in way and means, the Constitutions, however, remain very clear about what concerns the end of the missions: "to help people meet Christ, God's epiphany." Even today we have to assure ourselves, concerning a candidate for the Society, that he is desirous and "zealous for the salvation of souls. For that reason he should also have an affection toward our Institute, which is directly ordered to help and dispose souls to gain their ultimate end from the hand of God our Creator and Lord" [156]. Our mission, which is our consecration to Christ, is that of aiding "our neighbors to attain the ultimate end for which they were created [307] or, more clearly yet, "to attain to beatitude" [163].

Have not these words, which at first seem antiquated, found a new urgency? Through the postulates the Society has given new scope to the mission of coming to the aid of others and to this rejection of conquest. There is a rejection of stridency and publicity, of proselytism and of counting numbers of converts, and a thrust towards encounter and interreligious dialogue, towards broad collaboration with all men and women of goodwill, towards the promotion of justice and the defense of peace, of human rights and of the environment, by means of the dialogue of life and by common seeking for the truth, by insertion in difficult surroundings, and by the submerging that makes of our life a simple question, by the testimony also of him who inspires all these aspects of his mission among humanity and the celebration of Christian vitality. We are given a whole new range for the full living of this ideal which Father Arrupe summed up in these few words: "men and women for others," thus translating the Constitutions' "ayudar a las almas." Pope John Paul, as he calls us to a new evangelization, asks us to make serious efforts to discover and put into practice a new language, a new approach, a new way to respond to the new challenges and to the new stakes for humanity, which needs to be helped to become in the reality of our time in the image and likeness of God, as he manifested himself on the day of the Epiphany.

Father Arrupe dared to express this in a mystical manner when he stated: "[M]an, the first word of the Spiritual Exercises, is the point of departure of the spiritual experience which Ignatius lived and taught, and is also—when taken to its completion by way of excellence and development—the be-all and end-all of life when conceived as contemplation" (EE 430). This view only echoes the conviction of John Paul II, which has been frequently repeated: "The human person is the way of the Church, the necessary way for the Church . . . and this is . . . because the human person—every man or woman without exception—has been redeemed by Christ, because Christ has in some way united himself to humanity" (*Redemptor Hominis*, 14).

Have not the words of the Constitutions, when thus viewed, found a new vitality that calls out to us? It is fortunate that we are looking for a new terminology for our mission and for new theological motivation, but this depends on a revival of our missionary thrust; for from a weakening of this spirit, we can expect only the death of the Society. In the Society from its beginnings, this spirit was expressed on the practical order in a universal availability. We willingly identify ourselves as messengers, but the account of the Epiphany, as well as the stories of the other biblical figures, teaches us that a messenger should set out for the place that the mission calls him. He should, therefore, be able to leave what is familiar to him in every sense of the word and give up his certitudes and habits to become truly immersed in situations which are painful for human living, especially the situation of the poor to whom the Gospel was announced before all others.

This universal availability doubtless takes for granted an involvement and gift of self, but today even more—and this is an aspect of the new evangelization—requires the courage to be accepting, to let oneself be transformed with complete freedom, so that the good news may and can become clear. Without this universal availability, which is concretely lived out in mobility and the choice of priorities, the Society is no longer capable of helping others go forward on the road which is theirs to the Lord. "The Society of Jesus in its history has always been distinguished, through the many and different forms of its apostolic ministry, by mobility and the dynamism with which its founder infused it and which has made it capable of grasping the signs of the times and, as a result, of being in the vanguard of the renewal which the Church wishes" (John Paul II, Address to the Provincials, n. 6). It is understandable that this task will thrust us into painful situations, into the temptation of being content to provide others only with mortal bread and of abandoning the need to give them the bread of life as well, in efforts to open new fields of apostolic activity and to close what no longer corresponds to our present-day mission, in places where the decrease in the number and quality of our capabilities in manpower and resources runs the risk of exhausting energies which are already indispensable for mere survival. We can pretend to be giving up a position of strength and security, and there is hardly any doubt that the Society has today reasons to be proud of its surprising activity in almost all the world. It is an undeniable fact, but it only makes sense if all this activity is an expression of the purpose for which it was founded.

The general congregation will have to measure the Society's spiritual vitality, its life in the spirit; for, as Ignatius reminds us in the Constitutions,

> [f]or the preservation and development not only of the body or exterior of the Society but also of the spirit, and for the attainment of the objective it seeks, which is to aid souls to reach their ultimate and supernatural end, the means which unite the human instrument with God . . . are more effective than those which equip it in relation to men and women. Such means are, for example, goodness and virtue, and especially charity, and a pure intention of the divine service, and familiarity with God our Lord in spiritual exercises of devotion, and sincere zeal for souls for the sake of glory to him who created and redeemed them and not for any other benefit. [813]

In the Spiritual Exercises Ignatius rightly focuses the entire mystery of the Epiphany on the adoration of the Magi: they see just a poor infant and fall on their knees or, rather, before an Oriental they fall prostrate. The poor infant has remained the poor of God while being the resurrected Lord. And then the question is put to all of us: "But who do you say that I am?" (Matt 16:15). This general congregation has the responsibility not to give a ready-made response, presented in one of its decrees, but it should put itself in the presence of this infant and make a colloquy with Ignatius: How is it that, though he is the Creator, he has stooped to become human (*SpEx* [53]), being able again to say who he is, that is to say, what we are inasmuch as we are companions of Jesus for the life of the world? As a participant in this general congregation, on the brink of the third millennium, I ask myself, Who am I? and "[a]ccording to the light that I have received, I will beg for grace to follow and imitate more closely our Lord, who has just become man for me" (*SpEx* [109]).

C: On Our Law and Our Life

7 January 1995

We want for a few moments to recall how Ignatius and his first companions entrusted the Constitutions to us. It is well known that we are dealing with an original work, of such originality that a specialist from the Gregorian was led to assert, "This law is not a law, this code is not a code." While remaining true to himself as a pilgrim on the road to the absolute of God, Ignatius outlines the reality of the road to travel even in the legislation of the Society of Jesus. There is no need to repeat here the original development of the different parts of the *Consti-*

tutions, which were proposed as stages of a long journey to be made, from admission to the apostolic body of the Society up to the definitive incorporation, by which a personal commitment was bit by bit transformed into a union of hearts and spirits with those who wished to be made into one body, "nos reducere ad unum corpus." As Ignatius marked out the way to God for us, he took the seeming risk of ceaselessly repeating himself and in this way, according to the opinion of Nicholas Bobadilla, of creating "a labyrinth of great confusion."

Ignatius, however, does not repeat himself for the joy of repetition; he was very aware of the distinctiveness of each stage on this long journey. The obedience of a novice cannot be that of a formed Jesuit. The sense of belonging to an apostolic body cannot be the same for one who is sent alone on a mission and for one who fulfills this mission in the framework of a community. We can expect maturation, growth from life in the Spirit. In the Constitutions Ignatius wishes each to be able to advance towards God according to the particular demands of each stage, of each mission entrusted to him. In our sometimes exaggerated concern for equality for all, have we not neglected or ignored differences in experiences and individuals instead of appreciating their importance and letting this mature? Ignatius was not familiar with our temptation immediately and almost automatically to see all differences in terms of master and slave, or of striker and stricken. As a result, he was not afraid to have confidence in those "who will be men who are spiritual and sufficiently advanced to run in the path of Christ our Lord to the extent that their bodily strength and exterior occupations allow" in everything that concerns the life in the Spirit [582], with the assurance that those who are not yet sufficiently advanced will be able to discover in the Constitutions advice and instruction for making progress on the way.

The companion as Ignatius would like him to be and become is not an outlaw, but one who wishes to find in the Constitutions a help for progress and for thus giving greater service. Precisely because it is a matter of someone wishing to be helped in his desire, Ignatius refuses to give any orders and remains satisfied with making challenges along with their motivation: what it is good to do [280], what it is essential to do [284], what could be helpful [282]. Nothing is imposed from without, and even less under pain of sin [602]; everything is founded on the desire, or at least the desire for the desire [102], of going forward freely and generously on the way which Ignatius proposes. Should anyone wish not to go forward on this way, he is completely free to go away. For life in the Society is just one way among many others. It is this liberty that transforms itself into a gift of life for service to the missions that are entrusted; it draws from this interior law of charity and love what the Holy Spirit writes and imprints on hearts. For it is this law which should help and inspire more that any external constitution [134].

Always a realist, St. Ignatius acknowledges in the Constitutions that there will always be in the Society members who cannot fully live according to these views of liberty and responsibility; he limits himself to remarking that there should not be too many who are Jesuits in name only and remain such because of the advantages of belonging [657]. For too large a number would paralyze the proper functioning of the Society.

For those who are able to carry the burden of this vocation (*Formula* [4]), the Constitutions should open the way, thanks to the experience which is accumulated in them and which they hand on, while avoiding at the same time an extreme rigor and an excessive laxity, a demagogic permissiveness and a militaristic discipline [822]. They in no way negate the fact that every companion will live in a permanent election, in a constant discernment which will lead him to be placed with Christ, in order to be made by the Spirit capable of making in everyday life the decisions which Christ made, of making them here and now, today in our mission.

The Constitutions and the interpretations subsequently given them in general congregations should facilitate this discernment by pointing out the obstacles after many unfortunate experiences; by indicating, when necessary, the paths which experience shows lead nowhere; by establishing, for the extreme but always possible cases, limits by which one can be assured of taking the good way; but also by shedding light on the way by discernment of the signs of the times and by formulating responses to new challenges and involvements; and by preparing by precise and concrete decisions the apostolic body of the Society, and especially those involved in initial and permanent formation, for the new tasks to be accomplished on our way towards God. Without this book of challenges and reminders, our desire to go forward remains without perspectives and without energy. The legislative work which particularly awaits this general congregation will help the Society go forward with more clarity and greater unity.

It is important to learn from Ignatius's experience how to confront the eternal problem which brings the letter into conflict with the Spirit, the institution into conflict with the charism. St. Paul sums up the difficulty in a few words: "Without the Spirit, the letter kills . . . but without the letter that Spirit has no voice" (2 Cor. 3:6). All one has to do is to open up the book of the *Spiritual Exercises* and to leaf through the book of the *Constitutions* to come face to face with Ignatius and his great inspirations, his wide horizons, his worldwide measures; and also with an Ignatius who goes into the least detail and particulars of conduct and process. We do not have a double personality here, or two parallel records of activity. Ignatius allows himself to be taken over by the logic of the Incarnate Word in whom true infinity and actual finiteness are joined together. Ignatius make no choice between right and love, between vision and management, between letter and Spirit. As he contemplates the mysteries of the life of the Incarnate One, Ignatius sinks his gaze into all the density of the world and neither scorns nor neglects anything that lives or dies, but discovers and proclaims it in Christ, the beginning and end, dead and risen.

Should we be surprised, then, that the Constitutions were composed precisely after many Eucharists, in which the Infinite freely enclosed himself in the finiteness of this bread that is broken and this wine that is poured out for the life of the world? It is in this faith that Ignatius searched for confirmation of his discernment, the presence of the Spirit in this text of the *Constitutions*. For him, it is a question of life and death. For if the Society was not established by human means, it could consequently be neither maintained nor developed by them, but only by the all-powerful hand of Christ, our God and Lord [812]. Because the Society should be a body which serves God and which God can use for his work for the world (*SpEx* [236]: "God works and labors"), Ignatius desires the text of the *Constitutions* to be at the service of what the Spirit says to the Church, and that the Spirit may be able to use this text of the *Constitutions* to lead the people of God to all Truth.

Ignatius never wished to consider this work definitively ended. He did not wish to leave us a cut-and-dried system, a spirituality that was closed in on itself. Father Diego Laínez stated that Ignatius never published the *Constitutions* and that they were never brought to completion by him as if there were nothing more to be added to them. In every sense, since he conceived the Constitutions as a way toward God, Ignatius was unable to consider them as forever set and determined. On the other hand, since he wished to have the Constitutions share in the *magis*, in the greater service, Ignatius did not wish to limit their thrust, which was inspired by a loving wholeheartedness for the following of Christ. Father Laínez saw in this unfinished work of Ignatius a summons to a creative fidelity, to the Society's responsibility, when gathered in general congregation, to renew, enrich, and clarify, with new apostolic experiences, demands, and urgencies, the way pointed out to us by the pilgrim Ignatius.

May the Spirit guide us in our work on legislation, so that by the intercession of our Lady of the Way and of Ignatius the pilgrim, the interpretation that we are going to give the Constitutions may be in all and for all our Ignatian way towards God

3. Introduction of Father General to the Final Voting on the Society's Law

24 February 1995

Today we begin the voting on what is called our proper law. Inspired by the Second Vatican Council, an earlier general congregation called for its revision so that a return to our sources would renew our apostolic way of proceeding in light of the challenges of the new evangelization on this threshold of the third millennium. After passing through so many competent and expert hands, after being shaped by our experiences and hopes, the revision is now presented to this general congregation for the approval of the whole Society. May the Lord bless all who have given their very best to this revision and all who have contributed to it from near and far.

This revision could have been done in a totally different manner; it could have adopted other procedures or formulations. But it could not have had a different purpose. The confirmation of its creative fidelity is the fortunate concurrence between the goal of our revision and that formulated in the deliberations of our first companions here in Rome in 1539. After heated and laborious debate, those first companions established once and for always a threefold orientation for the Constitutions and for every subsequent revision:

• first, to be able better and more appropriately to accomplish their original desire that in every action they might fulfill God's will which placed them with the Son to continue his work and his mission, in the world and for the life of the world

• next, to preserve the Society more surely as a ready instrument that the Spirit gathers into one apostolic body, so that the same Spirit can then scatter its members throughout the world to serve the missions received from the Vicar of Christ

• and finally, to guarantee that each of the companions has what he needs spiritually and temporally in order to accomplish the mission he is sent to perform

It is precisely this orientation which determined the results of the first companions' deliberations. It motivated Master Ignatius as he drew up the Constitutions; and—under the inspiration and guidance of the Constitutions and all previous general congregations—it ought also to be the basis for our revision as we add and delete, complement and clarify, reorganize and rephrase in contemporary language what it means to be a companion of Jesus in his company, both for today and for tomorrow.

In this work or revision some amount of the arbitrary and incomplete can never be avoided, no matter how many precautions have been taken. It was Master Ignatius's express desire that there always be an element of the open-ended, of

691

an indispensable apostolic freedom, so that "God our Lord may be more served and glorified in all things" (*Const.* [824]).

Thus between openness and procedure, between faith and law, in writing the *Constitutions* Master Ignatius dared to run the risk of designing "a pathway to God" which would be neither a disincarnate spirituality nor a spirituality trapped in activity. Ignatius the pilgrim wants us to be constantly alert and in an attitude of faithful discernment and creativity with respect to the will of God. The risks of our Constitutions come from this balance—the risk of always aiming for greater service, of making ourselves available to the gratuity and unpredictability of God's fidelity, the risk of living in the contradictory tension of being contemplative in action, of being universally available in a work which is inculturated; and today the risk of having to discern and make decisions in the midst of today's confusion and among the many unknowns of our future. In our Lord and in his service we will have to accept all these risks; they are part of our vocation and mission.

At the end of February exactly 450 years ago, Ignatius was finishing that part of his spiritual diary which reflected his struggle with the very real risks contained in the sections of the *Constitutions* which deal with our apostolic poverty. This is why he sought confirmation from the Blessed Trinity. While we search, through our reflection and voting, to express our creative fidelity to the gift which Ignatius received for the Lord's Church, let us pray with him:

> Eternal Father, confirm us; eternal Son, confirm us; eternal Spirit, confirm us; Blessed Trinity, confirm us; our one and only God, confirm us.

4. HOMILY OF FATHER GENERAL AT THE CLOSING MASS

Almost three months have passed since our communal discernment began in the Church of the Holy Spirit. This unremitting labor of renewal of our way of being and of our always becoming better companions of Jesus comes to a close tonight in this act of thanksgiving.

The general congregation concludes before the image of our Lady of the Way who incarnates so well a spirituality which, as a way to God, passes through the street, through the joys and the sorrows, the anguish and the hopes of humanity.

It concludes also before the altar of St. Ignatius the pilgrim, who has constantly accompanied us in our deliberations and voting for the renewal of the Constitutions in creative fidelity.

It concludes, finally, before the altar of St. Francis Xavier, as we acknowledge that in the present state of the Society we have ever greater need of his missionary passion to announce with greater zeal and vigor the Gospel of the Lord, the entire Gospel, and nothing but the Gospel, as servants of Christ's mission.

To this undertaking this evening's Word of God brings full meaning. It is the Lord who comes to fulfill the law and the prophets. Jesus confronts what had been spoken to the men and women of old and what he speaks to us now. But this new law, this law of Christ, does not sweep away the words of Moses and the words of the prophets. Not a letter nor a stroke of the pen will be suppressed of what God our Father has revealed as law for his people. Jesus does not replace it with a better or superior system. If he comes to fulfill this law, it is to assume it personally as a new commandment of love which knows no limits or calculations; it is to live it fully in the paschal mystery, loving his own who are in the world until the end.

In the spirit of this evening's Gospel, nothing of the laws and *Constitutions*, of the decrees and declarations, of the *Complementary Norms* and *Notes,* in the measure that they are grafted on to this law of the love of Christ, nothing is negligible and all merits to be assumed personally in the Lord by each companion.

Everything the general congregation has tried so hard to elaborate needs to pass though our hearts, so that for today and for tomorrow in the service of our brothers and sisters we more effectively resemble the Lord Jesus, often by becoming in the eyes of our contemporaries fools and madmen for him who first became such for us (*SpEx* [167]) and who nevertheless labors only for life, the true life of the world.

It is by the side of the Son that the intense work of General Congregation 34 will really be accomplished. In fact the abundance of words and the multiplicity of texts conceal as under a bushel the lamp of a great basic desire for conversion. Through all the encouragement of or cooperation with the laity and others, through all the urgency of ecumenism and interreligious dialogue, the clarifications of the vows for our day, the renewal of our commitment to justice in the name of the Lord, through all the insistence on authentic "thinking with the Church" in the delicate context of our times—to mention only these examples—the general congregation is calling for a change of mentality, a greater transparency in our mission and a conversion of heart for "an offering of greater value" (*SpEx* [97]). Why try to delude ourselves? It is conversion or the absence of conversion which is the deciding factor for the living-out of this congregation, for the future of all that this general congregation has elaborated, clarified, and decided. That the general congregation was able to appeal to this conversion of heart by means of its decrees and its norms is testimony that the grace of holiness has not been abandoned, even if our examen has revealed that we carry this grace in very fragile vessels of clay.

We thank the Lord that he gives us this opportunity to begin anew to live the words and gestures, to bring to reality the choices and desires of Christ that our labors of three months have tried to recognize. And by the intercession of our Lady of the Way, let us ask in the words of St. Ignatius the grace that we may always know the most holy will of the Lord and that we may accomplish it perfectly.

5. Replies of the Holy Father

A. At the End of the Congregation

Vatican City

Secretariat of State

8 April 1995

Very Reverend Father Peter-Hans Kolvenbach, S.J.

Superior General of the Society of Jesus

Rome

Very Reverend Father General,

The Holy Father was very pleased with the message which you sent in the name of your fellow religious at the end of General Congregation 34 of the Society of Jesus.

His Holiness expresses through me his keen appreciation for the work that has been done. He exhorts you to persevere in the Ignatian ideal of service to the Church, and he asks you with confidence to continue the many initiatives of evangelization to which the Society has always dedicated itself. He reminds you that primary among these is the proclamation of the Gospel to those who do not yet know Christ. He recommends in particular the spread of Ignatian spirituality through the preaching of the Spiritual Exercises, which has brought so much good to souls.

The Holy Father sends his best wishes to all members of the Society, and asks the numerous saints and martyrs of the Society of Jesus to watch over you. He imparts to you and to your fellow religious his Apostolic Blessing.

I take the opportunity to extend to you my own personal best regards.

Sincerely yours in our Lord,

Giovanni Battista Re

B. On Points Which Touch Pontifical Law

Vatican City

Secretariat of State

10 June 1995

Very Reverend Father Peter-Hans Kolvenbach, S.J.

Superior General of the Society of Jesus

Rome

Very Reverend Father General,

In your letter of 6 May, you presented for the approval of the Holy Father the modifications, decided upon by General Congregation 34, of some points which touch on the pontifical law for the Constitutions of the Society.

I wish to inform you that His Holiness, on 8 June 1995, has approved the following proposed modifications:

1. The simple vow not to seek positions of honor is restricted to the episcopate and to the positions of Vicar General and of Episcopal Vicar.

2. To the superior general is granted the faculty of suppressing any house whatsoever of the Society that he deems appropriate, after hearing his council.

3. To formed coadjutors is granted the right to participate with active, but not passive, voice in general congregations (including those in which the superior general is elected) by means of an appropriate representation which is not to surpass in its totality, counting both spiritual coadjutors and temporal coadjutors, 10 percent of the members of the general congregation.

The Holy Father wishes to stress that such changes ought not in any way be interpreted as a weakening of the structure of grades and of the need for them; this would contradict what St. Ignatius wanted for his Society, which is based on two essential elements: the priesthood and the vow of obedience of the professed to the Supreme Pontiff.

His Holiness is happy with the good work accomplished by GC 34 in a serene climate of charity, of fraternal collaboration, and of devoted respect for the directives of the Apostolic See. Wishing you blessings from heaven, he willingly imparts to you and to all members of the Society an Apostolic Blessing.

I take the opportunity to confirm my own best wishes and regard for you.

Yours in the Lord,

Giovanni Battista Re

C.   On Receiving the Decrees of the Congregation

To Very Reverend Father Peter-Hans Kolvenbach, S.J.

Superior General of the Society of Jesus

You have very thoughtfully sent to me the official edition both of the decrees of General Congregation 34 and of the "Complementary Norms" to the *Constitutions of the Society of Jesus,* also the fruit of the recent general congregation.

I thank you sincerely for this renewed expression of devotion and ecclesial union; at the same time, I assure you that I am joined in spirit with you and with the entire Society of Jesus at this significant moment in the life of the Institute. I am certain that the general congregation which is now completed will provide every Jesuit with an important occasion for reflection and for a deepening of spirit in the face of today's challenges, enabling you to carry out with fresh energy your esteemed apostolic work in the Church and in the world.

At the audience for the delegates on 5 January, I recalled that "your general congregation certainly understands the particular importance of this present historical moment, since it is essentially dedicated to discerning the specific contribution your Institute is called to make to the new evangelization on the brink of the third Christian millennium, as well as to updating the internal organization of the Society of Jesus so that it can render ever more faithful and effective service to the Church" (*L'Osservatore Romano,* 6 January 1995, p. 5).

I wanted then to recall some points of reference, already well rooted in your spirit, to you who were desirous to receive from the Successor of Peter his "missions" and directives, "in order that God our Lord and the Apostolic See may be better served" (*Const.* [612]).

Now that the documents produced by General Congregation 34 have been published, I offer to the Almighty Lord, Giver of every good gift, a joyful prayer of thanksgiving for the enormous work accomplished and for the generous response given by the general congregation to the expectations placed upon it. Truly, Holy Mary, who sustained and enlightened your founder and whom I invoked with confidence at the beginning of your important meeting, has given you a mother's guidance and has helped you to keep before your eyes God, above every other thing, and then the nature of the Society of Jesus (*Formula Instituti* [1]).

My dear brothers, always be faithful to the genuine charism of Ignatius! What has been decided in this Thirty-fourth General Congregation of the Society must be implemented in fidelity to the spirit and original intention of the founder. The congregation's action can, therefore, in no way be interpreted as a weakening of the structure of grades and of the need for them, since that would be contrary to what St. Ignatius wanted for the Society, a sacerdotal order, which has an essential and characteristic element the fourth vow of obedience to the Supreme Pontiff.

Therefore, my hope is that all the members of the Society of Jesus may welcome with religious spirit the documents issued by General Congregation 34 and that they may implement them with faithful generosity, striving to be ever more authentic sons of St. Ignatius, living your original inspiration and charism to the fullest and without hesitation in these final years of the century.

With these wishes and invoking the protection of the Blessed Virgin and St. Ignatius on the entire Society of Jesus, I impart to you and your fellow religious a heartfelt special Apostolic Blessing.

From the Vatican

27 September 1995, the 455th anniversary
    of the approval of the Society of Jesus

John Paul II

MEMBERS OF THE 34th GENERAL CONGREGATION

(In Alphabetical Order)

President: VERY REVEREND FATHER PETER-HANS KOLVENBACH

Elected General on May 22, 1965

Last Name, First Name, and Province

Agúndez, Melecio	Castile	Bosco, A. X. J.	Andhra
Aizpún, José Javier	Gujarat	Boulad, Henri	Near East
Aloysius, Irudayam A.	Madurai	Bratina, Lojze	Slovenia
Alvarez Bolado, Alfonso	Castile	Brieskorn, Norbert	South Germany
Amaladoss, Michael	Madurai	Buckley, Michael J.	California
Amalanathan, V. Anthony M.	Andhra	Busto Sáiz, José Ramón	Castile
Arroyo, Edward B.	New Orleans	Cacho, Ignacio	Loyola
Assandri, Andrés	Uruguay	Cardó, Carlos	Peru
Audras, Jean-Noël	France	Carrión, Jorge	Ecuador
Azevedo, Marcello de C.	Central Brazil	Carroll, Peter	Zambia-Malawi
Azzopardi, Cecil	Dumka-Raiganj	Caruana, Charles	Malta
Baiker, Alois	Switzerland	Case, Francis E.	Oregon
Baptista, Javier	Bolivia	Cavassa, Ernesto	Peru
Barla, Henry	Ranchi	Chacko, R. C.	Hazaribagh
Barredo, Fernando	Ecuador	Chang Ch'un-shen, Aloysius B.	China
Bélanger, Pierre	French Canada	Changanacherry, Jose	Gujarat
Belchior, José Carlos	Portugal	Charlier, Jean	South Belgium
Bellefeuille, Jean	French Canada	Chemplany, Mathew	Patna
Bernas, Joaquin G.	Philippines	Cobo González, Sergio	Mexico
Besanceney, Paul	Eastern Africa	Coleman, John A.	California
Blanco, Benito	Antilles	Colomer Casanova, Julio	Aragón

Connor, James L.	Maryland	García-Mata, Ignacio	Argentina
Cornado, João Pedro	Bahia	Gellard, Jacques	France
Coumau, Bernard	France	Gerhartz, Johannes Günter	North Germany
Crampsey, James	Britain	Ghirlanda, Gianfranco	Italy
Cribb, Ian	Australia	Glynn, L. Edward	Maryland
Ćupr Josef	Bohemia	Gomes, Aelred	Calcutta
Czerny, Michael	Upper Canada	González, José Adolfo	Colombia
Da Costa, Ralph	Karnataca	Gonzalez, Buelta Benjamin	Antilles
Danuwinata, Franciscus Xaverius	Indonesia	González, Modroño Isidro	Castile
Daoust, Joseph P.	Detroit	Goñi, Alejandro	Venezuela
De la Marche, Marc	North Belgium	Gray, Howard J.	Detroit
Decloux, Simon	South Belgium	van der Grinten, Steven	Netherlands
Dideberg, Daniel	South Belgium	Guillemot, Jean-Jacques	France
Dijon, Xavier	South Belgium	Hampson, Joseph	Zimbabwe
Doan, Joseph	Vietnam	Harnett, Philip	Ireland
Donahue, John R.	Maryland	Hidaka, Ronald	Zambia-Malawa
D'Souza, Lisbert	Bombay	Howell, Patrick	Oregon
Earle, George	Britain	Ibáñez, Manuel	Baetica
Egaña, Francisco Javier	Loyola	Ilboudo, Jean	West Africa
Eguíluz, Jesús María	Loyola	Ivern, Francisco	Central Brazil
Ekwa Bis Isal, Martin	Central Africa	Jackson, Charles	California
Fagin, Gerald	New Orleans	Jerome, Rosario D.	Madurai
Falla Sánchez, Ricardo	Central America	Jeyaraj, Donatus	Madurai
Farias, Terence	Karnataka	Junges, José Roque	South Brazil
Fernandes, Julian	Karnataka	Kalathil, Joseph	Jamshedpur
Fernández, Franco Fernando	Gujarat	Kerketta, John	Ranchi
Fernández-Martos, José María	Toledo	Kestler, Theodore	Oregon-Alaska
Ferreira, Pedro Vicente	North Brazil	Kim Jung-Taek, Andrew	Korea
Fonseca, Conrad	Bombay	Kinerk, E. Edward	Missouri
Franke, Bernd	Upper Canada	King, Geoffrey	Australia
Galli, Agide	West Africa	Klink, Peter J.	Wisconsin
García Diaz, Mariano	Paraguay	Komma, Gerwin	Austria

Koso, Toshiaki	Japan	Mollá Llácer, Darío E.	Aragon
Köster, Wendelin	North Germany	Morales Orozco, José	Mexico
Koźuch, Mieczysław	South Poland	Morujão, Manuel	Portugal
Krapka, Emil	Slovakia	Mudavassery, Edward	Hazaribagh
Kubik, Władysław	South Poland	Murickan, Joseph	Kerala
Kujur, Angelus	Dumka-Raigan	Murphy, Laurence	Ireland
Kunnunkal, Thomas	Patna-Delhi	Naik, Gregory	Goa
Kurukula, Aratchi Peter	Sri Lanka	Ndolo, Muwawa	Central Africa
Lafontaine, James F.	New England	Nemeshegyi, Péter	Hungary
Lakra, Christopher	Ranchi	Nemesszeghy, Ervin	Hungary
Laschenski, Sigmund	Indonesia-Thailand	Nicolás, Adolfo	Japan
van Leeuwen, Hans	Netherlands	O'Callaghan, John	Chicago
Lo, William	China–Macao–Hong-Kong	Ochagavía, Juan	Chile
Locke, John Patna-	Nepal	O'Hanlon, Gerard	Ireland
de Loisy, Edouard	West Africa	O'Keefe, Vincent T.	New York
Lombardi, Federico	Italy	Opiela, Stanisław	Russia
López Rivera, Francisco	Mexico	Oraá, Jaime	Loyola
Lucey, Gregory F.	Wisconsin	Orgebin, Jacques	France
Mac Dowell, João	Central Brazil	Orsy, Ladislas	New York
Machín Díaz, Jorge	Cuba	Padberg, John W.	Missouri
Maclean, Eric R.	Upper Canada	Padiyara, Cherian	Calcutta
Madelin, Henri	France	Painadath, Sebastian	Kerala
Marshall, Guillermo	Chile	Pandolfo, Salvatore	Italy
Matungulu Otene, Marcel	Central Africa	Parkes, Joseph P.	New York
McDade, John	Britain	Pełka, Florian	North Poland
Menéndez, Valentín	Central America	Perekkatt, Varkey	Patna-Delhi
Merz, Eugene F.	Wisconsin	Perz, Zygmunt	North Poland
Metena, M'Nteba	Central Africa	Picó, Fernando A.	Puerto Rico
Meures, Franz	North Germany	Pietras, Henryk	South Poland
Minj, Patras	Madhya-Pradesh	Pittau, Giuseppe	Japan
Miralles Massanés, Josep	Tarragona	Pozaić Valentin	Croatia
Misquitta, Kenneth	Pune	Privett, John A.	California

Pšeničnjak, Franjo	Croatia	Sosa, Arturo	Venezuela
Puni, Emil	Romania	Steczek, Bogusław	South Poland
Putranta, Carolus B.	Indonesia	Sundborg, Stephen V.	Oregon
Randrianasolo, Jean-Baptiste	Madagascar	Tabora, Joel E.	Philippines
Rasolo, Louis	Madagascar	Taborda, Francisco de Assis	South Brazil
Recolons, Marcos	Bolivia	Taft, Robert F.	New England
Régent, Bruno	France	Tan Chee Ing, Paul	Indonesia–Malaysia-Singapore
Remolina, Gerardo	Colombia	Tejera Arroyo, Manuel	Baetica
Restrepo, Alvaro	Colombia	Tetlow, Joseph A.	Missouri
Rhoden, João Claudio	South Brazil	Thelen, Albert R.	Wisconsin
Riedlsperger, Alois	Austria	Tigga, Satyaprakash	Madhra-Prasdesh
Roberts, Anthony P.	Jamshedpur	Tojeira, José María	Central America
Rdz-Izquierdo, G.	Guillermo Baetica	Tuñí ,Josep-Oriol	Tarragona
Rossi de Gasperis,	Francesco Italy	Uren, William	Australia
Rotelli, Gian Giacomo	Italy	Valero, Urbano	Castile
Rotsaert, Mark	North Belgium	Váni, Emil	Slovakia
Royón Lara, Elías	Toledo	Vásquez, Noel D.	Philippines
Saldanha, Julian	Bombay	Villanueva, Alfredo	China
Salvini, Gian Paolo	Italy	Vitório, Jaldemir	Bahia
Sánchez del Río, Luis Tomás	Toledo	Von Nidda, Roland	Zimbabwe
Sarkis, Paul	Near East	Walsh, Maurice B.	New England
Saulaitis, Antanas	Lithuania-Latvia	Werner, Götz	North Germany
Scannone, Juan Carlos	Argentina	Wild, Robert A.	Chicago
Schaeffer Bradley M.	Chicago	Wobeto, Affonso	South Brazil
Schineller, J. Peter	New York-Nigeria	Zuloaga, Ismael	China
Seremak, Jerzy	North Poland	Zwiefelhofer, Hans	North Germany
Shirima, Valerian	Eastern Africa		

THE 35th GENERAL CONGREGATION

OF THE

SOCIETY OF JESUS

LETTER OF PROMULGATION
FROM FATHER GENERAL

To the Whole Society

Dear Brothers in Christ,

Pax Christi!

In accordance with the Formula of a General Congregation, *n. 142, and following the decision of General Congregation 35 taken during its concluding session on 6 March 2008, we have concluded all the tasks associated with the preparation of the decrees and documents of the General Congregation. This important and complex task was carried out with the wise counsel of the* Assistentes ad Providentiam *as well as other members of the Curia with the right to take part in the affairs of a General Congregation.*

The decrees of General Congregation 35 are effective as of today, the date of their promulgation.

On this occasion it is certainly fitting for us to pray in gratitude to the Lord who accompanied us during the time of the Congregation. These two months were marked by a sincere search for his will, deep communication with one another and fervent prayer. We were particularly blessed by our common morning prayer and our evening Eucharist. From our first session we implored the Lord for guidance and confirmation; we experienced his Spirit until the final Mass of Thanksgiving. At no time did we sense even a hint of resistance to what the Lord was asking of us. All of us in the Society are "Friends in the Lord" and "Servants of Christ's Mission," and the General Congregation has given us a clear witness of obedience to the Lord, to the Church and the Holy Father, and to our tradition and our way of proceeding.

The members of the General Congregation worked with unconditional dedication, a consequence, no doubt, of their awareness that in them the whole Society was truly present. The task now at hand lies with the whole Society. It is our responsibility to "receive" the decrees and to give them life in our ministries, communities, and personal lives. Our experience has taught us that the success or failure of a General Congregation does not lie in documents but in the quality of lives which are inspired by them. Because of this, I earnestly exhort all Jesuits to read, study, meditate on, and appropriate these decrees. Likewise, I encourage you to enrich them with the depth of your own faith and insight. General Congregation 35 began a spiritual jour-

ney. As Ignatius would say, continue this journey in the Lord, always guided by his Spirit and in communion with our brother Jesuits throughout the world.

Certainly the recommendations and suggestions of the Congregation will shape the discernment and decisions of those of us at the General Curia. I am deeply aware of the expectations which the Congregation has raised and I am grateful to its members for providing me with an excellent and highly qualified team of counselors and companions.

It is my earnest prayer that the Lord's abiding presence and the gift of his Spirit will help us to promote in the Society the way of proceeding which was experienced during General Congregation 35. I also pray that the process we have begun will produce abundant fruit in our ministries, in which we strive to bring the light of the Gospel and living hope to all our brothers and sisters.

Sincerely in the Lord,

A. Nicolás, S.I.
Superior General

Rome, May 30, 2008
Solemnity of the Sacred Heart of Jesus

HISTORICAL INTRODUCTION

TO THE DECREES

OF THE

35th GENERAL CONGREGATION

Historical Introduction to the Decrees of the 35th General Congregation

1.   Preliminary Stages

The aim of this historical introduction is to help us to understand the important elements and the development of this 35th General Congregation from its convocation on 2 February 2006 until its conclusion on 6 March 2008.

On 2 February 2006, the feast of the Presentation of the Lord, Father General Peter-Hans Kolvenbach wrote to the whole Society that "it had become more and more clear that the Society had arrived at a situation . . . which required a General Congregation."

Besides that, having obtained the agreement of His Holiness Benedict XVI and having heard the advice of the assistants *ad providentiam* and of the provincials of the whole Society, in accordance with the provision of Complementary Norms, 362 §2 for the resignation of a superior general, Father Kolvenbach decided that the General Congregation must also be convened to provide for the supreme government of the Society. Consequently, he decreed the convocation of the 35th General Congregation for 5 January 2008 and added that it was the responsibility of major superiors to convoke and prepare provincial congregations which should conclude by 1 March 2007.

a. Remote Preparation

There is no doubt that the preparation of this 35th General Congregation had begun several years before its official convocation. Here are some milestones:

In September 2003, the 69th Procurators' Congregation met in Loyola. For several days the 85 procurators had the opportunity to inform themselves about the lights and shadows of the universal body of the Society, thanks to the information given to them by the Superior General, the sectorial secretaries, the general counsellors, and the secretary of the Society. Once in possession of this indispensable information, the procurators were able to make a judgment on whether it was opportune or not to convoke a General Congregation.

The Congregation of Procurators has no legislative power at its disposal but it is perceived rather as a sort of enlarged consult of the Superior General. In

2003, it voted *non cogenda,* that is that it was not in favor of imposing the convocation of a General Congregation. Nevertheless, it formulated a large number of proposals addressed to the central government of the Society and some recommendations in view of the next General Congregation.

In November 2005, Father General convoked a meeting of major superiors at Loyola, a little more than five years after the preceding one. This was in conformity with what is stipulated by decree 23 of the 34th General Congregation, which asked the Superior General to convoke a meeting of all the provincials about every six years counting from the last General Congregation.

The purpose of the meeting in Loyola was to "examine the state, the problems and the initiatives of the universal Society as well as international and supraprovincial collaboration" (GC 34, D.24, C5).

The following themes were treated: the government of the Society, apostolic preferences, formation, and collaboration with non-Jesuits. After a week of examination on the state of the Society and after prayerful reflection and discussion on the different themes, the provincials made numerous recommendations (21 in all) for the whole Society, independently of a General Congregation. Five recommendations, however, were retained as more important from the perspective of a General Congregation.

In a letter of 23 January 2006, Father General communicated to the whole Society these five recommendations from Loyola 2005:

1. The creation of a commission to study the new structures of government in the Society
2. The creation of a commission to evaluate the implementation of the decree on collaboration with the laity
3. An examination, by the General Congregation, of the quality of community life
4. Attention given by general government to the coherence and continuity of formation
5. A study, by the General Congregation, of the question of Jesuit identity in relation to the mission in the Church and in today's world

b. Immediate Preparation

In his official letter of convocation of the General Congregation, on 2 February 2006, Father General indicated that no particular subject for discussion had been laid down for the provincial congregations, but it would be opportune if they should consider in their deliberations the five recommendations reserved by the major superiors at Loyola and also some questions raised in the allocution *De Statu Societatis,* especially at the end of that document.

The provincial congregations took place within the appointed time; they chose electors and formulated postulates.

In the meantime, Father General, having examined with his consultors the recommendations voted at Loyola, decided upon and announced, in a letter of 7 July 2006, the creation of five preparatory commissions for the General Congregation. The task of these commissions was to study the themes likely to be treated by the General Congregation. The five commissions were as follows: social apostolate, juridical questions, collaboration with the laity, obedience, and community life. It was planned that these commissions would finish their work by the end of the year 2006 so that the fruits of their studies might be used by the *Coetus Praevius* of the 35th General Congregation, which would have its first meeting in March 2007.

All this preparation for the 35th General Congregation took place in the spiritual climate of the jubilee year, which began on 3 December 2005 in Xavier, at the end of the meeting of major superiors at Loyola. This jubilee, celebrating St. Ignatius, St. Francis Xavier, and Bl. Pierre Favre, reminded the Society that, following the example of its founders and seeking evermore to live out the charism received from them, this same Society must have as its only desire to serve God our Lord, trusting that his Divine Majesty will be pleased to make use of it.

It is worth remembering here that the General Congregation which had been convoked was of necessity a congregation *ad electionem*. As indicated earlier, the Holy Father had given his *placet* to Fr. Kolvenbach and allowed him to set in place the procedures which would lead to the presentation of his resignation. The latter took advantage of the meeting of provincials in Loyola in 2005 to ask their opinion confidentially. They were unanimously in favor.

In order to help the future electors of the General Congregation to prepare themselves to elect a new superior general, Fr. Kolvenbach, having taken advice from his counsellors, wrote a letter on 29 June 2006 to all the major superiors suggesting to them some common rules of conduct for the time leading up to the General Congregation and for the election of the new general. He asked the moderators of the assistancies to meet with the major superiors and the other future members of the 35th General Congregation who had the right to participate in the election. In a climate of spiritual discernment, the profile of the future general would be initially outlined. Then Father Kolvenbach asked that the electors suggest the names of some Jesuits who are professed of the four vows and who might be considered capable of assuming the office of superior general. This was to be done in accordance with the profile and simply as some kind of indication, without entering into details.

One important clarification was communicated to the electors in February 2007 concerning the mandate of the new general. A letter of Cardinal Bertone, secretary of State, gave the answer of the Holy Father to the question which had been put to him: the mandate of the new general remains *ad vitam,* the norms concerning his right to submit his resignation remain in force.

On 20 February 2007, when all the provincial congregations had taken place, Father General convoked the *Coetus Praevius,* a commission charged with the immediate preparation of the General Congregation. The members of this commission were as follows: Father General *(ex officio),* and Frs. Lisbert D'Souza (general counsellor and coordinator of the *coetus*), Fratern Masawe (AOR), Eugène Goussikindey (AOC), Ernesto Cavassa (PER), Arturo Sosa (VEN), Peter Bisson (CSU), Thomas Smolich (CFN), Edward Mudavassery (HAZ), Stanislaus Amalraj (AND), Adolfo Nicolás (JPN), Daniel Huang (PHI), Mark Rotsaert (BSE), David Smolira (BRI). Father Pasquale Borgomeo, at the request of Father General, was present at all the meetings of the *Coetus Praevius* as secretary; he had previously read and classified all the postulates of the provincial congregations as well as those which came from particular groups or individuals.

c. The Work of the *Coetus Praevius*

This preparatory commission met in Rome from 15 March to 3 April 2007. Its principal task was to finish the immediate preparation of the Congregation by carefully analyzing all the postulates which had been received and by preparing some preliminary reports on the main questions which had been raised (*Formula of the General Congregation* [FGC] 12, 2). The different reports were put together in a booklet entitled *Relationes Praeviae,* which was given to the delegates before the General Congregation itself.

Three hundred and fifty postulates had been received by the General's curia and they were classified into three groups: those which must be passed on to the General Congregation, those which came within the competence of Father General (117) and those which were rejected (31). The first group formed the basis of the material prepared by the *Coetus Praevius.*

The postulates were classified into eleven themes and a *relatio praevia* was prepared for each theme. Within each *relatio* there was first of all a list of the postulates concerned with this particular theme. A summary stated what the postulates were asking for. Then the *Coetus Praevius* presented the state of the question, an analysis of the situation, an evaluation, and finally some recommendations.

The *Coetus Praevius* also suggested dividing the groups of postulates into two categories: those which the Congregation might deem likely to lead to a decree and those which could be discussed by the Congregation with a view to recommendations and mandates addressed to Father General and the ordinary government of the Society. The possible themes for an eventual decree were: mission, identity, government, obedience, and relations with the laity. The possible themes for ordinary government were: community life, formation, promotion of vocations, youth apostolate and JRS.

The *Relationes Praeviae,* translated into the three official languages (English, Spanish, and French), were sent to all the electors with a questionnaire so that they might think about them and answer the questions asked at the planned assistancy meetings.

The *Coetus Praevius* met for a second time in Rome from 21 to 29 November 2007 in order to finish its work of examining the postulates which had been received since March as well as the responses which had been sent to them from the assistancies regarding the questions which had been put to them. The *Coetus Praevius* also proposed a schedule for the General Congregation.

After this second session, Father General, sent to all the members of the General Congregation a letter dated 12 December 2007, in which he informed them of the work of the *Coetus Praevius.* The commission was proposing a plan for five decrees:

1. An inspirational document to express our Jesuit identity and our charism
2. A document on mission in order to reformulate the apostolic orientations of the 34th General Congregation (faith/justice, culture, dialogue)
3. Collaboration with others
4. Apostolic obedience
5. Leadership and governance

The commission then proposed a list of twelve subjects concerning ordinary government.

The commission also reflected upon the process and practical functioning of the Congregation so that the delegates' time might be put to the best possible use. It proposed a possible schedule, pointing out mainly that there would be two phases in the General Congregation: the first the election of the new general and the second the examination of some important questions affecting the universal Society and its mission. The first phase *(ad electionem),* devoted to the resignation of Father General, the study of the *De Statu Societatis* report and (once the resignation had been accepted) the election of the new Father General, would take about two weeks. During the second phase *(ad negotia),* regional assistants would be nominated, and the assistants *ad providentiam* as well as the admonitor of Father General would be elected. At the same time the *Relationes Praeviae* would be presented by the *Coetus Praeviae* and the Congregation would treat the questions proposed and would decide to vote on decrees or to give recommendations to Father General.

d. **Other Aspects of the Preparation for the General Congregation**

In the meantime, Father General had included the provinces in the work of the preparation of the General Congregation by sending them some presentations on the different themes studied by the *Coetus Praevius.* These documents, as Father Kolvenbach wrote in his letter of 4 September 2007 to the major superiors, aimed to allow communities to "participate in the preparation [of the General Congregation] by prayer and reflection."

Several other aspects of the preparation of the General Congregation which have not been touched on deserve to be mentioned here. Father Josep Sugrañes, along with his collaborators, fulfilled an enormous task by taking care of reception, accommodation, logistics and a host of other details, before, during and after the Congregation. A range of facilities was put in place for the debates in the Aula, for the translations, for the voting (a rapid and remarkably effective electronic system), for the distribution of texts (in three languages), and for communication with the provinces. All of this presupposed the competent dedication of many people. Rules had been adopted concerning the communication of information to the outside and a team was set up to help with this. The daily prayers and special celebrations were also carefully prepared. In due course, the evaluation of the Congregation will tell of the high degree of satisfaction which was experienced for the preparations done, for the smooth functioning of arrangements and services ,and for the dedication of those looking after them.

2.   Opening of the 35th General Congregation

a. The Opening Mass

The members of the 35th General Congregation arrived in Rome during the early days of January 2008. All were present on the morning of 7 January 2008 in the Church of the Gesù, the mother church of the Society, for the solemn opening Mass presided over by Cardinal Franc Rodé, prefect of the Congregation for Institutes of Consecrated Life and Societies of Apostolic Life.

In his homily, the Cardinal, having recalled the aim of a General Congregation and the prospect of the election of a new general, addressed Fr. Kolvenbach in these terms: "I wish to express to you, in my name and in the name of the Church, a heartfelt thanks for your fidelity, your wisdom, your uprightness, and your example of humility and poverty."

The rest of the homily was devoted to texts from the *Constitutions* and the *Spiritual Exercises* which treat of the Society's apostolic charism, of obedience to the Holy Father, and of *sentire cum ecclesia.*

The Cardinal concluded by issuing a strong invitation to the Jesuits: "Despite the urgent apostolic needs, maintain and develop your charism to the point of being and showing yourselves to the world as 'contemplatives in action' who communicate to men and women and to all of creation and orient them once again to the love of God. Everyone understands the language of love."

At the end of the celebration, Cardinal Rodé and Father General turned towards the altar of St. Ignatius, and before the statue of the saint, Father General lit a lamp which, during the time of the General Congregation, symbolized the prayer of the whole Society throughout the world.

b. The Official Opening of the 35th General Congregation

At three o'clock in the afternoon of that same day, 7 January 2008, the members of the General Congregation met in assistancy groups to prepare for the official opening which had been planned for 16:30. The task was to propose names for the election of members of the commission *De Statu* and for the positions of secretary of the election and his assistant.

The first session of the General Congregation was chaired by Father Peter-Hans Kolvenbach. Two hundred and six electors participated. In accordance with the *Formula,* the session began with the singing of the *Veni Creator.* Then Father General extended his welcome to the electors and explained to them the reason for his presence as chairman. Pope Benedict XVI had asked Father General to remain in office unti

l the moment when the General Congregation would accept his resignation, and to continue as his delegate until the election of the new superior general

At the invitation of Father General, by a majority public vote, the General Congregation allowed ten regional superiors to take part in the General Congregation as electors by right. These were the superiors of the following regions: Amazonia, Cuba, Malaysia-Singapore, Mozambique, Nepal, East Timor, Puerto Rico, Russia, Ruanda-Burundi, and Vietnam (the latter region having been established as a province after the convocation of the General Congregation).

Also, given the fact that the provincial congregation of Gujarat, which had the right to elect two electors, had only elected one, it was decided by a public majority vote to admit Fr. Fernando Fernández Franco as a second elector. He was the substitute for the first elector (FGC 35).

These eleven fathers entered the Aula, thus bringing the number of electors to 217.

The electors, in conformity with the *Formula of the General Congregation,* then decided by a public majority ballot that the Congregation could be considered as complete and legitimate. Father General then went on to the election of the secretary of the election and of his assistant. Fr. Orlando Torres (Puerto Rico) was elected as secretary and Fr. Ignacio Echarte (Loyola) as his assistant.

Father General indicated the names of the electors who formed the commission charged with judging cases of "ambitioning" for the position of general. This commission is composed of the most senior members in religion from the ten assistancies (FGC 54). Therefore they were Frs. Augustin Karekezi (Africa), Ramón Alaix (South Latin America), Jorge Ambert (North Latin America), José Changanacherry (South Asia), Adolfo Nicolás (East Asia and Oceania), Wendelin Köster (Central Europe), Elías Royón (South Europe), Peter-Hans Kolvenbach (Western Europe), Adam Żak (Eastern Europe), and Vincent Cooke (United States of America).

Next came the elections of the constitution of the *Deputatio de Statu* responsible for gathering information and for submitting a report on the "lights and shadows" in the Society. This commission included the four assistants *ad providentiam* and ten members elected by the General Congregation, namely: Frs. Eugène Goussikindey (Africa), Alfonso Carlos Palacio (South Latin America), José Morales (North Latin America), Mudiappasamy Devadoss (South Asia), Bienvenido Nebres (East Asia and Oceania), Stefan Dartmann (Central Europe), Elías Royón (South Europe), Mark Rotsaert (Western Europe), Adam Żak (Eastern Europe), Bradley Schaeffer (United States of America).

Father General announced that the commission de Statu would begin its work on the following day, 8th January 2008, under the chairmanship of Fr. Valentín Menéndez, one of the assistants ad providentiam.

The General Congregation was ready to begin its work. Father General then offered his resignation in these terms:

> With the blessing of the Holy Father granted the 20th of June 2005 and after having obtained a positive vote from the Assistants for provident care and from the Provincials of the whole Society on the seriousness of the reasons to resign, I present now to the judgement of the General Congregation my resignation as Superior General of the Society of Jesus.
>
> As stated in article 362 of the Complementary Norms, although the Superior General is elected for life and not for any determined time, he may nonetheless in good conscience and by law resign from his office for a grave reason that would render him permanently unequal to the labours of his post. I feel that the Society of Jesus has the right to be governed and animated by a Jesuit in full capacity of his spiritual and corporal gifts and not by a companion whose energies will continue to diminish because of his age—soon 80 years old—and because of the consequences of that age, especially in the area of health. Even if the *Constitutions* and the Norms do not mention it, may I add that the election of a new General will give the Society God's grace of renewal, or to express it with the words of Saint Ignatius "una nueva devoción," "nuevas mociones,"
>
> The discussion and the vote on the resignation will take place at the eve of the four days of *murmurationes* which will be determined by the deputation *de statu Societatis*. In a less formal and a more fraternal way the decision of the General Congregation will be communicated to the whole Society. So much for the resignation."

Father General read the letter of the Holy Father by which the Sovereign Pontiff gave his blessing to the General Congregation. The Congregation then accepted the proposal of Father General to assign to Fr. Jacques Gellard the task of giving an exhortation on the same day as the election. In conclusion Father General recited the prayer to the Holy Spirit.

The debate and the vote of the Congregation on the resignation were fixed for Monday 14 January 2008.

Everything happened in the presence of a statue of St. Ignatius given by the province of English Canada and placed beside the president's table. Thus the 35th General Congregation was launched, committed to discern, by the light of the Spirit, what must today "be determined for the greater glory of God."

3. Beginning the Work of the Congregation

From 8 to 12 January 2008, the commission de Statu carried on its work while the other members of the Congregation held meetings in language or assistancy groups to discuss the *Relationes Praeviae* of the *Coetus Praevius,* in preparation for the second phase *(ad negotia)* of the General Congregation.

On January 14, in plenary session, the Congregation submitted the resignation of Father General to the vote. First the signed letter sent to Father Kolvenbach by the Holy Father was read. Then Fr. Menéndez, the moderator, invited the electors who wished to do so to put questions to the four assistants ad providentiam on the reasons for the resignation of Father General. This time for questions was followed by a moment of silent individual prayer before proceeding to the ballot.

Father General, who had left the Aula during the ballot, was invited to return to learn the result of the ballot. The Congregation had accepted the reasons which had led him to present his resignation. Fr. Menéndez, in moving terms and in the name of the whole Society, thanked him for his 25 years as general at the service of the Society. In his turn Fr. Kolvenbach thanked the delegates and concluded:

> At this time before the election of my successor and before the choices which the General Congregation will have to make, I make my own the prayer with which St. Ignatius finishes his letters: "May it please the Lord by His infinite and sovereign goodness to grant us his perfect grace so that we may always have the sense of his most holy will and that we may fulfil it completely."

4. The Election of the Superior General

After four days of prayer, reflection, and consultation among themselves *(murmurationes),* the 217 electors of the 35th General Congregation were ready, on the morning of 19th January 2008, to proceed to the election of the new general.

Under the chairmanship of Fr. Francis Case, secretary of the Society, they concelebrated the Mass of the Holy Spirit in the nearby church of the Holy Spirit in Sassia. When this was over, the electors went immediately into the Aula of the

Congregation where there were enclosed. After the prayer *Veni Creator,* they listened to the exhortation of Fr. Jacques Gellard (assistant *ad providentiam*). Then in silence each of the electors continued in prayer until the end of the first hour of the session. Each elector then wrote, in his own hand, on a printed ballot sheet, the name of the one whom he chose as general.

By a majority of votes, Fr. Alfonso Nicolás was elected, from the province of Japan. Former provincial of Japan, he had been for three years president of the Conference of Major Superiors of East Asia and Oceania.

The decree of appointment was immediately drawn up by the secretary of the Congregation and signed by Fr. Peter-Hans Kolvenbach as delegate of the Holy Father.

The newly elected General approached the crucifix in the center of the Aula and pronounced the profession of faith.

The name of the elected was immediately communicated to the Holy Father.

Then, after Fr. Kolvenbach, the secretary and his assistant, all the electors approached the newly elected General to greet him. After this demonstration of respect and affection, the doors of the Aula were opened and the members of the community of the curia came to greet the General.

A Mass of thanksgiving was celebrated the day after the election, Sunday, January 20, in the church of the Gesù in the presence of a great number of Jesuits as well as members of numerous religious congregations.

Some days later, on Saturday 26th January in the morning, Pope Benedict XVI received the newly elected general in private audience. It was a brief and cordial meeting, in the course of which, according to the custom of the Society, Father General renewed his vow of obedience to the Holy Father.

5. The Phase *ad negotia* of the 35th General Congregation

a. Organization

As laid down in the *Formula,* once the election of the General has been completed, the Congregation started the second phase *ad negotia.* The Congregation began by electing a secretary and two assistants. Fr. Mark Rotsaert (North Belgium) was elected as Secretary of the Congregation, and Frs. Ignacio Echarte (Loyola) and Thomas Smolich (California) as his assistants.

Next came the elections to form the *Deputatio ad negotia,* a commission responsible for helping Father General to organize the work of the Congregation. Ten members coming from ten assistancies were elected: Jean Roger Ndombi (West Africa), Ernesto Cavassa (Peru), George Pattery (Calcutta), Arturo Sosa (Venezuela), Daniel Huang (Philippines), Janós Lukács (Hungry), Lluis Magriñà

(Tarragona), František Hylmar (Bohemia), François-Xavier Dumortier (France), and Thomas Smolich (California).

Three members of this *Deputatio* were chosen to be moderators of the general sessions: Frs. Ndombi, Huang, and Magriñà. A smaller coordinating committee was also set up: Frs. Cavassa, Dumortier, Pattery, and Smolich.

On January 23 the General Congregation clarified the manner of proceeding in order to treat the different themes in language groups. Twenty-one groups were formed in this way to treat the five themes of possible decrees proposed by the *Coetus Praevius:* ten groups for mission and identity, three for the theme of the government of the Society, three for apostolic obedience and five for collaboration with others. On January 24, the different groups sent a written report back to the secretary indicating the principal points raised in the discussion. Included in the report were a preliminary draft of a document on the subject discussed and an indication of the "tone" which the decree should adopt.

b. The New Team around Father General

After the election of Fr. Nicolás, the General Congregation devoted some days to the question of the constitution of a new team around Father General. First, the manner of proceeding had to be clarified. The 34th General Congregation, in its decree 23 (section E II) had adopted, on an experimental basis, a procedure for the appointment of general counsellors and for the election of assistants *ad providentiam.* It had also envisaged a revision of this procedure by the following General Congregation. Information was then given on the actual sharing of responsibilities and on the tasks of counsellors, regional assistants, and assistants *ad providentiam.* The electors exchanged ideas on this, and by a vote which took place on January 28, decided to maintain the system of government and the election procedure of the members of Father General's council adopted by the 34th General Congregation.

The electors of each assistancy proposed to Father General the names of three candidates who were members of their assistancy and who would be suitable to become general counsellors and to be appointed regional assistants.

Consequently on February 12 the following general counsellors and regional assistants were appointed by Father General:

Fr. Jan-Roger Ndombi (West Africa), assistant for Africa
Fr. Marcos Recolens (Bolivia): assistant for southern Latin America
Fr. Gabriel Rodríguez (Colombia), assistant for northern Latin America
Fr. Lisbert D'Souza (Bombay), assistant for south Asia
Fr. Daniel Huang (Philippines), assistant for East Asia and Oceania
Fr. Adam Żak (Southern Poland), assistant for Central and Eastern Europe
Fr. Joaquín Barrero (Castille), assistant for Southern Europe

Fr. Antoine Kerhuel (France), assistant for Western Europe

Fr. James Grummer (Wisconsin), assistant for the United States of America

Since a single assistant is now responsible for Central Europe and Eastern Europe, the number of regional assistants went from ten to nine.

On February 14 Father General introduced something new: the appointment of two general counsellors non-resident in Rome, Fr. Mark Rotsaert (President of the Conference of European Provincials) and Arturo Sosa (rector of the Catholic University of Táchira, Venezuela).

Finally, on February 18 the General Congregation elected the four assistants *ad providentiam* (FGC 130–137): Frs. Lisbert D'Souza, James Grummer, Federico Lombardi, and Marcos Recolons. It then elected Fr. Marcos Recolons as Admonitor to Father General (FGC 138–141).

Father General appointed two other General counsellors: Fr. Orlando Torres (Puerto Rico), confirmed as General Counsellor for formation, and Fr. Joseph Daoust, Delegate for the interprovincial Houses of Rome. Then Father General appointed Fr. Ignacio Echarte (Loyola) secretary of the Society, replacing Fr. Francis Case.

6. The Documents

a. The Method of Treating the Work

Independently of the appointments mentioned above, the General Congregation continued its work, still using the same method for dealing with subjects with a view to voting decrees. Commissions were set up to work on various themes and to present them in the Aula. Each assistancy then met to react, to prepare remarks, and to present them in plenary assembly. The commissions gathered and evaluated the suggestions and commentaries in order to draft a second report and a text for a decree. This was presented in the assembly and followed by questions for clarification and discussion. Eventually there came a final draft to which amendments in writing could be proposed. The assembly then moved to a final vote on these amendments and on the text of the decree in its totality.

In certain cases, after discussion in the Aula, the draft text had to be re-examined by an editing committee. A new presentation and a new discussion followed. In this way the Congregation as a whole worked together to improve texts by observations and suggestions presented in the Aula or sent in writing to the various commissions responsible for the drafting of the decrees.

b. The Decrees

Five commissions worked on drafting the documents which were voted on and accepted as decrees on the following subjects:

1. Identity: A fire that kindles other fires—rediscovering our charism

2. Challenges for our Mission today—sent to the frontiers

3. Obedience in the life of the Society

4. Governance at the service of universal mission

5. Collaboration at the heart of the mission

It should be further noted, however, that a sixth commission was set up to write and propose a response from the Society to the letter of Pope Benedict XVI to Fr. Kolvenbach (10 January 2008)—to which the latter had replied on 15th January—as well as to the Pope's speech to the members of the Congregation during the audience on February 21. This *ad hoc* commission worked in various stages and produced the document "With Renewed Vigor and Zeal," in which the General Congregation and the Society expressed their gratitude to the Holy Father for his esteem and trust as well as their response to his call.

c. Subjects Entrusted to the Ordinary Government of the Society

From the beginning, the 35th General Congregation, in harmony with the proposals of the *Coetus Praevius,* had expressed its desire not to produce a large number of documents. Nevertheless it touched on many other subjects which were not destined to be developed into decrees but which were presented by a commission, freely discussed by the delegates and sent to Father General, usually in the form of suggestions or recommendations, for the ordinary government of the Society.

The following are the subjects which were dealt with in this manner and which are presented together in another document: youth ministry, migrants, dialogue and religious fundamentalism, the intellectual apostolate, communications, ecology, formation, community life, finances, Africa, China, the Roman houses, Jesuit brothers, and indigenous peoples.

7. The Papal Audience

On 21 February 2008, in response to an invitation from the Holy Father, all the members of the General Congregation made their way to the Vatican and went to the *Sala Clementina,* where they were received in audience at 12:15 by His Holiness Pope Benedict XVI. Father General addressed to him some words of greeting and gratitude. The Holy Father, in his speech to the General Congregation, reaffirmed his trust in the Society and encouraged it in its present mission in terms which deeply moved the members of the Congregation:

> I very much hope, therefore, that the entire Society of Jesus, thanks to the results of your Congregation, will be able to live with a renewed drive and fervor the mission for which the Spirit brought it about and has kept it for more than four centuries and a half with an extraordinary abundance of apostolic fruit. Today I

should like to encourage you and your confreres to go on in the fulfilment of your mission, in full fidelity to your original charism, in the ecclesial and social context that characterizes this beginning of the millennium . . . the Church needs you, counts on you, and continues to turn to you with confidence.

8. Conclusion: The End of the General Congregation

On March 1 in the Aula, in a special ceremony which was simple and short but very warm, Father General expressed in the name of the entire Society the gratitude owed to Fr. Peter-Hans Kolvenbach for his almost 25 years of service to the universal Society as superior general. The whole assembly stood up and applauded at length, thus expressing their profound appreciation. The General Congregation also approved the text of a letter of thanks to Fr. Kolvenbach.

On Wednesday March 5, at the end of the afternoon plenary session, Father General thanked the assembly and formulated some recommendations.

On Thursday March 6, four members of the General Congregation gave witness to their experience of these two months of General Congregation.

Then the delegates voted unanimously to renounce the right to have three days for intercessions (FGC 125). After a pause, the assembly by a large majority voted the powers granted to Father General for the promulgation of the authorised text of the decrees, as soon as the necessary corrections have been made. Thus the 35th General Congregation officially ended.

Father General thanked the Brothers for their participation in the work of the General Congregation. He also thanked the translators, the two secretaries of the Congregation, the assistant secretaries, the moderators, the members of the *Deputatio,* the *ad hoc* commission, the liturgical team, the media technicians, the Treasurer's office, the infirmary, and the entire Curia staff.

On the afternoon of the same day, the delegates and all those who had helped them met once again in the church of the Gesù to celebrate the final Eucharist which had been carefully prepared by the liturgical team. The *Te Deum* was sung at the end of the Mass (FGC 143).

In his homily Father General said in conclusion: "We have lived a great experience and I believe we are all aware of it. But the word of God invites us to go to the source of that experience and to understand well that this transformation is not something which finishes here, but it is something which goes on; all of this becomes mission, a total mission which will go on producing fruit in others."

DECREES OF THE

35th GENERAL CONGREGATION

DECREES

DECREE 1

"WITH RENEWED VIGOR AND ZEAL"

The Society of Jesus Responds
to the Invitation of the Holy Father

I.   A Spiritual Experience of Consolation in the Lord

1/   1.   The 35th General Congregation experienced the deep affection of the Holy Father on two occasions, in his letter of January 10, 2008, and at the audience on February 21, 2008. Following in the footsteps of St. Ignatius and his companions, we gathered, the 225 delegates led by our Father General Adolfo Nicolás, as the General Congregation of the Society of Jesus, to be hosted by the Vicar of Christ and to listen with open hearts to what he would say about our mission. It was a powerful moment and a moving spiritual experience.

In his address, Pope Benedict XVI openly revealed his confidence in the Society of Jesus, as well as his spiritual closeness and deep esteem, in words that touched our hearts, stirring and inspiring our desire to serve the Church in this contemporary world marked "by many complex social, cultural and religious challenges."[1]

2/   2.   These two events gave new clarity to the challenging task of the General Congregation. After the election of our Superior General, the largest part of our work was actually devoted to issues concerning our identity, our religious life, and our mission. As is its duty, the General Congregation attentively scrutinized the situation of our apostolic body in order to provide guidance that will enhance and increase the spiritual and evangelical quality of our way of being and proceeding. First in importance is our intimate union with Christ, "the secret of the authentic success of every Christian's apostolic and missionary commitment, and especially of those who are called to a more direct service of the Gospel."[2]

3/   3.   Our effort to be completely honest with ourselves and with the Lord included much of the dynamic of the First Week of the *Spiritual Exercises:* it helped us discover and recognize our weaknesses and inconsistencies, but also the depth of our desire to serve. This required that we reexamine our attitudes and our way of living.

---

[1] Benedict XVI, *Letter to Very Reverend Father Peter Hans-Kolvenbach* (10 January 2008), §3

[2] *Letter*, §2

4/ 4. However, this experience could not lose sight of the perspective that grounds it: our mission. Indeed, the transition from the First to the Second Week of the *Exercises* is a change in perspective: the retreatant experiences how his entire life has been embraced with mercy and forgiveness, ceases to concentrate on himself, and starts to "gaze upon Christ our Lord, the eternal King, and all the world assembled before him. He calls to them all and to each person in particular."[3] Truly we are sinners and "yet called to be companions of Jesus as Ignatius was."[4]

5/ 5. For the delegates this was the spiritual effect of the allocution of the Holy Father at the audience on February 21. In presenting to us with deep affection a dynamic vision of our mission and our service to the Church, he seemed to say, Turn your gaze to the future "in order to respond to the expectations the Church has of you."[5]

II. Confirmed and Sent on Mission

6/ 6. With such powerful words, the Holy Father definitively placed the future of our mission before us, a mission expressed with complete clarity and firmness: the defense and proclamation of the faith, which leads us to discover new horizons and to reach new social, cultural, and religious frontiers. As Father Adolfo Nicolás noted in his words to the Holy Father, these frontiers can be places of conflict and tension that threaten our reputation, our peace, and our security. That is why we were so moved by the Pope's evocation of the memory of Father Arrupe. The Holy Father referred to his proposal that Jesuits be in service to refugees as "one of his last farsighted intuitions.[6]"

The service of faith and the promotion of justice must be kept united. Pope Benedict reminded us that the injustice that breeds poverty has "structural causes,"[7] which must be opposed, and that the source of this commitment can be found in the faith itself: "the preferential option for the poor is implicit in the Christological faith in the God who became poor for us, so as to enrich us with his poverty (cf. 2 Cor. 8:9)."[8]

---

[3] *Spiritual Exercises*, 95.

[4] GC 32, D. 2, n. 1 (11).

[5] Benedict XVI, *Allocution to the 35th General Congregation of the Society of Jesus* (21 February 2008), §1.

[6] *Allocution*, §8.

[7] *Allocution*, §8.

[8] *Allocution*, §8.

By sending us to "those physical and spiritual places which others do not reach or have difficulty in reaching,"[9] the Pope entrusts to us the task to "build bridges of understanding and dialogue,"[10] according to the best tradition of the Society, in the diversity of its ministries:

> In its history the Society of Jesus has lived extraordinary experiences of proclamation and encounter between the Gospel and world cultures—it suffices to think of Matteo Ricci in China, Roberto de Nobili in India or of the "Reductions" in Latin America. And you are rightly proud of them. I feel it is my duty today to urge you to set out once again in the tracks of your predecessors with the same courage and intelligence, but also with an equally profound motivation of faith and enthusiasm to serve the Lord and his Church.[11]

In a decisive manner Benedict XVI confirmed what our previous General Congregations have said of our specific mission of service to the Church.

7/   7.   In this light we can better understand why the Pope stresses so much—in his letter and in his allocution—that "[t]he Church's evangelizing work therefore relies heavily on the Society's responsibility for formation in the fields of theology, spirituality and mission."[12] In an era of complex social, cultural, and religious challenges, the Pope asks us to faithfully help the Church. This fidelity demands serious and rigorous research in the theological field and in dialogue with the contemporary world, cultures and religions. What the Church expects from us is sincere collaboration in the search for the full truth to which the Spirit leads us, in full adherence to the faith and the teaching of the Church. This help and this service are not confined to our theologians; they extend to all Jesuits, called to act with great pastoral sensitivity in the variety of our missions and apostolic work. They are manifest also in the institutions of the Society as a characteristic of their identity.

III.   The Response of the Society to the Call of the Holy Father

8/   8.   It is obvious that the Society can not let this historic moment pass without giving a response at the same high level as the ecclesial charism of St. Ignatius. The Successor of Peter told us of the confidence he has in us; for our part, we sincerely want to respond to him, as an apostolic body, with the same warmth and same affection he has shown us, and to affirm in a resolute way our specific availability to the "Vicar of Christ on earth."[13] The 35th General Congregation expresses its full adherence to the faith and the teaching of the Church, as they are

---

[9] *Allocution*, §2.

[10] *Allocution*, §5.

[11] *Allocution*, §5.

[12] *Letter*, §6.

[13] Formula of the Institute, *Exposcit debitum* (15 July 1550), §3 (MHSI 63:375).

presented to us in the intimate relationship that unites Scripture, Tradition, and the Magisterium.[14]

9/   9.   The 35th General Congregation calls all Jesuits to live with the great spirit and generosity that is at the center of our vocation: "to serve as a soldier of God beneath the banner of the Cross . . . and to serve the Lord alone and the Church his spouse, under the Roman Pontiff, the Vicar of Christ on earth."[15]

10/   10.   From the beginning of our formation and throughout our lives, we must be and remain men familiar with the things of God. Our desire is to grow now and in the future in the "interior knowledge of Our Lord, who became human for me, that I may love him more intensely and follow him more closely,"[16] especially in prayer and in community life and in apostolic work. As Nadal said, "La Compañía es fervor."[17]

11/   11.   As we know, "mediocrity has no place in Ignatius' world view."[18] It is therefore essential to give young Jesuits a human, spiritual, intellectual, and ecclesial formation as deep, strong, and vibrant as possible to allow each of them to achieve our mission in the world with "a proper attitude of service in the Church."[19]

12/   12.   To be authentically "contemplatives in action," seeking and finding God in all things, we must continually return to the spiritual experience of the Spiritual Exercises. Aware that they are "a gift which the Spirit of the Lord has made to the entire Church," we should, as we are called by the Holy Father, "focus special attention on that ministry of the Spiritual Exercises."[20]

13/   13.   We are aware of the importance of the intellectual apostolate for the life and mission of the Church today, as Pope Benedict XVI has told us on several occasions since the beginning of his pontificate. We have heard his appeal and want to respond fully. In this context, we encourage our theologians to carry out their task with courage and intelligence; as we have heard the Holy Father say, "This is not of course a simple task, especially when one is called to proclaim the Gospel in very different social and cultural contexts and is obliged to address

---

[14]Cf. Vatican II, *Dei Verbum*, 7–10 and the instruction *Donum Veritatis*, 6, 13–14.

[15]Formula of the Institute, *Exposcit debitum* (15 July 1550), §3 (MHSI 63:375).

[16]*Spiritual Exercise*, 104.

[17] Cf. erónimo Nadal, *Plática 3ª en Alcalá (1561),* §60 (MHSI 90, 296).

[18]Peter-Hans Kolvenbach S.I., *To Friends and Colleagues of the Society of Jesus, AR* 20 (1991) 606.

[19]GC 34, D. 11.

[20]*Allocution*, §9.

different mind-set."[21] Given the difficulties inherent in the task of evangelization in our time, it is important that they are disposed "in the most genuine Ignatian spirit of 'feeling with the Church and in the Church'—'to love and serve' the Vicar of Christ on earth with an 'effective and affective devotion' which must make them his invaluable and irreplaceable collaborators in his service for the universal Church."[22] To be missioned to this work at the new frontiers of our times always requires that we also be rooted at the very heart of the Church. This tension, specific to the Ignatian charism, opens the way to true creative fidelity.

14/ 14. In the light of Decree 11 of the 34th General Congregation and the final speech of Father Peter-Hans Kolvenbach to the Congregation of Procurators in September 2003, we call each Jesuit to consider "the proper attitude of service in the Church," which should be ours. This means recognizing, with honesty to ourselves and before God, that some of our reactions and our attitudes have not always been expressed as our Institute demands of us: to be "men humble and prudent in Christ."[23] We regret this, conscious of our common responsibility as an apostolic body. Therefore, we call on each Jesuit, with a resolutely constructive attitude, to strive with the Holy Father, to create a spirit of "communion" so that the Church can bring the Gospel of Christ to a world as complex and troubled as ours.

15/ 15. Recalling the Examen[24] and asking the Lord for the grace of conversion, we ask each of our companions to examine his own way of living and working at "the new frontiers of our time." This examination will include the following: the demands of our mission "among the poor and with the poor"; our commitment to the ministry of the Spiritual Exercises; our concern for the human and Christian formation of a complete cross section of individuals; "that harmony with the Magisterium which avoids causing confusion and dismay among the People of God"[25] about the "themes, continuously discussed and called into question today, of the salvation of all humanity in Christ, of sexual morality, of marriage and the family."[26] Each Jesuit is invited to acknowledge humbly his mistakes and faults, to ask the Lord's grace to help him live his mission and, if necessary, the grace of forgiveness.

16/ 16. The letter and the allocution of the Holy Father open for us a new epoch. The General Congregation gives us the opportunity to live "with renewed vigor and zeal the mission for which the Spirit willed it [the Society] in

---

[21] *Letter*, §5.

[22] *Allocution*, §7.

[23] Formula of the Institute, *Exposcit debitum* (15 July 1550), §6 (MHSI 63:381).

[24] *Spiritual Exercises*, 32-43.

[25] *Allocution*, §6.

[26] *Allocution*, §6.

the Church."[27] Conscious of our responsibility, in, with, and for the Church, we desire to love it more and help others love it more, for it leads the world to Christ humble and poor and announces to every person that "Deus Caritas Est."[28] We can not separate the love of Christ from this "sense of the Church,"[29] which leads "the entire Society to seek to integrate itself more and more vigorously and creatively in the life of the Church so that we may experience and live its mystery within ourselves."[30]

17/ 17. We acknowledge what the Lord calls us to be and to live with greater intensity, through the letter of the Holy Father on January 10 and his address at the audience on February 21. "In the spirit of the fourth vow *in regard to missions* that so distinctively unites us with the Holy Father,"[31] we want to express our willingness to achieve what he invites us to put into practice and what he encourages us to continue or to initiate. We express our renewed availability to be sent into the Lord's vineyard, for the greater service of the Church and the greater glory of God. In asking the Lord for the power of his Spirit to do his will, all of us unite our voices to that of the Successor of Peter in praying with him:

> "Take, Lord, and receive all my liberty,
> My memory, my understanding and my entire will,
> All I have and possess; you have given me, I now give it back to you,
> O Lord; all is yours, dispose of it according to your will;
> Give me only your love and your grace; that is enough for me."[32]

---

[27] *Allocution*, §2.

[28] Benedict XVI, encyclical, *Deus Caritas Est.*

[29] *Spiritual Exercises*, 352–370.

[30] GC 33, D. 1, n. 8.

[31] GC 34, D. 11, n. 18.

[32] *Spiritual Exercises*, 234.

DECREE 2

A Fire That Kindles Other Fires

Rediscovering Our Charism

Many Sparks, One Fire; Many Stories, One History

18/ 1. The Society of Jesus has carried a flame for nearly five hundred years through innumerable social and cultural circumstances that have challenged it intensely to keep that flame alive and burning. Things are no different today. In a world that overwhelms people with a multiplicity of sensations, ideas, and images, the Society seeks to keep the fire of its original inspiration alive in a way that offers warmth and light to our contemporaries. It does this by telling a story that has stood the test of time, despite the imperfections of its members and even of the whole body, because of the continued goodness of God, who has never allowed the fire to die. Our attempt here is to present it anew as a living narrative that, when brought into contact with the life-stories of people today, can give them meaning and provide focus in a fragmented world.

19/ 2. The continued narrative of the Society has provided, over the centuries, the ground for numerous experiences of unity-in-multiplicity. We Jesuits are frequently surprised that, despite our differences in culture and context, we find ourselves remarkably united. Through prayerful discernment, open discussion, and spiritual conversations, we have again and again been privileged to know ourselves as *one* in the Lord:[1] one united, apostolic body seeking what is best for the service of God in the Church and for the world. This graced experience reminds us of the experience recounted in the Deliberation of the First Fathers. Our earliest companions, even though they considered themselves weak and fragile and originating from many different places, found the will of God together amid great diversity of opinion.[2] What enabled them to find God's will was their "decided care and alertness to initiate a completely open way" and to offer themselves fully to it for the greater glory of God.[3] Thus they began a narrative; they lit a fire, which was handed on in subsequent generations whenever people encountered the Society, enabling the personal histories of generations to become embedded in the Society's history as a whole. This collective history formed the basis of their unity; and at its heart was Jesus Christ. Despite the

---

[1] Cf. *Constitutions,* 671.

[2] *Deliberation of the First Fathers* (1539), § 1 (MHSI 63:2).

[3] *Deliberation of the First Fathers* (1539), § 1 (MHSI 63:2).

differences, what unites us as Jesuits is Christ and the desire to serve him: not to be deaf to the call of the Lord, but prompt and ready to do his most holy will.[4] He is the unique image of the unseen God,[5] capable of revealing himself everywhere; and in a tantalizing culture of images, he is the single image that unites us. Jesuits know who they are by looking at him.

20/ 3. We Jesuits, then, find our identity not alone but in companionship: in companionship with the Lord, who calls, and in companionship with others who share this call. Its root is to be found in Saint Ignatius's experience at La Storta. There, "placed" with God's Son and called to serve him as he carries his cross, Ignatius and the first companions respond by offering themselves for the service of faith to the Pope, Christ's Vicar on earth. The Son, the one image of God, Christ Jesus, unites them and sends them out to the whole world. He is the image at the very heart of Jesuit existence today; and it is his image that we wish to communicate to others as best we can.

Seeing and Loving the World As Jesus Did

21/ 4. Fundamental for the life and mission of every Jesuit's mission is an *experience* that places him, quite simply, with Christ at the heart of the world.[6] This experience is not merely a foundation laid in the past and ignored as time moves on; it is alive, ongoing, nourished, and deepened by dynamic Jesuit life in community and on mission. The experience involves both conversion *from* and conversion *for*. Saint Ignatius, recuperating on his bed at Loyola, entered into a profound interior journey. He gradually came to realize that those things in which he took delight had no lasting value but that responding to Christ beckoning instilled peace in his soul and a desire to know his Lord better. But—as he came to see later—this knowledge could only be won through confronting the falseness of the desires that had driven him. It was at Manresa that this confrontation took place. There the Lord, who taught him like a schoolboy, gently prepared him to receive an understanding that the world could be seen in another way: a way freed from disordered attachments[7] and opened up for an ordered loving of God and of all things in God. This experience is part of every Jesuit's journey.

22/ 5. While at Manresa, Ignatius had an experience at the river Cardoner that opened his eyes so that "all things seemed new to him"[8] because he began to

---

[4] *Spiritual Exercises,* 91.

[5] 2 Cor. 4:4; Col. 1:15; Heb. 1:3.

[6] Cf. *NC* 246, 4°; 223 §§ 3–4.

[7] *Spiritual Exercises,* 21.

[8] *Autobiography* 30.

see them with new eyes.[9] Reality became transparent to him, enabling him to see God working in the depths of everything and inviting him to "help souls." This new view of reality led Ignatius to seek and find God in all things.

23/ 6. The understanding that Ignatius received taught him a contemplative way of standing in the world, of contemplating God at work in the depths of things, of tasting "the infinite sweetness and charm of the divinity, of the soul, of its virtues and of everything there."[10] Starting from the contemplation of the incarnation[11] it is clear that Ignatius does not sweeten or falsify painful realities. Rather he begins with them, exactly as they are—poverty, forced displacement, violence between people, abandonment, structural injustice, sin—but then he points to how God's Son was born into these realities; and it is here that sweetness is found. Tasting and seeing God in reality is a process. Ignatius had to learn this himself through many painful experiences. At La Storta he received the grace to be placed with the Son bearing the Cross; and so he and his companions were drawn into the Son's pattern of life, with its joys and with its sufferings.

24/ 7. Similarly today the Society, in carrying out its mission, experiences the companionship of the Lord and the challenge of the Cross.[12] Commitment to "the service of faith and the promotion of justice,"[13] to dialogue with cultures and religions,[14] takes Jesuits to limit-situations where they encounter energy and new life, but also anguish and death—where "the Divinity is hidden."[15] The experience of a hidden God cannot always be avoided, but even in the depths of darkness when God seems concealed, the transforming light of God is able to shine. God labors intensely in this hiddenness. Rising from the tombs of personal life and history, the Lord appears when we least expect, with his personal consolation as a friend[16] and as the center of a fraternal and servant community.[17] From this experience of God laboring in the heart of life, our identity as "servants of Christ's mission"[18] rises up ever anew.

---

[9] Diego Laynez, *Letter about Fr. Ignatius* (1547), §10 (MHSI 66"80).

[10] *Spiritual Exercises,* 124.

[11] *Spiritual Exercises,* 101–109.

[12] *Spiritual Exercises,* 53.

[13] GC 32, D. 2.

[14] GC 34, D. 2, nn. 19–21.

[15] *Spiritual Exercises,* 196.

[16] *Spiritual Exercises,* 224.

[17] Matthew 18:20.

[18] GC 34, D. 2.

Our "Way of Proceeding"

25/ 8. To find divine life at the depths of reality is a mission of hope given to us Jesuits. We travel again the path taken by Ignatius. As in his experience so too in ours, because a space of interiority is opened where God works in us, we are able to see the world as a place in which God is at work and which is full of his appeals and of his presence. Thus we enter, with Christ who offers living water,[19] into the dry and lifeless areas of the world. Our mode of proceeding is to trace the footprints of God *everywhere*, knowing that the Spirit of Christ is at work in all places and situations and in all activities and mediations that seek to make him more present in the world.[20] This mission of attempting "to feel and to taste" *(sentir y gustar)* the presence and activity of God in all the persons and circumstances of the world places us Jesuits at the center of a tension pulling us both to God and to the world at the same time. Thus arises, for Jesuits on mission, a set of polarities, Ignatian in character, that accompanies our being firmly rooted in God at all times, while simultaneously being plunged into the heart of the world.

26/ 9. Being and doing; contemplation and action; prayer and prophetic living; being completely united with Christ and completely inserted into the world with him as an apostolic body—all of these polarities mark deeply the life of a Jesuit and express both its essence and its possibilities.[21] The Gospels show Jesus in deep, loving relationship with his Father and, at the same time, completely given over to his mission among men and women. He is perpetually in motion: from God, for others. This is the Jesuit pattern too: with Christ on mission, ever contemplative, ever active. It is the grace—also the creative challenge—of our apostolic religious life that it must live this tension between prayer and action, between mysticism and service.

27/ 10. It is necessary for us to examine ourselves critically in order to remain mindful of the need to live faithfully this polarity of prayer and service.[22] However we cannot abandon this creative polarity, since it marks the essence of our lives as contemplatives in action, companions of Christ sent into the world.[23] In what we do in the world there must always be a transparency to God. Our lives must provoke the questions, "who are you, that you do these things...and that you do them in this way?" Jesuits must manifest – especially in the contemporary world of ceaseless noise and stimulation – a strong sense of the sacred inseparably joined to involvement in the world. Our deep love of God and our passion for his

---

[19] John 4:10–15.

[20] Cf. Vatican II, *Gaudium et Spes*, 22; also GC 34, D. 6.

[21] Cf. Peter-Hans Kolvenbach, *Sobre la vida religiosa* (Havana, Cuba: 1 June 2007) , p. 1.

[22] Kolvenbach, *Sobre la vida,* p. 3.

[23] GCs 33 and 34.

world should set us on fire – a fire that starts other fires! For ultimately, there is no reality that is only profane for those who know how to look.[24] We must communicate this way of looking and provide a pedagogy, inspired by the Spiritual Exercises, that carries people—especially the young—into it. Thus will they be able to see the world as Saint Ignatius did, as his life developed from what he understood at the Cardoner to the eventual founding of the Society with its mission to bring the message of Christ to the ends of the earth. This mission, with its roots in his experience, continues today.

A Life Shaped by the Vision of La Storta

28/ 11. Saint Ignatius had the most significant experience for the founding of the Society in the little chapel of La Storta on his way to Rome. In this mystical grace he saw clearly "that the Father placed him with Christ, his Son," as the same Ignatius had asked insistently of Mary. At La Storta, the Father placed him with his Son carrying his Cross, and Jesus accepted him saying: "I wish you to serve us." Ignatius felt himself confirmed personally, and felt the group confirmed, in the plan moving their hearts to place themselves at the service of the Vicar of Christ on earth. "Ignatius told me that God the Father imprinted these words on his heart: 'Ego ero vobis Romae propitius.'"[25] But this affirmation did not make Ignatius dream of easy paths, since he told his companions that they would encounter "many contradictions"[26] in Rome, and perhaps even be crucified. It is from Ignatius's encounter with the Lord at La Storta that the future life of service and mission of the companions emerges in its characteristic contours: following Christ bearing his Cross; fidelity to the Church and to the Vicar of Christ on earth; and living as friends of—and thus in—the Lord in one single apostolic body.

Following Christ . . .

29/ 12. To follow Christ bearing his Cross means opening ourselves with him to every thirst that afflicts humanity today. Christ is nourishment itself, the answer to every hunger and thirst. He is the bread of life, who, in feeding the hungry, draws them together and unites them.[27] He is the water of life,[28] the living water of which he spoke to the Samaritan woman in a dialogue that surprised his disciples because it took him, like free-flowing water, beyond the river-banks of what was culturally and religiously familiar and into an exchange with someone

---

[24] Cf. Pierre Teilhard de Chardin, *Le Milieu Divin* (London: Collins, 1960; original 1957), p. 66.

[25] Diego Laynez, *Adhortationes in librum Examinis* (1559), §7 (MHSI 73:133).

[26] *Autobiography,* 97.

[27] Cf. Mark 6:31–44 par.

[28] Cf. John 4:7–15.

with whom custom forbade him to speak at all. Jesus, in his outreach, embraced difference and new horizons. His ministry transcended boundaries. He invited his disciples to be aware of God's action in places and people they were inclined to avoid: Zacchaeus,[29] a Syro-Phoenician woman,[30] Roman centurions,[31] a repentant thief.[32] As water bringing life[33] to all who thirst, he showed himself interested in every parched area of the world; and in every parched area of the world he can thus be welcomed, for all who are thirsty can understand what living water means. This image of living water can give life to all Jesuits as servants of Christ in his mission because, having tasted this water themselves, they will be eager to offer it to anyone who thirsts and to reach out to people beyond frontiers—where water may not yet have welled up—to bring a new culture of dialogue to a rich, diverse, and multifaceted world.

30/ 13. To follow Christ bearing his Cross means announcing his Gospel of hope to the many poor who inhabit our world today. The world's many "poverties" represent thirsts that, ultimately, only he who is living water can assuage. Working for his Reign will often mean meeting material needs, but it will always mean much more, because human beings thirst at many levels; and Christ's mission is directed to human beings. Faith *and* justice; it is never one without the other. Human beings need food, shelter, love, relationship, truth, meaning, promise, hope. Human beings need a future in which they can take hold of their full dignity; indeed they need an absolute future, a "great hope" that exceeds every particular hope.[34] All of these things are already present in the heart of Christ's mission, which, as was particularly evident in his healing ministry, was always more than physical. In healing the leper, Jesus restored him to the community, gave him a sense of belonging. Our mission finds its inspiration in this ministry of Jesus. Following Jesus, we feel ourselves called not only to bring direct help to people in distress, but also to restore entire human persons in their integrity, reintegrating them in community and reconciling them with God. This frequently calls for an engagement that is long-term, be it in the education of youth, in the spiritual accompaniment of the Exercises, in intellectual research, or in the service of refugees. But it is here, aided by grace and drawing on whatever professional capacities we may have, that we try to offer ourselves to God fully, for his service.

---

[29] Luke 19:1–10.

[30] Mark 7:24–30.

[31] Luke 7:2–10; Mark 15:39.

[32] Luke 23:39–43.

[33] Cf. John 7:38.

[34] Benedict XVI, *Spe Salvi* (30 November 2007), see paragraphs 4 and 35, for example.

31/ 14. The Son's way of acting provides the pattern for how we must act in the service of his mission.[35] Jesus preached the Reign of God; indeed it was given with his very presence.[36] And he showed himself as having come into the world not to do his own will but the will of his Father in heaven. Jesus' entire life was a kenosis, and he approached situations by self-forgetfulness, seeking not to be served, but to serve, and to give his life as a ransom for many.[37] Thus incarnation and paschal mystery unfold in his life pattern; his life pattern will be ours also when we join with him. As companions with him on mission, his way is our way.

32/ 15. In following this way, Jesuits today affirm all that has been specified regarding the Society's mission in the last three General Congregations. The service of faith and the promotion of justice, indissolubly united, remain at the heart of our mission. This option changed the face of the Society. We embrace it again and we remember with gratitude our martyrs and the poor who have nourished us evangelically in our own identity as followers of Jesus: "our service, especially among the poor, has deepened our life of faith, both individually and as a body."[38] As followers of Jesus today, we reach out also to persons who differ from us in culture and religion, aware that dialogue with them is integral also to our service of Christ's mission.[39] In every mission that we carry out, we seek only to be where he sends us. The grace we receive as Jesuits is to be and to go with him, looking on the world with his eyes, loving it with his heart, and entering into its depths with his unlimited compassion.

In the Church and for the World . . .

33/ 16. Knowing ourselves to be sent with Jesus as companions consecrated to him in poverty, chastity, and obedience although we are sinners, we listen attentively to the needs of people whom we seek to serve. We have been chosen to live as his companions in a single body governed by means of the account of conscience and held together by obedience: men of and for the Church under obedience to the Supreme Pontiff and our Father General and duly appointed superiors.[40] In all of this, our aim is to be ever available for the more universal good—indeed desiring always the *magis*, that which is truly better, for the greater glory of God.[41] It is this availability for the Church's universal mission that marks

---

[35] *Spiritual Exercises*, 91–98.

[36] Cf. Matt. 12:28, Luke:11:20; 17:21.

[37] Mark 10:45.

[38] GC 34, D. 2, 1.

[39] GC 34, D. 2.

[40] Cf. *Spiritual Exercises*, 352–370.

[41] Cf. *Spiritual Exercises*, 23; *Constitutions*, 622.

our Society in a particular way, makes sense of our special vow of obedience to the Pope, and makes us a single apostolic body dedicated to serving, in the Church, men and women everywhere.

34/ 17. It is in its obedience, above all, that the Society of Jesus should be distinct from other religious families. One need only recall the letter of Saint Ignatius, where he writes:

> We can tolerate other religious institutes outdoing us in fasting and in other austerities that they practise according to their Rule, but it is my desire, dear brothers, that those who serve the Lord our God in this Society be outstanding in the purity and perfection of their obedience, the renunciation of their will, and the abnegation of their judgment.[42]

It is to the obedience of the *Suscipe* that Saint Ignatius looked in order to highlight what it was that gave the Society its distinctive difference.

As an Apostolic Religious Community . . .

35/ 18. Together with obedience, our Jesuit vows of poverty and chastity enable us to be shaped in the Church into the image of Jesus himself;[43] they also make clear and visible our availability for God's call. This availability is expressed in a variety of ways, according to the particular vocation of each. Thus the Society of Jesus is enriched and blessed by the presence of brothers, spiritual coadjutors, and professed fathers who together, as companions in one family—enlivened in particular by the presence of those in formation—serve the mission of Christ according to the graces given to each.[44] Thus we Jesuits live our consecrated lives in response to different graces. We minister sacramentally at the heart of the Church, celebrating the Eucharist and the other sacraments and preaching the word of God faithfully. We take this word to the very ends of the earth, seeking to share its riches with people everywhere.

36/ 19. The differentiation of roles and ministries of Jesuits finds its necessary complement in a life of companionship lived in community. Our life together testifies to our friendship in the Lord, a sharing of faith and life together, above all in the celebration of the Eucharist. Following Jesus together acts as a pointer to the disciples *en mouvement* with their Lord. Jesuit identity and Jesuit mission are linked by community; indeed, identity, community, and mission are a kind of triptych shedding light on how our companionship is best understood. This companionship shows how people different in background and diverse in talent can live together as true "friends in the Lord." Jesuit identity is relational; it grows

---

[42] *Letter to the Jesuits of Portugal* (26 March 1553), § 2 (MHSI 29:671).

[43] 2 Cor. 3:18.

[44] *Constitutions*, 511.

in and through our diversities of culture, nationalities, and languages, enriching and challenging us. This is a process that we enter upon as we join the Society, and we grow in it every day. As we do so, our community life can become attractive to people, inviting them—above all the young—to "come and see,"[45] to join us in our vocation and to serve with us in Christ's mission. Nothing could be more desirable and more urgent today, since the heart of Christ burns with love for this world, with all its troubles, and seeks companions who can serve it with him.

A New Context—To New Frontiers

37/ 20. Serving Christ's mission today means paying special attention to its *global* context. This context requires us to act as a universal body with a universal mission, realizing at the same time the radical diversity of our situations. It is as a worldwide community—and, simultaneously, as a network of local communities—that we seek to serve others across the world. Our mission of faith and justice, dialogue of religions and cultures, has acquired dimensions that no longer allow us to conceive of the world as composed of separate entities; we must see it as a unified whole in which we depend upon one another. Globalization, technology, and environmental concerns have challenged our traditional boundaries and have enhanced our awareness that we bear a common responsibility for the welfare of the entire world and its development in a sustainable and life-giving way.[46]

38/ 21. Today's consumerist cultures do not foster passion and zeal but rather addiction and compulsion. They demand resistance. A compassionate response to these cultural malaises will be necessary and unavoidable if we are to share in the lives of our contemporaries. In such changing circumstances, our responsibility as Jesuits to collaborate at multiple levels has become an imperative. Thus our provinces must work ever more together. So also must we work with others: religious men and women of other communities, lay persons, members of ecclesial movements, people who share our values but not our beliefs; in short, all persons of good will.

39/ 22. God has created a world with diverse inhabitants, and this is good. Creation expresses the rich beauty of this lovable world: people working, laughing, and thriving together[47] are signs that God is alive among us. However, diversity becomes problematic when the differences between people are lived in such a way that some prosper at the expense of others who are excluded in such

---

[45] John 1:39.

[46] Cf. *Globalization and Marginalization*, (Rome: Social Justice Secretariat, February 2006), pp. 16–17.

[47] Cf. *Spiritual Exercises*, 106.

a way that people fight, killing each other, and are intent on destruction.[48] Then God in Christ suffers in and with the world, which he wants to renew. Precisely here is our mission situated. It is here that we must discern our mission according to the criteria of the *magis*[49] and the more universal good.[50] God is present in the darkness of life intent on making all things new. God needs collaborators in this endeavor: people whose grace consists in being received under the banner of his Son.[51] "Nations" beyond geographical definitions await us, "nations" that today include those who are poor and displaced, those who are profoundly lonely, those who ignore God's existence, and those who use God as an instrument for political purposes. There are new "nations," and we have been sent to them.[52]

40/ 23. Recalling Father Jerónimo Nadal, we can say with him: the world is our house.[53] As Father Kolvenbach said recently, "A stable monastery does not serve us, because we have received the entire world to tell about the good news., ... we do not close ourselves up in the cloister, but we remain in the world amid the multitude of men and women that the Lord loves, since they are in the world."[54] All men and women are our concern for *dialogue* and for *proclamation* because our mission is that of the Church: to discover Jesus Christ where we have not noticed him before and to reveal him where he has not been seen before. In other words, we look to "find God in all things," following what Saint Ignatius proposes to us in the "Contemplation for Achieving Love."[55] The entire world becomes the object of our interest and concern.

41/ 24. Thus as this world changes, so does the *context* of our mission; and new frontiers beckon that we must be willing to embrace. So we plunge ourselves more deeply into that dialogue with religions that may show us that the Holy Spirit is at work all over the world that God loves. We turn also to the "frontier" of the earth, increasingly degraded and plundered. Here, with passion for environmental justice, we shall meet once again the Spirit of God seeking to liberate a suffering creation, which demands of us space to live and breathe.

---

[48] Cf. *Spiritual Exercises,* 108.

[49] *Spiritual Exercises,* 97.

[50] *Constitutions,* 622.

[51] *Spiritual Exercises,* 147.

[52] Adolfo Nicolás, *Homily on the Day After his Election as Superior General of the Society of Jesus* (20 January 2008).

[53] Jerónimo Nadal, *13ᵃ Exhortatio Complutensis* (Alcalá, 1561), § 256 (MHSI 90, 469–470).

[54] Peter-Hans Kolvenbach, Homily *Regimini Militantis Ecclesiae*, celebrating the anniversary of the approval of the Society of Jesus (27 September 2007).

[55] Cf. *Spiritual Exercises,* 230–237.

"Ite, Inflammate Omnia"

42/ 25. Legend has it that Saint Ignatius, when he sent Saint Francis Xavier to the East, told him: "go, set the world alight." With the birth of the Society of Jesus, a new fire was lit in a changing world. A novel form of religious life came about, not through human enterprise but as a divine initiative. The fire that was set alight then continues to burn in our Jesuit life today, as was said about Saint Alberto Hurtado, "a fire that kindles other fires." With it, we are called to set all things alight with the love of God.[56]

43/ 26. There are new challenges to this vocation today. We live our identity as companions of Jesus in a context where multiple images, the innumerable faces of a fragmented culture, compete for our attention. They seep into us, take root in the fertile soil of our natural desires, and fill us with sensations that flow through and take control of our feelings and decisions without our awareness. But we know and proclaim one image, Jesus Christ, true image of God and true image of humanity, who, when we contemplate him, becomes flesh in us, healing our inner brokenness, and making us whole as persons, as communities, and as an apostolic body dedicated to Christ's mission.

44/ 27. To live this mission in our broken world, we need fraternal and joyful communities in which we nourish and express with great intensity the sole passion that can unify our differences and bring to life our creativity. This passion grows out of our ever-new experience of the Lord, whose imagination and love for our world are inexhaustible. This love invites us to "participation in the mission of the One sent by the Father, in the Spirit, in an ever greater service, in love, with all the variants of the cross, in an imitation and following of that Jesus who wants to lead all people and all of creation to the glory of the Father."[57]

---

[56] Luke 12:49.

[57] Pedro Arrupe, "*Trinitarian Inspiration of the Ignatian Charism,*" §79, *AR* 18 (1980–1983):150.

DECREE 3

Challenges to Our Mission Today

Sent to the Frontiers

I. Reaffirming Our Mission

45/ 1. As servants of Christ's mission, we recall with gratitude the graces received from the Lord during the past years. In our lives together as Jesuits, we have experienced an ongoing process of renewal and adaptation of our mission and way of proceeding as called for by the Second Vatican Council[1].

46/ 2. Since the Council, the Spirit has led the whole Society gathered in General Congregations to the firm conviction that "[t]he aim of our mission received from Christ, as presented in the *Formula of the Institute,* is the service of faith. The integrating principle of our mission is the inseparable link between faith and the promotion of the justice of the Kingdom."[2]

47/ 3. Reflecting on our experience during GC 34, we discerned that the service of faith in Jesus Christ and the promotion of the justice of the Kingdom preached by him can best be achieved in the contemporary world if inculturation and dialogue become essential elements of our way of proceeding in mission.[3] We experience this mission as being part of the Church's overall mission of evangelization, "a single but complex reality" containing all these essential elements.[4] We want to reaffirm this mission which gives meaning to our religious apostolic life in the Church.

> Thus the aim of our mission (the service of faith) and its integrating principle (faith directed toward the justice of the Kingdom) are dynamically related to the inculturated proclamation of the Gospel and dialogue with other religious traditions as integral dimensions of evangelization.[5]

48/ 4. During the past years, the fruitful engagement of the Society in the dialogue with people belonging to different cultures and religious traditions has enriched our service of faith and promotion of justice and confirmed that faith

---

[1] Vatican II, *Perfectae Caritatis*, 2.

[2] GC 34, D. 2, n. 14.

[3] GC 34, D. 2, nn. 14–21.

[4] Cf. John Paul II, *Redemptoris Missio*, 41: "Mission is a single but complex reality, and it develops in a variety of ways." Cf. nn. 52–54; 55–57.

[5] GC 34, D. 2, n. 15.

and justice cannot be simply one ministry among others; they are integral to all ministries and to our lives together as individuals, communities, and a worldwide brotherhood.[6]

49/ 5. Our pastoral, educational, social, communication, and spiritual ministries have increasingly found creative ways of implementing this mission in the challenging circumstances of the modern world. Different ministries carry out the mission in ways that are appropriate to them. However, all have experienced mission as the grace of being "placed with the Son." We remember with gratitude so many of our brothers and collaborators who have offered their lives generously in response to the call of the Lord to labor with him.

50/ 6. In our desire to continue "serving the Lord alone and his spouse, the Church, under the Roman Pontiff,"[7] we find confirmation in the words the Holy Father addressed to the members of this congregation:

> Today I want to encourage you and your brothers to go on in the fulfillment of your mission, in full fidelity to your original charism, in the ecclesial and social context that characterizes the beginning of this millennium. As my predecessors have often told you, the Church needs you, counts on you, and continues to turn to you with confidence.[8]

51/ 7. In response to the challenging new contexts we face, we want to reflect further on our mission in the light of our experience.

II. A New Context for Mission

52/ 8. The new context in which we live our mission today is marked by profound changes, acute conflicts, and new possibilities. In the words of the Holy Father:

> "Your Congregation takes place in a period of great social, economic, and political changes; sharp ethical, cultural and environmental problems, conflicts of all kinds, but also of more intense communication among peoples, of new possibilities of acquaintance and dialogue, of a deep longing for peace. All these are situations that challenge the Catholic Church and its ability to announce to our contemporaries the Word of hope and salvation."[9]

53/ 9. We live in a global world. GC 34 already noted the "growing consciousness of the interdependence of all people in one common heritage."[10] This

---

[6] GC 32, D. 2, n. 9.

[7] *Exposcit Debitum (1550),* § 3 (MHSI 63, 375).

[8] Benedict XVI, *Allocution to the 35th General Congregation of the Society of Jesus* (21 February 2008), §2 (Allocution).

[9] *Allocution,* §2.

[10] GC 34, D. 3, n. 7.

process has continued at a rapid pace; as a result, our interconnectedness has increased. Its impact has been felt deeply in all areas of our life, and it is sustained by interrelated cultural, social and political structures that affect the core of our mission of faith, justice, and all aspects of our dialogue with religion and culture.

54/ 10. Globalization has also given birth to a world culture affecting all cultures; often this has resulted in a process of homogenization and in policies of assimilation that deny the right of individuals and groups to live and develop their own cultures. In the midst of this upheaval, postmodernism, mentioned also by GC 34,[11] has continued to shape the way the contemporary world and we Jesuits think and behave.

55/ 11. In this new world of instant communication and digital technology, of worldwide markets, and of a universal aspiration for peace and well-being, we are faced with growing tensions and paradoxes: we live in a culture that shows partiality to autonomy and the present, and yet we have a world so much in need of building a future in solidarity; we have better ways of communication but often experience isolation and exclusion; some have greatly benefited, while others have been marginalized and excluded; our world is increasingly transnational, and yet it needs to affirm and protect local and particular identities; our scientific knowledge has reached the deepest mysteries of life, and yet the very dignity of life itself and the world we live in are threatened.

III. Call to Establish Right Relationships: A Mission of Reconciliation

56/ 12. In this global world marked by such profound changes, we now want to deepen our understanding of the call to serve faith, promote justice, and dialogue with culture and other religions in the light of the apostolic mandate to establish right relationships with God, with one another, and with creation.[12]

57/ 13. In Luke's Gospel Jesus inaugurated his public ministry in the synagogue of Nazareth.[13] Reading from the prophet Isaiah and acknowledging being anointed by the Spirit, he announced good news to the poor, the release of captives, the recovery of sight by the blind, and freedom for the oppressed. With this action he rooted himself and his ministry in the tradition of the Jewish prophets who passionately proclaimed God's justice, the duty of the people of Israel to establish right relationships with God, with one another (especially with the least among them), and with the land.[14]

---

[11] GC 34, D. 4, n. 19-24.

[12] *Compendium of the Social Doctrine of the Church*, §575.

[13] Luke 4:16 ff.

[14] John Paul II, *Tertio Millennio Adveniente*, §§11–13.

58/ 14. In proclaiming God's message of love and compassion Jesus crossed over physical and socio-religious frontiers. His message of reconciliation was preached both to the people of Israel and to those living outside its physical and spiritual frontiers: tax collectors, prostitutes, sinners, and persons of all kinds who were marginalized and excluded. His ministry of reconciliation with God and with one another knew no boundaries. He spoke to the powerful, challenging them to a change of heart. He showed special love for the sinner, the poor widow, and the lost sheep. The kingdom of God, which he constantly preached, became a vision for a world where all relationships are reconciled in God. Jesus confronted the powers that oppose this kingdom, and that opposition led him to death on the cross, a death which he freely accepted in keeping with his mission. On the cross we see all his words and actions revealed as expressions of the final reconciliation effected by the Crucified and Risen Lord, through whom comes the new creation in which all relationships will be set right in God.[15]

59/ 15. Ignatius and his first companions understood the importance of reaching out to people on the frontiers and at the center of society, of reconciling those who were estranged in any way.[16] From the center in Rome, Ignatius sent Jesuits to the frontiers, to the new world, "to announce the Lord to peoples and cultures that did not know him as yet."[17] He sent Xavier to the Indies. Thousands of Jesuits followed, preaching the Gospel to many cultures, sharing knowledge with and learning from others. He also wanted Jesuits to cross other types of frontiers between rich and poor, between educated and unlearned. He wrote a letter to the Jesuits at the Council of Trent on how to behave and insisted that they should minister to the sick. Jesuits opened colleges in Rome and in the great cities of Europe, and they taught children in villages across the world.

60/ 16. We are sent on mission by the Father, as were Ignatius and the first companions at La Storta, together with Christ, risen and glorified but still carrying the cross, as he labors in a world yet to experience the fullness of his reconciliation. In a world torn by violence, strife, and division, we then are called with others to become instruments of God, who "in Christ reconciled the world to himself, not counting their trespasses."[18] This reconciliation calls us to build a new world of right relationships, a new Jubilee reaching across all divisions so that God might restore his justice for all.

61/ 17. This tradition of Jesuits building bridges across barriers becomes crucial in the context of today's world. We become able to bridge the divisions of a fragmented world only if we are united by the love of Christ our Lord, by person-

---

[15] 2 Cor. 5:19; Eph. 2:16.

[16] *Exposcit Debitum* (1550), §3 (MHSI 63, 376).

[17] *Allocution*, §3.

[18] 2 Cor. 5:19.

al bonds like those that linked Francis Xavier and Ignatius across the seas, and by the obedience that sends each one of us in mission to any part of this world.[19]

IV. Our Apostolic Response

62/ 18. As servants of Christ's mission we are invited to assist him as he sets right our relationships with God, with other human beings, and with creation. "Our world is the theater of a battle between good and evil," the Holy Father reminded us:[20] and so we again place ourselves before the Lord in the meditation on the Two Standards. There are powerful negative forces in the world, but we are also aware of God's presence permeating this world, inspiring persons of all cultures and religions to promote reconciliation and peace. The world where we work is one of sin and of grace.

Reconciliation with God

63/ 19. The *Spiritual Exercises* invite us to a renewed and deepened experience of reconciliation with God in Christ. We are called to share, with joy and respect, the grace of this experience that we have received and that nourishes our hope. Globalization and new communication technologies have opened up our world and offer us new opportunities to announce with enthusiasm the Good News of Jesus Christ and the Kingdom he proclaimed. Our ministries of the proclamation of the Word and the celebration of the life of Christ in the sacraments continue to be fundamental for our mission and our lives together as Jesuits. They must be seen as part of the threefold responsibility that lies at the heart of the deepest nature of the Church: proclamation of the word of God (*kerygmamartyria*), celebrating the sacraments (*leitourgia*), and exercising the ministry of charity (*diakonia*).[21] In fulfilling this responsibility, we search for new forms of integral evangelization to "reach the geographical and spiritual places others do not reach or find it difficult to reach,"[22] always attentive to the demands of the cultural context within which we carry out our mission.

64/ 20. Globalization has hastened the spread of a dominant culture which has brought to many people wide access to information and knowledge, an enhanced sense of the individual and freedom to choose, and openness to new ideas and values across the world. At the same time, this dominant culture has been marked by subjectivism, moral relativism, hedonism, and practical materialism leading to a "erroneous or superficial vision of God and of man."[23] In many soci-

---

[19] *Constitutions*, 655-659.

[20] *Allocution*, §6.

[21] Benedict XVI, *Deus Caritas Est (2005)*, 25.

[22] *Allocution*, §2.

[23] *Allocution*, §3.

eties people find themselves increasingly alone and struggling to find meaning for their lives. This has become a new apostolic challenge and opportunity for us. In all our ministries, we are called to a more serious engagement with this reality and to broaden the spaces of a continuing dialogue and reflection on the relationship between faith and reason, culture and morality, and faith and society, in order "to make the true face of the Lord known to so many for whom it remains hidden or unrecognizable."[24]

65/ 21. The rapid pace of cultural change has been accompanied by an interior emptiness as well as a new interest in popular religiosity, a renewed search for meaning, and a thirst for a spiritual experience often sought outside institutional religion. The *Spiritual Exercises,* which from the start have been a precious instrument in our hands, are today of invaluable assistance to many of our contemporaries. They help us to initiate and to progress in a life of prayer, to search for and to find God in all things, and to discern his will, making faith more personal and more incarnate. Our contemporaries are also helped in the difficult task of feeling a deeper sense of integration in their lives; the experience of the Exercises helps them achieve this by entering into a dialogue with God in freedom. We encourage Jesuits to give the Spiritual Exercises, "to allow the Creator to deal immediately with the creature and the creature with its Creator and Lord,"[25] to lead people to a deeper relationship with God in Christ and through that relationship to service of his Kingdom.

66/ 22. We live in a world of many religions and cultures. The erosion of traditional religious beliefs and the tendency to homogenize cultures has strengthened a variety of forms of religious fundamentalism. Faith in God is increasingly being used by some to divide people and communities, to create polarities and tensions which tear at the very fabric of our common social life. All these changes call us to the frontiers of culture and of religion. We need to strengthen and support those Jesuits and collaborators actively involved in the fourfold dialogue recommended by the Church,[26] to listen carefully to all, and to build bridges linking individuals and communities of good will.

67/ 23. We need to discern carefully how we carry out educational and pastoral ministries, especially among youth, in this fast-changing, postmodern culture. We need to walk with young people, learning from their generosity and compassion so as to help each other to grow through fragility and fragmentation to joyful integration of our lives with God and with others. Volunteer work with and for

---

[24] *Allocution*, §4.

[25] *Spiritual Exercises*, 15.

[26] Cf. GC 34, D. 5, n. 4: dialogues of life, action, religious experience, and theological exchange.

the poor helps young people to live in solidarity with others and find meaning in and direction for their lives.

68/ 24. Since Christ's death and resurrection has reestablished our relationship with God, our service of faith must lead necessarily to the promotion of the justice of the Kingdom and to the care of God's creation.

Reconciliation with One Another

69/ 25. In this global world, there are social, economic, and political forces that have facilitated the creation of new relationships among people, but there are other forces which have broken the bonds of love and solidarity within the human family. While many poor people have been lifted from poverty, the gap between rich and poor within nations and across national boundaries has increased. From the perspective of those living at the margins, globalization appears to be a massive force that excludes and exploits the weak and the poor, which intensifies exclusion on the basis of religion, race, caste, and gender.

70/ 26. A political consequence of globalization has been the weakening of political sovereignty experienced by many nation-states all over the world. Some states feel this phenomenon as a particular type of global marginalization and the loss of national respect. Transnational interests, unconstrained by national laws and often abetted by corruption, frequently exploit the natural resources of the poor. Powerful economic groups foment violence, war, and arms trafficking.

71/ 27. Our commitment to help establish right relationships invites us to see the world from the perspective of the poor and the marginalized, learning from them, acting with and for them. In this context, the Holy Father reminds us that the preferential option for the poor" is implicit in the Christological faith in a God who for us became poor, to enrich us with his poverty (2 Cor. 8:9)."[27] He invites us with a prophetic call to renew our mission "among the poor and for the poor."[28]

72/ 28. The complexity of the problems we face and the richness of the opportunities offered demand that we build bridges between rich and poor, establishing advocacy links of mutual support between those who hold political power and those who find it difficult to voice their interests. Our intellectual apostolate provides an inestimable help in constructing these bridges, offering us new ways of understanding in depth the mechanisms and links among our present problems. Many Jesuits in educational, social promotion, and research institutions, together with others engaged directly with the poor, are already committed to this work. Still others have helped in the growth of corporate social responsibil-

---

[27] *Allocution*, §8.

[28] *Allocution*, §8.

ity, the creation of a more humane business culture, and economic development initiatives with the poor.

73/   29.   Among the defining characteristics of our globalized world are new communications technologies. They have a tremendous impact on all of us, especially the young. They can be powerful instruments for building and supporting international networks, in our advocacy, in our work of education, and in our sharing of our spirituality and our faith. This Congregation urges Jesuit institutions to put these new technologies at the service of those at the margins.

74/   30.   Our response to these situations must come from our deep faith in the Lord who calls us to work with others for the Kingdom of God, for the establishment of right relationships among people and with creation. In this way we cooperate with the Lord in building a new future in Christ for a "globalization in solidarity, a globalization without marginalization."[29]

Reconciliation with Creation

75/   31.   Following the directive of GC 34,[30] Fr. Peter-Hans Kolvenbach commissioned a study and invited all "Jesuits and those who share our mission to show ever more effective ecological solidarity in our spiritual, communal, and apostolic lives."[31] This invitation calls us to move beyond doubts and indifference to take responsibility for our home, the earth.

76/   32.   Care of the environment affects the quality of our relationships with God, with other human beings, and with creation itself. It touches the core of our faith in and love for God, "from whom we come and towards whom we are journeying."[32] It might be said that St. Ignatius teaches us this care of the environment in the Principle and Foundation[33] when speaking of the goodness of creation, as well as in the *Contemplatio ad Amorem* when describing the active presence of God within creation.[34]

77/   33.   The drive to access and exploit sources of energy and other natural resources is very rapidly widening the damage to earth, air, water, and our whole environment, to the point that the future of our planet is threatened. Poisoned water, polluted air, massive deforestation, deposits of atomic and toxic waste are

---

[29] John Paul II, *From the Justice of Each Comes the Peace of All: World Day of Peace Message* (1 January 1998), 3.

[30] GC 34, D. 20, n. 2.

[31] Peter-Hans Kolvenbach S.I., *We Live in a Broken World. Introduction, Promotio Iustitiae* 70, April 1999.

[32] Benedict XVI, *Message of Peace* (1 January 2008), §7.

[33] *Spiritual Exercises*, 23.

[34] *Spiritual Exercises*, 230–237.

causing death and untold suffering, particularly to the poor. Many poor communities have been displaced, and indigenous peoples have been the most affected.

78/ 34. In heeding the call to restore right relationships with creation, we have moved anew by the cry of those suffering the consequences of environmental destruction, by the many postulates received, and by the recent teaching of the Holy Father and many episcopal conferences on this issue.

79/ 35. This Congregation urges all Jesuits and all partners engaged in the same mission, particularly the universities and research centers, to promote studies and practices focusing on the causes of poverty and the question of the environment's improvement. We should find ways in which our experiences with refugees and the displaced on one hand, and people who work for the protection of the environment on the other hand, could interact with those institutions, so that research results and advocacy have effective practical benefits for society and the environment. Advocacy and research should serve the poor and those who work for the protection of the environment. This ought to shed new light on the appeal of the Holy Father that costs should be justly shared "taking due account of the different levels of development."[35]

80/ 36. In our preaching, teaching, and retreat direction, we should invite all people to appreciate more deeply our covenant[36] with creation as central to right relationships with God and one another, and to act accordingly in terms of political responsibility, employment, family life, and personal lifestyle.

V. Global Preferences

81/ 37. In continuity with the recommendations made by GC 34,[37] and to respond effectively to the global challenges described above, this Congregation has emphasized the importance of structures for apostolic planning, implementation, and accountability at all levels of the Society's government.[38]

82/ 38. During the last years the Society has made a concerted and generous effort to increase interprovincial cooperation in a variety of ways. In this context, GC 34 stated that "Fr. General . . . in his regular contacts with Provincials and with the Moderators of the Conferences will discern the greater needs of the universal Church and will establish global and regional priorities."[39]

---

[35] Benedict XVI, *Message for the Day of Peace* (1 January 2008), §7.

[36] Benedict XVI, *Message for the Day of Peace* (1 January 2008), 7.

[37] GC 34, D. 21.

[38] GC 35, D. 5, nn. 12, 18 –21.

[39] GC 34, D. 21, n. 28.

83/ 39. While respecting provincial or regional priorities, these "preferences" indicate apostolic areas requiring "special or privileged attention."[40] In our present context, we may confidently say that they offer areas for the realization of the mission orientations provided by this decree. In consultation with the Conferences of Major Superiors, Fr. Peter-Hans Kolvenbach decided on the following apostolic preferences:

1. *Africa.* Aware of the cultural, social, and economic differences in Africa and Madagascar, but also conscious of the great opportunities, challenges, and variety of Jesuit ministries, we acknowledge the Society's responsibility to present a more integral and human vision of this continent. In addition, all Jesuits are invited to greater solidarity with and effective support of the Society's mission of inculturating faith and promoting more justice in this continent.

2. *China* has become of central importance not only for East Asia but for the whole of humanity. We want to continue our respectful dialogue with its people, aware that China is an important key for a peaceful world and has great potential for enriching our faith tradition, as many of its people long for a spiritual encounter with God in Christ.

3. The *intellectual apostolate* has been a defining characteristic of the Society of Jesus from its beginning. Given the complex yet interrelated challenges that Jesuits face in every apostolic sector, GC 35 calls for a strengthening and renewal of this apostolate as a privileged means for the Society to respond adequately to the important intellectual contribution to which the Church calls us. Advanced studies for Jesuits must be encouraged and supported throughout formation.

4. The *Inter-provincial Institutions in Rome* are a special mission of the Society received directly from the Holy Father.[41] Ignatius wrote that we should "treat the missions from His Holiness as being most important."[42] This Congregation reaffirms the commitment of the Society to the Houses and Common Works of Rome as an apostolic preference of the universal Society. To serve that mission most fruitfully, there should be ongoing strategic planning and evaluation by the institutions and by the Society.[43]

---

[40] Peter-Hans Kolvenbach S.I., *"Souhaits de Noël et de Nouvel An: Nos préférences apostoliques"* (1 January 2003), *AR* 23, no. (2003): 31–36: "[The choice of apostolic priorities] has been accomplished in prayerful discernment, identifying some of the most important and urgent needs, those that are more universal, or those to which the Society is being called to respond more generously."

[41] Benedict XVI, *Address to the Pontifical Gregorian University* (3 November 2006), *AR* 23, no. 4 (2006): 696–697.

[42] *Constitutions,* 603.

[43] Cf. GC 34, D. 22.

5. *Migration and Refugees.* Ever since Fr. Arrupe called the attention of the Society to the plight of refugees, the phenomenon of forced migration for different reasons has increased dramatically. These massive movements of people create great suffering among millions. Therefore, this Congregation reaffirms that attending to the needs of migrants, including refugees, internally displaced, and trafficked people, continue to be an apostolic preference of the Society. Moreover, we reaffirm that the Jesuit Refugee Service adhere to its present Charter and Guidelines.

84/ 40. We invite Fr. General to continue to discern the preferences for the Society, to review the above preferences, to update their specific content, and to develop plans and programs that can be monitored and evaluated.

VI. Conclusion

85/ 41. Our mission is not limited to our works. Our personal and community relationship with the Lord, our relationship to one another as friends in the Lord, our solidarity with the poor and marginalized, and a lifestyle responsible to creation are all important aspects of our lives as Jesuits. They authenticate what we proclaim and what we do in fulfilling our mission. The privileged place of this collective witness is our life in community, Thus, Jesuit community is not just for mission: it is itself mission.[44]

86/ 42. An apostolic body that lives in creative obedience and in which the members know how to appreciate their collaborators in mission gives a powerful witness to the world. Our ministries and institutions are the first place where faith in our Lord Jesus Christ, which we profess, should be incarnated through the justice of our relationships with God, others, and creation.

87/ 43. In this global context it is important to highlight the extraordinary potential we possess as an international and multicultural body. Acting consistently with this character can not only enhance the apostolic effectiveness of our work, but in a fragmented and divided world it can witness to the reconciliation in solidarity of all the children of God.

---

[44] Cf. Peter-Hans Kolvenbach S.I., "*Sur la vie communautaire*" (12 March 1998), *AR* 22 (1996–2002): 276–289.

DECREE 4

Obedience in the Life of the Society of Jesus

I. Introduction

88/ 1.   Obedience is central to the mission and union of the Society of Jesus, and a special bond of obedience links the Society to the Holy Father, "the successor of St. Peter and vicar of Christ on earth," as St. Ignatius was accustomed to call him. Therefore, the Society must constantly deepen and renew its life of obedience. The last four General Congregations of the Society have not been silent on this theme, and the Thirty-fifth General Congregation confirms their directives and norms.[1] In addition, we feel the need to add a word of encouragement and guidance adapted to our present circumstances and to respond to the request of Pope Benedict XVI that we reflect on the fourth vow.[2] To do so, we will begin, as the Second Vatican Council instructs us,[3] with a reflection on the Sacred Scriptures and the charism of our founder.

II. The Experience of St. Ignatius and the First Companions

89/ 2.   We find the origins of the mysticism of service of St. Ignatius and his First Companions in their experience of the Spiritual Exercises. In the meditations of the First Week,[4] they came into contact with the merciful love of God extended to them in Christ. Through the contemplations of the Second Week and especially the invitation of the Eternal King,[5] they felt called "to make offerings of greater moment . . . offering their whole selves for this labor."[6] In the Meditation on the Two Standards,[7] they asked to be placed under Christ's standard in order to "put into practice their union with Christ and his power as a grace of the Spirit of the Lord."[8] Each of them wanted to feel "that he thinks with Christ's thoughts,

---

[1] See *Complementary Norms* [*NC*] 149–156, 252–262; GC 31, D. 17; GC 32, D. 11; GC 34, D. 11.

[2] Cf. Peter-Hans Kolvenbach, *The Holy Father's response* (21 February 2007), Letter to all Major Superiors and Electors of GC 35, p. 803 below.

[3] Vatican II, *Perfectae Caritatis,* 2.

[4] *Spiritual Exercises,* 45–47.

[5] *Spiritual Exercises,* 91–100.

[6] *Spiritual Exercises,* 97, 96.

[7] *Spiritual Exercises,* 136.

[8] Jeronimo Nadal, *Orationis Observationes,* §308, Michael Nicolau (ed.) (Rome, IHSI, 1964), p. 122.

wills with Christ's will, and remembers with Christ's memory; that he is and lives and acts no longer as himself but completely in Christ."[9]

90/ 3. The First Companions' desire to accompany Christ and to wear themselves out in his service so that all men and women might be saved and freed from their suffering and slavery took on concrete form in the vow they took at Montmartre in 1534. If their plan to travel to the Holy Land did not come to fruition, they promised to place themselves at the disposal of the pope so that he might use their help as he thought would be for God's glory and the salvation of souls.[10] This offering of the First Companions was confirmed in the vision at La Storta, where through St. Ignatius the Eternal Father gave them to his Son as his companions and promised to be propitious to them in Rome.[11] In this way, God responded to their unceasing prayer, through the intercession of the Virgin Mary, to be placed with the Son.

91/ 4. When the pope decided to send the First Companions on various missions that would involve their separation from each other, they asked whether they should unite themselves as a body. According to the *Deliberation of the First Fathers*, they unanimously decided, after prayerful discernment, to become a body in which each would care for the others, strengthening their bond of union through mutual knowledge and sharing in each others' lives.[12]

92/ 5. Before their priestly ordination in 1537, the First Companions had taken vows of poverty and chastity. In 1539 they asked whether or not to take a vow of obedience to one of the group at the same time that they dedicated their entire will, understanding, and strength to carrying out the missions they received from the pope. Their answer to this question was also affirmative. After prayerful discernment, they concluded that vowing obedience to one of them would allow them "to follow the will of God in all things with greater certainty and with greater praise and merit."[13]

93/ 6. The papal bull *Regimini Militantis Ecclesiae* is the Church's confirmation of this foundational experience. That is why the only way the Society can be true to the historical and mystical experience of the First Companions is "to serve

---

[9] Jeronimo Nadal, *Orationis Observationes,* §308, Michael Nicolau (edit.) (Rome, IHSI, 1964), p. 122.

[10] *Autobiography of St. Ignatius,* 85.

[11] *Autobiography of St. Ignatius,* 96; Jerónimo Nadal, *Exhortationes in Hispania* (1554), §16 (MHSI 66, 313); Diego Laynez, *Adhortationes in librum Examinis* (1559), §7 (MHSI 73, 133).

[12] *Deliberatio primorum Patrum* (1539), §3 (MHSI 63, 3–4).

[13] *Deliberatio primorum Patrum (1539),* §4 (MHSI 63, 4).

the Lord alone and the Church, his spouse, under the Roman Pontiff, the Vicar of Christ on earth."[14]

94/ 7. The goal of the spiritual formation outlined in the Constitutions is to prepare Jesuits in formation for apostolic life in the Society and to deepen the apostolic life of the body of the Society on mission. The Third Part of the Constitutions introduces the novice to spiritual and apostolic discernment. It confronts him with the demands of a life lived in companionship at the service of the apostolate and offers him an opportunity to grow in faith and trust in the Lord, to understand the obstacles to human and spiritual growth, and to avail himself of the spiritual means to overcome them.[15]

95/ 8. The Sixth and Seventh Parts of the *Constitutions* address formed Jesuits and propose the fundamental virtues of apostolic life in the Society: *discreta caritas* and the *magis*.[16] The Sixth Part insists that passionate love for Christ must become incarnate in obedience to the pope and superiors in the Society whose commands the formed Jesuit should obey as if they come from Christ because it is for love of Christ that he obeys.[17] The whole Seventh Part is a demonstration of the foundational principle of obedience, the *magis*. Here the emphasis is on discernment, freedom, and creativity in seeking the will of God and engaging in apostolic activity.[18] Thus, fidelity to obedience becomes the way the Jesuit incarnates the values of the Gospel and of the Spiritual Exercises: availability for being at the service of the Kingdom of God and freedom to be a "man for others."

III. Theological Aspects of Obedience

96/ 9. Before all else, our obedience seeks to fulfill the will of God. Its foundation is personal love for Jesus Christ who has deigned to choose us as his companions. The Holy Spirit, who has freely poured this love into our hearts, inspires in us a desire to identify ourselves with Christ and gives us the strength to "let the same mind be in you that was in Christ Jesus."[19] This desire "to clothe ourselves

---

[14] Formula of the Institute, *Exposcit Debitum* (1550), §3 (MHSI 63, 375).

[15] *Constitutions,* 260; *NC* 45 §1; GC 32, D. 6, n. 7.

[16] *Constitutions,* 582.

[17] *Constitutions,* 547, 551.

[18] Ignatius's instruction to the Jesuit sent to be patriarch of Ethiopia breathes the atmosphere of the Seventh Part. "All this is proposed under the heading of advice. The patriarch should not consider himself obliged to comply with it. Rather, he should be guided by *discreta caritas*, taking into account the circumstances of the moment and the unction of the Holy Spirit which should be his principal guide in everything" (MHSI 36, 689–690).

[19] Phil. 2:5.

with the same garb and uniform of the Lord"[20] situates us in the mysticism of the Third Degree of Humility.[21]

97/ 10. Our religious vows place us with the Lord and move us to follow him in fidelity to the mission of announcing the Kingdom conferred on him by the Father. From the first moment of his existence, Jesus' life was oriented to the Father: "Here I am; I have come to do your will."[22] Jesus has "no other food but the will of the Father."[23] Knowing himself sent by the Father "that whoever sees the Son and believes in him shall have eternal life,"[24] Jesus does not act of himself but only does "what he sees the Father doing."[25]

98/ 11. Jesus' fidelity to his mission brought him into conflict with human sinfulness and injustice, and it led him to "death, death on a cross."[26] Conquering even his resistance and weakness, "Abba, let not my will but your will be done,"[27] Jesus became the source of salvation for all by fulfilling the Father's will. "Although he was Son he learned obedience through suffering and having been made perfect became the source of eternal salvation for all who obey him."[28]

99/ 12. To be joined with Christ as his companions in obedience to the will of the Father allows us to become servants of his mission of evangelization. Obedience frees us to give ourselves exclusively to the service of the Gospel. By freeing us from our own "affections, desires and interests,"[29] obedience lets us dedicate ourselves totally to what God loves and to those who are the object of God's special concern.

100/ 13. To be joined to Christ as his companions in obedience and in mission, in poverty and in chastity, makes us witnesses to the Kingdom and its values.[30] At the same time that we work for the growth of the Kingdom in this world, we await its fullness as a gift God alone can give. Renouncing the use of this world's goods as if they were our own, and putting our affections and our en-

---

[20] *Constitutions,* 101.

[21] *Spiritual Exercises,* 167.

[22] Heb.10:7.

[23] John 4:34.

[24] John 6:40.

[25] John 5:19.

[26] Phil. 2:8.

[27] Mark 14: 36.

[28] Heb. 5:9.

[29] *Spiritual Exercises,* 189.

[30] Vatican II, *Lumen Gentium,* 44.

tire freedom at the service of the Kingdom, we contribute to making the Kingdom we long for a reality here and now.

101/ 14. The incarnation of the Son of God in human history invites us to see God in all things and leads us to understand that he can make use of all things in carrying out his saving work. This is why our discernment must take into account our historical, social, and personal circumstances; it is in the midst of them that God calls us to fulfill his will.

102/ 15. When created realities have been distorted by sin and injustice, however, they can cease to express the goodness of God and can become impediments to our response to the Lord's call. This is why some degree of participation in Jesus' *kenosis*[31] will never be absent from our lives. Like Jesus, we spend ourselves day after day, trustfully handing ourselves over to the will of God who has shown us so many proofs of his love, even though at times he may seem far from us[32] or hidden from us by the effects of sin.[33]

103/ 16. By his resurrection, the Lord continues to be present in the Church through the Spirit, and through the Church he continues to make his voice heard. "Whoever hears you hears me and whoever rejects you rejects me."[34] The Church is the mediation of the Word of God and the sacrament of our salvation in spite of the imperfections of her children. It is through the Church that the Christian finds God, and we profess obedience in the Church in order to serve God. Within the Church, the Society is a privileged place where the will of God is manifested to us; it becomes our "pathway to God."[35]

104/ 17. We will only be able to live our vow of obedience as freedom and true self-realization if the mystical experience of passionate love for Christ, the one who is sent by the Father and who is obedient to the Father's will, remains alive in us, and if we daily renew our unconditional commitment to be his companions. It is precisely our love for Jesus Christ that will make our work in service to his mission fruitful, because "the means which unite the instrument with God and so dispose it that it may be wielded well by his divine hand are more effective than those that equip it in relation to human beings."[36]

---

[31] Phil. 2: 5–8.

[32] Matt. 27:46; Mark 15:34.

[33] *Spiritual Exercises,* 196.

[34] Luke 10:16.

[35] Formula of the Institute, *Exposcit Debitum* (1550), §3 (MHSI 63, 376).

[36] *Constitutions,* 813.

IV. Our Contemporary Context and Its Challenges

105/ 18. Many positive values prized by our contemporaries are essential to living religious obedience according to our Jesuit way of proceeding: respect for the human person and for human rights, willingness to engage in dialogue marked by freedom of expression, openness to creative alternatives, the desire to build community, and the longing to live for something greater than oneself. But our culture is also marked by a tendency to exaggerated self-sufficiency and individualism that create difficulties for the practice of religious obedience.

106/ 19. Faith in Jesus Christ teaches us that self-realization comes from self-giving and that freedom is not so much the power to choose as the power to order our choices toward love. At the same time, love for Jesus Christ and the desire to follow him call us to trusting commitment. Commitment to the Word Incarnate cannot be separated from commitment to the concrete mediations of the Word that are at the center of our lives, the Church and the Society which exists to serve the Church. At times, however, our desire to commit ourselves to the Lord in personal trust is not matched by our desire to commit ourselves to the Church or to the body of the Society and its way of proceeding.

107/ 20. An exaggerated desire for autonomy has led some to various expressions of self-sufficiency and lack of commitment: lack of availability to our superiors, lack of prudence in the expression of our opinions, lack of a spirit of cooperation in our approach to the local Church, and even disaffection from the Church and the Society. Some have used the language of discernment to excuse a desire to determine their own mission, forgetting that discernment in the Society is a communal exercise that takes into account a multiplicity of voices but reaches its completion only in the conferral of a mission by the superior.

108/ 21. The patterns of our contemporary world have their effect on the exercise of authority as well. The way in which our world prizes productivity can lead to overwork, and this can lead to distraction and lack of attention to the human person. The exercise of authority can be reduced to an exercise of power that marginalizes others or to a demand to be heard that is not matched by sufficient willingness to listen. We know these tendencies disfigure many structures and relationships in our world; we cannot imagine we will be immune from their influence when obedience places us in positions of authority within the Society or in institutions through which the Society carries out its mission.

109/ 22. These attitudes exist around us and within us. However, many of them are far from the spirit of the gospel, far from the spirit of obedience the Society wishes to foster in its members, and far from the ideal of obedience our way of proceeding presupposes.

V. Some Specific Aspects of the Practice of Obedience in the Society

110/ 23. The practice of obedience in the Society has its roots in the spiritual experience of Ignatius and the First Companions. Drawn together by the Spiritual Exercises, they came to have but one goal: to be sent on mission in the image of the Son and so serve the Lord in companionship. Therefore, obedience in the Society is grounded in the desire to be sent effectively, to serve completely, and to create ever stronger bonds of union among ourselves.[37]

111/ 24. These three strands come together in the account of conscience. For this reason, the account of conscience is essential to the practice of obedience in the Society.[38] A Jesuit reveals to his superior all that is happening in his soul, the graces that he has received and the temptations he has undergone, so that his superior can more prudently and confidently send him on mission. The account is repeated annually so that the Jesuit and his superior can evaluate and confirm that mission together.

112/ 25. This degree of transparency is possible because our superiors are also our companions. Ignatius wanted superiors to love their companions. To love is to act responsibly. Jesuits bear the responsibility to reveal themselves completely to their superiors; superiors bear the responsibility to hear their brothers attentively and to dialogue with them honestly. This is especially true when a Jesuit humbly represents to his superior any difficulty he has with the mission he has been given, a practice Ignatius valued and encouraged.[39]

113/ 26. The trust that marks obedience is mutual. Jesuits make an act of trust in their superiors when they obey; superiors make an act of trust in their brothers when they send them on mission. This trust is grounded in the superior's appreciation of the Jesuit he sends as someone who discerns; that is, someone who seeks familiarity with the Lord through prayer, desires freedom from disordered attachment, and thus opens himself to the guidance of the Spirit in an ongoing quest to discover the divine will.

114/ 27. Because Ignatius knew and trusted the prayerful desires of the Jesuits he sent on mission, he left much to their discretion.[40] Following the example of Ignatius, the Society expects that Jesuits will exercise creativity in carrying out their mission as they see circumstances require, that they will go beyond what has been asked in the true spirit of the *magis*.[41] Thus the superior's trust expresses itself in effective delegation, and the Jesuit who obeys knows he can rely on his

---

[37] *NC* 149–156.

[38] *NC* 155 §1.

[39] *Constitutions*, 543, 627.

[40] *Constitutions*, 633–635.

[41] *Constitutions*, 622–623.

superior's openness to creative initiatives he might propose.[42] This is why obedience in the Society has rightly been described as an exercise of creative fidelity.[43] It is creative, because it calls on the individual's freedom and resourcefulness. It is fidelity because it calls for a generous response to the directives of the superior whose duty it is to make decisions, "keeping in view the purpose of the Constitutions, which is the greater divine service and the good of those who live in this Institute."[44]

115/ 28. A consideration of the practice of obedience would be incomplete if it were limited to the relationship between the superior and the individual Jesuit. The community has its role to play. We obey our superiors in community so that our common life can effectively support our mission and become a sign of the possibility of human communion our world so sorely needs.[45] The community is also a privileged place for the practice of apostolic discernment, whether through formally structured communal discernment[46] or through informal conversation that has the more effective pursuit of the mission as its goal. Such discernment will help us not only accept our personal missions but also rejoice in and support the missions received by our brothers. In this way, our common mission is strengthened and the union of minds and hearts confirmed and deepened.

116/ 29. For Ignatius and for the Jesuit, obedience is both grace and gift. It is a path to which we are called by the Lord, and it is the Lord who enables us to follow this path in his service. A personal history of generous response to the grace of obedience allows a Jesuit to serve joyfully and effectively.

VI. The Fourth Vow of Obedience to the Pope with Regard to Missions

117/ 30. Ignatius and the First Companions offered themselves to the Vicar of Christ to be sent on mission out of a "desire to serve the Church in the most beneficial way possible."[47] By means of the fourth vow pronounced by the pro-

---

[42] GC 31, D. 17, n. 11.

[43] All of this clarifies the significance of phrases like "an old man's staff" or "*perinde ac cadaver*" that can be found in the Constitutions. The context makes it clear that to obey is not to become lifeless; rather, it is to offer oneself to be carried by the mission conferred by the superior. "For in this way the obedient man ought joyfully to employ himself in any task in which the superior desires to employ him in aid of the whole body of the religious order" (*Constitutions*, 547).

[44] *Constitutions*, 746.

[45] Peter-Hans Kolvenbach S.I., *"Sur la vie communautaire"* (12 March 1998), *AR* 22 (1996–2002): 276–289.

[46] *NC* 150–151.

[47] Benedict XVI, *Allocution to the Members of the Society of Jesus* (22 April 2006), *AR* 2^9, no. (2006), 677.

fessed, the whole body of the Society puts itself at the disposition of the ministry of the Successor of Peter "for distribution into the vineyard of Christ our Lord."[48] In this way, we achieve greater availability to the divine will and offer the Church better service.

118/ 31. The fourth vow, which Ignatius himself defined as "our beginning and principal foundation,"[49] expresses what is specific to the Society: total availability to serve the Church wherever the pope sends us. The fourth vow also makes clear the place of the Society in the Church. It gives the Society structural incorporation into the life of the Church by linking its charism as an apostolic religious order to the hierarchical structure of the Church in the person of the pope. It is through this vow that the Society participates in the universal mission of the Church and that the universality of its mission, carried out through a wide range of ministries in the service of local churches, is guaranteed.

119/ 32. According to the Constitutions, "the entire purport of this fourth vow of obedience to the pope was and is with regard to missions . . . for having the members dispersed throughout the various parts of the world."[50] This is the matter of the vow. But the Constitutions also invite us to distinguish ourselves in obedience "not only in the matters of obligation but also in others even though nothing else be perceived except an indication of the superior's will without an expressed command."[51] This is thoroughly congruent with Ignatius's ideal of obedience, which holds "that obedience is imperfect in which there does not exist, in addition to the execution, agreement in willing and judging between him who commands and him who obeys."[52]

120/ 33. The availability promised in the fourth vow is distinct from the Ignatian spirituality of "the proper attitude we ought to have in the Church" or "*sentire cum ecclesia*."[53] However, both are rooted in the love we have for Christ our Lord, a love that extends itself to love for the Church and for "the one who holds

---

[48] *Constitutions,* 604.

[49] *Declarationes circa missiones* (1544–1545) (MHSI 63, 162); Peter Faber, *Memoriale,* n. 18 (MHSI 68, 498); GC 31, D. 1, n 4.

[50] *Constitutions,* 529 and 605.

[51] *Constitutions,* 547. Although the reference in the Constitutions is to obedience to Jesuit superiors, the Thirty-first General Congregation applies the citation to obedience to the pope. "With all our force and energy we should strive to obey first the Sovereign Pontiff and then the superiors of the Society 'not only in matters of obligation, but also in others, even at the mere hint of the superior's will, apart from any express command'" (GC 31, D. 17, n. 10).

[52] *Constitutions,* 550.

[53] *Spiritual Exercises,* 352. Cf. GC 34, D. 11; final allocution of Father Kolvenbach to the 69th Congregation of Procurators (Loyola, 23 September 2003), *AR* 23, no. 1 (2003): 431–438.

the place of Christ our Lord for us."[54] This is why we speak of being united with the pope effectively and affectively. Taken together, the fourth vow and our ecclesial spirituality move us to offer the service asked of us by the pope.[55]

121/ 34. The Society is deeply grateful to God for its vocation to serve the Church and derives great consolation from the innumerable examples of generous Jesuits who offer their lives in service to the mission of Christ throughout the world, making themselves available for missions from the Holy Father and collaborating with local churches under the guidance of their pastors. In the name of the whole Society, the Thirty-fifth General Congregation asks the Lord's pardon for those times when its members have been lacking in love, discretion, or faithfulness in their service of the Church. At the same time, this Congregation affirms the Society's commitment to grow daily in love for the Church and availability to the pope.

VII. Obedience in Daily Life

122/ 35. This Congregation does not want to repeat everything set down about obedience in the Constitutions and Complementary Norms; neither does it want to repeat the directives on obedience to be found in the decrees of the most recent General Congregations. However, we do wish to offer some advice that can assist us in our present circumstances so that we can continue to distinguish ourselves in the perfection of our obedience[56], as St. Ignatius urges us.

Jesuits in Formation

123/ 36. The Thirty-fifth General Congregation invites Jesuits in formation to live their progressive incorporation into the Society with joyful hearts, reproducing the First Companions' fruitful experience of being friends in the Lord and committing their lives to generous service of all men and women, especially those most in need.

124/ 37. We encourage Jesuits in formation to grow throughout the stages of formation in the spirituality of obedience and in availability for placing their lives and freedom at the service of the mission of Christ. It will be good for them to take advantage of the opportunities for self-abnegation that community life, constant and rigorous dedication to studies, and other aspects of their experience will doubtless provide. Self-abnegation, "the fruit of our joy at the approach of the

---

[54] *Constitutions*, 552.

[55] *NC* 253.

[56] "We can tolerate other religious institutes outdoing us in fasting and in other austerities that they practice according to their Rule, but it is my desire, dear brothers, that those who serve the Lord our God in this Society be outstanding in the purity and perfection of their obedience, the renunciation of their will, and the abnegation of their judgment" *(Letter to the Jesuits of Portugal* [26 March 1553; MHSI 29, 671]).

Kingdom and the result of a progressive identification with Christ,"[57] is a virtue Jesuits need to accept peacefully the sometimes difficult demands of obedience.

125/ 38. We encourage *formatores* to help Jesuits in formation understand and live the mystical source of obedience: an unconditional love for the Lord which will bring them to a desire to serve him in fulfilling the Father's will. We ask *formatores* to help Jesuits in formation become progressively aware of the demands of a life of obedience: transparency with superiors, esteem for the account of conscience, the responsible exercise of personal initiative, and a spirit of discernment which accepts the decisions of the superior with good grace.

126/ 39. The spirituality and tradition of the Society require that Jesuits be filled with a spirit of obedience to the Holy Father as an essential characteristic of our mission and identity. Jesuit spiritual and ecclesial formation should emphasize availability for mission and "the proper attitude we ought to have in the Church" as established by the Thirty-fourth General Congregation.[58]

Formed Jesuits

127/ 40. The Thirty-fifth General Congregation invites formed Jesuits to grow in interior freedom and trust in God. In this way, their availability to go to any part of the world and undertake any ministry "of more universal scope and from which greater fruit can be expected"[59] will increase.

128/ 41. The Congregation encourages all Jesuits to strengthen their affection for the pope and their respect for the pastors of the Church and to correct any faults that might exist in this regard.

129/ 42. Similarly, the Congregation asks all Jesuits to recognize with gratitude the service local and major superiors offer the Society and to support them in their task.

130/ 43. It is of vital importance that all Jesuits consider the account of conscience essential for the practice of obedience and that they offer it according to the guidelines set down by Father Kolvenbach in his letter to the Society of February 21, 2005. Because "the mission is conferred, confirmed, or changed"[60] in the account of conscience, it should be given in the first place to the major superior. However, what the letter says in regard to opening one's conscience to the local superior

---

[57] *NC* 223 §4.

[58] GC 34, D. 11.

[59] *Constitutions,* 622.

[60] Peter-Hans Kolvenbach S.I., "*Le compte de conscience*" (21 February 2005), *AR* 23, no. 1 (2003): 558.

should also be noted: "A Jesuit may always open his conscience to his local superior—and indeed the latter would be permitted to request this if need be."[61]

131/ 44. We ask Jesuits to refer to the local superior all questions that lie within his competence and not take these questions directly to the major superior.

132/ 45. In our present circumstances, it is not infrequent that Jesuits find themselves serving in works of the Society under a director of the work who may or may not be a Jesuit. In either case, Jesuits owe directors of the work complete, loyal cooperation in what pertains to their office. Jesuits are to make every effort to contribute to maintaining the work's Jesuit identity.

133/ 46. The Congregation wishes to express its profound gratitude to formed Jesuits of advanced years who have given their lives to the service of the Church. We also wish to remind them that they are as closely identified with the Lord when they serve him with reduced energies or even in sickness and suffering as they were when they went about "proclaiming the kingdom in towns and villages."[62] Those whose primary task is to pray for the Church and the Society are truly on mission, and their contribution to the Society's well-being and its service of the Kingdom can never be overemphasized, for they provide an example of placing oneself entirely in the hands of God, which can only inspire and console their brothers.

Superiors

134/ 47. The General Congregation encourages major superiors to exercise their roles with confidence and joy, to assign Jesuits to their mission with clarity, and to show interest and care for the Jesuits they send on mission.

135/ 48. When major superiors name non-Jesuit directors of works, they should not only take into account candidates' professional competence but also their understanding and commitment to our mission and way of proceeding.

136/ 49. In the spirit of subsidiarity, we recommend that major superiors respect the scope for decision making that appropriately belongs to the local superior.

137/ 50. The General Congregation wants to emphasize once more the importance of the role of the local superior. Local superiors need to receive the formation and preparation necessary for their mission. In this regard, major superiors are responsible for offering regular and timely courses and programs to prepare local superiors.

138/ 51. The local superior shares with the whole community responsibility for the care and formation of Jesuits who have not yet pronounced final vows. Local

---

[61] Peter-Hans Kolvenbach S.I., "*Le compte de conscience*" (21 February 2005), *AR* 23, no. 1 (2003): 558; *Guidelines for Local Superiors,* 16, *AR* 22 (1996–2002): 369.

[62] *Spiritual Exercises,* 91.

superiors are asked to take special care to request the account of conscience twice a year, to provide for the renewal of vows, and to ensure a community atmosphere that encourages the Jesuit in formation to grow as a person and as a religious.

139/ 52. It is important that community life be governed by clear directives. Local superiors should collaborate with their brothers in working out and putting into practice a daily order and guidelines for common life. These practices should be evaluated at the time of the major superior's annual visit or other appropriate times.[63]

VIII. Conclusion

140/ 53. Along his pilgrim way from Loyola to Rome, Ignatius prayed unceasingly to Mary, our Lady, asking her to obtain for him the grace to be received under the banner of her Son.[64] In her expression, "Behold the servant of the Lord, let it be done to me according to your word,"[65] Mary shows us how to live in total availability and to place our whole lives at the service of her Son. In her instruction to the servants at Cana, "Do whatever he tells you,"[66] Mary points out for us the basic orientation that should guide our lives. For this reason, the Society has always seen in Mary a model of obedience.

141/ 54. Through the intercession of Mary, the Mother of the Lord, of St. Ignatius, and of the great company of brothers who have lived their lives of obedience with a love so profound that it has even led some to martyrdom, the Society rededicates itself to the practice of obedience "for the greater service of God and for the more universal good."[67]

---

[63] *NC* 319, 324.

[64] *Spiritual Exercises,* 147.

[65] Luke 1:38.

[66] John 2:5.

[67] *Constitutions,* 618, 622.

DECREE 5

GOVERNANCE AT THE SERVICE OF UNIVERSAL MISSION

Introduction

142/ 1.　General Congregation 35 establishes three principles to guide our consideration of governance in the Society of Jesus based on the experiences of recent decades and our apostolic mission:

> *a. Our governance structures and ways of proceeding should flow from a perspective of greater universality.* This is in keeping with the directions set by previous General Congregations[1] and responds to the accelerated pace of globalization, the transnational and multicultural dimensions of the challenges facing the Church, and our desires to work more collaboratively throughout this universal Society.

> *b. Structures of governance should be streamlined, modernized, and made more flexible where possible.* The Society is organized in function of its mission. We will serve that apostolic mission more effectively by simplifying some structures and procedures of governance, using modern methods of communication and collaboration, and introducing increasingly flexible structures at various levels.

> *c. Changing circumstances require a better articulation of Ignatian values and ways of proceeding in our contemporary life and work.* Such changes as apostolic collaboration with others, the separation between apostolic institutions and community, and the development of an inter- and supra-provincial level of some ministries demand certain clarifications about how to exercise governance so that it might continue as genuinely Ignatian.

Following from these principles, we offer some concrete directions for the different levels and organs of our current structure of governance.

I. General Governance

General Congregation

143/ 2.　The General Congregation directs and authorizes the General to undertake, in anticipation of General Congregation 36, a comprehensive revision of the *Formula of a General Congregation (FGC)*, and of the *Formulae* of the Congregation of Procurators and of the Province Congregation.

---

[1] Cf. GC 31, D. 48, n. 8; GC 32, D. 4, n. 81; GC 33, D. 1, n. 46; GC 34, D. 21.

144/ 3.   The revised *FCG* should be approved by GC 36 in its first sessions. After consulting with the Major Superiors and receiving the approval of the General Council by deliberative vote, Father General may approve revisions in the FCG that would take effect before GC 36, as well as any related changes in the Formulae of the Congregation of Procurators and the Province Congregation.

145/ 4.   The revision should, in accord with the principles enunciated in the introduction (cf. n. 1), aim at better facilitating the effective, responsible, and adaptable use of the rich diversity of human and material resources that are employed in the preparation and conduct of a General Congregation, for the service of the life and mission of the universal Society. The revision should also respect, among other things, the following:

> *a.* The threefold character of the General Congregation as

>> *a.1.* the body which elects the General and which has a major role in the choice of the members of the General Council;

>> *a.2.* the highest instance of giving expression to the self-understanding of the universal body of the Society at a given moment; and

>> *a.3.* the supreme legislative body of the Society.

> *b.* Given the traditional conviction that a General Congregation is an exceptional occurrence in the governance of the Society, its work should be confined to "matters of greater moment" (*FCG* 1 2).

> *c.* The importance of the whole Society's being represented in the General Congregation, especially in the Congregation *ad electionem.* In this context, at least two other matters are to be respected:

>> *c.1.* the number of elected members being greater than that of the appointed and *ex officio* members combined (cf. GC 34, d. 23 A, n. 1);

>> *c.2.* the presence of an adequate number of Brothers as electors.

> *d.* With regard to the duration of the General Congregation: the need to balance, on the one hand, a responsible use of limited resources, and, on the other, the creation of an atmosphere of Ignatian discernment in the proceedings.

> *e.* The need for a more thorough preparation of the General Congregation, especially in the work leading to the formulation of the *Relationes Praeviae* and the report *De Statu Societatis,* but without prejudice to the freedom of the General Congregation itself to determine the content of its deliberations. Such preparation may require the role of a Province Congregation in preparing for a General Congregation to be expanded.

> *f.* The rapid development of means of communication, as they affect both the preparation and the conduct of Congregations.

146/ 5. Of particular importance in preparing the General Congregation are the meetings of Major Superiors (cf. GC 34, d. 23 C, n. 4), of Presidents of Conferences (cf. GC 34, d. 21, n. 25), of electors of each Assistancy or Conference, and assemblies of various apostolic sectors. Each of these bodies could make a substantial contribution in the preparation of the General Congregation.

147/ 6. The Congregation of Procurators should be maintained, as representing the "rank and file" of the membership of the Society. As indicated above, however, its *Formula* should be reviewed along with and in consequence of the revision of the *FCG*.

Central Governance

Principle

148/ 7. The Superior General is a source of unity in the universal body of the Society.[2] The Congregation recognizes the rich diversity in the Society's membership and the inculturation necessary and proper for carrying out our mission within the universal Church and in an increasingly globalized world. As governance in the Society is always measured in an appropriate balance of union and diversity, the office of General must be exercised in a manner which respects diversity while placing it at the service of our universal mission and identity.

Reorganization

149/ 8. The General Congregation confirms the procedures to elect the four Assistants *ad providentiam* and to renew Father General's Council determined by GC 34, d. 23 E, II, 1.

150/ 9. In order that the General may have the most effective support for carrying out his responsibilities, he is directed by this General Congregation to undertake a comprehensive review of the central governance of the Society, with a view to reorganization for the service of mission.

151/ 10. Included in the purpose of this review is the provision of the resources and staff needed to handle the ordinary business of the Society, while allowing the General the opportunity to do comprehensive apostolic planning and to animate the whole body of the Society.

152/ 11. This review should take account of but is not limited to:

a. the framework provided by *NC* 380–386;

b. the need for communication among the various persons and groups mentioned in NC 380–386, as well as between these persons and the General;

c. the need for coordination and articulation of the functions of these persons and groups;

---

[2] *Constitutions,* 666, 719.

d. the importance of avoiding unnecessary "bureaucratization" or unnecessary multiplication of officials and secretariats;

e. the importance of developing appropriate job profiles, which would involve regular articulation of goals and expected outcomes, together with an effective mechanism for review and evaluation.

153/ 12.   The General is encouraged to look to ways in which finances might be used more effectively and equitably for the service of the international mission of the Society.

154/ 13.   A professional and comprehensive strategy needs to be developed to improve our internal and external communications, so as to facilitate governance, foster cooperation, and enhance the effectiveness of our universal mission.

155/ 14.   The General is encouraged, in undertaking this review of central governance, to make use of the best professional assistance that is available within and outside the Society.

Evaluation

156/ 15.   The General is asked to develop instruments and programs for assisting all those in governance (central, conference, provincial and local) to review the effective implementation of and accountability for their proper responsibilities. *Practica Quaedam* is to be updated to reflect these developments.

157/ 16.   A review of the progress made in these matters should be included in the agenda of subsequent meetings with Presidents of Conferences. A more comprehensive report should be made at the next meeting with Major Superiors.

Conference of Major Superiors

Principles

158/ 17.   Since we are aware that "today many problems are global in nature and therefore require global solutions,"[3] we consider the Conferences of Major Superiors—at present Africa and Madagascar, East Asia/Oceania, Europe, Latin America, South Asia and USA—to be a significant initiative in the governance structure of the Society.[4] While recognizing the authority of the General for universal mission, we hold the conviction that today cooperation among Provinces and Regions to realize the apostolic mission of the Society is an undeniable necessity.

159/ 18.   The Conferences are expected to continue to be structural means that foster in all Jesuits a sense of universal mission, while facilitating union, communication, a common vision among the superiors, and inter- and supra-provincial cooperation. In order that the Conferences may respond more adequately to these aims, the following principles should be observed:

---

[3] *NC* 395 §1. Cf. also *NC* 395–400.
[4] Cf *GC* 34, D. 21, nn. 21–28.

a. Conferences are structures oriented for mission and not mere instruments of inter-provincial coordination. They must continue doing apostolic planning at the inter-provincial level, taking into account the apostolic preferences of the universal Society. This apostolic planning is the result of discernment among the Major Superiors of the Conference, should be approved by the General, and should be evaluated and revised periodically.

b. Conferences are structures of cooperation among Provinces and Regions regarding specific inter- and supra-provincial aspects of mission (common works, formation centres, networking, inter-provincial teams, geographical regions, etc.). While Conferences do not constitute a new level of government between the General and the Provincials, they offer an opportunity to enhance the governance of Provincials by enabling them to care for the mission of the Society beyond their own Provinces.

c. Conferences have followed varying courses of development in the Society due to regional differences. The Statutes of each Conference should, therefore, respect those differences and take into account the following:

c.1. The Statutes are to be approved by the General and should include the following points: the membership, their rights and duties, the matters that come under the Conference's competence, the method of making decisions, internal structures, the authority and duties of the President (in accordance with nn. 19–23), and, in general, whatever is considered necessary for an expeditious and efficient functioning of the Conference.

c.2. Each Conference should adapt its Statutes in accordance with the orientations of GC 35.

d. Conferences should have the resources necessary to attend to the financial needs of works and houses dependent on the Conference.

President of the Conference

160/ 19. The General appoints the President after appropriate consultation with the Major Superiors of the Conference. He has the faculties of a Major Superior to carry out the specific responsibilities entrusted to him by the Statutes of the Conference.

161/ 20. The principles of unity of governance *(cura personalis, cura apostolica)*, subsidiarity, and sufficient authority to exercise one's office, are to be applied appropriately to the role of Presidents of Conferences in this way:

a. Assignments:

a.1. In the area of his competence as defined in the Statutes, the President has authority to request and to assign persons from the Provinces or Regions needed for the activities and works dependent on the Conference. A basic criterion to make these assignments is that, all other things being equal, the needs of Conference activities and works have priority over those of individual Provinces.[5]

a.2. Respecting the centrality of the account of conscience in missioning, any such assignment requires the consultation of the man's Major Superior, who is the one who makes him available for a mission in the Conference.

a.3. In those rare situations in which the President and the respective Major Superior cannot come to an agreement regarding an assignment, the matter should be referred to the General for resolution.

b. Decision making:

b.1. In the area of his competence as defined in the Statutes, the President is to make decisions as he sees fit, after having heard and considered attentively the views of the members of the Conference.

b.2. Although the President is endowed with the proper faculties to make decisions, it is necessary to emphasize the importance of his moral authority with the Provincials, which will enable him to propose objectives for collaboration and to promote discerned consensus among the Provincials. He himself needs to be an especially good leader, prudent, tactful, and considerate (cf. *Const.* 667).

c. Relations with Provincials and Regional Superiors:

c.1. The existence of Conferences with their Presidents, as well as their decision-making authority in the inter- and supra-provincial sphere, implies that Provincials and Regional Superiors are involved in a new way of interconnection and interdependency, and are oriented toward cooperation.

c.2. The President does not have any direct authority in the internal governance of the Provinces nor does he supervise it. Provincials depend directly on the General. They are accountable to him in what concerns the internal governance of Provinces; they are accountable to the President in the strict area of his competence.

c.3. In exercising apostolic leadership, the President should be involved, as appropriate, in the apostolic discernment of Provinces and Regions.

162/ 21. The President is also the Major Superior of the common houses and works of the Conference, which the General has designated as such. In this sense,

---

[5] The second sentence of GC 34, D. 21, n. 24 is thus modified.

a. the President, together with the other Major Superiors, has the responsibility to provide the human and financial resources needed for houses and works dependent on the Conference;

b. the President hears the manifestation of conscience of the Jesuits assigned on a stable basis to common houses and works;

c. the President has the responsibility for the ongoing formation and health care of the Jesuits assigned to common houses and works.

163/ 22. The President of the Conference attends a General Congregation as an *ex officio* elector.

164/ 23. The Presidents of Conferences shall meet together with the General at least once a year, or whenever called by him for consultation on important matters[6].

II. Province Governance

The Nature of the Province

165/ 24. While our vocation is to the universal Society, Provinces have been established for greater apostolic effectiveness and more effective governance, so that the specific articulation of a Jesuit's mission is the direct result of the animating leadership of the Provincial.

Essential in this governance is the manifestation of conscience, conducted in an atmosphere of transparency and trust that enable the Provincial to assign men to specific ministries after discerning carefully how the holy desires, needs, and gifts of his men meet the needs of the Province's apostolic plan and works alongside those of the Conference as well as the apostolic preferences established by the General.

166/ 25. Through the centuries, the structure of Province governance has had much to commend it in apostolic and administrative efficiency; respect for varied cultural, linguistic, national, and regional traditions; and the effective uniting of *cura personalis* with *cura apostolica.* Given today's globalized context within which Jesuits exercise ministry, sophisticated communications technologies, growing apostolic networks, and transnational realities, new challenges and new opportunities for ministry require reflection, formation, and concerted action that enables us to think and act across Province and even Conference boundaries.

This constantly evolving context calls for greater and better coordination and cooperation among Provinces (for example, in apostolic planning and financial administration) at the service of our universal mission. It also suggests a need for consideration of how Provinces can best be governed, including the regular evaluation and review of effective governance, apostolic plans, administra-

---

[6] Cf. GC 34, D. 21, n. 25.

tion of apostolic resources, and engagement with other Provinces through Conference structures (cf. *supra* nn. 19–20).

167/ 26. With a view towards better serving our universal mission, the General Congregation requests the General to commission a process of reflection on Provinces and Province structures which will lead to practical proposals for adapting this aspect of our governance to today's realities. This commission's responsibility should include a comprehensive review of the criteria for the establishment (cf. *NC* 388), reconfiguration, and suppression of Provinces and Regions. The criteria would include numerical and geographic size, age distribution, availability of effective leadership for governance and formation, financial viability, and capacity for developing a comprehensive apostolic plan which meets local, regional, and universal needs. The progress of this commission's work should be presented at the next meeting of Major Superiors.

Province and Local Church

168/ 27. It is particularly important that the Provincial actively pursue good communication and harmonious relationships with the Bishops of the local Churches in which we serve. This would include the expectation that local superiors and directors of works be encouraged to do their part in the fostering of such relationships.

Province Planning and Decision Making

169/ 28. The Society's law (cf. especially *NC* 354 §1) strongly encourages a participatory and discerning approach to decision making at all levels, including that of the Province.[7] So that this approach may be even more effective, care needs to be taken that:

a. it remain clear that it is the appropriate superior, not a consultative body, that makes the final decision (cf. *NC* 354 § 1);

b. there be sufficient clarity about the process for planning and decision making, with the specific roles of various commissions and officials being adequately communicated to members of the Province.

c. the role of the Province Consultors, as laid down in universal and proper law,[8] be respected. This role should not be eroded by the responsibilities rightly given to staff, officials, or commissions.

d. the Commission on Ministries (cf. *NC* 260 §1) be an effective instrument for apostolic planning and its review, especially as this relates to estab-

---

[7] Cf. *Guidelines for Provincials,* 30–35, *AR* 23, no. 1 (2003): 297–298.

[8] Cf. *Guidelines for Provincials,* 30, *AR* 23, no. 1 (2003): 297.

lished works and ministries of the Province, the creation of new apostolic works, and the ongoing apostolic formation of collaborators.

e. the legal and economic aspects of any decision should be considered.

f. there be structures for implementation and ongoing evaluation of the effectiveness of Province plans.

Apostolic Works of the Province

170/ 29. Another critical aspect of the Provincial's governance is comprehensive care for the Province's apostolic works, including a thorough evaluation of their contribution to the Society's mission and of their Jesuit character. These works should be visited regularly by the Provincial (or his delegate; cf. *NC* 391 §3), a report of which is to be included in his letters to the General. When the director of a work is someone other than a Jesuit, that director is expected to report on the work during the Provincial's visitation. A comprehensive articulation of the relationship between apostolic works (including international works of the Society) and the Province is expected and would include written agreements as helpful or required.

Training for Leadership

171/ 30. Leadership in the Society today is a very demanding ministry. The need for international cooperation, new structures for partnership with others, and heightened expectations about the quality of community life are only some of the factors that call for new attitudes and new skills in superiors and directors of works at all levels of governance. Specific formation for Jesuits and others in positions of leadership is needed.

172/ 31. Ongoing formation in such attitudes and skills will often take place at the Province level, although there will also be many occasions when Conference-wide programs will be extremely helpful. Critical areas for such training include:

a. principles of Ignatian leadership, including the practice of apostolic discernment in common

b. formation in an attitude that enables one to work as a member of a team[9]

c. principles of leadership in general

d. management skills in areas such as:

1. financial administration

---

[9] Cf. *Guidelines for the Relationship between the Superior and the Director of the Work*, 16, *AR* 22 (1996–2002): 386–387.

2. human resources

3. planning

4. conflict resolution

5. confrontation

6. conducting meetings

7. crisis management

8. media and public relations

   e. Skills required for effective membership of a board of governance.

173/ 32. In addition to leadership-training courses or workshops, there is great value in using forms of apprenticeship and mentoring. In appropriate ways potential leaders can be identified and be put in situations where they can learn from an experienced and wise leader.

III. Local Governance

Local Superior

Principles

174/ 33. The effectiveness of the local superior is critical to the apostolic vitality of the Jesuit community as a sign to the world of the Reign of God which we proclaim by our lives together. For Ignatius, love for the members of his community was to be the distinguishing mark of the Jesuit Superior.[10] From that starting point, the Superior can encourage the mission of apostolic men and ensure the quality of religious and community life that enables them to fulfil their mission.[11]

In a spirit of service, the Superior supports the members in their apostolic responsibilities and religious lives as servants of Christ's mission. These duties require an intimate knowledge of each man made possible by regular spiritual conversation and, where appropriate, manifestation of conscience. With such aids, the Superior can help each Jesuit to see how his apostolic work, assigned by the Major Superior, is properly integrated into the universal mission of the Society, promoting the sense of apostolic solidarity of all the community members, even of those who may be engaged in very diversified activities.[12]

175/ 34 . From his privileged place at the heart of the community, the superior is also responsible, together with each member, for developing its apostolic life. Concretely, this commits the local superior to lead his community in a Jesuit

---

[10] Cf. *Guidelines for Local Superiors,* 11, *AR* 22 (1996–2002): 368.

[11] Cf. *Guidelines for Local Superiors,* 33, *AR* 22 (1996–2002): 373.

[12] Cf. *NC* 403 §2.

common life characterized by the celebration of Eucharist, prayer, faith sharing, communal discernment, simplicity, hospitality, solidarity with the poor, and the witness that "friends in the Lord" can make to the world.

The General Congregation insists once again on the importance of the mission of local superior and emphasizes the relevance of the points described in the *Complementary Norms*.[13]

Challenges

176/ 35. Actual practice has not always followed the guidelines presented in the *Complementary Norms*. The General Congregation recognizes that several factors jeopardize the proper fulfillment of the mission entrusted to the local superior:

a. Communities are of different types: in some of them, Jesuits have received very different missions in a great variety of places; other communities are closely linked with the life of a particular apostolic work (directed by a member of the community or by another); other communities mix a number of Jesuits involved in the one apostolic work and other Jesuits whose missions take place in other institutions.

b. It is fundamental that every Jesuit be able to maintain a direct relationship with his Major Superior; but ready access to modern communication technologies can facilitate bypassing the local superior to directly communicate with the Major Superior in ways which undermine the proper relationship with the local superior.

c. It is often too easy to minimize the importance of decision making at the local level by concentrating too much authority at the provincial level, in apparent violation of the principle of subsidiarity in governance.

d. In some circumstances, relationships between local superiors and the director of the work, whether Jesuit or not, are a source of confusion and even conflict.

Recommendations

177/ 36. The General Congregation recommends that, in each Province or Conference of Major Superiors, formation sessions be developed in order to assist new superiors to come to an understanding of their mission and to learn practical ways of carrying out that mission.

178/ 37. The General Congregation recommends that Major Superiors set up regular meetings of local superiors, with the following objectives: to promote mu-

---

[13] Cf. *NC* 148, 151, 226, 323, 324, 349–354, 403, 406–407.

tual support among superiors; to encourage discernment among those in charge of apostolates; and to facilitate ongoing formation in the mission of local superior.

179/ 38. The General Congregation recommends that Major Superiors allow for proper application of NC 351 by assuring that the Superior's primary responsibility is the animation of the local community.

180/ 39. The General Congregation recommends that superiors acquire a good knowledge of the *Guidelines for Local Superiors.* They are to make a responsible application of the *Guidelines* (i.e., adapted to the local situation), with particular attention given to the proper use of the house consult.[14]

Superiors and Directors of the Work

181/ 40. The relations between superiors and directors of the work must be developed in accordance with the *Guidelines for the Relationship between the Superior and the Director of the Work;* these must be adapted to the local context in dialogue with the Major Superior.

182/ 41. The superior must have a clear awareness of his responsibility regarding apostolic works and be prepared to exercise it. The director of a work must know to which superior or Provincial delegate he is called to give an account of his apostolic action.

183/ 42. It is important for the Major Superior to consider ahead of time the ways in which the relationship between the director and the relevant local superior will develop[15]. Often this relationship will also be formed with those in charge of institutions which are under the jurisdiction of civil law. Account must be taken of the requirements of both civil and canon law, and the relations between the two.

---

[14] *Guidelines for Local Superiors,* 18, *AR* 22 (1996–2002): 369–370.

[15] Cf. *Guidelines for the Relationship between the Superior and the Director of the Work* 18, 19, 23, 26–29, *AR* 22 (1996–2002): 387–388; *NC* 406 §1–2.

DECREE 6

COLLABORATION AT THE HEART OF MISSION

Encouraging the Dynamism Initiated by GC34

184/ 1. When[1] Jesus wanted to teach his disciples about the power of the word of God, which every Jesuit ministry proclaims, he began, "Listen! Imagine a sower going out to sow."[2] He explained how some seed falls upon rocky ground, some among weeds, and other upon fertile soil, where it yields a rich harvest. In his allocution to the members of GC 35, Pope Benedict XVI stressed the importance of the mission in which we are all engaged: "[M]ake the face of the Lord known to so many for whom it remains hidden or unrecognizable."[3] He told us that the Church needs the Society, counts on it to "reach the geographical and spiritual places where others do not reach or find it difficult to reach."[4]

185/ 2. As men sent by the Vicar of Christ, we are led more and more to offer our gifts and to share with others the Good News of the Kingdom. Following the inspiration of the Second Vatican Council, the Society of Jesus has been transformed by a profound movement of the Spirit. Recognizing this, GC 34 approved the decree "Cooperation with the Laity in Mission," which both affirmed and encouraged apostolic collaboration, calling on Jesuits to cooperate with others in their projects and in ours[5]. GC 35, reviewing our own life and service to the Church, and noting how the seeds which have been scattered through the inspiration of GC34 are yielding a harvest "thirty, sixty, and even a hundredfold,"[6] renews our commitment to apostolic collaboration and to a profound sharing of labor for the life of the Church and the transformation of the world.

186/ 3. We are humbled and grateful that so many—inspired as we have been by the vocation of Ignatius and the tradition of the Society—have chosen both to

---

[1] "Collaboration in mission" is described in different ways in various languages across the Society: Ignatian apostolic partners, partnership in mission, companions, collaborators, co-workers, colleagues. The common aspiration is apostolic companionship based on discernment and oriented towards service. In this document, we have simply used the word "collaboration."

[2] Mark 4:3.

[3] Benedict XVI, *Allocution to the 35th General Congregation of the Society of Jesus* (21 February 2008), §4 (Allocution).

[4] *Allocution*, §2.

[5] GC 34, D. 13, n. 7.

[6] Mark 4:8.

work with us and to share our sense of mission and our passion to reach out to the men and women of our broken but lovable world. We are enriched by members of our own faith, but also by people from other religious traditions, those women and men of good will from all nations and cultures, with whom we labor in seeking a more just world. Rich is the harvest. In many countries, important Jesuit works depend largely on the generous, loyal, and skilled collaboration of women and men of diverse religious and humanistic convictions. As the Holy Father affirmed our ministry and mission, saying to us, "The Church needs you," we must in turn look to our collaborators in mission and say, with gratitude and affection, that the call we have received is a call shared by us together.

Challenges and Responses since GC34

187/ 4. Since GC 34 we have learned much. In some regions the development of collaboration has been limited because the participation of lay people in the local Church is minimal. In other regions, where Christians are in the minority, the challenge rests on bringing an awareness of the Ignatian charism to those whose spiritual experiences are often far different. Furthermore, in places oppressed by mass culture, the distractions of exaggerated individualism and consumerism have encouraged resistance to the powerful call of community and service found in our mission. Furthermore, our own uncertainty, born of the changing face of our ministries in a time of growing collaboration, has led to some hesitation and even resistance to a full engagement with the call of GC 34.

188/ 5. At the same time, the powerful spirit acknowledged and encouraged by GC 34 has not been idle, and for every challenge greater creativity and zeal have been the response. Numerous programs of Ignatian formation have grown up around the world, adapted to various religious and cultural contexts. The foundational grace of the Spiritual Exercises is more widely available and provides a common language and experience, in which collaboration in mission is rooted and inspired. Increasing numbers of Jesuit works are directed by committed lay people, by other religious, and by diocesan clergy. The members of the Society—priests and brothers, those formed and those in formation—have a greater awareness of shared responsibility with others for the mission and ministry of the Society. Further, the Society has been enriched by our encounter with diverse communities of dialogue and cooperation. Lay and religious, women and men, indigenous persons and those of different religious and spiritual experiences: all these have changed us and nurtured in us a greater sense of the God "in whom we live and move and have our being."[7] The grace of these years is reflected in both more extensive and deeper apostolic collaboration, which places all—Jesuits and others—with the Son.

---

[7] Acts 17:28.

189/ 6.   The seeds of mission sown by our collaboration have actually yielded a rich harvest, for the Ignatian charism serves not just the Society but the whole Church. We are aware of the contribution of this Ignatian charism in forming an apostolic laity, a development called for by the Vatican Council and identified by GC 34 as "a grace of our day and a hope for the future."[8]

Orientations for Furthering Collaboration

190/ 7.   While GC 34 recognized the Spirit's movement and opened for us fresh avenues to implement our mission through more profound collaboration with the laity, the current Congregation recognizes the more diverse community of those with whom we have been called to share this common mission. The seeds sown by grace are growing in many ways and in many lands, and we wish to support this growth, while also indicating some other ways by which that growth might be fostered.

191/ 8.   In this Decree we wish especially to reflect upon the way in which collaboration in mission calls us to a new and often challenging renewal of our ministries. This renewal demands that we address the following questions:

> 8.1. What constitutes a Jesuit work, and how might it be sustained with other than Jesuits in leadership?

> 8.2. What are the necessary elements of formation needed by Jesuits and others to ensure growth in the spirit and practice of our mission?

> 8.3. What bonds might appropriately unite us as collaborators in mission who seek to serve together, with deepening affection, the mission given to the Society?

What Constitutes and Sustains a Jesuit Work?

192/ 9.   The heart of an Ignatian work is the *Spiritual Exercises* of Ignatius. Indeed, any work may be said to be *Ignatian* when it manifests the Ignatian charism: i.e., when it intentionally *seeks God in all things*; when it practices Ignatian discernment; when it engages the world through a careful analysis of context, in dialogue with experience, evaluated through reflection, for the sake of action, and with openness, always, to evaluation. Such a work does not rely necessarily upon the Society of Jesus for its Ignatian identity, though it may affiliate with the Society in partnership through networks and other structures.

193/ 10.   An *Ignatian* work can be said to be *Jesuit* when it has a clear and definitive relationship with the Society of Jesus and when its mission accords with that of the Society by a commitment to a faith that does justice through interreligious dialogue and a creative engagement with culture. In such a context, the

---

[8] Vatican II, *Apostolicam Actuositatem*, 29; GC 34, D. 13, n. 1.

mission of the work, whether administered by a Jesuit or by another who shares this commitment, will be "ultimately accountable to the General of the Society through appropriate lines of authority."[9]

194/ 11. The leadership of a Jesuit work depends upon commitment for mission and can be exercised by Jesuits or by others. Such leaders must have a commitment to the mission of the Society as realized in the particular work, though they may be of religious or spiritual traditions different from our own. Clarity about the mission of each apostolic work and the respective roles of all parties prevents misunderstandings, promotes greater accountability, and builds teamwork. All those in leadership should understand and affirm these varied responsibilities in order to be better able to participate in the discernment and decision-making processes regarding matters of mission.

195/ 12. In developing a relationship between the Society and a Jesuit work, it is vital that Major Superiors engage and support those entrusted with leadership, whether Jesuit or other. Regular dialogue, conducted in a spirit of trust and with respect for appropriate subsidiarity, serves to promote discernment, accountability, and a clearer sense of collaboration for mission. Further, the Provincial or others should provide such leaders important information and directives from the wider Society of Jesus, thus encouraging a broader vision of mission and a better understanding of apostolic priorities and criteria.

196/ 13. The local Jesuit superior and local Jesuits do much to foster the connection between a Jesuit ministry and the Society. All Jesuits, but especially those assigned to a work, can help to foster a spirit of discernment and collaboration by their example and their willingness to share their lives with others. Likewise, our communities, as apostolic centers and not as mere residences, are called to explore how their hospitality may promote collaboration.

197/ 14. Recommendations:

a. We encourage Father General to revise the *Guidelines for the Relationship between the Superior and the Director of the Work* to provide effective support for all those in positions of responsibility, whether Jesuit or others, and assist all parties in the understanding of their various roles and responsibilities. This document should recognize the multiplicity of contexts and give parameters that foster unity while allowing appropriate diversity.

b. We encourage Major Superiors (and Conferences, where appropriate) to develop provincial or regional guidelines for endorsing and sponsoring Jesuit works.

[9] *Guidelines for the Relationship between the Superior and the Director of the Work,* 9, *AR* 22 (1996–2002): 385; *Instruction on the Administration of Goods,* 109–111.

    c. We encourage Major Superiors (and Conferences, where appropriate) to develop tools to evaluate the effectiveness of Jesuit ministries in accomplishing their mission.

    d. We encourage local Jesuit communities to explore ways of offering hospitality and support for the development of collaboration in mission.

What Are the Elements of Formation for Collaborative Mission?

198/ 15. Collaboration in mission has resulted in abundant blessings for the apostolates and the Society of Jesus. Being with apostolic collaborators in mission encourages us to live more fully and authentically our Jesuit religious vocation. Ultimately, we bring to these relationships our own identity as men of the vows and of the *Constitutions,* men whose experience of the Spiritual Exercises has bound us to one another and to a particular "pathway to God."[10] In collaboration with others, in respectful dialogue and shared reflection, in labor alongside those similarly engaged who walk a different pathway, we come to know our own journey better and to follow it with new zeal and understanding.

199/ 16. From the earliest stages of Jesuit formation and throughout our lives as Jesuits, training in collaboration must be experiential, not only informing our understanding of ministry but molding our identity as men for others who are also men with others.[11] The vital role of collaboration for our way of proceeding as Jesuit ministers has implications for the content and methodology of formation as well as for the role of *formatores.*

200/ 17. Likewise, the importance of collaboration in mission means that all Jesuits, as men on mission, must also be men of collaboration. Ongoing formation in this area should be encouraged and supported within provinces and throughout Jesuit conferences. When undertaken together with collaborators, programs of professional development and spiritual enrichment can help us deepen our sense of common vision and our unity in mission.

201/ 18. The formation of Jesuits for collaboration, however, must be accompanied by a parallel formation of those with whom we minister, so that they might deepen their understanding of the mission they share with us. Diverse programs that respect and draw upon the wisdom and experience of the participants allow for a personal appropriation of the mission of the Society. Respecting various levels of connection and understanding, these programs invite each person—whether employee or volunteer, newly arrived or veteran, Christian believer or member of another faith community, or person without a religious affiliation—into a deeper awareness of his or her place in the Ignatian and Jesuit mission.

---

[10] *Exposcit Debitum* (1550), §3 (MHSI 63, 376).

[11] GC 34, D. 13, n. 4.

202/ 19. Such formation should provide professional skills, develop a special understanding of Ignatian spirituality regarding mission, and include opportunities for growth in the interior life. Part VII of the *Constitutions,* the Complementary Norms, and the Autobiography of St. Ignatius provide important insights, although the Spiritual Exercises is always primary.

203/ 20. A final dimension of formation for mission involves programs of preparation and support for collaborators in leadership positions. All those in leadership positions have a special relationship with the Society of Jesus. Since their challenging work is important for the mission of the Society, they need ongoing support and care from the Society and one another. Furthermore, they should receive suitable formation in the distinctive dimensions of our way of proceeding, especially the integration of apostolic discernment in decision making.

204/ 21. Recommendations:

a. We encourage Conferences and Assistancies to examine the program of Jesuit formation to ensure that all men in formation have appropriate experience of collaborative ministry.

b. We encourage Major Superiors (and Conferences, where appropriate) to assist in the continuing development of opportunities and structures for the ongoing formation of Jesuits in collaborative ministry.

c. We encourage Major Superiors (and Conferences, where appropriate) to assist in the continuing development of opportunities and structures for the formation of others who collaborate in the mission of the Society.

d. We encourage Major Superiors (and Conferences, where appropriate) to ensure the development of opportunities and structures for the appropriate formation of those in leadership positions in Jesuit ministries.

What Connections Might Make Our Work More Fruitful?

205/ 22. As means of communication develop, the Society works more effectively as an international body and seeks synergies in service of its universal mission. Jesuits are often engaged beyond their province boundaries in national and international networks and in collaboration with a variety of persons, including other Jesuits. Some of these international networks such as Jesuit Refugee Service, Fe y Alegría, and the African Jesuit AIDS Network are works of the Society. Others are collaborative projects. In all such works, however, the good accomplished is multiplied by participation of the Society in collaboration with diverse parties united in a common mission.

206/ 23. GC 34 invited the Society to develop an "Ignatian Apostolic Network"[12] among persons and associations that share an Ignatian commitment

---

[12] GC 34, D. 13, n. 21.

to service in the Church. In those places in which the Society has responded zealously to this call, cooperation is growing in programs for formation as well as in the discernment, planning, and execution of common projects. These networks enable men and women with common concerns to share their experience and make use of their expertise. In this they realize the ever-widening possibilities of our networking. Moreover, the Ignatian tradition, when expressed by various voices—women and men, religious and lay, movements and institutions, communities and individuals—becomes more welcoming and more vigorous, capable of enriching the whole Church.

207/ 24. The Society desires strong relationships in mission with as many collaborators in the Lord's vineyard as possible. Those asking to be more closely linked with the mission of the Society[13] normally come to this desire through an experience of the Spiritual Exercises.

208/ 25. Among the many different forms of collaboration, GC 34 considered a specific "closer personal bond" between individuals and the Society, whereby a lay person could be missioned by a Provincial. This relationship implies mutual commitments by the Society and the individual.[14] Sometimes called a "juridical bond," this manner of collaboration was authorized and recommended by GC 34 for an experimental period of 10 years, subject to evaluation by GC 35.

209/ 26. GC 35 affirms that this experiment was meant to be spiritual and mission focused,[15] rather than legal or canonical. Over the last 13 years, the experience of this specific form of "closer personal bond" has not been widespread in the Society, nor was there much demand for it. Some individuals became devoted to our common mission in this way, and they have contributed much to it. Occasionally, however, misperceptions arose as to what mutual expectations were, and collaborators without such a relationship wondered whether their manner of collaboration was somehow less valued than those with the "closer personal bond."

210/ 27. GC 35 acknowledges with sincere gratitude the contribution that has been made to the Society of Jesus and its mission by these experiences. However, after reviewing them, the Congregation concludes that it is preferable no longer to promote the special kind of spiritual bond which GC 34 described in D. 13, n. 23–25. Those who already have entered into this closer personal bond with the Society should be able to continue in it as long as local provincials discern with them that it is the best way to proceed in mission. But this option for such a spe-

---

[13] Cf. Peter-Hans Kolvenbach, S.I., *"Concernant les laïcs associés"* (25 February 2003), *AR* 23, no. 1 (2003): 102–103.

[14] GC 34, D. 13, nn. 23–25.

[15] This bond between the Society and the individual "is by its nature spiritual and apostolic, not legal." Peter-Hans Kolvenbach, S.I., *"Sobre la 'vinculación jurídica' de los laicos a la Compañía"* (17 March 1999), *AR* 22 (199–2002): 530–533.

cific "closer personal bond" should no longer be open to new candidates. As we continue to accompany those desiring to work in the mission of the Society, we can encourage them to live their vocation in one of the many ways of collaboration with which the Church has been blessed, especially since Vatican II has so clearly spelled out the mission of the laity in the Church. Among these are an increasing number of associations inspired by Ignatian spirituality.

211/ 28. We note with gratitude and joy the many autonomous associations with whom we share a spiritual bond, the fruit of which is greater and more effective service to the mission of Christ in the world. Among these, the Christian Life Community has roots that are deep in the charism and history of the Society. We wish to continue to support CLC in its journey towards ever-greater apostolic effectiveness and collaboration with the Society. Likewise, other Ignatian groups, including Jesuit alumni/ae associations, various Jesuit volunteer organizations, the Apostleship of Prayer, the Eucharistic Youth Movement, and many others deserve our continued spiritual accompaniment as well as our support for their apostolic service.

212/ 29. Recommendations:

a. We encourage the Society's government at all levels to explore means by which more effective networking might take place among all apostolic works associated with the Society of Jesus.

b. We encourage the Society's government at all levels to explore with other communities of Ignatian inspiration, both religious and lay, ways to promote and support an "Ignatian Family" or "Ignatian Community" which will have a common vision of service, will promote networks of mutual support, and will foster new and closer forms of collaboration locally, regionally, and internationally.

c. We encourage Superiors, especially Major Superiors, to seek ways to support and accompany CLC and other Ignatian-inspired autonomous associations locally, regionally, and nationally.

Conclusion

213/ 30. In his day, St. Ignatius gave shelter to the homeless of Rome, cared for prostitutes, and established homes for orphans. He sought collaborators and with them established organizations and networks to continue these and many other forms of service. To respond today to the pressing needs of our complex and fragile world, many hands are surely needed. Collaboration in mission is the way we respond to this situation: it expresses our true identity as members of the Church, the complementarity of our diverse calls to holiness,[16] our mutual responsibility for the mission of Christ,[17] our desire to join people of good will in the service of the human family, and the coming of the Kingdom of God. It is a grace given to us in this moment, one consistent with our Jesuit way of proceeding.

---

[16] Cf. John Paul II, *Vita Consecrata*, 12.

[17] 1 Cor. 12:12 ff.

OTHER DOCUMENTS

1. Issues for the Ordinary Government
   of the Society of Jesus Studied at the 35th General
   Congregation

2. Letter of Thanks to Fr. Peter-Hans Kolvenbach from
   the 35th General Congregation
   of the Society of Jesus

Issues for the Ordinary Government of the Society of Jesus Studied at the 35th General Congregation

Once the election of Father General was concluded,[1] the 35th General Congregation began to deal with agenda, *negotia*. To do this they accepted the proposal of the *Coetus Praevius* to organize the postulates by topics and to consider two main categories. One category consisted of five topics which were proposed for decrees: mission, identity, government, obedience, and laity; the other category consisted of five topics which were proposed as possible recommendations or mandates for the ordinary government of the Society: community, formation, vocation promotion, youth ministry, and the Jesuit Refugee Service.

After gathering the suggestions which had been made by the electors in meetings according to Assistancy, the General Congregation added ten other topics which were judged appropriate for consideration. With these additions the list of topics proposed for ordinary government was the following:

Africa	Religious Fundamentalism
Intellectual Apostolate	Brothers
International Houses in Rome	Youth Ministry
Communications	Migrants and Refugees
China	Indigenous Peoples
Ecology/Environment/Globalization	Community Life
Finances	Vocations
Formation	

The Congregation decided to form commissions to deal with these topics. Each commission prepared a document which was then presented and discussed in a plenary session. After receiving reactions, the commissions made proposals for action on the part of the ordinary government of the Society. In other plenary sessions the opinion of the General Congregation was sought by means of a vote. Some of the approved proposals were included in decrees; others were presented to Father General for his government; still others were directed to the Provinces and Conferences of Provincials and are included in this document.

---

[1] The General Congregation decided that, together with the official decrees of the Congregation, a narrative document should be published dealing with the discussions of the topics for the ordinary government, without including the suggestions directed to Father General. This document was entrusted to Father General, with the deliberative vote of the Fathers of the Curia who have the right to participate in a General Congregation due to their office.

The following is a summary of the discussions in the commissions and in the plenary sessions of the 35th General Congregation.

Africa: The delegates of the African Assistancy to the 35th General Congregation asked the Society to join their efforts to promote a better understanding of the continent. The negative image frequently presented by the media must be changed. We need to foster respect and unified action.

In Africa good work is being done in Jesuit institutions and there are advocacy efforts to prevent the forced displacement of peoples and the exploitation of resources. These initiatives, however, are not well known.

The African Jesuits are grateful for the international collaboration which has been offered to them and they invite Jesuits throughout the world to continue to join their apostolic efforts. Even though their continent has many needs, they offer themselves to collaborate in the universal mission of the Society beyond their own borders.[2]

Intellectual Apostolate: As the commission assigned to study this topic reflected on the tradition of the Society and the recent urging of Benedict XVI,[3] it originally proposed a decree. In the end it made three recommendations.

First, young Jesuits should be encouraged to consider this apostolate and to be assigned to it. In spite of the cost and time involved, it is indispensable to promote special studies among them without neglecting care for their personal and community life.

Second, it is crucial that the intellectual apostolate foster every possible form of collaboration among persons, teams, centers, and journals, promote working in networks, and choose institutions which can ensure excellence in research.

Third, Conferences and Provincials should care for the conservation and preservation of our intellectual patrimony or its distribution.[4]

International Houses in Rome: After an introduction to the topic by Father General's Delegate, the commission met with the members of the CIP (Permanent Interprovincial Commission for the Roman Houses), which explained its program.

---

[2] Africa is one of the global preferences established by Decree 3, n. 39 (i).

[3] Benedict XVI, *"To the Members of the Society of Jesus"* (22 April 2006), *AR* 23, no. 4 (2006): 676–679; *"Discourse to the 35th General Congregation of the Society of Jesus"* (21 February 2008), pp. 803–806 below.

[4] The intellectual apostolate is another of the global preferences established by the GC 35, Decree 3, n. 39 (iii).

It is important to engage in planning which involves not only a general framework for these works but also a reorganization and integration of administrative structures, as well as an improvement in the networking among them.

There is need to design a relevant pedagogical plan which includes not only the formation of professors and administrative staff but also the recruitment of highly talented students.

The commission pointed out some ad intra tasks: the relationships between Superiors and Directors of the Roman institutions and between the Delegate and the Provincials, the type of religious community which is helpful to young professors and the reentry of retiring professors into their Provinces.[5]

Communications: The commission appointed to discuss this topic first pointed out how important the world of communications is for our vocation as evangelizers. Our whole history bears witness to the efforts that have been made to find better and more effective means to evangelize. We are, however, in a new world. Modern means of communication and new technologies demand that we adapt our way of proceeding to today's generation, which lives in a continuous process of change.[6]

The commission also spoke about concrete topics, for example, a review of the norms for publication and a possible broadening of them to include what is placed on the Internet. The General Congregation asked that communication be given special attention during formation and it urged Provinces and Conferences to promote creative and apostolic use of the Internet.

China: The 35th General Congregation discussed the situation of China because this country has become a global power which cannot be neglected.

The commission charged with this topic explained how experts on China view its economic power, its impressive rate of growth, the rapid decrease in poverty and areas of tension.

The commission spoke about advances in the area of religious freedom as well as the positive contribution which persons of different faiths have made to the construction of a better Chinese society. Finally, the commission mentioned

---

[5] The Roman Houses are another of the global preferences established by the Decree. The intellectual apostolate is another of the global preferences established by the GC 35, Decree 3, n. 39 (iv).

[6] Cfr. GC 35, D. 3, n. 29

the letter of Benedict VXI to Catholics in China[7] and the generally positive reaction which it received.[8]

Ecology/Environment/Globalization: The 35th General Congregation wished to discuss these topics as a whole and appointed a commission for this task. During the discussion which took place in a plenary session, reference was made to the magnitude and complexity of this phenomenon.[9] For this reason it is essential that we collaborate with individuals and institutions in establishing networks.

In collaborating with others, Jesuits must not forget the specific contribution which the Christian faith can make to this topic. It is sad that the contribution of the Society[10] in this area is too little known and made use of, even by Jesuits.

The General Congregation recommends that the Provinces draw up guidelines so that individual Jesuits as well as Jesuit communities and institutions may use their resources in an ecologically responsible way.

Finances: In a plenary session the General Treasurer of the Society presented the economic situation of the Society in the context of the world economic situation. He emphasized how this situation affects the resources available to many Provinces and the capacity of the Society to obtain and distribute them. He stressed the necessity of making decisions which would lead to a better use of the resources which are available. To achieve this goal Jesuits are needed who are competent in planning, administration, and accounting, and who can assure transparency and good management.

The General Treasurer suggested some concrete courses of action: the creation of adequate structures to obtain funds, the reinforcement of mechanisms for reaching decisions with the help of advisors and consultants, a knowledge and application of the Statutes on Poverty and the Instruction on the Administration of Goods, and the formation of men in administration.

Formation: In a plenary session the commission in charge of this topic presented the positive and negative aspects of formation in the Society. Among the successes are the excellent documents for all stages of formation and greater interprovincial collaboration. On the negative side, mention must be made of the difficulty in

---

[7] Benedict XVI, *"Letter to the Bishops, Presbyters . . . of the Catholic Church in the People's Republic of China"* (27 May 2007).

[8] China is another of the global preferences established by the Decree "Challenges for Our Mission Today: Sent to the Frontiers," no. 39 (ii).

[9] Cfr. GC 35, D. 3, nn. 31–36.

[10] Secretariat for Social Justice: "We Live in a Broken World," *Promotio Iustitiae*, no. 70, April 1999;

"Globalization and Marginality: Our Apostolic Global Response", February 2006.

adapting formation to the diverse candidates who come to the novitiate as well as of the rapid rate of cultural change which affects young men and hinders their integration into the Jesuit way of proceeding.

It is a challenge for formation to find not only adequate pedagogies but also a sufficient number of trained men who are able to work in formation. There was a consensus that the main "formator" is the body of the Society and that all Jesuits, therefore, must assume their part of the responsibility for formation.

Religious Fundamentalism and Dialogue: From the beginning this commission stressed the multifaceted character of fundamentalism. Jesuits have to make an effort to understand it in all its complexity. The 35th General Congregation reaffirmed the commitment of the Society to interreligious and cultural dialogue and recognized the work being carried out in this field.[11]

Now Jesuits are asked to accept the difficult task of expanding this dialogue to religious fundamentalism, of entering into contact with it, of improving activities in networks, and of cooperating with secretariats and organizations committed to dialogue.

Brothers: The commission appointed by the 35th General Congregation was composed mostly of brothers and presented several practical proposals in a plenary session.

The commission first proposed that the government of the Society always keep the brothers in mind when planning programs for studies for Jesuits in formation.

It was suggested there be some programs of formation specifically for brothers, as is already being done in some parts of the Society. The "Alphonsus Month" would be an example. Attention should be given to the ongoing formation of formed brothers.

Youth Ministry: Although only three postulates on this topic were received, the General Congregation decided to appoint a commission to study it. After reviewing the most successful experiences, the commission identified the principal points of youth ministry and the new challenges emerging since the 34th General Congregation.

The reality of young people depends on the geographical context. In some areas what is needed is listening to young people and promoting a deeper spirituality; in other areas the accent is on inviting young people to participate in social projects or in reaching out to and engaging young people who are not involved.

The Congregation suggests that each Conference consider whether it would be helpful to appoint a coordinator of youth ministry.

---

[11] GC 35, D. 3, nn. 3–4.

Migrants and Refugees: In a presentation during a plenary session, the commission noted that since the founding of the Jesuit Refugee Service in 1980, the phenomenon of "people in movement" has become more complex. Some migrants move to another country of their own free will; others are forced to move, sometimes to another place within their own country, because of war, natural disasters and even human trafficking. They are received with hostility, and weak legal structures do not protect their rights.

The General Congregation asks that the Society continue to support the JRS with the assignment of Jesuits and other resources and to promote close collaboration between the Provinces/Conferences and the JRS. It also urges all Provinces, through their institutions, to promote the integration of migrants into the society which receives them.[12]

Indigenous Peoples: The 35th General Congregation received numerous postulates on this topic. In a plenary session the commission which studied them emphasized the fact that today there about 370,000,000 indigenous people[13] spread throughout the world and that they represent a rich cultural heritage and an important legacy of civilization.

Because of various political and socioeconomic factors, the indigenous peoples are among the most marginalized and exploited. The process of globalization, which is partly responsible for environmental degradation and the pillage of natural resources, has a particular effect on them. In addition, climatic change continues to seriously harm them.

Since this situation threatens the very survival of these peoples, the Society should increase its commitment to them. The General Congregation suggests that in every area where this challenge exists, the Conference of Provincials form "work groups" of Jesuits working in this apostolate.

Community Life: The commission which was charged with this topic originally wanted to make a decree. Although the proposal was not accepted, the plenary session provided the opportunity for a rich discussion on community as a part of the mission of the Society and not merely as a locus for its members to restore their energies for the apostolate. It was stated that the Kingdom of God has need of clear signs in this world and that the quality of our community life is one of them. This presupposes grace, but also an effort to experience personal and community conversion, to share faith, to discern, and to adopt an austere lifestyle close to the poor. If Jesuit communities are not going to be mere residences but signs of the Kingdom of God, the office of Superior, according to the Ignatian way of proceeding, has to assume its crucial importance.

---

[12] This is another global preference established in GC35, D. 3, n° 39 (v).

[13] Cf. United Nations: *Permanent Forum on Indigenous Issues (UMPFII),* p. 1.

Vocations: The commission evaluated the implementation of Father Kolvenbach's letter on vocation promotion. It paid particular attention to the cultural changes which make the countercultural and lifelong commitment of a religious very difficult.

There has certainly been progress in this area. There is a growing awareness that all Jesuits are responsible for vocation promotion.[14] Stable structures have been set up for vocational promotion and follow-up. The Society has greater experience of and confidence in the pedagogy of the Exercises as applied to young men.

Some problems still remain, such as the lack of articulation between youth and vocational ministry and the lack of spiritual directors for young men. Some Jesuits, unfortunately, are not convinced and concerned about vocation promotion.

The General Congregation invites the Society to put into practice what has already been established on these topics and hopes that the treatment that has been given here will be an effective aid in the ordinary government of the Society.

---

[14] Peter-Hans Kolvenbach S.I., *"Sobre la promoción de vocaciones"* (29 September 1997), *AR* 22 (1996–2002): 158–161.

LETTER OF THANKS TO PETER-HANS KOLVENBACH FROM GC 35 OF THE SOCIETY OF JESUS

Tuesday, 4 March 2008

The Reverend Father Peter-Hans Kolvenbach, S.J.
Curia Generalizia della Compagnia di Gesù
Borgo Santo Spirito 4
CP 1639 ROMA

Dear Father Kolvenbach:
The Peace of Christ!

On the morning of Saturday, March 1, shortly before you took your leave of us, we had the opportunity to thank you in person for the outstanding contribution you made to our Society during your twenty-four years and more as Superior General. Our farewell came from the heart: both the warm words of Fr. Nicolás and our spontaneous and affectionate response expressed not only our sentiments but those of our brother Jesuits around the world.

We could not end this General Congregation, however, without providing you with this written record of our gratitude and esteem, one which gives brief and no doubt inadequate expression to our conviction that your years as General have been a great grace for us. For this grace, we now give God thanks as we shall no doubt continue to do for a long time to come.

Many of us have reason to know something of the burdens carried by those in leadership positions in the Church and of the increasing complexity of their work. As over the years we have set about our many tasks, we have been unfailingly supported by your own devotion to duty. This involved a daily schedule of work that would have taxed a man many years younger than yourself.

We have all benefited from your wisdom, your sense of humor, your precise attention to detail, and from your already legendary capacity to remember people and places in our provinces often better than we can ourselves. On a number of occasions during this Congregation, we have had reason to appreciate once again the fruits of your profound sense of *sentire cum ecclesia* and of your devotion to our vocation "to serve as a soldier of God beneath the banner of the Cross

. . . and to serve the Lord alone and his Church, under the Roman Pontiff, the Vicar of Christ on Earth."

Your governance was also always personal. Your many letters, your lunches with those visiting the Curia, and your visits to our provinces and regions, where you met so many Jesuits and collaborators, shook as many hands, and participated in numerous meetings, made the central government of the Society present to us in a way that has both inspired us and encouraged us.

The challenges that faced the Society in the years of your generalate were considerable. These were years of rapid change both in the Church and in the wider world, changes from which the Society could not be, nor would wish to be, immune.

It was your gift to motivate us to take up the opportunities for mission provided by these new contexts. As our work expanded on the new geographical frontiers of the Church, we also explored those equally challenging frontiers where many faiths and cultures meet. While it was always your way to support provincials in the exercise of their local responsibilities, you nonetheless challenged us to respond generously to the universal mission of the Society and to put our sometimes scarce resources at the service of the greater need. The development of conferences of major superiors, which you promoted, and the apostolic preferences for the whole Society, which you identified, will surely enable this more universal perspective to come to still greater prominence in the years ahead.

It was always your desire to encourage the Society in its life with the Lord and in its fidelity to the Ignatian charism. To this end, you wrote us many inspirational letters, on aspects of formation, discernment, poverty, community life, and the Eucharist, to name but a few. These were all the more valuable to us because they were clearly informed by your own personal prayer and reflection.

In these letters, as in your articles, addresses, talks, and homilies, you taught us to ground ourselves in the experience of the first companions. At the same time, you demonstrated an acute understanding of the challenges which face those who live our life today. What you have written will nourish the quality of our religious life for many years to come. The attention you gave to bringing the *Complementary Norms* to fruition, moreover, will long remain a sign to us of the care we should have for the Constitutions of our Society.

Meanwhile, you also encouraged us to be not only "men for others" but "men with others." You have seen, as we have, so much new energy and enthusiasm coming to our service of the Church from those many others who have also been called to follow the path of Ignatius and with whom we now more readily, and more constructively, collaborate in mission.

Nowhere has this collaboration borne more fruit than in our service of the poor, not least in our accompaniment of refugees and forced migrants. The work of the Jesuit Refugee Service has, with your unflagging support, expanded considerably during your years as General. It is just one of the many ways in which we give witness both to a faith that does justice and to our conviction that we cannot be companions of Jesus unless we are also companions, as he was, with those who have least.

During the Jubilee Year which you opened in December 2005, you reminded us that our vocation is above all a missionary vocation, as it was for Francis Xavier, which has its origins in that ever-deeper encounter with Jesus himself in the *Spiritual Exercises* of Ignatius. This vocation finds its expression in that warm and devoted companionship epitomized by Peter Faber: a companionship with Jesus, with one another and with those whom it is our privilege to serve as we engage in our mission of faithful service to the Church. This was the vocation you promoted amongst us and you did so, first and foremost, by embodying it yourself.

May the Lord bless you with safe travels, good health, and many years of happiness as you return to serve the Church and the Society in Lebanon.

While assuring you of our continued prayers, our very best wishes and our profound gratitude, we remain

Your devoted brothers in Christ

The Members of the
Thirty-Fifth General Congregation
of the Society of Jesus

COMPLEMENTARY DOCUMENTATION

(in chronological order)

1. Letter of Fr. General Peter-Hans Kolvenbach to Major Superiors and Electors of GC 35, Conveying the Response of Pope Benedict XVI (21 February 2007)

2. Homily of Franc Cardinal Rodé, C.M., to the Members of GC 35 (7 January 2008)

3. Letter of Pope Benedict XVI to Fr. General Peter-Hans Kolvenbach, S.J. (10 January 2008)

4. Letter of GC 35 Expressing Gratitude to Fr. Peter-Hans Kolvenbach (14 January 2008)

5. Letter of Gratitude from Fr. Peter-Hans Kolvenbach to GC 35 (14 January 2008)

6. Letter of Fr. Peter-Hans Kolvenbach Acknowledging the Exhortation of Pope Benedict XVI to GC 35 (15 January 2008)

7. Homily of Fr. Frank Case, S.J., at the Mass of the Holy Spirit (19 January 2008)

8. Homily of Fr. General Adolfo Nicolás in the Church of the Gesù, at the Mass of Thanksgiving (20 January 2008)

9. Words Spoken by Fr. General Adolfo Nicolás in the Presence of Pope Benedict XVI (21 February 2008)

10. Address of Pope Benedict XVI to the 35th General Congregation of the Society of Jesus (21 February 2008)

11. First Greetings of Fr. General Adolfo Nicolás to the Whole Society (22 February 2008)

12. Homily of Fr. General Adolfo Nicolás in the Gesù at the Conclusion of GC 35 (6 March 2008)

1. Letter of Father General Peter-Hans Kolvenbach to Major Superiors and Electors of GC 35, Conveying the Response of Pope Benedict XVI

Rome, 21 February 2007

Dear Father,

As material for your meetings and discussions in preparation for the 35th General Congregation, I would like to share with you a decision and a desire that the Holy Father recently communicated to me.

In accord with our Constitutions, last January 24 I submitted to the Holy Father the issue about whether or not to maintain the *ad vitam* mandate of the Superior General of the Society. This issue had been discussed previously by the commission on juridical matters in preparation for the General Congregation.

In his response of January 29, the Holy Father determined that the term of the Superior General remain *ad vitam,* while maintaining the General's right to resign in special cases after having first informed the Holy Father of his intention. The Holy Father's agreement then allows the whole process laid out in the Constitutions and the *Complementary Norms* for the convocation of a General Congregation *ad electionem* to begin. Thus the Holy Father has confirmed the present practice.

Furthermore, the Holy Father expressed the desire that the General Congregation reflect on the spiritual and ecclesial formation of young Jesuits, and also on the value and observance of the fourth vow for the whole Society. The Holy Father had already mentioned this concern in his address to the Society in the Basilica of St. Peter on 22 April 2006. The commission that is preparing a document on obedience in the Society will give this deeply Ignatian characteristic of our apostolic commitment its due importance. It merits our attention during this time of preparation. The Society, in effect, completely submits its judgment and its will to Christ Our Lord and to his Vicar (Cf. *Constitutions,* 606).

I assure you of my union of prayer and of work in the preparation for the upcoming General Congregation.

Fraternally yours in the Lord,

Peter-Hans Kolvenbach, S.J.
Superior General

2. Homily of Franc Card. Rodé, C.M. to the Members of GC 35

7 January 2008

Dear members of General Congregation 35 of the Society of Jesus:

St. Ignatius considered the General Congregation "work and a distraction" (*Const.* 677) which momentarily interrupts the apostolic commitments of a large number of qualified members of the Society of Jesus and for this reason, clearly differing from what is customary in other religious Institutes, the Constitutions establish that it should not be celebrated at determined times and not too often.

Nevertheless, it must be called principally on two occasions: for the election of the Superior General and when things of particular importance or very difficult problems which touch the body of the Society must be treated.

This is the second time in the history of the Society wherein a General Congregation gathers to elect a new Superior General while his predecessor is still living. The first time was in 1983, when the 33rd General Congregation accepted the resignation of the much loved Fr. Arrupe, for whom the exercising of the role of governance had become impossible because of a serious and unforeseen illness. Today it gathers a second time, to discern, before the Lord, the resignation presented by Fr. Kolvenbach, who has directed the Society for nearly twenty-five years with wisdom, prudence, commitment, and loyalty. This will be followed by the election of his successor. I wish to express to you, Fr. Kolvenbach, in my name and in the name of the Church, a heartfelt thanks for your fidelity, your wisdom, your righteousness, and your example of humility and poverty. Thank you, Fr. Kolvenbach.

The election of a new Superior General of the Society of Jesus has a fundamental value for the life of the Society, not only because its centralized hierarchical structure constitutionally concedes to the General full authority for good governance, the conservation and growth of the whole Society, but also because, as St. Ignatius says so well, "the well-being of the head resounds throughout the whole body, and as are the Superiors so in turn will their subjects be" (*Const.* 820). For this reason your founder, when pointing out the qualities which the general must have, places first of all that he must be "a man very united to the Lord our God and familiar with prayer" (*Const.* 723). After having mentioned other important qualities which are not easily found in a single person, he ends by saying, "if any of the above qualities should be missing, at least may he not lack much goodness, love for the Society, and good judgment" (*Const.* 735).

I join you in your prayer that the Holy Spirit, the father of the poor, giver of graces, and light for hearts, will assist you in your discernment and your election.

This Congregation also gathers together to treat important and very difficult matters which touch all members of the Society, such as the direction which the Society is presently taking. The themes upon which the General Congregation will reflect have to do with basic elements for the life of the Society. Certainly you will deal with the identity of today's Jesuit, on the meaning and value of the vow of obedience to the Holy Father which has always defined your religious family, the mission of the Society in the context of globalization and marginalization, community life, apostolic obedience, vocation recruitment, and other important themes.

Within your charism and your tradition you can find valuable points of reference to enlighten the choices which the Society must make today.

Certainly and necessarily, during this Congregation you are carrying out an important work, but it is not a "distraction" from your apostolic activity. As St. Ignatius teaches you in the *Spiritual Exercises,* you must, with the same vision of the three Divine Persons, look at "the entire surface of the earth crammed with men" (n. 102). Listening to the Spirit, the creator who renews the world, and returning to the fonts to preserve your identity without losing your own lifestyle, the commitment to discern the signs of the times, the difficulty and responsibility of working out final decisions are activities which are eminently apostolic because they form the base of a new springtime of being religious and of the apostolic commitment of each of your brothers in the Society of Jesus.

Now the vision becomes broader. It is not only for your own Jesuit brothers that you provide a religious and apostolic formation. There are many institutes of Consecrated Life who, following an Ignatian spirituality, pay attention to your choices; there are many future priests in your Colleges and Universities who are preparing for their ministry. There are many peoples from both within and outside the Church who frequent your centers of learning, seeking a response to the challenges which science, technology, and globalization pose to humanity, to the Church, and to the faith, with the hope of receiving a formation which will make it possible for them to construct a world of truth and freedom, of justice and peace.

Your work must be eminently apostolic with a universal human, ecclesial, and evangelical fullness. It must always be carried out in the light of your Charism, in such a way that the growing participation of laity in your activities does not obscure your identity but rather enriches it with the collaboration of those who, coming from other cultures, share your style and your objectives.

Once again I join in your prayer that the Holy Spirit may accompany you in your delicate work.

As a brother who is following your works with great interest and expectation, I want to share with you "the joys and hopes" (*GS* 1) as well as "the sorrows and anguish" (*GS* 1) which I have as a man of the Church, called to exercise a difficult service in the field of Consecrated Life in my role as Prefect of the Congregation for Institutes of Consecrated Life and Societies of Apostolic Life.

With pleasure and hope I see the thousands of religious who generously respond to the Lord's call and, leaving all they have behind, consecrate themselves with an undivided heart to the Lord to be with him and to collaborate with him, in his salvific desire to "conquer all things and thus enter unto the Glory of the Father" (*Spiritual Exercises*, 95). It is clear that consecrated life continues to be a "divine gift which the Church has received from the Lord" (*LG* 43), and it is for this very reason that the Church wants to watch over it carefully in order that the proper Charism of each Institute might be ever more known and, although with the necessary adaptations to respond to the present time, that it keeps its proper identity intact for the good of the whole Church. The authenticity of religious life is characterized by the following of Christ and by the exclusive consecration to him and to his Kingdom through the profession of the evangelical counsels. The Second Vatican Ecumenical Council teaches that "this consecration will be the more perfect, in as much as the indissoluble bond of the union of Christ and his bride, the Church, is represented by firm and more stable bonds" (*LG* 44). Consecration to service to Christ cannot be separated from consecration to service to the Church. Ignatius and his first companions considered it thus when they wrote the Formula of your Institute, in which the essence of your charism is spelled out: "To serve the Lord and his Spouse the Church under the Roman Pontiff" (Julio III, *Formula* I). It is with sorrow and anxiety that I see that the *sentire cum ecclesia* of which your founder frequently spoke is diminishing even in some members of religious families. The Church is waiting for a light from you to restore the *sensus Ecclesiae*. The *Spiritual Exercises of St. Ignatius* are your specialty. The rules of *sentire cum Ecclesia* form an integral and essential part of this masterpiece of Catholic spirituality. They form, as it were, a golden clasp which holds the book of the *Spiritual Exercises* closed.

You hold in your very hands the elements needed to realize and to deepen this desire, this Ignatian and Ecclesial sentiment.

Love for the Church in every sense of the word—be it Church people of God, be it hierarchical Church—is not a human sentiment which comes and goes according to the people who make it up or according to our conformity with the dispositions emanating from those whom the Lord has placed to direct the Church. Love for the Church is a love based on faith, a gift of the Lord which, precisely because he loves us, he gives us—faith in him and in his Spouse, which is the Church. Without the gift of faith in the Church, there can be no love for the Church.

I join in your prayer, asking the Lord to grant you the grace to grow in your belief in and love for this holy, catholic, and apostolic Church which we profess.

With sadness and anxiety I also see a growing distancing from the Hierarchy. The Ignatian spirituality of apostolic service "under the Roman Pontiff" does not allow for this separation. In the Constitutions which he left you, Ignatius wanted to truly shape your mind, and in the book of the *Exercises* (n. 353) he wrote, "we must always keep our mind prepared and quick to obey the true Spouse of Christ and our Holy Mother, the Hierarchical Church." Religious obedience can be understood only as obedience in love. The fundamental nucleus of Ignatian spirituality consists in uniting the love for God with love for the hierarchical Church. Your 33rd Congregation once again took up this characteristic of obedience, declaring that "the Society reaffirms in a spirit of faith the traditional bond of love and of service which unites it to the Roman Pontiff." You once again took up this principle in the motto "In all things love and serve."

You must also place this 35th General Congregation, which opens with this liturgy, celebrated close to the remains of your founder, in this tradition, which always been followed by the Society throughout its multi-century history, in order to show your desire and your commitment to be faithful to the charism which he left you as an inheritance, and to carry it out in ways which better respond to the needs of the Church in our time.

The service of the Society is a service "under the banner of the Cross" (*Formula* I). Every service done out of love necessarily implies a self-emptying, a *kenosis*. But letting go of what one wants to do in order to do what the beloved wants is to transform the *kenosis* into the image of Christ who *learned obedience through suffering* (Heb. 5:8). It is for this reason that St. Ignatius, realistically, adds that the Jesuit serves the Church "under the banner of the Cross" (*Formula* I).

Ignatius placed himself under the orders of the Roman Pontiff "in order to not err *in via Domini*" (*Const.* 605) in the distribution of his religious throughout the world and to be present wherever the needs of the Church were greater.

Times have changed and the Church must today confront new and urgent necessities. I will mention one, which in my judgment is urgent today and is at the same time complex, and I propose it for your consideration. It is the need to present to the faithful and to the world the authentic truth revealed in Scripture and Tradition. The doctrinal diversity of those who at all levels, by vocation and mission, are called to announce the Kingdom of truth and love disorients the faithful and leads to a relativism without limits. There is one truth, even though it can always be more deeply known.

It is the "living teaching office of the Church, whose authority is exercised in the name of Jesus Christ" (*DV* 10) which is the voucher for revealed truth.

The exegetes and theological scholars are involved in working together *"under the watchful care of the sacred teaching office of the Church, to an exploration and exposition of the divine writings (DV 23)*. Through your long and solid formation, your centers of research, your teaching in the philosophical-theological-biblical fields, you are in a privileged position to carry out this difficult mission. Carry it out with study and in-depth examination, carry it out with humility, carry it out with faith in the Church, carry it out with love for the Church.

May those who, according to your legislation, have to oversee the doctrine of your magazines and publications do so in the light of and according to the "rules for *sentire cum ecclesia,*" with love and respect.

The feeling of ever-growing separation between faith and culture, a separation which constitutes a great impediment for Evangelization (*Sapientia Cristiana,* proemio), also worries me.

A culture imbued with a true Christian spirit is an instrument which fosters the spreading of the Gospel, faith in God the Creator of the heavens and of the earth. The Tradition of the Society, from the first beginnings of the Collegio Romano, always placed itself at the crossroads between Church and society, between faith and culture, between religion and secularism. Recover these avant-garde, positions which are so necessary to transmit the eternal truth to today's world, in today's language. Do not abandon this challenge. We know the task is difficult, uncomfortable, and risky, and at times little appreciated and even misunderstood; but it is a necessary task for the Church. The apostolic tasks demanded of you by the Church are many and very diverse; but all have a common denominator: the instrument which carries them out, according to an Ignatian phrase, must be an instrument united to God. It is the Ignatian echo to the Gospel proclaimed today: I *am the vine, you are the branches. He who remains in me and I in him will bear much fruit* (John 15:15). Union with the vine, which is love, is realized only through a personal and silent exchange of love which is born in prayer, "from the internal knowledge of the Lord who became man for me and who, integral and alive, extends himself to all who are close to us and to all that is close to us." It is not possible to transform the world, or to respond to the challenges of a world which has forgotten love, without being firmly rooted in love.

Ignatius was granted the mystic grace of being "a contemplative in action" (Annotation to the Examen, MNAD 5, 172).[1] It was a special grace freely given by God to Ignatius who had trodden a tiring path of fidelity and long hours of prayer in the Retreat at Manresa. It is a grace which, according to Fr. Nadal, is contained in the call of every Jesuit. Guided by your Ignatian *magis,* keep your hearts open to receive the same gift, following in the same path trod-

---

[1] See also "In examen annotationes," *Epistolae P. Hieronymi Nadal,* Monumenta Historica Societatis Iesu (Madrid: 1905) 4:651. *–Ed.*

den by Ignatius from Loyola to Rome, a path of generosity, of penance, of discernment, of prayer, of apostolic zeal, of obedience, of charity, of fidelity to and love for the hierarchical Church.

Despite the urgent apostolic needs, maintain and develop your charism to the point of being and showing yourselves to the world as "contemplatives in action," who communicate to men and women and to all of creation the love received from God and to orient them once again toward the love of God. Everyone understands the language of love.

The Lord has chosen you to go and bear fruit, fruit that lasts. Go, bear fruit, confident that "*all that you ask the Father in my name, he will give you*" (cf. John 15:16).

I join with you in prayer to the Father through the Son and in the Holy Spirit together with Mary, Mother of Divine Grace, invoked by all the members of the Society as *Santa Maria della Strada,* that he may grant you the grace of "seeking and discovering the will of God for the Society of today which will build the Society of tomorrow."

3. LETTER OF POPE BENEDICT XVI TO FATHER GENERAL PETER-HANS KOLVENBACH, S.J.

19 January 2008

On the occasion of the 35th General Congregation of the Society of Jesus, it is my fervent desire to extend to you and to all those taking part in the Assembly my most cordial greetings, together with an assurance of my affection and of my constant spiritual nearness to you. I know how important for the life of the Society is this event which you are celebrating, and I further know that, consequently, it has been prepared with great care. This is a providential occasion for impressing upon the Society of Jesus that renewed ascetic and apostolic impulse which is wished by all, so that Jesuits might fulfill completely their mission and confront the challenges of the modern world with that faith in Christ and in the Church which distinguished the prophetic action of St. Ignatius of Loyola and his first companions.

The Apostle writes to the faithful of Thessalonica of having announced to them the gospel of God, "encouraging you and imploring you"—Paul specifies— "to comport yourselves in a manner worthy of God who calls you to his kingdom and to his glory" (1 Thes. 2:12); and he adds, "Indeed on account of this we continually thank God because, having received the divine word preached by us, you welcomed it not as the word of men, but as it truly is, as the word of God, which works in you who believe" (1 Thes. 2:13). The word of God therefore is first "received," i.e., heard, and then—penetrating all the way to the heart—it is "welcomed," and who receives it recognizes that God speaks through the agent sent to deliver it: in this way the word acts in believers. As then, so even today, evangelization demands a total and faithful adhesion to the word of God: adhesion first of all to Christ and to attentive listening to his Spirit which guides the Church; humble obedience to the Pastors whom God has placed to guide his people; and prudent and frank dialogue with the social, cultural, and religious appeals of our time. All this presupposes, as we know, an intimate communion with him who calls us to be friends and disciples, a unity of life and of action which is fed by listening to his word, by contemplation and by prayer, by detachment from the mentality of the world and by unceasing conversion toward his love so that it may be he, the Christ, who lives and works in each of us. Here is the secret of authentic success for the apostolic and missionary commitment of every Christian and, even more, of all those called to a more direct service of the Gospel.

Such an awareness is certainly well present among those taking part in the General Congregation, and I am eager to honor the great work already completed by the preparatory commission, which in the course of 2007 has examined the postulates sent by Provinces and indicated the themes to be faced. I would like to direct my thoughts of gratitude in the first place to you, dear and venerated Father Superior General, who since 1983 has guided the Society of Jesus in an enlightened, wise, and prudent manner, seeking in every way to maintain it in the channel of its founding charism. For objective reasons, you have at various times asked to be relieved of so heavy a post, assumed with a great sense of responsibility at a moment in your Order's history which was not easy. I express to you my most heartfelt gratitude for the service you have rendered to the Society of Jesus and, more generally, to the Church. My sentiments of gratitude extend to your closest collaborators, to the participants of the General Congregation, and to all Jesuits scattered in every part of the world. To all and to each should arrive this greeting from the Successor of Peter, who follows with affection and esteem the multiple and appreciated apostolic works of the Jesuits, and who encourages all to continue in the path opened by your holy Founder and walked by innumerable hosts of your brothers dedicated to the cause of Christ, many of whom are inscribed by the Church among its saints and blessed. From heaven may they protect and sustain the Society of Jesus in the mission which it carries out in this our current age, marked by numerous and complex social, cultural, and religious challenges.

Indeed regarding this theme, how can one not recognize the valid contribution which the Society offers to the Church's activity in various fields and in many ways? Truly a great and meritorious contribution, one which only the Lord will be able to rightly reward! As did my venerated Predecessors, the Servants of God Paul VI and John Paul II, I too gladly wish to take this opportunity of a General Congregation to bring such a contribution to light and, at the same time, to offer for your common reflection some considerations which might be of encouragement for you and a stimulus to implement ever better the ideal of the Society, in full fidelity to the Magisterium of the Church, such as described in the following formula which is well familiar to you: "To serve as a soldier of God beneath the banner of the Cross and to serve the Lord alone and the Church, his spouse, under the Roman Pontiff, the Vicar of Christ on earth" (Apostolic Letter *Exposcit debitum*, 21 July 1550). One treats here of a "peculiar" fidelity confirmed also, by not a few among you, in a vow of immediate obedience to the Successor of Peter "*perinde ac cadaver.*" The Church has even more need today of this fidelity of yours, which constitutes a distinctive sign of your Order, in this era which warns of the urgency of transmitting in an integral manner to our contemporaries—distracted by many discordant voices—the unique and immutable message of salvation which is the Gospel, "not as the word of men, but as it truly is, as the word of God," which works in those who believe.

That this might come to pass, it is indispensable—as earlier the beloved John Paul II reminded participants of the 34th General Congregation—that the life of the members of the Society of Jesus, as also their doctrinal research, be always animated by a true spirit of faith and communion in "humble fidelity to the teachings of the Magisterium" (Insegnamenti, vol. I, pp. 25–32). I heartily hope that the present Congregation affirms with clarity the authentic charism of the Founder so as to encourage all Jesuits to promote true and healthy Catholic doctrine. As Prefect of the Congregation for the Doctrine of the Faith, I had the opportunity to appreciate the valid collaboration of Jesuit Consultors and experts, who, in full fidelity to their charism, contributed in a considerable way to the faithful promotion and reception of the Magisterium. Certainly this is not a simple undertaking, especially when called to announce the Gospel in very different social and cultural contexts and when having to deal with different mentalities. I therefore sincerely appreciate such labor placed at the service of Christ, labor which is fruitful for the true good of souls in the measure in which one lets oneself be guided by the Spirit, remaining humble as regards the teachings of the Magisterium, having reference to those key principles of the ecclesial vocation of the theologian which are delineated in the Instruction *Donum veritatis*.

The evangelizing work of the Church very much counts on the formative responsibility which the Society has in the areas of theology, of spirituality, and of mission. And, really so as to offer the entire Society of Jesus a clear orientation which might be a support for generous and faithful apostolic dedication, it could prove extremely useful that the General Congregation reaffirm, in the spirit of St. Ignatius, its own total adhesion to Catholic doctrine, in particular on those neuralgic points which today are strongly attacked by secular culture, as for example the relationship between Christ and religions; some aspects of the theology of liberation; and various points of sexual morality, especially as regards the indissolubility of marriage and the pastoral care of homosexual persons.

Reverend and dear Father, I am convinced that the Society senses the historic importance of this General Congregation and, guided by the Holy Spirit, wants once again—as the beloved John Paul II said in January 1995—to reaffirm "unequivocally and without any hesitation its specific way to God, which St. Ignatius sketched in the *Formula Instituti:* loving fidelity to your charism will be the certain source of renewed effectiveness" (Insegnamenti, vol. XVIII/1, 1995, p. 26). Furthermore, the words my venerated Predecessor Paul VI directed to the Society in another analogous circumstance appear so very current: "All of us must be vigilant so that the necessary adaptation will not be accomplished to the detriment of the fundamental identity or essential character of the role of the Jesuit as is described in the *Formula Instituti,* as the history and particular spirituality of the Order propose it, and as the authentic interpretation of the very needs of the times seem still to require it. This image must not be altered; it must not be distorted" (Insegnamenti, vol. XII, 1974, pp. 1181–1182).

The continuity of the teachings of the Successors of Peter stands to demonstrate the great attention and care which they show toward the Jesuits, their esteem for you, and the desire to be able to count always on the precious contribution of the Society to the life of the Church and to the evangelization of the world. I entrust the General Congregation and the entire Society of Jesus to the intercession of your holy Founder and the saints of your Order, and to the maternal protection of Mary, so that every spiritual son of St. Ignatius might be able to keep before his eyes "first of all God and then the nature of this his Institute" (*Formula Instituti,* 1). With such sentiments, I assure you of a constant remembrance in prayer and in a heartfelt way I impart to you, Reverend Father, and to the Fathers of the General Congregation and to the entire Society of Jesus, a special Apostolic Blessing.

Benedict PP XVI

Vatican, 10 January 2008

4. Letter of GC 35 Expressing Gratitude to Fr. Peter-Hans Kolvenbach S.I.

Rome, 14 January 2008

Now that General Congregation 35 has accepted your resignation, it is fitting that this same Congregation gathered here today express, in the whole Society's name, its profound gratitude to you for your crucial service, as missioned by the Lord, to the Church and to the Society.

First of all, we wish to tell you how edified we are with your manner of submitting your resignation, namely, in that freedom of spirit that frames the Gospel and the Exercises. The example you give us today, of course, is very different from what commonly is found in a world characterized by the clinging to and fighting for positions of power and prestige. Our charism and legislation are not good merely because they propose beautiful ideals, but precisely because there are people who know how to embody and live them.

We are most especially grateful to you for the way in which you governed the Society following the difficult 1981 Pontifical intervention. Since then, you have known how to navigate the Society with serenity, recognizing how to balance fidelity to the Church with fidelity to our way of proceeding as expressed in our Constitutions and the most recent General Congregations. The words we heard in Cardinal Rodé's homily, which represent the thinking of the Church, clearly express the Holy See's esteem for you and your leadership during these past years.

We also appreciate the charism of union that you and your governance have represented for us, especially in light of the Society's ever greater plurality and cultural diversity. While living that freedom of spirit typical of our manner of proceeding and in the midst of cultural diversity, of varied ways of feeling and thinking, and through different historical contexts, you have maintained the union of the Society's corporate body. You have kept that union by being respectful of others, by means of your wise and balanced counsel, and by your inspiring presence in every province.

The trust that you have shown through your governance, not only to your curial staff but also to all of the provincials, has created a fraternal and collaborative setting. This broad setting has indeed affected the entire body of the Society and expresses very well one of our ideals, namely, to be, all of us together, companions of Jesus.

May our Creator and Lord reward you for your faithful service during nearly a quarter of a century. Additionally, we ask that the Lord continue to bless you in whatever new ministry he grants you for his greater glory.

In GC 35's name and that of the whole Society, and with all of our heart, we say: Thank you very much, Fr. Kolvenbach! We are proud of you and of your service during these difficult but exciting years the Lord has seen fit to give us.

5. LETTER OF GRATITUDE FROM
FR. PETER-HANS KOLVENBACH TO GC 35

Rome, 14 January 2008

Dear Fathers and Brothers:

Today the General Congregation has thought it well to accept my resignation as General Superior of the Society of Jesus. At the end of these nearly twenty-five years of service, I want first of all to thank the Lord, who—to use the words of St. Ignatius—has truly been propitious to me at Rome, in leading a Society he has called into service for his greater glory.

I am also most grateful for the privilege of having met and accompanied so many friends in the Lord, who in their many diverse vocations have always shown themselves to be true servants of the Mission of Christ.

No single Jesuit should feel himself excluded from this profound sentiment of recognition. Nonetheless, I would like to thank in a particular way those in the General Curia who have helped me day after day over many years in carrying out my responsibilities for the Society, as well as all the Major Superiors spread throughout the entire world.

Earlier I was able to express my great thanks to the Holy Father for his apostolic orientations which have allowed the Society to continue our mission "under the banner of the cross and under the Vicar of Christ on earth."

Let us be grateful to the Lord that despite a disconcerting diversity of persons and cultures, of desires and works, our union of minds and hearts has never failed and, despite an increasing fragility, the Society retains the capacity of apostolic dialogue before the challenges of the modern world in proclaiming the one Good News.

On this eve of the election of my successor and of the many decisions that the General Congregation will have to make, I unite myself with the prayer with which St. Ignatius finished his letters: "May God our Lord in his infinite and supreme goodness be pleased to give us his abundant grace, so that we may know his most holy will and entirely fulfill it."

Fraternally yours in the Lord,

Peter-Hans Kolvenbach, S.J.

6. Letter of Fr. Peter-Hans Kolvenbach Acknowledging the Exhortation of Pope Benedict XVI to GC 35

Rome, 15 January 2008

Most Holy Father,

The General Congregation has received with profound attention and gratitude the message that Your Holiness has addressed to the Superior General and—through him—to the whole Society of Jesus during this meaningful and important moment in the life of our Order.

Your Holiness has manifested once again the affection, spiritual closeness, esteem, and gratitude with which the Successors of Peter have regarded and see the Society of Jesus, continuing to expect the faithful service of the Society for the integral and clear proclamation of the Gospel in our time. While Your Holiness confirms that the intimate union with Christ should be the secret of our apostolic and missionary life, you recall the original charism of the Society of Jesus as defined in the *Formula of the Institute:* "to serve as a soldier of God beneath the banner of the cross . . . and to serve the Lord alone and the church, his spouse, under the Roman Pontiff, the Vicar of Christ on earth."

In continuity with the interventions of your predecessors—in particular Pope Paul VI and Pope John Paul II, on the occasion of the previous General Congregations—and with his other previous interventions, Your Holiness recalls the particular bond that binds the Society of Jesus to the Successor of Peter, as expressed in the "fourth vow" of special obedience to the Pope. The Holy Father underlines "the formative responsibility of the Society in the fields of theology, spirituality, and mission," asking "that the Congregation reaffirms, in the spirit of St. Ignatius, its own total adhesion to Catholic doctrine, in particular on the crucial points under attack today from secular culture," examples of which you mention explicitly.

The Society of Jesus affirms its own desire to respond sincerely to the call and demands of Your Holiness. The General Congregation will give them full attention in the course of its labors, a considerable part of which will be dedicated precisely to the topics of the identity and mission of the Jesuits, and on religious and apostolic obedience, in particular, obedience to the Holy Father.

The Congregation has set out to face its tasks with confidence and serenity, knowing that it can count on the affection and prayer of Your Holiness and your deep understanding of the difficult challenge "to announce the Gospel in the various social and cultural contexts, being confronted with different mentalities," as the mission the Society of Jesus demands today for the service of the Church.

With profound gratitude,

Devoted yours in the Lord,

Peter-Hans Kolvenbach, S.J.

7. HOMILY OF FR. FRANK CASE, S.J., AT THE MASS OF THE HOLY SPIRIT

19 January 2008

These days the General Congregation, in the persons of the Electors, is passing through a moment of profound obedience on behalf of the entire Society of Jesus. It has been and will be for many one of the most meaningful and memorable acts of obedience of your Jesuit lives. The word "obedience" comes from the Latin root *audire*, to hear or to listen. You have been listening to the Spirit of the Lord, both in personal prayer and in your conversations with one another. The election of a new Superior General today is a key fruit of this listening. It takes place here in Rome in the context of and in solid continuity with the Society's founding over four and a half centuries ago, so that we might "serve the Lord alone and the church, his spouse, under the Roman Pontiff, the Vicar of Christ on earth." It takes place also in the context of today's first reading from Paul's Letter to the Corinthians, describing the gifts of the Spirit to the Church we serve, gifts packaged in a variety of mixes in the men you have been considering these past four days.

In today's Gospel we see Jesus, after his resurrection, breathing on his apostles, giving them the Holy Spirit for the forgiveness of sins. This Holy Spirit, whom Jesus gives, will abide in the Church to remind us of who Jesus was and of what he said and did, and to guide us in carrying his message faithfully to all the cultures and historical epochs where the Gospel has been preached and is being preached today. In reminding us of who Jesus was and what he said and did, the Spirit keeps the Church faithful to her traditional roots in the revelation of God through the incarnation of his Son. The Spirit guarantees the Church's fidelity to its original inspiration and mission. In guiding us through diverse historical situations and cultures, the Spirit instills the Church's mission of evangelization with a creativity that puts the Gospel in words and images appropriate to so many diverse settings. This is the Church's mission under the Vicar of Christ, inspired by the Spirit.

The Spirit raised up the Society through Ignatius and his companions to serve this mission under the Vicar of Christ. Therefore what the Electors will do today, and what the Congregation will do in the following weeks, is squarely within the obedience we proclaim, an obedience of listening to the Spirit who reminds and guides, who inspires us to discern our paths in creative fidelity to our founding as articulated in the *Formula of the Institute,* "to serve as a soldier of God beneath the banner of the cross . . . and to serve the Lord alone and the Church, his spouse, under the Roman Pontiff, the Vicar of Christ on earth." If we listen to and follow the Spirit speaking in the Church and in our superiors, we can trust that our creativity will be faithful and our fidelity will be creative.

Besides reminding and guiding the Church in its spread of the Gospel, the Spirit also holds the followers of Christ in unity with one another. For our part, in electing a Superior General today, you will give the Society a new point of union of minds and hearts and of obedience to the Spirit as servants of Christ's mission at the core of his Church.

In the words of today's Eucharist Prayer, we pray the Lord: "Through the power of your Spirit of love include us now and forever among the members of your Son, whose body and blood we share."

8. Homily of Father General Adolfo Nicolás in the Church of the Gesù, at the Mass of Thanksgiving

20 January 2008

Above all I would like to say that this is not a message for the whole world. Rather, it is merely a simple homily; a prayerful reflection of today's readings for us Jesuits who are here this afternoon.

The first reading taken from the prophet Isaiah briefly describes to us Christians our mission in the world. The prophet Isaiah tells us that we have all been called to serve, that we are here precisely to serve. It is a clear message regarding our mission as Jesuits, as Christians, as the people of God. God has made us servants and, in so doing, God finds delight. The Spanish version of this first reading says that God is proud of the servant, while the Italian version says that God "is satisfied." I believe the latter is closer to what the Bible wants to say. The more we become as servants, the more pleased God is. I think this is an image we should all take home today.

Newspapers and magazines these past few days have been toying with a number of clichés, namely, the Black Pope, the White Pope, power, gatherings, discussions. . . . But it is all so superficial, so artificial! These are but crumbs for those who love politics, but they are not for us.

The prophet Isaiah says that serving pleases the Lord. To serve is what counts: to serve the Church, the world, our fellow men and women, and the Gospel. St. Ignatius also has written in summary form about our life: in all things to love and to serve. And our pope, His Holiness Benedict XVI, has reminded us that God is love; he has reminded us of the Gospel's essence.

Later on the prophet Isaiah describes the servant's strength. God is the servant's only strength. We do not have any other source of strength: not the external strength found in politics, in business, in the media, in studies, in titles, nor the internal fortitude found in research. Only God. Exactly like the poor. Not too long ago I spoke to one of you regarding something that happened to me while working with immigrants. It was an experience that deeply affected me. A Filipino woman who had experienced many difficulties adapting to the Japanese society, a woman who had suffered a great deal, was asked by another Filipino woman for advice. The second woman said, "I have many problems with my husband, and I do not know if I should get divorced or try to save my marriage." In other words, she wanted advice concerning a rather common problem. The first woman replied: "I do not know what advice to give you right now. However, come with me to Church so that the two of us can pray because only God really helps the poor." This statement deeply touched me because it is so true. The poor have only God in whom to find their strength. For us only God is our strength. Unconditional, disinterested service finds its source of strength only in God.

The prophet Isaiah continues today's first reading by speaking about health. Our message is a message about health, about salvation. A bit later he stresses what has most caught my eye about this reading; namely, that our God, our faith, our message, and our health are so great that they cannot be enclosed within a container, in any one group or community, regardless of whether or not the group in question happens to be a religious community. What is at stake is the Good News of salvation for all nations. It is a universal message because the message itself is enormous: a message that in itself is irreducible.

All represented nations are gathered here today. All, everyone, is represented here. However, nations continue to open up. I ask myself today which are those "nations." Indeed, all geographic nations are here today. However, there may be other nations, other non-geographic communities, human communities, that claim our aid: the poor, the marginalized, the excluded. In this globalized world of ours, the number of those excluded by all is increasing. Those excluded are diminished, since our society only has room for the big and not the small. All those who are disadvantaged, manipulated, all of these may perhaps be for us those "nations": The nations that need the prophetic message of God.

Yesterday after the election, after the first shock, there came the moment of fraternal aid. All of you have greeted me very affectionately, offering your support and help. One of you whispered to me, "Don't forget the poor!" Perhaps this is the most important greeting of all, just as Paul turns to the wealthier churches of his time requesting aid for the poor of Jerusalem. Don't forget the poor: these are our "nations." These are the nations for whom salvation is still a dream, a wish. Perhaps it may be in their midst, but they don't realize it.

And the others? The others are our collaborators if they share our same perspective, if they have the same heart Christ has given us. And if they have a bigger heart and an even greater vision, then we are their collaborators. What counts is health, salvation, the joy of the poor. What counts, what is real, is hope, salvation, health. And we want that this salvation, this health, may be an explosion of salvation that reaches out everywhere. This is what the prophet Isaiah is talking about: that salvation may reach and touch everyone. A salvation according to God's heart, will, Spirit.

We go on with our General Congregation. Perhaps this is what we need to discern. In this moment of our history, where do we need to fix our attention, our service, our energy? Or, in other words, what is the color, the tone, the image of salvation today for those many people who are in need of it, those human non-geographic nations that demand health? There are many who wait for a salvation that we have yet to understand. To open ourselves up to this reality is the challenge, the call, of the moment.

And we turn to the Gospel. This is how we can be true disciples of the Lamb of God, he who takes away our sins and leads us to a new world. And he, the Lamb of God, has shown himself as Servant, he who fulfills Isaiah's prophecies, the message of the Prophets. His identity as Servant will be his sign, the mark of our own mission, of the call which we try to respond to these days.

Let us pray together for this sense of Mission of the Church, that it may be for the "nations'" benefit and not our own—the "nations" that are still far away, not geographically, but humanly, existentially. That the joy and the hope that come from the Gospel may be a reality with which we can work little by little, doing it with a lot of love and disinterested service.

9. Words Spoken by Father General Nicolás in the Presence of Pope Benedict XVI

Most Holy Father:

I would like my first word to be, in my name and in the name of all present, a heartfelt "thank you" to Your Holiness for kindly receiving today the members of the General Congregation meeting in Rome, after having already bestowed on us the precious gift of a Letter which by way of its rich content and its positive tone, encouraging and affectionate, has most surely been appreciated by the whole Society of Jesus.[2]

Gratitude, indeed, and a strong sense of communion in feeling confirmed in our mission to work at the frontiers where faith and science, faith and justice, and faith and knowledge confront each other, and in the challenging field of serious reflection and responsible theological research. We are grateful to Your Holiness for having once more encouraged us to follow our Ignatian tradition of service right where the Gospel and the Church suffer the greatest challenges, a service which at times also lends itself to the risk of disturbing a peaceful lifestyle, reputation, and security. For us it is a cause of great consolation to note that Your Holiness is more than aware of the dangers that such a commitment exposes us to.

Holy Father, I would like to return once again to the kind and generous Letter which you sent to my predecessor, Fr. Kolvenbach, and through him to all of us. We have received it with an open heart, meditated on it, reflected on it; we have exchanged our reflections, and we are determined to carry its message and its unconditional words of welcome and acceptance to the whole Society of Jesus.

We wish moreover to convey the spirit of such a message to all our formation structures and to create—taking the message as our starting point—opportunities for reflection and discussion which will enable us to assist our confreres engaged in research and in service.

Our General Congregation, to which Your Holiness has given your paternal encouragement, is looking, in prayer and in discernment, for the ways through which the Society can renew its commitment to the service of the Church and of humanity.

What inspires and impels us is the Gospel and the Spirit of Christ: if the Lord Jesus was not at the center of our life, we would have no sense of our apostolic activity; we would have no reason for our existence. It is from the Lord Jesus we learn to be near to the poor and suffering, to those who are excluded in this world.

The spirituality of the Society of Jesus has as its source the *Spiritual Exercises* of St. Ignatius. And it is in the light of the *Spiritual Exercises*—which in their turn inspired the Constitutions of the Society—that the General Congregation in these days is tackling the subjects of our identity and of our mission. The *Spiritual Exercises,* before becoming a precious tool for the apostolate, are for the Jesuit the touchstone by which to judge our own spiritual maturity.

---

[2] Greetings delivered by Fr. General at 11:30 on February 21, when the members of the General Congregation had been received by the Holy Father Benedict XVI in a special audience. The Pope's discourse followed Fr. General's words.

In communion with the Church and guided by the Magisterium, we seek to dedicate ourselves to profound service, to discernment, to research. The generosity with which so many Jesuits work for the Kingdom of God, even to giving their very lives for the Church, does not mitigate the sense of responsibility that the Society feels it has in the Church. Responsibility that Your Holiness confirms in your Letter, when you affirm, "The evangelizing work of the Church therefore relies a lot on the formative responsibility that the Society has in the fields of theology, spirituality, and mission."

Alongside the sense of responsibility must go humility, recognizing that the mystery of God and of man is much greater than our capacity for understanding.

It saddens us, Holy Father, when the inevitable deficiencies and superficialities of some among us are at times used to dramatize and represent as conflicts and clashes what are often only manifestations of limits and human imperfections or inevitable tensions of everyday life. But all this does not discourage us nor quell our passion, not only to serve the Church, but also, with a deeper sense of our roots, according to the spirit of the Ignatian tradition, to love the hierarchical Church and the Holy Father, the Vicar of Christ.

"En todo amar y servir." This represents a portrait of who Ignatius is. This is the identity card of a true Jesuit.

And so we consider it a happy and significant circumstance that our meeting with you occurs on this particular day, the vigil of the Feast of the Chair of St. Peter, a day of prayer and of union with the Pope and his highest service of universal teaching authority. For this we offer you our good wishes. And now, Holy Father, we are ready and willing to listen and attend to what you have to say to us.

10. Address of Pope Benedict XVI to the 35th General Congregation of the Society of Jesus

February 21, 2008

Dear Fathers of the General Congregation of the Society of Jesus:

1.   I am happy to welcome you today as your demanding work is coming to an end. I thank the new Superior General, Father Adolfo Nicolás, for having conveyed your feelings and your effort to respond to the expectations that the Church places in you. I referred to them in the message addressed to Reverend Father Kolvenbach and—through him—to your Congregation at the beginning of your labors. I thank Father Peter-Hans Kolvenbach once again for the precious service he has rendered to your Order for almost a quarter century. I also greet the members of the new General Counsel and the Assistants who will help the Superior in his delicate task of religious and apostolic guidance of your Society.

2.   Your Congregation takes place in a period of great social, economic, and political changes, sharp ethical, cultural, and environmental problems, conflicts of all kinds, but also of a more intense communication among peoples, of new possibilities of acquaintance and dialogue, of a deep longing for peace. All these are situations that challenge the Catholic Church and its ability to announce to our contemporaries the Word of hope and salvation. I very much hope, therefore, that the entire Society of Jesus, thanks to the results of your Congregation, will be able to live with a renewed drive and fervor the mission for which the Spirit brought it about and has kept it for more than four centuries and a half with an extraordinary abundance of apostolic fruit. Today I should like to encourage you and your confreres to go on in the fulfillment of your mission, in full fidelity to your original charism, in the ecclesial and social context that characterizes this beginning of the millennium. As my predecessors have often told you, the Church needs you, counts on you, and continues to turn to you with confidence, particularly to reach the geographical and spiritual places where others do not reach or find it difficult to reach. Those words of Paul VI have remained engraved in your hearts: "Wherever in the Church, even in the most difficult and extreme fields, in the crossroads of ideologies, in the front line of social conflict, there has been and there is confrontation between the deepest desires of man and the perennial message of the Gospel, there also there have been, and there are, Jesuits" (3 December 1974, to the 32nd General Congregation, p. 380 above).

3.   As the *Formula of your Institute* states, the Society of Jesus was founded chiefly "for the defence and propagation of the faith." At a time when new geographical horizons were being opened, Ignatius's first companions placed themselves at the Pope's disposal "so that he might use them where he judged it would be for God's greater glory and the good of souls" (*Autobiography,* n. 85). They were thus sent to announce the Lord to peoples and cultures that did not know him as yet. They did so with a courage and zeal that still remain as an example and inspiration: the name of St. Francis Xavier is the most famous of all, but how many others could be mentioned! Nowadays the new peoples who do not know the Lord or know him badly, so that they do not recognize him as the Saviour, are far away not so much from the geographical point of view as from the cultural one. The obstacles challenging the evangelizers are not so much the seas or the long distances as the frontiers that, due to a mistaken or superficial vision of God and of man, are raised between faith and human knowledge, faith and modern science, faith and the fight for justice.

4.   This is why the Church is in urgent need of people of solid and deep faith, of a serious culture and a genuine human and social sensitivity, of religious priests who devote their lives to stand on those frontiers in order to witness and help to understand that there is in fact a profound harmony between faith and reason, between evangelical spirit, thirst for justice and action for peace. Only thus will it be possible to make the face of the Lord known to so many for whom it remains hidden or unrecognizable. This must therefore be the preferential task of the Society of Jesus. Faithful to its best tradition, it must continue to form its members with great care in science and virtue, not satisfied with mediocrity, because the task of facing and entering into a dialogue with very diverse social and cultural contexts and the different mentalities of today's world is one of the most difficult and demanding. This search for quality and human solidarity, spiritual and cultural, must also characterize all the many activities of formation and education of the Jesuits, as it meets the most diverse kinds of persons wherever they are.

5.   In its history the Society of Jesus has lived extraordinary experiences of proclamation and encounter between the Gospel and the cultures of the world—suffice it to think of Matteo Ricci in China, Roberto de Nobili in India, or the "Reductions" in Latin America—of which you are justly proud. Today I feel I have the duty to exhort you to follow in the footsteps of your predecessors with the same courage and intelligence, but also with as profound a motivation of faith and passion to serve the Lord and his Church. All the same, while you try to recognize the signs of the presence and work of God in every part of the world, even beyond the confines of the visible Church, while you endeavor to build bridges of understanding and dialogue with those who do not belong to the Church or who have difficulty accepting its position and message, you must at the same time loyally fulfill the fundamental duty of the Church, of fully adhering to the word of

God, and of the authority of the Magisterium to preserve the truth and the unity of the Catholic doctrine in its totality. This does not apply solely to the personal task of each Jesuit; since you work as members of one apostolic body, you must be attentive so that your works and institutions always maintain a clear and explicit identity, so that the purpose of your apostolic work does not become ambiguous or obscure, and many other persons may share your ideals and join you effectively and enthusiastically, collaborating in your task of serving God and humanity.

6.   As you well know because you have so often made the meditation "of the Two Standards" in the *Spiritual Exercises* under the guidance of St. Ignatius, our world is the stage of a battle between good and evil, with powerful negative forces at work, which cause those dramatic situations of spiritual and material subjection of our contemporaries against which you have repeatedly declared your wish to combat, working for the service of the faith and the promotion of justice. These forces show themselves today in many forms, but with particular evidence through cultural tendencies that often become dominating, such as subjectivism, relativism, hedonism, practical materialism. This is why I have asked you to renew your interest in the promotion and defence of the Catholic doctrine "particularly in the neuralgic points strongly attacked today by secular culture," some of which I have mentioned in my letter. The issues, constantly discussed and questioned today, of the salvation in Christ of all human beings, of sexual morality, the marriage and the family, must be deepened and illumined in the context of contemporary reality, but keeping the harmony with the Magisterium, which avoids creating confusion and bewilderment among the People of God.

7.   I know and understand well that this is a particularly sensitive and demanding point for you and not a few of your confreres, especially those engaged in theological research, interreligious dialogue and dialogue with contemporary culture. Precisely for this reason I have invited you, and am inviting you today, to further reflect so as to find again the fullest sense of your characteristic "fourth vow" of obedience to the Successor of Peter, which not only implies readiness to being sent in mission to far away lands, but also—in the most genuine Ignatian sense of "feeling with the Church and in the Church"—to "love and serve" the Vicar of Christ on earth with that "effective and affective" devotion that must make of you his precious and irreplaceable collaborators in his service of the universal Church.

8.   At the same time I encourage you to continue and renew your mission among the poor and for the poor. Unfortunately, new causes of poverty and exclusion are not lacking in a world marked by grave economic and environmental imbalances, processes of globalization, caused by selfishness rather than by solidarity, by devastating and absurd armed conflicts. As I had the opportunity to repeat to the Latin American Bishops gathered in the Shrine of Aparecida, "the preferential option for the poor is implicit in the christological faith in a God that

has made himself poor for us, so as to make us rich by his poverty" (2 Cor. 8:9). It is therefore natural that whoever wishes to make himself a companion of Jesus, really share the love of the poor. For us the choice of the poor is not ideological but is born from the Gospel. The situations of injustice and poverty in the world of today are countless and dramatic and it is necessary to try to understand and combat in the heart of man the deeper causes of the evil that separates him from God, without forgetting to meet the more urgent needs in the spirit of the charity of Christ. Taking up one of the latest intuitions of Fr. Arrupe, your Society continues to engage in a meritorious way in the service of the refugees, who are often the poorest among the poor and need not only material help but also the deeper spiritual, human, and psychological proximity especially proper to your service.

9. Finally I invite you to reserve a specific attention to the ministry of the Spiritual Exercises that has been characteristic of your Society from its origins. The Exercises are the fountain of your spirituality and the matrix of your Constitutions, but they are also a gift that the Spirit of the Lord has made to the entire Church: it is for you to continue to make it a precious and efficacious instrument for the spiritual growth of souls, for their initiation to prayer, to meditation, in this secularized world in which God seems to be absent. Just last week I have myself profited from the Spiritual Exercises together with my closest collaborators of the Roman Curia under the guidance of your outstanding confrere Cardinal Albert Vanhoye. In a time such as today, in which the confusion and multiplicity of messages, the speed of changes and situations, make particularly difficult for our contemporaries to put their lives in order and respond with joy to the call that the Lord makes to everyone of us, the Spiritual Exercises represent a particularly precious method to seek and find God in us, around us, and in everything, to know his will and put it into practice.

10. In this spirit of obedience to the will of God, to Jesus Christ, that becomes humble obedience to the Church, I invite you to continue and bring to conclusion the work of your Congregation, and I join you in the prayer that St. Ignatius taught us in the Exercises—a prayer that seems to me too great, so much so that I almost dare not say it, but which all the same we must always propose to ourselves anew—"Take, Lord, and receive all my liberty, my memory, my understanding and my entire will, all I have and possess; you gave it to me, I now give it back to you, O Lord; all is yours, dispose of it according to your will; give me your love and your grace; that is enough for me" (Ex. 234).

11. First Greetings from Father General Adolfo Nicolás to the Whole Society

Rome, 22 February 2008

Dear Friends in the Lord,

This is the first time I write to you since the election, exactly one month ago, on January 19. I think you can easily imagine the surprise, even shock, I received with the election. I had considered myself out of bounds because of my age, without entering into the long series of inadequacies and shortcomings that are well known to those with whom I have lived and worked.

Maybe the most difficult thing to explain is the experience we all went through on those days, searching in the fog, looking for the Will of God and the good of the Church and the Society. It was this intense, sincere, and open search that made it impossible for me to decline or refuse the choice. You cannot say no to people so sincerely looking for the Will of God. And now I assure you that I will give all my energy and person to the work of helping the Society move forward, supporting what is good, responding to new challenges, encouraging one another to face the difficult task of being consistent with and credible witnesses of the Gospel of Jesus Christ that we believe in.

The task is daunting, the service needed is unlimited, the pace of change in our world is dizzying; we could not even dream of contributing to the mission of our Society if the Lord were not with us, guiding, supporting, and comforting us with his Spirit. We will be led and supported by this Spirit and the love for the Church in all its different manifestations. We want to serve this Church with total dedication and depth under the guidance of and in fidelity to the Holy Father, and in an ever-friendly and trusting cooperation with the Hierarchy wherever we are.

The incredible support, availability, and spirit of service that I am finding in the General Congregation and at all levels of this Roman Curia is a source of joy and of hope. This convinces me that we Jesuits will be able to continue doing our best for others; and that we will take our humble position in the Church as servants called to share our lives, invited to teach and to learn, to search for depth and to pray with intensity and joy.

The weeks following the Election have been equally intensive in the search of a good team to help me with the Governance of the Society. We have almost concluded the task with the election of the Four Assistants *ad providentiam* and the *Admonitor*. I am deeply grateful to the General Congregation; they have given me an excellent team that will help me sleep better, with the confidence that I have the best possible advice and support. Even so I will probably make mistakes and will need your understanding and forgiveness whenever they happen. Be "generously" ready!

As you have surely read elsewhere, the new group of Regional Assistants and General Councilors is composed of the following men:

Africa: Fr. Jean-Roger Ndombi (AOC)
South Latin America: Fr. Marcos Recolons de Arquer (BOL)
North Latin America: Fr. Gabriel Ignacio Rodríguez (COL)

South Asia: Fr. Lisbert D'Souza (BOM)
East Asia and Oceania: Fr. Daniel Patrick L Huang (PHI)
Central and East Europe: Fr. Adam Żak (PME)
South Europe: Fr. Joaquín Barrero Díaz (CAS)
West Europe: Fr. Antoine Kerhuel (GAL)
United States: Fr. James E. Grummer (WIS)

I have also named two General Councilors who will normally reside outside Rome and come to Rome as needed. They are

Fr. Mark Rotsaert (BSE and CEP)
Fr. Arturo M. Sosa Abascal (VEN)

The four Assistants *ad providentiam* elected on Monday, February 18, are

Fr. Lisbert D'Souza
Fr. James E. Grummer
Fr. Federico Lombardi (ITA)
Fr. Marcos Recolons de Arquer

Also on February 18 I named Fr. Ignacio Echarte Oñate (LOY) the new Secretary of the Society to succeed Fr. Frank E. Case (ORE).

It is my pleasure to take this occasion to thank, on behalf of the entire Society, all who will soon be leaving the General Curia after the General Congregation. First of all, we all owe a deep and sincere vote of thanks to Fr. Peter-Hans Kolvenbach for his tireless, inspiring, and very wise leadership of the Society over the past quarter of a century. Likewise I want to thank the outgoing General Councilors—Fathers Joseph Nguyên Công Đoan (ASO and VIE), Jacques Gellard (EOC and GAL), Jean Ilboudo (AFR and AOC), Wendelin Köster (ECE and GER), Valentín Menéndez (ALS and CAM), Manuel Morujão (EMR and POR), and Ignacio Echarte (DIR and LOY)—and Father Frank Case, the outgoing Secretary of the Society. They have served the Church and the Society generously and well.

Other changes will be taking place in the Curia after the Congregation, of which I will be informing you in due time.

Finally, while counting on the accompaniment of your prayers during the coming months of transition, I also commend the remaining days of the General Congregation to your continued good prayers.

Sincerely in the Lord,

A. Nicolás, S.J.
Superior General

12. Homily of Fr. Adolfo Nicolás in the Church of the Gesù at the Conclusion of GC 35

6 March 2008

I shall deliver this simple homily in Italian. I do not know whether that will put you at ease or make you uncomfortable.

Right now we are filled with the experience which we have lived for the past two months. This morning, in a prayerful and grateful spirit, we heard some reflections on this experience, an experience of incredible diversity, perhaps the greatest diversity we have ever had in the history of our General Congregations.

Along with this diversity we have experienced a strong desire to listen to others, to be open with others so different from ourselves. We have also experienced the will to change. And, yes, we have changed. We have changed in our points of view, in the drafting of our texts and in our discussions. We have developed an attitude of greater attentiveness to others. In such a large and diverse community, we have rarely witnessed so much rejoicing in the joy of others and so much sadness in the suffering of others. We have prayed for one another.

The first reading of the day invites us to go to the source of this experience and to make it fully Christian. The logic of the Christian experience is very clear. God is love, and so we too love. God is mercy, and so we too show mercy. God is good, and so we too desire to be good. If we do not love, we really do not have anything to say. Here we discover, I think, the root and source of our identity and our mission. Here is our raison d'être. Why do we want to love the poor, to help the lonely, to console the sad, to heal the sick, and to bring freedom to the oppressed? Simply because this is what God does. Nothing else. As the Holy Father told us, love for the poor does not have an ideological but a Christological basis. It is the very essence of Christ. Christ has taught us how he acts, how he lives, how God loves—and we try to learn.

Another thing which John's letter tells us is that this is not something sporadic, something we do in a fleeting moment when we feel strong, even heroic. No, it is a constant in our lives. The letter invites us to "remain" in love. This word is repeated several times in the letter. In order for God to "remain" in you, you must "remain" in love. For Christ to "remain" in you, you must be united with others. There is a play of words as the concept of "remaining" is repeated several times.

The invitation which we have received in our Congregation and in today's liturgy is to become new persons—persons who "remain" with our insights and who "remain" with the contacts we have established with the Lord through one another.

In the document in which we considered our charism, we say that in looking at Jesus we understand who we ought to be. "Remaining" in him. We all know that it is not through guidelines or directives written for others that the Church and the Society will change. They will change if we know how to become new persons. The question is not what we wish to do in community, but what kind of community men we need to become in order to "remain" obedient men, men who know how to discern, men who are always companions, always. Not with some people whom we choose to be our collaborators, but to be companions of others always and everywhere—ready to serve, ready to offer solidarity. Men who live continually in love and in service. "To love and to serve in all things." How often we have sung these words in the past two months! In all things. This is not an act of heroism: it is a way of life. This is what we have prayed for these two months.

The Gospel takes us still further. It tells us that everything we have done is for mission. I did not choose the Gospel text for our Mass here in the Gesù. Others chose the mission of Christ as the text. At the very heart of the sending is the "remaining." We are sent, as you have discussed these days and indicated in the documents. We are sent because we have entered into Christ and it is Christ who has sent us. The mission has its source, its *zampilla,* as the Italians say, in our encounter with God; but it ends in others. It begins with Christ and ends with others—in their joys, in their hopes, in their sufferings. Then Mark tells us: make universal what you have experienced these two months during the General Congregation. This love and this concern for one another must now be extended to all we meet. This collaboration, this mutual help must become our way of life. This is not easy. Perhaps some of you are familiar with the power point which features letters written to Jesus by little children. One letter reads, "Jesus, how do you manage to love everybody? There are only four of us at home and we don't do very well at loving one another." We know what this means. At least we have accomplished it among the 225 of us. But how do we keep doing it in our local communities, in our Provinces, and with our collaborators, unless we remain in love?

The Gospel also indicates how we are to carry out our mission. I will limit myself to the most important points because the vision presented is very dynamic.

As I have already said, it is a dynamism which begins in us when we go out to others. Something happens in others and then it is beyond us. The results are there, not here. The vision is very modern. The fruit is not "input" but "output." First of all, go. Go to the whole world. We have spoken of frontiers, or the periphery. The Gospel tells us: Go, go. We have indeed gone and we have encountered many problems and made many mistakes at the frontiers. I could tell you about my mistakes, but I know that there have been other mistakes as well. We have come to understand that "going" does not mean simply getting on a plane, but entering into the culture, into the life of the people. "Going" means study, research, entering into the life of the people. Solidarity, empathy, inculturation, respect for others. Going to the whole world turns out to be more difficult than we had thought. We feel like children. Perhaps we have discovered the Kingdom of God.

We are then told, Go and proclaim the Gospel. We have done so—sometimes well, at other times not so well. But then we have understood that proclaiming the Gospel requires that the Word of God be visible. It is not enough to proclaim it with our lips. Visibility is necessary, visibility in our life, in our work, in our openness to others, in service, in forgiveness, in compassion, in reconciliation, in our capacity to help others become healthier, freer, more human. And the Gospel continues. Something happens. People have faith. Those who believe are transformed. This is where St. Ignatius can be a great help to us. Ignatius saw this. Faith is not something exterior. Faith transforms. Faith is something which has happened to each one of us from the moment we became Christians, from the moment we became Jesuits. This has been a process of transformation, an all-embracing process, a process which changes the person and a process which opens the doors to hope, to love and to the risk of caring for others. When the Gospel touches us, we change. Something happens and we all grow.

The Gospel goes on to say that this is salvation. It is not a matter of saying, "If I believe, I will be saved." That is far too external. If I believe, I am already saved. To believe, to enter into this process means to find salvation. Ignatius understood this very well. This is the very essence of Ignatian pastoral practice, whether in a parish, in education, in the spirituality of our houses. Salvation consists in interior change, in interior transformation. Ignatian pastoral care, based on the *Spiritual Exercises,* consists precisely in helping people to change interiorly. From this interior change of heart comes the change in feet, hands, service, work, and love for others.

The end of the Gospel states that there will be visible signs. These signs will be in those who believe, not in the missionary who may already have been forgotten. The center of attention, therefore, is those whom we serve. Believers will find that their lives have been changed. The signs are the result of faith, of a life that has been transformed. Perhaps our challenge today is to discern the signs of the Gospel. Nowadays we do not handle snakes! What, then, are the signs?

Justice, peace, compassion, solidarity, reconciliation, and human dignity. When these have become universal, when everyone has access to these most human elements of our lives, these will be the signs. The Gospel tells us that our mission is to go and proclaim the Gospel which transforms the human person. The signs will follow. In yet another passage the Gospel states that "by their fruits you will know who is true and who is not." Our question, then, must always be this: What signs do we need in our parishes, our schools, our services, and all our works?

Now I conclude for today. I believe that we are all aware that we have had a great experience. The Word of God, however, invites us to go to the source of this experience and to make sure that it is being transformed into mission, an all-embracing mission, a mission which will continue to bear fruit in others. To return home with less than this cannot justify the two months we have spent together, guided by the Spirit and seeking to find God's will in all things. We pray, therefore, that this experience as well as the Word of God we have heard today will bear fruit in transforming our own lives and the lives of others, so that the faith which we communicate may always be a transforming faith. This is what I ask for all of us.

MEMBERS OF THE 35th GENERAL CONGREGATION

In Alphabetical Order

Last Name, First Name, and Province

Abranches, William	GUJ		Boughton, Michael	NEN
Alaix Busquets, Ramón	BOL		Boynton, James	DET
Álvarez de los Mozos, Francisco Javier	LOY		Brown, Timothy	MAR
Alzibar Arrinda, Luis Maria	LOY		Buckland, Stephen	ZIM
Amalraj, Paramasivam Stanislaus	AND		Busto Sáiz, José Ramón	CAS
Ambert, Jorge	PRI		Bwanali, Peter	ZAM
Andretta, Edson Luis	BRC		Calderón, Gustavo	ECU
Anthony, Sebastian	SRI		Canillas Lailla, Carlos	PAR
Anthonydoss, Joseph	PAT		Cardó, Carlos	PER
Anton, Ronald	MAR		Cardozo Cortez, René	BOL
Ariapilly, John	DEL		Carneiro, Carlos	POR
Arregui Echeverría, Juan	LOY		Casalone, Carlo	ITA
Aste, Gerardo	PER		Case, Frank E.	CUR
Bafuidinsoni, Maloko-Mana	ACE		Català Carpintero, Vicent	ARA
Bambang Triatmoko, Benedictus	IDO		Cavassa Canessa, Ernesto	PER
Baranda, Guillermo	CHL		Chae, Matthias Joon-ho	KOR
Barla, Henry	RAN		Changanacherry, Jose	GUJ
Barrero Díaz, Joaquin	CAS		Chilinda, Charles	ZAM
Barretta, Claudio	ITA		Chojnacki, Gerald	NYK
Barros, Raimundo Oliveira	BNE		Cooke, Vincent	NYK
Bentvelzen, Jan	NER		Corkery, James	HIB
Biron, Jean-Marc	GLC		Cutinha, Jerome	JAM
Birsens, Josy	BME		da Silva, Anthony	GOA
Bisson, Peter	CDA		Daccache, Salim	PRO
Borrás Durán, Pere	TAR		Dacok, Ján	SVK
Bosa, Olivo	ROM		Daoust, Joseph	DET

Dardis, John	HIB	Idiáquez Guevara, José	CAM
Dartmann, Stefan	GER	Ilboudo, Jean	AOC
De Luca, Renzo	JPN	Jaramillo, Roberto	BAM
de Mello, Francis	BOM	Jeyaraj, Veluswamy	CCU
De Mori, Geraldo	BNE	Joseph Sebastian, Sandanam	AND
Devadoss, Mudiappasamy	MDU	Julien, Jaovory	MDG
D'Souza, Charles	KHM	Kalapura, James	JAM
D'Souza, Jerome	KAR	Kalubi, Augustin	ACE
D'Souza, Hector	KAR	Kammer, Alfred	NOR
D'Souza, Lisbert	CUR	Karayampuram, Joy	PAT
D'Souza, Anthony	BOM	Karekezi, Augustin	RWB
Dumortier, François-Xavier	GAL	Karla, Viliam	SVK
Dyrek, Krzysztof	PME	Karumathil, Joye James	KER
Echarte Oñate, Ignacio	CUR	Kejžar, Franc	SVN
Feely, Thomas	NYK	Kennedy, Michael	CFN
Fernández Franco, Fernando	GUJ	Kerhuel, Antoine	GAL
Fitzgibbons, John	WIS	King, Geoffrey	ASL
Follmann, José Ivo	BRM	Kiyaka, Isaac	AOR
García Jiménez, José Ignacio	CAS	Koenot, Jan	BSE
Geisinger, Robert	CHI	Kolling, João Geraldo	BRM
Gellard, Jacques	CUR	KOLVENBACH, Peter-Hans	CUR
Gendron, Louis	CHN	Koprek, Ivan	CRO
Gómez Boulin, Alfonso	ARG	Köster, Wendelin	CUR
González Buelta, Benjamin	CUB	Kot, Tomasz	PMA
González Modroño, Isidro	CAS	Kowalczyk, Dariusz	PMA
Goussikindey, Eugène	AOC	Krettek, Gerald	WIS
Grieu, Etienne	GAL	Kujur, Joseph	RAN
Grummer, James E.	WIS	Kuriacose, Thomas	DEL
Gudaitis, Aldonas	LIT	Lamboley, Thierry	GAL
Hajduk, Tadeusz	PME	Laporte, Jean-Marc	CDA
Holman, Michael	BRI	LeBlond, Daniel	GLC
Huang, Daniel Patrick L.	PHI	Lee, Patrick	ORE
Hylmar, František	BOH	Lee, John	CHN

Leitner, Severin	ASR	Orozco Hernández, Juan Luis	MEX
Lewis, Mark	NOR	Pace, Paul	MAL
Liberti, Vittorio	ITA	Palacio, Alfonso Carlos	BRC
Locatelli, Paul	CFN	Pallipalakatt, Varghese	DUM
Lombardi, Federico	ITA	Panna, Boniface	MAP
Longchamp, Albert	HEL	Pappu, Peter	DAR
Louis, Prakash	PAT	Parakad, Joseph	DAR
Lukács, János	HUN	Pattarumadathil, Henry	KER
Mace, John	WIS	Pattery, George	CCU
Madrzyk, Leszek Andrzej	PMA	Polanco Sánchez, Félix	ANT
Magadia, Jose	PHI	Prabhu, Vijay	KAR
Magriñà, Lluis	TAR	Priyono Marwan, Agustinus	IDO
Maniyar, Lawrence	NEP	Puthussery, Varghese	DUM
Marcouiller, Douglas	MIS	Quickley, George	ANW
Masawe, Fratern	AOR	Rafanambinana, Jean Romain	MDG
McGarry, John	CFN	Raj, Sebasti	MDU
Mcintosh, Robert	KOR	Raper, Mark	ASL
McMahon, Timothy	MIS	Recolons de Arquer, Marcos	BOL
Menéndez Martínez, Valentín	CUR	Regan, Thomas	NEN
Mercier, Ronald	NEN	Restrepo Lince, Alvaro	COL
Messmer, Otto	RUS	Rhode, Ulrich	GER
Morales Orozco, José	MEX	Riyo Mursanto, Robertus Bellarminus	IDO
Morfín Otero, Carlos	MEX	Roach, Thomas	MAR
Morujão, Manuel	POR	Rocha, Rosario	GOA
Mosca, Juan	URU	Rodríguez Arana, Carlos	PER
Mudavassery, Edward	HAZ	Rodríguez Osorio, Hermann	COL
Mukonori, Fidelis	ZIM	Rodríguez Tamayo, Gabriel	COL
Ndombi, Jean-Roger	AOC	Rohr, João Roque	BRM
Nebres, Bienvenido	PHI	Romero Rodríguez, José	BET
Nguyên, Công Đoan Joseph	VIE	Rosario, Jerry	MDU
Nicolás, Adolfo	JPN	Rotsaert, Mark	BSE
Ntima, Nkanza	ACE	Royón Lara, Elías	ESP
Orbegozo, Jesús	VEN	Rozario, Bertie	PUN

Ruiz Pérez, Francisco José	BET	Steiner, Marijan	CRO
Sajgó, Szabolcs	HUN	Sumita, Shogo	JPN
Sales, José Acrizio Vale	BNE	Tan, Larry	MAS
Salomão, Carlos	MOZ	Tata, Francesco	ITA
Sancho de Claver, Carlos María	ARA	Toppo, Amritlal	MAP
Sanfelíu Vilar, Federico	ECU	Toppo, Ranjit	RAN
Sariego, Jesús	CAM	Torres, Luis Orlando	CUR
Schaeffer, Bradley	CHG	Umba di M'balu, Joachim	ACE
Schmidt, Edward	CHG	Uribarri Bilbao, Gabino	CAS
Schultenover, David	WIS	Valenzuela, Eugenio	CHL
Scullin, Robert	DET	van de Poll, Jan	NER
Sermak, Jerzy	PME	Veeresan, Yogeswaran	SRI
Shirima, Valerian	AOR	Velasco, Luis Rafael	ARG
Sidarouss, Fadel	PRO	Venad, Thomas	HAZ
Silva Gonçalves, Nuno	POR	Vu Quang Trung, Thomas	VIE
Smolich, Thomas	CFN	Whitney, John	ORE
Smolira, David	BRI	Wisser, Gernot	ASR
Sonveaux, Daniel	BME	Zaglul, Jesús	ANT
Sosa Abascal, Arturo	VEN	Żak, Adam	CUR
Soto Artuñedo, Wenceslao	BET	Zollner, Hans	GER

INDEX OF TOPICS

General Congregations
31 through 35

INDEX TO THE DECREES
OF GENERAL CONGREGATIONS
31 THROUGH 35

Unless otherwise noted, the numerical references are to the consecutive marginal numbers of the decrees in the texts; these numbers are followed by slashes, e.g., 25/. Circled numbers indicate the General Congregation in which the references are found; e.g., ① = GC 31.

① = Documents from General Congregation 31

② = Documents from General Congregation 32

③ = Documents from General Congregation 33

④ = Documents from General Congregation 34

⑤ = Documents from General Congregation 35

Numbers preceded by p. or pp. indicate page numbers as found in this book.

58; —the Spir. Exerc. its wellspring, 87; —direct to individuals, besides structures, 89; —its three inseparable elements, 100; —coordination, 117; —review of A for action, 58, 101; —intellectual, 162

③ —difficulties today, 8; —adapting traditional A, 40; —attention to other A, 40. *See also* MINISTRIES; MISSION

Apostolate of prayer:
① —210, 492.

Apostolic end of the Society:
① —403; —encompasses all religious life, 204; —as principle of formation, 80, 141; —explains our vows, chastity, 248; obedience, 269; poverty, 288

② —character S.J. recalled by Paul VI, 5; —vocation in S.J. one but manifold, 31; —shared by Brothers, 155; —formation process, 137; —community, 26-29, 111-118; young Jesuits in ap. comm., 147-148; —dimension of our religious life and vows, 30, 65, 111, 113; —institutes: defined, 274; some questioned, 75; their witness to poverty reviewed, 97; attachment to them, 97; their poverty, 274-293; their suppression, 293; —message, 77; —options for today, 88-110; —poverty and efficiency, 265; —aim of non-priestly work, 128; —principle of unity of our communities, 113; —value of celibacy, 225

Apostolic organizations:
① —362

Apostolic schools:
① —533

Apostolic spirit:
① —of the first Companions, 4; —of the Society today, 15, 16, 24; —interreactions, 144; —of Brothers, 66-67; —to be instilled in the young religious, 79, 80; —in the novices, 105; —in the Scholastics, 122, 127; —to

be put into practice, 131, 139,144, 344; —supposes the spirit of prayer, 212, 213, 219; —necessity of permeating every aspect of religious life, 204; —and chastity, 247, 248, 259; —and obedience, 269; —and poverty, 288, 291, 299; —and community life, 313, 315, 327, 339, 340

Applied *(applicati):*
③ —as members of Province, 69

Approved Coadjutors:
② —formation, 155, 160; —tertianship, 188; —final vows time requirements, 196; —and diaconate, 194; —in Prov. Congr., 322. *See also* BROTHERS

Approved Scholastics:
② —promotion to profession, 192; —and diaconate, 194; —final vows requirements, 196, 197; —in Prov. Congr. 322. *See also* SCHOLASTICS

Arms Race:
③ —hostile to Kingdom, 38; —impoverishing and threatening, 49

Arca:
② —Seminarii, 299; —for Aged and Sick, 287, 299; —for Foundations, 299; —for Apostolic Works, 293, 299; —Charitable and Apostolic Fund of the Society, 288, 298

Arrupe, Pedro:
③ —resignation as Superior General, 1; —and Society's apostolate and spiritual life, 1; —and spiritual doctrine, 10; —and direction for formation, 22; —and plight of refugees, 48; —message to Society (September 3), Rel. Doc. 4, pp. 473-474; —homily at La Storta (September 4), Rel. Doc. 5, pp. 475-476
⑤ —memory of, evoked, 6, 83

Arts:
① —importance of:—533; —cultivation in the Society, 158, 555; —means of apostolate, 553, 554, 556; —formation of those who are involved, 558;

② —conscientization for justice of those in power, 109; —each province its program for action, 120; —its method and aim, 122; —of transcendent values, 154

Balance, emotional:

① —99, 100, 106, 108, 126. *See also* MATURITY

Beatitudes:

① —70, 395

② —how to express their spirit, 82; —proclaimed by our apostolic communities, 265

Believers and unbelievers:

② —ignorance and rejection of Gospel, 15-16; —and end of the Society, 21, 202; —collaboration with all, 39; —mission countries and lands of mission, 73; service of faith, 100-101; —evangelization and inculturation, 102-103; —apostolic formation to serve them, 137, 138, 141 b

Benedict XVI, Pope:

⑤ —messages of, to GC 35: —confidence in and encouragement, 1, 50; —fidelity to Jesuit mission, 6; —preparation for evangelization through theology and dialogue, 7; —importance of intellectual apostolate for mission of the Society, 13

⑤ —response of the Society to exhortations of, 8-17; — intellectual training essential, 7, 83

Benefactors:

② —and mendicancy: 260; —respect their wills, 291, 293

Bible: *See* SCRIPTURE

Bishops:

① —282, 371, 401, 407, 431, 446, 468, 473, 521

② —obedience to, 30; —we their helpers, 32, 33; —our leaders, 54; —Synods in 1971, 1974, 71; —consent to civic activities directives, 129

③ —cooperation with B, 7, 8, 50; —Synod of B, 32. *See* COLLABORATION

Body of the Society:

② —and local community, 26; —many members of one body, 31; —first band of Companions, 63, 64; —be aware of corporate identity and mission, 85, 114; —goes beyond the local community, 117; —younger members gradually integrated, 136, 139, 140; —all involved in formation, 136; —learn team spirit, 149; —unity of vocation in all grades, 191; —union with God base of its unity, 204

Brotherhood:

② —of all Men, 76-78, 86, 99; —worldwide B of all Jesuits in a common life, 19, 26, 112, 264; —Brothers and Friends in the Lord, 212-213; —brotherly communion, 212-225; —fraternal correction, 218

Brothers, apostolic vocation of:

① —66, 105, 204, 410; —offices, duties, responsibilities, 67, 520; —relation with scholastic novices, 101; —participation in consultations, 72; —at the Congregations, 72, 625, 629; —spiritual formation, 73, 520; —cultural and technical formation, 112; —apostolic responsibilities, 410, 452; —the theology of their vocation, 74; —experiments and suggestions, 74; —revise and adapt their rules, 74; —the Brothers in Rome, 568

② —apostolic call and mission, 31, 32; —Formation: equal to modern demands, 137; theological and technical, 155; according to need of Province and ability, 172; activities directed, 160; Church and Jesuit spirituality, 165; permanent diaconate, 194; implement 31st GC on this, 192a; —Tertianship urged, if overdue, 187; helps spiritual progress, 188; may join priest tertians, 188; time requirements for last vows, 196;

ress, 308; —scholarship and modern problems, 309-310

Changes:
② —rapid, 58, 74, 150; —our openness to Ch, 130; —influence and condition our formation, 133-134

Chaplains:
② —their remuneration, 301

Characteristics:
② —the Jesuit today, 41; —our response to the world today, 53-56; —our religious consecration, 65; the Society's mission today, 67; —today's apostolic task, 108-109; renewed poverty today, 270

Charism of Society of Jesus :
② —humble service, 39; —foundation, 41; —in our mission today, 62-72; —the same as the Church's, 62; —of apostolic team, priestly and religious, 64; —specially united to the Pope, 64; —vowed repudiation of world's idols, 65; in Formulas of Paul III and Julius III, 66; —in search of greatest need and more universal good, 88; —in social involvement, 92; —serve Christ poor, 258
③ —Ignatian C in Gen. Cong. 31 and 32, 41
④ —C of the Society, p. 663; —fidelity to the *magisterium,* p. 665; —fidelity to the Holy Father, p. 663; —specific way to God, p. 664. See also IGNATIAN TRAITS; IGNATIUS; JESUITS; SOCIETY OF JESUS

Charity:
① —love of God and of neighbor, 29, 77, 86, 126, 148, 216, 223, 45, 257, 267, 275, 290, 295, 317, 343, 345, 366; —fraternal, 81, 100, 131, 251 b, 282, 314, 675
② —internal law of Ch, 272; —works of Ch in the Formula of the Institute, 66; —Charitable and Apostolic Fund, 288, 298. *See also* DISCRETA

CARITAS

Chastity:
① —100, 315; —particular nature and importance, 245, 247, 264; —sign of the world to come, 247; —new problems, 243; —necessary requirements, 250; —associating us with the mystery of Christ, 249; —source of spiritual fruitfulness, 248; —friendship with Christ, 252; —supported by true brotherly love, 315; supposes mastery of the affections, 248, 249, 250, 255; —itself a source of apostolic force, 248; —means of preserving, 251, 315
② —frees us to be men for others, 30; —eschatological dimension, 65; —apostolic value of love and service to all, 225; —GC 32 confirms decree of GC 31, 225
④ —C and apostolic availability, 236-238; —and St. Ignatius, 232-234; —apostolic character of, 235-239; —changing views toward, 228; —cost of, 241-243; —criticisms of, 229; —harm resulting from failures in, 258; —matter of vow, 240; —meaning of, in Jesuit lives, 230; — guidelines and aids to, 244-272; —account of conscience, 263-266; —affective maturation, 259-262; —ascetical practices, 257; —care in admission and dismissal, 267-272; —community interaction, 250; —community life, 248-251; —discernment and self-discipline, 256-258; —familiarity with God, 245-247; —hospitality, 251; —life of ministry, 252-255.—professional conduct, 253-255; —spiritual direction, 261, 263-266; —watchfulness of superiors, 262, 269-272

China:
⑤ —important key to a peaceful world, 83

Choice:
② —Basic Ch of 32nd GC, 13, 19, 20, 22,

676; —with neighboring Provinces, 325, 344, 680; —missionary, 430-431, 441; —ecumenism, 456-462; —with the hierarchy, 371, 401, 407, 431, 446, 468, 473, 521, 573; —with religious, 332, 372, 431, 508; —with the laity, 373, 410, 440, 500, 526, 540, 541, 551, 578, 588; —with the parents of new students, 526; —with our separated brethren, 459-462; —with non-Christian, nonbelievers, 430, 506, 547, 583; —international, in the apostolate of education, 508, 542; —for the social apostolate, 460, 578, 579; —economical, 679

② —in execution of decrees, 10; —with Church universal and local, 54; —with Christians and non-Christians, 39; —with others in involvement, 86; —to avoid competition and duplication, 92; among professors for integration and reflection, 158; —for mobility in interdependence, 118

③ —with bishops, religious, clergy, others, 50; —mutual C with Christian Life Communities, 51; —with laity, 51.

⑤ —important for mission, 184-313; —dynamism of GC 34 encouraged, 184; —cooperation with laity affirmed and valued, 185-186; —challenges and responses to: —local circumstances differ, 187; —great progress already made, 188-189; —orientation toward furthering collaboration, 190-212; —lay leadership, 191; —means to sustain Jesuit work, e.g., Spiritual Exercises, 192; —definite relationship to the Society of Jesus and its mission needed for a Jesuit work, 193; —commitment to mission of Society essential, 194; —relations between provincial and directors of works important, 195; —example and edification of

Jesuits important, 196; —revised *Guidelines* to provide effective support of authorities, 197. *See also* ALUMNI; BISHOPS; INTERNATIONAL; LAITY; POPE

College
③ —authority to suppress, 84

Commandment:
① —of love, 45. *See also* LOVE

Colleges and Houses:
② —poverty, 267, 274; —suppression, 335. *See also* EDUCATION

Comfort:
② —love of, 4; —poverty, 30; —appetite for enjoyment and consumption, 259

Commission for the ministries :
① —379, 380-385, 507. *See also* MINISTRIES

Commissions:
② —Regional or Provincial for Formation, 163; —for Statutes of Poverty, 295-296; —for Inculturation, 132 note; —Prov. Cong.: for screening Postulata, 325, 326, 328; for study of Postulata, 326; —Gen. Congr.: 305, 310, 311; for screening Postulata, 308, 325, 326; —State of Society, 308, 309; —for revision of Formula of GC, 310; —on number of members in GC, 311

④ —appointment of, pp. 501-502

Commitment:
② —to serving the Church, 45; —to work for justice, 77, 90, 91, 96, 101, 266; —will lead to involvement and responsibility, 91; —of individuals and institutions, 97; —work not directly priestly, 127-128; —other contracts must yield to mission, 115; —other commitments to be reviewed, 96; —to social involvement: conscientization, 92; analysis of situation, 93; and discernment, 94; review, 101; solidarity and C, 123; in civic matters, 129; exceptional

④ —501-508; —assistants *ad providentiam,* 502, 504, 507, 509-515; —general counselors, 510-511, 514, 516-518;
—replacement of, 515-516; —terms
of, 515-516

Counsellors:
② —task of apostolic animation, 118;
for integral formation of Ours, 164;
for world cooperation, 130; for matters of poverty, 288. *See also* ASSIS-
TANTS; COUNSELLORS; CONSUL-
TORS

Counsellors, general:
③ —and membership in Gen. Cong.,
70; —and suppression of college/
professed house, 84; —assisting Father General re new Canon Law, 89-
92. *See also* CURIA, GENERAL

Counsels, evangelical:
① —126, 130, 203
② —30, 33, 34

Courses:
① —at regular intervals, of renewal and
information for Ours, 139, 477;
—for those who give the Exercises,
494; —taken by Ours, 161, 172
② —flexibility, 171; —unity in variety,
179, 182; — adapted to individual,
171; —and apostolic activities, 160,
181; —2 years Philosophy, 173; —4
years Theology, 174, 175

Creatures for man:
② —15

Credibility:
③ —prerequisites for C, 50; —and poverty, 52; —and justice in lives, communities, institutions, 53

Crisis:
② —of apostolic institutions, 75 b

Criteria:
③ —for action, 43

Criterion for choice of ministries:
② —90

Criticism:
② —of 31st GC, 3; —of one another, Fr.
General, Magisterium, Pope, 4; —of

traditional values, 75

Cross of Christ:
① —249, 258
② —Jesus carrying C, 3, 11; —Jesus crucified, 13, 209, 258; —death on the
C, 40; —rallied under C for common life and work, 41
③ —standard of the C, 54.

Culture
① —universality of mind and openness
needed in the Apostolate, 151, 375,
433, 503, 505-507, 526, 528; —and
faith, 503, 525; —esteem of all cultures, 426
② —variety, 36, 63, 86, 214; —identity and autonomy of C influence
our formation, 133; —formation to
confront C of today, 138; —inculturation, 85, 104, 109, 131, 132; —regional information, 161; —personal
insertion into C or region, 142, 177;
—languages for cultural communication, 178
③ —vitality in world's C, 39; —adapted
research into C, 40; — postmodern C:
④ —Christian mysticism as an approach
to, 105; —influences of, on Jesuits,
104

**Cultures and traditions, new and differ-
ent:**
⑤ —enrichment of the Society, 48-51

Cura personalis et apostolica:
⑤ —application of, 161, 166

Curia of the General:
② —central government, 330-333; —reorganization, 332 e; —vote of *ex officio* members of GC, 310, 315, 316,
322, 334, 337
③ —and adapting norms for Congregations, 71 —and preparation for
Gen. Cong. 34, 78; —and authority
over decrees of past Gen. Cong., 82;
—and authority over Formulas of
Congregations, 83; —and authority
over decrees, 87

cial order to be reviewed, 109
③ —as ministry, 47; —importance,. 47
—schools and non-formal E, 47;
—requirements as apostolate, 47;
—papal call to adapt, 40. *See also*
MINISTRIES

Education, secondary, primary, nonformal:
④ —416-419; —valuable contributions of
nonformal education, 419; —value
for disadvantaged, 416-417; —preprimary and primary education not
contrary to our institute, 418

Electio praevia **for a Prov. Congr.:**
② —317, 322

Election in the Spir. Exerc:
② —219

Election of officials, method followed:
④ —pp. 502-504

Electors:
③ —in Gen. Cong., 60-67, 70, 75:—*ex
officio,* 62-67, 70; —elected, 61-67

Emigrants:
① —apostolate for, 429

Encounter:
③ —with God, 11. *See also* EXPERIENCE

End:
② —of the Society, 11, 21; —of Man, 15.
See also AMDG

Environment:
③ —its destruction, 38
⑤ —care of by Jesuits, 75-80; —effect
on poor, 79

Epiphany:
④ —p. 676

Eschatological value:
② —of our common witness, 65, 265;
—of the Kingdom, 90; —freedom
and salvation offered in Christ, 82

Eternal King's call:
② —204, 269

Equality:
③ —of all Jesuits, 18

Eucharist:
① —vital center of our life, 98; —assimilates us to Christ, 251; —center

of life for our communities, 224,
338; —of our apostolic action, 392,
413; —makes of the community
one body, 267, 326; —favors ecumenism, 454.
② —center of community sharing, 28;
—E celebration bond of union, 112;
—for personal vital union, 141 b;
—furthers our union with God in
Christ, 210; —daily celebration, 235;
—concelebration encouraged, 208
note, 235; —Mass and thanksgiving, 236
③ —celebrating experience of God, 12
⑤ —importance of, 35. *See also* LITURGY; MASS; MYSTERY; SACRAMENTS

Evaluation:
② —of mission:—of apostolic
methods, 58, 101; of each province,
120-123; of performance of mission,
216; of apostolic decisions, 121, 122;
of apostolic works, 124-126,151; of
problems of our mission, 123; —of
formation: norms given, 134-135; of
apostolic activities of scholastics,
160; by regional or provincial commissions, 163; of formation experiments, 164; element of continued
formation, 151; implementation of
decree on Formation, 186; —of poverty, 263

Evangelical counsels:
② —make us free to serve, 30, 33; —E
poverty, 269

Evangelism, new:
④ —and a revitalized missionary spirit,
p. 692; —dependent upon spiritual
means, p. 683; —less strident, pp.
681-682; —new approach required,
pp. 681-682; —total availability required, p. 682

Evangelization:
② —inseparable from promotion of justice, 77, 79; —of the poor, 97;

—closeness to Christ of SE, 34;
—"labor with" Christ in serving
Kingdom, 34; —contemplating
world in SE, 37; —and discernment,
42; —as ministry, 46; —renewal
and laity, 51

Ex-officio right:
② —to a GC, 315, 316, 322 b, 334, 337 b;
—to a Prov. Congr.: 318

Expenses:
② —community, 282; —in formation,
166.

Experience: formative for growth in free
obedience, 84
② —of God in Christ, 37, 70, 100, 141,
158; —of Ignatius on poverty, 258;
—of the Exercises, 63, 107, 209,
242; —sharing spiritual E, 98, 208
note:—response rooted in E, 53,
55; —of living with the poor, 142,
261, 266; —apostolic E during studies, 153, 162, 180; —E reflection and
action, 122
③ —E of God, 12; —since Gen. Cong.
32nd, 34-35; —for review of ministries, 43; —for thought transfor-
mations. 43. *See also* CONVERSION;
ENCOUNTER; EXPOSURE

Experiences:
① —against the law of the Institute, 19;
—necessary before modification of
the Constitutions, 54; —in relation
to the brothers, 74; —in the adaptation of the tertianship, 191, 192; —of
closer bonds with the laity, 593; —of
inter-Province collaboration, 681

Experiments:
① —in the novitiate, adaptation of, 96,
97; —in the tertianship, 131-132, 170

Exposure:
③ —for discernment, 44

Externs:
② —their concern for the Society, 4;
—sharing resources with E, 285, 288

Faculties:
② —to dispense in matter of Poverty,

302; granted by GC to Fr. General,
334-337

Faith:
① —how to develop it, 30, 77, 78, 99,
127, 163; —the difficulties that it
encounters, 27-30; —example of,
584; —the pedagogue of, 472, 493;
—science and faith, 127, 366, 503,
547; —spirit of faith in obedience,
277, 281
② —inseparable from Justice, 12, 18, 48,
77; —its defense and propagation
end of S.J., 13, 21—our common
task, 36; —our mission today, 41;
—our priestly service of the F, 48,
67, 138; —proclaim, propagate, defend the F, 45, 100, 153; —in Form.
Instit., 66; —insertion in world
test of our faith, 84; —doubt about
depth of our F, 4; —F and hope
vs. unbelief and injustice, 84; —F
experience, 208; —F community,
210, 241; —creative effort of F, 75 a;
—F works through love, 77; —one
F, one baptism, one Lord, 233—dialogue between F and reality, 158;
—review our efforts to bring F to
believer and unbeliever, 101; —F
and Justice two inseparable ways, 18;
—injustice obstacle to F, 17; —integrating factor of all our ministries,
19, 96; —Jesuit contribution, 22;
—witness to F and J, 84; —studies
to be directed to this mission, 153;
—evaluation and discernment on
problems of F and J, 123, 125
③ —F and unbelief, 12; —and essential
ministries, 46; —one commitment
with justice, 45; —F–justice commitment and love, 45; —requires
promoting justice, 54; —F first and
last, 54; —and works of justice and
love, 54

Faiths, non-Christian:
③ —collaboration with those of NF, 50

Familiarity with God

① — in prayer, 98, 213, 216, 252; —in meditation upon Scripture, 215, 234; —in examination of conscience, 233; —in studies, 123; 182; —the goal of formation, 140, 141, 143; —its conditions, 99; —closer involvement in this world, 367; —means to help us with, 216

② —in daily prayer, 236:—need of personal prayer, 205, 221; —to be regained, 205; —familiar with spiritual sources of Church and Society, 165; —for community discernment, 220; —finding God in all things, 206

③ —and personal prayer, 12. *See also* UNION WITH GOD; WILL OF GOD

Family:

① —contact with, 106; —attendance at Mass of first vows, 201; —pastoral preparation of, 476

③ —solidarity of human F, 39

Father General:

① —powers, 23, 356, 357; —duration of office, 631; —resignation, 632-637; —and atheism, 40

② —criticized, 4; —call to renewal and rededication, 5; —has all power *ad aedificationem,* 30 c; —obedience to, 30c; —has support of all for real apostolic mobility, 148; —and permanent diaconate, 195; —publish summary of decrees of 31st and 32nd GC and his instructions, 255; —obtain dispensation on revenues, 302; —revise Formula of GC, 310; —reorganize Curia and Secretariates, 322, 333; —powers granted him by GC, 334-337; —promulgation of GC decrees, 337; —recommendations made to him: appoint Counsellor for world cooperation, 130; promote inculturation, 132; Formation Counsellor, 164; publish summary of decrees and letters, 255 a; commission on Statutes on Poverty,

295; revise formulas of GC and PC, 310-329; organize Council and Secretariats, 332, 333

③ —letter promulgating GC 33rd's decrees (November 30), p. 405; —letter to Society (September 14), Rel. Doc. 6, p.477; —homily (September 16), Rel. Doc. 7, p. 478; —homily (October 15), Rel. Doc. 8, pp. 479-480; —statement on Brothers (October 15), Rel. Doc. 9, pp. 479-480—homily at close of Gen. Cong. (October 25), Rel. Doc. 10, pp. 481-483. *See also* SUPERIOR GENERAL

Father General, activities of:

④ —pp. 495-498, 499, 503, 505

Father General, discourses:

④ —pp. 669-690

Father General, powers and mandates:

④ —522-534; —regarding chastity, 273; —regarding general congregations, 476; —regarding interprovincial cooperation, 461; —regarding interprovincial houses and works in Rome, 453-466; —regarding parishes, 429; —regarding priestly ministry, 193; —regarding province congregations, 499; —regarding secretariat for implementation, 217; —regarding superiors, 521; —155-157, 193, 217, 273, 297, 429, 461, 463-466, 476, 499, 521, 422-434

Father General, recommendations to, regarding:

④ —department for the study of religions at the Gregorian University, 156; —expansion of the Pontifical Biblical Institute of Jerusalem, 157; —secretariat for interreligious dialogue, 155

Fidelity:

② —to Magisterium, 4, 43-46; —to Pope, 4, 41, 43-46; —obligation and tradition, 44, 45, 68; —praise and regret, 45; —to apostolic mis-

tion and concern for the Society, 5; —our gratitude, 6; —Paul VI's suggestions to the GC, 14; —first Companions and Paul III, 23; —mission from him, 23-24; —Fourth Vow, 33, 34, 35; —fidelity to, 41, 43; —his leadership, 54; —atheism mandate, 68. *See also* POPE PAUL VI

Holy See
① —documents to 32nd GC, Section C; —faculty for permanent deacons, 195; —dispensation for use of revenues, 302

Holy Spirit:
① —docility to its movement, 124, 313, 401, 442; —persuasiveness of, 22, 182, 280, 404; principle of our brotherhood, 100, 273; —manifests its power in our chastity, 248; —guides us to Christ, 211
③ —service of Church in hearing HS, 9; —same HS in Christ and Church, 9. *See also* DISCERNMENT OF SPIRITS

Honor, positions of, restrictions in meaning of:
④ p. 692

Hope:
② —confidence in the future, 7, 64; —eschatological, 65, 82; —hopeful revival, 83, 84; —and human commitment, 79

Hospitality:
① —324, 327, 332, 486, 590.
② —249, 252

Hospitals:
① —493
② —visiting, 66; —chaplains' remuneration, 301

Household tasks:
① —for all, 72, 328.

Houses:
② —helping other houses, 286; —H consultations and discernment, 221; —in houses of formation: young Jesuits' integration, 147; —poverty, 280

Human Rights:
③ —attacks on HR, 48; —and threats to unborn, handicapped, aged, 48

Humanism, false:
① —13

Humanities:
① —158, 528

Humility:
① —32, 76, 78, 125, 128, 163, 194, 277, 368, 445, 473
② —respect to Pope's words, 6; —mindful of past shortcomings, 7; —subordinate, supporting, anonymous service, 39; —availability for meanest task, 40; —willingness to learn service, 87, 99; —courage to walk with the poor, 99; —serve Christ in humility, 209, 258

Hunger:
② —for God and His Word, 50, 69, 70, 82; —for bread, 70, 82; —for man's deepest needs, 82; —for freedom, 82; —for justice, 86
③ —massive H, 38; —for meaning and values, 48

Identity of a Jesuit:
② —Declaration "Jesuits Today," 8, 11-42.—personality of our own, 83; —availability for meanest tasks, 40; —relevance of our life and work questioned, 75; —corporate awareness, 85; —self-identity of nations and cultures, 102, 133. *See also* JESUITS

Ideologies:
③ —hostile to Kingdom, 38

Idols:
② —wealth, pleasure, prestige, power, 65, 78; —false images of God, 75 a

Ignatian traits:
② —at La Storta accepted, 11, 12; —indifference and "magis," 37; —examen of conscience, 218, 238; —manifestation of conscience, 116, 230; —spiritual discernment, 121, 208,

requires, 40, 48-49, 85; —guidelines toward, 118-127; —and formation, 122; —creation of inculturated churches, 126; —experience of other cultures, 124; —lifestyles of Jesuit communities, 120; —respect for cultures of the poor, 119; —present-day challenges to; —Christianity viewed as Western, 81; —dialogue with other religions and cultures required, 85, 87, 97; —hostility of modern secular cultures, 80; —readherence to native cultures, 83; —rejection of remaining colonial influences, 84; —urbanization and loss of traditions, 82

Independence:
② —in living, 4; —in acquiring and spending, abuses condemned, 264

Indifference, Ignatian:
① —73, 365
② —and the "magis," 37; —apostolic readiness for anything, 121; —required for community discernment, 221; —active I in poverty, 270
③ —for review of ministries, 43. *See also* EXERCISES, SPIRITUAL

Indifferent, grade of:
④ —can be reinstated, 220

Individual:
② —attention to I, besides transforming structures, 89; —initiative stressed more in diversity of ministries, 114, 230; —sense of mission and integration even if alone, 114; —I freedom stressed 214; —each one's contribution to community life, 250

Individualism:
① —how to fight it, 321
② —an obstacle in formation and life, 141c, 149
③ —transcendence of I and rhythm of life, 15

Infirmaries and their poverty:
② —280, 287, 299 b

Information in Prov. Congr.:
② —321

Informationes:
① —before admission to theology, orders, last vows, and government, 200

Initiative:
① —and obedience, 83, 102, 126, 280
② —and sense of mission, 114, 228, 230

Injustice:
② —prevalent today springs from sin, 16, 17; —institutionalized, 52; —its victims, 69, 76, 89, 98; —to be attacked at the heart of man, 81; —endangers man's sense of destiny, 70; —and false idols, 75 a; —and atheism, 77; —liberation and evangelization, 89; —affects our formation process, 137
③ —reality of I, 12; —situations of I, 48

Insertion:
② —among poor, 66; —into the region, 142

Institute SJ:
② —study in Tertianship, 289
③ —and expression of mission, 37-38; —religious and priestly 1 and promoting justice, 40; —the substantials and Canon Law, 90; —Formula of the I, 41. *See also* FORMULA OF THE INSTITUTE

Institutions:
② —apostolic I and communities, 267; —described in the Decree, 274; —no financial benefit to community, 278; —ruling for their poverty, 289; —functional character, 290,— in case of suppression, 293; —their promotion, 298

Instructors of tertianship:
① —133-136; —preparation of, 176; —adaptation of tertianship, 190-191; —revision of rules of, 192

Instrument united with God:
① —205, 269, 366

forts to pray, 207

Jesuit brother. *See* BROTHER, JESUIT

Jesuit mission:
 ④ —consolation and desolation criteria in, 88; —dialogue with other religions and cultures required, 85, 87, 97, 109, 154

Jesuit Religious Life:
 ③ —a help to renewal, 16

Jesuits:
 ② —Declaration "Jesuits Today," 11-42; —Companions of Jesus, 8, 11, 12, 24, 35, 87; —acknowledge sinfulness, 11; —committed to struggle, 12; —essentially a man with a mission, 24, 41; —in companionship under Christ's standard, 25, 41; —shares apostolic mission, 32; —in consecrated life of evangelical counsels, 33; —vocation tested and formed, 35; —availability for service, 40, 118; —identity formula, 41; —we stand in need of evangelization ourselves, 72; —formation for world-insertion, 84; solidarity in Christ with the poor, 87; —primacy of His membership, 115; —contemplative in action, 122, 190, 206, 211
 ③ —fidelity to Church and Pope, 8; —meaning of our life as J, 11; —witness of lives against consumerism, 29
 ④ —a diverse and worldwide body, 16-17; —and the new evangelization, 12; —Christ on mission model of, 7, 15, 25; —companions of Christ in hardships, 26; —Crucified and Risen Christ experienced by, 31; —friends in the Lord, 10-11, 15, 34, 227; —friends of the poor; 34.—Ignatius model of, in helping others, 5-6; —mission of, depends on grace of Christ, 27; —pilgrims ready to be sent on mission, 8-9. *See also* COMPANIONS OF JESUS; CONSTITUTIONS SJ; IGNATIUS; INSTITUTE SJ; SINNERS; SOCIETY OF JESUS

Jesuits, formation of:
 ④ —thorough and lengthy for professed, p. 667; —response to modern world, 315-323; —constructive criticism of Church, 317-319; —creative incorporation into Church, 316; —fidelity to Church, 324-325; —support of Church teaching, 320-323

Jesus:
 ① —knowledge of, 73-78, 117, 212, 469; —imitation of, 31, 281, 313; —following of, 4, 77-79, 117, 269, 299; —attachment to, 14; insertion in His Mystical Body, 203; —personal love, 79, 213, 249, 252, 256; —conformity to, 313; —mission of redemption, 80
 ② —sent by the Father, He sends us, 24; —His love in the Eucharist, 28; —His Sacrifice and Sacrament, 28; —His Heart, 41; —Jesus poor, 38, 97; —our mission to make Him known, 60; —His mission of service and life, 62. *See also* CHRIST

John Paul II, Pope:
 ③ —homily to members of Gen. Cong. (September 3), Rel. Doc. I, pp. 461-466; —confirming decree on poverty (November 3), Rel. Doc. II, p. 483;
 ④ —praise of decrees of GC 34, p. 693-694; —praise of work of GC 34, p. 691; —discourses of, pp. 663-668, 691-694. *See also* POPE

Joint responsibility:
 ② —94, 95, 117

Joy:
 ① —257
 ② —ready to pay the price, 95; —attracts vocations, 209; —celebration of life, 216; —in poverty, 270.
 ③ —at election of General, 1; —Christian J, 8, 14; —relaxation and J in rhythm of life, 15; —prayers for J, 55

Labor of the intellect:
④ —in history of Society, 394; —importance of, 395-396; —formation of Jesuits for, 396-399; —uses of, in modern world, 399-403; —theological reflection, 400-403

Laicized Jesuits:
② —and membership in Prov. Congr., 323

Laity:
① —interpreters of the modern world, 540; —their mission in the Church, 394, 581; —their help, 540, 582; —our responsibilities towards them, 394; —collaboration with them, 373, 410, 500, 526, 540-541, 588.
③ —strength from L, 51; —Ignatian spirituality and L, 51; —work with L, 51; —their responsibility and vocation, 51; —formation of L, 51
④ —future cooperation with L, 352-360; —apostolic network, 355-356; —assisting Church of the laity, 363; —closer personal bond to Society, 357-359; —lay leadership in works of the Society, 354; —laity, Jesuit cooperation with, 340-351; —in non-Jesuit works, 344-345; —in works of the Society, 341-343; —with associations, 346-351. *See also* CHRISTIAN LIFE COMMUNITIES; EXERCISES, SPIRITUAL

Languages, modern:
① —study of, 158, 423; —use of, 140; —use in first vows, 291
② —178

La Storta:
⑤ —influence on Ignatius, 6, 11, 60—and First Companions, 90

Law:
② —of charity, 234, 272; —L and Spirit, 269; —civil, 300; —vacation of, 337 e

Law of the Society:
④ —new revision, pp. 687-688; —a path through confusion, pp. 687-688; —arbitrary elements necessary, pp. 687-688; —Ignatius's objectives implemented, p. 687; —offering of greater value demanded, p. 690; —not a departure from original law, p. 689

Letter writing:
② —a means of communication among Ours, 216

Liberation of Man:
② —in the Formula of the Institute, 21; —Christ brings total L, 76, 201; —now, and fully in heaven, 79; —by transforming structures, 89

Liberty:
① —83-84, 148, 257, 281, 302; —evangelical, 315. *See also* FREEDOM

Libraries:
① —140, 172, 307, 482, 519

Licentiate in Ph and Th:
② —170, 185

Life:
② —of the Society in past decade, 1; —divine L, 62, 213; —human L, 69, 97, 100, 213; —of the Church, 103; L's testimony, 154. *See also* COMMUNITY LIFE; RELIGIOUS LIFE; SPIRITUAL LIFE

Lifestyle:
① —292, 296, 299, 329.
② —changes called for 97, 263; —frugal, 286; —to favor apostolic formation, 141 c; —approved budget, 268

Literature studies:
② —178

Liturgy and the Mystery of Christ:
① —71, 86, 98, 114, 116, 138, 152, 472; —in our life, 214, 224; —in our schools, 515; —and ecumenism, 457
② —and inculturation, 103

Living standard:
② —263, 264, 286

Local Ordinary:
⑤ —relation between LO and the Society, 168

Local Superior:
② —head of apostolic community, 112; in individual and community

hope, 65; —help them open to God
and Christ, 67, 101; —millions of
victims of injustice, 69; —hunger
for bread and the Word, 70; —God
not in public life 70; —transformed
by technology, 74; —God in human
adventure,—75 a; selfishly rejects a
better world possible, 76— injustice
rooted in man's heart, 81; —their
appeal to us, 84; —men and structures, 88-90; —men-for-others, 30,
109; —the whole person and every
person, 110. *See also* CONTEMPO-
RARIES; WORLD

Manresa, effect on Ignatius:
⑤ —and realization of true spiritual values, 21, 22

Marriage, Christian:
① —250, 261

Mary:
① —filial devotion, 79, 251 e, 471
② —places Ignatius with her Son, 11;
—devotion, 244
③ —Queen and Mother of Society, 55;
—M's intercession, 55

Mass:
① —224, 231; —summit and center of
prayer, 208; —source of holiness,
fraternal love, apostolic fervor, 214;
—daily in our schools, 532. *See also*
EUCHARIST; LITURGY; MYSTERY

Mass Media:
② —promote ability to communicate, 57,
109, 159; —reevaluation of traditional means, 58; —uniting us to God, 61;
—and secularization, 74, 75; —priority, 108, 109 d; —studies encouraged,
177; —funds allowed, 209

Master of Novices:
① —choice, aptitude, gifts, 89; —preparation, 176; —assisted by selected
men, 110-111; —solicitude for adaptation, 111

Materialism of rich and poor:
② —250.
③ —hostile to Kingdom, 38

Maturity, Christian:
① —affected by the entire formation
and for each one of the stages, 83-
84, 89, 93, 108-109, 126, 145-146, 158,
255, 260; —in the life of prayer, 230;
—in the life of the community, 100,
148; —by observance of the rules,
348-349; —obedience not opposed
to it, 28

Meaning:
③ —search for M growing, 39

Media, Social Communications:
③ —as apostolate, 47

Meditation: *See* PRAYER

Meetings:
① —fraternal, more frequent, of Jesuits,
81, 325; —on formation, continuing
renewal, 139, 477, 552, 559
② —of formation personnel, 161;
—on spiritual topics, 208 note;
—prayerful discussion, 237; —local
superiors in province, 254; —major
superiors in assistancy, 254; —men
of same apostolate, 254; —gatherings of area communities, 254

Memorabilia Societatis Iesu:
① —605

Mercy:
③ —justice and God's mercy, 35. *See also*
LOVE; JUSTICE

Migration and refugees:
⑤ —assistance of victims, 83

Ministry, priestly, of Jesuits:
④ —and lay ministries, 176; —stages of
individual Jesuit's ministry, 185-192;
—very inclusive, but must arouse
faith in Gospel, 172

Ministries:
① —their revision, 20, 361, 365, 379;
—the urgency to take on certain
ones, 375
② —Some priorities, 108-109; choice of,
124; —integrated in service of faith
and justice, 19, 270; —our present
M geared to F and J, 125; —some
presence in different fields, 127;

cations of faith in God, 37-38. *See also* COLLABORATION; FAITH; JUSTICE; LOVE; MINISTRIES; OBEDIENCE; PEACE; POPE

Missionary:
① —432-434.
② —Body, 111-118; —vocation and tradition of inculturation, 104
③ —call to adapted M Activity, 40

Missionary spirit of Society:
① —subject to confusion, *272*

Missions, foreign:
① —their history in the Society, 418; —dogmatic foundation, 414, 417; —urgency, 421; —availability of every Jesuit, 377, 422; —norms, 426-431; —special preparation, 432-434; —cooperation of the entire Society, 435-441; secretariat, 441

Missions of the Pope: entrusted to the Society:
① —5-7, 362, 376

Mobility:
② —117, 118, 138. *See also* AVAILABILITY

Moral theology:
② —158; ascetico-moral perfection, 260

Mortification:
① —251, 259. *See also* SELF-ABNEGATION

Multiform:
② —response to challenge of Mission, 56; —proclamation of Gospel, 85

Mystery of Christ:
① —86, 104, 127, 160, 249, 370, 470; —paschal mystery, 249
② —of Christ poor, 258, 260; —of poverty, 258, 260; —Christian M, 102; —Eucharistic Sacrifice, 235

Nationalism:
① —151

Needs of the world:
② —of bread, freedom, God, 82; —our answer is involvement, 84; —accommodation to, 13; —greater awareness and concern, 98, 141 c; —criterion of greatest need, 88, 90, 284-286
③ —N of People:—spiritual NP, 40; —NP for concern, 48

New:
② —challenges, 50-57; —instruments, 57; —opportunities, 74; —signs and symbols, 205; —international values, 105; —questions and knowledge, 150; —N heaven and N earth, 79, 261

Non-Christian religions:
② —methods of prayer, 208

Non-formed Jesuits:
② —participation in Prov. Congr., 322. *See also* FORMATION

Norms:
② —General N of Studies, 134, 138, 164, 169; —on Formation, 163-186; —on union of hearts, 235-255; —on Poverty, 272-293

Novices:
① —knowledge of them, 111; —confidence in the master of novices, 102; —formed in self-denial, 103; —awakened to their responsibilities, 104-108; —formed in knowledge of the Society, 105

Novitiate:
① —91-111; —twofold purpose, 92; —conditions for admission and remaining, 93-95, 109; —site, 107; —to test the vocation of the novices, 96-97; —to form them in the spiritual life, 98; —in community life, 100; —in charity, 102; —equality among scholastics, brothers, 101; —doctrinal and scriptural formation, 104; —relations with the world, 106-108
② —perpetual vows, 35; —ongoing formation begins in N, 138; —purpose: formation and probation, 144; progress of integration from N, 144-145; —instructed in discernment, 144; —may be common for Scholastics and Brothers, 144; —introductory course of Theology, 175. *See also* FORMATION

life to favor prayer, 216, 241; —renewal in Spir. Ex., 208; —contemplative in action, 112; —pray for authentic poverty, 269, 270; —forms and schools of P today, 208 note; —in non-Christian religions, 103, 208; —spiritual directors experts in prayer, 240; —trust in P, 53

③ —for familiarity with God, 12; —involved in discernment, 13; —for vocations, 24; —expressing search for meaning, 39; —and intercession of Mary and Ignatius, 55; —for strength and joy, 55. *See also* EXAMEN; ENCOUNTER WITH GOD; EXPERIENCE; EUCHARIST

Preaching: preparation for,
  ① —158, 476

Preferences, global:
  ⑤—81-84; —structures in Society to meet global challenges, 81; —interprovincial cooperation to achieve priorities, 82; —Africa, opportunities and challenges in, 83; —China, important key to a peaceful world, 83; —intellectual apostolate, renewed dedication to, 83; —interprovincial institutions in Rome, as missions of the Pope, 83; migration and refugees, assistance of victims, 83

Preliminary election of Prov. Congr.: *See* ELECTIO PRAEVIA

Preparation:
  ② —of a GC, 303-305; —of a Prov. Congr.: 313-314.

Priesthood, preparation of the scholastics for:
  ① —105, 118, 122; —activity of the Jesuit impregnated by P, 403, 413; —formation for the P, 538
  ② —essential character SJ: 5, 32; —training of priests, 157; —ordination, 189; —and apostolic activities of scholastics, 160

Priesthood, Jesuit:

④ —158-159, 170-184; —and episcopacy, 193; —central to Jesuit identity, 165; —characteristic priestly activities, 167-169; —exercised especially toward those uncared for by others, 168; —Jesuit priestly mission, 163-166, 183-184; —with relation to diocesan bishops, 160; —with relation to Jesuit brothers, 162

Priestly apostolate
  ① —the problem stated, 386-389; —principles of the Council, 390-395; —of the Institute, 396-399; —presuppositions, 400-405; —nature and mission of the priesthood, 406; —priest as representative of the Kingdom, 408
  ② —service, 32, 67; —training, 160 ; —character of the Society, 32; —hyphenated priests, 127-128

Priestly Order:
  ③ —role of PO, 34; —Pope and PO, 34, 40; —and promotion of justice, 40; —and Brothers in Prov. Cong., 81. *See also* BROTHERS, COADJUTOR

Priests, Worker:
  ③ —identity with, apostolate for workers, 48

Primacy:
  ② —of the spirit in our mission, 61; —of ministries in Formula of the Institute, 66; —of the Spir. Exerc. as wellspring of apostolate, 87, 216; —of our life's testimony over academic training, 154; —from grace force flows to work, 216; —of mission over other commitments, 115

Principle and foundation:
  ② —15

Priorities of ministries:
  ② —108-109, 124-126.

Prisoners:
  ① —493.

Privacy in our houses:
  ② —252

—in poverty, 269; —R in Church influences our formation, 133; —through continued formation, 150-152; —through the Spir. Exerc, 242; —a decade after Tertianship, 168; —a chance of apostolic R to all, 567

③ —options and R, 32 —cooperation in Church R, 40; —and review of ministries, 43; —of Ignatian spirituality, 51

Representation in conflict of conscience:
② —256 a

Research;
③ —call for adapted R, 40; —as ministry, 47; —its importance. 47; —requirements for R as apostolate, 47.
See also ADAPTATION

Research, scholarly scientific:
① —178, 409, 423, 459, 535
② —scholarly R in publications praised, 45; —demanding challenge, 84; —diagnose socio-political problems, 93; —experiment in vitality of adapted Spir. Ex, 107; —by formation personnel, 162

Residences:
① —defined, 478; —different names, structures, ministries, 479; —living communities not too large, set up according to works, 480; living conditions, 480-484; —style appropriate to poverty, 300, 485-486; —among working men, 487; —among more neglected groups, 487

Resources:
② —human, 38; —of the planet, 76; —spiritual, 112; —material and spiritual, 125, 167; —all for our mission, 53; —for institutes, 378; —for some apostolates, 299; —sharing R, 30, 284-288

Response:
② —to new challenges: total, 53; corporate, 54; in faith and experience, 55; —multiform, 56; —prerequisites for

our R to challenge of mission, 83-87; —of Ignatius and Companions to call of Christ, 63

Responsibility, encouragement of:
① —108, 146, 320, 351; —growth in, 320; —personal, in prayer, 216; —of all Jesuits with regard to the Society, 324; —with regard to the missions, 435-441; —mutual, in the spiritual life, 81, 329; —of the scholastics, 126, 520.
② —of subject, 231; —joint R for choices, 117; —for socio-political apostolate, 94-95; —during formation, 146, 147; —of formation personnel, 181

Retreat Houses:
② —role in service to F and J, 73 b, 125; —poverty of, 274; —fund for, 299

Retreats: *See* EXERCISES, SPIRITUAL

Revelation of God through Christ:
② —74, 75 a, 77, 141 a, 153

Revenues:
① —papal note, section C, pp. 239-240
② —of colleges and houses, 367; —forbidden to communities, 300; —apostolic use, 268; —allowed to apostolic institutes, 289; —of Society and Provinces, 297, 298, 299; —not from investment, 302 (and letter 3 in Section C, pp. 239-240)

Review of Ministries: *See* MISSION; MINISTRIES

Revision:
② —of Form. GC, 303-311; —of Form. PC, 312-329; —of Congr. of Proc. and Prov. 310 d; —of Curia organization, 332 c, 333; —of Statutes on Poverty, 272, 295

Rhythm of life:
③ —its meaning, 15; —sign of interior freedom, 15

and deficiencies, 10-13; —current difficulties, 1; —in the service of the Church, 14-16; —apostolic goal, 80; —renewal and adaptation, 17, 128, 543; —to know it, 324

② —foundation, 13, 21, 41; —its end, 13, 21; —four characteristics, 5, 30-34, 64, 191; —religious, 30; —apostolic, 31; sacerdotal, 32; united with bond to the Pope, 33; worldwide, 26; —unity in diversity, 161; S's body beyond local community, 117; —spirit and tradition, 2, 4; —S of love, 212; —take to heart Pope's words, 6; —humbly acknowledge failings, 6; —service to Church, 45; —gathered in 32nd GC, 13; —choice for F and J, 13; —specific contribution to F and J, 22; —inculturation, 105; —faculty to possess, 297, 298

③ —as body in service and life, 17; —for solidarity of rich with poor, 49; —for just peace and freedom, 49; —as international body, 49; —for just world order, 49; —and justice in lives, communities, institutions, 53; —and solidarity with the poor, 52

④ —Society a sacerdotal order: pp. 693-694

Society of Jesus, challenges of ministry:

⑤ —gratitude for past renewal, 45; —integrating principle of Society, 46; —inculturation and dialogue needed, 47; —fruits of inculturation, 48; —ways of implementing missions, 49; —dangers from dominant culture, 64

Society of Jesus, charism of:

⑤ —unity in multiplicity, 18-19; —companionship with the Lord and one another, 20; —experience of being placed with Christ, 21, 23; —mission of Ignatius to help souls, 22; —challenge of the Cross, 24; —friends in the Lord, 85

Society of Jesus, future course of:

④ —cultivate clear missionary spirit, p. 681; —practice new evangelism, pp. 681-683; —reflect strongly the God to be communicated, p. 680; —cultivate clear missionary spirit, p. 681; —practice new evangelism, pp. 681-683; —reflect strongly the God to be communicated, p. 680

Society of Jesus, mission of today:

⑤ —attention to global context, 37; —resistance to consumerism, 38; —evangelization of those unaware of God or misusing his name, 39-41; Jesus Christ, our sole inspiration and model, 43-44; —mission today, 60; —implementation of our educational and pastoral ministries in modern culture, 67; —ministries and institutions incarnate our faith in Jesus, 86; —potential of Society as an international and multicultural body, 87—mission of Society, proclamation of faith, 6; —service of faith and promotion of justice to be united, 6; —travel of Jesuits to little-served or difficult apostolates, 6

Society of Jesus, new context for mission:

⑤ —52-55; —obstacles to, 52; —interconnectedness, acceptance of, 53; —autonomy vs. solidarity, 55

Society of Jesus, response of, to Benedict XVI's exhortation:

⑤ —full adherence to the C Church, 8; —generosity and spirituality of Jesuits, 9-10; —inspiration from *Spiritual Exercises*, 12; —emphasis on intellectual preparation, 13; —communion with the Church, 14, 16; —adherence to the Magisterium, 15; availability for missions, 17

Society of Jesus, special responsibility of:

④ —dedication to mission of the Church, p. 249; —missionary outreach, p. 250; —new evangelization,

Teaching:
  ① —secondary, 525-531; —primary or elementary, 524; —in higher education, 177, 535-536, 561-563; —religious, 513; —in talking about atheism, 38; —active methods of, 166
  ③ —as ministry, 46. *See also* EDUCATION; SCHOOLS

Team work:
  ② —114, 149, 214. *See also* COLLABORATION

Technical schools:
  ① —529

Technology:
  ② —progress, 69-70, 74; —dazzling, 51

Temporal administration:
  ② —keystone to reform, 267; —goods, 271, 297-299; —Charitable Fund, 288; —instruction, 296

Temporal Coadjutors:
  ① —term abolished
  ④ —216. *See also* BROTHERS

Temptations:
  ① —262

Tension:
  ① —result of the necessity for adaptation, 20
  ② —in community and discernment, 94, 223; —relaxation of T, 216; —study-apostolate, 154; —rich institutions-religious poverty, 265

Territory:
  ② —in dispersed provinces, 314; —and Prov. Congr., 319

Tertianship:
  ① —esteem and value, 188; —current difficulties, 190; —renewal and adaptation, 188-189; —opportune experiences, 191-192; —spiritual formation, 133-137
  ② —in high regard by 31st and 32nd GC, 187; —if overdue, not to be postponed, 187; —Model A, 189; Model B, 190; —not later than 3 years after ordination, 190; —Instructor, 190; —approved forms, 190; —assignment in apostolic community, 190; —required for last vows, 197

Thanksgiving after Mass:
  ① —231

Theological reflection:
  ② —research, 84; —its importance, 108; —interdisciplinary and integrated in culture, 109; —and inculturation, 103, 132; —in apostolic reflection, 141; —integrate studies into life, 151, 153, 158; —and philosophical training, 156

Theology:
  ① —studies, 122, 161, 163-165, 177, 459, 548, 550; —schools of higher education, 536; —reading of theological works, 140; —courses for brothers, 116; —pastoral, 179; —preparation of Jesuits for spiritual theology, 476; —missionary, 434; —ecumenical, 447
  ② —solid academic formation, 154; —integrated, systematic, adapted, 158; —following Church laws, 158; —grounded on tradition and official teaching of the Church, 161; —moral theology, 158; —personal experience of Faith, 158; —language adapted, 103; —new questions, 150; —appropriate instruction for Brothers, 155
  ③ —call to adapt study of T, 40. *See also* RESEARCH

Thinking with the Church:
  ② —spirit of these rules valid today, 46, 233

Third World:
  ② —103, 130, 131

Thomas Aquinas, Saint:
  ① —184.

Time of Last Vows:
  ② —196-198; and ordination, 189, 190, 197